THE DESERTER

THE DESERTER

P. J. Gonzales

Library of Congress Control Number:		2016910123
ISBN:	Hardcover	978-1-5245-1119-7
	Softcover	978-1-5245-1118-0
	eBook	978-1-5245-1117-3

Print information available on the last page.

Rev. date: 06/17/2016

To order additional copies of this book, contact:
Xlibris
1-888-795-4274
www.Xlibris.com
Orders@Xlibris.com
738594

CONTENTS

The extreme nature of the story necessitates the importance of presenting this book as how it may fit individual beliefs due to the many reasons that has to be taken into consideration. There are documents, notes, and journals of the accounts of events in existence that can prove its veracity. However, as time heals the wounds of war, it is best it remains untouched to respect the will of the dead as it also suffices the living. Again, there is no intention to effect and become an initiating factor to raise claim of any kind for an individual, ethnicity, or organization[s] as they may find the book disturbing and contradicting by principles and opinions. In its entirety for itself to be written had also required logical adoptions of known facts [dates, places, and events] that had been a common knowledge for many decades. It is therefore a profound apology precedes in all manners that it shall not cause anyone to derive accounts therein that may contribute in confusion of thoughts, principles, and beliefs. **THE AUTHOR**

Unedited version, Feb. 2, 2012.
P.J. GONZALES Pelagio.pj@gmail.com

THE DESERTER
Based on a True Story

In memory of
Dominador and Niza Cabarles
Anna Cabarles

And all our heroes

"You don't need to [salute]. Once the liberation is over, we are back to nobody. My sufferings and struggle as an individual or a soldier in this war shall be a story worth telling under a tree on a lazy day. I had seen many deaths, many I buried myself. The only thing that mark their graves were pieces of rocks, a cross made of twigs. Who shall remember them? Perhaps those men who in some ways offered a little prayer and grieved for them, only to end up in the same fate. They are the ones worth every generation to be saluted, not me."

-(Dominador Cabarles, USAFFE)

PROLOGUE

I wished for heaven, and heaven came down to me. It was the happiest moment of my life. Then there came the tears; it was as if I had forsaken heaven to embrace my destiny, only to find out it was hell I had sent myself to—too late. I prayed for miracles; they came one after the other. In fulfillment of my promises to heaven, I was given strength. In my faith, I was refused by hell itself to take that one last step, one last breath to gasp in surrender—another miracle. I did not realize that the most important thing I have to wish for is yet to come.

A PENITENT MAN

Good Friday. Summer vacation has just begun. I could stay on bed, get more sleep as much as I wanted. At least that's what I thought it would be. My mother, always loud as she can be, was just a few feet away screaming. She wanted me to get up to simply run an errand. I was already awake; it was just that it was unusually too early to get up thinking there was no other person on their feet yet at the time. But her persistent yelling made me aware of what could be her next action. The consequences of pretending to still be asleep would make me regret it for the rest of the day. I knew where she kept the broom— close enough so that she could grab it before I had any chance to run.

I had no intention of ignoring her, but forcing myself in the early hours of the morning was not easy. I lazily dragged myself to the side of the bed inch by inch. I just went back to bed after complying with the morning rite of the family, which was pushing a jeepney to get it cranking. Luckily, it ran without much effort as we got help from a big guy.

"What shall I do?" I asked as if I didn't know yet what she wanted me to do. "It's still dark." I complained cautiously.

"Bring coffee to your *ninong* (godfather)," she repeated in a very firm voice what she wanted me to do for about the fourth time.

"Where is the coffee?" I politely asked, thinking it would be easy—just run across the street and everything will be over.

"You make it!"

Inside the chapel across the street, a silhouette of a man penitently reading verses from the book *The Passion of Christ* at the hymn of a song that is ordinarily heard during rites and in the mourning of the dead. Aided by the light of a candle that glimmered like it was dancing to the tune of his breath, his voice was loud enough to fill the space, reverberate against the concrete walls and tightly closed windows, and out through the fully open door of the chapel. As the voice passed and traveled through the humid morning breeze of the dry season, it sounded like a weeping canine that sang in duet with the crowing of the roosters in the darkness of dawn.

I was seven years old. At that age, I had learned so many things already. Starting a fire out of firewood and paper in our stone kitchen to boil water is not difficult. I had done it many times. Many days ago, I had discovered that the free-range chickens owned by our neighbor had generously laid eggs in our property, and since then I boiled eggs. Sometimes I sold them. It always yielded more than I could eat for many days; I was happy to find about a dozen of them. Although I had to fight with the hen in the process of incubating the eggs, I still managed to grab four and put them in the pot of water and started boiling them with coffee granules altogether.

It didn't take long. I went to deliver a cup of coffee to a person whom I was told was in the chapel. It was different inside where the seats were arranged facing the altar, so quiet except for the sounds created by a man who may not have noticed my coming. He was so solemn and serious, not aware that his reading sounded like a stray dog that was mauled by others of its kind, at least to my ears. He was alone, mumbling every word while making sure he didn't miss any page turning to another. He was my godfather; I could recognize him even in the dark. He was not wearing his wide sombrero, but I could tell it was him because of his white sideburns and square-top haircut; it could not be anyone else but him. I watched him a little bit fighting every word as he read; perhaps there was not enough light as I saw him trying to overcome the difficulties.

It was his self-imposed tradition in observing the Holy Week. Others would want to be nailed in a cross at worst. For him, for two hours or so, he has to read *The Passion* inside the chapel on a certain day of the Holy Week. He would read it at home during the whole period of Lent. I courteously got his attention about my presence, offering what I had brought for him. I could tell he was thankful through his smile, but he continued reading passage after passage. The style, like in the opera is not as bad standing closer as it hears outside the building. It's not as bad up close; however I built up my confidence to say I could do it a lot better.

The sun was coming up as its light came through the glazed windows, enough for the candle to be put out. My plan was only to get his attention that I had brought him something for breakfast. But I did not; instead I sat by his side and started to read with him his hymns. A little while later, I became comfortable, and as he may have thought that I can do it by myself, he turned himself to the cup of coffee and eggs that were starting to get cold while watching me read confidently to his amazement. All I wanted was to make him empty the cup so I could bring it back home and go back to sleep.

"You made me so proud, you can read as good as I am already," he uttered silently, making sure I didn't get distracted.

I looked at him momentarily; the compliment had to be taken for how it was said. Surely I could read better than him. In maybe five or ten minutes, the eggs were already eaten. He was sipping the last drop of coffee when I glanced to see a chicken feather that partially blocked his lips. He just spit it away, eyes still locked on me. However, I didn't have the courage to excuse myself when he got completely done. I felt that it would be disrespectful, so I had to wait until he could read back with me. Some elderly women came to take over half an hour after; to them, he expressed with pride and bragged about my reading skills.

Of course, I could read. At seven turning eight in a couple of months, I had finished my third grade already short of receiving my report card. I started first grade at five and accelerated a year. In the next school year, I would be in the fourth grade. I began attending school as a cat pupil to boost the numbers in the class. Our school organization was in its infancy, requiring minimum head counts to justify its continuance. A scream away from home, I attended school early also for the expectation that I can keep playing with my friends the whole day. That didn't happen. Our strict principal who also had his own reasons for letting me in school was also a friend of my father. I knew that both of them had connived with each other to keep me in the classroom after I had set ablaze to that little forest not too far away from our house.

I grew up calling my godfather as Ninong. His name was Dominador Cabarles, in his fifties, at a height that was unusually taller than most men in our community, and was respected for his patience and low-profile approach in dealing with everything and to everyone. He was known for being *kuripot* (Scrooge) because he never extended financial help to anybody including to his own relatives despite their tilling a large area of agricultural land that yield plentiful harvests twice a year. He was reputed to be actually avoiding people, so they say, except probably those he had trusted. There were not too many of them; a few include my parents. Needless to say, it was only me that became personified with him and his family.

He would always walk unusually fast as he was unusually slow in reading simple verses. We walked home together; it only took him to reach our yard a time equal to running the distance for me. My mother was sweeping the ground of fallen leaves from the old star apple tree. That very early in the morning, I got a pat on the back from my ninong and I had already accomplished an errand for my mother. The day began in my favor after all; it should be a day of no trouble, another day full of fun and adventures ahead.

"Good morning, *comare* (godsister)," greeted my godfather as he opens a conversation. I knew it will just be a short exchange of a few words, customary greetings between elderlies. No disrespect, but I passed them, thinking I could go back to bed undisturbed this time. I didn't heard what else they talked about.

"Good morning too, *compare* (godbrother)," my mother responded.

"I just stopped by to thank you for the coffee and boiled eggs—they were very good. I also want to remind you that we are sponsoring the Passion of Christ readings today. You know how it is done, it will be in my place," he said, extending the humble invitation in gratitude of my hospitality.

I was already lying in bed as planned. It wasn't even seven o'clock in the morning yet, plenty of time before I do the rest of my chores.

Lying on my stomach, I heard my mother coming in. She caught me off guard when I felt the swing of the broom handle that landed on my butt; it was too late to react to another one.

"Where did you get those eggs you fed to your ninong?" she screamed at the top of her lungs almost at the same time she swung the broom for the third time.

I suddenly realized my mistake. I knew I should have eaten all the eggs, but I was full. I thought it would be nice to share a couple to Ninong. The source of fresh eggs was my secret deal. I never thought it would come up in their conversation. I ended up under the bed with the threat of more punishment coming if I didn't tell the truth. But I didn't wait for that; as soon as I found a window, I took the opportunity to run and disappear from her sight.

GENES OF THE FATHER

It was about two o'clock in the afternoon when I showed up at the house of my godparents. I had been there many times, but that day was different as there was plenty of food. Many people were gathered, taking a little rest after an early morning of cooking and feeding a long line of people for the traditional observance of Holy Week that would become a feast. Lunch was over, and dinner would be served in a few more hours. A long dining table matched with wooden benches were set up under the shade of an acacia tree, its leaves overlapping a mango tree. In one corner of the property fenced by barbed wire to keep off animals that proliferate in the yard was a barn raised to about four feet above the ground by log poles and rusty corrugated tin sheets around, same as on the roofing.

That structure always gave me the creeps but also made me curious as to what was inside. I remembered the dark green boxes stacked on top of the other in the darkest corner. I would know what they were when the right time came. My curiosity always found satisfaction at the most unexpected time. I wondered what it was like to be locked in and left inside for a day. I was told it wasn't easy, and I was on the brink of getting it too. My ninong spotted me as soon as I passed that shed where one corner was noticeably lower than the others. The door was made of thin wooden planks nailed side by side;

it had started to rot and was tied up tightly with rusty steel wires to prevent the wind from blowing it open. But that was not the real door; there was another that was strong and padlocked.

"Where have you been, young man?" That was the welcome I always got from him, from any members of the family. Most likely he knew, for there had been so many times that I had been to his place where there was nothing else to keep me amused but collect spiders. The best and ugliest fighting spiders could be found in the woods close to his property. Seeing my untidy and hungry appearance, he eventually guided me inside the house where together with my godmother he served me food.

In a usual gesture, I greeted first the occupant of a chair in the living room just to let her know of my presence. I could tell her difficulty in hiding her excitement when she turned her head to respond. With a plate full of rice, meat, and vegetables, I didn't waste any more time walking past an open shelf full of pictures and figurines that I had seen so many times already. I always liked looking at them to appreciate how those things were neatly and carefully arranged. To the right were stacks of old illustrated comics and magazines on top of the counter and a small transistor radio that was tuned in to a soap opera in full volume.

On a rocking chair sat a girl by the widely open window made of wood and seashells. All other windows were also fully open so she could see the people coming and going throughout that day for the free meal. I chose to sit closer by her on a varnished wooden sofa, separated from a set that lined up by the windows along the perimeter of the living room. I could feel fresh calm air passing through. It had been an exhausting morning.

"Hi, Anna, you look great." There was an exchange of greetings again, and I noticed those straight long hair that was partially blown over her neck and chin by the gentle breeze. Her face, so pretty as always, became prettier with the thin layer of Johnson's Baby Powder spread uniformly on her skin. Maybe there was something else as she looked not as pale as she normally was on ordinary days.

"Where have you been? I've been waiting for you all day," she asked with an expression of sadness that the day was almost over and it was not what she had expected to spend. She had difficulty in every word she said, and she tried to speak clearer, which became harder and harder for her as the day went by.

My ninong and ninang came to us. Ninong Domeng was carrying a glass of water—for me, I hoped—while saying something, adding to the guilt that I already had. My ninang stopped by the radio and tried very hard to at least lower the volume. Her always loving and caring husband came to the rescue and did it for her. Afterward, he carefully placed his hand on her shoulder while apologizing and explaining to us that neither of them could not stay with us for there were so many chores that they need to attend to because of the occasion.

And then Anna and I were left alone again; I had not said anything more yet as the food was keeping me busy. I was hungry, and she must have noticed that. She was patiently waiting, watching me eating, until I found a chance to talk between handfuls of rice and meat that I put in my mouth one after the other. "Do you want something to eat too?" I said again.

She was staring as if she hadn't seen me for a long time, which was true. Maybe it was for a week or more; I could not count how many times her father had requested me to visit her. I didn't because I was always caught up with playmates or doing chores after classes. Except for that sweet smile every time I looked at her, she was barely moving. That beautiful face, eyes naturally shadowed with a rosy color around it, nose and cheeks were so pronounced that I compared her to a fully grown woman. Fully grown indeed for she was even taller than me. I just couldn't find words to describe her. All I know was she was as pretty like the leading actresses I had seen on television, especially when they were about to cry. Like her mother, my ninang, the most understanding mother who would never resort to swearing and violence like mine.

"You were spanked again, weren't you?" She was guessing, but more likely she had already known, looking straight at me. She must have noticed the traces of tears on my face and the swollen eyelids from my crying that morning.

"How did you know?" I responded to her question. I could not deny. I felt uneasy as I drank a glass of water ignoring the embarrassment that just came back to me. Suddenly, I was reminded that I still had some explaining to do when I come back home. I touched that part of my body where the broom handle landed. "Hmm." It was not painful anymore. I was not scared to get more if I could not avoid it, which is most likely to happen when I show up at home.

Her laughing made me feel a little better from my worries. I just could not help but laughed too, feeling better in admitting my guilt without actually telling I fed her father stolen eggs according to my mother. I chose not to contest my action.

"What are you two laughing about?" *Ate* Massey asked casually as soon as she joined us, grabbing a magazine from the very top of its pile on the counter. I said we were not laughing.

"He got spanked," Anna replied quickly, expressing pity in her voice.

"Oh, that. I know already," Massey responded quickly. Looking at me, holding more laughs or perhaps she had laughed enough already, she walked graciously and finally sat down by the window closest to us.

How did she know? I didn't care. It didn't bother me. Getting punishment was just like a part of me at home and in school. "You have a new chair, Anna. Are you comfortable?" Everybody knew it was new, but I was just trying to divert their attention to something else.

"Yes. My father paid someone to custom made it for me," she replied.

"It's beautiful, looks strong," I commented, slowly rocking the oversized chair while continually appreciating how fine it was made, adding how every part was connected to each other. "It is made of a fine and strong type of wood, not like the old one," I added.

"Better than the one that you destroyed, you mean?" Massey said with a smile and sarcasm, recounting a past event that was forgotten already.

"That one was old, squeaking, and weak. It's about time it got destroyed and replaced by a better one." I repeated her word *destroyed* to justify my participation on that past event. "It's good the other one broke. Look, aren't you happy? Anna is very comfortable now," I added carelessly, implying I may have done bad but it somewhat resulted for the good of her sister.

"Yeah, it may be good you broke the other one." She sighed, accompanied by a shaking of her head. It sounded like finally she was conceding in agreement with my rationalization. "But not when she was still on it. Be careful rocking that chair now!" she yelled.

She surely knew how to shut me up. But she was right. I was sorry about a past incident that may have contributed to the complications of Anna's illness. Ate Massey, the always loving and caring sister of Anna, was the oldest of three siblings. At nineteen, she was a perfect beauty. Being tall ran in the family. Her very fine complexion, build, and a little of those she put in her face; she was comparable to the models on the cover of every foreign-issued magazine she subscribed. She shared enough chores around the house and shared the sacrifices of the family living in an isolated place away from the center of the community. But as how my godfather said it, she spent more time in front of the mirror than anything else. Except for that, he had no complaint at all.

Massey had so many suitors that visited her from adjoining towns and far places. I remember when two of them almost axed each other because one had finished chopping all the firewood, leaving the other nothing left to show off. Yes, my godfather had no complaint because most of them helped voluntarily with fathers or relatives in tow every time he needed them, especially in the rice planting and harvest season. All young able-bodied men in the spirit of *bayanihan* (goodwill), all were trying to win the affection of Massey and of course the approval of the parents first and a brother, Ernesto, who had the advantage of them all for having a lot of breaks from hard work. The only time Ninong would disapprove of them was when they did tricks to discourage each other of their ultimate intentions that sometimes ended up in a fistfight.

She was really that beautiful. But what I admired most was her dedication in taking care of her younger sister. Nothing else was more important for her. I was a nobody but a nuisance young boy who will destroy just about anything if left unsupervised. I could tell she had joined us not only to attend to Anna's needs but to also watch me, making sure that nothing happened to her sister while I was with her. For sure, she had not forgotten when I fed Anna a big piece of chicken that almost choked her. She was always cautious when I was around the poor girl, making sure I didn't "kill" her, as she said it. I never contested that too. However, I don't easily embrace humiliation without payback.

"*Ate* Massey," I called to her while she was pretending to turn pages of that magazine I knew she had seen a lot of times already.

"What?" Her naturally sweet voice could not be hidden while she was pretentiously mad, eyes still on that page.

"Do you have suitors here today?" I asked while looking outside the window to the helpers that came for the occasion.

"Why do you want to know?" She looked straight at me; now I had really gotten her attention.

"I'm sick and tired of watching my spiders fighting with each other."

"So?" she responded curiously to what I was trying to imply. Her eyes went wider; she was thinking, what was the connection between my spiders and her suitors?

"I want to see real people fighting again."

"You little egg thief!"

We laughed and talked while teasing each other. Ernesto, who came and went and came again, only to be called again to run errands for that busy day, could not help it but just stay with us for the rest of the day and join the fun. A typical teenager, shy, and reserved, Ernesto more leaned toward spending his time daydreaming under the acacia tree. His teeth protruded out of his upper lip that made it difficult to keep his mouth close, perhaps caused by smoking that he learned at an early age from his father. He was dark and skinny but strong, used to the hard work of farming that he had grown up with while helping his father. He resisted going back to school since that first day. Massey told stories about him, about how he would only go to school when his father threatened him with a large bamboo trunk. "You too, *Ate* (older sister)," he would say, referring to Massey who also refused to go to school when they were younger.

There were so many excuses they had presented with each other, but both came to agreement that the main reason was their being too far from civilization, which was true. The closest school at the time was in the town proper of Bigaa, now Balagtas, and in Poblacion, Pandi. Both places were about fifteen kilometers from their house; the first ten was only possible by foot over the rice fields and meadows. The rest might have passenger jeepneys available if they were not fully loaded or if they had not missed the first trip. Otherwise, they would walk the whole distance in the morning and afternoon every day. However, they all managed to learn how to read and write, evident of those comic books and magazines. Ernesto could write love letters on his own. Frustrations of the father who never relent on encouragement by persuasion and by force or intimidation to some degree. So much frustration and nothing else he can do. It's on his genes.

GENES FROM THE MOTHER

The youngest, Anna, was the only one who had ambition and finished a degree like her mother almost did. Rain or shine, she wanted to go to school, with both parents and siblings always supportive of her if her physical condition allowed. There are no stories that can equal to her perseverance to accomplish that ambition. I would always keep silent all the time; no words can come out of my mind to the thought that anything I say may be offending when the topic becomes her. I have minimal recollection of her life when she was younger until she became my classmates. At twelve, she was in the second grade on the two-year-old school system in Malibo Bata. The chapel of San Isidro, which also served as our schoolroom in those years, became overcrowded when the second grade started. At the same year, construction of a real school building began, financed by the Nationalist Party leadership in 1967 at the height of the presidential election campaign between Ferdinand E. Marcos and Diosdado Macapagal. The architectural design and its bright green and yellow finish stood out when it was inaugurated. It was the best of all graces the community had ever received; in reality, it was the first ever grace that came to the barrio after the Japanese occupation of the Philippines.

With a beautiful landscape, large playground, spacious classroom, new chairs, desks, and blackboards that inspired everyone, pupils and parents alike, no one was happier than Anna to know that the new school with big classrooms had opened. She had yet to see it. When she began missing days in school in the second grade, I honestly thought that she just could not handle the brutal teasing and bullying of our classmates. One so demeaning was that she occupied too much space on the already crowded room for nothing, among others, causing her too many absences. Aside from being the oldest in the class, she was tall, unusually tall, that she had a special chair provided by her parents. Wetting that chair might be the other reason, but she wasn't the only one doing that. Our teachers, a team of a husband and wife who were more dedicated in making the life of their pupils miserable and scared, disciplined pupils according to them, were serious in keeping their reputation of being strict educators. They would give the pupils a hard time even in asking permission to go outside for personal purposes. Even though Ninang and Massey alternated in attending to her personal needs every time she was present in class, it was not that easy to avoid that kind of thing to happen. I always sat by her not because of the request of my godparents but because no one else wanted to.

Very shy in the beginning, she started to confide with me that she wanted to go do something personal. Her mother or sister would be sitting and waiting patiently in the porch of our house overlooking the chapel, always ready to assist her in case of emergency and the wetting of the floor under her seat would stop, at least for a while, a long while and then she just didn't show up in school again.

Until the new school building opened. I saw her one morning inside the classroom in an old wooden rocking chair fortified by a rope around it. How did she get there I didn't know yet at the time until later. I was just happy to see her again in school; she was also very elated and proud. But things never came to her favor. Aside from difficulties in talking, she just could not walk by herself anymore. Both parents and siblings were in rotation to attend to her special needs, and I was back to my role as her personal assistant inside the classroom. I was in third grade, and she was still in second grade so she was positioned in between two classes separated by an invisible wall so we could sit close together. Acquired new spirit, confidence always intact and mentally capable of the lessons after long confinement in the hospital or in bed at home, she was well aware of her physical condition but never lost hope that someday she would be better and can walk again. She didn't mind staying seated while watching other kids playing and having fun. She was like a normal child like every kid in school despite her age because of repeating the second grade many times. There were no traces of any complaint or dislikes on the way other kids were treating her. And her life moved on, for a week, months, although there were absences that I got used to. Everything became normal until the inevitable happened.

I did something bad, or I would rephrase it to I was wrongly accused of doing something bad. The principal discovered that his car had a flat tire after a morning recess. He was really mad. In his so-called educated mind and unquestionable authority of being the principal, he could allegedly pinpoint who did it, that no one else could have done it. Who would know how to release air from a car tire? That would be me according to him because my father had a similar clunker that made me the only one who had the knowledge and capability of doing such a thing. He pulled me out of the classroom for not admitting. I knew I would be punished one way or another but less if I remained silent. He made me stay out on the sun by the flagpole, both arms stretched sideways like a statue. That was only a warm-up for the real punishment I would get when I confessed to that "real bad thing" that I committed. An hour passed, longer perhaps. Until I saw all my classmates, en masse, running out of the classroom covering their noses trying to catch fresh air in unison.

"Someone must have eaten spoiled food," said one girl.

"No, I think she really did it this time," firmly corrected by another one.

Without hesitation, I went inside the vacated classroom to check on Anna. She was all red as she could barely look at me when I walked in. The foul smell got really bad as I got closer to her. I already guessed what had happened, but I didn't ask. Sweaty and smelling bad myself, I just didn't know what to do for a moment other than telling her not to worry until Massey came, equally embarrassed as her sister. The only thing we could think of was to get her out of the room and fast. No one should do it but us. And so we did. The rope around her chair was designed for carrying her in it with a long bamboo pole by two people, regularly by his father and Ernesto. Massey and I together had never tried until then that we had to actually do it on our own. She wasn't that heavy. She was maybe humongous, but she was skinny and light and we managed to bring Anna outside, carefully lowering her down in the shade of a small tree away from the school. There, Massey agreed to just bring her home upon my insistence on taking the opportunity to save myself from going back to punishment.

Walking down the road was easy, which was about five hundred yards over compacted dirt and dry path. A little rest again and think for a while of what we are about to do to get Anna home. Massey was never exposed to sunlight that long. She never carried more than the weight of her pair of shoes along the path that we were about to go through. I said I could and dared her. We had to move as Anna was becoming more uncomfortable and restless while saying nothing.

And then we went. The path was a narrow dike of hardened pile of dirt designed and constructed to contain the water of the muddy rice paddies. Both sides were filled with water from the irrigation canal that we had to cross too. Foot by foot with synchronized steps, we were able to reach that spot where we could be visible from their house and expect someone to see us, help us. Ninang did, and a few seconds more, she and Ernesto were coming for the rescue. But Ninong was nowhere in sight. After a little worried conversation about the condition of Anna came another problem. Who would be the second guy to balance the load with Ernesto? Massey might be big, but she was not used to any work and she was already exhausted. Certainly not Ninang. The men should do it. I was too small, but I kindly volunteered myself, requesting to stop, at times feeling the weight that had started to irritate my shoulder. Massey began to feel comfortable as we were getting closer to their house; so was Anna that both of them jokingly talked with each other, confident. All of us were, actually. We started laughing at each other, especially to that story where I was like a statue in the schoolyard. "I didn't do it," I said while really concentrating to every step I made. It was still too early to get out of the worries. I felt that the weight on my shoulder was not light than I had thought after a while and the dikes were getting slippery.

Twenty yards ahead was another irrigation canal. Anna, very thankful as to maybe of my effort of bearing her weight, started to jokingly touch my back with her toes. We were in a lowland, and the paddies were full of water collected from overflows from the higher paddies, making it look like a lake. I slipped my right foot on the edge of that path just after Ana touched my butt again by extending her legs, which was all it took to lose my balance. We ended up splashing on the rice paddies almost at the same time. Ninang and Massey jumped in too to the rescue. Ernesto regained himself fast enough to pull her sister from underwater, gasping for air, from the chair buried in the mud topped by two feet of water. The old rocking chair was destroyed.

That was the "past event" that became all my fault, the chain of events that led to some bruises to Anna that took a while before they healed. And since then she didn't come back to school anymore. However, we kept seeing each other. I visited her in their house often and admitted it was not always my intention to see her. Other reasons include free candy from Massey and listening to the continuation of many stories that always began to endings. Her condition became worse day by day as it was somewhat an incurable disease. Doctors, so many of them, said the same thing, as well as specialists and quacks alike from far places in Manila and the entire Luzon provinces—a hereditary disease that a person just succumbed to growing too fast until the body and mind cannot handle it anymore.

The memory and the guilt created on myself of that day in the pond of mud became funny every time we talked about it—at my expense, of course. I should have been more careful. Massey surely knew how to aggravate any incidents of my involvements, witnessed or hearsay, but in the end, she was always that responsible, caring, and devoted sister. With me too, as they had all accepted me as part of the family. Needless to say, she was also happy when I was around, someone to make fun with.

With the promise of imported candies from Massey and good fighting spiders from Ernesto, I became a frequent addition to their dining table. I seldom missed a weekend when Anna would be seated by the window so she could see me coming from afar. But what became more interesting was the relationship I had developed with my godparents, who, aside from constantly reminding me of concentrating on my lessons, had stories that were better than any schoolbook. Love stories, actions, and drama, I found them all very interesting to listen. Every chore was paused, all farm works set aside, and animals left unfed when I showed up at their place. Other than tending to the farm animals and that old horse that they usually talked with, there was not much to do anyway when planting season was over, especially in the summer. Sometimes Ninang would join us with her own biography to tell that would motivate her husband to tell accounts of their life together and that *"times of our life when we can only pray for each other."*

At the end of my fourth grade the following school year, before another Holy Week, a newly organized Parent-Teacher Association decided to celebrate the fifth year of the school's foundation. Guest speakers were invited, kids would perform their talents, and honors and special awards were to be given to those deserving pupils. I seriously practiced a lot of my dance number but missed it on the actual night of the programs. At the height of speeches of people I didn't even know, mostly politicians, I felt sleepy and found a very good spot under the stage to take a nap. I missed the rest of the program until someone woke me up; apparently a lot of people were looking for me. The program was over. I felt sorry for my godfather who was dressed up for the occasion to pin a ribbon on me up on the stage. I felt sorry for the whole Cabarles family who all came. Nonetheless, the teacher handed me that ribbon the next day and I put it in my pocket. Then I went to Ninong's place to apologize following the command of my parents for it was known that he never dressed up or felt proud that much. I disappointed a lot of people that night, most especially Anna who insisted on watching the event.

It had been more than two weekends that I hadn't visited their place anyway. For some reason, I was practicing my dance number that I didn't actually learn. When I came to the blue house, there again was Anna waiting by the window in her rocking chair, the best spot where she could see someone coming from the road. It wasn't a good sight. Something was different in her. I couldn't explain it. As Massey said, she requested to be seated when told I was coming. I couldn't think of any word to say; everyone around her was speechless too. All I could do was show her the red ribbon that was still in my pocket, crumpled but still colorful. Her eyes opened widely, sound barely came out of her throat in an attempt to sound very hard to be understood. Her arms no strength to hold anything, I pinned that ribbon to her dress as best as I could, failing to find words to say. She was very happy; she truly deserved it more than me. Everybody cried in happiness for that little sign of life and elated expression in her eyes. That afternoon and the following day, she willingly tried to eat some food. A few more days after, she passed away. Too much tears ended the hope for *one last miracle.*

"IT WAS AN ACCIDENT"

On a Sunday in June 1971, another summer vacation had just concluded. It had been a long vacation, and I was enjoying the last day of a casual morning, pushing my father's jeepney to get it started. The next day would be my first in high school. I was enrolled at St. Lawrence Academy in Balagtas, Bulacan, and arrangements had been made for me to stay with our relatives in Longosan. No one was more excited than my godparents; they said they would miss me a lot because I would have no more time to visit them.

"Be serious with your studies, no more gambling." It was the same old phrase I heard from my godfather on a regular basis. "Stay away from sin, so many pretty girls in that school. Do not look at them." The first time on that one. "Well, you are not circumcised yet, but just be careful." Teasingly, with a little sound of sarcasm, a lure to get me into longer conversation.

I couldn't help it, but it was a degradation of my manhood. "I'm circumcised already, a very long time ago," I said.

"Yeah, if only I can believe it." Jokingly again, that grin on his face and the lines on the forehead reminded me of the trap I was about to step in.

I responded with the same look. But it was too late before I could make a step to leave.

"What are you two talking about?" Ninang Inez asked. "Still very early in the morning, and you talk like we are still in our old house." She continued while holding back her jaws profusely in order to be comprehended, matched with an uncontrollable movement of her hands.

Her husband came quickly to her aid and assisted her in walking through the door until she was seated. "I just want to tell him to have dinner with us today," she said horribly like I was given a choice not to obey.

"That is a good idea, indeed," he said then turned to me. "Did you hear what she said?" he asked, repeating every word his wife uttered and more that she wanted to say. It left me no option but to stay and listen to them for a while.

The house standing about twenty feet from the road was made of bamboo and palm leaves all around except for the logs that supported the structure on four corners, which were visible as it stood about six feet from the ground. There was a large extension attached at the back side, overseeing their old blue house on the other end of the rice field toward the east. Roughly finished concrete floor on that area with furnishings also made of bamboo. Very creatively designed and constructed, many said that it eased up the hot and humid climate. I was so proud since I helped in building that house, mainly in picking up nails that Ernesto and his father dropped more than they actually hammered in. Massey, who constantly around to cook for snacks and meals, was appreciative of my effort and became comfortable as the house was finally done without any incident that I had caused.

Outside was equally relaxing; a lot of trees growing up by the fence were starting to bear fruits. Ornamental plants looked pleasing on their selected spot to grow; blooming orchids and cattleyas in the summer indicate that they are taken care of very well. The lawn, all green with bermuda grass with their natural stepping-stones that lined uniformly from the gate to the main door, was often complimented. From the street, it was truly a beautiful sight in its entirety. It was not even a year old since it was constructed.

It had been more than two years since Anna left the family. A year earlier was a happy celebration for Massey's wedding to a very nice gentleman from a well-known and respectable family. Massey strongly refused the idea of me being her ring bearer; she said I was grown up already. What I didn't understand then was she was begging for me not to be present during the occasion. With Massey starting a family of her own and the constant disappearance of Ernesto in a quest to find a mate of his own, Ninong decided to construct a house by the road due to the worsening condition of Ninang caused by complications of her suffering from Parkinson's disease.

"I'll be going now," I said, the time with them may be enough already not to be considered rude. Besides, I was coming back for dinner. I left them without looking back.

Playing heads and tail with my playmates while waiting for the others for the Sunday morning game of softball, I became too concentrated that I didn't notice my ninong standing just behind me while throwing coins in the air. I had been warned and scolded about that kind of activities. Everyone pretended it was just for fun, but it was my last money I just lost. I quickly pretended not to participate, but I went home broke and still early. I decided to do some chores by washing the dishes and doing the laundry. I would make my mother happy; later, I would easily be able to ask her for some change without hesitation. But she wasn't there.

I saw my father parking his jeep on the street and disappear. It was an old surplus US Army jeep with Willis four-cylinder engine; the body was modified to be long in order to accommodate more passengers. The roofing was a stretched black canvas reinforced with tubular steel. It was rusty and old, but still looked good and in working condition. My father had taught me how to drive a few times and was confident that I knew how already. Moreover, I had helped him done many repairs and maintenance works on that thing a lot of times. The key was there.

Looking around, I saw him coming with bundles of large burlap bags. The opportunity was very clear as the engine must be still warm. That vehicle for some reason needed to be pushed every morning to get started, and somewhat it would run perfectly afterward. It was just that the damn engine didn't want to be cranked after a night in the parking. I touched the hood, still warm, and I thought that a joy ride would be more exciting than playing ball. There was nothing to lose; with my father around, the only way it was possible was to ask permission very nicely.

"Sure, go ahead," he said. I wasn't sure if I was understood. "Bring the rice seedlings to your uncle loaded in it already and all these empty sacks as well."

I was running errands at the same time. Picking up all the burlaps, very quickly, before he changed his mind. I just threw them all inside with excitement. I climbed in, hands on the steering wheel, depressed the clutch pedal all the way down, right foot on the accelerator, and pushed the start button. One click as expected, the engine ran. I pushed the accelerator a couple of times harder than my father does it then released the clutch pedal very slowly. It didn't want to move, what could have gone wrong? The stick was in neutral. I finally got it moving after the engine stalled twice.

It would be the first time for me to be alone and unsupervised, also a little bit nervous. But I had the ability to overcome that feeling, especially when showing off. I could barely see through the bottom of that windshield while at the same time reaching the pedals. I knew the brake was in the middle of the two pedals where my feet were. I shifted to second, then third the last, testing how fast it could go, then getting ready to brake. Downhill stretching for about two hundred yards, it was gaining speed when I see a buffalo pulling a cart on the middle of the road. I slammed the brake pedal just like my father was doing it to slow down as a precaution all the way to the floor. Nothing happened; again and again, I repeatedly pumped that pedal as I was getting closer to that black monstrous animal. There was a man riding on it, equally nervous at that very moment I turned the steering wheel to the right to avoid a direct collision straight through a wire fence until for some reason it stopped with a loud crash.

"Oh boy," I said to myself. The house was very familiar; in fact, I was just there earlier that morning. Breathing profusely and heart palpitating, I could feel the beating of my chest all over my body. I didn't know how I got out that quick, but watching the structure squeaking and coming down in slow motion, I realized what I had just done. The vehicle crashed on the corner pole supporting the house and was now wedged under it, preventing the house from total collapse. The previously eye-catching lawn was like a tornado had passed through it when I dragged the wire fencing, pulling out all on its path from one corner of the property and around. But what worried me was how I was going to explain what just happened.

Everyone came out of the house as soon as they heard the crash, equally speechless while staring at the house that although settled was uneven for having a big assembly of rusted metal supporting its weight.

"What happened?" Ernesto was the first one out. Like he didn't know what he saw.

"Who's driving?" Jacinto, carrying a baby, was Massey's husband to come out next, in a hurry to investigate.

There was no one else there but me. I couldn't deny it was me on the wheel, but I remained silent. Massey and Ninong came after assisting Ninang to get seated in a safe place. Assessing the wreckage in awe, they just looked at me and the house alternately, waiting for an explanation.

"It was an accident. The brake didn't work and I lost control because of the buffalo." All that came into my mind was said at once. The owner of the animal added more on how he saw everything.

Then everyone recovered from complete shock, and finally someone asked me if I got hurt. I didn't feel any. It was Massey who showed extreme anger. Of all the people, she was the one who spent so much time and effort to make the place real nice. The rest were relieved that nobody got hurt. And before they could say anything, I already ran away to home. I was thankful nobody was hurt, but I felt real bad and disgraced.

At home, my father was still busy of the same thing when I left. "Why are you here, where is my jeep?" he asked right up.

"The brake didn't work, it's under Ninong's house," I said. I couldn't explain what just happened.

"Why did you leave it there? I need it." He didn't have any clue as to what happened yet.

"It's under Ninong's house," I repeated. "It went in there, and I don't know how to get it out," I added. Then came some people to clear what I meant to say.

For the rest of the day, I hid. My mother was screaming, and when she found me, she had keep on yelling how I almost killed my ninang. She was equally mad at my father for letting me drive that piece of junk, so mad she repeatedly hit my wooden bed with the broom handle until it broke because she could not reach me under it. For the rest of the day, I kept figuring out how I could get out of the trouble I had put myself into. Too many people were involved. The way I saw the destruction I made was immense, considering I really may have killed anyone in the house preparing food in my honor.

Before sundown, hungry and still afraid but overslept, I went out from hiding. It was so quiet, and I very slowly peeked through the door while carefully opening it to prevent it from squeaking. Other than the dog licking himself, there was nothing else moving. The clunker was parked in the garage. I went out of the house to check on how much damage I had caused on it. The bumper and fender were bent on the right side. The roof framings were crushed with a big gaping hole like it was cut intentionally. And the windshield was not there anymore; they were on the floor in pieces scattered on the seat and over the burlap bags.

Nothing to do, I began cleaning it. I looked for the broom and paused for a while, imagining how painful it could be if the handle got broken hitting me. I was almost done when something caught my eye—a thing wrapped with thick brown paper and tied up of abaca twine around it. Judging the size and weight, I guessed it was just a book. I didn't pay attention to it. It was getting dark. I placed the package together with others in the book shelf when I walked back inside the house. Hungry, looking for anything to eat, it reminded me of the roasted chicken, noodles, pork chops, and probably more that I should be eating. I had to deal with cold rice and salt, hiding from people.

Monday morning, wondering if they would still let me continue studying in high school after the mess I caused, I woke up so early. I cooked breakfast for everybody anyway, fed the animals, and did some chores again. I never did those kinds of things voluntarily unless I got yelled up or was repenting. My brother woke up next, greeting me of yesterday's incident and exaggerating on how I almost massacred the whole family of my ninong. "Almost doesn't count," I replied. The moment had come to face the worst of my transgression. My mother had calmed down overnight. Maybe she had enough breaking her broom already.

After hearing so much of the lectures, somehow I got over it. The heavily rusted piece of junk was running again after a good push that morning. My father drove it this time, dislocated frames and several dents. Just like my confidence, there was no reasonable sense that I should even say a word. Apparently, the brake was working, he said. However, I chose to keep my mouth shut hearing sounds that were definitely louder than it was creating before, especially when it began moving. He would send it for repair after dropping me off to my new school in Balagtas.

Traveling down that hill again, sunshine breaking, I saw Ninong's house amazingly standing again, looking good as it was. The fence was back on, and the juvenile trees were standing up. Except for the noticeable scars on the lawn with tire tracks still visible, everything else looked like nothing really happened. My father asked if I wanted to stop for a while for a customary tradition of blessings from my godparents, also to apologize before we proceed. I chose not to, saying they might still be sleeping, but only trying to save some face, ashamed of the trouble I had given them a day ago. I almost killed them all, I said in my mind. What could be worse than that to be forgiven easily?

St. Lawrence Academy was a big school. There were so many classrooms and a very wide grounds that served for the rendering of the National Anthem and Pledge of Allegiance every morning and Citizen's Army Training in the afternoon. In the change of environment, there was something that did not end. My uncle had his own story about the Japanese Occupation that also fascinated me, specifically about my godfather.

THE VISITORS

It was sometime in mid-September of the same year when I saw my godparents again. A respectable-looking couple from a far-flung province were looking for Dominador Cabarles, asking where they lived. Luckily for them, I was hanging out by the chapel that time. Somewhat that day became a happy reunion for all of us, especially to Ninang Inez to see me again and for Ninong with the said couple whose happiness at seeing each other were indescribable. Mystified and unconstrued, their revelations from the beginning of their friendship with Dominador Cabarles was a story I had heard many times already. However, they filled many gaps on important parts of the story that needed collaboration to be plausible. The whole event somewhat was a part of the never-ending accounts that renewed my interest at my ninong's story. Their names were Hombre and Myraflor Donono from Bicol; they said they were husband and wife that needed proof also to be believed in.

A very odd couple, the woman was in her early fifties and very pretty in her natural splendor condemning the husband seemingly in considerable jealousy, like a sister looking for help from the man they called Cab and *Kuya* (older brother). "Would you please tell him to stop seeing other women? I can't stop him from going to Polangui." She revealed her many disappointments with the man. Apparently based on what she was saying, he was truly her husband. Later, it would be known that somewhere in Polangui, a town in Albay Province, prospered nightclubs and strip joints.

It was interestingly fascinating to know the couple, every manners shown thereat they wouldn't spent substantial amount of time and fortune to find a man basically in hiding just to indulge marriage counseling. Myraflor revealed that she had given birth to nine children, one in their company, eight more left at home, all by Hombre Donono, who was proud as he blew smoke in the air feeling so much confidence that he was one handsome stud, the opposite of the character he was portrayed in the story that was narrated over and over again. Indeed, time had elapsed for more than thirty years. Myraflor disclosed that in the last ten years, they were trying to locate Cabarles in Bigaa (Balagtas). They actually had been in Pandi a couple of times; they had searched every barrio and met every barangay captain, but no one could actually know Cabarles dead or alive.

Finally, their quest had ended despite all odds and confusions. In the past decades, the town of Bigaa had changed its name to Balagtas. Pandi became a town, and Sitio Malibo became a barrio that split into two—Malibo Matanda and Malibo Bata. Malibo Bata is hidden in the vast agricultural and wooded land that lies in the boundary of Bocaue and Balagtas; not many people knows it exist except for the people who thrive in the place. The barrio is stagnant because of the deaths of its prominent residents, leaving their heirs—the Sandovals, Arandas, de Laras, and Agapitos along with many others—during the war. What was left were families and orphans who survived on their own, struggling while the population grows only reach by graces from the government come national election time. Overall, it was a community that time forgot. It wasn't until in the seventies that it began to be recognized by the town and provincial administration mainly because of the increase of registered voters. Also, because of the modernization of farming that yielded bountiful harvests, it prospered and somehow began to pursue knowledge and higher education by the younger generation.

Throughout my high school year, I concentrated more on attending classes on weekdays. I usually helped my father on his newly acquired farmland on the weekends but still found time to visit my godparents when I wasn't with friends experimenting and getting drunk with whatever brand of liquor we could buy from the store. One could say I am very accommodating and friendly to all people of different ages; I listen to their stories too over gin and bottles of beer. However, we had learned how to take it gently as we talked of our adventures, mostly stories inspired by radio dramas and action movies. Seldom would I visit my godparents that eventually stopped until Ninang died of so many complications to her deteriorated health caused by Parkinson's disease at the age of sixty-eight. From time to time, Ninong visited in Balagtas but seldom did we catch up with each other, indicative of the one or two pesos and messages passed to me by my uncle Adriano Guzman. And then I went to college in Manila. Ernesto found a very nice lady who became mutually infatuated to him. They got married shortly that made Ninong basically alone.

We hardly saw each other. He just could not help it, but he would become emotional every time at the memory of his wife Inez that always led to stories of his own, mostly a repeat of the past events he had already told quite many times. In my mind, they became dull as I had heard them a few times already. However, any which way, I thought that he was avoiding something that the absence of that part became unbelievable to the rest. I was like reading an old weekly illustrated adventure magazine and I had missed a lot of issues.

TIIE REVELATION

August 1984. I was on a month's vacation from working in the Middle East; nothing can equal to the feeling of being home again. Suffering from a severe headache caused by an all-night drinking spree with cousins and friends I didn't see for a year, I barely could not respond to my mother who had been waking me up that morning. Not as cruel as when I was young, she calmly kept waking me up to attend to my guest who was waiting patiently.

"Your ninong is here, he wants to see you," my mother said.

I really didn't want to get up. My hangover was unbearable from a bottle of Johnny Walker I had bought at the Duty-Free store followed by cases of San Miguel Beer. The mixture of those in my system was excruciating. "Can you talk to him for a while, please?" I said, begging. I just couldn't get up.

"I had been talking to him for two hours already. He has been waiting for you to get up since the dark of dawn. Here, have some hot coffee. Next time, don't drink too much, will you?" she rapidly said as became irked of my excuses. "Attend to him now. It seems important for him to see you now," she exclaimed softly.

"All right." I got up, and everything seemed to be moving everywhere I looked. But I didn't want to be disrespectful until I was finally on my feet. A sip of hot black coffee helped a little.

"I'm sorry to make you waiting for too long," I greeted while I took hold of his hands. *"Mano po."* I took hold of his hand for customary respect.

"I understand. I'm totally sorry to bother you, but I am really excited to see you again," he opened in a very soft-spoken tone that added to my guilt. His humility had never changed with time; he was holding an old sombrero with both hands, reducing my headache to see that he had aged a lot.

I offered him something to drink. "Coffee?" Even though I could see three empty cups by him.

"More blessings to you," he said, looking at me from head to foot as if he hadn't seen me in a long time, which was true. "You really look very different now. Single, an engineer, and a good job abroad—I'm so proud of you. I know from the beginning you will attain what we always wanted for you," he nicely said and so on.

"Thank you," was all I could say to his patronizing.

"I just hope you always find your way back to our place wherever you dare to go." These were meaningful advices I had taken for granted.

Maybe he meant visiting him in his place. I had been back to the barrio for several days and truly he never came up in my mind. "I'm sure I will. How are you?" I responded with similar enthusiasm to see him again.

He then described his life that was saddened by the loss of loved ones. Though he had grandchildren now, he still missed the likes of me that made me special for him particularly my childhood. There is nothing more unpleasant than the sight of a man in his category becoming emotional. The conversation was getting sad as it is so I excused myself for a second then handed him a carton of Marlboros when I came back. I knew he smoked as far as I could remember; usually he rolled his own.

"Thank you very much. I'm just happy to see you," he said while lighting up a stick I had offered from a separate pack, and we smoked together.

After a few more exchange of words, he said then apprehensively, "You know, the other reason of my seeing you is to ask a favor if you don't mind." He was grasping for words to explain what kind of favor.

"Anything for you, Ninong, I will gladly do it. Please don't hesitate to tell me." It was about time for me to do something for him, I thought.

"I got these papers from the municipal office." He pulled out an envelope from his back pocket momentarily. "They said it is about veterans' benefits, but it is in English. I certainly don't know what to do with it. I hope you can help me fill it out." He uttered soft and unassuming words that were quite different from what I knew him while unfolding the papers.

Puzzled with noticeable reluctance, I took the papers from his hands and carefully read them. The heading said, "Application for Veterans Benefits, for those who fought against the Japanese Occupation during World War II with the US Forces." It was a simple and straightforward application protocol. On the second page was required to state the name, rank or title, unit, and the commander in charge and below it to describe an event of direct involvement that would warrant or justify the application for the benefits.

I looked at him. I can write so many events he was involved in during the war from his personal accounts with me, the stories that never had a beginning, always an ending in the making. Any one of those would qualify and all those narrated to me by other people including my uncles Adriano and Ambrosio about him. All would highlight that half-a-page spot; even a hundred pages may not be enough to write all. I explained to him what the paper was all about. The first page was basically the procedure for application of the benefits and personal information. I quickly found a pen and began filling it up. I went on to the second page.

"You are being asked here of your serial numbers, what should I put here?" I asked casually, not remembering of any that was mentioned like that to me. On columns provided, I could think of a general's name, a few colonels, and many captains and lieutenants. I remembered them clearly from three decades of stories I was told. Anyone should do but must coincide to the accounts of battle or incidents that were really too many.

He continued to become quiet, looked down and back at me again, thinking very deeply for a name maybe. "Will those documents include disclosing my identity during the war and be connected at the present time?" he anxiously asked with hesitation before saying any rank or names.

"Yes, sir, definitely. I had already written your name in," I replied.

"You know, son, there were truly many battles and events I was involved with against the Japanese as a soldier. I already recollected with you about my war experiences countless of times." He stopped with some thought. "Can we omit those especially telling who am I then and now?"

He was nervous of something I had no clue to what and why he wanted to remain discreet about his direct involvement in the war. "There is something else I never told you," he added.

I was caught, mesmerized. All the mysteries of his life may depend on that information he had never revealed to me. It was maybe the beginning of a long chapter or an additional chapter that was missing substance and justification to the ending. He was telling me to fill up the form without putting the most critical information, his own name. I already did somehow.

"Why can't we?"

"Because I was . . . a deserter." It was one word that explained it all. After a long moment of silence clearing his throat, he was finally able to say it after a deep inhale and puffing smoke from a fresh stick of cigarette. "I doubt if anyone can justify my action, but do you think I still deserve to be called a soldier or a veteran and an officer after I deserted?" He stopped again, noticeably in refraining from that moment of his life that he had buried in his thoughts. But he continued like the old days. A greatest burden in his heart that inhibited his endless accounts was revealed.

"You know, son, I had attained the rank of captain and I never knew if it was official. I always say I earned being a captain and so I was told so be it. I may have earned more than that I always wanted to believe and told you, but I know I am not capable of carrying out the duties of an officer then and now. I was a soldier, all right. I took oath as a soldier, a foot soldier at least. Your ninang told me I didn't officially serve in the military because I was an undocumented soldier to begin with that justifies I didn't desert any military service.

If I deny that I was ever a soldier, then I am lying to you since you were a child. The truth is, I really cannot explain my situation. I am not educated like you. In fact, I only finished third grade in school, which I believed was not official either." A pause.

"I ask myself many times, bringing my life back on the moment I made the decision to desert my oath of duty as a soldier. Did I make the right decision? It was my heart and my thought that persevered. I can honestly tell you that was an easy decision. I have no regret what I chose. I also didn't tell you that all of my life I was scared, guilty, and ashamed of myself of being branded a coward and hiding like one." He was wiping off the tears that were about to drop.

I was speechless, unlike when I was younger when narrations involved suspenseful actions and adventures and bravery and heroism under all circumstances of many people. It was then I realized that there was also an enormous burden that was kept for a long time in his thoughts that he was trying to find an answer to and he couldn't resolve alone. I felt compelled to reach a mature status to give an answer that would give him a peace of mind or otherwise.

"Please tell me, son, you're an educated man. This is one time I ask you to be honest with me. You're an officer in the reserves, you're also a soldier. Do I deserve to claim I was a soldier while denying I was because . . . because I survived the war?" He paused again. "You fill up those papers and submit it to the authorities. I'm ready to face the consequences. It is not for the benefits I may receive but for the little time left in my life that I can walk with you and all the people on the street with honor and dignity."

Half a century was over, and WWII is only remembered by the famous "I shall return" of Douglas MacArthur. I don't understand what principle is involved therein; I say the war is over for so long and nobody is interested about the undesirable things of the past committed by an individual. Obviously not for him. If what it took was only filling up the papers that came his way by accident, then I will do it. I quickly wrote an event of a battle on the document, just one among many that I was told. It was finished in a matter of minutes. He laid down his sombrero on the floor, ran a hand through his short hair a couple of times, and checked the papers. All blanks were filled on the first page except for one, the serial number box. I explained it was not necessary; then on the next page, I showed him where to sign the paper. He couldn't do it. I signed the paper myself on his behalf. "You were a soldier and served your duty. Nobody can deny you of the privileges," I said.

He was extremely elated. He walked out of the house and went across the street to the chapel; what it was he intended to do, I didn't know. He was going to pray, I thought. He forgot his sombrero that became his namesake; I followed him inside the church and handed it to him. He said, "I won't be needing that no more, son. Thank you."

I didn't understand; it was barely used. I remembered the times he would wear a sombrero every time he set foot out of his house and thereafter. That day, he invited me to the old blue house or what's left of it. We squared over a bottle of Jameson and turned to full volume the Sony boom box I brought. He toured me around the vicinity, highlighting a few spots that somehow always reminded him of the war significantly. The stories continued; there were so many more I had yet to know.

"I will tell you these, son . . . Nothing made me at peace with Inez making an honest living while raising our children. A simple living plentiful enough to an illiterate like me. Nothing is the happiest of my life with the thought of her and the times we were together. The only regret I had was I can provide her of all the wealth and riches but chose not to because she had no desire of it either."

"What do you mean?"

"Your ninang was keeping a satchel—it belongs to me. It contained maps and documents way back to the time of war," he stated.

"What are those maps and documents?"

"I believe it can make us very rich. I heard people killing others to have those kind of documents. The one you had drawn for me was there too, if you remember. There were others," he explained. "Included in it are papers that will prove I served in the army."

"Where is that satchel now if you don't mind my curiosity?"

"We lost them. Inez was keeping them. I believed she used it to smoke the mosquitoes away. Well, I hope she did, otherwise I would have burned it myself. She had been telling me to burn it." Another cigarette was lighted up. "I really wished I burned them myself," he added.

"How about those old green metallic boxes you were keeping in your shed. What were those?"

"How did you know about those?" He was surprised but smiling. "I never told you about them."

I didn't answer. But I saw those boxes a long time ago. I never had a chance to actually see what was in them.

"Those were old rifles and Japanese money not worth anything—the termites ate them. I burned all of them including the shed after the declaration of martial law in 1972. I was afraid. When we were caught violating curfew in Barrio Batia, I told the Philippine Constabulary soldiers where I lived. Do you remember that day?"

"Yes, sir, I do." I remember that event very well; I was twelve years old. A soldier was about to shave his hair as punishment if I didn't open my mouth to say he was also a soldier. A veteran during Japanese occupation, I said. It was awkward because a part of his hair was cut already. The soldier was apologetic; he gave him a free haircut in the style of a soldier and escorted us till we were home.

"You said you're a doctor too at one time. How and when did that take place?" I became comfortable in probing his stories now that I had a chance. Somewhat the alcohol took over rapidly. I knew when he became a priest; it was a very long story too. I can relate to the events that followed our visit in the province of Cavite in September 19, 1972. I still needed more details to fill up the gap on the legend of Cab and the numbers of women who were all as pretty as my ninang in vague summary.

"I made promises to some people I met in Mindanao. You know I met a lot of women too aside from your godmother." There was bragging in his voice, something new to the usual humble tone. Maybe he had liquored up.

He started with his thumb counting; our talks could go anywhere without him looking over his shoulder anymore. "Without disrespect to the soul of my beloved wife, in Mindanao, I met a woman . . ." He began about an angel, counting his fingers with names to match. I didn't know how long I kept on listening to him that day until that night. I left and remembered about one named Rosalia Brown in Bohol when I woke up.

I didn't know what I was thinking at the time, but I made a promise that I would bring him to Mindanao one day. There was a long story about a certain Rhodora X that reminded him of the first imported liquor he had ever tasted. These were detailed memories that he kept in his thoughts at the first count of his fingers. I promised to give him company in meeting her again. He was thrilled. We would go the next night.

That night went awful, but it was enlightening. In Highway 54, also known as MacArthur Highway at the town of Marilao, existed two establishments at the time. They were Mindanao and, across, Zamboanga, both of which served beer and spirits by young women—and more for a price. It wasn't the Mindanao he wanted to see, but he went along. I said we should find Rhodora X inside. I was rebuked. He expressed anger to whoever owned the establishments for naming them Mindanao and Zamboanga.

We never spoke about that night again. We met many times more in the span of five years; the counting of fingers continued added with a name. Then it became frequent; for another two long years, I stayed in the Philippines, which coincided with the People Power Revolution against the Ferdinand Marcos regime in 1989. In 1992, I migrated to the United States.

"IT WAS ALL TRUE"

There was a new way of life that I had to start and get adapted to again. I had no job, no money after losing my last dollar at the casino in Atlantic City. The Filipino community in New Jersey were somewhat very supportive anyway. I found new friends, new drinking buddies, and established new connections. Shortly after, I found a job. And my life moved on, truly no more communication with him of any kind.

In the spring of 2005 in New Jersey, I decided to refinish our basement to convert it into a functional room. There were too many stored boxes that we had not touched anymore nor needed. The place needed to be cleared first before I could start the job.

Every piece of old clothes were folded neatly and tightly in large brown boxes. Pairs of old shoes that were just so many were carefully arranged and separated from the bad ones that could be discarded. Black plastic bags filled and were ready to be donated to make room for the newer ones.

"There is one more box, Dad." My daughter called my attention for one more look at a dark corner of the basement.

"I think they are my books, old books older than you. It can stay there." I knew exactly what could be in the box because I had placed it there a very long time ago.

"We should get rid of them too, otherwise we shall put it in the bookshelves," she suggested

"If you are willing to do that, help yourself." I could feel her persistence as she started dragging the box while complaining it was too heavy for her.

"I'll bring it upstairs and there you can do what you want with it," I said and did.

The old shipping box contained technical handbooks, references, and engineering reviewers that were sent to me about ten years ago from the Philippines upon my request to the plan of taking state license examinations. With the availability of new edition references and updated review materials in New Jersey, the box was never opened. It was still sealed with shipping stickers on it.

Giving free will to my daughter for the final demise of the box to conclude the last task of the day, I turned the television on and watched.

"Dad, this one looks even older than you. Can I open it?" She was referring to one item she was holding with curiosity.

"Yes, suit yourself."

She ripped the brown wrapper first. "It is not a book, Dad. It's an old leather satchel."

"Can I see it?" I couldn't remember any leather materials that ever belonged to me; I became interested too.

"Here it is." While handing me the thing, she waited with curiosity as I was undoing the big brass buckle that kept the overlap tightly closed. The smell of old leather was awful, but it didn't stall my curiosity.

The satchel, about fourteen inches on the sides and eighteen inches on the top and bottom, was made of thick leather with heavy stitches rotting out. The condition indicated that it had been heavily used by whoever may have owned it before it was wrapped and kept away. There was a long shoulder belt that became exposed when I turned the flap open. Stiff and heavily stained as a sign of its being stored for a long time, I went on to check the contents. One thin leather-bound pocketbook was still in good condition, notebooks of unequal sizes with loose papers inserted in every one of them adhered the pages. There was also a big brown envelope; the newest-looking one contained loose papers of different sizes and another letter was still sealed in a mail-size envelope decorated along its edges with a faded blue and red color. Still sealed with names and mailing addresses in pencil, it was impossible to read considering that the legibility of the handwriting was not good either.

Still not aware of what it could be or whom it belonged to, I picked up one loose paper, a lined regular pad paper, which I unfolded with the intent to read it. Written from a seemingly abused ribbon of a manual typewriter, it started with UNITED STATES ARMED FORCES OF THE FAR EAST, which was barely readable. My heart started pumping. I only knew of one person who would have connection with the USAFFE. I went on reading; it stated a promotion of Rodrigo Santos to the rank of captain for his gallantry and so on. It was signed by Randolph Pertig, General, USAFFE Twenty-First Artillery Division. The other paper bore the name of Dominador Cabarles. There was a pin of a captain and an old Zippo lighter among loose items with old paper bills in one envelope.

The thing belonged to my godfather; the paper should be legitimate considering how old it was dated—April 5, 1943. No doubt of any kind could arise on the authenticity of the documents. And it all came back to me while examining the rest of its contents—more old bills, maps, and short anecdotes of all sorts, with another leather pocketbook that contained the same in Japanese writings. I remembered some of his last words: *I think Inez used them as firewood, I hope she did* and *I wish I burned them myself.* More of that began to unfold in my memory and so much more including how I got hold of it. The satchel had been in my possession for about forty years. The rush in my mind of so many events that was recounted starting from when I was a kid just finally made sense.

I booked a trip to the Philippines immediately. All of it, especially the land titles and documents of property ownership, must be turned over to the rightful heirs.

It was a long trip. Though I had already decided on what my conscience dictated, I realized that there were many things to reconsider. First thing I did when I arrived in Manila was visit my godfather's grave alongside with his beloved wife in Pandi, Bulacan. The memory of times they shared to me were filled with sorrow and sufferings, yet their devotion to each other's triumph for the time they were given was a success. I uttered a little prayer; wherever they were, I was sure they were reunited again and were happy together.

From Poblacion, I went on to visit *Ate* Massey. I gave her all the documents that pertained to property ownership of her late parents. I was relieved to find out that they were all retitled and reconstituted legally in proper order, although maybe not all. I advised her to consult a surveyor. She was not interested about the rest though I spent time to explain all about the other papers.

"What am I going to do with it?" she said. Above all, she was just happy I had spent time to see her, reminiscing how close I had been with her parents. "They always loved you like the youngest son. I didn't know how they got into your possession, but I believe it's just rightful for you to have them," she stated.

I could keep them; it was all right, but I didn't know what to do with them either. The most important was that I had closed the immediate burden that I acceded in knowing that the contents of that old satchel included land titles.

A burden it was, and a burden that would be in my mind from then on. I was told of a story, a story that was narrated in three decades and buried in memory for another two. I came upon the fifth to discover the satchel and prove that I was told a real story; it was just too hard to ignore them all. Well, it really was; I always wondered why I kept dreaming of my godfather for so many years like I was constantly reminded of our times together even he passed away.

In another trip back to the Philippines a year later by myself, I couldn't help it but spent some time to be adventurous. The map that I had drawn when I was five years old was refreshed in my mind. It didn't interest me then, but it excited me upon discovery of the satchel. After a careful study of Philippine geography aided by a map drawn in crayons, I went to the place where it could possibly be. There it was, a spring. Still flowing in many directions covered with flora and fauna so perfectly arranged and blooming in the hot summer. It was now part of a modern resort where many people would enjoy the amenities it offered—swimming pools, wet slides, picnic areas, hotels, and restaurants that served exotic and delicious food with the best-looking view of hills and mountains. What could I say to the long lines of children and adults sliding that steep wet slides passing the top of the spring down to a crystal-clear pool? Should I say that there were people buried under it? Should I tell the owner that there was a possibility that something of immense value was buried in his property? The real and most possible scenario was only discovered during the development and construction of the resort. It was the right location, all right, that was what I wanted to believe. "What was I thinking to waste my time like this?" I said to myself. But I would not dare to come slide and swim on that pool nor go back to that place.

Shortly after, I flew back to New Jersey. Although I understood it would be a difficult feat, somehow it lessened my burden. I started writing. I finally understood that I was given a task that took unimaginable preparations. Dominador Cabarles essentially financed my education, and so much more I had learned from his principles. From the mind of an intellectually inadequate soldier lay the grandest feat and determination to find the answer to a burden that troubled most of his life. Was he a deserter?

CHAPTER 1

"TILL DEATH DO US PART," "SO HELP ME GOD"

There was a man I used to see—a rifle on his shoulder and a little girl walking with him. One day I'll be that man—a rifle on hand, shooting every moving thing I see. Shoot the birds that fly above beyond the reach of my sling.

THE WEDDING

8:00 AM
Saturday, December 6, 1941
Bigaa, Bulacan

"In sickness and in health, for richer and for poorer, till death do us part. I, Dominador Cabarles, accept Inez Sandoval to be my wife in the name of God." It was the happiest moment of his life saying those words. There was nothing more he could possibly wish for. Holding both of her hands while whispering words of promises to the bride was simply beautiful; she was equally full of joy. Kisses so tender he bestowed upon heavenly creation that came down for him is the fulfillment of his dreams.

A simple wedding ceremony, there was no lush celebration thereafter. In fact, only a few people attended the parents of the bride and groom, a few friends, and the accidental devotees who happened to be in the church for morning prayers who witnessed the occasion. When the priest motioned that they were husband and wife, they took a moment holding each hands and said a few more words with each other that only the two of them could hear. Afterward, they slowly walked down from the altar and welcomed the greetings of everyone, but not for too long. They continued walking through the aisle of the San Lorenzo Church directly to the waiting *carretela* (horse-drawn transport) just outside the door.

"Inez, careful . . .," hinted the husband to the wife as he assisted her in climbing the *carretela*. He could touch her now, hold her hands in public without fear of her parents getting mad anymore. He was naturally shy but resolute, shadowed only by his overwhelming affection for the very pretty lady who was now his wife. Their destination should be to a place they would share and begin their union as husband and wife with the blessing of God. It wasn't really; there was another important thing to do before the day ended.

"What time is the bus leaving?" Domeng asked as the horse slowly walked toward Highway 54.

"Usually nine o'clock. Don't worry, the bus station is not too far," Inez responded, understanding what was bothering the mind of the husband but slightly offended. Though the next events that were to happen that day was planned and agreed upon, she could not avoid worrying. If only she could convince Domeng to just return to Pandi and forget the trip, but she chose not to. Domeng's decision was certain; he needed to go to Manila, and she understood. He was now her husband; the love she bequeathed to him was a love that should not interfere with what would make him happy. She devoted many thoughts of the only man whom she would spend forever with in happiness, love, and faith; she knew of nothing else these man could offer but the same love, and she was also happy. A very simple gentleman, handsome and caring, she would stand by him in any way it would do best for him.

Still holding the soft hands of the wife, Domeng reiterated to the owner of the horse to whip the damn animal to at least walk faster if it didn't want to trot. For so many years that she adored Inez, the fulfillment of what the day brought to him was already tremendous. The pleasure of being with her at the moment could only turn for the best as the day transpired. Just a joy ride to Manila where he had never been to all his life, there could be no better feeling to do just that while drowning in the thought of a dream that came true. He just wanted to get it over with and come back home. Meanwhile, he had not the slightest idea what he was up to other than what he was told; his confidence depended mainly with Inez on that trip. It was simple—get some business done in the city then go back to the barrio at the welcome of relatives and friends who had prepared a feast in celebration of their wedding.

The trip to Manila could not be postponed. The groom, Dominador Cabarles, had to be there at a specific time. It was compelling and planned ahead; it was the wedding that was inserted. It was a Friday, and offices were expected to close early. He checked again that piece of paper in his breast pocket, which complicated what had to be done in rapid succession—the rushed wedding and now to their destination. It didn't bother Domeng what he was up to. He wanted to catch up on the last chance, be on time as he was told, and then can come back in the afternoon in the barrio. He wanted to hurry for the reason that he was thinking of several things playing in his mind already—well, for their first night as husband and wife.

"Please try not to hurry!" Inez said again.

"I can't help it. I'm sorry. I just wanted to go back home immediately," he said with an unusual smile on his face, disclosing his thoughts as he looked at the woman. He wanted to kiss her, but there were too many people on the street. Naturally shy that he may have overcome already with Inez but such gesture would mean disrespect to the lady of his life, He didn't want to do that. After all, they were husband and wife already. There was plenty of time ahead, all theirs together.

THE OATH TAKING

11:10 AM, Manila

Standing in front of the building at No. 1 Victoria Street, they were not sure if it was the right place, nor would they be attended to at that hour. The paper said to report at Fort McKinley in Rizal. Inez's father, who was presumed to know more than anybody else, had recommended to report at the USAFFE headquarters in

Manila instead. Inez basically lived in the city, and having been in Intramuros a couple of times, she was hoping that a few friends could redirect Domeng without punitive consequences of reporting late as the paper required. This time, she hesitated to enter the building, but a look on the anxious husband made her just say a little prayer and hold his hand as she led him through that big door. Domeng had no clue whatsoever what he was up to. As the urgency of the matter was becoming frantic, a man barely clothed on the sidewalk approached them in barely understood dialect that matched his skinny appearance of very dark skin and curly hair. He was obviously begging. The newlyweds, still dressed in matching all whites, could only extend natural kindness; they had food to spare, and Inez gave them all. To get inside the building before the offices close was the urgent concern they should not miss.

Inside, they were greeted by the yelling and screaming of an American officer to an elderly man standing at attention in front of him. Panic surged immediately to the farm boy who just realized he would be dealing with Americans. Nervous as he was already, he grabbed his wife by the arms so they could leave the building, but not fast enough when another man in khakis called their attention to the nature of their business in the office. Domeng handed him the paper hesitantly; the English-speaking man looked at it and passed it to the screaming Yankee who paused from his seemingly enjoyable moment of tormenting a Filipino that was doing the shining of the floor.

"What is this?" he said disgustedly, looking at the man taller than him still in all-white wedding clothes and shiny shoes standing with the most beautiful Filipina he had ever seen. There were two other Filipina ladies who were equally gorgeous that attracted his attention a while ago. He toned down his voice that was deliberately characterized to military conduct of a gentleman or perhaps he realized he must change strategy to impress the ladies and return to his barracks with at least one of them for the weekend. "You're late, soldier. You're supposed to report at Fort McKinley at eight hundred hours. Wednesday." Nice enough but still showing authority while shifting his eyes on Inez again.

There was another Filipino approaching, but this one came from inside an office across the lobby. "Sergeant Santos!" He was calling the soldier who was most likely on the way out.

"Yes, sir," politely complied the soldier he called a sergeant in fitted all khakis. He looked to have been acquainted with the screaming American already. After a gallant salute to the officer who displayed several stripes and colors in his khakis, he said in English, "What do you want me to do with them, sir?" He was looking at the man in white at the very moment joined by the little one who followed the newlywed. Very odd pair—he was seeing a tall, muscular-built man in all-white clothes and an almost qualified midget who was barefooted and sweaty while almost naked, standing side by side straight and chest out, both unaware of what was going on.

"Help me with him, he will be your man." He was only referring to the tall guy. Calm but commanding, he continued talking some more in English to the sergeant. They concurred with each other after a long talk.

In the lobby of the building where they were gathering was displayed the national flag of the United States of America. Santos explained to the man what he was about to do. Inez was motionless but understood the events that would follow; she translated every word she heard to Domeng in the presence of the small guy.

Standing in front of the US flag, Sergeant Rodrigo Santos, Dominador Cabarles, and the unknown man recited the Pledge of Legion repeated by an American lieutenant. The unknown man just stepped forward and joined them. He may or may not have known what was going on, for he seemed to be mumbling words too. People that had started to gather in the lobby paused upon hearing the recital of the oath. All on the way from a half day's work that day, ready to go home or whatever they planned to do that weekend, had captivated themselves of the ceremony. It wasn't normally done in the lobby, actually never until now. And then there was the Army Oath. The same officer led:

> I, Dominador Cabarles, do solemnly swear that I will support and defend the Constitution of the United States of America against all enemies, foreign and domestic. That I will bear true faith and allegiance to the same; that I will well and faithfully discharge the duties of the office on which I'm about to enter. So help me God.

And they were all congratulated immediately by the same officer. To the third man, he scratched his head. "Who are you?"

"*Don't no now eh,*" he replied. "*No, no eh,*" was all he could say.

"Sergeant Santos, he is your man too." The MSgt gave up; he could not understand the man who could only repeat what he said. "His name is . . . Don't Nonow," he added, still misconstrued, but he went along. It wasn't his first time to handle that kind of situation, being in the Philippines for a long time. In fact, he could speak Tagalog, greeting all the beautiful ladies present at the time. The Tagalog-speaking sergeant attended to the two of them, introducing the soldier.

Inez approached the ecstatic young husband, and after a sweet kiss, she uttered, "Now you are a soldier, congratulations." She was smiling while the jubilant inadvertent spectator started to clear the space. "Don't nonow eh" stayed by Domeng, captivated at seeing too many white people in one occasion.

The No. 1 Victoria Street building was the headquarters of the USAFFE, where the top brasses of the United States Armed Forces in the Asia Pacific Region held offices. No enlisted or drafted Filipinos had ever taken an oath in that building, but they did entertain walk-in recruits. It was usually done in the parade grounds in battalion or company at the army headquarters at Fort McKinley in Taguig, Rizal. The desk officer took the opportunity of having the new guys officiated before they could change their mind over the weekend.

He had taken care of two of them in the last minute; one who was commissioned as a sergeant was accompanied by two gorgeous girls. Another was accompanied by his wife; surely the army would lose both if they waited until Monday. About the third man, he didn't care. He was sure he made the right decision. On the other hand, he was uncertain of how to spend weekend liberty, but then he got an idea when Santos came in. Showing off to impress a couple of alluring Filipinas was very hard to pass. He took care of the man personally earlier from whom he found out his imaginations could be arranged. He should go out of the building with at least one of them. However, the entrance of Inez and the well-dressed man had changed his mode to a gentleman in uniform. As his show concluded, he didn't know what to do with the new soldiers, but he wanted to ensure they could not renege their oath as soon as they walked out of the door. Another officer passing through was a second lieutenant in complete officers' uniform. They knew each other pretty well.

"Lieutenant!" he called the attention of the officer. "Are you going back to Bataan today?" he asked after greeting each other.

"Yes indeed. I'm just waiting for my CO," replied the lieutenant whose attention was also taken by the equally alluring ladies more than the new recruits who were getting acquainted with each other.

"I have three good guys for you, one of them is a sergeant. Would you take care of them?" he was casually explaining his worries about them.

"Sure, I will." He glanced toward the cluster of young men and women. "They might take care of us too," he added at a glance primarily on the two ladies with deep red lipsticks similarly delighted with the coming of the Americans in uniforms.

The lieutenant approached the Filipino soldiers. Santos knew the drill; he alerted the other to salute also.

"Do you know how to shoot guns?" he asked the one in all whites. He wasn't understood. But it was all right; Inez filled in to translate.

THE POINT OF NO RETURN

0730 Hours
December 7, 1941

Enjoying the cold breeze of the foggy morning as they reminisced the good times of Friday night along Ermita's bars and joints were three officers of the Fifty-Seventh Scouts of Sixty-First Division, led by a captain who just got a promotion and new mission order. Smelling of cheap girly perfumes overwhelmed by the strong scent of alcohol, each one tried to top the satisfaction of the other from all-night adventures on the pleasure strips of Manila. Talk of a master plan to do it again sometime resulted to laughs that drowned the noise of the boat engine as it cruised Manila Bay.

Sergeant Rodrigo Santos, who got most of the commendation from the officers on his first duty as a soldier, was equally smelling like vomit. He was known as Rod; Domeng would call him sir. According to him, he owned a trading business with offices in Ermita. About twenty-three years old and single, he knew every strip joint in Manila where entertainment and pleasures were cheap. He bragged that the place was his territory. Truly, he was well known in that area. Last night was just like every night for him; as he said it to the Americans, the company of officers somewhat increased his reputation among patrons of his businesses. He was truly an influential man that night. He just hoped none of the Americans contracted any disease.

Originally from the Visayas region, he finished his BS in commerce in Manila. A reservist in the Philippine army, the call for duty became difficult for him to make a decision with the kind of life he was enjoying. A college graduate and a second lieutenant, he was demoted to sergeant for not reporting on duty at the time he was called up. He worsened his credibility by not having any actual training as a soldier. In fact, he only attended a couple of Saturdays in the Reserve Officers' Training Corps in college. How to stand straight in drill formation and salute a ranking officer were all that he knew as a soldier. He thought that bribing his drill commander at the beginning of first training attempt would do and a lot easier to acquire his bar. Nevertheless, he didn't extend enough enthusiasm to be a soldier as the calling of somewhat equally rich friends was definitely more stimulating. However, his exceptional skills in diplomacy and concession was an advantage; he was reinstated to lieutenant over a bottle of whiskey before the night was over. He made the American officers happy in the game he knew best; it led him to become an important ally who knew Manila very well. He bragged that he actually owned businesses in Ermita that included strip joints and beer houses.

As he droopily moved his eyes around the boat that would ferry them to Bataan, he just could not impute himself but concede; he was also nervous as hell that could not be erased by the memory of previous night's escapades. Well, certainly nothing more satisfying for him than the streets of Manila. That was where he spent most of his life. On a boat again, this time he was not going back home in Iloilo nor on another pleasure journey to a private island. He was on a trip to complete his officers' training somewhere in Bataan to be reinstated as a lieutenant officially. Unlike Cabarles who should have reported for duty three days ago or earlier is shooting in the air what awaits him. Santos's pretext was sealed in association with the officers.

He was wealthy, handsome, and single. Reporting for duty was given a lot of thought and preparations with serious consideration while understanding information on the ongoing war in Europe and the Japanese military expansion in the Pacific. Japanese occupation of the Philippine islands was imminent, and he knew it. Demoted a rank for turning AWOL several times, he had learned the consequences of reneging his oath the hard way added by the humiliating effect that he was just another cowardly loudmouthed gangster in the streets of Manila. In fact, only the influence of his connections made him reinstated as a soldier. So much to say he was serious this time.

Cabarles did not say a word while he sat staring at the dark silhouette of Manila from the western bay. He resigned looking back when he can no longer see people on the dock. He sat flat on the deck, hugging both legs that were bended, which made his knees touch his chin like it was feeling too cold. On his mind was a long six months in combat training until he could be reunited again with a woman he cherished. He could not believe what had just transpired. All he wished for and dreamed had come through, all he desired was at hand by all accounts. What was on his mind to disregard the realization of his dream in its entirety to embrace uncertainties? Should he disregard the call of duty that emerged in a very untimely date? He was not after honor nor glory; he just didn't like the consequences of disregarding the call of duty. He could not live the rest of his life being penalized for cowardice.

"Are you all right, Cabarles?" Santos said in Tagalog, with an ironic smile knowing what else must have happened the previous night—an attempt that he might tell details to break the monotonous morning until they disembark on land again. "Hey, Cab," he repeated. The man was in deep thought; apparently his mind was left on land. He wasn't noticed; he wanted somebody to talk with about anything to be relieved of apprehensions. Santos could only sympathize with the man who was noticeably unsettled to face their destination. So much to say he was similarly afraid.

Domeng was truly in an intoxicated state; his intelligence could not comprehend it just yet, and never would he. Any which way he does, no logical answer could he grasp in mind. His limited rationalization dictated that his wish was granted with conditions and he was taking it with the hope of endless happiness in the end.

Only the ocean could decide his fate at the moment, and he was allowing it. He had not much of a choice to back out anymore from that one step he made from the dock to the boat.

"Can you bring me back to the marina?" Cabarles requested to Santos.

"I think that's not possible anymore," Santos replied. "We are in the middle of Manila Bay already."

The sound of diesel engine and the occasional splash of seawater brought Cabarles back into pretending he was only going on a fishing trip; he didn't say goodbye to Inez. Her tears broke his heart as the time they were supposed to share with each other very intimately suddenly became no more. He had not foreseen such a situation, and his promises to her that had to find satisfaction and fulfillment yet had become suddenly unclear. Sad to say, it was summarily broken at the first sunrise after their wedding.

On the other hand, it was a continuation of the feeling of indescribable joy since he had already won her heart. It was a night when he must have all of her imagining he could have done more; she was his wife anyway. Nonetheless, he was thankful to the Filipino sergeant who spoke with the Americans for the guest room he and Inez slept together in at the Manila Yacht Club while the Americans drifted in and out of the strips of Ermita Avenue.

He finally responded to Santos, smiling, lips stretched as much as possible but shaking his head. The thoughts and emotions he and Inez had bequeathed to each other when he left her on the marina alone and crying was unconceivable. None of them had expected that the calling of being a soldier would be constrained right away. They had only been married yesterday, and all the assurances and promises he made did not appease his expectation that they would be able to go back in Bulacan. This was not only what he vowed to God with her, but he also made an oath as a soldier on the same day. "So help me God," he said again and continued praying quietly.

The little man who always responded "Dontnonow eh (I don't know)" whatever he was asked of by the Americans became Hombre Donono. It was Inez who started calling him Hombre (a boy). He was given a new name as no one could actually pronounce his name the way he said it. He would be known also as the Little Don. He said he was from Tayabas (now Quezon) and had walked all the way to

Manila for days to become what fate had brought him into as long as there was food. He liked Cabarles a lot, maybe because of the white shirt and pants. He liked staring at the Americans too. He was allowed to come on the boat because he could stand guard over it all night. For reasons he tried to explain but which none understood, he followed Inez and Domeng wherever they would go; somehow Domeng was the only one who could communicate with him. He spent the night supposedly with mosquitoes on the dock while guarding the *Seven Seas* to make himself useful—*Seven Seas* was the name of the boat as it was painted on the outer sides—relieving another American soldier for the night. However, there was something that made his night comparably exultant possibly because of the food the boat had to offer. He was wearing nothing but a piece of cloth just enough to cover his "dingdong," which was kept in place by a string around his waist. He also displayed an unusual necklace and scars around both of his upper arms.

The Americans, all from the Sixty-First Infantry Brigade, had found a good use for the Filipinos, especially for Sergeant Santos. He communicated well in English and spoke Tagalog, and he was fluent in the southern dialects. Not Donono's dialect yet. Most important, his knowledge of the best night spots and entertainment in the city was what they liked the most. They should do it again. Donono was very good in following orders, especially in cleaning the boat and moving stuff. He was happy guarding the boat and equipment; his loyalty was established as soon as he tasted an apple. Still, they had to see what the neat-looking guy had to offer. He seemed shy, quiet, and perplexing. Who wouldn't be after leaving his bride alone in tears?

ACCIDENTAL SOLDIERS

MSgt. Lance Casey was the navigator. He was blond and tan, shirtless most of the time. He had been in the Philippines for years with the established reputation as an instructor and combat trainer for the Philippine army. He thought he had seen it all from the many Filipinos he had trained over many tours. Today, he had three new recruits that would be added to the bunch of bare feet he already had. One was definitely smart and dependable in many ways but aware that he might run AWOL again. He had no problem with him. The other was a tall, muscular, and above-average Filipino; he could be a great soldier if he could only talk. He was not counting the small guy who was giving him the creeps; Dononoeh always stared at him sitting down like he was taking a dump, both arms over his knees while busy wiping the deck.

"Throw him an apple, you'll get his attention," the lieutenant suggested.

Well, he did. To his amazement, he caught it like it was nothing before the fruit went overboard. "Hey, LT, look at this," he repeated, this time closer to the edge of the boat and it was caught and another one farther, only to go overboard. Donono's instincts showed that he would jump in the water to retrieve the apple if not for the quick reflexes of another man who had grabbed him by the leg while airborne and pulled him back to the boat. The mute man finally talked, explaining to the little man that he could die. He put him back to where he was, and they both munched on the red fruit he had collected.

"That was incredible reflex," Casey murmured in amazement.

"Yes indeed," the LT agreed.

"If you want to give him apple, make sure it doesn't drop on the water while the boat is moving," Rod Santos yelled who was awakened from snoozing. He didn't like what he saw.

"Yes, Sarge," Casey complied. He knew Donono would be most likely eaten by sharks even before they could turn the boat to retrieve him. He apologized for his action with a box of apple handed to them this time.

1100 Hours
Subic, Zambales

The trip took longer as they passed the northern points of Bataan Peninsula and around to Subic Bay. At the port, the officers embarked immediately and disappeared on a jeep ride. Master Sergeant Casey L. W., who was also the boat captain, had to stay to make sure the boat didn't disappear while refueling. Santos, Donono, and Cabarles should have been dropped off at a training camp in Mariveles at the same time they were going to pick up combat-trained units of elite soldiers for an unknown mission. Constrained by time again, the Americans chose to sail straight to Subic Naval Base at the order of the CO for another meeting in Fort Stotsenberg. They would get rid of the Filipinos on their way back later.

Apologetic for his previous action that almost killed Little Don, Casey redeemed himself by using his connections at the navy yard. Cabarles and Santos were given pairs of combat uniform, boots, and caps. Enfields were also handed the same. By afternoon, the new recruits were displaying new haircuts, new pairs of boots, and were looking good in their uniforms, complete with canteens belted around their waists, which was the most important. No one was more thrilled than Donono who was the most proud in carrying his pair of boots around the neck instead of wearing it. Everything he was handed were all oversized. Only the candies sufficed his needs.

The trio were given orders to stay on the boat until 1830 hours when they were ready to sail back on the ocean again. Casey would frolic around the base, taking advantage of the base supply. Meanwhile, the Filipinos were delighted with the instant acquaintance of civilian employees in the shipyard who seldom saw local soldiers. Having Sergeant Santos in charge, his sweet talking became very beneficial. Food packages, apples, oranges, and candy bars were handed to them by their new friends. Whether stolen or rejects at the officers' mess hall of Subic Naval Base, there was nothing bad or good; they would take them all as they came. The word that Filipino soldiers were on a mission trip spread rapidly. Sergeant Santos was a truly convincing and effective talker. Food supplies by the boxes arrived more than they needed with a pledge of more if they can tell what else they wanted. When he wanted liquors, they came. Soap bars, more chocolate candies, ham and canned foods, cigarettes—they all came with another plan in mind. He could sell them back in Manila.

For about six hours, they waited. Sergeant Casey came back on a US Navy truck loaded with three drums of diesel fuel and boxes of more food and supplies. It didn't take too long to load them on the boat.

The *Seven Seas* was ready to sail again. Casey could only be understood by Santos. There was a change of plans, he relayed. The captain and the lieutenant decided to stay overnight, but he would wait for them somewhere else until the next day.

At 2030 hours, the boat slowly docked into a hidden cove designed for a small fishing vessel. Vegetation covered the place, and through the darkness, Casey gave orders, speaking in English that none understood by Cab and Donono. They relied on Santos who translated to them in Tagalog. The cove made by nature seemed just to fit the bulk of the *Seven Seas*, which was a good hiding place for the boat as it was used by some soldiers on unofficial night trips as they pleased since it was rehabilitated from a hulk of junk by the marines in Corregidor. How the army got hold of it was unknown.

The journey back to Manila that night was canceled; the bases were on high alert. Japanese reconnaissance planes were spotted a few days ago. The higher command suspended all leaves. Without liberty permission, catching the happy hours that night did not appeal to anyone. "Some other day, if there's another," Casey said.

"Everyone come with me," Casey ordered the soldiers with a hand motion. They still had to be delivered in Mariveles, but they had to wait for the commanding officer who was tied up on a confidential meeting somewhere, he explained. For the meantime, they would be spending the night in a nearby gun battery. From the shore, they climbed up the narrow path of a limestone hill to a small clearing. It was more than an hour's walk at Cab's estimate through bushes and trees until they reached small clearing. It was dark, but the view of Clark Air Base on the north lit with electric pole lights was beautiful from their position. Less than a mile from the end of the runways were planes and hangars that were visible on the far end. He looked around. There was a small concrete building on his left, close to a structure with no walls, wooden benches, and a table in it. There were heavy nets on the roof and covering another spot. Most soldiers were congregating on a lightbulb powered by a small generator, listening to radio broadcasts.

There was a bulk of steel on the shadow about twenty feet away and two separate bunk holes with bags of dirt in four layers around it at the edge of the hill as it gently sloped down overlooking the air base. Antiaircraft weapon and .50 caliber machine guns decorated the clearing manned by the marines.

With nothing to do, they picked a spot close to one of the holes under a leafy tree and sat down on the grass. Donono requested Cab to continue the crash course about his rifle. The guns were old. Cab commented that his Springfield at home looked a lot better. Santos was similarly enthusiastic but not for long as he fell asleep. He sure knew how to fire a gun. Shortly after, they were joined by Casey who likewise took the opportunity to slumber after watching the fresh soldiers practicing how to get ready to shoot. He offered some pointers but to no avail; he left them shaking his head. Not a word he said was understood. However, he was thrilled upon seeing that the bigger guy seemed to know about the weapon better than anyone he had trained. He closed his eyes on the same grassy depression on the ground close by.

December 8, at 0530 hours in the morning, Cabarles was awakened from his dream, embarrassed to find out that it was the little guy he was hugging and fondling. Disgusted at what he might have just done, he smacked the poor guy in the face hard enough for him to be abruptly awakened, wondering what just hit him. Donono saw Cabarles drinking water from his tin as his face looked at the first light of the morning through fog that enveloped the hill.

"What's that for?" He was stroking the irritated part of his face; surely it was Cab who did it to him.

"Good you are awake." He ignored what else Donono had to say; certainly he wasn't happy.

Donono was confused; the man who had been so nice to him had suddenly become hostile. He did something bad, he thought. The white part of his wide eyes were so pronounced that they were the only visible part of his body. So dark was he in his entirety that he could blend in with the background unseen.

"Let's see how we can make coffee here."

Cab continued pretending that nothing had happened beyond the normal. At the same place where the marines were busy fortifying their cover, they met two locals who were already brewing coffee. Chatting followed and not too long they were all having hot coffee while getting acquainted with each other. One introduced himself as Rufino San Pedro. The other one wanted to be called Cabo, as he was close to being promoted to the rank of corporal for being there the longest, he said. The new recruits were attentively listening; they were all ears in believing every word of the two fellows. They said they were from the nearby province of Pangasinan and had been with the marines for three months.

San Pedro narrated his own experience, which was not much but run errands for the Joes. He was in charge of the meals, mainly boiling water every morning that includes fetching freshwater supplies for everybody. He said he was also a very good cook, which made the Americans like him. Their long stories concluded, however admitting that they were only utility boys in the gun battery. The talking stopped when a marine jeep drove in through the rough road from Clark beeping repeatedly and waking up everyone else to their feet. The Japanese had attacked Pearl Harbor three hours ago, ordering the soldiers in full battle position, and he disappeared again, hurriedly leaving six more marines with advice to keep their radio on. "Bring it on, Sarge. We're ready," one of them said.

Eight hundred hours. No one was sure, but this should be it. The marines certainly knew what to do in high alert. Cab and Donono didn't; they kept having coffee and eating what San Pedro and Cabo offered them. They had no clue what it meant when one marine yelled, "Take cover, men!" Soldiers were scuffling around wearing their battle helmets. San Pedro would translate it for them: "*The Japanese are coming. Hide!*" he said. And they hid. Cab saw Santos waving for them in the fortified hole where Casey was also calling their attention. Both preferred to hide with Santos.

"What are you doing there?" Santos asked.

"Having coffee," the big guy replied.

"Don't you know it's war already?" he said, scratching his head.

"Yeah, that is why we are hiding already," Cab replied.

"Lock and load, enemy is coming any minute," Casey commanded. All he could do was shake his head to a conversation he could not understand.

"What did he say?" Cab asked.

Santos briefed them of what high alert meant, saying they could not leave the place until their commander showed up. Cab subsequently understood also what "lock and load" meant. And he did to the watchful eyes of Sergeant Casey. He was impressed how expertly he dealt with the Enfield.

Donono had a problem; he wasn't given a gun, and he liked one obviously. He was eyeing the .50 caliber. He moved closer to it and stared at the gun. "You know how to fire this baby?" a marine on the gun asked, noticing how Donono was stupefied by its size. He didn't answer.

They all immediately got a crash course on the machine gun on the spot from Casey. Donono was thrilled at the size of the gun and its rounds. He certainly was too small who looked smaller when he got his hand on it. Some of the marines were indeed amused for a while. He was obviously having trouble with a standard rifle; he would definitely be thrown away once he let fire that gun. Just his appearance alone wearing oversized uniform was already laughable.

"Who will be our enemy?" Cabarles innocently asked, breaking the silence, having no indication of hostilities just yet.

"Should be the Japanese," the equally battle virgin Santos replied.

"Where are they?" Donono giggled, making an act with the .50 mm.

"They are coming, I hope not," the sergeant answered silently, not sure of what the situation was at the moment, peeking over the sandbags. He heard vehicle coming.

The vehicle stopped at about ten yards. The lieutenant, confirming the Japanese attack was imminent, gave orders to carry on battle position. Ordnances had been laid out. Machine guns were ready to fire, so were the three ins. antiaircraft positioned about thirty-five yards behind them manned by the marines. The Americans were talking; the army would take over one of the foxholes. In fact, they already did. They saw planes leave the Clark Field and come back; nothing serious just yet. The tension of the morning hours decreased as everyone finished their chow. Pedro and the Cabo surely knew how to take care of the marines. The LT, Stevens R. S. as it read on the brass nameplate pinned just above the right pocket of his khaki shirt, left again after talking to Casey for a while. The marines could not help it but suspected that something was cooking with the armies squatting in their holes.

Speaking of Santos and Cabarles, they were on the brink of battle on their thirty-sixth hour as soldiers. They were sitting silently in their foxholes, aware of the impending battle but not knowing how it will happen. "The Japanese will attack from the air," Santos spoke. Cabarles understood finally; he had never fired a rifle to an airplane, but it would sure be a big target. Nobody knew from what direction the enemy were coming, but they were ready.

At past noon, they saw planes coming from the east overlooking Pampanga, American fighter planes from Nichols Air Base in Paranaque flying low through slightly cloudy sky. Casey boasted that they were the welcome party for the incoming enemy. Every soldier shouted in jubilance watching them disappear from their sight to the cloudy sky.

GREATEST FEAR

0800 Hours
Manila

The desk officer at the lobby of USAFFE headquarters was busy and tense every second; weekend was too short. Inez went back to the place trying to send a package or at least get an instruction on how it can reach to her husband presumably in Corregidor or Bataan. It was nothing serious, just personal items like a letter and prayer booklet. It was distinctively not a regular morning; she had waited enough already and had waited by the table for the guy to finish his conversation on the phone. She noticed the papers that were on the very top of his garbage container; they looked very familiar as to how they were folded and stained with sweat, but she wasn't sure. Actually, the officer did not appreciate whoever left those papers on his desk, and the absence of the individuals named on it made him just throw them away without hesitation as he tidied up his office. She approached him again.

"Miss! I advise you to hold on to that until later," he told Inez even before she could state her purpose. "The war has broken off."

Inez was shocked, and blood rushed to her brain. She was informed that the Japanese attack was imminent and there was no way she could be entertained at the moment even. She and a friend went directly to Quiapo Church to find relief for the greatest fear in which they had succumbed themselves. They understood what was happening. In her heart and thoughts, it was all about her husband that she was praying for. Two hours later, as they walked back to the dormitory at Espana Avenue, the rumbling sound of passing airplanes in formation added more terror to her already weakening lucidness. The rapid succession of events from becoming one and followed by being apart the next day was really not a pleasant thought for what else was coming. She just didn't know what to do. She wanted to go back to Bulacan, but the empty streets would make her think otherwise. No public transportation of any kind was visible; in fact, she had to walk from Espana to Intramuros that morning only to be confirmed of what she had heard from the radio. The resulting frenzy among the people about the news had added confusion to her nervous disposition. Should she remain in Manila and try a few more days to establish a means of communication to her husband? She didn't have much of a choice, knowing that the same man who gave her most of the reason to come back to in the *barrio* was not there anymore. She should stay, hoping that the boat in which he had embarked on would return any day. She was also worried that Domeng would not know how to find his way back to Bulacan alone. She decided to stay in Manila.

The world seemed to stop spinning. Children stopped playing while people refrained from walking as they tried to grasp what would be the impact of United States' declaration of war against the Japanese while its forces were being mobilized against Germany in Europe. Many people would have different assumptions; some could only guessed based on what they heard. Many who were following Japanese atrocities in the territories they had already occupied in the Pacific region were most troubled. Inez was one of them although in her mind, the troubling effect revolved around her husband for a day. She knew it was the first time in Domeng's life that he had traveled out of town. The destination might be clear, but his being alone in the sudden change of situation was very disturbing. The man who only had acquaintances with horses and carabaos aside from immediate families, the man whom she loved and cherished, whom she vowed a day ago to be her husband in a faith they both believed in was giving her too much concerns to think about. The simple beautiful life they planned and dreamed together has ended even before it has begun.

1225 Hours

San Pedro joined the group where he was understood well enough. All eyes were directed to the north where humming sounds were coming from, becoming louder by the second. A couple of minutes, an air-raid siren went off, and a few planes managed to taxi on the runway and take off. The sky above the Clark Air Base became dark as hundreds of planes began to drop their loads while flying above the airfield. Loud explosions started just about when the lead planes flew overhead. Three-inch guns started firing, so did the .50 calibers in the bunker. One Zero was hit as it exploded in the air to the eyes of Japanese pilots behind him. Half of them veered to the right and the other half to the left as it circled around, dropping more bombs on the airstrip. Five planes dove to their position as bullets started to strafe down at the slope right where they were. Another Zero just lost control of his smoking plane and plummeted down the thick forest behind them. But more were coming, bigger and flying higher, hailing of continues fire from the ground. Cabarles was reloading when he heard a loud shout from the other bunker to take cover. Before he could fire again, loud blasts that were too close started in succession that he was thrown down to the bottom of a pit. Countless more exploded everywhere on their position.

As Cabarles described the event, it was like "the sound of a bag of firecrackers thrown in a campfire and another bag right after, only a million times louder and powerful." The ground was shaking in simultaneous explosion; it was so loud that he became deaf for about three days with the humming lasting too long that he could not remember when it stopped in his ears. And it wasn't the worst:

> The aftermath was unspeakable. When we regained consciousness, the whole area was obliterated, gun batteries no more. Even trees had fallen and were burning. No more shed or structure of any kind other than craters and smoke on the ground, and the burning smell was horrifying. No sign of any other living soul aside from us that were spared from direct hit. Flesh, metals, and fallen trees everywhere. We were saved by sandbags that collapsed inward, literally buried us alive after long minutes of shock.

Eight Marines and few Filipino soldiers died. I don't know what is waiting for us now as we sail the West Philippine Sea. (From Sergeant Rodrigo Santos's journal, entered Dec. 24, 1941).

The raid continued. Donono and Santos helped each other in trying to recommission the "baby" that was knocked down from its pedestal. Casey was bathed in blood and was down; he was yelling orders that were in vain. The machine gun was repositioned over sandbags, and Santos fired to a target about half a mile away over the runway to spend remaining rounds randomly and only to disclose their position. Cab had retrieved his Enfield, aimed to a leading Zero as three were coming fast, closing in and firing machine guns at the same time. Cabarles took aim; it would be the first bullet he would fire, then he emptied the cartridge rapidly onto a plane that flew overhead until it plunged to the upper hills. Santos and Donono up again occupied the big gun as the surroundings was rained down by displaced debris. Cabarles joined them and tried to help, discarding his emptied rifle. Finally, everyone nodded that it was ready again. Donono was tapped to position himself on the trigger, which he did without hesitation. No more enemy in sight, but he fired anyway shooting planes flying away as fast as they appeared. Two men were holding the gun for him. Casey had better experience with the gun supported a little by a man's weight immediately from behind. Donono kept on cursing and daring the Zeroes to come back; at least that was what everybody thought he was saying.

The bomb raid didn't take too long except for a few planes shooting each other from afar that ended as fast as they saw it begin. Later, two landed on the severely damaged base as it continuously gave off large volumes of thick smoke in different places. Santos would not let his hands off the "baby" as he waited intensely. He was damn sure there were many more, but where were they? Donono would realize that he was sitting on someone; his attention was also caught by moving bags of dirt at the corner of the pit. Someone was moaning. They scuffled to remove piles of dirt on top of him. He was San Pedro, who dove in for cover when the bombing began. A few minutes later, at Sergeant Casey's lead, they all came out of the hole and looked for the others and the possibly wounded. There were none. He reassessed the area and said, "It was a miracle we are still alive." No one heard what he said.

Before dark came the captain and Lieutenant Stevens with a squad of marines coming by foot because the place was not accessible by motor vehicles anymore due to the many holes and downed trees. Wrong timing. They were welcomed by a stray of bullets from the .50mm still manned by Donono. His fascination with the big gun was not satisfied previously in strafing trees and more branches, but the back force and recoil were more than he could handle with him firing it alone. He was thrown back a few feet as he landed on the sandbags that caved down the foxhole. Santos took over immediately until the soldiers downhill identified themselves and moved forward. Donono swore he would never touch that gun anymore.

"Where are the marines?" an officer looking for his unit almost instantaneously asked a bunch of temporary deaf and "no English" soldiers. But even if some of them could hear or understand, they could not find the words to say. They saw them before the air raid, but they didn't know where they were after that? The marine officer was also fuming mad for being fired at by the machine gun. He clearly showed he wasn't happy about that.

Nobody answered. Even he shouted at the top of his voice, he still didn't get a response. He just walked around and found them himself in disbelief. He was left alone in vengeful grief; many who died were his men and friends. Meanwhile, the army had a different mission to carry on. Casey, wounded himself, called the attention of his battle-tested men by motions of the hand and body for them to follow him. Donono would carry the .50 mm, Santos taking all rounds left. Cabarles made sure it was the same rifle he had. Another survivor, San Pedro, was still in shock to follow what he was told to do.

In Manila, Japanese bombings continued nonstop. The resulting effect was shocking though most of the bombs were dropped at Nichols air base, and selected targets, many places in the city, suffered extreme loss of life in which large numbers were composed of civilians. As soon as the last enemy plane had disappeared in the sky, Inez returned again in Intramuros. The Japanese invasion force was on its way to Manila.

CHAPTER 2

THE SOUTHERN SEAS

Sailing on a boat that goes nowhere to see where the river ends. Find new friends and places. Far away from ponds and meadows that becomes green and a short period of golden color until it becomes brown. Sorely dry to wait for the rain, the grace of heaven that sometimes a long wait to come by, only to begin green again. Like the sea, we seek refuge because the land become hostile to find another land that shall take us. No more places to go. Only guns can keep us going. The rifle on my hand, seldom it rested on my shoulder because at any moment there are enemies who keep their fingers on the trigger.

IN THE SEA WE SEEK REFUGE

On the third day after their oath taking, the recruits were sailing again. They were still shouting to each other, but none were in shellshock anymore, just deaf. Their first taste of the war was not easy to forget; the gallantry they had shown in the mismatched battle had acquired them great respect for each other while entrusting their life on individual capabilities: Santos, with his skill in leadership and communications; Cab, with his cool and corroborated marksmanship, who also possessed unbelievable bravery; Donono, the astonishing little guy who didn't even blink the whole time they were under attack. Sergeant Casey was dumbfounded. He told of what he had seen to his officers; it was not flabbergasting, but he said he believed there were none that could top the bravery of the men they already had.

"They are not like we thought they are," he said to his superiors, ending his tale. And San Pedro, who likewise didn't lose competence of his assumed duties as the "supply officer," grieved the demise of his best friend, who without him he was totally lost. He settled in the company of Donono and newfound friends while remaining in the unit led by Americans, the army this time. Later, he confided that he and the late *Cabo* were moonlighting as utility boys to the marines in the hope that they could help them immigrate to the United States someday. They were dishwashers and part-time cooks at Clark's officers' mess hall.

The Japanese were advancing from the north and the south by sea and land after the bombing of Clark, Nichols, and other American airfield and military installation throughout the country. Cab tried very hard to drop him off at the shoreline by the Manila Bay so he could go home, but he wasn't successful. Rodrigo promised he would get him a woman when they got to Iloilo where he grew up. Cab declined the offer.

Cruising out the vast West Philippine Sea, their destination was unknown yet. Santos repeatedly suggested Iloilo to the Americans while they were already navigating to that direction. Plenty of fuel and food on the boat. Peaceful, other than occasional drizzles of seawater that reminded them of hot clay and pebbles that rained down on their foxhole two days ago. There was nothing else they can do but rest and let faith take over. Donono just continued eating apples and oranges; his appetite on the fruits had kept him busy all day while San Pedro expertly skinned them for him. Cab remained quiet, still not believing what he had been into. It wasn't any of what he had in mind after his wedding. Four days had passed, as he counted it with his fingers. He was back thinking about his wife the whole time he was sitting flat on the deck.

It was only two weeks ago when he was handed a letter from his father; it was in English. He didn't know how long the old man had it; he said he asked a couple of people what it was all about. Don Pepe, a respected and educated resident of the barrio and living nearby, had translated the paper for them in context and the possible consequences and punishment if he ignored the calling of being a soldier. Inez said the same too when he showed her the letter. In the obedience to the best of advices and his own decision, Dominador Cabarles would report for duty in the army. Nothing serious, the best scenario as he was told would be a training of few months after which he could go back home thereafter. In the barrio, nobody gave attention about the role of United States in the war in Europe. Most people would listen to soap operas on the radio than current events. Philippines was an American territory by annexation and therefore Japan would not dare to show hostility against the islands. Being a soldier was an experience and distinction. As he understood, the training would merely involve how to shoot guns, which he was already good at, and therefore it would go easy and he could be back home in a short period of time. Truly he could not afford the humiliation of not reporting; instead he could take advantage of it as it would change his reputation from a nobody to somebody.

Not before he got caught kissing a submissive beautiful woman in his life that led to the sudden wedding. That and the anticipation of Domeng leaving for the army had made his in-laws insist on the early nuptials. No way could they let him took advantage of their daughter and leave. The existing customs and tradition of the community did not permit that kind of perspective; whether they liked it or not, they had to get married. After all, the only person who would reject him in fulfillment of his dream was actually the one insisting to marry his daughter. Of course, Domeng liked it very much. He welcomed the idea with all his heart like he was in heaven. He could set aside everything else. He and Inez would the take vow "till death do us part." There was nothing more he could wish that would make him happy, not considering the long period of time he was obliged to slaving himself to prove that he would be a perfect husband for Inez too. The talk of the wedding eventually became a priority, but in no way could reporting for duty be set aside before it expired.

It was more than five years of chopping firewood, fetching water, tending to the horses, and helping in the farms. All throughout that period he could only take a glimpse at the beautiful young lady from a distance and daydream about her. Now they were married, but the short time they were allowed with each other was never what he had hoped for. In the vast ocean, in the middle of nowhere, all he could comprehend was the humming in his ears that could be attributed also to the sounds of the diesel engine of the *Seven Seas*. He was a soldier serving a country at war in the front line. The fear that yielded from his first taste of battle was over, and nothing but being together with Inez was all that occupied his mind, again only in his imagination—the thought of her soft skin touching his, her lips so tolerant of his, the feeling that had been only in his dreams. When it came true, he walked away.

CHANGE OF PLAN

December 16

While moored in an uninhabited shore along Guimaras Island, they had to assess the damage on their boat from enemy fire. The plan to stay over in Iloilo didn't materialize as the island was under siege from the Japanese forces who would shoot anything moving within their sight, as how the residents described their brutalities. Which was true because when they encountered a company of them on the town of Guimbal, it was clear they were no match and decided to retreat back to the boat from the unwavering persistence of the enemy to eradicate them. They were joined by eight soldiers, remnants of army regulars or policemen that sustained severe casualties defending the islands from enemy attack on Southern Iloilo. Corporal Rolando Bantigo, the unit commander, was thankful for the timely arrival of the group for their rescue; however, the minimal number of soldiers from Bataan could not halt persevering Japanese. They retreated altogether back to the ocean. The Ilonggos reiterated the endless gratitude for the new pals stopping by as they were already overran by the Japanese into sure death. On the other hand, they were welcomed by the Americans and the Filipinos to join the Fifty-Seventh Scouts while regrouping into guerilla combat unit. Bantigo complied; joining forces with a well-armed and supplied unit was hard to pass aside the leadership and ample time for his wounded to recuperate. He refused to the proposition of establishing a guerilla camp in Iloilo. He said that there was no place in the island safe to hide from the Japanese. The enemy showed off their might and superiority to every living thing they saw that defied their presence. The Ilonggos had proven it the hard way. Many in his troops had surrendered; otherwise, they would have died in the firefight when the Japanese landed on their island.

Change of plans, Negros must equally be under siege. The best decision was made to continue cruising to the big island of Mindanao, where the captain wanted to go in the first place. Considering its size and more rugged terrains and mountain, there was no way the enemy could occupy the whole island. There should be plenty of space left to regroup and organize a guerilla company. The food were still plenty; otherwise, it would not be a problem with the ocean full of fishes that were large enough that one would sometimes jump right into the boat. The fuel was still enough for the chosen destination.

From Guimaras, they docked on a hidden cove in Lugait then cruised to Cagayan before dawn. In the mouth of a river close to the border of the Lanao province in the north, they disembarked on a virgin shore of unknown vines and trees thriving abundantly. About twenty yards from the embankment of the river, they spotted a small clearing. They could not imagine what happened on the place as cogon and cattails were down to the ground like wild animals had rambled in the area. Blood was noticeably everywhere that it was poured around in unexplained fashion. Just a fresh evidence that a group of people had camped and spent the night on the place while eating their hunt. The natives from Iloilo had advised everybody to leave immediately as they said it wasn't safe to stay there too long. They were afraid not from the Japanese but from the headhunters inhabiting that part of Mindanao. True or not as to the story about human-eating tribes on this part of the island, they all left the area without saying any word. They maintained silence and alertness as they sailed about fifteen more miles into another cove. Any farther would not make any difference. Whoever inhabited the area could be found elsewhere. They were ready to shoot while crossing the vast woods and grassy hills of western Mindanao.

December 27

Walking through swamps of thick palms and vines for a day, they didn't stop until they decided to take five on a rocky plateau. Food supply was dwindling; it was consumed faster in land than on the boat. Cab realized that the palm tree variety growing in the place was the same also to the ones that grew wild in Luzon. He cut a cluster of nuts and started eating the soft and sweet meat inside after chopping them in half like coconut. And they all ate, resting for a while and letting another night pass through at the same spot. It was about sunrise when they started hiking again until they crossed a narrow trail that indicated of inhabitants in the area. They just hoped they were not the dreaded tribes of headhunters. They picked the trail going south with only one thing in mind—to establish contact with the residents. They could see wild animals; surely they would make for a very good meal, but the only way they could eat them was to shoot them first. Not a good idea because gunfire would give their location to the Japs or the hostile tribes they were more scared of. Frogs were abundant, but there was also the poisonous kind according to Donono. He had munched on the last candy bar, and like others, he was longing for meat. Fives became tens; just shoot an animal and to hell with whoever heard the gunshot.

In December, it was always hot and humid during the day and cold at night. Morning dews were available to collect droplets of water to drink when they woke up in the right vegetation. With fourteen people to quench the thirst equally, it was not enough. Sometimes there was nothing, but it didn't pose a problem because there were many rivers and streams they could see along their path. Three days on foot deep in a virgin jungle, there were no more wild animals on sight to shoot when it became the only option left to fill their bellies. There was just thick vegetation around canopied by tall trees with visibility so vain they could not even see each other at a few feet away. Donono would show his skill in climbing a tree to the top, but only it was the same scenery he could see around—just the top of other trees. They kept moving on another day to a small rocky clearing. They could only guess where they were, changing destinations to the south, which was too difficult to maintain because of the many obstructions. They moved southeast to the Bukidnon base on a map the officers kept on looking. Trekking the wilds for fourteen days already, and they had not seen any sign of other people yet, with no Japanese either. Cabarles had no idea where they were going; he had lost count of how many days since he had left Inez, but he was sure of one thing: he was so far away from her. Very far away.

CHAPTER 3

LEGEND BEGINS

Bravest men side by side, destination unknown. My life depends on every steps they are making and the words they are saying. I wanted to go back, go home. No one listens to me, no one knows where we are.

THE SOUNDS THAT TELL TIMES

By sundown on the fifteenth day on land, the unit reached a rough road. The condition and signs of tire tracks revealed that motorized vehicles constantly passed through it. With walls of green vines shrouded by branches of tall trees and bamboos on both sides, they continued walking southwest, cautiously taking advantage of undeterred steps until it got dark again, real dark. Only the sound of insects and owls could be heard occasionally. A bleak light presumably from a kerosene lamp suddenly appeared within their sight as they continued walking, indicating local residents finally. They didn't expect there would be enough food that could be provided for fifteen hungry men, but any information they could get was very important. They went up a gentle slope past the house for about half a kilometer, picking a spot with few trees growing just below the rocky top where a bigger one thrived boastfully and leading back to the jungle. With the officers talking, Sergeant Santos was all ears awaiting orders. They all agreed to make contacts early in the morning to avoid scaring the occupants. For the meantime they would be spending the rest of the night right where they were. Donono could only voice out his discontent depending on the growling of his stomach. How he got hungry so fast was justified by the .50 caliber that he and San Pedro was carrying alternately. He had not seen coconuts for a long while. Everyone was starving, and the only hope he could see was to beg for food from whoever lived in that house. His unusual metabolism always bothered him that he wanted to check the place immediately. There were signs of farming activity around the area, but the land was so dry the plants barely thrived awaiting for the rain.

"Cab, can we go now?" pleaded the small guy to Cabarles. Of all the people, he only confided to Cab about his empty stomach. He had developed trust and respect to the man from whom he would get his approval first before making any move, even before carrying orders from the officers. He only listened to Cab, and there was not a moment that he was not by his side.

"Just drink water for now, will you! You have to start training your worms not to eat sometimes," Cab suggested while making himself comfortable for a nap.

At the first crowing of the roosters, Donono was awakened. There was only one thing in his mind—food. His senses knew where the sound was coming from, just down the hill where the house was. His movement alerted Cab, who guessed instantly what was bothering Donono. "Get permission from Sergeant Santos first before we go," Cab suggested, thinking he had not eaten chicken meat for a long time either.

Santos, equally starving to approve the suggestion, said he was coming too. Waking up the corporal from Iloilo, they walked down to the direction of fowls that could also tell time in the morning. There was a small house made of local materials, old, and crumbling. They knew somebody lived there for sure; they must be sleeping yet. Bantigo, on the lead accompanied by Donono, called in Ilonggo to get the attention of who may be dwelling in the house. Cab and Rod Santos were in the dark. Not long after that, a man peeked through the window. The soldiers identified themselves and forthright stated their purpose, cautiously requesting to the man to spare them water to drink.

The man woke up his wife in excitement after identifying Filipino soldiers on their doorstep. Although nervous and afraid, they welcomed the visitors inside the house hurriedly. The woman started boiling water for coffee right away as they knew already what to do. Sweet potatoes on a big pot already cooked, it seemed the couple knew they were coming. They were excited after learning that more soldiers nearby were equally starving. The man pulled a bag of milled corn from one corner and also a few personal items for themselves through the watchful eyes of the soldiers. A few live chickens were taken out from the cage, leaving its door open to plenty more. Donono was sure one of them was crowing earlier. The man said he had a cow somewhere if they wanted it. But what they didn't understand was why the couple were also packing a few of their own personal things while offering everything they had that might be useful to the soldiers. Bantigo asked for the reason in their dialect.

"Wherever you are going, we will go with you, and we have to leave now," replied the woman firmly like they had planned and waited for the opportunity to come a long time ago.

The man said his name was Jesus Marfil; he and his wife Katerina had no choice but to come with them. Many Japanese and local collaborators would stop by their place for chow at sunrise, and they had nothing left ready to offer. Sunrise was only a few hours away. They disclosed their fear, having a very bad experience on the first encounter with the enemy. The Japanese took their only child, a fifteen-year-old daughter, whom they wanted to find. To add insult to injury, they had been cooking and feeding the enemy who kidnapped their daughter and God only knew what the Japanese did to her. They had been discussing to evacuate in Davao but had never found the courage to do it by themselves. Every morning, they were afraid of the Japanese patrolling the area who would stop for food and become aggravated if they had nothing cooked for them; the threats that would be beaten terribly was very hard to live by. Jesus described the horrors of the first day of their encounter with the enemy only five days ago when they took their daughter. Since then, they would come in the morning and disappear during the day, moving back south.

"Anything else you may found useful for you in the house, take them," Jesus said again. "We are coming with you and we shall leave now." He continued explaining that the Japanese definitely could come at any time and surely they were outnumbered.

They had no reason not to believe the couple. Not wasting any minute, they hurriedly started abandoning the house to relay the information to their commanding officers. Still sleeping like babies,

Santos commented that if they were the enemies to see their comrades, everybody should have been dead already. All the information provided by Jesus and his wife were very valuable. However, it was too late for them to know that they were in the path of the advancing enemy troops heading north.

NO RETREAT

The information provided by Jesus could not be disregarded. They moved rapidly at about a kilometer heading to the jungle northward. Dawn was breaking when they reached the place to see the surroundings, dismayed to see another clearing over clusters of trees. They were in an endless wilderness for many days that they wanted to go back in, but they had to run for it this time. Certainly, it was the sound of engines they could hear from the south. The captain observed with his binoculars.

"Yeah, positively the Japs, and there are troops on foot too. They are heading this way," He said. "We can be seen if we keep moving. There are at least two companies down there, no way through west either, look." He uttered to his lieutenant who confirmed seeing more that was coming from the other direction.

"We should have listened to them to move out at once," Lieutenant Stevens replied while sitting, scouting the direction his commanding officer just said. Daylight was spreading. If they could see the enemy moving, they must see them too if they moved out through the same clearing.

"Why?" the captain asked.

"Look yourself seven hundred yards straight down."

With his binoculars again, the officer carefully scoured the area from their position. Between rows of corn seedlings about a foot from the soil and an occasional cluster of thick vegetation, nothing was different except that some of those clusters of dark leaves were moving forward. They were walking toward their location. By the river, lined by the walls of bamboo trees and vines, was another Japanese patrol where they would meet them by the riverbank if they sprinted the distance. Running back to Marfil's place was not an option as there could be real mad Japanese at the abandoned house already. They heard gunfire back where they came from. The shots alerted every Japanese on foot to move faster to where it was coming from. "They will miss us about fifty yards," one of the Americans estimated.

They heard only one clip, and it was over. The Marfils disclosed that the sweet potatoes and chickens belonged to the Japanese with specific orders to cook them all for that day. That was what they had been doing all night.

The Filipinos knew the situation already; they were surrounded by the enemy. Though none of the enemies were aware yet of their presence, it was only a matter of time. Jesus has informed them that their exact position was also the favorite snoozing place at daytime of the Japanese. Under the shade of trees, a big one stood out, the leafy shade it offers very relaxing. The rock formation with thick short grass around was really a perfect place to hide and rest. Evidently, the enemy had already claimed the place as theirs before them, as what the carvings on the trunk of the biggest tree said, that they had been there. Dark clouds forming, indicated that it was going to rain soon as the sun rises.

Rarely does it rain in January, but in Mindanao, no one can predict the weather. Cab admitted that he has prayed for it earlier for the plants, but he didn't know it would come with the Japanese from all directions as the drizzle began. Sergeant Santos was waiting for command, but clearly, nothing was most logical than staying down and getting ready to fire. "It's a pleasure knowing you, gentlemen," he said to the Ilonggos. The Iloilo gang must have known what they were up to. They had already experienced in combat against the Japanese taking position on the north end where the enemy was expected to show up. After a handshake to each one of them, he crawled back in the center, a box of bullet with him. San Pedro was with the Americans on the other end who had taken over the machine gun from Donono.

Santos joined Cab and Dono in the middle, who were having conversation with the local couple. Cabarles found out that they could speak Tagalog and were also aware of the situation. He was upset to learn that Mindanao was not connected by land to Luzon, thus walking back home was impossible. The immediate concern that arose at the moment was clearly he could not go anywhere without being shot at. Boxes of ammo were opened and ready by clip. The only thing left to do was pray. Jesus Marfil indicated that the Japanese were advancing north from Davao and were caught in the middle of their entire forces.

Santos and Cabarles resorted to talking about their women as they did every time they were whispering to each other. Cab was truly thinking about Inez; he was done praying over the imminent situation of seeing the enemy coming that should put his skills to test. Not to games and tin cans but other human beings who could shoot back and attack at the same time. He looked at the Japs as a lot bigger than birds and which can't fly; the problem he had seen in Iloilo incidents was they didn't get easily tired up when provoked to a firefight. He also observed that the enemy whether they were on a plane or on foot was determined to kill them all. He found himself as the quail this time, exactly like the flightless bird who stays put rolling eyes when it senses danger.

Donono was the calmest among them. As long as his belly was full, he should be all right. San Pedro didn't have his own gun; he didn't like to touch one for some reason. But unlike Donono whose attachment to the group was by his own choosing, he always displayed courage amusingly in any given situation. San Pedro's ties with the soldier was by mistake, and everybody knew it. He could only show his usefulness by seemingly what was best to cook the chickens. Under frightening situations could he only turn his attention to the chickens. Donono had taken position alongside with Cabarles while Santos moved over with the Americans, convening a strategy to get out of the situation undetected. There was nothing else to do but stay down and let the Japanese pass.

The remnants from Iloilo corresponded but conceded that running has come to an end as Corporal Bantigo saluted everyone. From Iloilo to Mindanao, they took a hitch with the soldiers from Bataan; together they found that the Japanese was everywhere, leaving them no place to settle for a bit of time. Time to make the enemy know they could not do that; he said the Japanese couldn't just come to any place or any island and mark every spot, claiming it their own without a fight. So much for getting their asses kicked out of Iloilo. The only other option was to surrender, and sure thing as hell, they would not do that by coming to Mindanao.

The Americans could only keep their cool to learn that surrender was out by all; it meant looking for a hole they could get through to escape but to no avail. They have accepted that there was none unless they made one. Anywhere down and around from their location, one could easily spot the enemies' location. They were everywhere. Casey approached and made clear to Santos about the battle plan they had formulated. He replied, "Very well." No surrender, but no one would fire until it was imminent of being discovered.

Jesus had one story to tell to enlighten the soldiers, as if he hadn't said it already. Facing northwest, looking down directly to the pile of enemy troops, Jesus said that they were the ones looking forward for hot chicken soup he and his wife must prepare earlier, and they were joining those that were already in the house, usually the truck drivers and passengers, five or six most of the time although there could be more. He added that the livestock were not all theirs but belonged to the Japanese who would be very mad to see them uncooked and running loose instead.

To their left, at the American side, was another group moving closer to a level trail winding around their location and leading to Jesus's place. The leading platoon must have been in the vacant house already, enraged that there was no food or water waiting for them through the hospitality of the couple who used to live in that house. Gunshots were heard again. They assumed that they were actually shooting the rest of the chickens that was let loose; perhaps they thought that the people who were expected to cook for them were just hiding nearby and they could scare them out too. It was absolutely nothing at all of what they expected.

Katerina said, "They always fire their guns every time, it's just longer this time. They must be real mad." She sighed.

Two Japanese broke up from the pile, camouflaged by fresh vegetation attached to their bodies, slowly hiking the hilly path up to their marked post, straight to the obscured Americans who had already seen them and coming. The Americans motioned with their hands to get the attention of the foot soldiers close to them, indicating that they would take care of them. In a few minutes, the two Japs met their sudden and quiet death from the hands of overpowering combat-trained officers. They had proven that size mattered too, whispered Dono to Cabarles. The Little Don was startled that the enemy was camouflaged, with leaves on twigs stuck around them. He had finally seen the enemy up close, how they looked like. Santos likewise was amazed to what he just witnessed. He regretted not reporting early on duty when he should have learned that kind of skill too. "What do you think, can we get out of here alive?" he casually asked Cab.

"We will know for sure when this is over. Otherwise, only them (the enemy) will know," Cab whispered to Santos, who became voiceless to what the big guy responded while Cab pointed to the rest of the Japanese changing direction toward their position. He clearly understood what he meant. The order was clear: The Americans must shoot first. Only at this time would they know that the battle had begun.

BAD LUCK, GOOD LUCK

To all they had been through together, they learned how to confide with each other without inhibitions. The recollection of the Japanese attack in Clark was not easy to forget. The brutality of the enemy had no difference whether they were on the plane or on foot. The experience in Iloilo where they ran away from the enemy even without actually seeing them was not acceptable to their individual pride. At least they would not be blown to pieces, that's what they thought. Their silent conversation were cut short.

"Hey, guys, how are you doing?" Sergeant Casey moved over as he noticed that the three odd friends were occupied with nonsense conversation like nothing was ensuing by the second.

"We are good. What do you want us to do?" Santos asked, upset by the slow and faltering decision of the officers.

Casey elaborated the plan, whispering, "The enemies are coming. Fifty yards and coming closer in our position."

"What did he say?"

"He wants us to kill all of them," Santos replied, translating the order.

Thirty yards away, the Japanese had no clue to what awaited them when someone started firing. In less than a minute, they were all lying lifeless. Nothing to use as cover except their dead, their scattered formation on the clearing became an easy target to the awaiting barrel of assorted rifles and submachine guns. Some of them didn't even have the chance to take their weapons off their shoulders. Down by the riverbank, another platoon of enemy started coming faster about a half-mile distance. The shooting had alerted every enemy in the area as far as the gunfire could be heard. Those by the road the closest to them were idle. Perhaps the had been used to having no armed resistance since they began mobilizing their invasion troops to northern Mindanao.There was no noticeable activity of an immediate attack, but those from the house set out from the bushes and trees to investigate. They were the disappointed and hungry members of the platoon who were firing randomly a while ago whose actions might have created mistaken belief among the others that the latest volley of gunfire were from their own troops. It was quiet again.

The hill had a wooded area on its peak that extended a trail leading down to the road Around it was a vast clearing, a mile of dying cornfield northwest to south altered by a line of green trees, presumably a river coming inward at eight hundred yards to the eastern side. Other than about ten acres of farmland and a selected area from the road with unknown crops growing timidly, the hill generally was covered by thick brown grass as it sloped down. Many new depressions on the vegetation indicated trails leading to the top, evident of previous activities that they didn't see at night. They didn't even know there was a river nor a bridge ahead. According to the resident couple who had joined their unit, the Japanese only came in small patrols on unannounced days and disappeared. "Today is entirely different." At about ten o'clock, thick clouds above turned to drizzle again, and eventually heavy rain followed and the ground became muddy and slippery.

"Don't eat that!" Cab yelled at Don as he was about to take a bite of a candy bar out from the pocket of a dead Japanese.

"Why?" Donono asked in surprise. He was known to have no discrimination to food. Cab would not allow him to even take a bite of that candy.

"Bad luck. That is a dead man's food. Never eat nor use anything that belonged to a corpse." He made sure Donono remembered that. "Eat the *camote* (sweet potatoes)," Cab suggested.

"You can eat the chicken too if you want, otherwise let them go." He pointed to the hens and a rooster still tied up on their feet.

Donono grabbed the hens; he let them go but not the rooster. He repeatedly stroked gently over its wet feathers, obviously uttering something.

"What's that for?" Santos curiously asked, thinking it strange kindness for a man who sees everything as food.

"For good luck. Come and do the same too," he replied, moving nearer with the rooster, demonstrating the proper way of rubbing down on its feathers so the luck would work.

Sergeant Santos and Cabarles submitted themselves to the suggestion of the little guy. It was the first time they heard of such a thing, but they all carefully kneaded the rooster altogether until they let it run away. The two looked at each other afterward; a similar question arose on the veracity of what they just did. They then looked at Little Don who turned his hunger to the *camotes*. They concluded that they were sure duped like a couple of idiots, but neither said anything. There was nothing to lose; sure they need luck, more than just luck.

The heavy rain stopped, but the formation of heavy clouds from the horizon implied of pouring rain coming again. Wet and dripping, Cab changed his pants to his own that he kept with him. He said he was not comfortable with the heavy marine uniform; it took time to dry and it was tight in his crotch. He took his boots out too that were just soaking his wet feet and heavy as dirt got stuck on the soles; then he grabbed his rifle again. The old single-action Enfield might be not as good as the Garand semi automatic Santos had, but he sure could hit a target at a far distance better. Donono like the Browning; it was shorter and compact, but the truth was he didn't like the teasing when the butt of a rifle was almost touching the ground when he carried it hanging on his shoulder. Sergeant Santos was nice enough to switch weapons with him. The recoil force may be too much for his size, but he said he was sure he could handle it.

The Japs had discovered their fallen comrades; however, before they could take cover, they were sprayed with bullets of unseen adversaries hiding in the rock formation and bushes of formerly their outpost. Those that made it out alive retreated only to get hit. The brave ones continued exchanging fire then again met the same fate from the vindictive Ilonggos. The volley of fire confirmed hostile forces on the hill. There must be too many of them, a company or more with machine guns. The Japs swarmed in no time and attacked from the left in unknown numbers with many blind shots to unseen adversaries. There was no more enemy in sight on the vast cornfield where someone suggested they could run and retreat, but the chances of getting spotted as soon as they ran was real as they were dead in a matter of time. The Americans immediately adjusted the plan of escape and held their position until dark. So far, they held the Japanese where they were.

The Americans kept covering the eastern plank where more of the enemy were expected from the road. Half a kilometer away, they could see clearly amidst the dark sky. They could also see the enemy start scaling the slope, and they were advancing fast. Santos joined them. Southwest lurked the remnants of the company they had been engaging earlier. Their advantages over the hill had halted the Japs, keeping them tightly down if not dead at a hundred yards. Cab and Donono helped the defending Ilonggos who suffered immediate casualties. The Japs had managed to get too close to them before it was too late. They could blend in along the bushes while others were hidden flat on the grasses and it was so difficult to see them until they were really close. Cab took his position by crawling higher up between a boulder and a little tree. There, he could see them all; no one was hidden for him. He started targeting first those that were clearly visible and moving in with a rapid succession of firing and reloading. Donono only saw the Japanese when they fell. His rifle started jamming for he can't remember how many times it was fired consecutively. The Japs retreated again, realizing the large casualties in their position, their camouflage were not as effective as they thought it would be.

"I can see more of them moving. Get me another rifle," he instructed Donono who handed him his semiautomatic almost immediately. "I want a rifle, any rifle, hurry up." He fired the Browning anyway until it stopped.

The little man came back with a loaded 1903 Springfield with ten shots magazine. "Where did you get this?" he asked, noticing the beautiful rifle for not having a scratch and cold while he aimed it at his target.

"From one of the guys. Don't worry, he is still alive," Donono replied cautiously, peeking above the rocks trying to locate where the enemies were. At the very moment, the Japs returned fire again; he got hit on the head, knocking him down. Cab had established his aim, and as he pulled the trigger, the enemy slowed down, firing back as they fell one by one. He saw a few more remaining, running in retreat. However, they were chased by bullets from Bantigo and his men down the trench who were equally busy. The firefight was intense on their end, and it was the same on the American side. Santos would yell for help in the middle, and the enemy just kept on coming.

"Donono, where are you?" He was looking for the guy who had just started regaining consciousness with blood gushing from his face.

"I got hit," was all he could say, touching a part of his right forehead. Cab pulled him down back on the trench and checked his wound. Not a bullet wound as it started to swell but by a rock most likely, the blood was oozing out badly. He dragged Donono down for cover and told him to stay there. Jesus and Katerina attended to him.

Cab thanked them very much and hurriedly joined Sergeant Santos alongside with Casey. "There are so many of them and they keep on coming," Santos uttered.

For about two hours already of firefight, the Japanese were suffering heavy casualties and must have been regrouping, as could be noticed by the silence in their positions. No holes to get through yet. On the far end were the captain and Lieutenant Stevens, poised with .50 caliber, bravely holding the enemy down and retreating before running out of ordnance. The rain stopped; it seemed that even the wind had become very quiet suddenly. Trucks were on the road, and they could see immediate activities as more enemy troops joined their comrades. There was a little breathing time on their side. Cab joined Santos while inserting bullets in his rifle.

"I'm glad you come," replied Santos as he took a pause to reload and at the same time verify the situation on the left. He was told that Donono was wounded, but nothing serious. He was being helped by the local couple. About the enemy, Cab said with attestation to the gallantry of the Ilonggos, "Those who can still run, they ran away already." The information was relayed to their commandant.

"Very good, men, I'll make sure you all get promoted," the captain said.

"What did he say?" Cab looked at Santos for help; there was not a word that he understood.

"Nothing, he must be daydreaming." Santos disregarded it because it was not a concern at the moment. Getting out of the current situation alive was. Who would want a promotion when you are dead? "Take over my spot, I'll check on Donono," he uttered as he crawled toward the location of the little guy.

"Bring back more ammo," Cab said as he took position.

The effort of the USAFFE officers had kept the enemy over a hundred yards at standstill with a good cover, but many were moving and crawling. It took Cabarles a while before he could locate them. On a grassy hill, their camouflage perfectly blended with vegetation. Santos was right—there were "many," but not "too many" as he saw them moving in closer again, crawling like monitor lizards coming out of their holes that he used to hunt on the Sandoval properties. He picked the first five, the closest side by side, and started firing until his rifle discharged no more. Another cartridge was emptied and another one sent those that were not hit on foot and retreated to the eyes of the Americans who at first wondered what he was shooting at. Indeed, they fired at them too before they could take cover again.

Santos came back with nothing but a piece of sweet potato and Donono. "He is all right?" he asked.

"Just a bump on his forehead, nothing serious," the sergeant whispered.

The greatest threat was coming from the east that seemed to encircle them around over two hundred yards. The captain was looking with his binoculars while Cabarles, Donono, and Santos kept shooting, Cabarles most of the time.

During the fifth hour since the first shots were fired, they were still holed up. They also suffered casualties on the rank of the Ilonggos, some wounded. Lieutenant Stevens was also wounded and needed medical attention. The gunshot on his lower right jaw was somewhat given first aid to stop the bleeding by his fellows, but everyone knew it was serious. There was no medic on their unit; the captain had tried all that he knew to stop the bleeding. San Pedro and Casey assisted him to a comfortable spot. Jesus and Katerina also came for aid as much as they could. Donono had clearly recovered from getting knocked down earlier, disappointed of himself to be knocked out by a splintered rock. He surely learned his lesson very well. It was only a few more hours to getting dark.

The first barrage of mortar fire from the road was all missed. But they were getting closer to their position at every explosion. Everyone took cover as they could. The Japanese would not accept defeat. They were determined to regain control of their outpost with the nonstop shelling. Almost an hour when they became tired, Cab had his right leg aching, also bleeding somewhere above his torso; the humming in his ears was also back. It was the same situation for Little Don, bleeding everywhere on his head and body. He took his clothes off, ripped, and tied them up to the head now with the fresh wound. Doe complained of something embedded on his lower back. A piece of metal, he pulled it out and used the rest of the cloth to stop the bleeding. He then crawled back to Santos and the Americans. The lieutenant was hit again seriously and obviously dead; Casey was still alive but incapacitated. Being on the same spot, the captain and San Pedro seemed all right together. He could not see Sergeant Santos anywhere. Four or five minutes later, they heard the Japanese shouting "Banzai!" repeatedly in their language while they hurriedly started to attack them. A load of Springfield held them back, followed by automatic fire from the captain and Pedro who had somehow picked up a gun.

"We are retreating, men."

Cab was at a loss to the command; he didn't have any clue to what it meant. He looked at San Pedro for help. The poor guy translated in Tagalog. He understood eventually, but no one else was capable of running other than the two of them. Santos was nowhere in sight. The Ilonggos were so quiet at their positions, and only Donono could be seen barely moving with Casey.

"I'm staying. Go, you two must go. I'll cover for you." He looked behind where the little man was again; Santos was still nowhere. He was thinking of running too, but he could not just leave them. Cab thought of the possibility in making it alive anyway if someone would keep firing on the enemy crawling and hiding near the end of the meadows bounding the cornfield. If someone would try to run, it must be right that minute while shelling was still in progress.

San Pedro translated again, now from Tagalog to English. Somehow the captain understood, shook his hand, and said more that Cabarles didn't mind at all. The last gesture of the officer leaving him his khaki hat was not of importance though he put the hat in his pants pocket instinctively. He quickly resumed aiming his gun and fired at a target he had already identified. The captain and San Pedro sprinted the clearing until they were partially hidden by the cogon grass at the northwest end of the cornfield while Cab shot at every moving leaf. His disposition and spirit was back when Santos joined him. Neither said any word. They just spent the remaining ammunitions of every gun they could get their hands on randomly. The rest of the Filipino soldiers just did the same on their position. The shelling became intense again, longer. When it stopped, the last of the tree fell down. It could not get any more punishment than it had accepted already. Santos admitted defeat with the empty gun; he was exhausted and bleeding. Only Cabarles was capable of moving, but he was also wounded. "I will find Little Don, stay here for a while," Cab said hurriedly.

PROMISE TO JESUS

Cab crawled to where he had last seen Donono; he knew he was still alive. Halfway there, someone grabbed his arm. It was Jesus with his dying wife, holding up his last breath, saying something in mixed Tagalog and local dialect. He said, "Please find and save our daughter. We know she is still alive." He repeatedly said while his hands got tighter, "Promise us, in the name of the Lord, please help her."

"Opo, opo, ipinangangako ko." Meaning "Yes, I promise." He may not understand all of what the poor guy said, but he knew at the moment that he could not deny him of what he thought the man wanted.

"Her name is Myraflor Marfil, she's only fifteen," Jesus murmured with difficulty, seriously wounded and dying. He sounded as if he was saving up his last breath for that last moment to come along.

"Thank you very much, the Almighty will help you," the woman said, struggling also to be understood, trying to move her hand to reach him.

He had thought she was dead already. He took her hand, and almost at the same time, Cab felt their demise and repeated his promise if he lived. The rain was now pouring stronger than ever. There was nothing else he could do but leave them after carefully covering the couple with white long-sleeved shirts nearby. So much for the memory of that shirt, as well as the pair of pants he was wearing covered with blood and mud. He paused a little bit and checked its pocket for a piece of paper. It was soaked as it was stuck inside; it got destroyed and simply melted on his soiled hands.

Donono was pinned down under a collapsed tree. He crawled under the branches and leaves that now covered the ditch. In fulfillment to what he wished for and prayed at the moment, the man he was looking for answered his calling, still alive, barely visible through the cover of twigs and leaves as the rainwater flowed down, filling up his location with reddish and soiled water from every direction.

"Cab, is that you?"

He answered while struggling to reveal himself out from a dark corner, "Yes, get out of there! You're going to drown yourself." The water was starting to collect, and there was no sign that the rain would stop. The sound of a loud boom made them squeeze each other down again until they realized it was thunder. Inch by inch, Don tried very hard to a point where Cab could just pull him out; he was moaning and cursing.

"Stop cursing, it is bad." Cab didn't know what he was saying in his dialect, but he took it as cursing, figured to just get his friend out and let his belief in God take over. Still breathing though dragging their feet, they managed to walk to a higher ground past the bodies of the kindhearted couple who met their final demise by just being with them.

Donono remembered how they helped him stop the bleeding of his wounds. He began ranting, taken to mean in his dialect as his offering prayers for all their casualties and all the death he had seen in such a short time of war. Although his fascination about guns were fulfilled, the subsequent effects to his existence was becoming a nightmare. He just wanted to get awakened. Even if it meant being back in the province of Quezon picking and splitting coconuts.

"I said stop cursing," Cab commanded.

He was awake, all right, but not from the threat of whipping by the masters of the coconut plantation he used to work for but the vengeful point of bayonets by the screaming Japanese. He had no more strength to spare; he could not even raise his hands to surrender. He wasn't even sure if the beating of his heart he was listening to was his own. His desire to live and the purpose of his miserable life were contradicting. He was giving up his life, but with the determination of a man who was sustaining the last of his strength and spirit. With remaining strength and a heartbeat he could hear, Donono believed Cab was not just a man. "I don't know who you really are, but I thank you for making me feel there are more to benefit of my existence." Donono was mumbling, maybe praying or whatever, but it was in his dialect.

"I said stop cursing."

He kept on praying, only it was in his delirious thought as his face was close tight to Cabarles. His eyes rolled down to the pair of pants soaking of mud and blood. It wasn't white no more. More gunfire brought his senses to reality. The sudden and forceful effort of Cabarles accompanied by his begging halted the shots. He yanked Santos as fast as he could but carefully from where he had fallen until he was up on his feet. There were two more bodies that might have a little more life left before the Japs could shoot them mercilessly; he had no more arms to spare for them. Casey was a good man.

His efforts may not be necessary; he knew they would die. He had no more hands to raise for surrender, only knees to kneel and face death. Rod Santos was embracing the same man with Donono, and coming back from the shock of second shelling had incapacitated his left leg from a rolling rock. He must have been hit also by shrapnel, obviously by the sight of his bloody khakis. Though both of his legs were injured, the numbness had helped him to put pressure on it little by little as the pain started to subside. He did the motion to surrender to the Japanese officer who became sympathetic of their appearance. The enemy could possibly let them live as long as they made it down to the road, which he could not.

Ten soldiers and two civilians were accounted for among the dead. It was not possible that the Japanese only lost thirteen soldiers that lasted a day and caused them countless casualties and wounded.

There should be many more who had managed to retreat. Where did they go?

Donono was easy. He pointed to the north when asked. He had an available hand to respond. However, he would not have been given the name of Donono if he really knew what he was being asked in a foreign language.

He lowered his hand down a little bit when screamed at. Up again at another, then lowered again in between screamings of the Japanese. He didn't know he was being interrogated to tell where the rest of their company went. To the north as he had indicated.

Among those captured, only one was clearly a soldier, one in a light-colored pair of pants and shirtless who looked to be an American by size. The only one whose appearance does not seem justified to be called a soldier whatsoever was cooperating. Who would call him a soldier with him being so little, with no pants, and wearing an oversized shirt? Altogether, they were a vital source of information on the whereabouts and strength of depending Allied forces against the Japanese. They would let them live for now, regain their strength, then kill them later. The trio knew there must be a lot of dead or wounded around the hills. The Japanese should have discovered their comrades who were massacred at the cornfield down the other side of the hill. How many more around, they didn't know, they didn't want to know. Without a doubt, the Japs were equally horrified by the numbers of their casualties as they were with their own. For sure, every breath they were still making was absolutely at the mercy of their infuriated captors; it was only a matter of time before someone will shoot them.

More than a half a kilometer walk was not easy being surrounded by screaming Japs whose fingers remained on the triggers of their rifles while pushing the surrenderees with their bayonets. They were paraded on the road to the eyes of many more soldiers passing a dozen cannons and hundreds more of shells. The rain had stopped, leaving a very muddy road. They were told to stay by the roadside kneeling and facedown with hands overhead, leaning with each other shoulder to shoulder; a hard kick had disentangled their bodies. After an hour of more kicking and numerous rifle butts that landed on every part of their bodies, a truck stopped by them followed by a military jeep. A Japanese lieutenant and a few subordinates came down immediately to join the others waiting for the final resolution of their captures. They were talking, noticeably in disagreement, until they yelled the prisoners to climb the truck. They were sensing all kinds of pain as they could hardly stand up by themselves. Donono got in first with help from Cab. There was one Japanese who was increasingly enraged by their sluggish motion and had become more eager to just kill them. They would lose the opportunity to do so when their prisoners got into the truck. A slightly wounded young officer coming from the hill—in his mind playing the horror of the number of their casualties and dying in the battle—would find anyone to avenge their death. The shame of losing his command wasn't acceptable without immediate retribution.

"Cab, hurry up!" Donono yelled to his fellows while witnessing the furious Jap shooting civilians. What the civilians were doing with the Japanese he didn't know.

Cabarles picked Santos up like an overgrown child to load him in with Donono who was also putting all his efforts on the difficulty of the process. Santos might not be too big, but his wet, slimy, and powerless body was causing the trouble. The excruciating pain that he felt in his incapacitated legs and wounds somewhat didn't help either. Three of their captors were just behind them when the mad officer laid eyes on them momentarily and stopped from screaming, and before anyone could react, he had pierced his sharp bayonet on the back of the barefooted soldier with incredible force and anger. The weapon penetrated from behind, went through the chest of another man, and added to the pain and horror of Donono and Santos who saw it coming. The last remaining strength of Cabarles was overwhelmingly spent to get Santos in the truck; then he fell on his knees.

"Cap, get up, give me your hand quick!" Donono screamed repeatedly as the truck moved away. Cabarles tried to raise his arms, trying to reach Donono, maybe to say goodbye. The last thing he could see that last moment he saw Cabarles was a bayonet I the air that would surely kill him. Santos closed his eyes; he refused to see how Cabarles would die. It was beyond horror for him to grasp, and he passed out. Donono remained calling Cabarles to get up. "Cap, Cap!" shouted as hard as he could. Hard kick and rifle butts quieted him down.

CHAPTER 4

THE CAPTAIN

DIAGNOSIS WITH AMNESIA

"*Le, iie, kare wa twatashi, no taichodeshu* (Halt, he is an officer, don't kill him)." A Japanese standing by stopped his comrade from giving that final blow, realizing that their prisoner was addressed as "Cap," a captain. Something else would lead him to believe that he was an officer. He explained to the soldier to let him live so he could give them information on the whereabouts of the rest of the enemies. An important prisoner, he ordered his men to load him in his jeep and brought "the captain" in the hospital himself. Cab was shivering and delirious but unbelievably alive.

On the forty-sixth day of his wedding and as a soldier, Dominador Cabarles was in a hospital in Davao. Unconscious but his pulse stable, the doctor who attended to him had said that there was nothing that he could do anymore. The blood lost by the young officer was massive, and the complications from the hypothermia was incalculable that any medical expert wouldn't be able to say he is going to live. He could not survive with the extent of his wounds alone. Although a direct blood transfusion from a donor in the hospital had kept him breathing, he didn't know if all medicines could suppress the infection from his numerous wounds. All he knew was that the captain's heart kept beating and to his astonishment just didn't want to stop. However, he kept on taking care of the man as much as he could and as much as he was allowed and as much as he was not to. Medicine was becoming scarce and could only be dispensed with Japanese permission.

On the fourth day in his care, the doctor visited the soldier on his sickbed somewhat to give him unconceivable elation; yet he believed that the will of this soldier to live was what kept him breathing incessantly. He swore he would attend to this man until he opened his eyes. Since the war began, all he had attended to was the rich Japanese civilians and the high-ranking officers who would come to the hospital even for simple scratches and colds. Although Davao Hospital had been designated exclusively for the Japanese elites with their own doctors, they retained the service of the local practitioners, nurses and employees alike, who could roam freely in the compound.

> The Japanese Imperial Army was in the process of enjoying the outcome of their Philippine occupation, structuring a new government that was being taken care of while expanding control to adjoining provinces in the island of Mindanao. Identifying who will embrace their presence and execute those who will not is what is keeping them busy. Many locals became loyal; and in a short period, orders in the province were attained. However, they categorized the Filipinos as an expendable race and forced them to bow on the Japanese. For those who didn't suffered humiliating punishment, mostly a slap in the face and kicking; those who chose to run scared were shot like stray dogs. That was not the worst of it. After the Japanese had found and made the final count of their casualties on the battle in Bukidnon, their atrocities had increased multiple folds. They bow to hunt down all the escaped Americans and Filipino troops who slaughtered their forces on that firefight. They began burning villages while civilians were forced to evacuate from their homes.

Cabarles, who didn't even know his rank, was a very important prisoner. He was put in a private room, his sickbed guarded by soldiers, which was manifested by the hierarchy of the Japanese Imperial Command who constantly visited him daily. The same lieutenant who had brought him there was losing his patience already as the last time he checked on him, the prisoner was said to be alive. The officer thought he could wake him up by slapping his face several times. He became impatient of the soldier getting a first-class treatment and still no use for them. He was guaranteed by a doctor and nurses to give more time as he would be waking up eventually.

On the fifth day of "the Captain" on his sickbed, the fast healing of his wounds inspired every staff in the hospital. A soldier who had no hope to survive whatsoever was recuperating very well. Being an ally, the Filipinos were enthusiastic of his development, yet afraid of what awaited him in the hands of the enemy when he woke up. He was a prisoner bound for execution as many conjectures had already been established from the unusual treatment he was getting from the Japanese. He had the best accommodation, all right, but getting screams and slaps while unconscious was conclusive of that what awaits for him is unimaginable.

About four o'clock in the afternoon of the same day was the regular visit of the nurse whose own blood and kindness had contributed to the healing of the soldier's wounds. She had developed a personal attachment to the young officer while mending and taking care of him.

"If you can hear me, I suggest you remain asleep until the war is over," she would say most of the time. The compassion that grew in her heart every time she was by his bedside had been the same when he was delirious and dying. She could feel that he would wake up anytime, but she wanted to be there. The fear of him waking up back in the hands of the furious Japanese is not a good thing to think about. Sometimes she would fall asleep in the room while holding his rough and calloused hands. "I'll be leaving you again, but I'm coming back," she would whisper every time she got done with her routines. But this time, she left without noticing that the eyes of her patient just opened. The room was getting dark, and the yelling of the restless guards to get her out of the room was making her nervous even though she had learned how to deal with them already.

Cab had finally awakened, the jumbles of nightmares and dreams of angels and sinners still on his mind. In fact, he just saw an angel leaving the room. He remembered her holding his hands whispering words that he didn't understand at all. He had no clue to where he was, but he remained quiet, the stiffness he felt on every part of his body was unbearable. The most important though was he was not by the gates of hell like in his nightmares. It could be heaven, but the angel had just left and the only voice he could hear was the Japanese guards talking on their own language. Perhaps they were waiting to show him the way to hell, this time for real.

He was back to his senses just like that, but he remained lying in bed. His body didn't want to respond to the command of his brain even if he wanted to get up. He started to move his fingers, imagining those hands that he felt holding his a while ago. The right hand for sure was Inez's, softer, who was always there. On the left was another but only in his dreams; they were equally thoughtful, caring, and all synonymous terms he could not simplify that pertains to that kindness. All throughout that night, he was awake trying to shift or move his arms and legs little by little correspondingly while recollecting his thoughts about his loving wife whom he swore was by his side all the time and had never left him. It must be a dream, but he thought it was real. He might still be dreaming as the room was getting darker and he was trying to grasp what place he was in when he woke up.

SHE IS AN ANGEL

It was still fresh in his mind the first time he was able to touch her hands or his by hers when he handed her a bucket of water. It was unintentional, but the intimacy that was already there with each other led to a closeness that they had created to themselves. For all the years he had dreamed about the most beautiful Inez who was now his wife, it was not a good feeling to think that they were apart. He wanted to turn the times back on their life when he was happy just by watching her sitting by a bench on their yard reading her schoolbooks while he was chopping firewood or doing something else. He may have had a good chance to know that Inez likewise adored him earlier, but he always found his tongue stuck to his throat and he couldn't say any word that would open his feelings to her even though the lady was giving her all the advantages; actually he truly had all the advantages, being almost literally living in their place and seeing her every time she was in the barrio. Inez was a student in Manila of whatever degree she was taking. He was not interested in what she wanted to be, but the clear discrepancies of his bearing to fantasize for her affection was practically impossible to win her heart. Inez was the only daughter of a rich, well-respected couple, intelligent and educated like her parents. She was modern and the most beautiful of them all that he had ever seen and among her classmates who sometimes spent a weekend at their place. He never thought she would equally be amorous to him. All he was sure was he was just happy looking at her and not expecting any in return.

Another morning, the Japanese guards were all alerted by the difference in the patient inside the room they were guarding. The occupant was not lying flat but was on his side; conclusively, he had moved by himself. A few hours later, the attending doctor in the company of some people came in.

"Good morning, sir," greeted the kindhearted doctor. His next move consisted of taking the vital signs of the obviously awakened fellow.

Astonished and overwhelmed by the sudden presence of many people around him speaking of different languages and dialects that none he could understand, he chose to keep quiet. In addition, he didn't know where he really was; he had no idea who they were except the Japanese soldiers in uniforms with weapons, one even having a long blade hanging by his waists. It didn't take too long for them to push everyone out of the room. They couldn't allow the prisoner to have any further civilian contact until they could interrogate him; they had been waiting for this moment for a long time. Later, someone brought some food, and he was encouraged to eat but which was cut shortly.

"Captain Maish, we are derrighted (delighted) to see you awake," a Japanese officer who just entered the room said, coming in slowly until he had settled himself standing by the bedside. "You should thank the kindness of the Japanese Imperial Army for keeping you alive and healthy," he continued.

The "captain" was unresponsive, mesmerized by not knowing what anyone was saying. In Japanese, in English, or in local dialect, he really didn't know. Even if he wanted to respond to anyone whom he was sure was talking to him, he didn't know what to say. "Aahh, . . . uhmm," was all that came out of his throat followed by pretentious coughing. Nervous and afraid, his rigid body could truly allow little movement made worse by people talking obviously to him. He acted not hearing any word at all and turned his eyes around, looking at a few waists that displayed pistols. He settled his eyes on the ceiling. He really didn't recognize anyone. He was seeing a Japanese soldier up close and he was not shooting them. The lady in a white dress was familiar, but no one else he could concentrate his mind but her until he closed his eyes after a deep breath.

"He may be having temporary amnesia," the doctor explained to the Japanese officer. "He is still too weak and most wounds are not fully healed yet. Give him more time to recuperate." He added this in a voice that could be heard by all the guards, hoping he would be understood clearly.

"All right, but you have to tell me when he started talking," the impatient officer ordered. He just could not wait any more time for the information he was going to get from the "captain."

"Yes, sir, I will." The doctor was compelled to concur, thinking that if this man was truly having lapses, five days should be enough for him to regain his memory as well.

The lieutenant left but made sure he would be back soon. The guards became more strict that sometimes would not allow anybody be with the prisoner without them watching close by.

"I am Dr. Angelo Penafrancia," the doctor introduced himself while examining the soldier again. "Very good, all your wounds are healing fine. You really are an extraordinary man, no one will ever live with injuries like you had." He was evaluating his psychological condition.

"I don't speak and understand any language but Tagalog, sir," the soldier spoke in a timid voice, hoping that the respectable-looking man must know the language.

Dr. Penafrancia suddenly became confused. The foreign-looking man, identified as an American officer speaking clearly of the language of mainland Luzon, somewhat changed his amnesia theory.

"What is your name?" he asked immediately in Tagalog, knowing that he had finally solved the mystery of the muted soldier.

"Dominador Cabarles *po*, from Bulacan." He was thrilled at finally communicating with somebody. "I have two companions, Santos and Donono are their names. Do you know where they are?

Please tell me where they are if you know," he asked, taking advantage of the moment, concerned that his friends were also severely injured when they got separated as he explained further.

"Don't worry about them for now, you will definitely see them again if they survived," the doctor responded with his honest opinion. "So you are not Captain Ernest Maish? How did you get his cap?" He was referring to the officer's hat with the double bar insignia and the name of the real owner written inside. "You were sent here without anything to identify yourself except that hat." He was still baffled and mystified by the young soldier. "It was found in your pocket."

"The captain gave it to me during an encounter with the Japanese," he answered after realizing what hat the doctor was telling about.

"Where did that encounter happen?"

"I don't know the place, I am from Luzon. I don't know where I am," he answered, almost whispering. All that he could remember that day were atrociousness from both sides. He added more about the savagery at the foot of a bridge.

"That was six days ago, you've been here for five days already."

He didn't say a word after that. He had heard about a certain battle from the locals. It may not be accurate, but there were rumors that there were hundreds of casualties on the Japanese side, not counting the wounded. He uttered more prayers in his thoughts. He chose not to talk anymore, but for the last time, the doctor said, "I advise you to remain Captain Maish. However, I believe you were promoted as captain on the spot and you deserved it. I wish you more good luck. I will try to hold you here as much as I can, but that's all I can do for you." He remained quiet until he left the room.

There were so much questions to answer. The Japanese began the interrogation as if they could not wait. Well, they were nice, but he could not understand what they were saying. The ordeal that he had to take began on his sickbed. The doctor maintained that he was incoherent and could not remember anything and needed more time to recuperate.

The news that the young and handsome officer had awakened made the populace in and around the hospital happy. Though visits were not allowed, they became contented by just peeking through the window until it was totally forbidden. Many days passed, and the rumors began that he wasn't there anymore. He was transferred to a place only the Japanese could hear him talking. His food was inserted through a small opening, and things started to get bad, real bad for days. He was visited many times by the Japanese, sometimes by good ones; only a few could maintain to be nice.

"Good morning, Captain, how are you today?" They would say that all times they visited me in my cell. The head cap they found with me was used to slap my face over and over. Then it would be bare hands I would feel. They were the nice ones. I started to miss them when the bad ones took over. They showed me a map; I don't know what they were saying. I don't know what to say because I just really don't understand what they wanted. They made me drink a lot of water. I said no more because it was getting in my nose, but they wouldn't listen. Then they started pulling my nails every time I pointed at a spot on the map. "English, *bakero*!" I could only guess it was what they were speaking. I laughed when they laughed; when they got angry, I cried in pain. And then I thought it was over because there were no more nails to pull from my fingers. Days in the hole, they fed me; whatever it was, I ate them.

The worst was yet to come.

CHAPTER 5

DAVAO PENAL COLONY

Pains, I prayed. Afraid, I prayed. Dying, I can't pray no more. I was in hell.

IN THE NEW PLACE

The sudden change of his accommodations happened so fast he didn't know where he was. All the hours that ensued were spent in the dark. He had lost track of the time and days much more to know the places he had been. To be thrown into a little dark space with nothing other than walls of thick wood and bamboo in the middle of the night could not be another nightmare. He was sure of that as he started hearing that unusual humming in his ears again. It was bugs, crickets, and mosquitoes that became his friends, most times his food. During the day, it was flies, and they were many. He prayed while rubbing his ears, feeling the pain on his face that received more slaps and blows of hard objects. Fresh blood would drip again, but the pain in his jaws was more painful and traveled to his ears.

> Would it be my fault that the damned Japanese didn't understand or believe any words I said to them? I don't know what else I should do to appease them. My fingernails are gone, I have more on my toes. I only hoped they don't see them.

There was not a moment they had wasted since he was taken from Davao City. Only the travel in a truck at night over rough roads, he remembered. In the morning, he met the welcoming party of the Japanese in the new place. There were no more nice ones among them, they made sure of that. He closed his eyes, attempting to divert his mind. On the first day, he was taken in a warehouse and put back in his cage again in the afternoon. He was still musing about the other angel whom he had felt the most unselfish kindness he had only seen from his mother. *"I will be needing you again."* And he whispered prayers again and again until he could feel the same caring hands holding his.

But fate was clearing the way for him. He pretended not to notice what just happened, but it took his attention like an encouragement of doing what he was supposed to do. Although it might be accidental when it reflexively no more, the soft touch that he felt had drawn his sensitivity that he wanted to be in that regards for as long as it could be. He gently made his move, binding his own to that hand that submissively consented the adoration they had mutually felt for each other for a long time. No words came out from either one; the assuring glimpse and smile had tempered an understanding they had and would cherish and share with each other. Together they prayed and listened to the homily, though not as audible as they sat distantly from the pulpit; nothing mattered anymore. The Catholic church of San Lorenzo where it happened, where Inez and her parents attend mass every Sunday was in the town proper. Too far that with the absence of motorized vehicles the only means of transportation was the horse-pulled *carretela*. Only the rich could own them. Mr. Fernando Sandoval, a government employee of high position and office in the provincial capital of Malolos, owned two horses, one of which has given birth and grown to a healthy stallion, all in the care of Domeng. His personal attachment with the horses was special because they were the only animals among many others that the Sandoval family loved most, especially Inez. And for Inez, he would do just about anything that would make her happy. She would come home from Manila where her dorm was and excitedly attended to the young "stallion" every weekend.

"One very lucky stallion," he said, to be given such kind of attention from the most beautiful girl in the world as he slightly tightened his grip at the smooth and fine skin of her hand against his rough and callous palm.

The parent horses were from the finest breed used by infantrymen of the Spanish American War. The animals were either traded or slaughtered or given away as gifts to prominent Filipinos who had helped in the success of the American campaign in the archipelago. Along with the weapons of war, rifles, and pistols that were later sold in the black market, Filipina women also were obtained either by force, mutual respect, or for money. Nevertheless, the peace and prosperity that followed were enjoyed by all citizens and became a paradise for the US officers, servicemen, and civilian personnel who chose to stay in the Philippines. From the Malay race of the natural charming beauty of the Filipina mixed with four hundred years of Spanish occupation somewhat produced offspring of exquisiteness but who still remained true to the customs and traditions of simplicity and humility. Needless to say, in that long period, marital unions could only be done with the parents' intervention matched with the wealth and social status between families. A practice inherited from the Spaniards, the wealthy would become wealthier.

Dominador Cabarles, whose family ancestry was unknown, somewhat bore the genes of the so-called mestizos but remained in the poorest class, having nothing at all with regard to the wealth and prominence, could not say he was good enough to advance his dream to reality. In fact, he was only a servant of the Sandoval family. Instead, he was just being happy of being what he was and what he was good at, especially with his exceptional abilities to adapt himself to any situation without forgetting the status he belonged to the best of his abilities, which he learned from his folks. Short of any kind of formal education, he didn't know how to read nor write. The highest number he could count was the same as how many fingers he had in both hands. Over ten, he would say, "many," "so many," or "much too many."

Cabarles led a simple life that depended on belief in God and the laws of nature and the teachings of his father based on both. None beyond that could intricate of what he had wished for. He was granted the impossible—heaven it was—when he and Inez got married. He had to go through hell for walking away and hurdling over many obstacles, and none was easy. So far, he must survive it all before even thinking of a way to go back to her.

Well, it was really not easy being back from daydreaming. He could spend a night in a horse shack or under a tree but never be deprived of freedom to find comfort in choosing a better place to lie down and daydream. He could sustain his endurance for many days of hard work, but being beaten to death alternately by people without remorse was entirely different. A small damp room he was thrown in, it was clear his world was becoming smaller for him to fulfill his promises. However, his hope was always replenished by the morning sunlight passing through the planks of wood and bamboo in his cell when he opened his eyes.

"Cap, I'm glad you're awake," someone was calling his attention. Perhaps his new neighbor was awakened when he kicked the wall to test how strong it was. "James Feldman, LTJG US Navy, sir." The poor soldier gallantly identified himself to the presumed senior officer. A wall of bamboo separated them. He could peek through to see the outline of another human being in the duplex cage they had.

Though it took his attention, Cab just looked at the American, only saluting awkwardly in response. Trying to understand another language was the one that was giving him the most of a problem, how much more of waking up in a small space with an English-speaking guy? Much more to his dismay, he didn't know how to shut him up. Maybe the same technique when he tried to pacify down the horses would work. "Sshh." To his surprise, the soldier stop talking.

Only Donono called him "Cap" because for some reason, he could not pronounce his name right either. He was a good man. Cab didn't know what place was "Tayapas" (Tayabas), where he came from, where he also said there were a lot of pretty *papae* ("babae" in Tagalog, "ladies" in English). True to his intellectual limits, he knew he was a nobody, but getting a harsh punishment evidently much more than this officer who should be more deserving when it came to ranks, he would not take advantage of what the doctor advised. Fresh wounds and swollen face with dry blood was not big of a deal at the moment, but a dialogue with another person futile to his comprehension was what he feared the most and he didn't know how to overcome that feeling. He had undergone endless torture since he had awakened from that hospital.

The only advantage of being mistaken as an American captain was being saluted by another American, nothing else. The Japanese was definitely mistaken that he was an officer, as the doctor explained to him why he was let to live. They kept insisting he was, but he didn't know what to say to tell them that they were mistaken. He didn't know what rank he had to begin with. His limited rationalization directed him to be who he really was, and if becoming an officer was giving him so much punishment, he didn't want to be one anymore. He picked up the hat on the floor and tried to wipe his face of the blood or whatever it was on his face. He looked at it, saw blood, but that hat was what he wanted to get rid of for a long time and which always found its way to his hand. He inserted it between the spaces of the wall to the American prisoner and closed his eyes again. He missed the people who called him Domeng. Most especially the one who touched him also with her lips, with whom he shared memories of tender kisses with and could make him smile under any condition.

> The first time she held my hands had made the throbbing of my heart; the trembling of my knees were analogous to a newly born brood. It took a while before it could stand up by itself on his four feet. Inez had become so excited of the new life she saw as it tried to stand up on its own to express his joy that way. But the feeling of her warmth as her body rubbed with mine was a memory I shall treasure. I made that horse felt my gratitude by giving him the best care I could give, making it know of my pure intentions to the young woman as I encouraged myself that there was a chance to the impossible. However, it remained a dream that could only be revealed to the horses while growing up, whom I would not mind telling my thoughts and desires to. To whom I could express my fantasies freely without reservations. I don't mind when the mare is listening. I don't know why my tongue retracts in front of Inez; I have a feeling that even the horses are all making fun of me.

His abilities in making a decision of what he could be depended on wherever he could find himself in desperation, when he had no time to contemplate but act rigorously; when the first option is futile, then he would remain in silence. Most circumstances come what may, he depends on faith and of what he was told to do. The choice of remaining a captain as he was advised was taking a toll. He tried to tell the truth several times, but nobody would listen. He was a Filipino soldier, which he really was; the result was just the same—he would receive punishing blows and tortures. They were coming again.

"Captain Maish! Have you been rested very werr (well)?" a Japanese guard said to him mockingly as he opened the door to his cage.

"Our commanding officer is inviting you to his office," said another one.

Whatever they said he knew the drill very well already—get up and follow which way he was led to. They were obviously referring to him; the point of bayonets made sure it was him they wanted, no one else. He had learned the name of the real captain already, now his alter ego. He just hoped he made it alive back when they were done. As to his friends Sergeant Rodrigo Santos and Hombre Donono, wherever they were now, he always believed he would see them again.

The meeting with the commanding officer went well. He was intimidating, but not as much as the other two Japanese who stayed standing behind him. It went well to the sense that he was only yelled at until he was put back in his cage. Came another morning.

"Good luck, Cap!" his neighbor said. Somewhat he misheard him being called as "Cab." He made sure he was the same man upon a quick glance as he nodded confidently that he would get over another day. Only a few people call him by that name, and some of them were dead. He wanted to believe that they were not all dead. "Cap" or "Cab" they called him; those names were cursed or if they were for luck it is giving him, he doesn't know. He clearly remembered how the last time he was called by that name. There were also bayonets just behind pointing at him, pushing him.

He knew he would not survive another bayonet getting through his body. He walked to wherever he was directed, the same place during the daytime—a structure made of corrugated sheet metal on the roof as around the wall, his first impression was of a rice mill, but it wasn't. Inside was empty other than stacks of building materials on one corner and agricultural tools and plows along the wall on the right. The only way out was where they went in, a double door that opened and shut close immediately as they entered. At the middle was a wooden chair where two more Japanese were waiting.

"Nice to see you again, Captain Maish," one of the soldiers politely greeted him while telling him to sit down. A sign language made by the point of a rifle made him understand what they wanted. "I was told our commanding officer is not happy on his meeting with you last night." The Jap continued not getting any response from him whatsoever. He smiled too when they smiled, and he laughed when they laughed.

A robust slap on his face followed immediately by the butt of a rifle on his shoulder made him sure that what he had in mind was not what they meant. He chose not to respond anymore; it might help, but he was always wrong to guess what they were saying. Otherwise, he thought that the Japs were going to kill him another day if he would just remain quiet. The screaming of the soldier became louder as they got angrier. Cab absolutely had no idea what they were screaming about; all that he could think of was he had shot and killed a lot of Japanese and he was suffering the consequences. He had no clue that the furious soldiers were just asking his name. They tied his hands up with a long rope and looped it around the crossbar above the roof's frame. For two days, he was hanging by his hands, feet barely touching the ground. He would be left alone only when they tired of hitting him with a hard piece of bamboo on his back or when he passed out.

THE STUBBORN "CAPTAIN"

Two days of getting inconsistent yes and no answers on the same question somewhat started the Japanese interrogator to question his own proficiency in English. They brought in a translator, another Japanese in plainclothes with a white band of one big red dot around his arm. There was no way an American could not understand and answer a simple question with all the pain and punishment the prisoner had already suffered, which was very unusual unless he was keeping a lot of information. It didn't work; he was thrown back to the same dark space he was in before. How could he be understood when he was almost dead already? Nobody cared if he was dead or alive; they just pushed his unresponsive body into the cage; a hard kick on his shin that blocked the door concluded another day. Hungry and petrified, he remained on the only position he could make until he rose back at a time with just enough daylight to see that he was alone. He feasted on whatever was on the plate that was left by the door. The thirst and hunger he felt was way too much to pass up on that blessing of which ants had already started to get their share. His body so stiff again that if he moved any part of it resulted to an unbearable pain mainly on his jaws and shoulder bones. The rest were just numbed. His endurance to remain, kindled by unassuming stipulation, perhaps enhances his tolerance to pain and degradation. He admitted that the severity of retribution from the Japanese was definitely lack of ability to communicate, being illiterate.

I grew up on the rice paddies, tilling lands that was not even ours. Short of luxury of any kind in a farming community reachable mainly by walking. There was a road but seldom used in transportation of any type. The grasses that grew on it were taller than whoever tried to walk through, leading to a dead end but a bamboo bridge across a river. Neighbors were a mile apart to the closest, and the only time we could have contacts from each other were planting and harvest season of the crops and occasional family celebration that welcomed everyone. And of course, the main topic of conversations were always farming, sometimes a new birth, which gives the same enjoyment if it was a human or animal. A self-sustaining community abundant of natural food resources, there was really not much of material need. Diseases and untimely death are always put to the will of God. No real doctor was available except for the practicing quacks. The expensive costs of higher education could be attained only by the very wealthy, the elementary public school was about twentyty miles distance by foot and by horses through winding road that only the rich could afford. Sure it was not easy to even think of any ambition other than having a plentiful harvest to a land tenant like my own folks.

I could not remember, however, of having any interest in education. No one has told me of the benefits, or whatever there might was not necessary to the kind of life we were accustomed with. From boyhood until the time my heart started longing for a dream, what I had learned in life was my own with the utmost guidance of my parents based on their views of peaceful living short of irrelevant formal education. Just be happy where we belong, they would say. I was always happy of what I was, what I became capable of, physically and mentally. The respect and unselfish devotion in the family that I was taught of and extended to others became synonymous with my other abilities. It never occurred in my thoughts that time would come when I would be wanting for surreal desire that could only be attained by imagination. But faith sure knows how to guide me the way when it became clear that my dreams have come true.

"Hail Mary, Mother of God, please keep giving me strength. Let me fulfill the promises I had given into thee." It was the prayer he kept on saying to himself.

No one bothered him the next day and another night. He would fall asleep then become alerted of someone opening the door for his food. He had reoriented himself to his normal senses though the pains in his back was hard to ignore. He was visited again by a group of Japanese, but he chose to pretend he was sick and delirious as he lay down on the ground, still needing more time to recuperate. Water and food ration became doubled since then, and no other prisoner was with him in the cage. Sometimes he would look outside through holes on the walls where he could see Japanese soldiers walking in drill formation, with civilians—men, women, and children—from far in the east. There should be at least one of them who knew how to speak Tagalog with whom he could communicate with. There must be a kindhearted individual somewhere around who lived in those houses from afar. There were also tall fences with barbed wire on the other side and a guard tower. At night, it was always quiet with only the light poles that indicated there should be many people who lived around.

He didn't wait too long to be relieved of his boredom. He was taken again and brought back to the same warehouse. He didn't like it there anymore; the horrors of the previous time he was there had inflicted into his mind the dreadful thought that he might not make it out alive anymore. He tried to resist stepping inside, but to turn around would be a suicidal choice so he was sitting again on the same chair. This time he was tied up as soon as he sat down.

"I have to be clear to you, Captain. If you still refuse to talk, we will kill you. Understand?" the same Japanese officer made sure he was heard with his loud voice as close as possible to the prisoner's ear. "Tell me your name, your rank, and where your company is hiding," the lieutenant continually asked and said more of the threat that he would do.

The interpreter in civilian clothes repeated the question one at a time. An officer in the Japanese intelligence, he was frustrated of getting information from their vines of spies around the island of Mindanao to the whereabouts of the American company that massacred the Japanese soldiers in Bukidnon. The prisoner, believed to be the commanding officer of that company, should know where they retreated to.

"What is your name?" He didn't get an answer. "Your name!" Trying to hold his temper, he pointed to the nameplate of the uniformed soldier standing by him.

Still, the foot soldier didn't understand, but he guessed. "Dominador Cabarles, no Americano." Scared of what they were about to do, he just said his name as luck would have it if he answered correctly to the query of the seemingly more accommodating Jap. But he was learning as he realized that yes and no are two different words, one the opposite of the others from the last affair with these people. He had practiced saying his name in the cage, but with a rank unknown, he added his identification as not being an American. He was never told nor assigned a rank or number like how it was drawn on the Japanese uniform. As far as he knew, he was a soldier, simply given a gun to shoot the Japanese. Well, that was he was told, and he just did it as many times as he could. If only he learned more aside from that and it wasn't Inez that was in his mind all the time when not shooting the Japanese, maybe he wouldn't be punished this much.

Notwithstanding, a forceful smack on his face from the same guy sent him down to the floor. From where he fell down, he was raised again, immediately with the rope keeping him in place. "Dominador Cabarles, Filipino. No English," he said the same every time when asked of anything. He looked at the ununiformed Japanese; he thought he was nice. Well, he wasn't. He was the head honcho of the dreaded Kempeitai spreading atrocities among civilians in Davao.

"No, you are Ernest Maish, an American officer. A captain," the frustrated Japanese kept on saying. "Where is your company hiding?" He would keep asking furiously and signal to the other guy for more whacks from behind. He was left hanging up again that night clinging to whatever left of his sanity.

The next morning, an American was brought in to identify or claim whoever this guy was impersonating an American officer. At first look, he concluded that he was a Caucasian, but the horrible condition of the bloody soldier made him question the inhumanity of the Japanese not allowed in the Geneva Convention. The Japanese began to suspect that their prisoner was not a soldier but a common criminal who had killed so many of their men, who also had committed a crime on the American rank by posing as one of their own. He was forced to ask a few questions but to no avail. He only got the name; he must really be a local recruit. He recommended to get a Filipino interpreter, but he would not leave until he had also found out who that man was.

A local guy by the name of Ruben Pablo was brought in, working double for the Japanese favor aside from his regular job; he was cooperative, but bigheaded. He did not even blink or was regretful of the half-dead human being in front of him. *They want to know your name, tell me?* steadfastly asked the arrogant translator in local dialect.

"Dominador Cabarles, Filipino," responded the prisoner, head nodding down and eyes tightly closed. He surely had become comfortable saying his name. Actually, he didn't understand what the proud brown fellow asked. Some of the words were familiar from a similar situation, his senses dictating him of a little curiosity to wake up. "Please take me down, I cannot take it anymore," he begged in Tagalog. He begged the man who was yelling at him in the only language he could speak and understand. Finally, someone he could talk to without getting beaten so much.

A string of questions followed immediately. Bragging of his own status and intelligence in Tagalog for a moment, the local interpreter turned to the Japanese rendering his extra usefulness and carried on with what he was supposed to do. "He said he is a soldier of USAFFE, Fifty-Seventh Scout Division from Luzon. His commanding officer was Captain Maish, presumably escaped or dead. He doesn't know what happened to him."

More questions were translated and replied to. The Japanese may have believed that he was left commanding a unit; however, the story of thirteen men against the might of an entire invasion force of Japanese in Davao was unbelievable. They still wanted to know how many of the company had escaped.

"There was no two company, only two people had escaped," Cab repeated what he already said.

DEATH BY PUNISHMENT AND STARVATION

In total disappointment, one of the Japanese soldiers picked up the already fragmented piece of bamboo and beat the hell out of the prisoner over and over that it broke the chair eventually. He just could not accept the fact that they took care of a lowly soldier for too long, the same soldier they believed for a long time was a company commander who let his men retreat in the heat of the battle. He was so furious that there was no one else he could turn to for his revenge. The American soldier felt that the prisoner could not take any more blows and he would die; he hugged the man to take the lashes by just turning and covering his face to accept the punishment in behalf of a comrade. He was sent back to POW compound, Cab, to his cage; he was still breathing. The Japanese was not done with him yet.

The enemy command decided to give the worst of the death sentence for their prisoner, unbeknownst to the barefooted soldier, a captain or whatever rank that he should die. But killing him while unconscious would not give them the satisfaction; henceforth, shooting him would just be too easy for all the detriments he had caused to their forces.

Cabarles knew that he was in a Japanese prison camp. He wasn't sure; it must be hell. Raised as a devoted Catholic, the first of the Ten Commandments had given him a lot of thought. It was not worthy to justify the reasons of suffering anymore but keep holding up, hoping it would end eventually. He had given serious thought to the hell he was in and surrender to the punishment he also thought he deserved. He really had committed unimaginable sin multiple times. "Much too many." His count were all of his fingers plus Santos's and Little Doe's twice altogether. Maybe more, counting again based on how many times he had loaded a ten-shot magazine and the five-bullet cartridge in his rifle and all the weapons he had aimed at every Japanese he saw moving. All of those he was sure had hit his target; maybe not fatal at times, but never had he missed his aim when it came to those rifles, especially when the targets were large and near. However he tried, he could not make an exact count; what it meant was he didn't know how long he would stay in hell. He didn't even know how long he had stayed already. He gave up on his computation but made a momentous resolution—he would be able to get over it. Weak and agitated, he was scared and doubted if he would be able to handle any more of the beatings. What more may come next? He refused to just die.

There are angels to shed tears for me because I can't anymore. There were two, one always on my side holding my hands graciously, always adorable and charming like the one that sometimes disappear. My delusions had riveted my grip from reality that I had learned how to transform my unbearable situation to the opposite. I always see them, one pleasantly healing all my wounds while the other making all the pains go away. Terrifying visions of death had already consumed my body, only hindered by inspirations and encouragement from both to my declining consciousness. And they would help each other carry me to familiar places I always wanted to be. I don't know who may be the other angel; in every dream, she was obscured. Her thoughtfulness and sincerity in caring had been on my mind that can be compared to Inez. Just like Inez.

And so it happened in the most unusual way. Perhaps fate could not decide if I really deserved what I'm wishing for or the horse could not take any more of my hopeless incoherence. However, it may still be fate in motion when the young stallion pushed her to my direction that we both lost our balance, falling off to a thin stack of hay on the ground. It was embarrassing to my masculinity to fall down that easily, but feeling her partially on top of me was a moment I didn't want to get. As close as it can possibly be, short of touching her lips with my own, my arms were around her, feeling her breathe into my face while our eyes locked up with each other. It was an awkward feeling to me, taking advantage of the incident, but one of us regained from the inevitability fast enough. It wasn't me as I was still pondering, lying on the ground, heart pumping, profusely filling every bit of my veins with blood as much as it could. Her smell and the softness of her body against mine had carelessly revealed my desires; the limitations of my only function to her had been breached. A bit later, I just found myself holding her hands that I didn't want to let go. A few moments more, her arm were around mine and together we were overjoyed at how the young horse had become a handsome stallion. Not too many words were spoken, but it was then how a mutual compassion and understanding began between us. After that, I became closer to my religion, too close that I attended mass every Sunday. Even some extra days.

Though his concerns were more focused on his own survival, he was also frightened of the effect of war in Manila. The only way that would expunge his worries about Inez and relatives was not to think of them. His determination was so engrossed on how he could tighten the grip of his own self and be with them again at all costs when the chance was forgiving. Drained of strength, it would not be easy. He would have to stay breathing and thrust aside all what may come ahead. He knew it very well as he could not remember how many times his pulse had stopped already. Sometimes he would hold his breath as much as he could, testing himself of how much more punishment he could handle, and he would catch his breath, profusely filling up his chest to the greatest pain he could tolerate of his hapless body.

Then it ended for what it seemed. His blood dried out from fresh and old wounds. Even for the little benefit he must expect from the Japanese, none came in the days that followed. For one last time, he was fed and there was no more after that. Left alone to die but to no avail, he would be back to life. He wasn't given food at all for many days nor was visited by anybody.

What sustained my residual strength were a few drops of water collected every morning from the rusting roof of the cage. For some reason, sweet potato vines and leaves were growing just outside the wall even if it was dry season. Later, I found out that an open drainage ended close by, watering the plants that grew generously. The water didn't taste good, but it filled up a depression on the ground at uncertain times of the day. I had devised a tool on how to collect them in— piece of cloth from what I was wearing tied to a stick to reach the canal, but it wasn't enough to regain my strength. I became skin and bones until miraculous events happened—thunderstorm, followed by rain and strong winds that blew down my bamboo cage. I feasted on the water from heaven that were pouring like it would not stop. And the wind didn't relent its might until the cage just disappeared. It was in the dark of the night, too dark that I got more concerned that the wind would blow myself away either holding tight to a little bush while munching on its leaves and little fruits. Escaping wasn't a choice; I was too weak, and I didn't know where to go. In the morning, people found me cold and shivering from exposure, and my cage was gone. It seemed like a vague vision, but I could still see them around me. I was sent to a nearby compound fenced with barbed wires fortified with strong poles and bars by the people who found me.

THERE IS A PLACE BEYOND HELL

Inside the building were rooms of equal sizes, big enough to fill many people. Some were empty. I didn't know how delirious or sick I was, but the last step I did able to make was few more too short to fall on the ground. I was pulled and thrown into a space adjacent to occupied ones. They were not Japanese. I heard quiet commotion, but my mind was not responding anymore to who could be around me. My head was just circling in motion, made worse by persisting visions beyond my wildest dreams. I saw sinful people glowing in orange like they were in flames inside steel bars. Flames everywhere, on the walls, and on the grounds. Could it be real hell? There were images of horrifying faces walking in single file summoned by soldiers with horns protruding through their heads with intense fireballs coming out from their shoulders. And they all kept coming and going in choreographed motion; it was a busy day in hell. Rats roamed freely as they became bigger every time I looked at them. I didn't waste any effort to scare them away; the truth was it was me who was terrified. Terrified of how my death would be. I was in hell already, I was sure, but what else it was, like a dark hole? It was pulling me inside, a dark space sloping down with sharp blades arranged systematically so that I would be in pieces sliding to the bottom, to the waiting mouth of a monstrous rat. I may have been dead already, but I refused to be meal for that animal.

I was able to hold tight, dragging my stiff legs to clench firmly on a railing. But the horror I had didn't make me feel safe to just stay holding tight. I wanted to climb that wall as high as I could and fast. I did it so fast that when I reached the top, I noticed that had I left my body on the ground. I could see it so clearly. It couldn't be; I had to come back for it. I felt the cold floor and started shivering again.

It was the most terrifying ordeal I had ever fought for in my life. I had no more hope to live while silently saying sorry to all the people I knew that kept popping on my mind. I was in hell; what else did I need to prove to myself that I didn't deserve to be in hell or beyond? "Please, God, let me stay in hell for a while more," I prayed. I had no more strength to find my source of hope. My soul had literally separated from my body.

In hell, there would be a kindhearted soul who would alleviate my tormented spirit from so much suffering and hunger. The touch of warm hands on my arms at the moment my soul decided to leave my body for good fused them together again. Flaming people and fresh voices, I was given food fed directly into my mouth by so many hands alternately extended through and behind one another. Real food, rice balls, pieces of bread, or whatever and the warm water passing through my throat was like new spirit that had succumbed to me. Blankets were wrapped around my half-naked body; there were voices of people calling, saying to hang on tight as they joined the lines of flames. I was so grateful, but the surroundings were just too faint on my vision even with my eyes wide open. I started not to recognize anything until it became nothing at all, till the last that I felt was someone holding my hand.

Dominador Cabarles passed out with the "comforts" of the new place. Warm, spacious, and the most important, he knew he was in friendly company before he lost all senses. The residents of hell were accommodating, and the warm welcome they had shown somewhat transformed his feelings like he was in heaven. He saw colors other than the orange and darkness. It transformed suddenly into breathtaking sceneries, traveling on the most beautiful landscape, of endless blooming flowers and greeneries that he only saw in paintings. Of the golden rice fields and meadows full of wild blooms of different flowers in the month of June, where every living thing could thrive without much intervention until they became food for the others. Where he would join Inez and together they would enjoy and appreciate how nature could frame itself to such spectacular sceneries.

The most beautiful of feelings. The mood that doesn't end to be just as beautiful. It seemed like an endless splendor when my wishes would be rewarded then I could ask for more. It all came spontaneously. Her genuine kindness, absent of any influence from being a wealthy heir, educated, and being the prettiest did not became a deterrent to the affection that she had shown to me. However, the happiness on my part was always rejected because of my known identity. The poor and illiterate tenant of their ownership, notwithstanding to be even thinking of such bond with Inez. I acknowledged where I stood; it was not a question of claiming what was mutually mine. It was the trust that her parents had given me, and they deserved the respect be it known to them of my good intentions for their only child the best I promise to thee. That was what troubled me all the time; I had nothing but myself who could not even find the right word on the many instances of normal conversation with anybody. How much more to discuss about my promised commitments with their daughter? How much manhood would I need? I knew that the more I withhold would mean the more I disrespect them. I did not betray their trust, but how could I prevent myself from touching heaven? Would it be a good excuse that every time I found my courage, they would make me run an errand? The principles of decency and honesty that I was taught of were easily intimidated by inferiority in every level. What I could not do by words, I would show with diligence, but definitely it was not enough. Being accepted into a family whom I had taken advantage of with my freedom and gain the utmost confidence by doing what I should not have done was . . . I was just a man.

The hell had ceased on flaming when his eyes opened in the afternoon. There wasn't a picturesque view around. No holes on the floor nor rats. Just plain people dressed in bright orange shirts coming back from the details of the day. They were convicted criminals of the local justice system serving time in the Davao Penal Colony, a prison system that had been sustaining itself of its livelihood even before the war. The population had been reduced to the only able-bodied prisoners by sending the weak, sickly, and old to Iwahig Penal Colony in Palawan not long ago. Taken over by the invading forces, the compound was adapted to become the headquarters of the Japanese command in Mindanao to house the prisoners of war. The offices were converted to billet the officers, a storage building used as punishment and interrogation room where Cabarles stayed the longest period of his time yet. But most other structures were used for their original purposes like the hospital, the diesel powerhouse, the mess hall, and the chapel. Perimeter fences were fortified and additional towers were constructed to house a .50 caliber machine guns with twenty-four hours of Japanese guards on duty. Somewhere within the compound were thousands of allied prisoners of war—Americans and the insignificant little known foot soldiers, the Filipinos.

The main building that accommodated the convicts and was the oldest of the structures had its own perimeter fences. Cabarles had no interest just yet of what else were beyond those fences. He had enough of the ordeal he had suffered; surely he could not take any more. The tormenting experience of pain, hunger, and humiliation had afflicted his senses, and his physical endurance had long been on its edge. He himself believed he had died so many times already. But even in his constant refusal to totally concede every time he was on that edge, he believed the end of his story was not his to decide.

Just as how he was left on the ground, he was exactly of the same position when the *colonos* (convicted prisoners) came back in the afternoon.

"My name is Roberto dela Cruz," a gentle approaching voice broke the silence of the room. It was the same man who was the last to leave in the morning and the first to come back.

The convict got no response, noticing that the man held in their cell was still holding tight on the steel bars, his eyes blinking, staring at him like he had forgotten how a human being looked like. He was alive; it was just that he must be still in shock of most horrific experience. He offered him water, but it was almost impossible to drink without spilling the water. In a few more minutes, the rest of the inmates came, and they all helped an unknown fellow to be more relaxed and entrusting to let go of the railings. The offering hands and words he could understand clearly from Dela Cruz became an assurance that this occurrence was all real. He drank the water and ate more of the rice balls and fruit smuggled inside the prison just for him. Every inmate in the cell had contributed to the effort of bringing in an extra food. He had not said a word yet, just eating whatever they handed. Someone had taken off his shirt and attempted to help with each other to wear it on the weak and barely clothe man. None of them were prepared to what they saw around his body when they took the old one off. It could not be described, and it was sickening. All of them became speechless and shocked. Traces of wounds on top of the others that healed and more that became infected. How much of a wrongdoing can a person do to deserve this kind of retribution and abuse? How much of it can a person withstand and still live?

"Who has a clean shirt?" the older one was able to regain from his shock and realized that his sweaty and soiled clothes would not be appropriate for the healing wounds of the man.

He passed on an order that all stashed medicine be made available immediately. Not long after, an assortment of pills were put into the sick man's mouth. His unusually high temperature indicated he had a fever caused by infection from his wounds and prolonged exposure to weather. All of them struggled to attend to the well-being of the still-unknown man that could only be a prisoner. They cleaned his wounds first carefully with warm water; someone had a bottle of alcohol too, and they used it. He was attended to the best of their own skills on medicating oneself. They didn't want him to be sent to the hospital because he would only be left to die; no sick convict was ever treated in the hospital anymore. It was only for soldiers; for this man to be sent there, he would be as good as dead.

IN THE REIGN OF TERROR

Since the takeover of the Japanese on the colony, the life of the inmates were never the same. They were not the ones who decided the toughest among themselves; they must all be tough or at least look like one who could handle the hard labor under new authority. It was not survival of the fittest anymore; they must work together, plan together, and take care of each other regardless of whatever crime one has committed. The soldiers would not discriminate anybody except for a collaborator wearing their flag pinned around their upper arm. However, they were required to bow also at the Japanese like everyone else. Those who could do were the ones who were likely to survive, and the best of the best to do it was most likely a collaborator. The last inmate who was bowing one too many to the Japanese had died of snakebite in the rice field, and another had died in his sleep. Since then, everyone just avoided getting a close encounter with the Japanese.

The self-sufficiency in operating the colony was adapted by the Japanese from the previous administration of the prison. Under the new management, prisoners were forced to work equally to at least ten times of their daily consumption or more to support the food supplies of the entire Japanese military in Mindanao and the adjoining island provinces. There were no use for inmates who could not sustain the hard labor, and those who defied orders and weak were sent somewhere else. Local guards and officers who did not embrace the new management were the first of the prisoners of war in Dapecol. Those who had sworn loyalty were recruited to the network of the Japanese Kempeitai (agents of the devil, according to Cabarles) or became a local government official under the control of the military. Sustainability depended mainly on agriculture and labor supply to logging and plantation owners associated with the Japanese command.

Planned and studied even before the occupation of the Philippine Islands by the Japanese military spies, the only hindrance was how to control the hardened Filipino convicted criminals who would dare to fight to the death when provoked. The solution was easy—systematic elimination of the true fearless by executing them and creating trepidation among the rest. They also reduced the population to a manageable level of abled bodies by getting rid of the useless weak and sickly, and they did. The prison cell, though still crowded, could spare a space for one more.

The red dot became the symbol of terror and atrocities among the civilians, but what the Japanese didn't count was the courage of the Filipinos themselves, being worn down by foreign occupation—four hundred years of the Spaniards and forty years of the Americans themselves may only look like defeated, but the fight goes on.

It is a common knowledge that the priority of the Filipinos begin with the family's well-being. In times of hardship, pride and dignity could be set aside to let faith take over and be fulfilled of what they can be the next day. "Bahala na ang Diyos" (God's willing) was a saying originated from hopelessness and extreme poverty, also adapted heavily to make excuses for laziness and the inability to face the consequences of their own actions or the powerlessness to dispute what they rightfully deserve and own. However, this perception contradicts the position of the wealthy and educated whose precedence is how they can keep their riches and the greed for more even to the annihilation of their own race. From their class were born the so-called "Makapili" and the "Sakdalista" whose individual prominence and social status of their leadership became a figure to be supported by many and embrace the invading forces. Makapili was derived from the full word *MakaPilipino* (patriots). The word was subjugated to describe the undecided but which obviously lean toward collaborating the enemy. Sakdalistas are those who have shown alliances by deeds and principles.

The local government in Davao was restructured by retaining those who had immediately turncoat upon the invasion. The rumors there was that it had been organized even before the occupation. Majority of Filipinos bravely showed their resistance amid the dreadful force by the Japanese. It was also said that inmates put up a good fight individually against the belligerent Japanese invasion to instant death. But the effort was proven futile as the retribution mercilessly involved the cautious with an unconceivable ratio of casualties—a blatant waste of human life to a temper that could be withhold. Surely they learned a lesson as everyone had lost a friend or cellmate with brutal resolution.

THE COLONOS

The sun shone again with intense bright rays reduced by the shades of towering coconuts and trees that did not help to ease the discomfort of a humid morning. Cabarles woke up sweaty but better to the sight of another man whose hands held his. He could feel the warmth of a convict who chose to spend the night lying down with him on the floor. The solace of body heat transmitted to him at the time of shivering from extreme cold had helped tremendously, not to mention the arms that embraced his body like a terrified child being comforted by a blood relative. He believed that it wasn't only the body heat that had been transferred but life and spirit. He was so thankful that he tightened up his grip to the equally callous hands before he let it go. He retrained his aching joints and muscles, whatever was left on them, bending them in all directions as he tried to stand up with the help of the railings. He only made it to a kneeling position. His movement had caused everyone on the cell to be awakened, all happy to see him back to his senses.

"I don't know how to thank you all. I don't know what to say for helping me to another life," he said, full of emotion, tears dripping as he wiped them off, crying profoundly. He knew he was not that strong yet, but the gratitude he wanted to convey to these people who pulled him out of hell was very much sincere.

None of the prisoners found a word to respond. Silently, one gave him water to drink. They knew that what this unknown man had suffered was beyond belief, and what they may have done to help him was not enough, would never be enough. His endurance and courage to extend his own life was what kept him alive. They all knew that.

"I am Roberto dela Cruz, Berto" the man also kneeling in front of him introduced himself for the second time while trying to hold his hands to pacify the unfortunate prisoner from weeping.

"Domeng, Dominador Cabarles, from Bulacan. Thank you very much again. To all of you," he humbly responded while acknowledging everyone in the room.

"I was also born and grew up in Bulacan, in the town of Malolos," the elated Berto disclosed immediately, proud to know a presumed soldier from his home province.

The rest of the inmates close by introduced themselves too: Vicente Terso, Pablo Domingo, Marcos Terzo, and more in a cell overcrowded with hardened criminals sentenced to certain years' minimum to life of different crimes from simple carabao rustling to killing another human being before the war.

There was a sigh of disbelief in learning more about a soldier detained in isolation without food and water. Up to what extent must a soldier do to deserve unimaginable punishment from the Japanese and left for dead? Normally, the Japanese would just shoot anyone who had wronged them; this soldier must have done something else. Still, no one asked anything, but one commented that he should not be with the "*colono.*" He must be in the POW camp with his fellow soldiers, not in jail. They started to get worried for their own safety. However, they took care of the forgotten soldier very well until they could figure out what to do with him. Given a short time, Cab and Berto spent times to know more of each other while the soldier was taken care of like a VIP in the convict population.

On the eleventh day under their care, the presence of a soldier in the quarters of the inmates was secretly relayed to Juan Arcenas, the jail superintendent and Lt. Col. Chuck Cumberton, then the highest-ranking POW and camp commander. The remaining inmates of Dapecol had already identified who can be trusted among the ranks of civilian employees. Moreover, they had already developed a communications system among them when the information required secrecy. There was a rumor that an American captain of great interest to the Japanese intelligence had escaped during the storm and they wanted him to be captured again. However, the Japanese Imperial Army had been massively expanding their control over the islands against the defending Allied forces in Mindanao and the Panay Region; they didn't have the likelihood of pursuing the alleged soldier in question. The colonos quietly disputed that the prisoner they were taking care of was a USAFFE soldier who was found wandering in the compound after the storm while maintaining that he was an American. Only an American could raise concerns from the Americans, and somewhat they enjoyed better status in the camp compared to the Filipinos. Whether Cabarles was an officer or just a barefoot soldier with no rank or a lost vagabond, they intended to ensure his safety from the Japanese. And the safest for him in the meantime was to be among the ranks of prisoners of war. At the demand of Lt. Colonel Charles Cumberton who had already known that an American captive by the name of Captain Ernest Maish was in a makeshift cage somewhere in Dapecol, the information relayed by a captured navy lieutenant who had shared a detention cell with an army officer and verified his existence, Domeng was eventually handed over to the POW commandant. Jun Arcenas played a great role in the facilitation of the transfer. The confusion among Japanese ranks to identify the forgotten prisoner led them to believe that he was just an insignificant soldier and does not need much attention in the time being. In so doing, he would just be inside the inescapable POW camp when they needed him.

THE EARLY BIRDS

In the morning of April 3, 1942, at the muster formation of the American and Filipino prisoners of war at the Davao Penal Colony entered another one to add to their population. A common view since the camp were established, the difference was that this one was coming from within the colony.

Assisted by the head jailer himself, Arcenas and a few Japanese guards, his arrival had already caused confusion as there was a lingering tale about a man who was sentenced to death by punishment but just didn't want to die until the Japs had given up and eventually left him to die by starvation. On the other hand, there were a few civilians trying to locate a certain POW inside the prison itself who just disappeared. Normally, any deaths in the compound were accounted by name; Maish or Cabarles was not listed, but there were people who said that Cabarles had died in a battle a long time ago, accompanied by stories that were hard to believe but verified by the same people who had seen it happen. There was a soldier whose heroism and courage in battle was witnessed beyond belief, who had defied the odds and disregarded shelling while ensuring that his fellow soldiers would survive. He didn't take a clear chance to retreat but ensured that the others could while remaining to fight against the enemy, seriously wounded but who still managed to save the others. The legend continued of an American captain whose gallantry led his unit against a swarm of enemies and was severely injured but who still managed to escape, only to be captured. In his refusal to cooperate with the enemy, he was presumed executed after prolonged interrogation and punishment.

The Filipino version was a detailed account; he was described as a barefoot soldier and exceptional shooter who led a unit of lost soldiers fighting the Japanese to the last round of bullet while being shelled out. In the end, his last breath was dedicated to save fellow soldiers. The colonos' version was short but added confusion to the story; there was a man rescued by the convicts who must be an army officer who was disoriented and lost during the storm. Speculations about his origins were that he may have been from the POW camp blown out by the storm over the fence; otherwise, he had risen from the grave. Both were hard to believe, but not for those who could not come up with realistic explanations.

Conflicting stories only led to confusion on who wanted to believe. The Americans and the Filipinos claimed he was from their ranks. On the Japanese version, no such person existed and lived; whoever talked about him would die too. From the Filipinos who attested to the truth of the story, their hero had died but confirmed that he was a Filipino. For the Americans, it was just unbelievable that he could be a Filipino though they knew an account of the same battle, which was true—the commanding officer was an American captain who was captured but eventually escaped from a Japanese hospital. He was recaptured and executed, as the story went.

The civilian community had another edition that originated from a hospital in Davao. The colonos who actually met the man somewhat had their own to add to the legitimacy of the tale. They believed it was the same man in their care.

"My honor to meet the famous captain. Welcome to Dapecol," greeted the camp commander himself, standing along with a young navy officer and many more American soldiers behind them.

Cabarles just stared at the colonel momentarily and continued to focus his eyes to all the soldiers in detention, but the real thing was to divert his mind from being called a captain. He wanted to respond and disown the rank that he wasn't actually a captain, but he didn't know how to tell on the swarming English-speaking soldiers. Mistake on the rank may have saved his life in the beginning, but it was also the cause of the unimaginable punishment he had suffered. He was sure it was the primary reason; otherwise, he should have been dead already. Was he thankful? Should he be? The conflict of his rationalization on what he became and its resulting effect as a soldier in so short of a time was beyond he can assent. His mind and body was fixated to just surviving, nothing else, trying real hard every moment.

After a word of confirmation from a US Navy junior officer who shared a cell with the soldier, Colonel Cumberton took the opportunity of his silence to put on him a hat—the same hat that kept finding its way to his possession. He saluted the "captain" afterward, and everyone followed. Cabarles's heart was pumping, and he was outright disoriented of what was transpiring, his attention diverted to the Filipinos coming forward to check what was going on, the pair of Filipino soldiers who never wanted to be left out when food was possibly being distributed. They were not sure what was going on, but it was worth checking out.

Cabarles rubbed his eyes to make sure he wasn't deceive by his vision again; the Americans thought he responded to the salute. But the truth was, he just couldn't believe what he was seeing. The sight of the little man and a taller Filipino soldier had made him trembled like he was going to lose his balance from tremendous exhilaration. He had momentarily forgotten what he had been through.

Likewise, the two soldiers were simply speechless at seeing the ghost of their long-presumed-dead friend. Was he really alive? They were not sure yet. They came closer to the thin, long-haired and bearded soldier. One of them slightly uncovered the face from long sticky hair held tightly by a cap. They could not be mistaken.

"Cap! Cap! Is that really you?" Hombre Donono was bewildered, but certainly he wasn't mistaken. He hugged his long-lost friend and just cried. Though he knew the man very well, he could not believe the look of his formerly neat and masculine friend. Naturally talkative of a man, Donono could understand when Cab remained in silence; he felt the horrific transformation of the soldier who took a stab of bayonet while making sure he would be loaded on that truck first. It wasn't the same torso of firm body he was hugging this time. It was still firm, but literally it was only bones that he could feel. Covered by a sagging shirt courtesy of the inmates, what he felt inside of it was literally rib cage. He just could not avoid it, but he cried considerably at the presence of the confounded prisoners of war present at the time.

Sergeant Rodrigo Santos, perhaps overwhelmed by the resurrection of Cabarles or from extreme disbelief, just stood straight up in awkward salute, unaware of his own tears dripping. Cabarles noticed him eventually and gave him a real salute in difficulty, with a smile of greatest excitement. The reunion was full of emotions but was cut short. Everyone knew that time was constrained when the siren was heard.

The "captain" was directed immediately by the sergeant and Donono in their formation. The Americans were in protest but let them go for now as the Japanese were becoming wary of the delay in the muster. Details of prisoners haven't been established yet, but amidst the yelling and screaming of drill sergeants and details supervisors, everyone's attention was locked on the new prisoner assisted by two of their comrades. The insignia on his hat had made the pile of the lowly Filipino soldiers proud, but it wasn't what they had reservations about. Could he be the legendary soldier whose story of unequal gallantry and valor in battle had proliferated in the camp? But he was dead, verified by the POWs who fought the same battle with him, the same two soldiers who verified the truth of the story and among the early prisoners of war in Dapecol.

Surrendered or captured, whatever may be the right words to warrant their captivity by the enemy forces, they were the remnants of the Davao defenders from enemy invasion on December 20, 1941, and the period that followed. They were the lost souls whom many had no recollection of how they got in there, known as the early birds in the cage.

All prisoners, especially their captors, would stand and salute the flag of Japan while it was being raised at exactly the same time every morning. The Filipino soldiers were housed separately from the American prisoners. However, they occupied a large area in the compound with makeshift shelters or tents they made on their own at single or dual occupancy that they had managed to put together. By character, the Filipinos wanted to congregate on their own with several respect. First by province or islands of origin and dialect they spoke, they were divided in groups and the group is slash to buddies down to a couple of trusted friend or just by an individual who doesn't want to be bothered or rejected by general population. All together, only a few came from Luzon and not many could speak Tagalog. The Americans were occupying the few barracks, Americans, Britons, Australians, they were all the same. Discipline still intact into their ranks. However, there were some Filipinos who were able to secure space in the overcrowded barracks. They were the elite group of Filipino soldiers. They were officers, and importantly, they could speak English.

Though perimeter security was made tough to deter an attempt to escape, the prison compound was actually within the perimeter of a vast compound of Dapecol. Strong structures of wooden walls and raised floors with corrugated sheet metal roofing housed the POWs. And some more in construction were lined up in rows to the fifth and sixth that was not completed yet.

"*Doon tayo* (That's where we belong)," said Santos, pointing in the direction of a tent fit for two people made of old military canvass on the top and abaca weaving formerly used as rice sacks noticeably just put together not a while ago like the rest of them. Santos explained they had a better one until the storm blew it away.

Cabarles could not help but ask what the other compound was for? About a hundred yards on the northwest isolated from all the buildings, fenced by a full length of bamboo trunk high up side by side surrounded by tower guards erected outside overlooking the inside, it was like his former cage, only that this one was humongous. The inside was obscure of fresh bamboo trunks around, also newly constructed. From the north and around the west side were towering trees and coconuts visible from afar.

"That's where we came from until we got detailed to building the American barracks," Santos calmly answered and continued narrating. "It is a special POW camp. Inside are prisoners, mostly elite civilians of Davao who refused to cooperate with the invading Japanese Imperial Army. Not a good sight to see, but those tower guards were enjoying the view. Visitors were allowed, but never enough food to provide to the live ones. Starving and sick detainees never get medical attention until they die; it is hellish. We erected and fortified those fences as our daily detail for a long time since we were transferred here from Bukidnon."

According to Santos, his being a sergeant and proficient in English and the local dialect had earned him a position in the construction detail. He pulled Little Don with him, telling the Japanese and prison supervisors that he was a carpenter. Together, along with a platoon of Filipino POWs he personally handpicked, they earned the reputation of being the master builders of Dapecol prison camp. The detail was not easy, but it earned them three meals a day and the opportunity to have extra food and supplies, privileges entitled only to the Americans.

Still weak and looking confused, Cabarles was temporarily placed on the American sick bay in Barracks 4 for the rest of the day. Santos and Donono thought it would be the most comfortable place for him until the end of their detail. Being with the sick, injured, and dying soldiers was madness he should take aside in his own delirium. Reminded of so many deaths he had already seen, it would have been better to be killed in action than live in excruciating pain until they die. He was also thinking about Santos's description of prisoners on the inside of the bamboo fence perimeter. Cab recalled a story where there was a very small version of that prison. He was in it for so long and left for dead and forgotten that somewhat he had developed a phobic reaction to such kind of structure. So many horrible imaginations were playing on his thoughts that he wanted to sleep, but the crying and moaning of the others in the quarters made it impossible to do so because many topped his own weeping.

The smell of sweat and rotting flesh in the room and the effect of the extreme heat and humidity on his still-hallucinating mind was not helping. It brought him back to the vision of sharp blades and edges in a downward arrangement that he had refused to be thrown in. There was a hopeful difference this time; he was watching lines of soldiers going down one by one willingly.

Wide awake and should have been aware of his whereabouts, Cab was essentially having trouble in identifying reality from his delusion. They just kept coming back to his mind. There could be no more frightening than watching a fellow human being surrendering to death. He had been in hell; this must be the purgatory where people must spend time in agony until someone decides what kind of hell they have to go to. He had adhered on such delirium, and all efforts to reject it always found himself in the same situation. His vision seemed to pull him into the darkness again on a bright day. Going back and forth from hell to hell, he knew now there is a purgatory and it is just a walking distance in between. He looked around, adjusting to the new place, struggling to divert his attention from the poor occupants of the building who may be gasping their last breath, the last moan. He looked upward on the roof whispering a short prayer for them all, and downward, there he saw through the gap in the wooden floor where wild vines and grasses were still thriving despite huge obstructions from the sunlight. Trying to crawl out from the dark, a spectacle of nature he had observed and was explained to him several times. The meaning was becoming clear to him literally.

Santos and Donono took a break from detail to attend to Cabarles. Every stashed food were collected and passed to them secretly from other POWs and was given to Cabarles. They knew the consequences of that actions may lead to severe punishment by the guards, but they didn't care. The well-being of the long-lost friend was their priority; they knew he was also imprisoned all those times since they were separated, in the most horrifying prison no one knew existed. Where? They would never know but they were told it existed somewhere within Dapecol.

Almost unrecognizable from the newlywed Dominador Cabarles they first met in Manila compared to what he had become as they saw him again after believing he was dead, somewhat they thought it would have been better if he was dead already as they had presumed. However, Sergeant Santos and Donono said they prayed genuinely for his safety and for this time to come that they would see each other again; to that effect they were happy and swore they will be at the service of the friend for the rest of their life.

"Hey, Cap, are you all right?" Donono asked immediately as soon as he located him in the dark corner of the sick bay. It was his turn to check on him after an hour ago when Rod Santos delivered a handful of rice for him.

Still looking down between the spacing of the wooden floor, long hair concealing his face, he said, "Yes I am, Dono, thank you." The voice barely heard that Donono started to worry.

"Here, drink some water. I have food too. Is there anything else you want?" Dono made sure he was understood.

"I feel like I'm getting completely crazy here. Would it be all right if I stay outside for a while . . . with you guys?" What he said was true as he really was getting close to losing his mind. He was longing for company, but not with people who were struggling against imminent death. He could feel some who might have given up already, most likely the one who refused a bite of sweet potato he had offered. Just staring at him, eyes maybe blinking, but no movement whatsoever. Cab was fed well by the colonos the whole time he stayed in their jail cells; however, he had yet to recover from the psychological effect his past ordeal had inflicted on his sanity. The barrack was spacious to lie down and he could stretch his legs out, however, the only position he made since he took that spot was sitting flat on the floor, his chin resting over his knees bent tightly with both arms around them.

"Anything you want, Cab. Let's go."

Outside the barracks, Santos was coming also to get them. The midday ration was about to begin very soon, and the line was forming. Unaware that he was still wearing a hat with the decor of a captain, everyone they crossed paths with saluted as they carried a bowl. He was given one; someone also handed him a piece of dried meat as they lined toward the two giant pots. The line was long already, even the food distribution hadn't started yet. Prisoners were still coming, but what caught his interest was the one walking with the aid of a stick. From the farthest end of the compound, he could see the hardship of the soldier to reach the ration as he stopped and walked again. Surely something very painful was bothering him; he couldn't walk normally. But he chose not to ask that would disrupt the nonstop talking of Santos and Donono explaining all the rules that pertained to the food line. Rules, they explained, were violated outright; they cut the line right in front. None complained among the early birds.

Finally, the food distribution started, which consisted of a measured amount of mousy rice and boiled vegetable soup as word was passed to the end of the line. They always acted surprised to know what they were getting for meal, but the truth was there never was a change in the menu. Still not a word from Cab, who was keenly observing, enjoying the meaningless talk from everyone who would say a word of admiration to the captain. It was a rank that no Filipino had held yet and seen before until now. There was also laughing, a sound he had not heard for a long time that was renewing his grip on reality. If prisoners could laugh for any reason thereat, then life in the camp was not too bad after all. Renewed spirit was building up. He was given double of the ration by the kitchen detail. "Long live, Captain, *mabuhay* (welcome)!" the soldier said.

"Who is that guy?" were the first words that came from his mouth as the line moved forward.

"He is Abu Benghalid, a Moro," Santos replied.

"What happened to him?" The curiosity in his mind noticed that nobody even wanted to pay attention to the poor soldier despite his hardship to walk to the food line. The head was banded with a piece of cloth, probably to contain the long hair, but he understood it may also be part of the customs and tradition of the Moro. The man was heading their way for food while struggling in so much pain to reach the end of the line that kept getting longer.

"The Japs shot him on the foot for allegedly helping prisoners to escape. He refused treatment for his wound," Rod explained.

"Are they successful?"

"No, they were all shot to death."

Though nothing could terrify him anymore of what the war had caused to every one of them, a reason there was to be wounded had initiated a serious thought. The man may have a different faith, but still he had a precious life to hold on and clearly he was fighting for it whatever it took. The determination of the soldier to reach for a little food was tearing his heart apart and at the same time inspiring him. He remembered how he was taken care of by the inmates, how he was timely rescued when his soul literally was abandoning his body. It was also a similar situation he came across on the sick bay. He surely knew that he would have died already if not for the kind people who helped him. It was not just him who needed the same kindness. Many were sick and taking their place when they died in the compound and not many cared about them. He was briefed of the situation in the camp already. It was survival of the toughest, and he already knew how tough one should be to see the light of day after every night.

As soon as he got his food ration, he walked straight to the Muslim soldier who was still about fifty feet to the end of the line. Holding the stick with both hands to keep his balance, the man may have noticed his rank and authority when he attempted to salute while holding unimaginable pain caused by the swollen foot. Cab held his hand instead and emptied his bowl to his. No words were said between them except for what was expressed in their eyes. Cab assisted the man in sitting down on the ground. The gratitude was vague of pain from a bleeding foot. Fresh blood over unattended wounds forced to walk a distance for mushy ration. It didn't take too long to empty the bowl to fill an empty stomach. Not enough, clearly not enough.

Rod Santos and Dono who had joined them would not say a thing. The man's kindness was in his blood even if there was not much left of it. He had never changed despite the fact that his own looks clearly indicate that he had been deprived of food for a long time. They could not understand why he did it when he needed to eat the most among anyone else, why he offered his ration for a person he didn't even know. Truly the real Cabarles without doubt as how they had always known him. Eventually, they were joined by a few soldiers who were introduced one by one by Sergeant Santos.

Dono and Santos shared their rations too; both had long sworn to look out for each other. With Cabarles surfacing alive, the pact was amended for the benefit of the man. They were dedicating the rest of their lives for Cabarles; after all, he was the captain. They may have never known how he became an officer, but as Santos put it, Cab had been in hell and must have gotten his promotion from hell. He was bound to obey his orders whatever it took. It was put to a test right up. He was told to find any medicine for the Moro man's foot. The order was also voluntarily complied by prisoners who wanted to show alliance to Cabarles. Each one came back with a few rice balls and dried meat. One brought in a small bottle of *tintura de yodo*, a liquid mixture that has the same color and texture of soy sauce; he said it was for disinfecting wounds. Surely he cannot defy an order from an officer when Cab told him to clean Abu's injury. The man, who was hesitant for some reason, indeed submitted himself to the order of the "captain."

The soldier was suffering from a bayonet wound that went through his foot; some said it was a gunshot. He was not expecting any help; why now when he was wounded many days ago and nobody cared and instead it was all abomination that he had received? He had caused the wound to himself, as others would say so. For reasons unknown to Cab yet, Abu was avoided by the general population; no one wanted to be associated with him.

The afternoon was dedicated to a remedial healing mission. Cab was cool, observing the turn of events. Many just wanted to meet him but took the opportunity for a drop of rare medicine to their stubborn wounds that didn't want to heal. Many were afflicted by skin diseases such as *alipunga* and *buni*. In the busy afternoon, they became medics for the wounded soldiers. Santos and his crew of skilled carpenters had joined together on the effort seriously. A concoction of boiled guava, banaba, and other known medicinal leaves were used for precleaning wounds before applying the precious liquid. One foot was multiplied; taking advantage of the effort, others just wanted to meet the man who had been known among prisoners even before he had set foot in the compound.

"Thank God there's no more." Santos sighed. Darkness was falling.

"There's one more if you don't mind," Cab muttered.

"There's no one else," Santos insisted. "Don't worry, he doesn't have any injury," he added, referring to another POW coming to join them.

Sergeant Guido Agustin, sharing an abode with Santos and Dono, spoke Tagalog very well. Santos knew he did not even have a scratch. He hastily dumped the contents of the pot of brew nearby that were the nasty residue of the leaves.

"Don't worry about him, he may only have a cut on his finger," Santos said, telling the approaching soldier that he was an ally moonlighting as a barber after detail. But as soon as he had finished what he said, he looked at Cab, stupefied to the failure of not considering him to be the "one more."

"You?" A little nod was enough to say that he was. Dono boiled a fresh batch of medicinal leaves right away even before Cab could tell where his wound were. There was plenty of time until total darkness.

Guido offered everyone Lucky Strike cigarettes he had jacked up from the Americans. Eager to meet the man who had been the usual subject of unbelievable stories of bravery, he saluted the man before he sat on the ground, and he was introduced as a trusted soldier and friend.

"It is my honor to meet you, sir. I am Sergeant Guido Agustin of the Sixty-First Infantry Regiment, Philippine Army, at your command, sir." He was humbled to what he heard about the man in front of him. Agustin was a true soldier, combat trained, and battle hardened who earned his stripes in his long stint with the army. The respect and admiration to this man had built up extraordinarily when he was dead. The fact that he was alive made Agustin honored to know the man, personally expressing his loyalty in the kind sworn in by Sergeant Santos and Dono if Cab had lived. Cab's legend as a soldier could not be reversed by his humbleness and his simply not commenting on many accounts attributed to his name. It was truly unbelievable to shoot the pilot of a flying Zero as it was sworn true by the same soldiers who survived to tell the tale. Many more accounts highlighted the battle in the hills of Bukidnon, and there was an incredible story of how he died. Now the story was conflicting because the legend was alive. How he survived required rational explanation otherwise.

In prison, many tales of miraculous survival was common among Filipinos, not just about Cabarles. Individual stories, true or had been exaggerated to top another account were usual topic of conversations. The incredulity close to a real miracle was given to Cabarles. Indeed, Santos believed it was a miracle to see Cabarles alive. He and Dono were sure he was real, but neither would want to know how he survived, not yet. Their concern was in bringing the man back to full recovery.

There was a barber in the house; the opportunity was hard to pass. It took a while but he was white sided and clean shaven before another pot of water had boiled.

Donono just came back from his own errand of gathering wild plants and leaves. Having many scars of his own even before the war, he was also known and proven to possess skills that could assist in the healing of wounds.

It had been a long time already, but he could still remember. Santos also knew by heart literally. It was the end of January when they were separated. In March, all the wounds they incurred at the time had healed already. However, having known that Cabarles was the most injured among the three of them, considering they had no knowledge of what else Cab had gone through since he was presumed dead on that muddy footbridge, what was left unhealed should be superficial. The man indicated he had wounds to look at, then it would get the best attention.

Cabarles started unbuttoning his shirt, courtesy of the convicts. He knew that the lingering pain on his back that caused him discomfort and prevented him from lying on his back must be clean and treated until it healed. Upon the advice of convicts, it needed continuous cleaning until it healed. That was two weeks ago after the storm. Although he felt considerable relief of pain since then, he was taking advantage of the moment when a trusted friend could look at it.

The reaction of the soldiers to see those horrid marks were no different than the inmates. Donono started to apply a self-concocted cleaning agent on certain spots that refused to heal. It had been a long time since they got there, but the infection on some places were severe that without proper medication, it made the healing slow. Though most of them had healed, as Dono removed dried flesh over previous wounds, the horrible mark had left his skin indescribable, but that was not what bothered them. It was the pain they imagined to be while those massive scars and wounds were perpetrated. Sergeant Santos could not help it, but he cried again; he would never forget one of those, the one that went through and left a mark on himself and saved his life.

Cab didn't know what was going on behind him, he could feel stiffness of the skin but not much anymore. His tolerance to pain had increased a thousandfold by the process it was inflicted.

Two American officers came, and they too could not believe what they saw. One spoke to relay a message. "The camp commander is inviting the captain to report to his office, but I see it's not possible at this time. Please do so at any time comfortable for you, sir," LTJG

James Feldman politely said. "Would there be anything I can do to help?" he added, realizing that the "captain" was getting medical treatment at the moment.

"Yes, send a doctor here right now," Santos profoundly demanded. It was impossible to attain because no doctor attended to Filipinos, but he said it as he just could not keep his hands still while assisting Dono. No part of his wide back were clear of scar. The doctors and hospital in Dapecol were exclusive to Japanese and Americans. With voice broken and tears dripping, he could not bear to look nor continue what he was doing. Dono's expertise was enough; for some reason, he had many scars of his own even before the war. His ability to treat wounds was bragged about and proven effective. Santos could attest to his skill; the methods maybe unusual, but it worked in many ways. He could also make the scar protrude or disappear depending on how the wound were inflicted.

"It actually feels a lot better now, I don't need a doctor," Cabarles said as a sign of gratitude to the soldiers who were still wordless, quietly crying. He was given a cotton shirt by Agustin who also gave him a sombrero. He was assisted in getting back to his feet; at the moment, he did try to stretch his joints and body. The feeling was a lot better, scratchy, all right. It was really a nice feeling to be with the only two people he knew would take care of him. "You have the hands of an angel, Donono. You could be a doctor," he voiced out his appreciation to whatever was done on his back.

Feldman came back as pledged, a medic with him. He was told to attend to the swelling foot of a man still sitting on the ground. The Muslim was told not to walk just yet; otherwise infection would prevent the healing that could lead to the amputation of his foot. He was advised to recuperate in the hospital, which he strongly turned down. His foot was treated and dressed professionally.

"The colonel would like you to know you're welcome to billet in his barracks, Captain," Feldman relayed additional messages from the commanding officer.

Cab shook his head, smiling to hear English again; he admitted he could not get away from the curse of the captain as long as he had it. The American took it as turning down the offer with Santos just nearby translating.

"I'm fine with my brothers. Would he take this man in his quarter instead?" Cab replied, pointing to Abu. "What I need is a barracks that will shelter all Filipinos sleeping on the yard, at least for the wounded and sickly. Please tell that to the colonel," he added.

"I will, sir."

PROUD FILIPINOS

In mid-April 1942, there were about one hundred Filipinos scattered on the campgrounds, from the rank of sergeant down to the minuscule soldiers as Hombre Donono or as insignificant to a wounded Muslim or those dying somewhere in many shacks that could only provide shade from the sun. The irony was real because it was from the Filipino ranks that came the labor force building the barracks that began in January. It was told that Americans would start moving in even before completion, kicking out any Filipinos who would like a space within. Ridicule did not end in such kind of discriminations. Filipinos in the rank of lieutenants had secured themselves with a privilege of an American enlisted. They would show their presence only when there were complaints of lost personal possession that was most likely to be retrieved from the Filipinos. As American POWs kept on coming in, so did the overcrowding of accommodation rose. The Filipinos kept on building; the GI Joes kept on taking over when it was done. Barracks No. 6 was not completed yet, but it was occupied already. An order from the commanding officers to vacate Barracks No. 6 was made the following day. One hundred Filipinos moved in and settled by sunset.

Before sundown, as word spread, the rumors that started after the storm suddenly became a reality. The colonos didn't fabricate what they added to the story of the unknown captain. Only one thing was left—establish his true identity once and for all for the Americans and Filipino officers. In fact, there was never a Filipino commanding a company in battle. At least none whatsoever came from the rank of the foot soldiers who could not even speak English. It had never happened yet. Well, he was known to be a captain, captured, and interrogated as a captain and respected as a captain, so be it.

"Be it known he is a Filipino as he said he is. He is a USAFFE officer and a gallant soldier. It doesn't make any difference if he is an American or a Filipino, we are prisoners of a common enemy after all," the colonel said.

Santos had explained to Cabarles the importance of an order to report to Colonel Cumberton. Cab only shrugged his shoulder, becoming uncomfortable at the thought of talking in English. Obviously, back in his normal state of mind, he tried to disregard what the commandant wanted. But after a couple of days, he reported to Cumberton's barracks with Santos. The colonel was very kind and accommodating; Santos was finally reinstated as a Lieutenant. Donono officially became a soldier and a corporal. Cabarles had to keep the rank of captain. They had described their participation in the battle at the boundaries of Davao and Bukidnon, confirming that it had actually happened that resulted to the beginning of a legend. The fate of real Captain Ernest Maish was unknown, but it was attested that he was able to escape with a Filipino guerilla before their troops were overran by the Japanese. "He gave it to you. Keep it and give it back to him when you see each other again, Captain Cabarles," the colonel said, referring to the hat as Cab attempted to surrender it to the colonel.

"I believe it had caused me a lot of trouble already, I won't be needing this no more," Cab insisted.

"As you wish. You can keep the decor, you've earned it." He pinned it to the collar of Cab's shirt then saluted the captain.

It was a noteworthy affair; the POW commanding officer was after all a conscientious officer, a "very nice person." Donono was the happiest as they were given gifts of canned foods and candy bars fit only for the meals of the Americans on special occasions.

However, there was never a happy ending on any given day just yet. Intimidating Americans accompanied by a Filipino officer were looking for their shirts among others of their missing belongings. An immediate inspection failed to locate the stolen goods that usually turned out in a flash. The three newly promoted soldiers enjoying the imported cigarettes would cross paths with them. Donono hid himself immediately behind the big guys. He knew what the Americans were after. Cabarles was wearing it.

There was reason to be afraid for Donono. He stole it. Aside from that predicament, to see the officer again who were used to belittle and yelled at him and other prisoners all the time was not a good sight. In Tagalog, what was usually said were much harder to swallow than an American who could humiliate them summarily all day in English and nobody would understand a word. At the sight of double bars pinned on Cab's collar, the dreaded LTs could only salute the captain than reclaim their stolen shirts.

"How can I help you, soldiers?" Cabarles asked in Tagalog.

"Nothing, sir," one replied, sidestepping to give way. Cabarles's confidence increased as he knew more of the people spoke Tagalog.

It was the first time he valued the rank. Somewhat he wasn't cursed because of it; maybe it was just the filthy hat that he didn't have anymore. Self-esteem surged up. The consequent honor he was given by fellow soldiers in Barracks 6 was tantamount to a celebration; candies and Spam were cut into pieces to let everybody get a taste of them. In all accounts, that night became a memorable one; however, humility remained intact. What did the captain do in terms of duties and responsibilities? He didn't know. Lt. Rodrigo Santos would always be on his side to tell him.

CHAPTER 6

IN THE BEGINNING

Running errands, following orders. It's just the same. I believed I was a good son. A good soldier. I cannot remember there was any time I disobeyed a command. For all the knowledge and wisdom in life I was passed on, I was thankful and proud. Should I need to say to you that I have never set foot in an educational institution? You know I can barely read; I can only write my name. I have trouble counting more than my fingers and toes. That is the reality of my existence. We are poor, the poorest you can imagine, but I never had regrets.

GROWING UP

"Look at them, son, see what they are trying to do." He suddenly remembered his old man referring to the grasses left underneath the hut they just built in the middle of a meadow. "They become yellowish and start dying, but they are now leaning toward the light." His father always started the conversation in parables. Who cares about the nuisance grasses and wild plants when they were everywhere?

"Because we deprived them of important nourishment, of their source of life. They may look dying, but you will notice the new stalks growing as they creep away from the dark. They want light, and when they get through, they become green again, enjoying rewards of perseverance." He never understood what his father was trying to say about the insignificant grasses that even farm animals refused to munch. On the same day, he uprooted every one of them under and around their hunting shack, thinking that was what he meant.

He was mistaken indeed. The old Cabarles wasn't happy to see their formerly ambiguous shack standing clear on the meadow. He spent another day listening to his so-called wisdom and experiences because he scared away quails and herons, rendering the hut useless for the sole purpose it was built. His father kept a rifle, and he was very good at it, an old .22 caliber. Domeng, as he was called by family and friends, was a good listener; surely he never repeated the same mistake over again. He had proven that advices and perceptions of his father are encouraging to pursue as he always seemed right. His old man was really very good in what he does, always finding time to pass to the young son all the lessons in life that he had learned by himself. Very hardworking, possessing many skills that he always bragged about, as far as Domeng could remember while growing up, his father was his teacher.

Cab was five years old then. When the consequences of his actions came short of his father's expectations, revisions of what already been discussed would be repeated endlessly to prove that he was right. Especially at instances when dinner was at stake like that day. The old Cabarles left to go fishing instead, leaving the young Domeng alone with specific errands to comply, to clean and take the rifle back home. Though he was taught how to aim and fire a rifle, he sure knew he could hit a target if he was allowed to pull the trigger when it was loaded. Bullets were expensive, and availability was scarce at the time.

There were always plenty of game birds on the meadows; he found it hard to believe that clearing a small part of the field would send the birds away. He could see them, but they were truly far at the distance his father used to shoot them. There were many movements obscured by vegetation on the ground close enough; he just had to identify and pinpoint its exact location. He took the rifle, orienting himself with the target through the sight of the barrel. He had located a fat quail, its color perfectly adapted to the brown grasses, and it was confidently walking and feeding. The rifle was cocked quietly, and he made aim. He studied the movement of the bird meticulously, how it disappeared momentarily and blended in with the shrubbery, somewhat giving him a different motivation than killing the poor bird for dinner. He pulled the trigger anyway to find out if it was empty for a sure shot. He was expecting that, but eyes still locked in on the bird now joined by bigger ones similarly concealed by blending the color of their feathers wherever they turn themselves to. For a long time, he had watched the flightless dinner on their nesting and feeding ground, which led him to doubt what his father said. They actually walked under the hut confidently, under him joined by little ones scouring on the bare dirt for grubs. It was a family of quails, and he was amazed that he didn't see the smaller ones until they actually came out of the overgrowth. For the rest of the time, he observed the birds as they multiplied in number. Different kinds, "so many" he thought the birds knew he was just one harmless kid. Too bad he was left with a useless rifle; he see some black birds too, bigger, which was a lot easier to see and shoot. All day his attention was in learning more about what he had discovered. At dinnertime of catfish, he would challenge his father. The meal could have been a delicious game bird if the rifle was entrusted to him with bullets. It was not a year after when he was allowed to fire that rifle.

But those were not he really wanted to recall. If he was given a chance to attend formal education, what would he become? He knew that their meager family income was not enough to support sending him to school. He could not remember either of being personally interested to the idea of attending school since his young age. In fact, he refused to attend free classes of Don Pepe, a schoolteacher who conducted free lessons for the community children who doesn't know how to read and write. At least he would know how to write his name on his own.

At seven to becoming a teenager, he was just happy wandering in the prairies and running errands for family needs. Hunting, fishing when not working in rice paddies until sundown; tending to animals, taming water buffalo, and training them for plows—that was mainly what occupied his world during those years. Never in his mind did he have of any intention to learn no matter what else to know beyond the river in the west and woods in the east, vast rice fields and meadows as far as he could see north and south. He was already very good with his father's old rifle that even the old man could not believe how good he was with it. One shot, one kill. Whether the bird was in hiding or flying, it would become dinner, then he pulled the trigger of the old gun. As the years went by, the harvests become plenty and the income of the land increased. The landlord was happy. Eventually, the unaffordable became easier to come by.

His shooting skills was turned to sports with the same enthusiasm and interest of the landlord that became fond of him. He may had been given advice on the benefits of education and thought upon the idea of going to school, but none transpired whatsoever. Too late for that, at seventeen when he started to regret that the only thing he knew was basically shooting a rifle. So much to say he had never seen a pen in his entire life until he was signing a marriage contract at twenty-one.

Dominador Cabarles was the oldest of four siblings, the youngest a girl who died of unknown reasons that was blamed to earthly causes, speculations common among the old folks especially when the deceased was a young pretty girl. And if someone got ill, it was the witches to blame. But life went on eventually; no other things he could ask for. With plenty of food, life was easy, as he may say it was. Everything was just there for grabs when you get hungry, just be conscientious and diligent. Those were two most important qualifications for a person to prosper, according to his father. "Do not abuse your skill, guns are made to do harm. It is a gift of nature to your existence that you are very good at," his father would say, conceding that the son was exceptionally better than him on the target range. "We have only one lifetime to live, it's always too late when we realized that. Never complain of sacrifices and pain as there is no such thing." Those words became the core of his principles in dealing with any endeavor. So to speak in all other instances, aside from what he became good at, the rest was dealt with by fate accordingly and in many cases he was somewhat inadequate. He could make a very nice pile of hundred sacks of rice, but he could not tell how many it was.

"Do not start anything you cannot finish, but always start on something. Never contradict your own plans, put it into action, and be sorry when the result isn't of your expectations, and always share if you prosper." And therefore he grew up humble and responsible. The simple life rotated mainly around one season of rice planting and harvest for their landlord. The humility that ran in his genes had led him to become a well-liked young man in the barrio. Handsome, hardworking, helpful, and respectful. His adequacy to be caring and assiduous in good faith and conduct toward others overshadowed his illiteracy.

The limitations in his inherited way of life would not come into notice in high regard in the coming days and then to the rest of his life beginning when he was seventeen less few days. He would start to regret having no formal education at all and would seize his so-called existence into a standstill. Dreaming was the only way he could make the days turn in his favor.

The landlord came home one weekend; there was nothing out of the ordinary except that there was another passenger on his carretela other than his wife. It was the most beautiful creature he had ever seen. The gracefulness and her beauty somewhat transformed him into a momentary trance that usual tasks became difficult to accomplish.

By the end of school year 1935–1937, the sixteen-year-old Inez Sandoval, the only daughter and heir to the vast agricultural land and real estate in Bulacan, was staying home for the summer. She had freshly graduated from high school at a prestigious preparatory school in Malolos run by nuns, the capital town of the Bulacan province thirty miles away. She had only been home in a few occasions, but never had Domeng laid eyes on her since she a little. So did the now college-bound girl to see him again.

Filling up on the responsibility of his father who was the official farmhand of the Sandovals, routine work in the summer included mainly tending the farm animals and horses, not much to do in general. Then Inez came home to stay for a while; a heavenly creature came into the land to satisfy the void caused by the hot and humid summer. He never thought he would get to be within an arm's distance to such splendor. He was shy and nervous to even come closer knowing that the last time he took a bath was days ago, still wearing the same soiled and sweaty shirt and pair of pants. Literally he was smelling like horse manure as it was what he did all day, hauling manure to fertilize the rice paddies. Suddenly he became aware of his appearance. He became awfully wordless the whole time. That day began a courtship that would only be known to himself and probably to the horses for a long time, the start of endless daydreaming that he knew there would be no fulfillment, as it was an impossible dream.

His father was slacking down on the hard work already laid down for him as his inheritance; he had entrusted to him most of the personal functions to the landlord. It was one errand in the beginning that became a personal responsibility multiplied to almost everything else. Naturally hardworking and obedient, he may have missed some routine works on many cases, but excuses were attributed to getting new experiences with childhood friends and new acquaintances while growing up. He had seen many young Filipinas of exquisite beauty, but none had excited him so much like seeing Inez Sandoval in a less conservative dress provocative enough at the current period. Very alluring, she smelled so good that even the perspiration that built up in droplets reflected by sunlight seemed like many little stars had gathered to glow in her very fine skin, adorning a creature that was already blessed with so much beauty and lavishness.

Nothing else had complicated his simple outlook in life since then. He knew his place and was determined to keep it that way; however, many impossible thoughts would progress as the days went by and he would wish to the falling stars every time he saw one and every one of those that stayed in heaven. The affection that blossomed in his inadequate mind brought inspiration that was never thought it would come in an unexpected moment. He didn't know how to handle that strange feeling. Overwhelmed by the rapid beating of the heart, he was speechless and confused; there was no easy way to overcome that feeling that magically ended a day of labor still so inspired and vigorous. He was willing to live with it as it would be his destiny. A way of life strengthened by faith and family bond and people that were sometimes very unsupportive, he was not comfortable revealing a desire that he knew would only cost him total humiliation. He just kept on imagining.

THE EIGHTH OF APRIL

It was a special occasion; he remembered none of the date came in a year no *pansit* (rice noodle) was cooked for that day. Chickens were bled to death, this time suggesting there were invited guests. He was turning seventeen, and in the family ran a tradition that the birthday celebrant could take it easy while everyone else prepared for a special dinner. It had been eight days since he laid eyes on Inez, and he had not adjusted yet to the fact that the girl he could not get out of his mind only lived nearby. His mother Monique and sisters Loretta and Selina would take care of the cooking and other chores; it was simply just another day for him, but he was taking advantage of the day to continue what he had started—a day of dreaming with no one to bother him for an errand.

Nothing could break his thoughts of such good feeling; he still had to visit the animals under his care for the landlord even though his father made it clear they were taken care of already. It wasn't the real reason obviously; in the big blue house was a girl he wanted to see again, otherwise let her know that he did not always smell of manure, nor was muddy all year round. At least once a year, he was in his best pair of clothes and wearing a pair of shiny footwear, and his hair was not always sticky of sweat and sludge. He spent time and money for a jar of Tancho Pomade for the hair that just kept sticking up no matter how much he applied. By all descriptions, he somewhat looked very good to feed the horses that day. Out of excitement, he didn't realize that on Sundays, the Sandovals went to church. There were no horses also as they were taken to pull the *carretela*. Frustration immediately enveloped his thoughts that Inez would not see him feeling and looking handsome.

He should be attending the church too, but he had slept so late he could not get awakened by his sisters. He chose to just keep dreaming until the rest of his own family came back. At the time, missing mass on Sundays is a sin. He grew up in a family with a firm belief in God. None whatsoever could be more important than fulfilling the obligations of their faith, and there was no excuse. He was sorry to his parents and siblings, promising he will make it up. He was forgiven anyway provided he keep his words.

There was nothing he could do for the rest of the day. It was his holiday after all, as he was reminded by his siblings. "*Maligayang kaarawan, Kuya* (Happy birthday, brother)," they greeted him one by one.

His old man could care less. He had a plan of his own for his son. "Come with me to the target range," he said while carrying a long skinny thing wrapped in brown paper; he surely knew what was in it.

At the makeshift range back walled by thick layers of bamboos and hays, where he always practiced shooting the overused .22 caliber rifle on empty cans of sardines, some targets had already been set up. There were three rows of the small cans in groups of three at different distances. The farthest he knew was too far at the range of a .22; he would need luck to hit it at almost three hundred fifty yards in its new location as someone had moved it back. The closer range of about one hundred was already difficult especially when it was windy. The closest at fifty would be easy, considering he put the bigger cans at that distance. On a .303, he could knock them all down without a miss; his father knew that very well, but they did not own that caliber rifle. He was only able to fire those kinds of rifles while testing weapons he was cleaning and fixing that belonged to the landlord's arsenal.

Something unusual was in the making. Normally at any given day, he could practice shooting alone. "What is he thinking now?" he uttered to himself, baffled at the intent of the old man. He knew it was maybe a test of his skill as the poor old man was ridiculed countless of times they competed at shooting, but never gave up that easy. His father was always trying to regain the title.

"Here is the deal, son." The father broke into his thoughts, guessing at what could happen. "You can see all those targets very well, right? Now if you can hit all those, you can have this." He continued boastfully while unwrapping a rifle.

It was a handsome 190A3 Springfield, presumably used already, but hearing that he could have it by just shooting down the tin cans made him drool already. He assessed the targets carefully; he knew the farthest ones surely would take a longer time to aim, and the closest could be hit even by just throwing a stone. But there could be something more to his father's condition; never had he made anything easy for him, especially with what was at stake. He was sure of that. He politely asked to explain his terms out clearly, and he complied.

"At the count of fifteen, you must displace all the targets from where they stand by shooting them with the twenty-two. If you do that, 303 is yours." He handed him the dark maroon rifle that he loved immediately as soon as he laid hands on it. "Well, let's do this to your advantage. You can use it if you want," he added.

However he looked at the weapon, it was in flawless condition at every part and angle, perfectly matched to his grip. What else could there be to his father's mind to let him own the rifle that easy? It had already happened before, and he was confident that he could effortlessly do it. His father knew it too for sure. He examined the bullets; the old man had tricked him with blanks before and definitely it will not work again.

"All right, let's get started. You can start counting now," he confidently said to his father after he inserted one of the five rounds of cartridge, cocked the rifle, and positioned himself over a log taking his aim.

"Let's wait a few more minutes, relax. I am not the one who will do the counting this time."

"Who will?" he asked, knowing there was nobody else around and never was there someone around at any time they were in the shooting range. He was excited already to own that .303 rifle that could only be afforded by a rich sportsman in the whole province. "Let's just get this over with. I am ready, start counting now." He knew he could knock down all the tins, and his father was not done yet counting to ten. Plenty of time for fifteen. Why couldn't he just hand it to him without conditions?

The count would be fifteen to knock down nine cans; as far as he knew, fifteen were more than ten—even better. "Whoa!" he uttered, realizing the count would be up to fifteen. He knew they were both not capable of counting over how many fingers they had in both hands, so he paused. "Who will do the counting again?" he quickly clarified in protest, but it was too late.

"She will." The old man pointed to the landlord coming to the scene with his daughter. The interest in the Springfield was suddenly nullified. It was all in his imagination to see her again up close; in actuality, it really made his knees tremble. She was so graceful, alluring—and coming closer.

Totally becoming speechless as he felt his tongue recede again to not finding any word to say, he just bowed a little at once as a sign of respect to the owner of the land he was standing on. But it wasn't caused by him. It was his beautiful daughter that was also making his heartbeat palpitate louder than usual, even faster as she smiled in greeting to him and his father. The sweetest smile from a girl who had changed his world, who made him start being conscious about personal hygiene and appearance. He was neat and well groomed unlike their first meeting. He had finally redeemed himself of the previous embarrassment. He was sure he didn't look bad, but he had to find his tongue just yet in front of Inez. Suddenly, he felt cold. He could feel the breeze through the leaves of trees and bamboos. He was sweating while standing still.

After more of the customary compliments and brief conversations, all attention came back to Domeng who had not recovered yet to the surprise of his father's test to his manhood and resilience. He sure knew how fast Mr. Sandoval could count to fifteen; it was very fast. He didn't need to look at his fingers nor his toes. It was the effect of Inez nearby and watching that what made him so nervous. Just a glimpse of her was enough to throw him off into a trance, much more to hear her voice again. So much more if she would really be the one to do the counting.

She didn't belong in the range. What she was doing on the men's cove could not coincide to what was happening. It was a setup; his father had no plans of letting him own the .303A, considered to be the most powerful rifle at the time. He felt like he was going to pee in his pants. He thought of going for cover in the trees, but he could not definitely do it when Inez was around, even at the cover of the thickest bushes. He knew too very well that he had to adapt and be a man enough to show off and impress the girl. He didn't know how to do that. But clearly, he could not turn his back anymore from what had already begun. As much as he wanted to have the Springfield was how awful his feelings was.

The old man had noticed his son's unusual behavior—absurdly quiet and looking very troubled. He was sure Domeng could hit all the targets, but the change in his condition was that he was smiling. He had a chance to regain his title. He did it first with two cartridges, hitting targets on the first two rows easily and missing two of the farthest ones. There was no counting involved.

Domeng must have the fifteen counts because there was something at stake; his father made him understand the condition. The coming of the landlord was not an accident; he was carrying his own rifle too, so he was clearly invited to the occasion. Being a shooting enthusiast himself, he came to practice his own skills at the same time to see how good the young man who was bragged to be better than his father, the only man better than him in rifle shooting. Someone else was better than the man who was better than him. He was there also to practice in rifle marksmanship in preparation for the coming competition against Bulacan province's elites. Inez was not supposed to be in the range.

"Are you ready now?" the elder Cabarles asked, with a grin on his face for he could guess already what bothered his son.

"Sure," was all that he could respond. Actually, the only thought that was in his mind was the beauty of the landlord's daughter. Another thought that bothered him was that he would not know how long he could hold himself; he really needed to pee.

On April 8, 1937, Dominador Cabarles was seventeen years old. At the dinner table where special foods were arranged at best, prepared by the loving mother with the help of his sisters, sat the special guests, the Sandoval family. Joined by the elder Cabarles and Domeng himself, the topic of the conversation was not about shooting and rifle anymore. The mestiza beauty of Inez had shrouded the competence of Domeng with .303 at the firing range earlier. Though he was happy to win the Springfield fair and square, his tongue remained retracted in his throat even though the special dinner was prepared for him. The presence of special guests was causing the tension, made worse by unexplained palpitations of his heart. He was pretending to have a good time of his own while avoiding not to reveal his feelings to anyone, much more to a girl in front of him that was also causing him sleepless nights.

Being in a Catholic school and a boarding house also managed by nuns, Inez was appreciated for her very refined manners and upbringing with a complexion not fit to stay in the barrio, where all kinds of insects and animals especially stray and possibly rabid dogs could cause harm to anyone without discrimination.

"We want her to learn also the life that we are accustomed to," Mr. Sandoval would say, seconded by the wife unquestionably. "She will stay with us this summer then she will pursue a course in medicine in Manila next school year," the proud parents revealed. Having a pretty and smart daughter were enough reasons to be proud, but emphasizing that she wanted to be a doctor was more than Domeng could take. Did he ever think of what he wanted to be? Every day in his life, he only wanted to finish what he started during that day and none beyond.

Domeng suddenly felt a difficulty to swallow the food in his mouth. He could not talk, now he could not eat. Hearing those kinds of conversation made him an insignificant being not suitable at all with regard to Inez's attention. Only in his dreams absolutely. Quietly sitting on his own opposite Inez, hiding anything that would divulge his affection for the girl to avoid further embarrassment, he could dream, imagine things—certainly that was all he can do. Impossible to reach, but in his imagination, he could turn things any which way he wanted to be. Tilling farmland and shoveling manures was the bulk of his pitiful existence. Had he attended school, he might have been given the chance to be liked by Inez, moreover by his parents for her. Too late for that, truly to attain his dream was just to keep dreaming, and he would not deny himself of that. As his father always said, "In the mud we belong but we are not forbidden to look up in heaven." Heaven was unreachable, too high, yet she was just across the table at arm's reach and smiling. He conceded in being happy daydreaming the best that he could. That smile inspired it all as it had already begun since the first time he had seen her.

Then as unpredictable as it could be commanded by fate or by grand design, Mr. Sandoval commissioned him to advance his own skill in 1903A. An avid sportsman with an already exceptional competency, he was preparing for an upcoming shooting competition in the province. The added task could not be turned down, more so as it will increase his chances of having a glimpse of Inez more times in a day. Though Inez never showed personal interest in men's pursuits, she displayed fondness for the horses, which were also under Domeng's care, talking to the animals had also began. Indeed, the self-imposed hard work he exerted for the benefit of the Sandovals did not go unnoticed. Aside from being gratified for his contribution in winning a competition, his effort in rendering other chores around the house was recognized way over the elder Cabarles was doing for them. Chopping firewood, fetching water, and upkeep of the yard were among the tasks, added by a generous sharing of the best catches from the river or the sweetest tropical fruits from basically anywhere he could find the best yield. That summer was the happiest despite him never having a word said to Inez the whole time; just a glimpse of her was enough to make his day complete. Simply, her presence was an inspiration. Eventually, that summer ended rewarded by a delightful smile he was bestowed by the young lady. Nothing else could top that feeling. The college-bound girl would take up dorm in Manila, and he expected not to see her again for a long time. That smile, however, was enough for a tremendous inspiration that was perceived by his imagination while maintaining good relationship with Inez's parents. Talking to the horses continued. He started to wish and include in his prayers that she come back to the barrio. If ever there was a wish that truly comes true, Inez came back in the barrio after a week and every weekends thereafter. She liked horses very much.

FRIENDLY PEOPLE

That was about seven years ago. Reminiscing how it began and thereafter was what kept him going; he was aware of that. Finding himself in a prison compound well guarded by an enemy who would not spare to think a second in shooting prisoners by slight provocation was a realm to keep in mind at present. By presumptions, he had survived the worst. Everything else would be easy, as he would think so. With food to eat better than nothing added by being reunited with Rod Santos and Little Don, the chance of surviving to reunite with Inez was great. However, the responsibility he was given or what he had created involuntarily was hard to disregard. He had overcome the curse of the hat, but his association with it remained—he was the commandant of a company of Filipino soldiers regardless of disarray and individual delusions just like he had.

Recovering from a severe deprivation of nutrients, he acknowledged that regaining his strength to how it was would take a long time. The most important he said was being able to hold on to his sanity. His capacity of thinking revolved only on fulfilling his promises, to honor words that was spoken bequeathed by the love for a woman that kept his heart beating. He had emancipated himself by turning his back as soon as that wish of love was realized promises he had forsaken, and he was paying for it dearly.

He and Inez would rejoin at all costs and be the husband and wife that they were destined to be. No pain and suffering nor bullets and bayonets could hinder. He would reclaim heaven and live happily thereafter. Would he be given another chance? He admitted that God only knew what happened to Inez in the heat of the Japanese occupation in Manila. Most of the worries that had been mounting in him every moment were always about her. He knew it would be a long shot, impossible to get to her alive. Nothing was impossible anymore. The greatest of hope lay that she was safe; he devoted prayers for the meantime until he found a way to amend his sorry thoughts.

Exactly seven years had passed when that first smile overwhelmed his gullible heart, also five months when his love was bestowed with a vow "till death do us part". The difficulty of swallowing watery food could not be as worse while remembering those moments. In prison camp, the degree of survival was very little, especially to detrimental Filipino soldiers discriminated by both enemy and American allies made worse by distrust with each other. Should he settle to daydream again? The situation was entirely different; he would not let fate take its course this time to feel that kiss again. He must make a decision and work it out as soon as it was probable. Any delays might be too late. The only problem was that what he was thinking would need an elaborate planning and was deemed impossible. Many had tried and paid with their life. Even if he successfully escaped the POW camp, how would he get back to Luzon? He conceded to impossibility for now.

By the third week of May 1942, the Japanese Imperial Army had taken over the rest of the Mindanao provinces. The delay was caused by the battle in Bukidnon just outside the provincial border of Davao in the first week of January, where they suffered heavy casualties, where they captured Cabarles, the seriously wounded "Cap" whom the Japanese had punished to death for three months while still recuperating from battle injuries. Instead they recalled their troops and concentrated their strength in Davao, taking revenge with dreadful effect onto the prisoners and civilians, suspending patrols in company and abandon immediate plan to occupy the whole island of Mindanao. That was the first major loss they suffered since occupying Davao on December 20, 1941. They became cautious to expand their military campaign beyond after that incident. They had proven that their numbers was no match against American forces who were maintaining their stronghold just outside the province of Davao. They chose to postpone immediate occupation of the rest of

Mindanao until more troops arrived. After three months, however, waiting for an attack that didn't happen, they resumed field patrols. Only a massive reinforcement would ensure success of expansion, and they intend to wait just that. They concentrated their presence in Davao, showing unbelievable atrocities and murderous authority among the civilians avenging their losses.

The long-awaited reinforcement came, with a vengeance. The Japanese First Division easily overpowered Cotabato, the first island on the way to Davao on April 29, 1942, and then to Macajalar Bay in the North. Ensuing battles had defeated the defending forces eventually. It may be hard to believe for the Japanese to discover that in some encounters, they only fought soldiers armed with bamboo spikes. But still they were given great impediments as a whole before they subdued the island under their control. The population in Dapecol had started to increase by the hundreds starting June until its peak in October 1942. Attested by the fresh Filipino prisoners, the Japanese were simply brutal. Filipinos who defended the island in the front lines suffered most casualties. Barely armed and starving, accounts of survivors said that they were being shot at randomly even when they have already surrendered. In return, the Filipinos would chop a Japanese soldier into pieces whenever they captured one. Also began the legend of the headhunters with witnesses to attest they exist.

The early prisoners were caught off guard. The sudden scarcity of food however didn't become a serious problem to the Filipinos who had devised so many ways to cope up with the changes. Some groups had already established a covert entrepreneurship. They had been smuggling food and supplies inside the prison compound long ago. They didn't run out of ideas how to bring in food and medicine while stomachs were full before coming back from detail. In so doing, Cabarles had totally recuperated and regained strength in no time, capable of full-day detail. He maintained a white-side haircut and a shaved beard that was prominent to most of the soldiers in Dapecol. The sombrero made of *buri* (anahaw palm) leaves became the trademark of officers as it was hard and expensive to procure for penniless prisoners. Anyone wearing a hat would be known to be an officer otherwise leading a faction with influential connection, and there were not too many of them.

Cabarles was enjoying high the legend of his name among his people including the civilians; he was wearing his hat always slightly down, overshadowing his face for some reason. However, not many people could actually confirm who he was, only those who knew him personally as he was transformed from filthy skin and bones to one clean shaven and none of the traces of malnourishment. Though close buddies still called him Cab, he advised them not to because it was easily mistaken as Cap, short for captain as pronounced in the local accent. It wasn't that easy; the high regard to his courage and gallantry didn't allow him the obliviousness. He also became known as Kapitan Domeng that started outside of Dapecol. As the number of Filipino POW increased as fast as the Americans, somewhat the name Kapitan Domeng became synonymous to the leadership and humility in the rank of the Filipinos. Lt. Rodrigo Santos and Sergeant Guido Agustin would always be on his side to render tasks he was not capable of. In most tasks, there was because Cab had renounced distinction as an officer by admitting difficulty in communication. He only spoke Tagalog.

Little Don, proud to be *cabo* (corporal) also held and maintained a self-assigned job, being in charge of the food stash and resources while directing a unit to do what they had proven to be very good at—stealing from Americans and selling them back to other Americans, sometimes even to the Japanese guards. His name became synonymous to a pest among American prisoners that many times they complained, only to be told to watch their own personal things if they didn't want them stolen. Dono could not be responsible alone for rampant theft inside the compound of about four thousand prisoners. As Donono had mastered how to say "I don't know," he firmly denied allegations of stealing even from the Americans. The Filipino populations rose from below two hundred to six hundred at its peak. Taking advantage of the booming "business," the demand increased, requiring supplies that was never enough. Dono was ordered to give up the duty of master thief, delegating his command to more a ambiguous personality, Corporal Rufino Dominguez. Very intelligent and having trusted contact among civilians, he was chosen fit for the job while taking advantage of knowing the local dialect and Tagalog fluently. His resemblance to Cab was startling. In fact, he was proud to be called Kapitan Domeng and many times would accept the identity and title boastfully. His dealings in pretending to be the captain was tolerated as the advantage it brought to Cab was indeed very favorable.

Lt. Rodrigo Santos had to assume many duties when the less tiring carpentry detail was taken over by the Americans. As an executive officer reporting to Cabarles, he was directing orders and discipline among Filipinos that showed great improvement especially on the muster formations. Later, his task was turned over to other officers, legitimate soldiers fresh from battles or from other POW camps around Mindanao and the Visayas region who were briefed immediately of the ongoing systems among the Filipinos. Nothing complicated, only one rule existed that violation of such could cause death—do not blabbermouth against your own people. Seemingly daring and fearless, new prisoners had one too many a story to tell about their heroic exploits against the constantly loathed Japanese. Santos must stay in the sidelines adapting Cabarles's approach toward associating with fresh prisoners of Dapecol that kept on coming. With the overcrowding of the camp, it was clearly impossible to contain the attitude of everyone, it became survival of the fittest so to speak.

Cabarles would remain soft-spoken, quiet, and reserved. His reputation, which already precedes his presence in the camp, would extend all over Davao though no one could actually confirm that he was alive. Only his heroics would be repeated by many mouths despite the many "Kapitan Domeng" in wide sombreros that were seen to proliferate among the local ranks. As he explained to Rodrigo Santos who would agree to any of his assertion, he said he was not capable to put orders in hell as he himself depended on the lieutenant to keep surviving. He stated that he would remain subordinate to Santos just like how their brotherhood began no matter what being a captain meant.

Another Kapitan Domeng was Sergeant Guido Agustin, a native of the town of Lasang in Davao; his family were among thousands of evacuees that camped along the narrow road leading to the entrance of Dapecol. His role and loyalty to Cabarles and Santos would extend beyond mere friendship. Aside from being a good barber servicing POWs, he was very effective in intelligence gathering. Well-mannered but funny, he spoke Tagalog fluently and could communicate in

English aside from the many dialects that he knew. Unlike Rufino Dominguez who did not disclose having relatives close by, Agustin had been a trusted allied of Santos and Dono along with dozens of others that comprised a group initially imprisoned and treated in a field hospital by the Japanese in Bukidnon. The men that comprised the unit who built the prisoners' barracks had long established their camaraderie with each other. Among them were Lt. Luis Malvo and Sergeant Mario Rabong of the Twenty-First Infantry Division.

A character who was adopted into their fold despite his stubbornness was Abu Benghalid, a Moro from Lanao belittled by his own people for causing the death of many Muslims in the camp. He was said to be the major planner of an unsuccessful attempt to escape Dapecol, the first ever by a group of Muslims. The result was disgraceful for the Moros. Abu, who was shot in the foot so that he won't instigate nor be able to escape himself, was still nursing his wound. Little Don had made it an obligation to attend to Abu's injury while the Moro returned the favor by entertaining the pint-sized soldier about his skills, so many he could not do because of the foot injury. However, lessons about women was the subject Donono would like most to hear at all times. In addition, Abu also exerted considerable effort in managing and disposing stolen merchandise. He was the front man in doing business with other prisoners all day because he didn't do detail.

There were other allies, proven to be trusted and could provide the needs as requested. Outside the POW compound, the colonos led by Roberto dela Cruz was always all ears whatever messages and errands reached him from his *kababayan*. Likewise, as communications was also established as far as outside Dapecol, Roberto would find many ways to get in touch with Cabarles. In so doing, a clandestine communications system was created and expanded beyond Dapecol with major participants fully understanding their role and consequences if discovered by the Japanese. The convicts suited well in the effort because they retained the privilege to be visited by relatives right in their cells. First order of business was sending gratifications to Dr. Penafrancia for the life he saved. Though it was not easy surviving afterward, Cab had reserved his gratitude he was denied to express personally before he was taken by the Japs from the hospital. He owed him his life, and he conveyed his appreciation with extreme sincerity to everyone who in some ways took care of him while dying, especially the other "angel" that he was sure was a real person. She had yet to be known. The only person he knew personally was Dr. Angelo Penafrancia among the civilians in Davao.

Others mentioned were Tatang Abrina and Ruben Pablo. Both were agricultural supervisors at Dapecol even before the Japanese took over. They retain their jobs under the new administration; both were presumed collaborators as dictated by their reputations and influence. Though Abrina's dependability and loyalty would remain in check, there were underlying factors that he may not be a collaborator, giving precedence to the Americans who liked him. In fact, he could be seen cavorting regularly with the GI Joes as often as with the Japanese and showed disconcert about the Filipinos. On the other hand, Ruben Pablo had shown his true colors long ago. The man moonlighting as a translator for the Japanese Kempeitai owed a twin slap on the face from Cabarles. Feared by his own people, a demoted jail superintendent had been the subject of loathing and threats from the convicts and POWs alike. Rumors indicated that there were many more of his kind visibly romping with the Japs and civilians around Dapecol. Cabarles had long been advised to avoid people who could be possible spies. In fact, Agustin had already kept a long list that kept on adding. Abrina and Pablo were included.

As it will be written in the history of the war in the Philippines, the effect was unimaginable. However, the devastation in infrastructure all over the country was minimal because there was not much standing to destroy as compared to other countries especially in Europe. The real condemnation of the Japanese occupation led to an inconceivable loss of human life and atrocities to the American and Filipino forces alike; it was the civilians who had suffered the most casualties. It was witnessed that a whole community would be massacred simply because they were helping the defending forces particularly the guerilla units that remained fighting against the Japanese. Similar incidents were also happening in Mindanao in the outcome of enemy occupation. As frightening as it was, information brought in by new prisoners inflicted a severe demoralization among the Dapecol population; they came to think that the enemy may forever rule the Philippines. What would happen to the POWs was a big question mark although the Japanese command had regularly announced that any prisoner who was willing to work for the side of the enemy would be given special privileges and be ensured of a long life of prosperity. The program had started since the beginning of the war, and they were becoming successful as they could see former soldiers wearing white armbands displaying the red dot to support orders and security in the camp, proudly proliferating in the compound displaying a considerable change of behavior, showing authority like Japanese soldiers. Later, it was learned that they were forced to act in moderation, afraid of constant threat that they will be murdered. In fact, a POW had tried to strangle one of them in broad daylight but was meted out with sudden death from the Japanese guards. A similar event was said to be successful outside the camp, especially in details where they could be easily be bitten by venomous snakes or poisoned by accidentally touching certain frog species.

Those incidents didn't bring a favorable outcome to the prisoners. Throwing away the armband but maintaining allegiance to the enemy, an individual could blend in with the loyal without being identified as a traitor or collaborator. An opposite situation of the civilian employees of the prison was that many of them were not actually collaborating with the enemy but forced to display the Japanese flag because the other option would mean they would be interned and punished for disobedience. They conceded that working for the Japanese was the best choice. They were originally rehired to continue on their position in the supervision and management of Dapecol operations; many were demoted, but the money they brought home meant there was food on the table for their family. Therefore, it became difficult to know who was who. The three amigos from Luzon were forewarned of the situation; they could not risk being caught off guard just by not being nice to an unidentified spy or speaking in vain against the Japanese. Moreover, Cab and Donono didn't understand the dialect of Davaoenos and the Visayans; without Santos, they were completely lost in translation. Esteems were extended to Abu, Agustin, Dominguez, Malvo, and Rabong, all of whom would speak Tagalog in full respect of Cabarles and Little Don's deficiency. All would stay out of from associating with the general population, but they were actually steering clandestine operations benefiting the Filipinos. In their company who would be seen staying in one place most of the time was Abu Benghalid, only because the Moro man had a hard time frolicking around due to his foot injury. Guido assumed the role of public relations officer. He became a common sight among every group with a verbal promotion of being a master sergeant in the Filipino ranks.

Dominguez, who would be more famous as Kapitan Domeng to be known inside and out of the camp, was given full command of the night raiders of American barracks. He also had contacts outside the base who were helpful in smuggling dry goods like shirts, cigarettes, rolling papers, and occasionally canned foods to be sold in the black market. When the outbreak of diseases began, many civilians were very effective in employing different methods of sending in pills and liquid medicine to the Filipinos inside the prison, at least for the benefit of those who were running the schemes. Distributions and retails required extreme caution; newcomers who had earned the trust of the schemers got the goods in the open, sometimes for free. Everybody else must pay at prevailing price.

A THOUSAND SOLDIERS PLANTING RICE

Prisoners' duty on farming details became seriously enforced when the rainy season began in April 1942, in preparation to the first planting season in Mactan rice field under the eyes of the Japanese. Previously, it was the colonos' job while serving prison terms. In the coming of POWs and under the new management, they were happy not to be recalled in hard labor. The workforce they previously provided in Dapecol would not be necessary as the Japanese came with their own breed of prisoners. With tall, healthy, and big Americans, the supply was endless to suffice the need of labor in the entire Mindanao. Healthy in the beginning but deprived of proper nutrition while in manual labor, they rapidly lost weight under tropical weather, not to mention all kinds of diseases they succumbed to in no time. Although easier duties such as basket weaving, furniture making, and tending to farm animals had been going and available, rice planting needed extreme hard work and sustained strength of a full day's labor for the prisoners who never had enough food. For many, there was an arsenal of excuses to resist being slaves by their captors—sick of contagious disease, injured, weakened, or just developed laziness inside the camp for the long summer. How would they produce on a detail having no idea how it was done? Many simply just refused to cooperate by principles. Sick bay became overpopulated every day to avoid details. The recruiting process to rice paddies was never easy for the agriculture supervisors. Intervention of the Japanese was always necessary, threatening that no food would be given to those who would not work in the Mactan rice field but will increase for those who will.

On another case, when the prison commandant promised daily pay and extra food for those who would volunteer, hundreds of Americans lined up. Big and healthy soldiers took advantage of the offer. They were happy and excited to earn a few dollars while being fed decently in captivity, which was not bad at all. Three hundred required were filled up quickly, only to find that they were being transferred to another camp to do logging details and to man the lumberyard. The promise of extra food was provided, but it did not compensate long hours of work and energy spent in hard labor. Another two hundred more were distributed in pineapple and abaca plantations, in the mining industry, and road repairs. No excuse was good enough to stay in the barracks all day.

The sickly and old were assigned to light duties, taking over building constructions from the Filipinos who were sent to rice paddies and cornfields. Santos and his crew had been working at the expansion of the chicken coop where they had been breaking the necks of egg-laying chickens. There was mutual benefit among the evacuees, convicts and POWs, in such a scheme. Dead chicken would fly over the fence, then hours later it would come back clean, sometimes cooked. Groups of Filipinos coming back in from coop detail would have at least half a chicken over their head concealed by their sombrero. It had been going on for quite a long time with the connivance of civilian caretakers. This went all in the good days, to be missed when the Japanese guarded the farm heavily.

It didn't end however; the Filipinos passed on the scheme to the Americans taking over the completion of the encasement of the coop perimeter. The Japanese had long suspected that unproductivity of the chicken layers and substantial decrease of its numbers was caused by thieves. The Filipinos were the prime suspect but yet to be caught; they never were caught until they were just kicked out of the prestigious coop detail although rampant smuggling of food and supplies had stopped eventually at the apprehension of an American who was lashed many times in punishment. It could have not been a serious offense, but being caught with chicken meat in his possession was very bad, which was previously announced as punishable by death. Strict compliance against bringing anything in food kind inside the camp was enforced dramatically.

In new details, food was also available in abundance. Snakeheads, catfish, snails, rats, and even the real snakes were everywhere that can suffice the daily food requirements of the Filipinos. It compensated the timeout from fresh chicken meat, all they could eat amidst the danger of the presence of Japanese guards who never had any clue as to what was going on when someone was burning something. As the days moved on, the Filipinos had devised many more clandestine ways to smuggle almost anything inside the prison compound, many instances at the assistance of the colonos who were reinstated to teach the POWs in rice field details. Who needed chickens and eggs? Rat meat just tasted the same. Bird eggs were equally nutritious.

With the start of farming season also came the recommissioning of the old bamboo sledge designed to be pulled by water buffaloes; new ones were eventually made to suffice the need of a massive farming operation. Every hollows of the bamboo trunk used in the mainframe became a compartment filled with food and other goods every time it crossed the main gate of Dapecol. But that didn't last long. Eventually it was discovered as a smuggling transport aside from its intended use of hauling fertilizers, seedlings, and firewood. Americans who could not stand hard work in the rice paddies volunteered on taking care of the chicken that HAD started laying eggs again. Surely they enjoyed fresh eggs, but it didn't last long either because they were caught, causing them several days of no food at all in solitary confinement. The care of the chicken farm were left mainly with the civilian employees and the Japanese. The hope of real chickens vanished.

By August of 1942, in their new details of pulling nuisance weeds out of the rice plants or cornfields, the inseparable Cabarles, Santos, and Donono would always look busy but not in the work they were supposed to do. Most of their times were spent catching slimy fishes in the flooded rice paddies. Though it was difficult to catch them by hand in the deep mud and water, from a distance, they looked busy like they were doing their assigned work while collecting lunch. The detail instructors who were mainly colonos in orange shirts would cover up for them as much as they could from the guards and collaborating supervisors. In general, food was never a problem in Dapecol. Cab had long regained his original built and strength, and the company of trusted friends at all times had added to his confidence to just about anything. Life in prison, though not what they wanted, was no other choice but to live with it. By October, the number of POWs was at its peak. About four thousand Americans and over five hundred Filipinos that were constantly diminishing in numbers for many reasons therein.

Despite the reluctant acceptance of their fate as POWs, Kapitan Domeng would be famous as he had been at the beginning of his life in Dapecol. He would remain as a captain, however, he had established himself as just another prisoner. There were bolder prisoner who claimed he was the man only to find another one being called by the same name. Yet there would always be another faction who wanted the leadership, and there would be equally more who didn't want to be led by Donono. One of the groups who would be known for their intense bravery even in captivity was led by Abu Benghalid. The band of Moros whose adherence usually ran amok at a slight provocation, they also maintained defiance to bow to the Japanese and reject the Catholics. Benghalid, whose injury never healed and became accustomed to walking with a cane due, had remained calm and loyal to his benefactors as he was loyal to the Muslim community. He played a great role in the cooling off of the heat between the Moros and Christians.

There were a few lieutenants, however, said to be graduates of the military academy, who were entrusted the discipline of the soldiers that were divided into three companies. The remaining early birds of one hundred stayed at the command of Lieutenant Rodrigo Santos, rumored to be the real Kapitan Domeng or the man who was close to the captain. He had managed to suppress the legend of Cab as he was instructed to do so. The man died in a battle as far as he can tell the story.

Along with the sudden influx of prisoners came the increase of unattended injuries and sick soldiers, so as lingering illnesses spread, it resulted to more deaths in the camp. There was not just enough of about anything to support the well-being of the prisoners. The continuous buildup of evacuees outside the camp did not help either. In general, Dapecol was inundated by so many mouths to feed that the Japanese commandant had ordered the eviction of the civilian evacuees from the camp and reduced the food rations among the prisoners for the second time. Chaos due to food shortage worsened, and the increase of soldiers caught smuggling food inside the camp became a common sight at the gate. Even at the Filipino ranks, there was considerable difficulties to bring in extra food and medicine to spare to their sick fellows who could not do details. The number of collaborators increased to the promise of more food. And from bad, everyone felt the worst situation in and around camp. Though Cabarles had proven he would live over extreme hunger, he would not let himself be into the same torment again. He would rather be shot than punished to death by starvation. There were many things going in his mind but had yet to be revealed, things that he could not comprehend and do alone. His rib cage and backbones were still aching, and so did the nightmares of pain and the long ordeal from the hands of the Japanese. He just could not sleep well through that experience again; otherwise it reminded him only every time he saw a Jap. On another thought, he could not justify putting the life of friends in ultimate danger for personal intent. Any possibility, however, he could not plan alone. He also knew ten prisoners who would be executed for one escapee.

BETSY AFFAIR

By the end of September 1942, when all crops were growing and everywhere was abundantly green, the detail of weeding became the most boring to do. What could be more boring when almost everyone were just acting like doing something but actually chasing a mudfish or frog that requires tremendous skill and agility to catch by hand. The Americans would not dare to go hunting anymore due to the increased probability of getting lost in the forest. The edges of the rice fields were bounded by tall trees and wild vines that grows overwhelmingly in the rainy season provides frontage of lush greeneries as it gets thicker getting in on a flooded wilderness. In many spots, bayonets could be waiting and were ready to inflict at any moment.

The Americans turned their boredom to an albino carabao tied up on a tree and quietly grazing. One joked that it was the first time he actually saw a native of the land that resembled their own race by color and who therefore must be friendly. He named the animal "Betsy" after his girlfriend back in Texas—voluptuous, young, and sexy—joking about the name and his longing for a real American blonde. He tried to come closer with the intention of mounting the animal, but to his disappointment, it jumped and ran away the moment he laid hands on it. He was left cursing and moaning at the refusal of the animal to let him even come any closer. The laughing and comments from his buddies promoted a challenging reaction, unaware that the animal could be very aggressive. He had seen many carabaos used in tilling paddies submitting to anyone. This one should be no different.

"How can a blond girl like that tied up in this part of the world refuse you?" said sarcastically a marine officer, one of the three who would instigate an unimaginable determination to torment the animal.

"One peso, I bet you I can get my ass on it," a challenge from the other soldier who would go over the limit of break time just to see his buddy being mauled by the white buffalo.

"Call," he said adamantly as he knew that most of the same animal used in the plow can be mounted. This one surely just needed a little introduction of himself, let him know his master. He whispered something as if he was understood and jumped over without warning to the frightened Betsy. He got his butt dropped flat on the ground at the laughing of his buddies.

He failed over and over again and didn't want to give up; one peso was a lot of money to lose until the other one wanted his turn for another peso who would also give up when he was thrown away by the now extremely apprehensive animal. But the two soldiers would not pay unless the other guy himself could only be successful in getting on top of the animal himself. It was a winner take all, so they say, while deliberating the rules to the already furious Betsy. There were only three attempts to make increasing the bet for five pesos. Any more than that would mean another five pesos. The guy who started it all agreed, thinking that the animal was already tired and he could get it done easily. He thought wrong when it charged at him like a raging bull, sending him to the ground with an aching rib cage. When he was able to get back on his feet, he heard the loudest laughing of his fellows. He declined to do it again.

Dapecol kept a large herd of water buffaloes. They were used in cultivating soil for new seedlings, mainly in rice paddies and cornfields. The majority were tamed and easily restrained to do what they were supposed to do. As they bred, young ones were separated for training to augment usable animals by a few who dared. Supervisors and the Japanese were all aware of it and consented to any method to train buffaloes for agricultural use. Many times, the animal was just too stubborn and had to be tamed first before it could be trained for farmwork. The albino was regarded as untamable.

The fun and commotion had attracted the attention of other soldiers having a snack nearby. They checked out what was going on; most of them became thrilled to know that there was money involved. They wanted to try but had no money to put in the pot. Few had hurriedly borrowed cash from others, and the pot money that built up to one hundred pesos easily became too tempting, and more got tempted that the money collected at the end of lunch break that day went up to two hundred with a promise of everyone to try again the next day. A lot of the stash money were unsewn from their shirts and pants to put in the pot. A lot of them too were walking back to the camp at the end of the day either limping, with aching joints, or bleeding. A marine said that it was the best fun he ever had in the camp other than the thought of breaking the neck of a Japanese or a collaborator in a wrestling match.

Another day in Mactan was concluded. No one was successful to take home the prize that went sky high as everyone wanted to win it. The rules were amended so that a first timer must hand over ten while a repeater can do it for five. The three Texans who started it all assumed the duties of judges on a percentage of total prize; nothing was official unless they were present on what they called the "Betsy Affair." On Sundays, details were not enforced, except for the colonos and select POWs who did the feeding of the herds. Cabarles was among them. At the end of the same day, he spoke his interest on the money to Santos.

Santos had seen them all, so did the Little Don. The fun of tormenting the albino carabao didn't make Donono happy especially seeing that it was restrained to a tree. Cabarles told his buddy to provide ten pesos for him ready at lunchtime the next day. He wanted to end it all before they actually did real harm to the animal. He was warned of the viciousness of the animal, that he could get hurt seriously if he tried to mount it, which would mean more broken bones for him, so they said. Nothing could change his mind. On the said Monday, he was sent into the cornfield with Guido Agustin, and there was nothing he could do about it. He had to be detailed in the cornfield about three miles away where Betsy was tied up. His buddies had prearranged the sudden change to avoid the predictable consequences to Cab's plan. Worried of any injury that the event might inflict to himself, they had seen what damage Betsy can do to humans who dared to bother her peace—she just became more ferocious. Not worth any money. Let the Americans have their fun.

"It is money in the pocket, we can buy a lot of medicine out of it. I advise you to bet on the side at any amount you can," he told Santos in secrecy.

Lieutenant Santos had seen how many could not walk and had to be carried back to camp on Monday, which increased his concerns. Even the strongest-looking American was thrown out by Betsy with the head bleeding when it was hit by her large pointer. He was unconscious when brought back to camp, maybe dead. The aggressiveness of the animal could not easily be dismissed with all he had witnessed and the injuries it had caused to the prisoners. It was a lot more violent than an angry Japanese soldier. That same night, he disclosed what Cab wanted to Donono; Guido's judgment was also heard. Ten pesos they were not worried about. It was broken bones or the worst, they thought, to a skinny man. Well, that was what the captain wanted; they could only do much to prevent the foreseen outcome.

On Tuesday, Cab was back on the weeding detail on the paddies, so with the Americans with ten pesos or more in their pockets. What was happening in the rice field was not known in the general population, only a selected few, and those with influence can attend the events. The Japanese guards had known about the events and were happy to win money by betting for Betsy on the side. They had won a lot already that caused them to castigate the event even more.

The first competitor of the day was a large POW, fresh from the lumber detail. He heard of the fun in Mactan and signed up for paddy detail as well. It wasn't a good day for him. At least for a few days, he would be nursing broken bones. The Japanese had lost all their winnings. The rest of the chances they would stick to betting for Betsy even if the odds went down half to one.

The next one was thrown more than ten feet away and was lucky enough to land on the bushes, but he was certainly not capable of continuing. The third just got afraid and backed out. The buffalo noticeably became more furious as she was already; there was no more to challenge her savage power. There was only a half hour in the morning break, and three challengers was as many as could be accommodated. No one was successful to mount Betsy as expected. In an effort to win back their money, the Japanese picked up random prisoners and forced them to ride the buffalo.

Before lunch break, they were the first on the spot to anger the animal and increase her viciousness, thus ensuring their winning streak again. Laughing as wide as their mouth could stretched, the first one, a marine, ended up ten feet away on the bushes. They had more to celebrate when a guy from Australia who was reluctant and afraid at the start did it anyway. He found himself clinging to the branches overhead when he was thrown upward. It took a while before he regained his guts to jump down and escape the awaiting horns of the carabao.

None wanted to challenge the Betsy anymore; one more had signed up over the weekend, but he had not shown up yet. There was still plenty of time till end of break. The Japanese guards were busy counting their winnings, challenging everyone that they would bet all of their money for the animal. Then came another one when it seemed that there was none anymore. Santos and Guido thought he had listened to their advice. All sides bet for Betsy; the odds were five for ten. Who cared, it was a sure win anyway. Santos and Agustin bet on the thin guy, and they were very nervous.

The Americans and the Japanese alike were adamant that the Filipino guy would end up dead on the spot due to the increasing aggressiveness of Betsy. They had made the animal real mad, and it definitely could not be domesticated for farm use. She was most likely to be slaughtered for meat.

"Who will do it?" asked one of the three who had invented the game.

"He will," Santos said, pointing to Cabarles quietly smoking the cigarette he had just lighted, walking with a bunch of fresh grass on the other hand, sombrero down a bit.

"Okay, let's get started!" shouted the same guy.

As the nervous Santos gave him the nod, Cab slowly walked behind the animal, facing the spectators who were holding their breath, equally waiting for what would happen next. Side bets had been placed also at equal odds that the man would be knocked down on the first round. The four-legged animal showed excitement at once, and the screaming began.

From behind the tree, Cab pulled the rope, aware that the carabao might really go crazy so he thought that the tree trunk would give him cover. As he took the attention of Betsy away from the screaming POWs, Cab slowly pulled the rope, untying it from the tree. He gestured his hand with the fresh grass as he put it closer to the animal's mouth. She ate them.

"Sshh." He made the sound very calmly as the animal started chewing the food, then he easily mounted the submissive animal at his command, walking past the mesmerized spectators.

"How in the world did he do that?" commented the bewildered Australian cowboy who was violently thrown up the tree earlier. He finally found a chance to come down.

Not a word could be said among the rest of the men, either because of amazement or because they had lost their hard-earned money. Whatever it was, it was the end of amusement that had definitely also left many prisoners to nurse broken bones and swollen limbs.

"All right, gentlemen, see you on the next game," Santos, holding all the money, broke the silence, with Guido collecting the pot. The Japanese had never seen such a kind of thing; they were mystified as well but were more concerned about their money. Though they had lost all their winnings, they did not actually lost any but enjoyed the show. They acted like true gentlemen, but when they had regained from astonishment, they started yelling in anger for everybody to go back to their details. Santos immediately handed them all four equal amounts that pacified them a little. All in all, the three Americans who made it all happen were the most baffled. They had seen how crazy Betsy from the beginning; it was unbelievable for her to just submit to that man like she had been tamed for a long time.

"Who was that man anyway?" uttered one soldier.

"I don't know, first time I see him," answered the second one.

"I think he was the one they call Captain Domeen in the camp," wondered the third one.

"I had fun. Didn't you, guys?"

"I have no money, but yeah I had fun too. I feel great for a while."

"Yeah, I had fun too, but no money. Two broken ribs and dislocated shoulder, I feel like a moron."

The next day, they found another buffalo tied up on the same tree. They named him Murphy but didn't dare to even get closer to the black animal. He was bigger and grisly just by the looks of him. In a week, they were completely shocked to see the same skinny Filipino riding him.

CHAPTER 7

THE PEOPLE I MET IN DAVAO

NOTED NAMES

One of the men who would do just about anything for the well-being of the Filipino prisoners was Sergeant Guido Agustin; he could also cover for Cab at a moment's notice. They could switch details if one didn't feel like working on the assigned duty. Their build and mannerisms were similar, the height almost the same. Their skins both looked dark and handsome except that Guido had a nose like a potato and he could be very talkative at times. It was very distinctive to anyone who had known both personally. Kapitan Domeng would be known to detail only at the cornfield and no more, but physically, he was in the rice paddies with Santos and Donono. If he had been seen somewhere else, the man wasn't him, or was he?. They both wore the wide sombrero as though it had become a symbol of leadership and personality. Another one in their fold was Luis Malvo, also a sergeant who spoke Tagalog. He was a very serious soldier and clearly well educated to the likes of Santos.

There were others wearing the same hat as it was locally woven and very common. Some could be short, tall, or of any other appearance. It didn't matter; they could be Kapitan Domeng too. Guido did details in the cornfield most of the time as a lead man of a crew of ten. The recruitment process of details were done every morning by the agriculture supervisor who would just shout loudly, "Rice paddies, 200; coffee field, 40; cornfield, 100" and so on depending which supervisor was calling for certain requirements. There were a lot to be assigned for duties, from chopping firewood to farm animal care, to repair of buildings, and the countless cultivation of other experimental crops in the colony. If nobody stepped up, whoever selected had to fill the number required.

Tatang Abrina had been playing a great role to ease the hardship of labor duties among the prisoners; he usually doubled the manpower needed in agriculture under his management. Only a person like Cabarles who grew up in rice farming could attest to that. He knew that a single rice pad didn't need twenty people to finish weeding in a day or two. On a good day, he knew he could finish one by himself. Privileged information he shared and disputed by Santos and Agustin in an effort to get Abrina out of the "list" they kept. Cab contended that being detailed in the rice paddies presents many amenities especially in food kinds. However, his rationalization was opposed by maintaining that the prisoners could just stay in the barracks doing nothing instead of being subjected to hard labor. There were really some details that required a great deal of strength to get it done, and just walking two to five kilometers to the work site was exhausting enough. Cab could only get the backing of Donono. Abrina was a common sight inside the compound, most of the time in the rank of the Americans to whom he was known as Pop. Though he was working for the Japanese interests, he had developed camaraderie with the Americans as a trusted ally. His management of the agricultural affairs of Dapecol leaned toward the advantage of prisoners but noticeably concentrated for the benefits of English speakers.

Another Filipino of authority, Ruben Pablo lived in constant threat of being killed by the convicts; in fact, he had eluded a few attempts already and never went out of Dapecol anymore without the company of the Japanese. He was also rumored to disclose the identity of defiant civilians including his former boss to gain special privileges from the Japanese. One unforgivable sin he made was assisting the Japanese in transferring numerous convicts to Palawan. He was known as a translator but also attested to recruiting collaborators and spies among Filipinos. There was another by the name of Juan Canlas; he took care of the animals and agricultural equipment for what they knew.

The Japanese didn't care who's who to work where. A list of names and the total counts of prisoners on certain details was all they cared for. Heads counted as details went out of the compound and must come back the same number. The guards did the head counts, making their group leader responsible but maintained threats that they will all be shot to death if someone was missing.

Sergeant Rufino Dominguez, who was said to be a veteran soldier, have yet to earn the trust of Cab and Santos. He had a habit of talking in the native dialect even at the presence of Cabarles and Dono who could not understand and was heard belittling Filipino POWs as untrained and cowardly like Donono to whom he was dealing with most of the time. He was suspected of skimming profits of business and suspected of disclosing to the Americans that Donono was the thief among the population when he was caught selling stolen goods. Truly Dono was, but he was never caught and could deny such accusations with a captain and a lieutenant to back him up.

"We all have a responsibility by priority. His family needs to eat too as much as we do," Santos would say about Dominguez. He suggested distancing themselves from him but still play being nice while giving him the liberty to continue the business on his own. Having a competition would not affect them. Cabarles maintained that they would stay out of any actions that could single them out from a lineup.

Abu Benghalid had sworn his loyalty and support to the chain of Filipino command whom he despised in the beginning because they were all Christians. His usefulness was jeopardized by his firm refusal to get medical treatment from a real doctor from Dapecol Hospital. Being an elderly, he valued the respect he regained by associating with soldiers from Bataan, whom he also looked up to because of the known bravery and courage of the men in battle aside from their kindness and when they value his opinions on many things. Among the Moros named were Abu Mudal and Digos Amal; both became synonymous to smuggling schemes inside the base. They could produce mats and mosquito nets for sale not to mention dried meats and bull's penis and testicles. Name it, if it's available in Davao, they can produce it.

Outside Dapecol existed an unknown entity who would facilitate the appeal of Filipinos for more quinine and medicine; sometimes they would smuggle it in on their own. Roberto dela Cruz was most trusted in facilitating connections with the civilians. He was in the best position to relay important messages because relatives were allowed to visit the colonos. He had an established conglomerate of suppliers that spoke Tagalog and the local dialect aside from English; his skills in that department were very beneficial to the soldiers. He would deny ever knowing anyone among the POWs. His known association with the soldiers involved mainly in rendering his duties as instructor in the rice paddies. He himself avoided any kind of conversation, remained looking loyal to the Japanese while being likened by select Filipinos at the same time, just keeping his job. Who would be leading the helping hand outside the camp would remain unknown for the meantime. Only a chosen few knew they were there to help in desperate times at a moment's notice in providing special orders.

Hombre Donono had relented his skill he was proven very good at—stealing. He was linked to many missing personal belongings of the soldiers especially the Americans who would be mad to find that a certain thing of a soldier was sold and in the possession of others. A new source of supplies like cigarettes, candies, and items for personal hygiene to sleeping mats and mosquito nets could be made available and sold at a boosted price. As prisoners learned to watch their belongings also began the monopoly of almost every smuggled good that passed hands, a very clandestine operation that was established with the knowledge of a few Japanese themselves. Filipinos surely could make it available, even rubbing alcohol. The sale of locally made products like mats, cups, and bowls made of bamboo and sombrero could be procured easily. Mosquito net was the most wanted but hard to smuggle inside the camp. Dominguez's name became noted as the man to approach. No food and medicine was for sale where the bulk of profit goes; it would be spared to the sick Filipinos who could not walk to take the ration. It was the best time that Cabarles could say that life in prison is not too bad after all. The most important was someone out of the compound who could give instructions in treating illnesses on their own. However, diseases were just hard to control as there was always a new one to afflict the population. Sexually transmitted diseases were one of many affecting Japanese guards involved in smuggling conspiracy with the colonos. It created an atmosphere that needed to be resolved immediately because who the ones to take the heat were the people who arranged a tempting kind of bribe that was so hard to refuse. That man was Lt. Rodrigo Santos with the participation of a few evacuees.

FAIRY IN THE CORNFIELD

Taking advantage of a half day of duties, inside the barracks, Malvo and Cabarles were busy writing a letter. One was supposedly writing while the other one dictated. Both of them knew that it would never reach to the intended person; they did it anyway having nothing else to do. Lt. Rodrigo Santos nearby was also writing in his journal, seemingly in a sincere mode. The solemn ambiance in the room had been purposely imposed for the time being as ordered.

"My dearest Inez, my angel," Cab started and paused, a long pause. He had so many things in mind to say in the letter, but every time he did he got blanked. This was not the first time he tried, but for some reason, he just could not find a word to say. However, his mind never stopped thinking, mainly worrying about her beloved wife at all times.

"If you let me, I will write it myself and then I'll read it to you," Malvo suggested as they both had on the same situation many times, becoming frustrated having written nothing yet for many hours.

Entered Guido Agustin from the cornfield detail. Tired or enchanted, he had yet to figure how he would begin his story out of excitement. He knew exactly where to find Cabarles; they shared the same spot in Barracks No. 6.

"Cab. There was someone looking for you in the cornfield, a very beautiful fairy," he said, almost whispering

Guido always had a story to tell—fairies, earthly beings, and ghosts. This one had made him really excited for some reason. Usually, he would relay in private a short one and anything that may need confidentiality. He knew the drill. He seemed to have been enchanted or just exposed to extreme hot weather and having a compulsion of some sort, but what he wanted to tell was true; he said it needed immediate attention. He looked serious or was maybe losing his mind, but he was determined to find a listener. His persistence finally got some attention as he created a disturbance among the people who were all concentrated on their personal matter.

"Calm down, Guido," Malvo said, concentrating on the body of the letter he had already started for Cabarles. "This is serious, I need complete silence," he continued.

"What is it?" Guido asked, noticing that they really looked serious while Cab remained quiet and uninterested to his fairy story.

"A letter to his wife," Malvo said, getting frustrated as he was disrupted in finishing a paragraph.

"Write that my love for her is forever, that I always think of her alluring beauty," Domeng reminded his scribe from the deep silence of thinking. The contents of the letter should be written indicating his eternal love to the wife, he reiterated again.

"None of you interested in the most beautiful lady? I tell you, with that beauty, she must be a fairy," Guido insisted that his story was worth all the attention.

"You should see his wife," Donono said to Guido, indicating that no one could top the beauty of Inez, not even the fairy he was describing while keeping a pencil moving over a piece of paper on his own. He really was on fire and looked like was very concentrated to what he was doing.

Guido must have been missing too many meals. Or possibly he had seen the night girls from Davao City who sometimes roamed around the base in the afternoon selling their merchandise, promoting their establishment, or when lucky, providing samples anywhere at reduced price. The common customers were the Japanese; the guards at the gate sometimes got it for free. There was a bigger market if they could pass through the gate. He had that story one day when he saw a soldier pants down on top of a local woman in broad daylight. It was certainly true, but this one was about a fairy—a fairy in a heavily guarded prison colony where only atrocities exist.

"I'm telling the truth, sirs. She knows that Captain Ernest Maish and Captain Dominador Cabarles are one person," he uttered the names quietly just enough to be heard by the people in front of him.

Almost at the same time, he got the attention of his senior officers and confidants. Santos kept his things back to their hiding place almost at once, and at the same time, his eyes locked on Cab with a question. Cab equally showed a sudden interest to hear the names of the captains as Santos did. Someone out there knew about their commanding officer who may still be alive or someone who knew Cab as a captain at the same time.

"All right, tell me the story about the fairy," Santos submitted himself to Guido. He knew that sometimes the man misfired on his information. Concern arose that the fairy was a real person.

"Wait a second, Cab, hear this if it's good for you," Malvo called the attention of everyone for a moment and read. "You are the only one in my heart, and my love for you will be forever. My longing for the memory of that night we share together will always be on my mind while feeling the warmth of your body, which inflicted a desire that I promised to do over and over as soon as we reunited . . ."

Something is not right, too bold maybe. But he kept it in his mind; he was only asking for a favor. "All right, keep going," he said out loud, turning his eyes back to Guido. In truth, he just wanted to give the man something to do for he never stopped talking the whole afternoon and a letter already written may come handy in the future.

"I'm telling you, I've seen her. My eyes won't deceive me," Guido was still trying to prove the authenticity of his own story.

"So what did she tell you?" Santos asked casually on purpose that may reduce the excitement of Guido.

"Believe me, sir, she is young and so beautiful. She said her name is Rina, Rina Penafrancia. She is happy to hear you are alive. In fact, she was very disappointed to find I wasn't you in the cornfield but me instead," Guido explained.

"The name is familiar in my mind, but I had never seen her yet," Cab said while trying to remember seeing any other beautiful girl.

"She wanted to meet you, Cab. And she really knows you very well, she said," Guido continued.

"Donono, are you hearing this?" Calling Donono's attention, Santos was insinuating about another girl who may be linked to faithful Cab at a time they were separated with him.

Don responded, "Yeah, I hear, very clear. Love letter to an angel and a fairy to meet." He paused sarcastically, shaking his head.

"I may not know you very well personally, but you're very good, Cab, very smooth. Do you think you can hide her from us? I met the angel, I want to meet that fairy too," said Santos teasingly.

"I really could not remember her, but it will help if you tell me more about your meeting with her," Cab demanded more substance to the story. He was truly interested to the fairy.

Cab had a strong feeling she was the same woman who took care of him that led to his salvation. She could also be the same one anonymously sending supplies and medicines from outside the camp as indicated by Bert Santos. Over a long period of time, the Filipino POW had established communications with the civilians; a certain message through the colono must have reached the intended persons of interest. Otherwise, nothing was worth taking that kind of risk for a woman as pretty as she was described. What was she doing in the cornfield was yet to be determined; it must be an important matter that needed immediate attention. All kinds of threat even from a POW lay in the place. Convicts, vicious Japanese soldiers, and collaborators proliferated in the cornfield.

"What else did she discuss with you?" Cab asked.

Guido, who just realized he wasn't able to speak at all times on the alleged encounter with the beautiful fairy, admitted he was caught in astonishment, enchanted by her beauty.

"I didn't have a chance to ask. She just appeared and disappeared even before I could talk." He paused. "So she is a real person. I thought I was losing my mind. Thank God." Guido must have been doubting himself on the veracity of his own story. Truly she didn't belong in the cornfield if she was real.

"She might have known me from the hospital in Davao. The doctor who took care of me was Dr. Penafrancia. She has a daughter, also a doctor or a nurse. I had never seen her, but I was told she was the one who devoted most of her time and effort to take care me. Yeah, it should be her," Cab concluded, thinking about the kindhearted doctor whom he hadn't been able to express his gratitude and to the daughter too most especially.

It was an unexplained feeling inspired by the fairy or whoever she was who wanted to see him. Since regaining his full physical capability and the confidence promoted by the Betsy affair, he had begun a thought of a few things he wanted to do. If what he thought about the fairy was confirmed, then he could sustain an effort to fulfill a promise that was already initiated through Bert dela Cruz and his cohorts. Though the convict was trustworthy, Bert was as inutile as he was considering they were both prisoners, only differing on the orange shirt his *kababayan* wore. He motioned to go outside the barracks.

"What are you planning now? Should you meet her?" Lieutenant Santos asked frankly.

"Yes, but it will need careful planning. She saved my life. I don't want to endanger hers in return," Cab replied, whispering. "I have a feeling whoever was sending those medicines to us is the fairy herself. Including those personal items that we are using."

"What do you want to do?"

"We shall meet her. I don't know how, it's really too dangerous for her in the cornfield."

"She must have known that already. I will find another way," Santos stated.

"We need to talk to the courier. Do we still have money we can spend?"

"Yes, proceeds from Betsy is untouched."

"Good."

"I have to ask you something, Cab, if you don't mind." Santos was still serious.

"Yes, what is it?" Cab replied, lighting a cigarette.

"Why didn't Betsy maul you like the others? How did you make her submit to you that easy?"

Cab smiled then laughed before he replied, "Who do you think tied her up to that tree? I had been taking care of her, taming her long enough. I didn't know the Americans would make fun of that poor animal," he replied.

Cab stood up and walked to the direction of their barrack slowly. It was getting dark, and soon enough, siren would be heard indicating for there to be no more prisoners on the yard.

Santos laughed. "You made me believe you have a certain talisman that make animals to submit to your command."

"No, not of that kind."

"What are we going to do with the money?"

"Keep it. We will spend it when we get out of here," Cab whispered.

It quashed more questions by the response he heard. Santos understood that "out of here" required the utmost secrecy. He remained quiet as they entered the barracks greeted by Abu and

Donono. He instantly got excited while having an eerie feeling; he had toyed of the words himself a long time ago. The chances to be successful was too slim; many had tried and all failed, but the rationality of the situation was just the same—as only luck was keeping them alive at the present. At any given time, the Japanese were always ready to shoot them considering their shadowy activities prohibited in the base could cause them extreme punishment or death if got caught. Escape was certainly possible if planned better, but there was no conceivable way at the time to being successful. Having an indication that Cab was thinking the same, it was about time to deliberate on the possibility. If Captain Ernest Maish had survived, no doubt they would be welcomed back in his command, but that information had yet to be confirmed.

CHAPTER 8

THE PEAK SEASON

Thousand men in surrender, hundred ways to perish.
Angels in flesh conspiring. Another day to hold on,
keep hoping we live another day.

THE ART OF SURVIVAL

By the end of October 1942, prisoners had overcrowded Davao Penal
Colony at its highest peak. Evacuees tripled in numbers; the Filipinos
were in complete disarray. Americans who would be closed to four
thousand were also in chaos. The resourcefulness of the Filipinos
didn't do much as disorders and fighting within their ranks became
common. Monsoon rains added the difficulty of days being confined
in the overcrowded barracks. Only mosquitoes would find that
the best place in the world to live and reproduce was Dapecol, a
smorgasbord of blood they can suck, endless lines of bodies awake
and asleep to feast on. They preferred those who were motionless,
numb, and bedridden as they kept getting squashed on skin of those
who were conscious and remain strong. Dengue and malaria spread
subsequently to already disease-stricken populations. Added to
weakness from starvation, it was just hard to maintain calm and
peace individually, not to mention the hardship that was also felt
in the highest level. The Japanese were also suffering from food
shortage. All of them looked forward to replenishing the supplies
that the crops had yet to produce.

The fight for survival to live another day, for a little space to settle
at night, or for a little extra food to fill the stomach was part of a life

unthinkable to live another day. It was hopeless to continue with the good deeds, but the kindhearted ones tried to keep on going up to the last good deed they could spare. There were mixed reactions and comments about who would do such a thing to show concerns to lowly Filipinos. They can only be each other. The busiest was the one who assumed the role of a priest, the one who would keep on tirelessly reading passages from the Bible to every delirious and unresponsive person until he was buried. A makeshift hospital was established to house those rendered inutile by crippling illnesses. Whatever disease and injury they may have was just hard to describe. The most common was losing their sanity. Those who would have no strength would succumb to silence, lying down on their sickbed, eyes wide open and still breathing but good as dead as they could not move their bodies. They can no longer cope with the truly maddening situation. Some would just be found in the compound with a similar affliction. Some would seek an easy end to their sufferings by attacking the guards. Deaths reduced their numbers steadily as fast as it peaked to the highest.

It may be right to say what became of our life is our destiny. Slow death, we will die in the camp. On any given day, that suddenly become dark caused by severe hunger and pain from unknown diseases. If I try to get up from a night of agony and despair only to see how many will be buried at the end of the day, there is no more that can equal to horrifying deaths. What else can we do when I myself is losing hope? A dozen more to the likes of Cab and a dozen more of Donono or Sergeant Agustin sure would help and a lot of those unknowns who will find ways to give us relief. I don't know how many would be enough of them to alleviate the desperation and madness; I don't know how long it will last. Will there be an end? I amended what Cab always says, "*The hell is only a walking distance from purgatory. There is a choice to go back and forth until you make up your mind where to stay.*" I have to rephrase, it's only a step . . . no, it's only a blink of the eyes and there is no way back.

Shallow grave awaits. (From the notes of Lt. Rodrigo
Santos, Oct. 24, 1942)

Duties in the crop plantations had reduced to a minimum while
waiting for the harvest season. Golden sceneries indeed as vast grain
fields were ready for harvest very soon, but they didn't belong to them
nor could they expect a handful share. Besides, the Japanese were not
dumb to send hundreds of starving prisoners to the cornfield bearing
soft and fresh kernel or in the sweet potatoes and bean plots. They
were not allowed to harvest edible crops straight from the stem and
vines. Extra food hardly found its way in, and basically at a standstill,
any amount that could get through were consumed at once; the stash
of dried meat had long run out. Even the pinches disappeared around
the barracks. Rats were rarely seen. Hombre Donono had already
adapted himself to not eating at all sometimes.

"This is the last piece of the meat we have," Donono offered the
buffalo jerky to Cab, Santos, and Guido. Together they were forming
a circle while having the afternoon ration.

"You can have it," Cab replied to the pint-sized soldier whom he
had spoiled like his own little brother.

Dono tore the meat in half and to smaller pieces about the size
of a quarter. "Are you sure you don't like any?" he repeated the offer,
looking to the other two who shook their heads in response.

Donono had been sick for many days. The sudden change in the
diet of plenty to almost nothing was the only thing attributed to his
illness, friends would agree to say. Santos suggested that the worms in
his system had started to feel the same hunger and panicking in the
beginning. After his recovery, he said Don should be eating less as the
worms had eaten each other down to one left. It may be true; the little
man could care less about food. Instead he gave a piece to each soldier
passing nearby without saying a word. He said they can make a joke
out of his worms, but they cannot play with his conscience. How he
would enjoy the pleasure of eating when every time he attempted to
place it in his mouth, the big guys would open their mouths at the
same time too.

"You know there's a lot of them in Mactan," Cabarles suggested
in desperation.

"Yes, I know," Santos agreed. "What are you thinking about them?"

"I'm thinking of one roasting in front of us right now," Cab stated.

"Is it Betsy?"

"No, I like Betsy."

"How do you do that?"

"Do what?"

"You barely ate and seems you are full."

"Practice and preparations, I had learned a lot from experience. I drink a lot of water from the rain."

"I do too. How long do you think will it last? We are basically not eating for days already. I heard that details in Mactan is halted another month, only colonos are allowed there now. Details available are fixing roads and lumberyard." Santos was worried.

"I wish I can share with your thoughts. Are they delicious?" Agustin asked, referring to Cabarles imagining a whole buffalo on the roasting.

"Yes, it is. One may be not enough for us. I'm thinking of two or more."

"How can you do that? I don't know. I just can't." Agustin needed coaching.

"Let's ask the colonos, maybe they can help us."

"What is really in your mind? I don't understand." Santos had adapted on how Cabarles thought, but he was really caught wondering this time.

Dapecol may be literally surrounded with food but not at idle time when harvests were still limited. The monsoon weather was punishing. As prisoners, there was really not much they could do about it. The influx of more prisoners that come in hundreds per day in the already crowded compound had cause the worst of the situation even to the most resourceful. The Japanese command who also had their own food shortage problem became so strict and impatient, and security in the camp had tripled with a new breed of guards. They were more intimidating and did not play games; they did what they said they would do. However, there was always something for grabs as long as you have the skill of not getting caught. In most covert operations, having the right people to execute the job is critical. There lay the usefulness and cooperation of the convicts and jail masters at desperate times. The Moros must be alerted too.

The Japanese had agreed to resume the detail of prisoners to Mactan fields. Cabarles, Santos, Donono, Rabong, and Malvo were arranged to be chosen among others to work with the inmates on special details in the Mactan rice fields.

Guido and Rufino Dominguez and the Americans to the cornfield on another group to work with the civilians, he was also told to keep an eye on the "fairy." Their job was to rid the cornstalks of harmful caterpillars and other insects by hand but were warned not to eat the produce. The convenience of the cornfield detail was the anticipation of ready-to-eat food; they were already laid down on the path courtesy of the civilians. By the time they reached the greeneries that morning, the lucky ones had already chewed up on rice balls and boiled bananas. The insects themselves have replenished the emptiness of stomachs all day. Forbidden to touch the hearts, the cornfield offered an easy source of nutrition. However, they just had to tolerate the caterpillars still kicking inside their mouths even if the heads were already taken off. The other downside of the cornfield detail was that they were heavily guarded. Many were happy, and there was new hope among them at a time of extreme starvation. The meticulous and boring insect details were called upon mainly for diversion.

On another place, the view of the vast green turning to a golden color of rice crops was the best sight. In a month or so, it would require a lot of details for a long period of harvesttime. The Japanese could have the grains that still needed milling before it could fill stomachs. So much to look forward for that. One more month or so with basically nothing to eat at present was the problem they had to address with utmost seriousness; Filipino prisoners were dying already, and no one cared other than themselves.

The season of severe starvation could only come to worse before it was over. On the other hand, the predicament that the harvest would be shared to the Filipinos equally as the American POWs enjoyed were clearly not a thing barefooted soldiers would like to think. They knew it would never happen. It was a known fact that they were systematically harassed and underfed to expire from hunger and diseases since they set foot in the camp. By any means, they were insignificant soldiers who could just die. For a long time, they were having boiled beans lucky for anyone to see a piece of the vegetable on their bowl. For that matter, Filipino officers could not be blamed to embrace the fold of Americans. Surviving was more likely to be attained lining up on American food rations. Cabarles and Santos were welcome to do so, which they do only to spare their food to then sickened Donono and the invalid Abu Benghalid.

The resumption of Mactan details was carefully planned and initiated with the involvement of the colonos, so to speak. Work would include fortifying the corral of the water buffaloes that escaped a night ago in herds. The animals had made considerable destruction on the plantation and needed to be herded back to their abode.

"Good morning, sir," said a familiar-looking man in a bright orange shirt, grinning proudly to express a mission accomplished.

"Good morning, Bert," replied Cab, Santos likewise.

"I had received your message. As you can see, it is taken care of," Bert spoke proudly to a grand idea he was let to implement long ago. "It took a while before we could think of how to do it without making the Japs suspicious. Mr. Arcenas himself gave us the go." He implied that the jail superintendent himself had instigated the plan.

"Does it need to murder a man?" Cab seriously asked.

"Definitely, that man was stubborn. He would reveal our plan to the Japs than cooperate with us," Bert sadly replied.

"How did you do it? I heard he was bitten by a snake. Are there really cobras here?" Cabarles asked. He was afraid having to wander around barefooted while venomous snakes were actively seeking for food too. He didn't want to cross paths with them.

"I haven't seen one myself, but there's one now for sure," Bert replied, smiling.

Cab understood very well what Bert implied. He had known his kababayan as a kindhearted man, but now it was proven that he was capable of slaying a fellow human being in cold blood while denying the same reason why he was serving a life sentence.

"Smart, very smart," Cab stated while grasping the ingenuity of the idea.

THE GREAT BUFFALO STAMPEDE

Separated from the POW compound, the colonos had the privilege of being visited by almost anybody. Any information from outside the base and vice versa could be relayed through the inmates who had established a clandestine communication to the soldiers and the concerned group outside the base.

As starvation caused considerable uncertainty among prisoners who had run out of every other option in their arsenal, Cabarles and Santos had long been eyeballing the buffaloes that were completely visible from Zamboanga Road where they had been detailed for months fixing the road. If they could not be switched to other details aside from hauling gravel and dirt, he knew they would not last long. As he sent messages to Bert requesting immediate help, together with the connivance of trusted inmates and wanted bandits, they concocted an elaborate plan. If Cabarles wanted buffalo meat, then he should get it. At the time, it was the only place where there were plenty of animals left in Davao maybe inside Dapecol. Well coralled like the POWs, the animals were well fed, fat, and reproducing. Part of the fence was tampered days ago. It took a while somehow before the animals found their way out and now they were everywhere and ruining the rice field and other crops. They had to be brought back in containment.

In so doing, the animals were not expected to be recaptured in all. Most of them must be wandering in the deepest part of the forest already; also at the time, at least a couple of them had been slaughtered already. How its nutritious meat could find its way inside the camp may be easy, but still needed ingenuity and courage. For several days thereafter, there would be plenty of *chicharon* (fat crackers) cooked out of carabao skin that would be peddled in the refugee camp.

Since the inmates failed the important duty of taking care of the herds by losing more than ten, not counting the destruction it made on the crops, tending the farm animals were entrusted to the Filipino soldiers as it was prearranged by conniving individuals. Betsy, the albino carabao who was made sure to be spared from massacre of her kind at the request of Cab, was never found. With many available tamed animals suddenly in his care, he commissioned one buffalo that responded well in general command. It became a common sight inside the POW compound, and therefore, a constant flow of food found its way into the mouths of starving soldiers though it was never enough. *Careta* was reintroduced to bring firewood and local materials in the handicraft department, mostly bamboos. In the following days, Filipino details feeding the herds were rotated in a group to the supervision of either one of the original Fifty-Seventh Scout survivors and sergeants Agustin, Malvo, and Rabong. The cobra scare also began in a more threatening level as another collaborator died. In effect, even the Japanese would think twice to venture at the edge of the Mactan rice field. Every group must be aware of their job other than feeding the animals and themselves. They must bring back food to spare for those who were not capable of doing detail work.

JUST ANOTHER POW

One of the bedridden and who became seriously ill was Abu Benghalid, whose foot injury had worsened to a severe inflammation that turned blue up to his leg. He refused any more medication; malingering didn't help at all to relieve the pain he was suffering. Since he became a trusted ally of the Fifty-Seventh Scout soldiers, his life was only prolonged through his association with the especial care of Dono. Having heard many interesting events of his life story, the little dark man always found time to listen. How he became a soldier was an account he revealed unpretentiously in the manner of the Christian faith. He was confessing to a man despite of their unlikely camaraderie. His decision making, often based on pride or religious belief, never helped his condition nor eased his pain. Now he could not walk at all, and his foot was swollen blue. He refused adamantly to be treated in the hospital even at the constant advices of his fellows. He said he would rather die than cut his leg off; he wanted to die intact, which he knew wouldn't be long. In his stint with the Tagalog-speaking allies, he had revealed himself and all his knowledge about Mindanao and the adjoining islands. He was proud to convey that his old man was a *datu*. If by any chance his comrades would make it to Cotabato, he said to just mention his name and they would be welcomed like brothers.

Abu Benghalid was the firstborn of the first wife of a *datu* in the Lanao province, and he had worked in the lumber dock of Lasang in Davao as a security guard. They were pinned down by the invading Japanese forces while defending the island together with a few policemen and army regulars of whom only a few dozen were armed to a battle that didn't last long. He always boasted that they killed a lot of Japanese together with his fellow dockworkers. As the invasion of Davao ended, he was traced by his relatives in Dapecol who planned and arranged their unsuccessful escape from Dapecol that also cost the lives of many POWs. Remorseful of such careless move of undermining the Japanese warnings to those who would try to escape, the embarrassment and injury he incurred to himself gave him no other choice but to remain in prison. Nearing his death, his last wish was not to be buried like the others but for his body to be given to the brothers and wives who were blending in with the evacuees, brothers and wives who were part of the smuggling schemes and cattle rustling around Dapecol that also benefitted the POWs. All must have given up trying to extract Abu out of prison. They resorted to raiding the corn and vegetable plantations at night with the cooperation of caretakers and conspiracy with the agricultural supervisors of Dapecol. Their deeds extended farther away from Dapecol to the western provinces of Mindanao while becoming a nuisance not only to *hacienderos* (plantations owners) but also to the Japanese themselves. They were eventually hunted down as a band of thieves and animal rustlers. Rumors followed that they had retreated away to their home province in Cotabato; some said they were still around just cooling off. The Japanese said they were annihilated, which coincided with the end of the disappearances of many domesticated animals in the vicinity of Dapecol. A few of them were met by Cabarles and Santos; an offer to escape the prison was made outright, but the fear of many others being executed in effect did not make the idea pleasing at the time. Meanwhile, the pledge of loyalty and assertion that they would be around when needed was very encouraging to the prisoners.

The Americans who were also suffering heavy casualties due to illnesses had to stomach the general situation. Though they were equally taken care of with regards to food by the Filipino POWs as much as they could spare for a price, the hope of Red Cross packs alleviated their extreme dislike of the ration in addition to the food spared for them by the locals. However, they enjoyed a lot better condition and treatment than the Filipino soldiers. For the Japanese, they were the real POWs, not the expendable brown colored; for the Davaoenos who would lean more to helping the Caucasians than their own kind for some reasons extended their hospitality not only in food kind. Throughout their captivity and by the end of the war, children of noticeably foreign fathers would be born around the vicinity of Dapecol.

Filipinos simply resisted being sent to the hospital for medical treatment as there were rumors of insufficient medical skills of whoever should attend to them—an attestation made by many who buried the dead. Any Filipino willing to be confined in the facility should be better off leaving their important belongings to an ally with their last will, for no one came back alive. Abu Benghalid must have known his end was near as someone kept telling him it was time to get treatment in the hospital. Not yet, he would say most of the time.

Malnutrition and common insect bites that would progress to severe infections to symptoms of dengue and malaria were always taken for granted until they became worse. They believed that self-medication was proven to be more effective. Many quack doctors also found their usefulness in healing illnesses until they themselves become afflicted of the same diseases. Delirious or unconscious, one breath away to the hospital, the destination of one out of three patients was directly to the burial grounds; the other two were just luckier to wait for a few more days. The Americans enjoyed a higher survival rate. Many lived to tell the tales in otherwise more horrific stories to discourage the local soldiers in coming for treatment. Medicines were always in short supply, which were allotted in priority for the Japanese.

On the other hand, there were the so-called positive effects of giving up the last breath in the hospital facility. The sight of nurses and employees would do the trick to die peacefully. It was rumored that beautiful Filipinas comprised the attending personnel of the Dapecol hospital. It may be true to the perception of Dominador Cabarles as he was taken care of one he still maintained as an angel, downgraded by Agustin as a fairy. Either one, she was described to be of overwhelming beauty, and he actually described how peaceful it would be to know that angels were around while catching the last breath. Benghalid refused to believe in angels, neither be brought in the hospital.

Truly, many young and beautiful ladies were commonly seen not only in the hospital premises, but also everywhere except in the POW compound. Diseases from such escapades became an addition to the so many that spread uncontrollably. Difficulties in urinating and lingering rashes became common. Most of the afflicted were Japanese guards, whether paid, part of a bribe, or in exchange for a favor. The sale of the white pill became a lucrative business for the Filipinos, who definitely contributed to the spread of disease by selling compacted baby powder moistened by saliva in the process of production to desperate ones.

THE TALE OF COTTON BALLS

In the beginning of August until November 1942, the American prisoners from all over the Panay Islands were consolidated in Dapecol. The many additions were from Negros, Cebu, and Camp Casisang in Malaybalay, Bukidnon. Aside from Dapecol, the Japanese maintained a labor camp in Mindanao to supplement manpower in the logging and wood industry, mining, and crop plantations owned by the enterprising Japanese who had established their businesses even before the war. The demand for cheap labor increased as owners expanded production and profits, grabbing land for its mineral resources they claimed as their own, expanded at the nod of the commanding general of the Japanese Imperial Army in Mindanao. American prisoners of war would disappear from Dapecol by the hundreds and reappear in two or more months exhausted and sickly. Many of them would resist another tour of hard labor by pretending to be afflicted with whatever disease, only to find later that they really had it. The congestion of prisoners in detention camps around the country was resolved in such process—Dapecol would get the able-bodied prisoners from Manila Bilibid Prison and as far as the POW camp in Cabanatuan in Northern Luzon while letting those deemed inutile to die or be transferred to another prison. Soldiers could not die easily. Diseases were just difficult to contain.

Sometimes after the great buffalo stampede in October, POWs were caught off guard when the Japanese ordered inspection of the barracks. As the morning muster was in progress, the Japanese raided each and rounded up all prisoners who could not attend muster anymore, weak and strong alike. Sick, wounded, pretending, or just refusing to salute the Japanese flag, they were rounded up and assembled in separate places. Fortunately, Abu Benghalid and Donono were frolicking in the morning sunshine when that happened; he made the muster even before it began. There was no room for any prisoner in Dapecol if they could not do details. They were hauled in Lasang Pier with a promise of better accommodations, The destination Iwahig Penal Colony. About three hundred of POWs were rooted out in the second shipment of prisoners to another prison system; no hard labor thereat to give hope of recovery, which was very encouraging to those who made it to the boat and remained alive.

Rumors began after a week that on the shipload of prisoners sent to Palawan, the prisoners were lucky if half of them reached the destination physically. Rumors also arose that most of the kinds of fish caught in the Sulu Sea and Zamboanga Peninsula to Palawan would be found loaded with human flesh and bones. There were also tales of bloodstained cotton balls, the kind used to lepers, that were also commonly found on fish stomachs, even on smaller ones like the abundant yellowtail snappers that were commonly caught in schools in the Sulu Sea.

In November of 1942, hundreds of participants of the Bataan Death March arrived in Dapecol who were happy about the promise of a good chow only to be dismayed by another death march to endure while making sure they didn't aggravate the impatient Japanese. The chance of reaching Dapecol was slim. What else could they expect but take the opportunity better than just wait for inevitable death? From Cabanatuan, they finally reached the last leg of their journey. On their march from Lasang Pier in Davao of about twenty kilometers' distance to their new home, they couldn't help each other but toyed on the idea of escaping and hiding in the thick forest of centuries-old trees so close along the road. The only problem was how to get there without being shot at. A few weeks later, the US Marines and Army Rangers from Luzon found themselves actually in it, cutting those trees guarded closely by the Japanese. In Mindanao, there might be plenty of food, but they had learned how to be careful what else they wished for. In addition, they would know that Davao Penal Colony was a prison compound in the middle of nowhere, simply inescapable.

CHAPTER 9

FAILURES AND SUCCESS

PRIDE AND CONFIDENCE

Halfway in November and disease free was only true to Cabarles and company who kept advising Santos and Donono to keep in shape. The harvest season finally came progress to most crops in the 150 square miles of the mostly agricultural land of Dapecol. Things were looking better for the POWs. Food rations were brought back to regular as bragged to be plentiful by the Japanese quartermaster who had been running his own scam, scheming on the food supplies for the POWs. Prisoners were back to details in the crops, only this time there was plenty to munch on and extra to save, as long as they didn't get picky. Tropical fruits became abundant aside from the tended papayas, sweet potatoes, corn, and vegetables. The Japanese camp commander himself was happy as the situation came to his favor, and he desired to rebuild a reputation of a kindhearted officer after all the atrocities he had allowed. For reasons unknown even to his subordinates, he showed leniency on security; he abruptly changed, leaning toward developing relationships with civilians and prisoners in diplomatic ways.

His previous rejection of evacuees building up around Dapecol had somewhat turned to a more humane conduct. Formerly strict and atrocious especially to Filipino families who evacuated around Dapecol, the sudden change of behavior by Major Takeo Maeda was attributed to the good harvest. Others would say he may possibly respect the spirit of the incoming holiday season in essence. Only a few would know exactly the truth behind the changes. Not his normal style of managing the camp, he was seen many times coming in and out of Dapecol in his sequestered car, assumed to be rendering official military duties. Life in Davao seemed to look in order, not counting the guerillas fighting on the outskirts of the island that kept on harassing the Japanese. Mindanao was generally under control.

"The resistance is contained. Just don't waste our time with them anymore," he said as he spoke about the guerillas and bandits. "How can they reorganize and fight against us when we already killed almost every one of them? Those that were left alive are our prisoners and working for us," he continued with pride and confidence, and he might be right. There was no significant guerilla activity that challenged their rule since September. He would confirm his evaluation about the resistance as thieves and bandits to his commanding officer, an aging general in the First Division of JIP.

Major Takeo Maeda was known as a merciless commandant of Dapecol. He was also known to have a special fondness for Filipina women. In reality, he had never fired a single shot of his side arm since his troops landed in Davao. His orders and silence were enough for his men to do all the brutalities that followed in the invasion of Mindanao. Though the battlefields were commanded by tactical and combat officers that led to the ultimate bloodshed and casualties on both sides, his role in winning the war in Southern Philippines can be traced back by a few people who had known him better. It was said that he had caused and orchestrated most of the deaths of the Americans and Filipinos far beyond any combatant officers of the entire JIP in Mindanao. He was reputed to be the architect of the systematic eradication of sickly, old, and lazy colonos out of Dapecol to Iwahig, Palawan, while taking in healthy prisoners from other parts of the country. Maeda's brutality runs through a chain of command also blamed for the deaths of soldiers who were merely defiant to hard labor while getting rid of the sickly and weak from Dapecol. It was a tale foretold over and over that not too many of the prisoners transferred to Iwahig reached their destination.

So much to say that his revised stratagem was necessary to improve governing authority and status as people friendly. He knew it would be hard for him to redeem himself for the civilians to support his personal ambition and his country's vision to the Philippines. Before the war, he was said to be a young lieutenant frequenting Davao and the nearby provinces, envisioning how to win the war and ultimately how to rule the island in the name of the Japanese empire. He came back as a combatant captain and was subsequently promoted one rank up after successfully conquering Davao with only a few hundred men.

Nonetheless, the failure to expand his success outward was suppressed by a bloody battle with the lost Fifty-Seventh Scout Unit from Luzon that he maintained he fought a thousand well-armed Allied soldiers. It was outright demeaning to his reputation. He admitted that expansion could not be achieved without reinforcement. His cowardly decision to repudiate a battle plan that he put together and failed costly by many casualties in his troops caused him to be as ruthless as he became known.

Who else could he lay down his frustrations on? Only to the prisoners and civilians. One who had suffered most of such brutality was Dominador Cabarles, interrogating a captured "captain" who really had no idea what they were asking for in all languages and dialects would not yield any information. The time he consumed in tormenting a man who didn't even know how to read or write had given time for the Allied to arm, train, and organize. In early April of 1942, Mindanao was attacked with massive forces through the west in Cotabato and from the north in Cagayan. The island was depended intensively by Filipinos in the front lines armed only with bolos and bamboo spikes. In general evaluation of the bravery of the islanders, they fared equally as ferocious as the invaders resulting to the undetermined casualties on both sides before the Allied surrender.

The Japanese came out victorious eventually. Maeda's reputation was nonetheless scarred in the process. He lost his battle command and was reassigned to rule Dapecol instead, reporting to other senior officers and to an aging general who became the supreme commander of Southern Philippines. Strategically precalculated, assuring many benefits to take over the prison colony in Davao with about two thousand inmates, he was certain the functional concept of the Dapecol operation would be more productive if managed by the Japanese military. He found himself actually implementing his plan, undermining personal ambition to become the supreme authority of Mindanao. In his vision, the presence of Japanese forces in the Philippines could be supported out of the rich resources of the island alone. Many unforeseen consequences in the aftermath of bloody victory added up to the failure of his conception for the second time. Free labor from uncooperative colonos and starving POWs was not productive at all for several reasons. Convicts would attack a Japanese soldier when yelled at without regard of the consequences. Many would just refuse to work under new management, many others excusing themselves for being sick even when they were not. Those who complied may look busy working, but it would take a prolonged time to finish a job. Countless evacuees were also unexpected. Civilians displaced by the war migrated in Dapecol, arriving by the hundreds. In no time at all, there were over ten thousand men, women, and children begging a share of Dapecol food resources. Too many mouths to feed that some resorted to stealing even supplies allotted to Japanese soldiers. Guerillas and groups of bandits also presented a clear setback. They raided haciendas and businesses with known association to the Japanese; therefore it was difficult to maintain order in the colony, especially when disease began to spread. He had resolved the problems as it may appear on the POWs, but never on the evacuees.

In general views however, he was still the same officer respected by his men and definitely despised by the Filipinos. As order in Dapecol was seemingly restored, Maeda noticeably switched to diplomacy while demanding productivity. Substantial rewards were offered to those who could turn in or cause the extermination of anyone or group that did harm to the Japanese and its interests. It seemed to work when many turncoats showed their true colors promptly in exchange of employment and rewards in the new authority. Maeda may not have given up personal ambition to rule Mindanao, but there was another desire that he never relented to pursue. In his authority as a high-ranking Japanese officer, he would do whatever it took to get what he wanted most.

FINISHING THE THIRD GRADE

Confidence in the rank of Filipinos were upheld for the meantime; nothing to do after details but chat, they resumed on interrupted businesses. Earlier fervor put in progress. It started when it became known to Rod Santos that other than being incomprehensible in

English, Cabarles didn't know how to read nor write either. He decided to begin teaching the captain, and he did it seriously. The same extended to Donono who was found to be good at drawing but could not write either. In a short period, Santos was proud to say that Cab had already attained the comprehension of a first grade as he could write and sign his name legibly. He was given a handwritten certificate signed by Santos jokingly but accepted by Cab, who was happy and proud. An opportunity he was denied when he was younger, he took advantage of it to its full extent. He was made to learn the alphabets then was taught how to read and was given a book to practice on reading. Shortly after, the two pupils that Santos had were joined by many more illiterate soldiers that they actually developed a learning system with serious commitment on the effort. Volunteer teachers also willingly and patiently contributed their time that they named the last bay of their barracks as Elementary School of Smelly Foot, as a majority of the pupils could only sat on the floor extending their feet. Mostly were afflicted of certain bacteria that thrived between their toes, causing it scratchy, moist, and smelly rashes called *alipunga*. Charcoal was used by the teachers to write on cardboards that also served as sleeping mats at night. Pencils and papers were donated and smuggled inside the compound. Indeed it really became a learning school. They also conducted a common English-Pilipino translation class.

By November of 1942, almost ten months since he was reunited with Santos and Donono, Cab could read the entire book he was assigned to read with the extra time devoted to him by Santos and Agustin and with his own incredible initiative. He had issued the third-grade certificate, sixth grade when someone changed his mind after a minute that he gladly accepted at the sarcastic amusement of his friends. He could also count to a hundred but admitted that arithmetics was very hard to comprehend. He himself was amazed at his accomplishments to say it was the only good thing to remember in Davao aside from the brotherhood they had developed with each other. With the newly acquired talent, he didn't stop to advance what he had learned. He kept studying, reading, or writing most of the time on his own and was seldom seen hanging out with anyone after details unless on businesses he was directly involved. There was a dozen of Kapitan Domengs however that the Filipinos could rely on a daily basis, all of which were capable of subduing a frenzied soldier and all of whom were highly respected to mitigate a fistfight and soften offended pride. Meanwhile, Donono was just too hard to comprehend in most of the lessons. He was stuck on learning the alphabets, but his exceptional ability in sketching was augmented by the availability of papers and pencils. Armed with the ability to recognize the amount indicated on paper bills, so much to say in truth he could hardly comprehend what was written on a note and information board by himself.

The first meeting with the fairy of the cornfield was arranged, and of all places, it would happen in the corn plantation where she was seen the first time. The meeting was necessitated by a personal favor Cabarles would request from the woman in fulfillment of a promise that had been lingering in his mind. He also wanted to express his gratitude personally to the presumed angel who took care of him. These were very important subjects that must be discussed to extend her helping hand.

The fairy in person was confirmed to be Rina Penafrancia. Before the war, she was also pursuing a degree in medicine to follow the footsteps of his father when the war interfered. Devoting her time helping to his father's occupation, she exerted more effort in helping the underprivileged in health care and disease prevention on her own while defying the odds of getting apprehended for helping the prisoners. Developing sympathy for a man who refused to die only to be taken by Japanese soldiers, she had dedicated herself in an effort to find the captain whose blood it was that extended his life belonged to her. The only place to look was Dapecol, and in that place, there was a thousand more that needed her blood. In a volunteer capacity, she also moonlighted as a nurse at Dapecol Hospital since Cabarles disappeared from the Davao clinic. Rina extended the same struggle in caring for sick people as much as she could despite the danger inspired by acquired commitment to the captain's recuperation. Her failure to find Cabarles at Dapecol Hospital led her to believe that he had died at the hands of the Japanese.

Through the colonos, she was informed that Cabarles lived at the time she lost all hope. Her known line of work subsequently became a cover for other things she did thereafter. Little was known to everyone that Rina ran a communication and supply network that helped the POWs in Dapecol. Her access in Davao Hospital and having a family clinic of their own, she was in the greatest position to do the deeds. Her natural kindness like his father who would accommodate patients for free without recognition of any kind would be maintained with the utmost secrecy. There was not a single person she trusted but his father, and there were individuals who would do anything for her. Wealthy, aristocratic, and beautiful, she would not be the kind to spend time mingling with the evacuees much more being in the middle of acres of an insect-infested cornfield to meet a Filipino soldier.

"No civilians beyond this point" was painted on a board at the gate of Dapecol. Cab knew it had been there since the first time he entered the compound; he was glad he could read and understand what it meant at a glance. The normalcy of the situation in Dapecol had somewhat reduced the security; the rumors had been that the Japanese soldiers were sent to reinforce battlefields and were busy chasing guerillas and bandits in the outskirts. The security manning the compound were new and untrained soldiers shipped from Formosa just recently. It wasn't long to find that they could be easily bribed and manipulated. They shared common weaknesses as the ones they replaced—money to spend in the city at liberty. It wasn't long for them to know that the most they wanted in the city could be made available right in Dapecol for a favor. It was women; nobody knew who carried contagious diseases, but there were willing cohorts who became part of business deals with the Japanese guards. It didn't take long to learn either who to approach for a special pill that should relieve their difficulties in urinating.

"MEETING THE FAIRY"

As meeting Rina Penafrancia necessitated urgency, it was arranged in a venue that remained discreet the first time. The cornfield was the only place it could be done. The meeting was definitive of a certain subject matter that should be taken care of in lieu of anything else. Rod Santos was disappointed that Rina did not remove the piece of cloth covering her face the whole time in disguise of a male accompanied by a few locals to avoid detection and deter the burning sunrays. The voice of a woman no doubt, absent of the heavy accent of a Davaoeno, but the words were assuring and exact to the subject of the meeting.

Perhaps Rina was still embarrassed of her actions on the first attempt to meet Cab as described by Guido Agustin. Though she was sure it was the same unconscious man she had let her blood flow in his veins the first time she had seen him, she could not understand her heart that kept on beating like it wanted to give more for this man that had occupied her thoughts for a long time. Pity or something else to reason her longing, Rina knew she could only hope for survival of them all. She always had more blood to offer as long as her heart kept on beating. In blood and prayers that gave her strength, what she had done she could offer again and again. Life at POW camps was just too harsh it could change a handsome man to a skinny and old-looking man. Whether his name was Cabarles or Maish, certainly he was the same man she had devoted endless thoughts and prayers to, and she was thankful to the Lord that she was heard. She meant only business this time while preserving her elation. No woman of her status would meet a group of men on dangerous grounds just to show her looks. Cabarles could only reiterate his gratefulness to the many help the woman had done for him, most importantly for saving his life. Santos did the talking about the rest. As discreet as the meeting had transpired, Rina disappeared the same way.

"Very pretty indeed . . . and brave, no doubt," Santos stated. Obviously he was also enchanted.

"How do you know? You had seen only the eyes," Cabarles responded.

"Yeah, very alluring those eyes are. Isn't she? Guido was right. She definitely likes you. She won't show herself in this place for you if not. You know, I can rewrite your letter for Inez. How did you meet her again?" Santos brooded over an idea to ease the man's sorrow about his wife.

"She's just naturally kind . . . to all of us. Yeah, she's very brave," Cab uttered, disregarding what Santos had insinuated.

Both men were left to realize that they could not still identify the "fairy" in a crowd. However, it all went well, and they ignored the whines of disappointment of Donono for not seeing Miss Penafrancia even when he was told that the woman disguised as a man.

"You know, the only woman I met since leaving Manila was Katherina." Little Don sighed. "And she's dead."

"You had seen Betsy many times before she disappeared, didn't you?" Santos joked.

"I was truly saddened that she vanished. I hope no one does any harm to her."

"Good, you know, we don't want the fairy to abandon us too. We need her very much," Santos replied, which pacified Donono to silence.

Donono was reminded many times if he hadn't insisted to visit the place of the late couple for food. They could have just moved on, and the Marfil should still be alive at least. It happened a long time ago. Images of death lingered in his mind, only that moment he could not alleviate the culpability it created. It was truly hard to forget.

There were so much to look back. Superstitious or just being a man of his word, Cab reiterated that a promise made to the deceased couple must be resolved first; otherwise, they should face only bad luck with their plans.

THE REVELATION (ACCORDING TO HOMBRE DONONO)

Back to the first week of November 1942, the rest of the day was spent talking and jesting. Donono always asked questions. "What would be our life in Davao if we are not prisoners?" he would say, daydreaming, that he could stay in Mindanao, find a girl, and live happily ever after.

"We would still be killing Japanese, if not dead. To find a good life here forever, you have to kill them all (Japanese)," Rod answered immediately.

"Why?"

"Because they always wanted to kill us."

"Should it make any difference in Luzon? There should be a lot of enemy there too, you know," Don said in a casual tone but insinuating his longing to suffice a certain desire.

"Yes, it is true. But if we make it back alive in Manila, I can provide you any girl you want," Santos teased the little guy.

"All right, you just made up my mind." Don had kept silent afterward. He definitely wanted to go back to Luzon.

Though it took Donono a long time to be enlightened that the Americans were just another people not to be worshipped, he had proven it to be true that they could also die in starvation and illness like him. What they ate was what he also ate in prison, a situation totally different from the way of life he grew up in where he slept under a coconut with meals different from the masters he had grown up with. He had told his life story countless times which was not much involved aside from long stint in coconut picking. There was an unfortunate event that made him fled to the big city only to follow a newlywed couple in whites that showed him compassion and after which he became a soldier. He never thought he would become a soldier. The one who baptized him Donono had educated him so much as a human being to be treated like one. Spending more time with Santos, he was also taught about military disciplines. The lieutenant made him understand that the duty of a soldier was to follow orders from senior officers. Other than that, he had been equal even with the American.

Donono was from a village where everyone only thought of food to eat and how to raise their young. He grew up adapting to the culture shock brought in by the Americans when they took over the Philippines from the Spaniards. It wasn't clear why he left his village, but he revealed he would come back one day with guns and shoot some people he hated. The death of his father had caused him to stow away and wander in the streets of Manila. For him, Inez was an angel truly deserved to be adored and loved by Cabarles to whom he shall forever do whatever he wanted him to do. With a word from Santos, he could find a mate in Manila where he had been once already. He looked up to Santos as his father, the same person who could tolerate his passion in eating and appreciating his other talents. He had truly learned many things in the company of the soldiers and became one in the principles of Santos and Cabarles.

As Donono eventually understood the concept of soldiering, he was somehow still confused by the way he was treated by Santos and Cabarles. There was no sign of military discipline but a brother in the tradition of family. His association with Lt. Rod Santos and Cab was the one he was most proud of. A warrior he had become, he couldn't understand what responsibility came with the rank of a corporal. One thing he learned very seriously was not to get caught in the act of stealing. With them, he became part of legendary, brave, humble, and the most noble endeavors he could not believe himself taking part in if only for a hearsay. With them, he was not a lowly coconut picker or an insignificant being who deserved nothing. He could stand straight and head up even with the Americans, the white people he used to worship. They all had to live in constant threat to be punished or killed on the same act of defiance against the command of their captors. He had gone too far since he ran away from home.

Though he truly wished of coming back home with a loaded rifle on his shoulder, he gave up that thought long ago. He was given a new family, and he intended to keep them until they said it was time to die, until their "powers" weakened and could no longer sustain the hardship and struggles of being prisoners.

Donono believed Cabarles must have magical powers to make astonishing women yield to him. He confirmed his belief to see how Betsy behaved instantly at Cab's command. Neither of the two had disclosed to him that they had any of that kind. Donono came from a secluded village where all in whites or whites moving were worshipped and thought to bring good luck. Also intact in his memory, Cabarles was in all-white clothes with an angelic-looking woman the first time he met them. Very kind couple, he was given food while many denied him. Cab must have possessed something that even a female god would succumb to him, even a fairy. Cab was just an ordinary man as he was told repeatedly, but surviving death that he had seen with his own eyes could not change what Dono thought about the man.

Also, where he came from, a man enough could only have a woman to marry at the consent of the parents and that was after he had submitted himself to painful rituals, which explained the methodical scarring in some parts of his body. When he became a soldier, a few more scars were added from real battle; it was about time to fantasize about having one of his own. With a thousand men, the competition was too much with only a few he had seen on the other side of the fence and barbed wire. It was not possible.

"It wasn't about the scars, Dono," Abu Benghalid made him understand. "It's just that we are all prisoners that need to find the way out first."

In his association with Benghalid, Donono listened to Benghalid's story many times before and after the establishment of the Alipunga Elementary School. The man revealed he had three wives. Clear skin and almost similar in appearance to Donono, only taller, he was reminded of an amulet the Muslim had given him just a day ago. When he wore the thing, he was advised to never take it off to allow its power to work as he was told it could charm the most beautiful woman at any place and any time. According to the previous owner, he could also have three wives if he chose. "With your looks, you will be needing it," he said this to him before they fell asleep that night. Donono suddenly realized what he meant. *That silly man, I look better than him.* He sighed, smiling in submission to what Abu insinuated.

"Hey, Don. Time to go back to work," Santos cut Donono from deep thought. Agustin's reminder also distracted Cab from his usual state of mind—thinking about Inez.

Together, Donono, Cab, and Santos spent the rest of the day collecting grasshoppers in the intense heat and humidity. Each were eased by the usual run of the imagination. There were plenty of corn hearts almost ready to eat. The crop must have been sweet and thirst quenching; however, they were aware that it was forbidden to touch. Discouraged by the plantation bosses, most of whom were the colonos in oranges, the attitude of the Filipino details toward the yield was in consideration of not pushing their luck that was already spent during the day by accomplishing an important objective of meeting the fairy. The Americans, however, should have been full by then, either of the corn grains or grasshoppers. Benefiting also at the end of the day were the civilians. Locust was nutritious and tasted a lot better when fried. It became a delicacy many would say delicious, but maybe there was just nothing else to eat.

There was a system going in mutual benefit. Many children could be seen regularly in the path to the cornfield, cheering and singing. A few were Agustin's and Dominguez's children. They were not there for the details to just hear their voices. The awkward renditions of lullabies and Christmas songs were not in all just to entertain the POWs, but they were to get the insects collected. Only extremely hungry Americans would dare to eat them, but they were kind enough to pass their catches to the kids. Other usefulness of the children was providing drinking water, which was allowed without intervention by the guards. Some of them also served as middlemen in most items POWs would like to buy. They also preferred to intermingle with the Americans who would be more generous to share their hard-earned money and savings if not carelessness to leave corn hearts for them. A more pleasant relationship developed, adding to the longstanding partiality to American POWs than the Filipinos. Being the majority of the population in Dapecol and the common patrons of tobacco products, Americans were also regular buyers of luxuries like shaving blades and creams, toothpaste, soap, and more per order. Sometimes smuggling them inside the camp was part of the deal, but it would be more expensive. Donono and Cabarles were very intrigued to see that those children could take note of orders easily at a young age that were certainly difficult for them to learn. Many of those lists would end up going to Abu. Together they monopolized retail and distribution of assorted merchandise sold to Americans. Stolen within or smuggled in, to them the profits ended.

JUST ANOTHER DAY IN THE LIFE OF PRISONERS

At the end of the day, Santos couldn't help but notice a peddler along Zamboanga Road. *"Anting-anting, agimat, talisman, juju . . .* lucky charm." All meant the same in different dialects. He was definitely selling merchandise that was not peddled regularly. Knowing Donono was dying to have something of such a kind, Santos went to buy one for him.

"This the kind you want, I want you to have this?" Santos told Donono.

"No, thank you. I already have one," the young man responded while proudly displaying his gift from Abu.

"Where did you get it?"

"I can't tell you. Abu said for it to be effective, I should not tell anyone he gave it to me."

"What's it supposed to do?"

"I can't say that either, but I won't be needing your help to . . . you know," Donono said, smiling smugly. He emphasized what he meant by pumping his hips forward a couple of times.

The amulet was wrapped with a black string. It was tiny, and its obscurity from being heavily worn gave him the creeps. None of its kind was being sold.

"Let me see it." Santos was skeptical of the strange thing Donono had hanging on his chest.

"I should not take it off, otherwise it will not be effective," Donono replied, remembering the instructions of the man who personally knotted it around his neck. Donono couldn't understand why the thought kept coming back in his mind like someone was whispering it into his ear every second.

"Well, here is another one," said Santos.

The pioneers of Dapecol, Abu and Little Don, became close friends when the white animal worshipper started attending to the Moro's foot injury. The wound would heal and be relieved of pain, but then the swelling would come back again. The swelling became worse lately that it went up to his knees. Abu could not walk on the muster ground for many days already. He had to be carried out.

November 6, 1942, a Filipino soldier died on his sickbed. In fact, there were two deaths in a single day. From a distance, leaving the gate was a familiar sight of four men carrying a bamboo-made stretcher with another lifeless body. It was heading to the burial grounds.

Clearly visible from the long lines of cornfield, details were coming back in double files—local soldiers in front, Cabarles, Santos, and Donono in the file of about one hundred walking on a narrow path leading to the gate of the POW barracks. They were used to seeing such a view, except that it was Sergeant Guido Agustin escorting, indicating that a close ally was on his way to the burial grounds. Behind were two more souls carrying a pike and shovel and another two with their bayonet-laden rifles. The appearance of images against the bright-red canopy of western sky added to the horrible sight. The view of dancing fire absent of the orange glow visible only to the eyes of delirium distorted the panorama in the distance, dissipating while the sun came down over red clouds. One American would say, "The camp is burning," only to be discredited by another saying, "No, it's not. It's what hell looks like from a distance and that's where we are heading back."

The long walk from the corn plantation was hard labor itself; thirst and hunger of the already severely emaciated prisoners of war contributed to the weakening perception of reality. But for many, as they silently walked the path, their eyes were concentrating on the ground toward the pair of bare feet ahead of him. Lost in thought or maybe hoping they would be led in a different direction, they looked ahead only to find that the person in front had suddenly stopped.

The soldiers led the file, which was halted to give way for the approaching comrades in sorrowful details. It was a double funeral, one of which was the man who would always read passages from the Bible to the dying. His final day came to being carried in the poorest of a funeral repugnant of a human being much more of a soldier. The second one, without asking, could be clearly identified by a few. The deceased was Abu Benghalid, as revealed by his foot that was partially exposed. The unsolicited words from Guido also confirmed it. The following motions of every individual appeared like it was rehearsed. Santos and Cabarles stepped to the side and stood in salute to clear the way. This was followed by the rest of the POWs. Donono took off his marine uniform and laid it over his Muslim friend. He then took over one of the pallbearers. Santos seized the front from Sergeant Agustin who grabbed the shovel from another soldier. Santos stayed behind where he was then was joined by Cabarles after he put his sombrero on the face of the "cleric" on his way to the final destination.

With shovel and pike on their shoulders, the men stood up as straight as they could and started walking at the order of the impatient Japanese guards. They kept walking, passing individual soldiers from details who saluted gallantly in honor of the dead soldiers. No one had the courage to talk. Silence took over from the plain sadness that they felt after the loss of another two soldiers under hopeless conditions. However, the honor and respect that the dead deserved was bestowed with pride. Afterward, one American with tears in his eyes would say, "It was the most honorable rite of a dead befitting a soldier I had ever seen."

No more man of faith to read passages from an old *Reader's Digest*. He just died, the most common cause of death in the camp. Agustin could not help it, and out of his tongue he started reciting a poem, the "Huling Paalam" ("The Last Farewell") by Dr. Jose Rizal, the poem he specifically made Cabarles practice reading three months ago. Poetic as the words rhymed, he began.

As he thought, it was nothing special, but it became a tradition. In the absence of someone to rant in mourning to honor his buddy, someone had to do it. After two sentences, he was lost for verses, and Cab of all the people fed him the next word and a few more until Agustin was totally adrift. That left Cab alone to continue loud and clear with the accent and tradition of a true *makata* (poet). So much time and effort had Cab devoted on his assigned lessons that he had been able to memorize the entire poem without actually learning how to read each word. The credit went to the heavy tutoring of the pallbearers including the bodies they carried. And of course, Agustin, the one that had the shovel alongside who handed him the book, a compilation of works of known Filipino poets. Agustin was greatly impressed as Cab went on confidently.

About a half-kilometer walk to where they needed to go, just recently, Maeda had allowed for the deceased to be claimed by their relatives as they wished. They knew the Muslim man had families among the refugees. It was not long until two women walked toward them and then a third one followed by numerous children, and then the whole community started to show themselves from makeshift houses that lined along the Zamboanga Avenue on the North side entering Dapecol.

The information about the identity of the dead soldiers traveled a lot faster than they walked. An elderly man in the lead told them to leave the bodies in their care and promised that the non-Muslim one would be given proper burial as well. A moment of mournful silence was concluded with the salute of soldiers. The crowd whispered that it was Captain Dominador Cabarles himself they were seeing, Lt. Rodrigo Santos, and the famous little man as well who had been characterized in many tales of bravery and kindness. The old man expressed that he was indebted to the soldiers for taking care of his son to the end. In the loss of his firstborn came the birth of them all, promised all assistance in their benefit that someday they may be needed.

"I am as proud as my son to meet you all," he stated. The short condoling conversation was cut short by the guards, and they quietly walked away back to the barracks.

Donono could not wait. "Who is the wife of Abu among all those women?"

"All of them," Damal answered almost surely as he was the one doing the talking with the women the entire time because he understood the dialect very well.

The death of Abu was felt. He was an intelligent man, funny. The tasks he assumed for the betterment of POWs was inspiring. No more a homeroom teacher, he was a great adviser of basically all the things they did and planned ahead. Though Abu was alleged to exhibit more loyalty to the Christians from Manila than to his Muslim brothers, he had redeemed himself long ago by the selfless deeds he extended to his people in the manner of a Catholic while maintaining his own belief. He suggested that his allegiance to the officers did not characterize religion. In a letter to his father, he revealed that none actually observed their faith in exception of the little man who worshipped a white pigeon that nested on their barracks.

> I am a soldier. I am proud as you will be if you knew them better, just pure heart and loyalty with each other they had extended to me at difficult times when I was denied by our own. They will die for each other. I decided to die with them as a soldier. I can only preserve my honor with honorable men who do not acknowledge honor and glory. To die in their arms, I will leave this world in peace as an honorable man in the tradition of our clan. ABU BENGHALID

In true essence, religion was rarely mentioned in their camaraderie. The survival instinct of one man may embrace another's faith in time of despondency, in the silent hope that there was more hope to hold on to. A rationalization considered by Santos, being in the land of Muslims, he had nothing to lose but considered the Muslim faith. Faith just comes randomly in a time of hopelessness. Abu was left by himself to do his thing during times of worship. No one bothered him. In his last days, Donono or Cabarles would assist him in getting up from bed for that reason. In another case, Santos would forbid anyone to catch and eat the white pigeon for Donono's sake; it had disappeared long ago, coincided at the time when Donono was sick.

The loss of Abu also terminated the source of many of their products. Important contacts outside the base in the person of

Abu's wives and relatives had considerably affected the coming of important supplies. No more to concern about the camp of equal importance, the Benghalids were assumed to return to their home province in Lanao where Abu would be buried. Returned to the fold was Sergeant Rufino Dominguez, who would attempt to deal with the Fifty-Seventh Scouts to avail of their skills. He had established his own outfit, and his dealings recently doubled. He needed partners to bring in the products. His offer was turned down outright. The short supplies caused the black market pricing inside Dapecol to increase. Santos could not easily forget Rufino's wrongdoings. Simply, he could not be trusted.

Abu Benghalid was among the first POW to attempt to escape from Dapecol, he was made a living example of the consequences by the Japanese after executing participants. His life was spared to serve as a constant reminder to others. Shot or bayoneted in the foot, his courage remained until his death. At one time, he ran amok for unknown reasons. He would challenge anyone who crossed his path, even absent of a functional left foot, looking for a slight reason to get even with all those who regularly degraded his already impaired dignity, which explained why nobody bothered about him the first time Cabarles saw him walking in pain.

Instituting his camaraderie with Cabarles, he eventually calmed down, keeping himself busy with an important duty he was given. He was instated as sergeant in the Fifty-Seventh Scout Unit to be the brain of Donono when it was found that they could understand each other. The promotion were made "official" by the captain upon recommendation of Santos. Proud to become a real soldier from being a security guard, Abu took his duties very seriously. He would be at the muster every morning, earlier than the rest, wearing a stolen US Army uniform. His attitude became calmer as he was ordered to do so by "Captain Cabarles" himself. Being a sergeant, his initial assignment would be to promote discipline in the Filipino ranks. That was the time when his injury seemed to be healing with heavy doses of medicine and regular cleaning. Sad to say however, it never healed. In the end, as the Japanese commandant was changing tactics to diplomacy, Abu was one of severely ill prisoners given the liberty to walk out of the camp to his relatives, which he refused. Because of his inept condition behest of uselessness to the Japanese's work for food policy, he categorically insisted that he belonged to the lines of POWs as he was a soldier. Profoundly, he said that he would die as what he had signed for—a soldier. "Just give them my body," he said repeatedly. "If at that time you are still here."

In the mind of Lt. Rodrigo Santos, the promotion was only to prevent Abu from alienating himself from the others, from disappearing only to be found under the barracks alone, and most of all to regain his self-confidence, summing them all up in the true sense of intention, to gain his full loyalty. Abu's acquaintances with them started about the same time he and Donono were reunited with Cabarles. The arrival of Cab had also changed Rod's own behavior, extending his leadership toward the others. He still remembered all discriminations Donono had to overcome from the POWs simply because of his size and looks. However, Abu's situation was different. He was extremely despised and humiliated resulting from an unsuccessful escape attempt. The resulting impact to the morale of the Filipino soldiers was devastating.

Abu was a smart man, proven effective in the execution of their covert activities. He would walk the morning muster despite his excruciating injury. He was also critical of the establishment of a communications network with the guerillas and bandits alike who would provide a steady supply of dried beef or buffalo meat. As he showed renewed conviction of his existence as POW by "officially" becoming a soldier with stripes, he had regained his self-respect eventually. In addition, his comical antics and personal adventures that he shared was somewhat untiring and could make anyone laugh, forgetting their situation even if only for a short time. A dedicated soldier they made out of Benghalid. From him they learned the geography of Mindanao and many more that they should know about if they were thinking of escaping. And it was the thought of it that bothered them equally at the passing of Abu Benghalid. Luis Malvo wrote on the wall, "Abu Benghalid lives." For self-redemption justified the special honor they gave to the man, a friend and truly a hero. Abu Benghalid, staff sergeant, Fifty-Seventh Scout Unit, Sixty-First Division. USAFFE. Deceased. November 6, 1942. To the general population, he was just another dead soldier.

CHAPTER 10

IN FULLFILLMENT OF PROMISES

Forsaken promises, I vowed in faith. In hell, I made another. Sworn in blood to the souls departing. Mine shall stay.

THE POLITE GUESTS

In November 1942, the guerilla campaign in most part of Mindanao had declined. There were no serious infractions of peace other than thievery. The harvest season had begun producing plenty, but never enough.

In Davao City, some businesses had long opened back to normal as it may seem. Vendors slowly flourished with common merchandise, exotic fruits, dried fish, and vegetables tending to whatever was left in the population. Private and public employees had retained their jobs toward normalcy. The Davaoenos had somewhat embraced a life amid the presence of the Japanese military and the governance of a puppet administration headed by collaborating Filipinos with their Japanese counterpart. Davao City was also the sanctuary of the largest concentration of Japanese military in Mindanao, the Kempeitai, and the worst, Filipino peacekeepers who carried Japanese-issued identifications. Many of them wore armbands indicating that they took an oath of allegiance to the big red dot. At sundown, only the brave, collaborators, and Japanese patrol could be seen confidently frolicking the business district. Civilians were all in a hurry to go home or find refuge at least for a night, beating the last minutes they were allowed on the streets. However, there were a few establishments that didn't get bothered. One building was noticeable when its colorful lights switched on and served as a signal to others that soon it would be time for them to turn off their own lights. It was the Paradiso de Oro. The lavish display of different-colored lighting in front was tantamount to the elite nature of its business as compared to other thriving few. The establishment was open all day, but the real fun began in the night that coincided with the curfew hours enforced in the city. It also served the best cooking and delicacies, fit only for the wealthy *hacienderos*, politicians, and known individuals connected to the Japanese. An exclusive nightclub that served the best entertainment of its kind in the whole city even before the invasion. Under the new management, it was business as usual.

On a busy intersection, a reputable man in his midforties befitted a suit only the wealthy could afford was lighting up a cigar. He proceeded cautiously, probing the surroundings through the farthest his eyes could reach. A block away to his destination, a peculiar feeling he couldn't understand was jumbled in his thoughts. Afraid or embarrassed, turning back was not an option.

The timing was specific. At five thirty, he would be entering the door of Paradiso. The guards had let him right in as expected at a quick glance of his appearance in the dissipating light of day. Presumably they recognized the first customer of the night.

"*Buenos tardes* (Good afternoon), Doctor," greeted respectfully the man in black pants and white long-sleeved shirt that clearly indicated a turncoat just like him in appearance.

The white armband over white punctuated by the dreaded red dot was scary enough while smiling with sarcastic enthusiasm. The doctor may have been seen in the company of the Japanese but never in a night spot, much more at wartime considering the establishment was run by the Japanese. He was wearing the same band anyway, which made the employees of the place comfortable to welcome him inside with incredible politeness and hospitality.

"Good afternoon likewise. I want to taste your famous cuisine for supper, you know . . .," the doctor replied, trying to justify his presence in such a place with his good reputation that was now not too good anymore in the eyes of the few people who may have recognized him going in.

He was Dr. Angelo Penafrancia. Though he knew of the existence and the kind of services the place offered at night, he didn't have that much experience in a place like it. He was a little nervous as he stepped in. An attractive young woman welcomed him. Equally polite as everyone else and so beautiful at quick glance, she was dressed in a tight colorful dress down below her knees, which revealed the shape of her soft body that was intentionally rubbing to his. It was a delightful feeling to get seated in such manner. The man began to love the place immediately.

"Can I offer you a drink, sir?" she asked. The sweet voice added so much excitement to her scent. It justified the other warnings he was given by her own daughter. "My name is Rosie, I can be with you temporarily."

"A glass of water for now, please," he requested as his thirst deterred the clarity of his speech caused by the long walk and apprehensions that were relieved outright.

Paradiso was definitely better inside. Beautiful in its entirety, everything was just captivating, a very calm atmosphere made engrossing by soft music that filled the room in the ambiance of colored lightbulbs. But something else had his interest already. He was charmed by the young woman instantaneously that his eyes watched her every motion at leisure.

"I came here for a good supper. What would you recommend for me, Rosie?" he asked, regaining his thoughts to the true nature of his visit to the place. His asking was to engage the lady for an entrusting conversation. On the other hand, Rosie didn't have a plan to leave him alone just yet. She was entertaining a very polite man whose kind seldom visited the place. Usually arrogant politicians, collaborators, and the Japanese officers themselves were regular guests of the place, all those who could spend a ton of money for exclusive entertainment that the place was known for. She knew her job very well, and for a seemingly very wealthy customer at the tip of her tongue, he could get whatever he wanted for it was her job. She even sat closer to the man as she sipped the drink she made for herself. Alluring as she was, naturally stunning, the doctor couldn't help but yield to her charm while watching her talk, calculating her every word. Every which way he turned his mind, Rosie occupied most of it. He had forgotten why he was sent to that place.

"Please don't look at me like that. In a few more minutes, there shall be many to look at who can entertain you for the rest of the evening," Rosie uttered.

"I am already overwhelmed by your presence by my side. If it's not too much, I wish you could stay with me for a while," the man replied.

"I am flattered, sir. I will. Would you care for food now? We offer the best cooking here."

"Sure, Rosie, what would you like?" He thought he could get away with just a glass of water and leave. It wasn't going to happen. Truly he had to be very careful, but personal interest was taking place instead. Rosie was very accommodating. She alluringly erased all the fear that was nesting in his chest. It was still pounding, but he knew it was for a different reason.

The night had just begun. On Mondays, the concubines did not expect a lot of guests. Regular entertainers were still busy with their personal rituals, taking their time somewhere inside the building. He may have found Rosie enjoyable to be with, but he just couldn't be trusting that easily. Likewise, the reservations must have been the same. Rosie could also be a spy. Clearly, he was.

"Are there many Japanese who come here?" The answer was known, but he asked anyway to indulge the young lady in a conversation she knew best, a topic she could relate easily. Acting imprudent should allow the girl to overcome her discomfort toward him who displayed the enemy flag on his upper arm.

"Yes, they run the place . . . They own us here," Rosie stated. There was a loathing in her tone.

"Don't you like them?"

"You are seem too nice of a person, what would you do to me if I said no?"

"Nothing, I'm sorry if I offended you."

"Obviously, you'll like talking to me better if I said yes. Right?" Rosie asked as she took a quick glance to his armband then back again to look directly at his eyes.

"Would you be more comfortable without it?" He was measuring her.

She would have, but she didn't reply. Penafrancia took advantage of the moment, pretentiously waiting for a genuine answer while revalidating his impression. She was smarter than he thought she was. "Oh boy, she's beautiful." He almost it aired out of his mouth. Once and for all, he must know her true color as time was running out. He sensed weakness in her silence. The only way he knew best was to get her talking again. "You're so beautiful." This time, he made sure he was heard. "I think I'm falling in love again," he added.

"Yeah? I hear that all the time from men like you."

"I know, can you blame us?" he quickly responded.

"No, but in a few more minutes, I'm sure you'll say it again to someone else."

"What do you mean?"

Rosie smiled, waving to a couple of young girls who were just seated by a dim-lighted wall. With the many more vacant in the line of chairs, anyone could guess that more were coming. The music was louder than it was to signal that the place was in business as usual. Rosie politely excused herself to attend to other customers coming in. She walked away almost immediately then looked back after a few steps, smiling.

The doctor was left alone thinking about that smile of a woman gracefully attending to another man in exactly the same manner it was to him just moments ago. All he could do was relight his cigar. Well, there should be plenty of chance to be with her again. He almost forgot the reason why he was in Paradiso. He looked back to the wall where more seats were taken. One girl immediately took his attention, interrupted by the coming of food Rosie had chosen for him. He looked at her again; she was busy. She couldn't come back to him anytime soon while shooting the breeze out of two Kempeitai.

"Would it be possible to let one of those girls join me?" he asked the waiter.

"Sure, which one would you like, sir?"

It seemed so easy. The girl was on his table before he could give Rosie another glimpse. Very young and pretty, the place was true to its reputation. Only the best-looking girls could be found in Paradiso de Oro. As young as the girl was, she may be the one he was looking for.

"Her name is Lora. Enjoy your evening, sir."

"Thank you."

A different name, not even close to what he was told. "What is your full name, Lora?" he asked a personal question outright as soon as the girl was seated. He couldn't waste time being intimate to every one of them. He may be looking as a proud collaborator, but he was not; the other two in Rosie's courtesy must be real Japanese spies.

Even before the girl could answer his query, Rosie cut in, apologizing. The girl was already requested by another customer she couldn't disregard. A very important person, she tried to explain the situation. She didn't need to. Angelo wanted to get acquainted with Rosie rather than with anybody else. He let Lora go.

"I told you, you can fall in love here every minute," Rosie reiterated.

"Would you stay with me for a few minutes? If only a minute I should be allowed, so be it. But I want to spend that time with you if you let me."

"I'm starting to like you too . . .," she stated with gratitude. Normally, people that came in would not just give up a girl seated at their table. It was "first come, first serve" and Rosie knew it very well. Being seen in the club for the first time, this man was very polite, well conversant, and not demanding unlike the other two visitors who would turn berserk for any reason. "Who are you? You are not one of them."

"You'll know about me, but it won't take a minute," Penafrancia said.

Between sitting with him and welcoming the guests, Rosie made sure she spent more time with the man she barely knew, so much to say she was easily drawn to his charm even before she knew the man. She found herself initiating the story of her life.

She was originally from Tagbilaran, Bohol, an employee at a shipping and travel agency next door when Davao was invaded by Japanese. "Here now is where I am, and the rest of us work for the comfort of people who come here." Noticeably becoming uncomfortable, she playfully broke the round traces of condensation on the table with her finger. She wasn't happy of what she had become.

"Why don't you go back to Bohol, with your family?"

"You don't understand, we are here against our will. We are prisoners."

"Where do you stay?"

"Right here. There are rooms upstairs where we sleep during the day."

"Together with them?" he asked, referring to the back wall that was starting to fill up with nicely dressed young ladies. Equally appealing, another one stood out as being the youngest at first look.

No, the other one looks better. Wait, I would like the other one on my table later, he said only in his mind this time, but remained calm in disbelief that the most beautiful girls in Mindanao were assembled in a cage for the pleasure of the Japanese and collaborators. What would it be if he met one of them first before Rosie? He may have mourned the death of his wife for so long or had taken his profession so seriously to forget that Davao was the home of the most beautiful women in the islands. All the chances he had before the Japanese occupation were lost in their coming. As it appeared, all of them selected like fruit at its best right from the tree were all gathered in one place for the Japanese and their allies to see and touch.

"Yes." The sadness that had fully shrouded her face and revealed more of her formerly erotic beauty was now altered with emotion, and the eyes full of self-pity. "Would you take one of them to your table? I cannot be sitting with you." She may have just realized that more guests were coming in.

"I only came here for food, I would prefer spending more time with you, but I understand. Would you let me do that without making you jealous later?" It was a playful statement said to retain her precedence over other guests that kept on coming.

"Sure, help yourself." Rosie started to walk away again, leaving him with a smile from perfectly shaped lips.

The man with the good heart unknowingly followed the young woman with his eyes and concentrated on her as she turned her back. Very graceful, curve to perfection as her dress was tightly fitted from the shoulders down below her knees, he let her mingle with the rest of the people that were starting to build up. His imagination played; she was getting prettier everytime he looked at her. He knew he could not stay long; he needed to attend to priority with constrained time to follow through his mission.

"Holy Mother, forgive us sinners," he uttered to himself realizing what he had been thinking. He turned his attention to the rest of the girls. Of course, he was interested with the youngest-looking one to talk with on his table. There was another; she matched the description of the girl he was looking for.

It didn't take too long; the girl he asked for appeared with no hesitation when notified and started walking to his direction. She was assisted by another lady. He could not help it, but he started to fall in love again as the girls came closer, not to the young entertainer, but to another lady who took her out from the rest of the girls. The dim lights stirred with different-colored light bulbs that slowly rotated around the ballroom back and forth. Rosie was right; he was falling in love every minute with every woman he saw.

"Dr. Penafrancia! I'm sorry I didn't notice you," the woman said. She obviously recognized him from previous associations.

Of all places, the doctor did not expect to see Rhodora in Paradiso de Oro. She should have been in a faraway place and safe. At the very least, Rhodora should not be working for the Japanese managing their concubines, assisting young Filipina women directly to the guests of the establishment who had only one intention at any given night. Though the chance meeting was short, it could have been longer if she had chosen to stay with him, but she didn't. He was left alone with the young girl now seated close to him after a brief greeting with each other. As much as he wanted to reacquaint with Rhodora, he wanted to talk to the young girl too.

"How are you, Myraflor?" the doctor greeted the girl with a name already stuck in his mind while stunned by another who bolted away. If he was wrong, then she could definitely provide the information about Myraflor Marfil, the person he was looking for. But as advised, he should remain discreet: *Who you talked with might not be who they are anymore.* They could be collaborators indeed.

"My name is not Myraflor, sir," the girl said.

"Oh, I'm sorry, you just remind me of someone," he responded to the young girl who had no clue at all she was called by that name on purpose. She could be the one or maybe not. It didn't matter. He had already established contacts, and one of them clearly had mutual interests in him. The other woman he met again by chance, Rhodora, was best friends with his daughter and surely Rina herself could find a way to establish communication with her. The night was getting very interesting in sad ways; he couldn't even imagine how Rhodora ended up in Paradiso.

"So you're a doctor . . . Dr. Angelo Penafrancia," Rosie stated, taking another minute to sit back with the man.

"He also knows Myra," the girl cut in, sipping on her glass of fruit juice, before he could reply.

"Hmm, so smooth! You know our stars here already," Rosie replied, her words full of cynicism. She was a little disappointed. So it seemed, Angelo was just like any other rich collaborator that frequented Paradiso on a privileged status. However, the impression that lay on her mind about the man she just met was of admiration. He behaved like a real gentleman. Most guests of the club would make every penny worth of their bills with all kinds of rudeness. Curious, she might have still believed he was a natural gentleman, but evidently he liked real young girls. She excused herself again and let the man be entertained the way he wanted. After all, that was what he came for obviously.

Another soft music filled the air. Before she could step back, Rosie could not refuse an invitation to dance with another guest, a civilian speaking in Japanese. Angelo brought his attention back to the teenage girl—about sixteen years old, he would guess. He may be lucky if she was the girl who had been the subject of a clandestine search for so many days. "So how old are you, Myra, what's your last name?" he asked decisively with the likelihood that his quest would end in Paradiso. He knew young girls could easily be manipulated.

"I'm sorry, sir. I am not Myra. My name is Leonor. I'm eighteen," she responded.

Angelo knew that what she said about her age was a lie, but he rode on. He just wanted to make sure she and Myra were not the same person. He didn't know who Myra was or how she looked.

"If you're not her, where is she?" he questioned, looking directly at her eyes, expecting a definite answer. He made sure he sounded with authority and couldn't be lied to. Hearing the right last name, he was able to confirm that the girl he was looking for was somewhere in that building if she was not the one he was talking with. Maybe Leonor was a cousin or Myra herself.

The girl stayed in silence. She didn't know who she was really talking with and was starting to get nervous. A guest with unexplained interest toward Myra. The man had obviously never seen Myra yet.

"All right, don't get shaken, Miss Myraflor Marfil. You have no reason to be afraid of me." He smiled out of great pity at the pretty girl. "I am Angelo Penafrancia, there are other people who cares about you—very kind people."

"How do you know my real name?" the girl asked.

"I am not the right person to tell you. Like I said, there are very kind people who are concerned about you. Don't be afraid of us. I'm very glad to finally meet you."

"Thank you, but I'm confused. Who are they?"

"You will know them at the right time," Angelo responded. "I shall be going now, I'm very happy to have finally found you, Myra."

"I don't know you, sir, but I'm glad to know there are people concerned about me."

"Yes, there are. You will hear about them, but please be cautious to let other people know."

"Should I tell Mama Rosie that you're leaving?" the girl teasingly diverted the conversation to him, noticing how he always took a moment to look at Rosie or find Rhodora who had just disappeared.

"Don't worry about it, I'm sure we will see each other again. Would you mind arranging for my check please? I cannot stay longer."

"Sure."

On the way home to beat the curfew, the doctor realized he had benefited from such an experience other than the fact that the quest for Myra had ended. There was no explaining to do for her daughter in going back to Paradiso de Oro. She was actually the one who persuaded him to visit the place. "You're the only one with the reputation to be admitted in that place," Rina said to him when he refused in the beginning. For sure he wouldn't mind going back. The whole time he didn't feel any danger from the Japanese other than those he saw patrolling the streets.

Except for the unusual behavior of Rhodora toward him who was his daughter's friend and who frequented his home before the war, the night experience was successful to the very reason he visited Paradiso. Was Rhodora really working for the Japanese and contributing to the oppression and indignation of young Filipina women? So many thoughts he had come to wonder that they needed enlightenment. The only person who could give him answers was his own daughter, Rina. It turned out that Rina would not know anything about the fate of a friend. The situation needed to be verified before further pursuit of their objective. Rhodora could present the greatest obstacle or she could be a great asset. Angelo had every good reason to question allegiance of Rhodora based on how he had known her before the war.

THE DECEMBER AFFAIR

In the Philippines, the birth of Christ is observed normally when October comes. The hardship and struggles in previous months may hinder, but not when it is December already. The Christmas spirit cannot be ignored in the minds of every Filipino, especially the children who have started to make and display *parols* (paper stars) on their homes. It is a representation of a shining star made of a bamboo frame and usually wrapped in bright and colorful assortments of paper. There were parols that adorned the line of houses along Zamboanga Avenue; this time, they were not colorful. Shanties were poorly built considering their existence among the bigger structure that was now the residence of Japanese officers surrounding the POW camp.

The spirit of holiday season was everywhere; even the Japanese had become slack to the security, and it seemed that strict implementation against smuggling food and necessities inside the camp were tolerated. A prisoner made his own *parol* out of hay, the earliest one inside the camp to hang in Barracks 6. "Christmas is in the air!" exclaimed one soldier.

Troubled minds may be relieved by the good news, but more concerns arose as it seemed. The recent development and intelligence Cabarles had received added to the blessings. Myraflor Marfil was located in an exclusive club that also housed Japanese concubines. The place was heavily guarded. They could proceed to plan the next step.

As early as August 1942, a plan to escape from Dapecol was set in motion by a small group of Filipinos. Many things were learned from Abu Benghalid who planned the first ever attempt to escape Dapecol, many mistakes that should not happen again. A group of Muslims that were blending in with the civilians were at constant alert at a moment's notice for another bold and aggressive plan, a do-or-die strategy that was expected to be a bloodbath. The lead planner, Abu Benghalid, was crippled and reneged himself on a plan that was not much of difference from the disastrous first attempt. Aside from the timing that was uncooperative given by the monsoon season and the coming of more POWs in the camp, there were so many other issues to consider. The plan must establish an escape route to as far as the main island of Luzon, and that would be close to impossible. Abu had ensured however that if they were successful, they must head to Lanao. He vowed he would arrange their transport at least out of Mindanao. But Abu had met his demise, and his Muslim brothers were branded as bandits and being chased by the Japanese to extinction. The escape route through Lanao was considered no longer viable until it could be reestablished with extreme reliability of the participants.

To that effect, Lt. Rodrigo Santos had reassumed the task of studying the feasibility of other options. Born and raised in the Central Visayas province of Iloilo, he had great experience in seafaring, but the difficulty lay entirely on being able to disappear from the prison camp undetected and allowing as much time as possible to get as far as they could before being discovered. Getting out of Mindanao was simply unthinkable just yet. Meanwhile, as many options were being deliberated, the search for the fate of the daughter of Jesus and Katherina Marfil, dubbed as "MM," was taking in effect for a long while. Cab had insisted it must be done at all costs before they could leave Davao. The main part of the meeting on November 6 with Rina Penafrancia in the cornfield discussed the progress of such undertaking. Before the end of the month, a message confirmed that MM has been found. They were sad to learn that she was also a prisoner and was not allowed to walk out by herself. No one could just walk away from the Japanese.

NO MORE TEARS TO SHED

Monday, December 7, was another stint in Paradiso for Dr. Angelo Penafrancia, but this time, he had company. A colleague in the profession was how he introduced him to a chosen few who would like to know. One of the few was Rosie, who was elated that Dr. Angelo Penafrancia was back as he said he would be. Rhodora sat with them too after greetings and introductions. Myra came to the table as prearranged. The other doctor quickly stood up politely and greeted the young lady as she introduced herself.

"You're the daughter of Jesus and Katherina Marfil?" the man asked, almost whispering.

"Yes, sir. How do you know my parents?" Myra asked, suddenly becoming excited. She was longing for this moment. Finally, someone had contact and knowledge of her parents since she was turned over to Paradiso.

"We met but only for a short time. Sad to tell you, they are no longer with us," he responded in a mellow voice as how it was rehearsed.

"What do you mean, sir?" She understood what the man said, but she wanted to hear exactly what he wanted to say. What exactly happened to her parents?

"They died . . . together. They died with one thing on their mind at the last breath—your safety. Your most loving parents," Cab replied.

So innocent to suffer an unimaginable fate, yet her courage remained. In this far end of the world, it could happen to a young girl; thinking the worst where he came from was too much for what he could bear in his mind.

The young girl silently wiped off her tears. The hope about her parents surviving had just vanished. She hoped that a day would come when her parents would rescue her, telling her she was going home. Now, there was no more to hope for. The death of her parents was too hard to believe and accept, but she remained calm, not saying a word.

"I have sisters your age too. It has been a long time since I've seen them. I share your feelings," the fake doctor said. "You are as brave as your parents as I had known them in only the very short period we were allowed."

"Where are your sisters?" Myra asked, as expected.

"I don't know, it's been a long time. I can only pray for them, for my parents, for all of them," he replied. "All I always think about is us who are still surviving to see the end of our hardship while we are still breathing with our remaining loved ones. Do you have relatives you know that might have survived?"

"Our family came from the Bicol region. I would like to think they are safe. They are too far away," Myra hopelessly stated.

"How do you like this place? Would you rather stay here or be with your relatives in Bicol?"

"We are prisoners here. Perhaps you know already how the Japanese had been treating us. If only I can get out of here and go back to Bicol. They beat anyone who tries to leave."

"I made a promise to your father and your mother on their last breath. I'll take you to safety, but it won't be easy. Will you trust me? There are many people helping us."

"Yes, sir, I do."

He turned to the real doctor who was listening. They needed to leave while he needed to remain to the point. Here was a young girl who had no more to hope for, and he was adding more to her grief if he talked more. "You will be hearing from us from now on. But I must remain unknown even to you, to anybody."

"Yes, sir, I understand."

"We should be going now. Keep your courage and be strong."

Before anyone could say anything, a loud clapping of the hands were heard twice. "Soldiers."

Obviously, a high-ranking officer was coming in for an unscheduled visit. The concubines knew the drill. They filed up by the door to welcome very important guests. Myra and Rosie had bolted out to join the line.

On Monday, it was unusual, but it was too late to leave the place. They had to bow like everybody else until the soldiers were seated while being assisted by the girls they had grabbed. The doctors froze on their seats, one purposely hiding his face down, but with his eyes rolling. He recognized the Japs immediately; they were from Dapecol. The officer was Maeda himself and Lieutenant Hiromi, the commandant of the chicken coop. They were seated and acted like real gentlemen, absent of cruelties somewhat that was so different when they were inside the base. It was surprising to see that they could be gentle in treating a human being. There was no yelling and sudden bursts of anger that could lead to the beating of an individual. On a separate table, Hiromi and two more soldiers began to enjoy the company of Myra and three other girls, Rosie with Maeda. Not a moment wasted, a few of the girls danced, which took the attention away from the two doctors enjoying their food across the ballroom. One girl stood out among the rest. She was tall and very elegant who sat with the major by herself after greetings and they talked. Usually, a concubine would sit directly on the lap of a Japanese to avoid troubles; she seemed aloof and sad. Clearly it was not their first encounter as it may look, but the young lady was not well disposed like the rest of the girls; she was not happy at all. Rosie left them to make sure that the rest of the soldiers were happy. She knew exactly what was going when Maeda was in Paradiso.

Who would be happy to a man that had imprisoned her parents? They talked decisively, but it was Maeda who did most of the talking. After two more rounds of drinks till another music ends, the Japanese were screaming happily except for the Dapecol commandant; he was clearly not pleased. His anger, however, was held back. It was clearly noticeable he was upset and then later he calmed down. They were leaving.

The doctors were glued to their seats after being informed that there were bunches of soldiers outside the building also; however, they knew the drill. They stood up and bowed again as the dreaded Japanese were heading their way out. Lieutenant Hiromi stopped for a while and eyed them, but Rosie interfered, showing the best of what she does in Japanese language. Surely anyone could get distracted at the feel of her breasts and soft body while the merciless officer was assisted on the way out.

Rhodora was left alone on the table, fists closed tightly as if she wanted to scream to let out what was in her thoughts, what she had become in the time of war, and what she would be from tomorrow. She wanted to kill herself, the only other choice to evade what was settled between her and the major.

Rosie came and sat beside her; without saying anything, she knew what was bothering the woman. She had always confided of the situation in Paradiso, much more of her personal affairs and decisions. Strong will and defiance had no place anymore to resolve the situation. The only way was to kill herself and end it all. She really was about to kill herself. With the loss of her one true love, here came a very persistent Japanese who resorted to any which way in his authority to win her. Though Maeda had tried to be a gentleman from the beginning, he realized that so much time had been wasted when he could actually get what he wanted at any time. The last of his patience had ended after feeling that he was being played with by the lady, the object of his desires even before the war. But defeat was hard to accept when the beautiful Filipina had turned him down for another Japanese, to his underling. He vowed then that Rhodora would be his no matter what and by any means. The time had come when he ran out of patience to take her by decent means.

"He let my parents free already," Rhoda revealed while breathing profusely, calming herself, clearing her mind.

"What are you thinking now?" Rosie asked, sharing the worries.

"I don't know." She really didn't know but requested a bottle of whiskey and a knife; she wanted to do it herself, but she was still shaking. She felt as if a big rock was pinning her down on the seat.

Rosie came back with a bottle of whiskey—no knife.

Not too far from another table, the doctors watched them alternately drink the liquor straight from the bottle. It was time to go. They approached the two distressed young ladies. "It seems you two are busy. Pardon our interruption, but we shall be going now," the real doctor said. He actually just wanted to have a little time with Rosie.

Rhoda knew the business of the men in Paradiso; she was foretold and subsequently became a new addition to the Filipino network of covert activities in the fold of Rina Penafrancia. As their friendship was impeded by the outcome of the war, it wasn't hard to regain trust with each other. The doctors were not after the kind of entertainment they did; she knew them, at least one of them well enough. She had known the other one from Rina to meet him that night as arranged with her and Rina directing the show. In the next hours, all four of them had found mutual trust with each other. The spirit of the bottle was partly responsible, enhanced with the great desperation of a woman looking for a shoulder to cry on. Rhoda knew Dr. Penafrancia well enough to trust him with all her heart. She revealed her situation, mitigating the right thing to do. Though several were laid out, the ultimate choice was left to her, and that was embracing the option that seemed the only way she can get away of the burden, which is only by killing herself. The other choice was to take advantage of the situation, an ultimate sacrifice. After all, the major was trying to be a gentleman, promising all she wanted to make her happy, otherwise all in his power as a Japanese officer to make her life miserable to begin with his family very soon. Rhodora could not allow that to happen.

Maeda was apparently still madly in love with her or he just could not accept defeat.

Before the war, Maeda and another Japanese named Minoru Wada were prominent visitors in Davao. Both had shown serious interest to win her heart, posing as legitimate businessmen with genuine interests to invest in Davao like other Japanese who had prospered in Mindanao provinces. The hideous reality of their purpose was never known until he reappeared in the city as an officer of the Japanese occupying forces. They were in fact preinvasion spies of the Japanese Imperial Army. In the events that followed showing himself a decorated soldier while renewing his supposedly serious interest to Rhodora-san, he was turned down again over Wada. Takeo made it clear to Rhodora that he would never accept defeat at all costs. Minoru Wada didn't come back for her; instead it was Maeda with an army who was not contented to win the war over Mindanao. He had to pursue his desire over Rhodora-san.

Thirteen days before Christmas, back in Barracks 6 at about the same time, some prisoners could not sleep. Santos and Donono kept on whispering with each other, so did a man who didn't belong there at all. He was made to sleep with the POWs for a night to complete the head counts of details going back from another day of labor in the cornfield. Though they expected Cabarles would be coming back the next day, the worry was unimaginable. Cabarles could be dead already. If caught by the Japanese, it could only mean either of the consequences of swift death or punishment by starvation to death including the participants. Shot to death most likely. The camp was quiet; sleeping it off until morning was all they could do.

In Paradiso, the fake doctor was Dominador Cabarles. He looked good in his borrowed suit, but evidently he was not in his true profession because of his complexion that was severely exposed to harsh conditions. Inside the Paradiso ballroom, nothing of that concern mattered, with only the yellow teeth to worry about that contrasted with the dim red, blue, and orange lighting. He really looked handsome in his all-white suit and hat. However, the doctors couldn't help but take advantage of the night, developing friendships made swiftly by the spirit of liquor. Cab found himself dancing with Rhodora in a slow tune of foreign music in Mindanao. For the first in his lifetime and the second time to smell the scent of a beautiful and alluring woman to the class of his Inez, his heart palpitated just like the first time. And to whatever his senses dictated amid the amount of Hennessy he had taken, he was enjoying. Somewhat he liked the feeling of a warm beautiful woman hugging him tight. He had forgotten the pain in his feet, caused by the undersized pair of shoes he was wearing.

"I heard a lot about you, Captain," Rhoda whispered, her face closer to the man as both of her hands were around his waist too.

"Good ones?" He felt distress every time someone called him Captain; he knew that trouble usually followed. She smelled so damn good, so carefree. It brought trouble upon him, and he couldn't run away. He stayed cool and submitted to what the moment was allowing to happen. A moment he had forgotten that he was a prisoner of war.

"Yes, I can feel the kindness in your heart, your courage . . ." The woman had tightened up her arms as she moved closer, looked at him straight into his eyes before she submissively laid her head on her shoulder.

"We all have strength. It's easy to end our life when there's no more reason to live. I keep on praying that the reasons I live are also alive. My faith never discourages me to keep on hoping," he replied while he made her feel the embrace of his arms. Let her feel she was not alone in times of desperation.

"I know why you're here. Very brave and kind," she whispered.

"It is not an act of kindness. I have my own reason and compelled to do what my conscience dictates."

"When the time comes, would you take me too?" Rhodora whispered.

"Sure, I will."

"I honestly feel the comfort in your arms. I wanted to think that tomorrow never comes."

"I share your fear. Every day I have learned to live with it. Among us, the worst fear is not seeing tomorrow, but the most terrifying sight is to watch your fellowmen denied of seeing the next daylight and that someday it will be me."

"Will I see you in the camp?"

"I believe it can be arranged if we choose not to see the next daylight afterward."

"Then let's take advantage of this night. Please don't go yet."

"Yeah, can we take a seat now?" Cab said. In so short of the time that he knew Rhoda, essentially a prisoner of war that was made worse by her past. She really had a very difficult decision to make.

"I really wish I can have you to watch me for the rest of the night," Rhoda whispered in desperation as she really was looking for someone who could give her comfort until morning. "Would you? Please," she whispered very sweetly in his ears.

"I wish I could, but I put a lot of people in danger by coming here." The curse of the captain was back in his mind. No one talked until the music ended.

The objective was just to meet Myra, and it had concluded many hours ago. He let himself loose from her embrace but kept hold of her hand as she led her back to the seat. Rosie and Angelo were stunned—two people who were totally strangers yet found comfort with each other. Something had truly transpired in so short of a time. Two people who just met somewhat connected themselves intimately. Rhoda was known to be aloof to men and could not be manipulated that easily by any man. But who was seducing who? There was a short moment of silence, the two of them waiting for the other to talk first.

"My invitation still stands, and it is just for this night you know because there might be no other night," she alluringly said, the temptress of the night she was.

Cab had not that much of experience in dealing with a tease, an incredibly alluring tease. Inez was all that his imagination revolved about a woman. He started sweating; it wasn't his choice to make a decision. He looked at the doctor for help; they had to leave.

"I'm afraid we have to stay anyway, curfew time had started," the doctor said to him. "It must end in the morning before sunrise."

Six more hours to go, he was really worried. What were they going to do for the rest of the night? Another bottle of whiskey came up. There were no more other guests in the dance hall that had been emptied hours ago but for a pair of man and a woman who met for the first time. The other pair remained seated. There were so many stories to talk about. Cabarles started one in between shots of whiskey, devising a plan on how to get out of Paradiso safe and back to Dapecol on time. The night got deeper. He said that if avoiding curfew would mean an experience of a lifetime with Rhodora, then he would not mind seeing tomorrow; he was getting drunk. Those were all that Cab would remember that night. All that would keep intact in his mind was a kiss of goodbye with each other when they left. "Take care of yourself. Don't forget your promise." These were words from Rhodora; he was trying to remember what they had done together for the rest of the curfew hours. And he made a promise again of something he could not recall what he had promised for. His head was spinning.

On the twelfth day before Christmas, a file of prisoners on the way back to camp from the cornfield was starting to assemble. Cabarles joined them while preliminary head count was in progress. One in the line bolted out immediately and disappeared in the cornstalks like nothing happened. Santos, Donono, and Guido were all quiet like they didn't see anything. They just held eye contact with one another while approaching the main gate of Dapecol by way of Zamboanga Avenue. At least they were out of the agonizing hours since the morning break when he was expected to come back. The switch might have been spotted by the guards, which worried them all. Lagging the line, they must rendezvous with the guards on the road for another head count in their group. For reasons unknown just yet, they were ordered to stay away from the road. A car was coming through followed by truckloads of Japanese troops, noticeably a high-ranking officer, Maeda himself, that would require all of them to salute. Through the window of a vehicle, they could see the passenger, a beautiful woman seated at the back together with the camp commander.

That woman was the one Cab was with all night till morning. Their eyes locked in like a passing wind breeze that made him catch a deep breath in an emotion he could not explain. Rhodora chose the devil's lair, an unimaginable sacrifice. His body shook, his fists clenching. Suddenly, he felt drained of strength while the woman loathed by others could only settle for the sight of prisoners as much as she could be allowed in the distance. She would never know how much pity he felt. Pity it was for a woman of reverent courage and selflessness that stunned his comprehension. Coldness enveloped his senses, yet so thirsty; the scent of that woman was still fresh over his skin. Her cry for help was without tears but a smile to grant the last of her dignity to a man like him. He could only remember a kiss that somehow forged the memory worth another lifetime to tell.

Helplessly, Cabarles fell down to his knees. He was praying it may seem, but the truth was he wanted to scream her name and set her free. He felt that he had no more strength; he needed incredible strength and courage, but there was no more he could spare, only pity. Another helpless soul that disappeared in bright daylight to the same destination. Would he met her again? To abet, to give him comfort in that despicable moment, all of his brothers expressed their endless abomination of the same woman he revered. So much beauty, they said, only to be burned in hell for embracing the devil himself.

What could he say to discredit their impression? A woman cuddled by the commandant was the same woman who had sacrificed enough yet was offering what was left of herself into the lair of hell for the noblest of intentions. The information was privileged, even to the most trusted one. Let them curse about her for now because the effect of revealing the truth over the ears of many was not a fact he could substantiate on his own grasp. He was not enough of a man to stand by her side.

"Do you have water to drink, please?" He was so thirsty, exhausted after running and crawling about ten kilometers at daylight. Soak and wet of sweat, breathing hard. As much as he wanted to begin, he couldn't tell where he had been to just yet. Donono handed him a water container.

"My feet are hurting very much," he replied. A whistle blew from nearby, signaling for all details to begin walking back to the camp. No time to rest yet, but he was relieved they made it to the compound without incident.

All went well; however, his silence could only take as much time to keep from eager individuals who participated in that run—Santos, Agustin, and Donono. As it was freedom for him, it was death for them. They deserved to know. All facts in his recollection was primarily about Myra Marfil and the miles he ran to reach back in time. Yes, he met Myraflor Marfil. He had talked to her. She was also a prisoner in a facility that collected concubines after the Japaneses kidnapped and abused her. The girl was in the safekeeping of Japanese for the pleasure of their kind.

"A lavish place maintained and secured by soldiers and collaborators," he said. Despite a lengthy story detailing what transpired that night, he remained quiet about one that involved the woman they saw that same afternoon.

SWIFT ADAPTATIONS

There were many reasons to be thankful on the eleventh day. It may be just an ordinary day to fulfill back in detail but not for each one who had knowledge of someone who literally got out of Dapecol and came back. The fear they held in their chests a day before was relieved though it was said in repetition that Cabarles must have taken the opportunity and to hell it was; everyone else could take the consequences. Cabarles had created another burden for himself in the process unknown to his trusted allies. Some details of his escapade remained untold.

Ten days before the birth of Jesus and every night since then, four people that were usually comfortable sleeping at night couldn't do it anymore. One became restless. It was almost impossible for people who used the warmth of each body to sleep at night when one kept moving. Sleepless nights of so much dreaming was inspired by new thoughts, complicating a previously singular mind. He had seen Rhodora again, and as much as he wanted to forget the soft touch of her alluring body, it was her nakedness that filled his thoughts instead.

Many days after the meeting with the fairy in the cornfield, it was insisted that the promise to Jesus was a word to be uphold. Cab constantly said that he would rather stay in Dapecol if he disregarded the sole intent of a man and wife who died together in his arms. "It's bad luck" was the only explanation to describe his apprehension. He didn't discount that caressing a white rooster may cause them good luck as Donono claimed, but he also suggested it was the spirit of the local couple that kept them alive. He should uphold his promise as a priority before they decided the next step.

"The first of kindness we received in Davao and caused their life, it is just too hard to forget. I always believe a chance given to keep my own life is for us to succeed in our plan," he said.

Dono was taking the blame as Cab insinuated he should also take responsibility and Santos the most to blame according to the man absent of literacy but offers many eccentric belief.

"Why me?" Donono cried, refusing to take the blame.

"If it wasn't for the worms in your stomach, we could have just moved forward without bothering those couple. You had to insist going back for food. They would have been still alive today and we never would've met them," Cab stated. "You too." He motioned to Santos.

"What's my part in all that?" Santos interfered to clear his name. So many times the event was talked about but none in the way that caused the involvement of a girl they didn't know about.

"You cleared the order. You were there too. We literally ransacked the house leaving nothing," Cab replied.

"You were there too. As I remember, you ate as much as we did," Santos protested.

"Yes, all three of us ate as much as we did. So you must share my burden about the girl," Cab wrapped up his argument.

Santos was left thinking, somewhat Cabarles was right. He spoke in Donono's view of having full stomach at the time sustain their strength. "If we didn't come to that house, I believe we would've still engaged in a battle against the Japanese," he contested.

"Yes, I believe so either. We must all be dead too no doubt. Something in that succession of events that changed our luck." Cab sighed, waiting to be enlightened.

"Must be the white rooster, do you believe it was?" Santos suggested.

"You mean the chicken? I believe it was a lucky rooster too, we didn't have time to cook it." They both looked at Donono, thinking the same. "Somehow it may be true." Cab agreed.

"Yeah, I lean in believing it too. We should have better luck if we ate it. Look how he recuperated rapidly when we fed him the white pigeon," Santos complied.

"What pigeon?" Donono quickly cut in.

"Nothing."

So much with talk of chickens, so many white of them at the chicken coop. Donono must be worshipping anything white that breathes, but he loved that white pigeon, which explained his unusual admiration toward the Americans. But since he had witnessed they could be blown into pieces too, that belief changed considerably a long time ago. He had much more to learn that he could steal belongings from them. The number of white creatures subject to his adoration reduced to four-legged animals and birds that could fly, he firmly believed that the pigeon played a great role in his recovery before it disappeared; it was absolutely true.

Christmas was coming on the ninth. Donono was explained that it was the day when Jesus was born. Jesus died with his wife as far as he knew. He was so confused why everyone seemed to celebrate the coming of the day he was born. Cabarles was extremely worried about the daughter of Jesus. He had met Jesus himself. It took him another day to comprehend a little. He had to be told of the whole story of the Nativity.

On December 19 and 20, Red Cross supply was distributed. It was rumored that it came many weeks ago held in a well-guarded warehouse. The timing it was received by the prisoners supplemented the leniency of the Japanese toward the general population, noticeably a laidback approach in enforcing security in the camp. Among the noticeable changes was that the Americans were allowed the use of the baseball grounds. The ball was a coconut in the beginning and a bamboo pole as bat. There was nothing else they could enjoy much but playing the national pastime in the most crude way at the watch of the Japanese ready to fire a machine gun from the guard tower. However, the fun was great that even the guards laughed when the coconut was shattered by an impatient batter who liked to show off his skill in the game.

Six more days and counting, abaca twines were rolled tight and sewn inside an old sock that was dropped and rolled in the diamond from over the fence. It was light but would do the job for the many hours they were allowed to play. The strongest prisoner would need to be really healthy to hit the ball over the bases. The idea it was made was plain and simple. The next day, it was modified to be better and the real fun began. Fun that even the Japanese with better understanding of the ball game would enjoy watching over their bayonets; other prisoners would stay on the sidelines while waiting for their turn. On the other side of the fence were Filipino civilians, employees, and relatives of convicts watching. Kids mostly, they were denied of the use of the playground since the Japanese took over Dapecol. Adults too. One stood out, one who would have other interests other than watching skinny prisoners scattered on the field. He had important information to relay through the fence.

In four more days before Christmas eve, the Japanese joined the fun. They could hit the ball way farther than the thinly built Americans. "It's the ball they are hitting, works for me," one GI commented, looking dark skinned for the many days of detail in the rice paddies.

There was a man over the fence, and the message he carried must reach the person of interest. He was after eight nervous people who were not coming out of the barracks anymore waiting for Christmas Eve. The very urgent and critical message must be relayed at all costs.

Two days before Christmas Eve, the message needed to be delivered, but it was so secret that it required the source himself to speak personally with the person concerned. As part of the many graces the month of December was bringing in, local health figures were allowed to conduct a health mission in the prison compound. An event that was the first of its kind to happen should not be missed. The announcement came by loudspeaker two hours after the details were dispatched. Dr. Angelo led the group of kindhearted medical professionals to station at the mess hall for a day. The motivation to wait long lines was to see the fairy in person once and for all. Donono was excited. He was not sick nor qualified to be undernourished; it was just the way he looked. In front of the line was the fairy of the cornfield, undisguised. Cabarles and Donono were missing details for so many days for it appeared that Cab was sick.

"It's not possible on Christmas eve. They are not ready," Angelo muttered. "Miss X is very afraid of the implications it will create the next day," he added with engaging thoughts. "She suggested postponing until we can think of a viable plan."

"I agree with her, what do you suggest?" Cab replied.

"Wait until we can think of another way for a less bloodbath."

"I don't know if there's such a way, but you're right. I'm also having a bad feeling about it."

"We hope to see you again on Christmas Day," the man said.

"I'll be here, I rely on you."

There was more to say, but it was cut short by soldiers coming in. Whatever a Japanese officer was screaming about, instinct dictated to follow what everyone did—stand in attention. Salute, bow, and listen. VIPs were coming. He could only pretend to be listening. Rhodora was among the people who came. "God, she's so beautiful in her dress," he murmured.

There was an announcement from the camp commander himself who wanted to take credit for the humanitarian deed going on. He made sure he did. Everyone's attention was taken. Cab was the most among those caught by surprise, but only by the woman with the major, the unforgettable moments they shared together. In the dim light of midnight happy hours, in the morning sun, or past noontime, she was a woman blessed of such beauty that would make the son of the devil tone down his atrocities. She was a lady who stepped in hell. In hell, there was nothing abundant to play with but fire, and it seemed that she was enjoying it. He felt her eyes locked on him, a little change in her lips, which was noticeably conveying a word every time he glanced at her. Cabarles was sweating cold to extinguish the blaze he felt caused by Rhodora's actions toward him in the most dangerous situation. A suicidal woman full of hatred, now she could smile. Swift adaptation, shiny colorful dress in Japanese design matched with folding fan on hand slowly waving back and forth gracefully on herself and to the Major as he kept on talking. Only Cab could feel what she was going through; he could not look at her any longer.

God, please bless this woman. He did not even notice that the speech was over until an apparent jubilation started. There must be something good from whatever he said that excited the prisoners.

"Attend the Christmas Eve program, they will be there," Angelo uttered in conclusion.

WHAT TO DO IN PRISON WHILE STILL ALIVE

The commandant promised increased food ration starting immediately. He had so much to brag about that it had already begun before he did the announcement. Agustin, who should understand what the speech was all about, would translate and explain later in exultation. On the other hand, he had a reason to be upset to learn that the many days of planning and preparation would not push through. Malvo, Rabong, and Damal were equally dissatisfied; more to learn that someone else was calling the shot that Cabarles must adhere. Not the Moros anymore.

The program would showcase Filipino civilians, Japanese as well, and of course the Americans in the ball park. A day before, they learned that the celebration could only accommodate the POW officers for security reasons. Starting that day, every soldier wished and prayed for heavy rain on Christmas. For some, deep breathing was sufficient as they had prayed too much already in preparation for Christmas Eve. The plot of simultaneous escape from two prisons that would take place on the same evening was recalled in the nick of time. A few hours after lunch break at the coffee field, dark clouds were forming in the horizon and it didn't take too long for it to start raining. It started as just a drizzle that wet the dusty ground, but it got heavier that it was almost like a shower. Absent of soap and shampoo, they scrubbed their faces and bodies from thickening dead skin. The program venue was decided to be at the prison chapel because of bad weather.

Around 1900 hours, two good-looking Filipino soldiers braved the rain, freshly shaved and displaying a new haircut. The program had already started when they arrived, but the timing was planned so that everybody should be focused on the performances. Since it was standing room only, two civilians must give their space watching whatever a fat Japanese was doing on the stage. Cab and Rod would say later that when every Japanese laughed as they guessed it might be funny, they laughed too and clapped their hands also as everybody did when it was over. There was a standing ovation for the presenter who said his name was Namura. For Cab, it was still fresh in his memory. Seeing Namura again was a reminder of the many slaps in the face and smacks on the head that he received from the same man, also from the rest of those sitting in the front rows. He was the same man who also pulled his hair many times as he screamed a language he didn't understand while spit was coming out of the mouth. Not having seen him for a long time, he thought that Namura was dead already. His performance was very intriguing; he just could not believe the same guy could also be entertaining as much as tormenting. Literally, Namura was like a crazy monkey deprived of a mate in rendering a dance number that gained a standing ovation.

The next number was of another Japanese carrying a samurai onstage, followed by two young girls in heavy makeup behind to occupy the altar. Someone whispered from behind, "MM is the one in red, Rosie in yellow." He quickly let Santos know. In his comprehension of what the speechless show was about from a seemingly happy beginning of unusual music, Cab's attention was taken by the one in yellow and red and a little green. As much as Cabarles wanted to take her out of his mind, the only reason he attended the program was to see her again.

In the traditional Japanese dress of a woman, Myra was grotesque looking from where they stood, just like the other in yellow. Obviously the makeup was concealing her real face. Adorned with glitters while holding a folding fan that she opened and closed to the melody of gongs and drums, she exquisitely motioned her body to an expressive action to the tune of instruments that kept on spooking his imagination. At last, it was a moment that every POW could appreciate and applaud to when the man with the samurai apparently stabbed himself at the end of their show.

"Why can't every one of them just do it for real?" referring to all the Japanese around, he uttered to Rod Santos as they were both disappointed when the man stood up alive again, bowing to the audience.

The following performances were mainly the Americans who would sing and dance to the sounds of their own. The show was basically taken over by the Joes and Johnny-Be-Goods who for the meantime had noticeably forgotten that they were POWs. Meanwhile, behind, a civilian kept on whispering to Cab's ears, aware that majority of the attendees were Japanese soldiers, armed and treacherous. Not much to say, but he had identified who among the civilians were the trusted and the dreaded collaborators. Santos had someone to loath about again, the gorgeous Filipina sitting along with Maeda and his officers on the first row, every time he saw her in the company of the commandant. She was Rhodora X; she was an interpreter, and the major's mistress.

Before the whole show was over, Cabarles had a chance to have eye contact with Rina. She shook her head slightly; he understood what she implied. This time, she was well dressed and displaying red lips too. Both Cab and Santos agreed that she could really be mistaken as a fairy, a very pretty one. She was surrounded by children. Pops Abrina, Mr. Arcenas, and Ruben Pablo were among people they knew.

Still drizzling when they reentered the barracks, Donono and Guido were still awake and waiting. Their patience was rewarded, happy to know that they had their own gift boxes in addition to so much food that they brought with them courtesy of the Filipino civilians. It was shared in the barracks of about two hundred men. Some of them were also given fresh shirts, linen, soap bars, and anything Donono and Guido handed to them. Cab had retained a few gift boxes carefully wrapped and marked "from X."

The Christmas celebration continued, and even in the dark, men chorused on a holiday song, enjoying graces that rarely came. The men in other barracks were definitely having fun of their own.

Waking up in the morning was the most difficult. Santos confirmed discreetly that the entire plan was revoked. At the end of muster, no detail for the day was announced. A good meal waited for them instead as rumors spread. It was a nice day except that the ground was muddy. What a day to find themselves still in prison. A new plan was hatched for another day, and one day it would happen. Cabarles and Santos walked around talking. It was a holiday; what would have been the consequences when eight prisoners were missing on Christmas Day? They would have been far away by now if they went after the plan. Cabarles knew that Santos had a reason to be disappointed on the wasted opportunity and long planning though he didn't discount they would be hunted by now.

"The only way we can be successful is if we turn up dead when it happened." Santos sighed in resignation. "No one will be missed in the head count," he added.

Looking for matches to light up a cigarette, Cab didn't know much about arithmetic but Santos did very well. "Abu Benghalid lived and everybody knows he is dead. Well, he was dead, all right." Cab became ecstatic over the idea.

"Sir, lighter," a man standing outside the fence called their attention, among the crowd building up in anticipation of Americans to play baseball. Guards were in place.

They came closer, recognizing the man. It was him they called Romo, the same man he switched for a night to sleep in the camp. He was dressed nicely, fitted for a funeral. "Merry Christmas," Romo greeted while throwing in a Zippo lighter over the fence.

"Merry Christmas to you," the prisoners greeted as well.

Romo was excited to see them; in truth, he was made to scout any disturbances inside the POW camp that morning. Nothing was unusual; in fact, he was talking to the very people who should create such predicament.

"It's good to see you again," Santos responded.

"You can keep it, sir. Consider it a gift. I'm glad to see you too." Then he left.

"Very fascinating man."

"Indeed," Cab agreed.

Eventually, more people showed up on both sides of the fence. In the early hours of the day, the children started singing an awkward rendition of "The Star-Spangled Banner" to begin their own show, then Christmas carols ended by one last song in the local dialect. It was a little show that amused the prisoners for a little while. "USA, USA!" Cheering followed as the Japanese on foot showed up. A baseball match would begin any minute.

"Hey, Muryong! *Canta ka ng canta d'yan natigok 'yong tatay mo, pinauuwi ka ni Ima.* (Stop cheering, your father died, your mother wants you home.)" A kid who just came into the scene yelled.

Evacuees inundated the vicinity of Dapecol. Death among them didn't pick a day either. "If only they can walk inside the barracks before they die . . ." Santos sighed.

"What are you thinking?" Cab was desperate.

"How can we make eight dead bodies walk inside the barracks?"

"You know, I am having trouble in arithmetic. Let's do it two at a time, it may be possible."

The most bizzare idea to initiate a grandest plan. By the end of the day, Cabarles would learn better in arithmetic without the aid of his fingers and toes. Better yet, another plan to escape Dapecol was carefully taken into consideration. It was just that for Santos, the idea was unattainable—dead people could not walk out from the grave. For Cabarles, it was a good plan. For a desperate man, truly nothing was impossible. If meant to die, then they should die.

CHAPTER 11

RHODORA X

There is a woman despised by men, she is a venom they said. A devil she embraced in hell, in hell she will rot. She can smile, very graceful. A masquerade, beneath are sadness, courage. Tell me your heroes, she is one of mine. I don't know how she can still smile. . .

CHILDREN OF WAR

In a time of peace and prosperity, when every American would describe the Philippine Islands as a paradise and as a place to go to for tour of duty other than Hawaii, it really was, as writers and poets of local and foreign descent alike call it the Pearl of the Orient, a tropical group of islands clustered in the Pacific, which the United States had seized from Spain. Despite the escalating resistance of the Filipinos against the oppression of the Spanish, somewhat they welcomed the Americans in liberating the Philippine Islands from four hundred years of Spanish oppression. The Americans' true intentions, however, was to maintain check and balances of power with Communist China and take advantage of the almost paralyzed military might of Spain after a devastating loss in WWI. In so doing, the United States can also avail of the strategic military locations of the Philippines and establish domination in the Pacific. The American-Spanish War that took place in the Philippines was only fought in three years, from 1899 to 1902, but winning the war didn't end there. The Filipinos had awakened into just another oppressive foreign presence and started a revolution against the American. Though most of the ensuing battles were fought in the countryside, mostly in the Visayas and Mindanao areas, it sure created a hindering effect on the minds of the Americans about the bravery and courage of the Filipinos who would keep attacking despite the hail of bullets from their firearms. The effect of the revolutions was just the same on the results of every war written in history—death and to those who were left breathing, stripped of dignity and strength, they had nothing to choose but regroup and wait with their courage intact. In four decades of US authority over the Philippine Islands, guerilla warfare was introduced around the period when the .45 caliber handgun was invented. The most undermined war the United States fought was against the Filipinos that also left so many deaths unaccounted for in history. Most of those who lived were orphaned boys and girls whose minds could only grasp on their instinct to survive.

One of them would be a boy found wandering and begging for food in an American field camp in Mindanao. The boy who would wander inside the camp, naked but for an old shirt, became a constant sight on the American camps. Searching for scraps that could alleviate the hunger and thankful for graces that the soldiers could spare for him, the child had no name nor could understand foreign language. The only identifying characteristic credited to him was the unusually large thing hanging between his legs. He was dubbed as "the boy with the big penis" and later named Johnny Penis by generous Americans. At the conclusion of the Filipino revolution against another foreign incursion was only then did the boy learn to wear pants. His second name became permanent to him as he grew up to the care of an aging American officer who was happy in the company of Johnny till the end of his life. In a time of peace, as the Filipinos had tired up on the resistance against the Americans who had resorted to diplomacy on the general populations, the boy grew up, had friends of his own, and attended school bearing the same name. He became a handsome young man and found a good use for that big thing between his legs other than for the pleasure of his benefactor. In 1918, he bore a child of his own. For heaven's sake, it was a girl. She was baptized in a Catholic church with the name Rhodora Penis. The child grew up fed on a silver plate of wealth inherited by his father. Having genes inherited from his mother who was a half-bred Spaniard, she grew up amazingly beautiful, loved and guided by kind parents into Filipino customs and traditions.

So much to say that the girl grew up without worries. In the Philippines at that period, especially in Davao, Spanish was the tongue of choice for the wealthy. English was in its infancy, and no one cared about learning the language. So much to say that no one would care about her last name except for one who had knowledge of the male anatomy. When she began attending college in Manila, she realized the effect of her last name to her personality. There was nothing much she could do but just be happy to be called Rhodora X. Beautiful, intelligent, and rich, she finished a degree in business science, to return eventually to Davao, taking advantage of the booming travel and tourism industry. She established and operated her own business. Though her last name was not entirely an impediment to her business operations, it was an embarrassment vanity-wise in the elite society where she belonged. The nature of her business that could easily be mistaken to offer something else insinuated by her last name made her to retain the X. She was also Rhodora or Rhoda in plain acquaintances, and she would be known as Rhodora X to everybody while developing a very intimate liaison with a Japanese.

Since she appeared in Dapecol, she was loved and despised. To the commandant of Dapecol, she was Rhodora-san. For Cabarles, he was confused. He had love and pity for the woman who could dictate them both of what she wanted. It was Rhodora X who halted the plan escaping out of Dapecol on Christmas Eve.

One who would despise her was Lt. Rodrigo Santos. A "wasted beauty," as he would say every time he saw her in Dapecol. Confirming she was a Filipina and working for the Japanese presumably as a collaborator might be explainable, but clearly the mistress of an enemy officer was giving him a despicable viewpoint to her existence. He was not alone in loathing on her. In the group of eight he belonged to, Santos was among the six who cursed on Rhodora X; Donono never cared. One loved her, but his association with the mistress of the Dapecol commandant could not be divulged for how it transpired also caused him perplexity beyond what he could explain. So much was at stake, but he had yet to reveal as the impact would create a perilous effect while planning an escape.

Back two years ago before the Japanese invasion, a fresh graduate from the University of the Philippines in Manila, Rhodora was welcomed back in Davao by the proud parents. It didn't take too long for her to learn the import and export enterprise of the family. At the time when many foreign nationals were seemingly interested in business investments in Mindanao, mostly Japanese, she formed a travel and tourism office that equally succeeded providing services to tourists who wanted to see the whole Mindanao, places of interest that were as far as Zamboanga and the neighboring islands of Negros, Bohol, and the rest of the Visayan islands. Rhodora's parents were vocal to the constant abhorrence against Japanese investors who rapidly expanded their businesses at the expense of the local landowners. In short, her parents loathed the Japanese, but their resentment did not stop her from having a relationship with a young Japanese national, a handsome gentleman who simply fell in love with her, being caring with thoughtful gifts every time they saw each other, which somewhat developed into a mutual feeling.

With the time they spent together and seemingly sincere promises, the young lady made her choice over others including Maeda who was the most persistent. She disobeyed the father's advices and became involved emotionally with a Japanese named Minoru Wada. A few months before the war, she was devastated and heartbroken when the man sadly said goodbye for a reason he did not explain but promised he would see her again. Though the reasons for leaving her back to mainland Japan became explainable when the war broke out, the fulfillment of the promises she was given became a dim hope. As clear as she defied to submit herself for the pleasure of another Japanese exhausted of his patience over her constant refusal, it came a situation she had to choose.

When the war broke out, too many more sad things happened to Rhodora X—no more business to run, too many deaths to relatives and friends and more that she witnessed caused by the atrocities of the enemy. Her parents disappeared; later she would learn that they were among the prominent locals and nonmilitary Americans who would be interned in the special POW camp. She may be happy to know they were still alive, but the hatred the Japanese major had incurred in her mind was more than just Lt. Rodrigo Santos could imagine who hated them both. What she was doing on the lap of a Japanese officer?

A lady so graceful, innocent looking, a beauty that
makes his race proud. Beware she was thorny, no soul
to forgive, wide eyes to see blindly. Only a face angelic
as the fairy, how she sleeps at night.

A truly spellbinding beauty, Rhodora was the object of many
suitors in Paradiso. For that reason, she created dispute among
many men. With a Japanese officer who wanted her to be his own
exclusively, the competition was either dead or afraid. He was Major
Takeo Maeda. For a long time, he had been trying to impress Rhoda
with gifts and the offer of a job in Dapecol. The young lady kept
on refusing. Her former lover may be a Japanese also, but he was
completely different by looks compared to the arrogant major in all
angles. Rhoda could be seen accommodating the advances of the
officer but loathing after, even in her sleep. She had no other choice
but to use the situation to her advantage, for the good of them all in
the house of Japanese concubines.

WELCOME TO DAVAO

Paradiso de Oro was already what it was when the war broke out,
situated about five kilometers from the heart of the city and ten or
more toward Dapecol. The main door was closed during the day and
opens just before dark. An extension of pleasurable experience the
city offered during the day, they said that the real fun began when
someone switched the red lights on. The comforts it offered was
unlimited, from imported fine wine and whiskey to exciting and lively
nights of loud music that catered to those looking for entertainment
and pleasure. A block toward the city was a small building adjacent
to another one of decent size. Rhodora owned the property that was
now a Japanese detachment. Past them were lines of small businesses;
stores, hotels, and restaurants. The city was booming on its own as
a prime destination for tourist and businessmen from Manila, as far
as Britain and America, too many from Japan, China and Formosa.
"Welcome to Davao, Seeing Paradise Starts Here" was written in
bold lettering. An identical signboard was also displayed close to

Davao (Lasang) Port where she managed the main office with Rosalia "Rosie" Brown.

Though the enemy landed not exactly at Davao port, the occupying forces easily overpowered the loose group of defending civilians and a few law enforcement officers. The news of the Japanese invasion forces quickly advanced and took over the city. The decisive and choreographed incursion was somewhat already a success before the Davaoenos could eat their breakfast. The city capitol building was already under enemy control, and many civilians were made to stay on the lawn at the point of Japanese rifles and bayonets when the sun shone. Among them were the mother and father of Rhodora. In another area of the city, groups of women were thrown in Paradiso de Oro, convenient enough for the Japanese as many complained of the long walk. They were left guarded and unfed for as long as the survivors could remember. A few more days after the siege of Davao City, Dapecol was taken over from the correction officers basically unopposed. The defending American and Philippine army forces were easily toppled as majority of their troops retreated to the northern provinces of Mindanao in small scattered units with the mother base camp in Casisang in Malaybalay, Bukidnon. Rhodora and Rosie found themselves among others held up in the spacious ballroom of Paradiso.

In a sudden leap of fate, they found themselves among a group of equally scared women, hungry and ultimately losing hope due to starvation and atrocities of the guards. An initial negotiation to free the young and the elderly remained futile until the guards agreed to let the elderly go. Rhodora and Rosie, both fluent in Japanese, discovered they could use their charms to free more prisoners; on their irremediable part of the deal, they found themselves dancing erotically for the entertainment of Japanese soldiers. Paradiso de Oro was back on business again. In the so-called normality of the situation in Davao City under the new authority, they were left supervising the place housing captive Filipina women that were just too young and beautiful to be shot after abusing them, dancing and all catering to Japanese elites and wealthy collaborators as concubines. Beginning December 22, 1941, to the time Dr. Angelo Penafrancia visited Paradiso, Rhodora X was also a prisoner.

CHAPTER 12

THE ESCAPE

Places I had been, I don't know where. Pure kindness and courage of people thrives there. Tell me your heroes, I have many of them. I can tell you how great their hearts. I can describe their faces but only when sad and afraid because that's all I'd seen on every one of them.

IN THE BROKEN ROAD

December 27, 1943. Another day in Mactan rice field had concluded. Agustin and Little Don were quietly leading the line with their most trusted buddies. They were told that the escape plan would be reassessed with considerable changes on the manner it would be executed; it was still a go, only it would be a matter of when.

Along Zamboanga Avenue, a vehicle displaying the Japanese flag broke down. No convoy of military was behind it. The timing was so perfect, as the lady inside was quietly sitting alone on the backseat. Japanese guards commanded the prisoners to push the car after a short talk with the driver. Previous eye contact already established a need more than just a glimpse of each other.

"I just talked to Dr. Angelo, he is fine with it. Anytime you're ready," she said, almost whispering out of the partially opened window. "Good luck," Rhodora ended.

Two days after, on a Wednesday, two prisoners were found dead. There was no need to establish the cause of death. Many times a prisoner just died in the rice field. Exhaustion, heart attack, or gunshot, how they died did not matter. They went directly to the burial grounds if they died while on detail. This time, the snake was to blame because two strong prisoners were found dead for no apparent reason. The bodies were buried, subsequently creating fear among details that it was not only the guards to avoid. Snakes were commonly seen in the paddies. The last known death of an animal caretaker from the same cause was long ago and only hearsay; this time it was proven that poisonous snakes were really frolicking just about anywhere when the snakes hit again before the week ended. Two more prisoners died on the same spot.

Four more to die of snakebites, who among them should be the next two created serious deliberation. To make them die all at once was not possible logistically. With the message they received, only two bodies at most could be provided at any given time. Cabarles and Donono could not be together; they both needed a translator of the local dialect that Santos and Agustin possessed. However, the little man had proven his skills in the jungle; he said he should be partnered with Cabarles who would get lost instantaneously in the thick jungle and marshes. Santos, by all definition, was just the same; he was good in seafaring, but not in the jungle. Cabarles wanted to be the last. Santos insisted they go together or be the last. Donono did not present the ability of coordinating the plan as it progressed; he should go first no matter what but conceded only with either Cabarles or Santos. In the end, it was Donono and Santos together, provided that Cabarles and Agustin would follow the next day.

The opportunity was ascertained at the time it was coveted. Cabarles felt that the longer he was in prison, the sins building in his thought was surmounting. There was a woman that had caused him many moments to think about if he stayed. The other in his thoughts whom he really wanted to be with was so far away. Either one he chose was impossible to attain; it would mean death, slow death. He had seen hundreds of ways to die; none was a good sight if it wasn't Japanese. Slow death was something he would not allow himself to get into again for Japanese satisfaction. Such likelihood was imminent as he felt that Rhodora was becoming bolder; she wanted him to decamp one more time from Dapecol to a place they could be together again. He had to make up his mind before Rhodora X bore a child that didn't look Japanese. He could not imagine what would happen to him if he got caught having an affair with a woman also having an affair with the head honcho of Dapecol. Quick death he was visualizing for both of them. On the other hand, there was no guarantee he would find Inez exactly how he prayed about her though he never stopped hoping for it to come. He truly preferred the one where his heart belonged.

The conditions were cooperating; less guards were being assigned on duty with the details. The escape would be through the revitalized route to North Lanao. Four had gone, assumed to have been successful for they had heard nothing about them. Four more people would brave the odds with the help of a few individuals. Each knew very well what it would mean to all of them if they got caught. The math of disappearing eight prisoners from Dapecol without affecting the head count was proven to work. Two taken away two equals to zero; an added two again does not change the total sum of thousands. However, the major participants still bore the weight in mind as the date became closer for another two on January 15, a Friday. There was always a drawback; there was an intelligence report that raised suspicions that the escape was compromised.

"Americans are planning to escape, Tatang Abrina is working on it," Roberto dela Cruz whispered quickly to Rod Santos as they crossed paths in the rice field.

"Are they serious?"

"Seems like it."

"When?"

"I don't know yet. I will know for sure."

Even before the message was relayed to Cabarles, Lt. Rod Santos had already thought of the matters for important consideration. Only days to count, less than fingers. There was no other way to escape Dapecol but run from any point to the jungle. Americans must have thought over the consequences that should arise even if they were successful. Many had tried; they all got caught and were executed. The Japanese had maintained the strictest rule on escaping from camp. Shoot to kill, punish all conspirators to death, kill ten prisoners for one escapee. Any which one to happen was hard to imagine; they knew it from the experience of Abu Benghalid. But the most dreadful was starving the population as a general punishment with the certainty of atrocities that came randomly. To that effect, Santos felt their chances getting slim; they must go as soon as it deemed fit at any given day. He needed to discuss his concerns to Cabarles. For some reason, Cab was taking his time.

"We hear of escape from every one of them all the time, don't we?" Cabarles said, attempting to discredit the American determination.

"They are firm and decisive this time. Some brave marines from Cabanatuan, Pops Abrina is involved," the lieutenant replied.

"How many are they?

"Ten possibly."

"Do they know what they are thinking? They can escape, I wish they do, but it's just the same result either way," Cab commented. "The last American escapee was caught." They all know what happened to him.

"I'm sure they are determined. Pops said they can radio Allied submarines and the headquarters in Australia to send American forces to liberate Dapecol," the convict stated.

"What is your stance at this time?" Santos asked.

Cab remained in silence, confused of the words *headquarters* and *submarines*. He assumed Santos will consider the information to the highest regard; they would be liberated if the Americans were successful. If ten Americans escaped the camp, one hundred in total would be executed. The probability of getting picked up for execution was very high. They belonged to expendable USAFFE soldiers. Santos maintained they must go.

Cabarles relied on the intelligence of Santos. Santos should do whatever Cabarles decided. Two weeks had passed since Malvo and Rabong were "bitten by snake," six days gone since they buried Damal and Damueg. There was no noticeable disturbance on the base that could raise attention not to proceed. There was some details that raised concerns; whoever was dumping bodies in Mactan said it was difficult to find one close enough to the description of Donono. The decision for the time being did not change any of the plan getting out of Dapecol and as far as they could, and they would do just that. A little more time he was asking from Santos. On the other hand, they had to make sure the Americans had a good chance of the same objective.

"Shall we let the American come with us? Certainly we cannot let them go ahead of us." Agustin was seriously worried the GI would bolted out any given time.

"We cannot let them come with us. Most likely we would get stuck in some hills under heavy fire. At the very least, they will lead us to nowhere fighting for our life again," Santos replied, reflecting on the past.

"I agree with you there, sir," Cab responded. The point was taken loud and clear as the pressure was mounting.

Santos was in silence momentarily. "Don't worry, by tomorrow we will have the details of their plan and see how it looks." Santos sighed. He backed off from pressing Cabarles to disregard the GIs. He knew it wasn't the reason why Cabarles was hesitating. There was something else, Myra Marfil for one. Santos and Agustin knew it was Rina Penafrancia and his father helping them from outside the prison. They were informed that two women were coming with them to meet in a certain rendezvous. One was definitely Myra, the other unknown.

"You and Donono are going as planned." Cab sighed, realizing he must make a decision. "Do you think Abrina can be trusted?" He wanted fresh information from the detail supervisor.

"We have to consult Dela Cruz, I never trusted Abrina," Santos replied.

"Yeah, me too."

Tatang Abrina, as observed by the Filipinos, was a sucker, branded a leech working both ways. He showed loyalty to the Japanese by day and the same to the Americans before the sun went down. Both equally liked him; he always had stories for the amusement of the prisoners. His comical antics and fabricated information about the war outside Dapecol as far as Europe made him gain friendly reputation of himself for the Americans who would believe whatever he said. He was a walking entertainment; his broken English spoken in heavy Spanish accent was a reason enough to make a Joe laugh. His loyalty with the Japanese involved mainly in retaining his job, showing expertise in agriculture and manpower management. By what many said about him, he just could not be trusted. However, it had been proven that he could be reliable; one should only be aware that everything he said wasn't true.

Cabarles and Donono didn't like him at all because he spoke the native dialect even if he was told to speak in Tagalog. Sometimes he also spoke in English in front of them and other Filipinos, showing off his alleged linguistic ability. He even referred to Donono in the past as a lost uncircumcised kid wandering in Dapecol; he only stopped upon learning that Little Don was a combat-hardened soldier in the same unit with Captain Maish and Lt. Rodrigo Santos. He distanced himself from the Filipino POWs when rumor spread that he would be nailed on a cross if he was proven collaborating or spying, more so if he didn't change his attitude toward the Filipinos. He toned down upon learning that the rumor was true when a big cross made of logs was subsequently erected on the path to the chapel; it was called Abrina's cross. Since the great escape of domesticated buffaloes in September, he had redeemed himself substantially about his true color. Not to Santos yet who built the Abrina cross himself.

Said to be working with the American marines for a daring plot to escape from Dapecol, the timing was unreal because it coincided with the Fifty-Seventh Scouts that was already in motion. It was so kept a secret that only Roberto dela Cruz knew about it. Even the extent of participation by Rhodora X was never mentioned; she actually remained the subject of expletive comments of many soldiers including Santos. The only possible source of leak might be the Moros, but Abrina had absolutely no communications or knowledge they exist anymore among evacuees since the death of Benghalid and two more recently. If there were still a few that remained, Abrina was avoiding them. He was the source of the rumors that the Muslims were all killed by Japanese troops while he denied betraying them in the disastrous first ever attempt to escape Dapecol. There was a need to reevaluate the current situation as compelling doubt had arisen that it may have been blown. Cabarles arranged a meeting with his *kababayan*.

Tomorrow came. In the middle of a pepper field overlooking the chicken farm, they convened with Dela Cruz. Visibly, a construction was going on for a large extension at the end of the plantation along Zamboanga Avenue. It was very convenient for stealing eggs and chicken, lucky for those working on it. Berto arrived with a pocketful of fresh eggs at chowtime and joined the prisoners in an obscured spot from the guards. Short greetings were exchanged. Everyone knew what had to be discussed.

"I was asked to be their guide when the time comes," he responded to Cab after greetings.

"By whom?"

"Abrina. I figured we won't be here by then, so I accepted the job," Berto answered.

"Are they serious, or is Abrina just bragging to beat the tide?" Agustin asked, wanting to be reassured.

"Yes, they should be serious. I think Pops is serious too."

Deep breaths followed as eye contacts of a silent question between the soldiers.

"When?" Cab asked as he turned to Berto.

"There is no definite date yet, but sure I will know. The marines are still recruiting who wants to go with them," the convicted felon replied.

"We have reasons to believe our plan had leaked out and this may be an attempt to fish out and sabotage our plan." Cabarles expressed his worries.

"I haven't thought of that, but I am sure it isn't," Berto replied, reassuring there is no leak on his side. "What should we do?" He continued.

"We cannot postpone. Play it by ear for now until the last hours. There are others involved, and they rely on us." Cabarles made it sound he was really worried.

"Don't worry, sir, my loyalty is yours," he reiterated his allegiance to Cabarles.

"I know, you saved my life once. I'm still depending my life on you, our lives. Tomorrow shall be another day. Please send a message for me to the fairy. Tomorrow, two of us are going as scheduled," Cabarles confirmed.

"Who?"

"Lieutenant Santos and Sergeant Agustin."

Roberto dela Cruz had a life sentence; surely he always wanted to get out of prison. But the status quo changed almost entirely. He was a man of words and action, proven loyal without any doubt. That loyalty would be tested more beyond his own belief.

Back to camp the same day, Little Don and Santos were ready. There came another problem that caused great concern. Earlier, a known courier of the fairy had informed them that extraction of MM faces a big delay for reason not disclosed while confirming that a pair must go at all costs, coming with news that a tribesman had passed away. There was not much they could do; the order of who go first was already decided. Nothing changed in the manner it should be done; sure as hell they were ready. Santos would only go with the reassurance that Cab and Agustin follow as planned without deterrence of any kind. An intense moment of reckoning, one of them was worried about a girl. Another one who still believed that the successful American escape was more important than theirs had to justify his undermined rationalization in a settled argument about the matter: "If they (the Americans) had no regards at the consequences of their actions, then why should we." Santos conceded after learning it was the same group that was favored in the construction of the chicken coop extension by Abrina.

THE COBRAS STRIKE AGAIN

Another tomorrow, the camp was calmed and nothing out of ordinary happening. Normally, one being dead or more began the talk of the morning. None yet, however, a few knew that two should die sometime that day, a common occurrence among prisoners that should not raise any more attention than it was. The same morning, the marines were confirmed to be escaping. Reliable sources maintained that they were determined and motivated soldiers, bold and brave. There were no indications that they would back out when the time came, at least eight of them. February 22 was the chosen date. Santos and Donono should be long gone before that date. By noon break, every detail of the American plans were known to the Fifty-Seventh Scouts; there wasn't a plan at all but just to walk out of the camp and run.

In the morning of February 12, two more dead bodies were found in the rice paddies by the colonos. Subsequently, they were identified as Rodrigo Santos and Hombre Donono as the height and clothes they were wearing indicated they were. Unlike Americans, who displayed dog tags, they could not be mistaken as an American soldier even in civilian clothing dead or alive. Filipino soldiers may have been carrying a piece of paper for identification, but it could only last for a certain period of time. To identify their bodies was never important; no one cares except for a buddy who would be in grief upon their death. Bitten by snakes most likely and no one noticed. Who found them was Roberto dela Cruz. Having no known relatives among the evacuees, they went straight down to the burial grounds loaded in a bamboo sledge pulled by a buffalo. Guido Agustin had shown his seemingly sincere devastation to the loss of his friends as he tried real hard screaming their names along the way. Onlookers were Americans and Filipinos alike. For many, the annoying thief diminutive of a soldier was finally dead. Those who had known Santos was saddened. He was a good man. The Filipino community mourned the death of another two in their ranks, Cabarles showing greatest sorrow among all when he learned the sad news. "They should be in a better place already." He accepted the news quietly. His turn to die was what worried him. It could be for real.

Cab was sick and stayed in the barracks during the "death" of Santos and Donono. At worst, he was afflicted of an illness similar to those who would just die as it appears, a dengue fever among others that was giving him trouble for days. It wasn't all, there were other kinds of disease that can caused imminent death attributed to him. He also had rashes around his necks and arms, some on his face visible enough that most prisoners had to stay away from him. Even Sergeant Guido Agustin had discourage anyone who would come close to him. He had to wipe off some of the red dye because it was applied excessively. In the morning more than a week since Santos and Donono were buried and despite the numerous deadly diseases he visually had, Cab stepped forward for the Mactan details. By the gate, a man peddling bright mats and hand-sewn products was standing at his stall, Romo by his side; together they gave him a nod from a distance.

"You are not coming back alive in the camp, are you?" one American mockingly said to Cabarles.

"You got that right, my man." An answer barely came out from Guido Agustin.

"Yeah, it will be the greatest service being a soldier for you to just die," the other one said. He was serious.

"If he dies, you will be next," advised another one not to get too close to Cabarles.

I have no plan to die just yet. This time, he said it only in his mind. Maybe he was looking real bad.

"Tell your pal to burn your body when you die. Otherwise I'll do it," suggested the third one directed to Cabarles. A convenient advice, but it was already thought off.

"Don't worry, I'll do it myself." This time, Guido made sure he was heard.

Leading the line of seventy-two prisoners by a dozen in single file that morning, Cabarles had made sure he would be seen in a condition so sickly with an unknown affliction. Severe skin rashes were visible on his neck and half his face. He deliberately slowed down as prisoners of war started to keep walking past them. The impatient guards slowed down too until the next group had caught up with them. One of the rules in the rice paddies was whoever came first got the nearest spot in progression to the last who should walk the farthest to work off the remaining spot. Cabarles and Guido found themselves close to the edge of the field gathering rice stalks spread out for the sun to dry. It was exactly on the location where the cobras struck two days, ago killing two more prisoners. Even the Japanese would not dare to get too close in that area.

"I'm all set, Cab, but we have a problem. I'd only seen one body." The first step to get busy in the morning, Agustin expressed his qualms coming back from exploring the bushes and cattails that bounded the rice field and the jungle.

There should be another one placed in that vicinity the previous night, but they couldn't find it. They needed two.

"It's all right, we have to go. I'm ready," Cab said while taking off his long-sleeved shirts as the morning started to heat up. No more time to waste as they had to catch up with Santos and Donono who were supposed to be somewhere far in the jungle by now. It had been forty eight hours since they were gone ahead. Before morning break, smoke could be seen in Mactan. No one bothered because it was a common sight every day, apparently to scare snakes. The cadavers was courtesy of Dr. Angelo Penafrancia. "In times of war, there are only two things plenty everywhere—the dead and the dying." He remembered what he was told. Something went wrong; they found only one.

They had located a marked trail farther inside the bushes, and after saying a short prayer together, they went into the woods, the point of no return. They made sure that all those markers that were left for them on the path was taken out as they went. About a quarter of a kilometer, they were supposed to meet two civilian guides, but they saw no one.

Earlier that same morning in Davao City, Rhodora had apparently spent the night one more time in Paradiso as she was seen in a car speeding away from its vicinity at dawn. An hour of driving from the city along the provincial road to the north, there were two more passengers: two women who helped each other change clothes inside the car to white uniforms. A Japanese checkpoint was getting near the city limit going to North Davao. She had been through that checkpoint a few times with the commandant, and she was confident she could get through again without any problem. The situation was different; she hoped no one would recognize the nurses as the stars of Paradiso de Oro. If any of the Japanese manning the roadblock had been in the concubine house, to the very least, they would've seen Rosie and Myra.

Back in the jungle, Cabarles and Guido were quietly tracking the trail where people had gone through already; they couldn't find any. Both men were unsure if they were still on the right path. Bushes and vines were so thick they could not even see each other at four steps away.

"I think we are lost," said one of them.

"Yeah, I know. I just hope there's no real venomous snake here. Let us find our way back and start from there again," the other one replied in agreement with a suggestion.

"Yes, you go ahead, I'll follow you this time."

About one hundred feet walking back, they heard some noise coming just ahead. They hid themselves almost at the same time, and both jumped on the man, pinning him facedown on the ground. Obviously he was not an enemy as he spoke Tagalog in a familiar voice. Cab had identified him, immediately loosening his grip on the equally surprised convict. He was Dela Cruz; he led the way, telling the escapees to follow him. No more words were spoken; cautiously, they tried not to make any noise as they all knew the Japanese patrol may be nearby. In fact, every accidental clearing must be observed first before they went through; otherwise, they had to walk through the swamps. They also knew the enemy had resumed the daily foot patrol and could be anywhere. About an hour long of very slow advance to nowhere, Guido started to doubt the reliability of the man they were following.

"Do you still know where we are going?" the army sergeant whispered.

"Shh . . . Yeah, it's just that you two drifted too far away from the trail." The convict motioned to keep utterly quiet while pointing just down on a clearing about two hundred yards southeast. Japanese soldiers, some may be having siestas, taking a break on half-buried rocks where freshwater was flowing through it.

The Japanese had resumed the security patrol around the Dapecol area of responsibility. The commandant would not like anybody stealing grains or cows and carabaos alike. He had doubled the patrol on the south to west of Mactan where many trails had been created leading to the city areas. There they were in battalion, ready to swarm any moment agitated. They were encamped deeper in the woods to the city as explained by the less guards in Dapecol.

"Follow me, the Moros should not be too far from here." Dela Cruz sounded confident that he was on the right track.

Eventually, the trio joined two restless armed men patiently waiting for them, the same men seen standing at the gate of Dapecol as details dispersed in the morning. Disoriented escapees finally came, both speechless realizing they followed a track that was actually leading to a Japanese field camp. They all kept moving northeast deeper into the jungle.

Earlier, Roberto dela Cruz was watching from a distance waiting for cue to do his part. He had seen Cab and Agustin going into the woods in the opposite direction. His hunch was right; the two were lost to begin their escape from Dapecol. A convict godsend to Cab and Guido, he disappeared shortly to go back in the Mactan rice field. He had to finish his part, set a decaying cadaver on fire at the snake territory.

Another four excruciating hours of trekking the path barefooted on a jungle that every step they made seemed that they were going around in circles. The escapees conceded that it wasn't just a hearsay on how the colonos described the jungles around Dapecol. It was really close to impenetrable that anyone could easily get disoriented. The soldiers finally found a moment to express their gratitude to the guides; they would've been lost again if not for them. One of the guides was also the same person selling bright-colored mats and other handicrafts from Cotabato and Lanao provinces. He also provided Cabarles the red dye he rubbed on himself a few days ago. Bandit by night, merchant by day, in reality he belonged to a guerilla group based in Lanao. He said they didn't know how to take the dye out from human skin, but it should dissipate eventually. It was true, the sweat he exuded all day had cleared some of it out. As soon as they reached the rendezvous where Santos and Donono were waiting across a shallow river, Cab took a little time to scrub himself off that eliminated all of the dye from his skin. He had to look good again like a doctor. Later, he joined the group in a good meal prepared for them by locals living in the village. The worries they created to show two days' late than expected was relieved with happy greetings.

Two days' late on schedule, there was only one available body. Its advanced decomposition posed a discovery that could put the secrecy of the escape at risk. One more should be needed, and the total dissimilarity of the cadaver to Guido or Cabarles by its condition necessitated the burning of the body. Out of respect to its unknown identity, later they would know it was a fat Japanese unburied two days ago in Davao cemetery that took two abled bodies to bring it to Mactan.

There was another factor that posed an apparent impediment—the Americans. In three days, determined ones would break out in a daring plan expected to create retribution among prisoners at an unimaginable level. If they could not accommodate them, they needed head start as far as they could. The decision to maintain secrecy was made because of facts already discussed. One was that the Joes could be extremely stubborn at times, and Santos would not mind yielding to stupid ideas as long as it was from one of them. More issues were raised by the Moros; for specific reasons, they didn't like the Americans. By the long history of their existence on the land, they didn't like the Christians either. They had an unfinished business with both of them, but hatred for the Americans that started about forty years ago was still fresh in their minds and they intend not to forget about it just yet. Whatever they meant, it was pretentiously understood and taken without arguments. The Catholic soldiers from Luzon would not jeopardize a fragile relationship with new allies just because of difference in opinions and beliefs.

CONFUSED AND AFRAID

About twenty kilometers from the burning rice field that was set on fire, the escapees could see smoke on the sky miles away. Lt. Rodrigo Santos and Corporal Hombre Donono could not express their elation enough to see Cabarles and Agustin again.

On February 19, back in Dapecol, conflicting stories began, which resulted to an uncontrolled brush fire west of Mactan that revealed a body beyond recognition. Even before the details could come back to prison camp, rumors spread that Dominador Cabarles had died of his affliction even before the fire started. It was definitely him the Japanese found in the place where he was supposed to be. Whatever disease he was afflicted with, he died with it in a very painful way. One was not accounted for—Sergeant Guido Agustin. It would take another day to find another burned body in Mactan.

The escape from Dapecol was successful; somehow there were glitches caused by several factors that arose. The fire that was only intended for a certain spot spread in the vastness of forest surrounding Mactan. No harm was done to the rice field. It was just that if there were really venomous snakes where many prisoners "died" at, the fire had scared them away to basically any place. It could be anywhere.

Each one agreed that it wasn't easy to carry a cadaver in the middle of the night and place them where they needed to be. Besides, who was brave enough to do so? Even the escapees could not imagine there was really such a man who would actually do it. They also knew that it was not every day when people died among evacuees. Where the bodies were coming from, they didn't want to know.

The Moros were not notified that more escapees were coming. "There are two more, we have to wait for them before we can move out," Cab declared.

The people who actually made their escape happen amid all the risks presented given the conditions could be mentioned freely. Rina Penafrancia was not just a fairy, but she was also an angel. An angel of death partially, and all of them waited for the chance to meet the woman in a better situation. Myra should be one of two women in the party yet to come. They were not going any farther without her. Santos was excited imagining Rina to be the second one; he had expressed his admiration for the fairy, but it was revealed to him that she wasn't her. Cabarles had so much to worry about but was also excited. He spent the time dipping in the nearby river. He knew for sure it wasn't Rina, and the lieutenant deserved to know who would be the other.

"It's not Rina coming with us. Hold your heart, I'm not so sure either, but you also know her," he began.

"Who else is it?"

"Rhodora X. Maeda's translator."

"What!"

"Yes, she is."

"Now you're really getting me confused."

"I really don't know how to tell you that in Dapecol, there is another prisoner in the worst situation. Like you said, I don't know either how she sleeps at night," said Cabarles in deep emotion. He was having trouble grasp for words.

"I need enlightenment. As much as I wanted to believe you that she will show up here to come with us, I cannot imagine the implications it will create if she disappeared in Dapecol."

"Yeah, I know. For herself too, her parents are held hostage by Maeda for her."

It was all that Santos needed to hear to share in the compassion. "I'm sorry, I truly hated her so much. I thought Rina is the 'X.' How do you know Rhodora?"

"There were many other thing she did for our benefits since she walked into Dapecol."

"How do you know her?"

"I wasn't able to tell you all that happened that night when I met Myra Marfil. I want to believe it was a dream or one of my nightmares. Knowing Rhodora is the greatest honor and privilege or an ultimate burden, maybe something else because I think of her like how I think about Inez. Honestly, I don't know what to do if she comes with us."

"Are you serious?" Santos could not believe what he was hearing.

"What should I do? She had sent me a feeler confirming her decision to come with us. I'm thrilled looking forward to it."

"I'm starting to believe you're really cursed. I thought it was Rina that was causing your cold feet of getting out of prison. I'm sure she's loving you, otherwise she won't brave the cornfield just to see you. She's so caring and thoughtful."

"She's very pretty too, isn't she? I know you like her."

"Yeah right. What about Inez?"

"She's the only one in my heart, I'm keeping my promise to her no matter what."

"I don't know what to tell you. You're more complicated than your superstitions."

SMOKE IN THE SKY

The first to come was unexpected; he was Roberto dela Cruz. Though his part was accomplished very smoothly, no one had taken into consideration his personal agenda. Every prisoner's desire was to get out of prison, and he was one by all definitions.

Dela Cruz had built up reliability as a scout in the expanded guerilla spy network in Davao. By all categories, it was initiated and established. It began through his efforts to give aid to his *kababayan* in an adjacent prison only a stone's throw away. Cabarles's well-being was the subject of his concern that became personal since their first acquaintance inside the iron cell that softened his compassion. Without Cabarles, he was just another insignificant felon doing his time in prison. He may not have a plan to escape all the way to Bulacan, but the opportunity was very hard to pass. Also in his thoughts, escaping in the company of the Fifty-Seventh Scouts with Cabarles specially made him feel a better person, not as a fugitive but like a soldier to remain in the fold of great soldiers who trusted him as one of them. He was credited of all the functions he played on the planning and execution of the escape; he was damn sure to be welcome and join the journey farther away from prison. His *kababayan* would take him no doubt.

He had to go back. If they let him come with them, then no one would steer the Americans. He had another important mission to do, and it could not be discounted. He had to make sure that the Americans could find their way out of Davao, and that should be in two days if they did. Otherwise, they would all be lost in the jungles of Mindanao and become helpless prey for the Japanese.

"The Americans postponed to another date, maybe next week. I was informed this morning," he repeated to Cab and the rest of the group as he explained his intention to join the party.

It wasn't the case; he would be needed at any time of notice by the Americans, and that was a job he agreed with the planners. No one else had the experience and courage to do it. He spoke English well, knew the local dialect and geography of Mindanao, and was also trained on first aid. He knew how to work in and out of the prison compound and beyond as he himself had successfully escaped Dapecol already before the war. Too bad he got caught again while boarding a ship to Manila. Santos had explained to him the importance of the success of the escape of Americans from Dapecol, much more that the planners included former prisoners from Cabanatuan. The information they could relay to Allied headquarters should be vital to the outcome of the war, for the general situation of the Filipinos and all POWs in Dapecol.

"What does it mean to a convict like me? The war may end, POWs sure would be freed, but convicts like me would stay in prison. I have a life sentence," Dela Cruz responded after Lieutenant Santos's long dialogue.

"We are expendable soldiers, we don't exist anymore. You come with us and we survived, you will remain a fugitive hunted by the authorities. With the Americans who put you in jail, with God's help, you may be pardoned."

Dela Cruz looked at Cabarles in the eye; he was very quiet. The convict was waiting for his opinion, but none had come up. Santos explained the best for his situation. Cab was indebted to him; there was no doubt he could not be denied of the opportunity. Only Cab must say the word, and he should follow.

Lieutenant Santos continued. "You're a guerilla soldier now, all of us. Your mission is not over yet. Only you is in the best position to lead the Americans away from Dapecol."

"You know I would like you to come with us." Cab was forced to say something. "Whatever your choice would be fine with me. The lieutenant has given you an order. If you comply, you're a soldier. If you don't, you're a fugitive," he continued.

"You're going back to Dapecol, and that's an order," Santos reiterated before the convict could respond.

"Yes, sir, I will," Dela Cruz replied. He was twitched by the loud voice of the lieutenant; perhaps he had wanted to reply in the opposite.

Cabarles did what he did best—follow up to agree when the situation was settled. "Please do us another favor. Lead the Americans away from us."

"Yes, sir, I will." He saluted in conclusion. Somehow he felt different to be recognized as a guerilla soldier.

"I thank you very much. I owe you my life and there are more depending on you."

FAREWELL TO THE ANGELS, GOODBYE DAVAO

In a cluster of five houses lived families dependent on a corn plantation owned by the Penafrancias, tenants and caretakers who were tilling lands for a percentage of the harvests. Other vegetables and tubers were also grown; most were cassavas and sweet potatoes that were more susceptible to drought. With a kindhearted landlord, they were happy what they could do for him much more that they had given prior notification to extend hospitality to the people that should pass through their village. Help to Filipino soldiers, however, was something they would be proud to do on their own. The food they prepared was equal to a peacetime feast. There was plenty of boiled corn. For the first time in over a year, the soldiers had eaten and refused to eat more. Donono was advised not to eat too much because it would slow him down to the next leg of their escape, which would be very soon. The families, men and women, had alternately offered advices on how to handle the rugged terrains and jungles especially at night. The escapees were also given a crash course on how to use the heavenly bodies to guide them in the right direction.

"Avoid taking rests on an isolated tree or a cluster of trees on a meadow or being seen in it because it is most likely where an enemy nests." They knew that one already by experience. Everyone in essence were repeatedly given encouragement and good luck on their long and dangerous journey ahead. But the escapees were not completed yet; they were waiting for more people who had been expected to show up a day ago. The Moro man who was patiently waiting with his merchandise that he brought with him from the gate of Dapecol would be their guide, patiently having a conversation with Donono and Agustin. Romo had left as soon as the last escapees from Mactan reached the village. There was more on his part to undertake and confirm before the ghost soldiers could begin their journey out of Davao. He was a very busy man.

Though the sun was shrouded by clouds of smoke that drifted to the west and the ground was shaded by towering coconuts and *molave* (hardwood) trees, still it was a long wait to be alerted to who would come next. They could not discount that a Japanese patrol may come upon the place. The taste of freedom and plenty of food that they had been denied of for a very long time was so much to enjoy in the company of brothers to whom they owed so much gratitude. The people of Davao were very kind indeed, very polite and alert to notify them that people were spotted coming to their location. They were at an enough distance to see five people coming out from the brown cornfield about two hundred yards down a grassy path. Two people rushed in assistance to their landlord and company who were having trouble with their loads.

Greetings and acknowledgments by everyone followed. The people were two young ladies disguised as men with native-made sombreros obscuring their face and two others in their natural looks. They were delightful beauties on whom were glued the attention of everyone as they gracefully responded to the warm welcome of the people. Santos was getting the shock of his lifetime to recognize one of the women; she truly was Rhodora X. He had been foretold, but the feeling was different when all perception becomes clearly opposite from what he had known her. He had despised her endlessly; the guilt and pity was now tremendous in knowing her part in their escape. Agustin and Donono were shocked to see her.

Santos had known Rina already. Very determined and aloof, she was in Dapecol; she was very accommodating, respectful, and truly admirable to meet her in a forgiving place.

"Lieutenant Santos, I'm glad you made it. Please meet Rhodora, you should have seen her in the camp already," Rina said.

"Yes indeed. In bad times and confusing situations."

"What do you mean?"

"I was kept in the dark about you. I regret despising you for a long time. I apologize."

"He never told you?" Rhoda cut in.

"He did, just a while ago. I understand he has a reason."

"What else did he tell you?"

"Not much. He said he might just stay in Mindanao if you come with us. I don't know how to thank you for helping us, ma'am. The same to you, Ms. Rina," Santos stated.

"Where is he?" Rina must have heard enough.

She paid no attention to two others. She wanted to see Cabarles.

Donono just nodded a bit; he didn't know all of them, and he was nervous as hell in either seeing Rhodora X or seeing women in general. He just stayed quiet looking at them, noticeably drooling to watch the other ladies taking off a piece of clothing that partially covered their faces. Guido was likewise confused to see the translator or whatever she did for the commandant of Dapecol. He could not explain the presence of Rhodora X with them far away from the prison compound when every time they saw her was in the company of the dreaded Japanese major or in a vehicle marked with the Japanese flag. Much more of the thought they were escapees from Dapecol, a known collaborator in their fold at this hour was a scary thought. A beauty venomous as a snake, he would not forget the last time he saw her. She was seen watching in contentment while a soldier was beaten up by Japanese guards along the main entrance of Dapecol. It began an impression of one lady to be scared off inside the camp much more to learn later she slept with Maeda.

"Where is Captain Cabarles?" Rina asked, intended for anyone who would know.

Cabarles was made aware of the arrival of the rest of their contingent from the other prison. Someone called his attention inside a cogon hut having a conversation with his *kababayan*. Always a dramatic entrance on the scene, he went out of the house with an unfinished conversation with Dela Cruz.

Rina passed the time assisting his father who was attending to the welfare of the people in their domain, mostly relatives of Romo and help in their plantation, taking time with an elderly man, also making sure all were prepared as told. The doctor was assured that all had been taken care of precisely as he wanted.

"Well done, Captain," Rina said as soon as she saw Cabarles approaching. "I understand you are all set to go." Rina was not one to play games; she was very decisive.

"Yes, we cannot thank you enough. I wish we have time to know each other better. I can only hope to see you again."

"Yes, I do too."

She may not have heard at all, as Cabarles's eyes were directed to Rhodora almost immediately. The man remained quiet, a casual expression of greeting on his face. Rina stepped closer. No time to preserve femininity, she embraced Cabarles for a long moment while uttering words he could barely hear.

Angelo Penafrancia could only look the other way. He knew how much care and effort her daughter had devoted to Cabarles since they had known him. She deserved a little time with the captain as little as they could allow for themselves.

As what it appears, the dangerous gathering had also divulged the real identity of all major participants in the escape of eight Filipino POWs undetected from the prison camp. The manner it was executed was so vague that not many people would know it actually happened. Rina had introduced Santos, Guido, and Donono to his father too. However, they all knew it wasn't a gathering to celebrate.

There was another man the escapees owed too much, Romualdo Paredes, whom everyone called Romo. He was known as the man who collected all the cadavers that ended up in the Mactan rice paddies, the same person who spent a night to sleep in Barracks 6 when Cabarles was in Paradiso de Oro posing as a doctor. Rhodora was occupied by two afraid young ladies, hugging each other in tears of farewell.

As there were no Japanese soldiers yet, Donono and Guido were ultimately relieved at the turn of events and forgot the fear that rushed in their head a few minutes ago. However, they were still confused at the presence of Rhodora X. They needed an answer, a damn good one. Santos should know.

"What is she doing here?" Guido whispered to Santos as he could not wait anymore. He had to know now.

"She is coming with us."

"What!" The most unexpected reply needed clarification.

Cabarles was relying on his personal conversation with Rhodora. It was a long time ago. When he was given the heads-up that Myra Marfil would not be alone, he was quick to assume Rhodora had confirmed her coming. He held her word and couldn't blame her. He just could not understand what his mind suggested imagining to be with her again. Since the night they shared, so much was in his thoughts, that he should have done differently. Looking forward to arousing thoughts to spend days and nights with her, he was afraid. Very afraid that his knees were trembling he could not get them straight. He prayed. *Dear God, lead me from temptation.*

Constrained by time, the guides cut in to remind them that they should get going.

Accommodating and sweet, opposite to the woman most people knew as a collaborator and mistress of Maeda, her actions revealed her to be with great regards about her affection to Cabarles. How it happened was not important, and she didn't regret what transpired between them. She would offer more than herself for the passion she had realized with him. Knowing more about Cabarles from Rina only increased her affection as she revealed them to Rosie. She had given a lot of thought to leaving Davao, and it only ended in an unimaginable outcome. She had decided not to come.

It would be her best friend, Rosalia Brown. She was going to take her chances back in her island province of Bohol where her family lived. Myraflor Marfil should be in her care for now, but the end of destination was undecided. She said the only relatives she knew were living in the Bicol region, which was too far away.

Meanwhile, the father and daughter who took care of Dominador Cabarles from the beginning were becoming emotional. They made sure that Cab and the others would have a place in Davao should they choose to stay or come back when the war was over. Rina was the most poignant. Her personal dedication to the well-being of the unknown and seriously wounded prisoner in the Davao hospital to his incarceration at POW camp was coming to end, beyond her reach. Cab was going back to a woman she remembered hearing the name so many times. The same man she offered unselfish devotion to help him fulfill all the promises in his realm. In so doing, she could not help but admit to herself that she also had fallen in love to this man, envious of the woman whom Cabarles endlessly fought so hard with his life just to be with her again. Envious of another who had a chance to show that same feeling for him, and sorry for both of them. Only a few moments were left before they would never see him again.

"If ever you come back to Davao, you will find me waiting and still caring for you. You will remain in my heart and mind," she said, taking the very last moment tearfully without holding her feelings that she had kept to herself. There was no sense to hide those feelings now. Her warm and tight embrace had made it known the sincerity of that affection.

Cab had remained wordless, not finding anything to say but hold her in his arms momentarily as if he wanted to tell her that she had also earned a place in his heart. He made it known to her that at a time when he was losing hope to live, she was the angel who held his hands when the other was not around.

"There is another angel who would want to say a few words with you," Rina whispered. She let him loose from her arms.

The last of the daylight under the shade of the trees, Rina led Cab to Rhodora who made him froze a while ago. Her arms were around Cab as they walked a short distance. "I already know what's between both of you, and I'm so proud of loving you too. Please stay the gentleman that you are," Rina whispered.

Cab didn't understand what she meant, but it must be good with that smile Rina had shown while clearing her eyes of tears. "I'm sure you know each other very well. I'll let you two alone," Rina said while getting the attention of Rosie and Myra to come with her.

Their eyes locked almost immediately, but even before Cab could say anything, the mistress of Dapecol commander had put her arms around him just like Rina did, laying her head on his shoulder for a little while.

Rhodora had other things in mind; she held Cab on the chin to make him look straight at her then touched his lips with a tender kiss, enough to send him afloat. "You really are so easy to fall in love with, Mr. Cabarles," she declared. "I wish you all the luck and the happiness that you pursue. I say my farewell now, sorry I could not come with you. I really wish I could." She maintained the same sad look Cab had seen the last time they said goodbye with each other.

"What will happen to you?"

"I shall remain Rhodora X, a honey to my nightmares. If my life exists for that purpose, so shall it be."

The difference this time was dealing with a determined woman who was not under the influence of spirits. There was no sign of regret and surrender, only courage to the unimaginable sacrifice she chose.

"I have to say my farewell too, but I can't do it. Would you let me remember this moment that I have given a chance with you one more time? It is a great honor to know you, Ms. Rhodora X, if you let me . . ."

"As you wish, Captain Cabarles. Keep in mind that you'll bring what's left in my heart with you," she said. She felt a tender kiss close to her lips from a man who was offered all of her. It was the greatest feeling of such farewell, with a pure heart and kindness, to feel so much love he felt devoted by another woman. "I hope and pray that you find her (Inez) safe."

He breathed deeply; Inez had slipped from his mind for a moment there. Otherwise, it was her that he kissed. He pictured in his mind the same eyes full of tears. "I can only say that I have been given the chance of knowing you. I respect your decision of not coming with us."

"Would you still take me?"

"I already told you I will. It doesn't change."

"Thank you very much. I wish I could."

The whole moment didn't escape the watchful eyes of Santos, Donono, and Agustin, all whose attention never let go from the scene that transpired intimately. They were still insufficiently perceptive of what was going on, much more of seeing them kissing each other. Rina had revealed to them who Ms. Rhodora was and what role she played on their escape, so with the sacrifices she indulged for the general benefit of the POWs. Kindness and courage the woman had put herself since the beginning of the war. She also described the nature of her relationship with Cabarles. She sounded jealous as she ended her words seeing Cab and Rhoda coming.

"You have a lot of explaining to do Cab," Santos said with sarcasm to his tone. He was seconded by Dono.

"Gentlemen, meet Rhodora X. I don't know how to begin telling you what she did for us, but I promise you will know them all." Cab understood the guilt of not confiding X's identity to his brothers, but he had problems of his own to address about her.

Dr. Angelo Penafrancia had finished giving a crash course of emergency medical responses and treatment of malaria and common injuries. He pointed what and which about a bagful of medicines was for. He also attended to health evaluation of his domain. One was found to have pneumonia and was given proper medication. Truly kindhearted he was, he instructed all his tenants that they were all welcome for any medical consultation in his house.

The pregnant woman got most of the attention despite Rina visiting her one time with other purposes, of course, on the side confirming them to expect and prepare food for the coming of several guests. And they did with open arms and hospitality that surpassed the anticipation of the escapees.

A prayer altogether was requested and led by an elderly couple. Thereafter, the escape party began another beginning to their journey. The doctor had a few more words to say. He took off a leather satchel from his shoulder and presented it to Cab. Nothing could be so meaningful as this. "I have my revolver inside, it might come in handy on your travel. There's only one bullet in it, put it to good use," he said. "And please take care of the girls." He was clearly worried about Rosie. Then he simply said, "Good luck."

"I don't know what to say. You have been so good to me. All of you." he said.

Where was Roberto de la Cruz? He was standing nearby waiting for a moment with Cab. The whole time, he was struggling to write a letter. "I have chosen to stay indeed, just do me a favor. Make sure this letter is received by my mother if I'm not able to catch up with you." A few more words were said, and they hugged each other afterward. Soon enough, Cabarles joined Santos and Donono and the rest who had started their first steps heading out of Davao already.

In the silhouette provided by dark smoke billowing from afar, at the last turn of their heads from where they began, they were shown a waving of hands by the good people of Davao. The rich and famous, prettiests and not so pretty, pregnant, the elderly, and children. The picture that they formed against the background of thick and dark vegetation was the panoramic view that represented the whole Davao. Little children in front, young boys of different ages in awkward salute, girls waving, all together formed a line side by side. Behind in the middle was an aristocratic-looking man wearing an expensive hat then a convicted felon, and men and women standing next to each other. A nurse in a white dress and a Japanese mistress held hands, both beauty that shared in the sacrifices of everyone without expecting any in return. They offered their hearts to the same man but remained compassionate to let what that man desired. On both ends were couples standing in pairs.

Only one was not waving a hand, a father with a boy on his shoulder alongside a woman holding hands with another child. It was Romualdo Paredes, the enigmatic man who carried out the unthinkable, apologizing that he could not come any further because his wife was pregnant.

All stayed still until they saw no more of the men and two women whose survival could only be decided by their own determination and endurance. "God have mercy on them." One sighed followed by the others.

"God have mercy on them," Cabarles prayed as he made another step into the jungle.

CHAPTER 13

IN THE NO-MAN'S-LAND

Beautiful faces among them, just the same within. I can't forget each one. As I met them bleeding, I say farewell in tears. A village of tribesmen, very kind people even in unknown places. I can say again they exist in the farthest places.

OVERVIEWS AND ENLIGHTENMENT

In about an hour, they passed the clearing of a rocky meadows that only permitted the growing of wild plants and grasses up to the knees. They took a short rest to discuss what was ahead. The guides had estimated before darkness fell that they would reach another clearing, and only then could they take a rest and camp for the night. Otherwise, they would go around south of Mount Apo to Kidapawan where the Japanese maintained garrisons and active patrols day and night. Though the route planners were given advice to consider the women in the group, it was on the first leg that lay many obstacles that they had to get through. In their company were women who were only used to walking across a dance ballroom for over a year. Dancing, eating, and lying in bed were mostly what they were used to. Crossing rugged terrains and mountains to Lanao and beyond by foot wouldn't be easy. They had to face difficulties with every step and get used to it.

Long hair tied tightly covered by a piece of thin black linen around faces, only their eyes were exposed, the women in tow quietly following the pace of the soldiers. They said they were not bothered by mosquitoes because there were many of them also in the place they came from. They revealed they were afraid only of bloodsucking bats known to attack at night in the forest. Aside from those bats, there was no other reason to be frightened. For six hours of non-stop walking up or down hills and boulders of rock and through thick thorny vines, they reached an obscure spot to eat and rest for a while. The full moon that barely got through to the ground aided them to see each other in the dark. At three o'clock in the morning on February 22, they were in the middle of nowhere where the escapees had no choice but to let faith take over again. There were no known inhabitants in that area by the border of Davao and North Cotabato, just lost hunters and possibly migrating tribes. Even the Japanese patrols never dared to go deep into a forest that even sunlight barely got through the canopy of giant trees. Talks over supper did not discount the tales about the headhunters. The rumors of such tribe existing on this part of Mindanao was as frightening as encountering Japanese patrols. But then they could talk freely without looking over their shoulders.

Though escape from POW camp was motivated by a forsaken vow, the secrecy it was carried out couldn't be all credited to an incoherent captain, and he was aware of that. Lt. Rodrigo Santos and Sergeant Guido Agustin executed the most critical part of planning as willing participants became known. It began in the search for Myra Marfil.

In general perceptions of the Japanese, having no events of encounters and insignificant antagonists to challenge their authority was noted that diplomatic approach to maintain controls of Davao and adjoining provinces was effective to the benefit of both sides. Japanese casualties from firefights was minimal since October 1942. Deaths were entirely due to illnesses and accidents of their own doing while on patrols. Not known to the Japanese, it was part of a grand scheme to ease their patrol and security around Dapecol, punctuated by the snake scare that began upon the death of the buffalo caretaker. The aborted escape plan of eight Filipino POWs on Christmas Eve with makeup-laden concubines was taken as a blessing. Disclosed that it was called off by Rhodora X and not by Cabarles, the escapees could only repeat a thankful realm of the chain of events that avoided a bloodbath. Having given time to raise the idea of simple arithmetic applications, it became an endeavor no one would believe it ever happened. Though one Filipino soldier was not immediately accounted for, one more burnt body found in Mactan was presumed the missing POW. As a result, there was no significant disturbances in Dapecol other than the wildfire that also burned a portion of the Mactan rice field.

There were no guerilla actions against them for a long while. However, cattle rustling resumed as soon as the last of escapees were confirmed "dead," evident of bloody spots on bushes that could be mistaken as a furious battle that was fought in that place. The facts thereat was that a cow or a carabao was slaughtered on that spot. Raids of plantations with edible yields especially bananas and pineapple were reverted to the unstoppable. They were commonly attributed to starving civilians, nothing serious; in large quantity, there was reason to be alarmed. The population of Mindanao may have embraced the presence of Japanese, but never the problem of hunger had been contained. It actually got to worst. In general view, the pause in guerilla offensive was made because of the holidays. It was true in some ways, but the so-called cattle rustlers were led by people who benefited from their deeds and were very well alive. Upon the "deaths" of all prisoners from whom they carried orders, they were back to what they did best. Thieveries and banditries resumed, and stubborn refugees returned to raiding crops around Dapecol. Civilian peacekeepers were commissioned and reinforced with regular soldiers to contain escalating problems. In just a matter of weeks, atrocities and merciless killing returned with civilians affected the most.

Having no communication from Dapecol, the ghost escapees could not tell if the Americans had already broken out of prison. Although the Americans would be guided to the care of another guerilla group operating in the northeastern provinces, it didn't mean that the angry Japanese would not look for them in the northwest where they were heading. Their objectives remained—to get as much head start as far as to where the Muslim peddlers would lead them. Meanwhile, the American escapees couldn't be led all the way to the eastern part of Mindanao. There was nothing there but marshlands, lakes, and rivers full of giant crocodiles and pythons a hundred times more dreadful than Japanese soldiers. Eventually, they would turn up to northwest provinces with the Japanese on their tail.

ONE TOO MANY

Equipped of homemade bolos to use in clearing paths when necessary, the distance they traveled for three days was not fast enough than what was expected. The escapees had turned the experience into an adventure safari that was causing the delays. Well, there were also women in the group that could take a long time to take five for personal calling. Every waterfall they stopped at, every top of the hills they paused a moment on, looking back south. In fact, they learned to appreciate the beautiful surroundings. Large and colorful birds roamed around freely, and endemic animals could be seen watching them as they watched them too. On the fourth day, Donono worriedly told Santos that they were in an inhabited land; he said he was seeing signs that people had been in the area just recently. Maintaining position behind the file, one of his job was to keep head count of the total number of the party all the time, and so far so good. Being inside thick vines and bushes could easily cause disorientation and dizziness. Donono firmly believed that at one instance he had counted two more heads over their total number. Eight in all, he could have been sure there were nine ahead. Sometimes he thought there were more behind him. He was starting to get scared.

"Do you have more water left?" he asked. It was an excuse after getting Myra's attention accidentally.

"Sure," she said, handing him a jug of water.

There was plenty of water, but food was running out in the four days of walk then one more. By the end of the sixth, they resigned for the evening on a location that was estimated to be twenty more kilometers the mat peddler was leading them. Donono hoped they were not lost, but that was the least of his worries. He was born in the wilderness, and there was no trail so treacherous that he couldn't cope up. Where he grew up, he also wandered in the forest to hunt for food. What he had seen along the trail were real people no doubt, and he was aware they may not be friendly.

In a small grassy clearing where they had to wait till morning, he had to ask again if the others had seen what he kept on seeing. "Are there any people alive in this place?" he questioned Guido, taking their turns as lookout together.

"Yes, I'm sure there are. I had seen footsteps on the trail."

"Who do you think are they? Could they be eating people?" he uttered softly, avoiding to get the attention of the others.

"I do hope myself they are not."

"Why did you say that?" Don took a deep breath to get assured that his hunger was not affecting his vision again.

"Because they are staring at you right now," Guido answered.

"Yeah, I know. They are also behind you. Don't move," he warned

Guido and Donono were surrounded by yet unknown people, a few with bows and arrows but mostly carrying a thin pole with pointed ends. It sure was going to hurt if they were stabbed by one of those. The rest of the party may not have noticed the presence of half-naked people; at twenty feet away in darkness, they could only see the silhouette of their own. Though there were no signs of aggression, they could not discount the fact that they may be the dreaded headhunters. A few of them had somewhat shown an unusual interest to Donono. Dark skinned himself and almost the same height, he was touched and looked at closely by a few of them. Whatever they were saying, none understood. They just let them do what they wanted while checking him out in the moonlight, his scars, ears, hair, everything. After peeking through the hole of his nose and mouth, they stepped back and disappeared. He believed he would be cooked first, and like a kid, he took refuge between Cab and Santos. He said to let Guido be the watch alone for the night. After all, whoever inhabited the land already knew there were other people in their territory. Guido confirmed they were not alone, telling what just happened and what they did to Donono.

"They know we are here, I had been trying to tell you all day. I think I will be cooked first," Donono whispered.

"Please don't say that," one of the girls said, frightened already as she was and more to think if one of them was eaten and so with the rest of them.

"Don't get afraid, I'll die first before they can touch you," he said, trying to divert his mind but taking the chance to finally start a conversation with the girl. At least before he died.

Myra could burst into laughter but chose not to. A smile was sufficient to be thankful hearing there was a man who would die for her. "Thank you, that's very sweet, Dono," she said.

Since they left Davao, only a short introduction had taken place between them. Donono was more focused on the task he was assigned, making sure no one drifted away from the group or no one was left out every time they took a rest.

The ladies could only express their sorry to the soldiers; however, they all understood they could not keep up with the pace of the soldiers. Known for their bravery and courage under extreme conditions, kind, conscientious, and loyal with each other, they were brothers in a true sense of the word. Myra may have reason to fear almost everything for not knowing where they were heading. For six days, she was cared and respected like she was a little sister, and all her worries disappeared. Rosie was always on her side too; thank God, she said, otherwise she would have died of worries alone from Donono who kept staring at her.

All fears were gone. Despite the physical ordeal she put herself into, no complaint was heard from her. However, for what she observed, she was starting to doubt the fearlessness of Donono. She would say he was unusually built for a soldier—short and ugly and always falling behind. He was a corporal, all right; how he became one she could not understand. He looked agile, but called on many fives that slowed down their travel, thanks to him for that. There was more to be grateful, however, because he was always at her side caring, attending to her and Rosie on the difficult trail and terrain.

On the other hand, Myra had an outstanding beauty that made Donono look like a beast. She wouldn't be the star attraction of an exclusive nightclub if she didn't.

Donono had to distance himself from Myra at the beginning. He sure he wasn't blessed of the looks of the tall and handsome Cabarles or Santos and no sense to even think about Myra actually liking him and accepting his mediocrity in physical appearance and intellect. But he had the "thing" that would make any girl like him. And if it worked with what it was supposed to do, then he preferred Myra from Rosie who was way bigger than him.

Dono never told his age nor did anyone bother to know. He may be sixteen or in his twenties or thirties; he just damn looked mature for a kid. He conclusively halted growing upward at five feet and a fraction of an inch. He was shy about two inches compared to Myra barefooted, and she was only sixteen. Where he came from, as long as the man was proven he can provide and scarred enough, a mate was not a problem even a sister. Why return in his realm in that regard? There were two right at arm's reach and he only wanted one. He understood that Myra was regarded as their own sister; she had suffered enough and may never recover from the effects of war to her family and herself primarily. Donono's concern for the time being was not to die for real or get eaten, but there was a longstanding desire he would uphold. He fell asleep with that thought. For all he knew, where he grew up, a brother can truly marry a sister and he intended to stand by it.

Another morning in an endless wilderness, he woke up to see what he could do for breakfast. Cab and Santos always wanted hot brew in the morning. There was plenty of firewood around to gather. He got the surprise of his life upon getting up in full view of smiling tribesmen. All the men were of the same skin and build, some with colorful headdresses. He froze at the sight of the same people who touched him last night. They were touching him again. He cried for help; he wasn't too far away from the big guys.

"Let them, they are friendly," the guide said who was also awakened by his cry.

"Who are they?" Cab asked, immediately waving for Myra and Rosie to come behind them.

"The T'bolis. We should not be far from their village," one said.

"They will not do any harm to Donono, right?" Santos wanted assurance.

"No, they must be thinking he is one of them."

"Sir, please help me, they are going to cook me for breakfast!" Donono screamed as the new company were consulting with each other; they were truly interested in Donono. He eventually regained senses to thwart off the natives and tried to hide behind Agustin.

It was the T'boli tribesmen, all right. The Moro could understand their dialect to no avail aided by sign language. From what it appeared, the inhabitants expected their coming. They yielded to what it seemed the natives wanted them to do, for them to follow. The trail was getting bigger, and the inhabitants of the land multiplied eventually, surrounding them with hunting weapons ready at hand. They were intriguingly celebrating, happy.

"Where are they bringing us?" Dono whispered, seeking enlightenment.

"I don't know yet, but don't worry, they seemed friendly," Rod Santos assumed.

"How do you know that? They keep touching me, checking me out like they could eat me raw." Donono was frightened.

"Relax, our guide seems to understand what they say. Don't provoke any aggression," Santos responded.

"What are you planning? We are unarmed."

"It's all right, Cab has a handgun. If he is calm, we must be calm too. I think they like you for a different reason."

"Yeah, what is that?"

"Look at them. If you have the same haircut, you're almost one of them," Santos commented.

"I guess what they are talking about is you will be good roasted than boiled." Myra spoke up. With only her eyes showing, she could be mistaken as very serious.

Agustin played along. "Don't worry, Dono. They may like you raw."

The T'boli tribe was known to be hostile to anyone who dared to step into their territory. The dialect they spoke was hard to comprehend, even to their Muslim guides. Spoken slower, Myra could grasp some words she could understand, most likely Agustin also who could speak fluently in Ilonggo, Cebuano, and partially of any other dialect spoken in the southern region. Both remained playful of Donono's worries. By physical distinction, the little man truly had many similarities to the hosts though his hair was curly. Displaying an army cut from Guido's scissors, he could put half a coconut shell over his head and he could become a T'boli. He could sense Agustin and Myra making fun of him otherwise upsetting him more. He walked faster to be with Cabarles, the man with a concealed gun in front of the file, and kept his mouth shut. He felt safer and confident with Cabarles all the time, forgetting his assigned tasks. But he still had unanswered questions in mind. Being born and raised in the tradition of tribesmen, he knew of many rival clans that could be hostile without provocation. He was also aware that headhunters was not a folktale and he had heard many stories about them.

"Who do you think these people are?" he asked Cabarles when he could not take his qualms anymore.

"Guido didn't tell you?"

"No, they said I will be roasted and eaten first," Don replied.

"They were just kidding. These people are the T'boli, and they are expecting us," Cab replied. He continued to share of what he knew so far about the tribe and what they should expect farther down the hill.

"That is why I always like you the best," Donono declared, clearing his thoughts to another unrelated question, taking advantage of the moment.

He was calmed down, all right. However, there were other things in his thought that required immediate resolution. In the village he was raised, they were adapted to divergent customs and traditions. If a man had completed certain rituals of scarring on his skin, he was considered capable of having a family of his own. His assisted scars by traditional merit did not qualify him for a mate, but certainly the addition of real battle scars was tantamount to the honored privilege of picking out the prettiest in the village even if she was a relative, anywhere, anytime at any situation as long as the moon is round. All he needed to do was express his intention.

"Would you let me marry, Myra?"

"What? Why do you want to marry her?"

"I like her. She keeps smiling at me."

"It doesn't work out that easy, have you seen her already?" Cab became ecstatic from what he was hearing. By the tradition he knows, marrying does not happen that easily and surely he had no authority to do so. He took it as hunger taking its toll on Dono's head again.

"I'm serious, I want her to be my wife." Donono was assertive. He knew exactly what he wanted.

"You have to know if she likes you too."

"Why did you say that?"

"Because that's the way it is and it should be."

The talk might have continued if not for their attention taken by a clearing with an array of houses ahead. Donono was carried up by the tribesmen after he was fitted with a headdress. They were welcomed immediately by more T'bolis and a band of armed men. Two stood out and looked very familiar—one was Sergeant Rabong, the other was more known as the leader of animal rustlers in Dapecol, Abu Mudal. Rabong was partnered with Malvo who were known dead by snakebite a long time ago. Keeping his allegiance to the arriving party, Rabong was remarkably thrilled. He disclosed immediately to his former barrack mates that Malvo had proceeded on the mission as planned. Rabong stayed close to direct the route and ensure they would not really be eaten or slaughtered by hostile inhabitants. He was here to welcome the party with a few armed men they had already met before in Dapecol. The escapees were greeted and welcomed as very important guests in the village.

There were fish, dried and fresh alike on banana leaves, but the more plentiful was meat, which indicated that they butchered a large animal. In the remotest of places in Mindanao somehow lived a tribe who would welcome them as prominent people, a place so remote there was a feast prepared in honor of the ghost soldiers. The hospitality had somewhat surpassed the Davao experience that mostly involved nervous tensions, sad and endless goodbyes. Unknown to the group of Fifty-Seventh Scouts, their reputation of bravery and courage precedes them, especially of the leadership and goodwill they incurred within the Filipino POWs, the evacuees, and the guerilla organizations. Their escape had unified and created an unusual communications system of extreme clandestineness not only around Dapecol but as far as the wilderness of Mindanao. Reminiscing how the escape progressed, Agustin described how he cried for Donono and Santos. There were reasons to be cheerful and grateful for being reunited again. Known to be dead, they knew all of them were forgotten in Dapecol.

Here they were in the middle of nowhere after having a satisfying meal in the morning while discussing the continuation of their journey. The man who wanted to be married seemed to have forgotten his fear as there was a lot of food. Confidently, he won't be cooking anymore; instead he got the most of attention fitted for a king. Donono had somewhat realized he was related to the tribe by his looks, and to them, he was the most welcome. The pride of their kind he was fitted with especially crafted headdress and colorful clothing to wrap around his waist while people congregating around him. Girls lined up waiting for his attention that amused him for a while, a long while. Myra and Rosie found time to attend to their sore feet. To some extent, they had less to worry bearing in mind they were far enough from the Japanese and within the village they could take off what was covering their faces. Donono was in a trance to see her again, much more to be given a sweet smile.

By afternoon, the sound of a gong and drums began to signal the best of what the tribe could offer for the visitors. Men and women in colorful costumes, mostly unsold items of a peddler he brought with him patiently as a gift to the tribe, danced to the tune of the instruments. Donono, enjoying the feeling of being honored, showed that he would not announce he was fit to marry a girl for nothing. He could dance in the same tradition of the villagers. The former concubines had reasons to be merry too, and they joined in the celebrations.

The next morning, resupplied and rested, they had to keep moving. They were assisted by more than a dozen T'boli huntsmen adept to the place and were guided by six riflemen. Abu Mudal had briefed them of their destinations and bragged that the lavishness they had seen from the T'boli was nothing compared to what was being prepared ahead for them. For two days, they reached another tribal community along the edge of water palms and mangroves. A marshland where water had receded because of the dry season. Fish drying on display in front of the houses indicated that they were caught in abundance. Natives had offered them water to drink and boiled cassava and bunches of rice balls wrapped and boiled in palm stalks. They were hugged and greeted, especially the ladies by the women and children. Donono took the most attention again. A new group came with them carrying paddles and fish pouches made of bamboo. An indigenous people of distinct characteristics from the T'bolis, they were made aware that people would be passing by that needed assistance in reaching a certain destination. Though contained in a community away from civilization, they could not prevent that sometimes in their secluded way of life people must come through their village. As they seemed harmless fishermen and occasional hunters, to fully understand what they say was not important. The ghost soldiers were assured of certainty in their destination with trusted people on the lead.

BEYOND MOUNT APO

Days of walking, days of talking. The hard life in Dapecol was a constant topic, but what their camaraderie had created a year had also established a network of communications in many ways and directions. As a result of the atrocities of the Japanese, inhabitants were pushed in deeper into the jungles. Many found themselves in Dapecol known to yield plenty of harvest, but it didn't mean they gave up contacts with their relatives. To that effect, information changed ears that benefited the guerillas and POWs in great extent. Tribal members or plain settlers and refugees were viable means of carrying messages in collaboration with the resistance.

It was believed that while a single gunshot could be heard a hundred miles away from Dapecol, a whisper could also reach as far. However, there was a downside. Most of the time, information was exaggerated significantly until it was received. Far away from Dapecol, the soldiers were told that the POW camp had burned to the ground, which could not be true. Also many times the information died along the way with the carrier. With Rabong, Mudal, and company speaking, the most reliable were men that frolicked a long distance with carts powered by domesticated animal, merchants who sold bamboo and woodcrafts that could reach far distances from Misamis, around Davao to Bukidnon, and back around again. They comprised long-distance carriers, sometimes letters and packages. They could be seen everywhere including the gates of Dapecol blending in with the evacuees. Sometimes they congregated together in market areas, presumably talking about their merchandise but in reality many of them carrying homemade handguns concealed in bamboo hollows.

In what it appeared, there were handicrafts that reached the village that were also available in Dapecol. Clearly, the villages they passed through were not hostile tribes to be afraid of. Skillful in communications and unafraid of armed men, the escapees were told it wasn't the first time they were accommodating guerillas.

Reaching another village that remained thriving and untouched by the atrocities of the Japanese increased their confidence. Situated along the shoreline of a lake, they could only stay a few hours to take advantage of the hospitality. The first one hundred kilometers of very slow pace over all kinds of land formation and many obstacles was a journey enough to take many days of narrating under the same acacia tree:

> *In a land so far away, many days I stared at a view of a mountain high. Over barbed wires, through round red they said it was the rising sun, how long they shall stay maybe forever. And then I was beyond to see eagles soar. Black birds also flew in circles up high.*

THE POET

The journey to wherever continued. There was a lake to go across by *bancas* (wooden canoes). In summer, water could recede far away from the banks. The inland bodies of water were fed by constant streams of freshwater from brooks in the highlands, creating a sanctuary for many species of birds and animals that sustained the villagers and settlers of important nourishment. Lake Sebu offers a rich source of food.

A few *bancas* were waiting but not enough to accommodate the large party, only the women. The men must walk one kilometer along the shore to a rendezvous through marsh. Led by natives on the trail was truly punishing; they could only imagine how difficult it could be for the women. For the soldiers that were denied food for a long time, even in plenty, unusual critters in the wetlands became food to their eyes. In a small dry land hidden around thick vegetation and a few coconuts, the men were directed in a clearing where the boat party had started to get busy. The natives didn't waste time; men gathered firewood, and women were cooking the catch of the day in the afternoon sun. A while later, they were eating broiled fish and steamed crustaceans fresh from the lake along with the food they carried. It was a satisfying meal. By the light of the firewood that was maintained to keep insects away, they took advantage of the early darkness of the night to reminisce again the escape experience with emphasis on the people they left in Davao. Cotabato was a big province; the hurdle of going across had begun the moment they stepped on it. Somewhat it was a camping literally with supplies sustained right on every stop they made, an adventure for Rosalia and Myra.

As the night progressed over a campfire, the host extended their hospitality. It wasn't known what tribe they were. In the hands of Rabong and Damal left their fate. Wherever he was bringing them, only the promise of a grand welcome was waiting. For the meantime, they were told to be patient, reassured that they should reach their destination eventually. Nobody was in a hurry; concern lay on how much more the ladies could cope with. A time of fun initiated by the host was too hard to disregard. Rosie and Myra contributed English love songs this time. Guido had sung "Matud Nila." Santos did an old Tagalog song, and a few guerillas had shown their talent also in group singing. A request intended for the shy Bulakeno to sing did not push through because he didn't really know how. In spite of the situation, Santos boasted to everyone that he was born where poetry was spoken on a regular basis. He was from Bigaa, Bulacan, where Francisco Balagtas (famous Filipino poet) was also born. He was not downright shy because he had already begun it in his thought.

Emerging from persistent demand, he concocted a phrase that rhymed in his mind and one more that followed; he then began reciting a poem. It was a selection of segments from his own life that started the day his eternal love of a woman began to becoming a soldier. The poem ended justifying a desperate longing to be with that woman again no matter what obstacle was on the way. Somewhat to everyone, much more to those who understood Tagalog among the listeners, the poem was heart pounding. The accent of a true poet was carried on, and he was given applause by everyone after a moment of silence. No one knew however that it was derived from his true life other than Santos and Donono. Both also knew that what kept this man alive was primarily because of that woman, who was tearful and helplessly alone as they sailed away that morning from Manila Bay. He was applauded. Rosie and Myra knew of a similar incident that made them question the faithfulness of his poetic rendition about his true love. However, they felt a commitment that remain unchanged. Donono put his attention to the leftover food, immediately anticipating that he should be next, and he was right. Of all the people, it was Myra, seconded by Rosie, to show what the king was made of. Santos just advised everyone to rest as the night was not young anymore. The guerillas agreed; the marshland dwellers had come back from setting the traps, and not long enough, the darkness was left to the sounds of bats and owls.

The next morning was no different other than the natives being long gone. They would join with them on the other side of the lake after collecting the catch of the day. Locally processed cocoa were already boiling on a pot attended by a woman with Myra and Rosie. They were learning. For almost two weeks, all they had contributed was a duet in a song that only a few could understand. The girls found a good use for themselves by helping in the preparation for the morning chow. Donono was with them too, making sure as always that Cab and Santos were taken care of. While observing him carrying two cups of hot brew in the direction of still-sleeping friends and officers, they looked at each other as they both agreed there was a natural kindness in his heart despite his looks. On the other hand, Myra had a lot to worry about Donono. He really kept staring at her, and she was beginning to get afraid.

"Hot cocoa, it must be very good," Donono said as he offered them.

In a few moments, two more cups followed in Myra's hands, Rosie with sticky rice balls. The ladies were more comfortable dealing with the soldiers now after last night when they were having fun like longtime friends. Whether they admit it or not, at the beginning of their journey, their difficulties in walking was doubled with fear because they were in the company of men they had never met before with the exception of Cabarles. Relieved of apprehension, they observed genuine respect and act of many kindness with each other, extended to both of them with thoughtful concerns.

"How are you making out so far?" Cabarles casually opened a chat with the girls. "Is Don taking care of you good enough?" he continued.

"Yeah, he is very kind, I'm very grateful," Rosie answered.

Donono remained sitting nearby, attempting to discuss his interest to marry Myra with Santos, but the chance was botched by different matters.

"He is at your service and so do I." Santos made it clear.

"I am all right, thank you. He is helping us in many ways I could not imagine how we reached this far without him," Rosie replied.

Since the T'bolis' welcome affair and in the company of friendly inhabitants in this far land, Myra had noticed that Donono was good looking somehow. In a very amusing change of events, Donono was getting a lot of attention from many other girls, and he was enjoying it. He was actually getting the most courtesy than any one of them. Rosalia had implied that Donono was actually the most handsome man, well it was true, among T'boli tribesmen.

Both women preserved great respect for Cabarles. In Rhodora's views, he was a real gentleman who could keep cool under a very tempting situation. Confided of the details of the short time they spent together added to his reputation as a soldier, Rosie didn't think twice to escape Paradiso on the chance she was given. In Myra's young mind that transformed to sudden adulthood, she herself had thought to escape, but where was she going afterward if not caught? Her prayers were answered—a big brother was sent down from heaven to her rescue. She could only pray to what fate awaited for Rhodora X who had chosen to stay.

CHAPTER 14

THE GENERAL AND THE COOK

*I was in a domain where people severed wanderers'
heads. They received us like prominent men. I am not
scared, too late for me to get scared.*

FAMOUS DONONO

They crossed Lake Sebu in no time. They waited for each other then
walked again to a bamboo bridge made above the water level of the
marsh. Thick vegetation of palms and an assortment of wild plants
that ended up another fishing village overlooking a vast cornfield in
the sunset. Farm tractors were waiting in the town skirts of Banisilan.
Trailers were hitched on each one with a few people standing by.
Cabarles never cared about the name of the places they went through,
especially for Donono as long as there was food to eat and Myra was
taken care of. He must have given up on trying to understand what
the people were saying. Like every inhabited places they pass, every
people would be happy to meet them with warm welcome and gifts
they were thankful to receive. A five-gallon container was loaded to
the wheeled platform. Cabarles didn't have a clue to what the guys
were saying about its contents. He guessed it must be diesel fuel.
Santos and Guido were occupied with fresh people taking the ride.
Donono was back to being Donono, staring at Myra most of the time.
He had seen her quite many times with bare face, and he didn't want
to miss the chance when it happened again.

About fifteen people were crammed in each trailer until it just had
no more space to accommodate hitchhikers. The escapees occupied

the first one. A man started pouring the liquid from the container into a bamboo cup. He drank it straight like cold fresh water then poured again and offered it to Cabarles. It should be drinkable, not the tractor fuel as he thought it was. "Thank you very much." What else could it be? Nobody drank diesel. As soon as he tasted it, it was rejected fast by his mouth, spilling what didn't go through his throat. It was vinegar, but it would mean disrespect that might offend the host by refusing. He should drink too. What they eat, he should eat; what they drink, he should drink. In this part of the world, they were used to welcome guests with *tuba*. *Tuba* is a liquid extracted from palm trees, sweet and thirst quenching if fresh from the source; but let fermented for a few days, it becomes an alcoholic beverage, which smells so bad but tastes so good to people who were used to getting drunk with it.

"What is this?" he asked Santos right away as his taste of the liquid was truly vinegar, good only for cooking.

Santos laughed at his reaction but regained his posture to say it was fresh coconut wine.

"Does it really taste like this, too sour?" Cab asked again.

"Yes, I thought you know. You have to drink it so they don't get offended."

"But it's too sour." Cab hesitated to drink the rest of the wine.

"It's the special, aged exclusively just for us," Guido explained.

Cab believed Santos and Agustin; he didn't want to offend the hosts by not drinking the rest of the wine. He emptied the cup immediately and returned it to the guy. "What is your name if you don't mind?" he asked.

"Piang, sir," the Moro humbly replied.

"Piang, thank you very much," he said in Tagalog. Santos was quick to translate.

Santos was next. He could not help it, but he agreed with Cabarles. Then it was Donono's turn.

"What are you two talking about? It's very good," he said, boasting right up to the big guys with stories comparing how good it was to drink *tuba* again like he was home. Apparently he had too many stories in the production of such beverages to amuse those who could understand him.

Agustin lit up a stick of Lucky Strike from a fresh pack, then let it go around to everyone. So as the drinking of the "vinegar" continued, the slow-moving vehicle timidly followed a road clearly no other had driven through except for a similar tractor. At first dark on the last day of March 1943, the ghost soldiers with the two Japanese concubines in tow had fully defended their lives with the Moro guerillas and civilians. Some of them were also the hunted bandits and animal rustlers seen in Dapecol. They were all drinking coconut wine and smoking Chesterfields, Camel, and Lucky Strike. Life was getting better, a lot better.

Travelling to an unknown destination of constantly changing topography, the fear of the Japanese encounter could not be ignored. Many hills and deep creeks enveloped by darkness on narrow dirt roads, many kilometers ahead to nowhere but dark shadows of trees and mountains, the fear was wiped away by the shots of sour wine that kept on coming in overflowing cups. Everyone kept on drinking anyway. In about six hours, they entered an alley between limestones and trees. Cab lighted up another cigarette; he started breathing normally as darkness allowed no more to see in the distance. His head began spinning too. The tractor slowed down to a halt; they must have reached their destination. Pitch black around, the moon had yet to shine to reveal how the party had multiplied along the way. He could not even locate Santos or Agustin among the people. Some questions needed answers, but they were detracted by another cup of wine. They were just on his side, had never been away. Something was happening to him. He could hear Donono, but he just could not see him. People lined up on the road, some animals too. Just like in Dapecol when evacuees would line up to watch prisoners coming back from details. He was losing his orientation, like the effect of severe starvation but with his belly full—well, mostly of *tuba*.

There were a few Tagalog-speaking individuals drawn by the screaming and waving of hands of excited people. It was just too dark to recognize each other. Again, food was handed over. What they didn't understand was they kept hearing their names shouted among the crowds. "Donono!" He was the most famous of all. They all disembarked to hug or salute back to people who made them think about who would know Donono in this place, he could not be that famous. They recognized a few who said they had been in

Dapecol for some time, maybe as evacuees or peddlers and traders. The reunion was emotional but also happy. The encircling of the tuba cup continued. A lot of stories and anecdotes would be told in between for the next three hours from the remnant soldiers of the Sixty-First Field Artillery Regiment of the Philippine Army. Not many as they identified themselves. Among the group was Pvt. Aldo Damueg to reunite himself with the escapees. A Muslim and best buddies with the late Abu Benghalid and Hombre Donono, they were all accomplices of the Fifty-Seventh Scouts in the disbanded unit branded as impertinent thieves by the American POWs. Donono described them as the best of his gang that could provide almost about anything there was in Dapecol to sell. Americans must have been very happy and relieved when they "died." Damueg had informed them that the *Seven Seas* was found in Kauswagan in northern Lanao province.

"Where is Sergeant Malvo, I haven't see him yet," Cabarles had to ask again the whereabouts of another escapee. He was concerned about Malvo as it was to him that was assigned the most important aspect of their journey.

"He must be waiting for your coming, sir. He should be back in the camp by now. We are happy to see you all again," Damueg said, so proud.

"How is the Japanese doing around these area? Are there many?" Cabarles asked before another shot of wine again.

"Yes, there are many. They move in convoys but only on the main roads from town to town and between garrisons," Damal answered. "Nobody bothers them as you ordered."

"Collaborators, are there any?" Santos said this time.

"None in this part of Mindanao, all these men that you can see are recruits of the reinforced guerilla group operating in Lanao. There are more waiting to welcome your coming, sir," Damal said. "So feel safe and secured, we are all going to die first before you. We are all honored to serve in your command," he declared to the drunk soldiers.

Santos knew he was starting to feel differently too, but his senses remained intact. Cabarles felt that he was going to puke. Donono was overly talkative, but they just kept on drinking. All the people had their eyes on them, trying to understand what they were saying

About seventy kilometers were taken out in the convenience of tractors for three hours. They were led to the foothills far north of Mount Ragang. From the shadow created by moonlight were assembled huts along the lines of trees and boulders of rocks on the background. The long journey was over before midnight, for the meantime.

The escapees had multiplied in number to over two hundred men, which also included three Americans. They were attempting to salute or shake hands with obviously tired or drunk soldiers who couldn't even keep their legs straight as they tried to salute back. Only Guido Agustin could walk by himself. Cabarles had to be assisted by Santos on the two hundred yards they must walk. Donono passed out immediately as soon as he saw a flat surface to lie on. Rosie and Myra stayed with Cabarles. Having a prior experience in attending to Cab in such condition, Rosie took off extra clothes from her personal gear and wear it on him. The night was still young for a many other souls that remained awake; the soldiers had all fallen asleep.

Cabarles would express a vague memory when he woke up in the morning. "I slept very well, I thought I was in heaven," he said.

"Yeah, I heard that one already. You were not with Rhoda last night," Rosie replied.

"I swear I smelled her perfume all night, I really thought I did."

"You're wearing her blouse."

He didn't respond to check himself but smelled both sleeves of the shirt, confirmed the scents of Rhodora on him. He closed his eyes and lay down again.

"Cab, are you all right?" Donono asked, who had just awakened, still groggy and discomfitted.

"Yeah, I am," he replied while beginning to ponder on what suddenly came to his mind.

"You look different," Donono exclaimed.

THE SCENTED BLOUSE

Sitting all together in a long bench, all four, still recovering from the effects of tuba, had no idea they were being diverted from the planned route to satisfy an invitation. The comfort they had, being reunited with the trusted allies from Dapecol, was the reason they were overjoyed and confident. Their reunion progressed around a rectangular bamboo table, full of gratitude and jubilation, reminiscing the idea that using the dead would work beyond anyone's imagination. The bold lettering, "Abu Benghalid lives" that was written by Malvo on the wall of Barracks No. 6 started the idea. "If he died and lived, we can do it too." It sealed the plan of making the dead walk in Mactan.

Letting four other prisoners escape ahead had resulted to the greatest advantage of them all. A safer route was established with Myra and Rosie to consider. With covert coordination that also required the utmost camaraderie, the partakers had maintained and continued on ambiguous tasks that other routes remain viable for the benefit of those who were also planning to escape—the Americans.

Discredited by certain guerilla troops in the mountain range of Mount Makaturing as another group of misfit Filipinos, they were most likely to die even before they could execute their escape plan, like those who had already tried. The reason to abandon the plan on Christmas eve was primarily caused by futile effort to seek armed support from the guerillas known to exist in Mindanao. An escape party with a tail of entire Japanese forces in southern Philippines could not be given support and seek refuge in an American camp nor facilitate assistance for safe passage to their territory that may jeopardize the secrecy of their camp. Rabong and the Moros had resorted to seeking help from civilians and known tribes in Lanao. It was twice the distance but safe for unarmed and slow-moving escapees.

Coordinating an escape from two different prisons simultaneously were deemed possible, but the planners could not discount the vulnerability of women to sustain an unguided journey to an unknown destination provided they got out of prison. Rhodora X had insisted on planning to include a less-challenging route while avoiding firefight with escapees from Paradiso in mind. The escape was celebrated as successful and ingenious. However, it could only be done exclusively within the Filipino ranks with the meticulous coordination of serious participants. It would never be retold as no one could actually confirm it happened nor was it believable in the manner it was executed. In Dapecol, no one had yet ever escaped and lived to tell the tale.

Cab, the man who initiated and directed the escape was overwhelmed by the complications of the succeeding events he incurred to himself since he spent a night in Paradiso. He was tormented of leaving one behind. How could he let Rhodora stay?

"Do you miss her?" Rosie wanted to know.

"Yes, I do. The same feeling since I met her. I cannot stop blaming myself for letting her stay. I may not have persuaded her enough to come with us, and it's bothering me," he confided to Rosie.

"She made up her mind only that day. I believe she would have come if you insisted. I missed her too, very much," Rosie stated.

"I can't get her off my mind, I love her more than I thought I do. I had seen her smiling, I don't know how she can still do that."

"Because she loves you too. I know because she confided in me. But there are so many things to be considered. Your competition is very powerful. You should know how much influence Rhoda had made to ease the sufferings of the prisoners. Not just for you, not for Myra and me or her parents, but also for all those we left in prison."

"Yes, I am aware of that. I worried about her so much that whatever I do she's in my mind. Should I be telling you this?"

"You're as complicated and confused as she is. Rhoda knows you're a married man, Rina told her. Yet she truly cares for you."

"I should be very ashamed of myself."

"You shouldn't be."

"You don't understand what I meant. When I left my wife, she was also in tears, forgiving and understanding that I left her in vain. It's over a year I don't know what happened to her. I cannot imagine how much longer until I see her, maybe another year or no more. I left Rhoda just the same. Is it love or pity I feel for her? It was not important, but it was a chance I should have redeemed myself of my mistake the first time. I shouldn't have left without her."

"There's so little you know about her and yet you talk like you truly love her. She's truly beautiful and kind that she offered herself to you. How much more do you think she can take in breaking her heart? Should you find her on your side now, would you be happy while thinking somewhere else there's someone waiting for you? How would she take it?" Rosie paused for a while.

"I am glad she is still capable of the feelings she bestowed on you, but don't make it too hard for yourself than it is for her. You're not the only one, there is Maeda. There are many more who will do just the same you said you will do for her. I believe she can find peace to continue what she did for us and to others. She's very pretty, all right, but she is also courageous and intelligent. She will survive." Rosie paused again.

"I don't know if I will see her again. I'm afraid I will not see her again, and I am longing for her." Cabarles sighed in resignation.

"Very nice blouse, Cab." Santos came back from associating with the people of Lanao.

Cabarles did not respond. He smelled it but he was unaware how it looked.

What changed the mind of Rhodora X could only be regarded as the ultimate sacrifice. Cabarles admitted he was not man enough to disclose who she really was. Her involvement in their escape had proven there's no better way it could have been done.

The communications network implemented in secrecy while in prison was not a secret anymore as it had reached the town of Bayabao in Lanao. In this far land from Dapecol, there were people who also took part in their escape. Or at least there were people who said they took part one way or the other. Cabarles reiterated that there was not enough words to express his gratitude.

It may only be pity or a random act of kindness that began in saving the life of a dispensable soldier, but the subsequent outcome inspired serious support to the same man seeking redemption for promises he had forsaken. There was a father, and a daughter. He was not sure if he thanked them enough, he would always said that his gratitude cannot be expressed by words.

The resulting effects of an escape of the prisoners must remain unknown to the Japanese and the entire POW population left in Dapecol. The only people who knew eight soldiers who died in rice paddies were alive consists all extraordinary civilians who had a chance to say goodbye to them in person. The kindness they gave existed everywhere they go. Their story ended just like the others—a tale to tell that will fade in time. In Dapecol, when a dead gets buried, their legacy ends. The legend of Dominador Cabarles was short-lived. His body was burned in a wildfire that took three days to extinguish itself. He was alive, sure, all he needed was to keep it that way.

THE OFFICER IN COMMAND

Santos was talking with known acquaintances from Dapecol when he was approached by the American soldiers for the second time. Their eagerness to meet the ghost soldiers were always held with inattention. The thrills and excitements did not include their presence. The guerillas and escapees were noticeably avoiding them because of the language variation being one of the reasons, there were others that they must worry about seriously. Santos and Guido were nice enough to respond when approached. In their understanding, the Americans came a day ahead from an unknown place.

"We traveled a long ways to meet you here, soldiers," said the leader, introducing himself a lieutenant through another soldier who was translating. Everyone was listening. "Our commander gave an order for all of you to report immediately in his command. Our mission here is to secure your safety and redirect you to our camp." The officer showing authority by no means also showed aggravation for not getting any attention despite the kinds of weapons they were carrying.

Lieutenant Santos and Guido, consulting with each other, reluctantly replied, "We are also pleased to see you here, gentlemen, especially to know you're concerned for our safety now." Santos finally spoke in English. "I know what 'long ways' mean, that's how we got here too. Please calm down . . . too early in the morning to get aggravated," he added.

"Very good, someone speaks English here. Are you the officer in charge?"

"I am Lt. Rodrigo Santos, Fifty-Seventh Scout Group, please come with me."

"Lt. Lambert Stanford here, Lieutenant Santos." He saluted the Filipino officer that was comply right up before they eased up. "My privilege to meet you, Lieutenant. My commanding officer will be very happy to meet you and your men in our camp." He noticeably toned down when he learned that Santos was also an LT. He was speaking to an equal rank.

"The decision is not mine, Lieutenant. I am not the officer in command."

"Who is?"

"Captain Dominador Cabarles. Come with me," Santos replied.

Cabarles and Rosalia were still having a serious dialogue about who really was Rhodora. What the X about?

"Nice blouse, Cab," he said as he entered the shack. The Americans were behind him.

Cabarles may have something more to say in personal disclosures with Rosie, but his attention was taken outright by Santos.

Wearing a blouse that couldn't be mistaken it was owned by a woman did not worry Cab nor Santos. It had hand-embroidered laces adorned with a little ribbon around the neck.

"Looking good, Cab, looking very good," Santos commented.

Though skinny, the said blouse fit tight and showed his belly button when he stood up. Cabarles scratched his chin to gesture that he had not shaved for Santos to comment that he looked good.

The Americans looked at each other; the persevering impatience was worsening to conclude that they were being railroaded. The man they were about to meet did not characterize a soldier to be the officer in command of a thousand men. Cab momentarily displayed an unusual smile to react on the remarks of the lieutenant. The alarming situation they put themselves into increased with a little amusement. A man truly in a blouse and a diminutive man fit the description of the tribesmen they had seen many times, lazily trying to get up to the voice of Lieutenant Santos. Maybe Donono was surprised to see Americans again. He rubbed his face few times. Then Myra came carrying another cup of cocoa that took his attention.

"There are gentlemen here who wanted to see you, Cab," Santos stated.

Around eight o'clock in the morning, the sun was so bright through the shade of layers of coconut leaves. The captain was still reminiscing his dreams, otherwise enjoying the soft and fragrant shirt he was wearing. He slept well on it that it inspired uninterrupted pleasant dreams, better preserved the scents till it last. He took it off to change into his old one while conversing with the ladies. Behind him five feet away were the soldiers; to see him shirtless was more shocking. They ridiculed him for wearing a blouse; they could not look at him without it.

"He is my CO." Santos walked over to inform him of the presence of the Americans and their mission. He briefed him a little about the purpose of the people who wanted to talk to him.

Cabarles opposed outright, Santos concurred. The motivation to escape prison was not to join a guerilla command. The objectives remained the same, and it did not include yielding at the command of anybody.

The Americans would have known also that in this part of the Philippines, they were hated as the enemy of the unforgotten American-Filipino war fought fearlessly by the Moros. The Moros never forgot. An American who would dare to enter the domain of predominantly Moro people in arms against a new breed of enemy was a brave American. They needed no time to waste but get to the bottom of their brave mission. Cabarles and Santos snubbed an order from a colonel who was the same officer who denied them help when they asked for it. The GI Joes left to go back to their camp in Mount Makaturing. The escapees could not be recruited as they also refused to walk halfway back.

The cold acceptance from their host was understood; however, the Americans were impressed by the sheer number of guerillas assembled in one place. If given arms and proper training, they were enough to liberate the whole island of Mindanao from the Japanese. The assembly of guerillas was made through the efforts of sergeants Rabong and Malvo, both serious and intelligent soldiers whose mission was very specific—to be let out of prison ahead of time, to recruit and organize forces that could suppress Japanese pursuits if ever needed.

Four soldiers went ahead; they were tasked initially to reestablish contacts with any armed resistance that could reinforce the escapees in a bold plan that hatched in October. The only group at hand were the cattle rustlers at the time whose loyalty was recognized during the mass buffalo escape from Mactan. Joined by Abu Damal and Damueg shortly, Malvo and Rabong kept their orders to find a viable route for the rest of the escapees while seeking assistance from known guerilla organizations in the area. Rabong had accounted that they were rejected outright in trying to communicate with the Americans known to exist in Makaturing, said to be in several hundreds. Instead, the soldiers were suspected as spies solely for a reason they could not prove they were escapees themselves.

Though the aid of the bamboo runners was proven effective and there was no other dependable means to turn to, the option that was left was to utilize the inhabitants. It was a good idea, but an underlying problem existed—they were secluded and hostile people already pushed in deeper into the wilderness from the foothills of Mount Makaturing and Ragang. However, learning that a tribesman was among the party who would pass their village, described as a valiant huntsman and soldier wounded in many battles, the T'bolis proudly yielded for all the assistance they could give. They were not lied at; that soldier was Hombre Donono. That explained why he was treated like a king by the natives.

Donono's tribal origin was unknown. Though he was adopted by the T'bolis as their own, he could only describe himself as *kaibigan* (friend), which signified a unifying factor. And with his close associations with the Moro in Dapecol, in Lanao, he was already famous even before they set foot out of Davao.

Another problem that should be eliminated was that Dominador Cabarles, Lt. Rodrigo Santos, Guido Agustin, and the Paradiso escapees were all Catholics who were trying to gain access to Muslim land. They must be accompanied by Muslims while crossing the province; otherwise, they could get their heads cut off along the way no doubt. Abu Damueg made sure it would not happen.

March 16, 1943, the disappointed Americans were gone. More people were coming in groups, men and women, a few dragging stubborn cows in short ropes. Others might have come earlier or were residents in the area; all together, they were greeting each other. One who also came in a nicely dressed entourage was Datu Benghalid.

"I'm honored to meet you again, gentlemen," he said.

Bragging immediately that he had an army by the thousands, the datu repeated that the escapees were in a safe place and protected under his domain. The Christians became at ease to spend a few days in the land, having confirmed that a few cows were to be killed in their honor. Evidently telling the truth of having an army by the thousands, the datu admitted they were not capable of waging war against the Japanese as they had no weapons to equal the Japanese arsenal. The shortage of material supplies were not important; Moros were used to being barefooted and half naked at any weather condition. Indeed, the need of rifles to warrant a soldier was overwhelming. Training was already ongoing, with weapons of bolos and mainly relying on the old guerilla tactics learned while defending against the Americans. Training somewhat was not a problem; Rabong was adamant that firing a gun could be learned at anyone's backyard provided they had the weapon. The arms and ammunition could only come from one source—from the Americans.

As Lieutenant Santos viewed the situation, the Americans at Mount Makaturing did not want to join forces with the Moros; to unify with them would mean training and arming them. They could not allow that to happen in anticipation that they can turn against them at any time. For them, the Moros were opportunists and could not be trusted; the sentiments were mutual. In addition, the Moros also despised the Luzonians particularly the Tagalogs for easily embracing the Westerners and their way of life. Pure Tagalog and a Christian, Cabarles was aware that he could get his head cut off at any time in this part of Mindanao. Without Santos translating the dialect, he would not know what they were saying.

Aside from the datu himself, there were guerillas waiting for their chance to get acquainted with the escapees. A few identified themselves to be from Bohol, sailing across the sea to escape relentless pursuits of the Japanese in their province.

Cabarles and Santos was happy with what the advanced party of their escape had accomplished. Their only intention of giving specific orders to them was only to make sure their escape route would be safe and to pay respect to the gratifications to a datu and his factions who had maintained an invitation and expected them at an earlier date that they didn't make. While doing so, the orders also included advising every guerilla organization to suspend all campaign against the enemy. The hideous reason was to lessen Japanese incursions against civilians and cease chasing bandits and guerillas, hence minimizing a chance encounter with the enemy while the escapees were running in the middle of nowhere. While out of action, the guerilla leaders were told to carry out orders reinforcing and recruiting while considering a unified battle force that could match the might of the Japanese. Orders were given by Kapitan Domeng though nobody knew he even existed. Admittedly, they went overboard undermining the loyalty and capability of Malvo and Rabong, so did with Damueg and Amal.

Miniscule of intelligence in military planning and strategies like the educated and trained combatant officers of USAFFE and Philippine armies in front of him, he was totally at a loss moreover when he is addressed as "Captain Cabarles." In addition, he didn't have the incisiveness of these people who called him "sir." He had no clue how to deal with the situation, but in the presence of Lieutenant Santos who would translate the discussion followed by his own opinions, it could lead to firm decisions.

FIRST MAN ACCOUNTED

Enter the scene is Luis Malvo, jubilation paused all arguments about collaborators in very dramatic way. The first of the escapees was accounted in person, brave men in tears of elation, which altered the atmosphere in expressive emotion without considering that they were supposed to be brave men. No one should cry. Luis eventually regained his composure to reveal that his mission had been accomplished; then he introduced the new faces in his company.

Among the group was Lieutenant Joselito Makalintal under the command of Caprain Macario Peralta of the Sixty-First Infantry Battalion based in Negros. He sailed from Negros after receiving a message from Lt. Luis Malvo, who was a personal ally. They had fought together against the Japanese attack in Macahalar Bay in northern Mindanao and had lost contact since then. Malvo had managed to communicate with Makalintal in mid-January while in the shores of Iligan Bay at the town of Ubod while working on a boat. Makalintal was a dedicated soldier and well-respected officer currently heading a guerilla operations in Panay Island. He had decided that the message he received was too important; it involved escapees requesting assistance and indicating interest to join his command. The message verified through reliable sources, he was ecstatic to reunite with Malvo who convinced him to journey deeper in Lanao. He was proud to meet the escapees. Cabarles and his group were still recovering from sleep deprivation and muscle pain or the effects of *tuba*. Cabarles and Santos found themselves dealing with a difficult situation that resulted to undermining the intelligence and capability of Malvo. The concept of aiming one bullet to hit two targets backfired. Malvo and Rabong were given multiple tasks individually. One survived was sufficient; both survived and able to accomplish all the missions they threw at them was not projected. Makalintal expressed that the escapees were welcomed if they chose to settle in Negros.

Datu Benghalid presented his clan as a unified guerilla organization in the whole Cotabato and Lanao province to the leadership of Kapitan Domeng, which consisted of about ten thousand combatant Muslims. That was most likely including elderlies and probably children to justify the numbers. He voiced out his intent to avenge the painful death of his son caused by the Japanese. The old man wanted to go back to Davao and raid Dapecol.

Cabarles realized that the responsibility on his shoulders is beyond what he is capable of acheiving and comprehending. Just resolving the issues he saw around of about one thousand who came for firearms was not attainable; he was reminded of the revolver in his satchel. Santos explained that to arm the entire Benghalid clan and themselves, they would need resources that only Americans can possibly provide. Moreover, they needed the influence of a general to arm and command a guerilla force of ten thousand. "Then you shall be a general," the datu declared to Cabarles, recognizing that he could unite Christians together with the Muslims. They had a good chance at sending the Japanese back to their country of origin. But it wasn't that easy explaining the situation to an old man citing their own battle against the Spaniards and the Americans in the past.

A veteran fighter in the previous American-Filipino war, the elder Benghalid rose to an influential and prominent authority in the Moro lands of Mindanao. Having three wives of his own that ran in his bloodline, just the number of his family and immediate relatives was close to a thousand. He said that all of them were ready to fight any foreign forces that kept on meddling over their way of life. Perceptive that Cabarles had his own sentiments against the Americans and in fact known to avoid them all throughout his detention in Dapecol, the datu reiterated that he would rather be at Cabarles's command than be a subordinate to Americans. They would fight with the same weapons they used to wage every war against invaders of their land;

if bolos and bamboo stakes they have, so be it. But he had to be reminded that the modern weapons the enemy had in their arsenal could wipe out an attacking thousands in a matter of minutes from a distance. In addition, the retribution of the current enemy, even to the oblivious civilians, is unimaginable. They must consider patience and opportunity.

Makalintal had agreed, coming to like how calm the escapees were in handling the situation. Having been disclosed that Cabarles was a captain in rank and in disguise as a lowly soldier, he was also briefed on what this man was capable of and had gone through to become a living legend. He revealed that a certain Col. Randolph Pertig was based in Ozamiz, and intelligence sources indicated that he kept a lot of ordnance in storage. He could be contacted to affiliate the Moro and Scout Command with his forces.

The name was familiar to Santos, who remembered Pertig from the time of Capt. Ernest Maish in the beginning of the Japanese attack way back in Luzon. He was a major then; they could not believe that he also made it to Mindanao. He should have hidden himself well because his name did not surface with all the intelligence they gathered, nothing was mentioned about him. The explanation was carried out by Luis Malvo. The Moros may have known his existence, but it was the pride that persisted to seek help from an American who didn't want to come out from his hiding. A light suddenly came to Santos's brain to get themselves out of the situation, at the same time preserving their honor without reneging the call of duty.

Turning down an offer to travel in Negros Island, Luis Malvo and Digos Amal together with Makalintal volunteered to find ways and establish contact with Pertig. In the morning, they left in small contingents carrying messages. They had to do it as soon as possible, taking advantage of Japanese slack on field patrols that would not be for long when the marines in Dapecol broke out. In retrospect, the message indicated, "To General Randall Pertig: Escapees from Dapecol to report for duty with ten-thousand-strong guerillas combat forces. Please confirm respond." The message sender were Captain Dominador Cabarles and Lt. Rodrigo Santos.

SERIOUS SOLDIERS

A colonel having no command of his own except for a radioman and a civilian cook who fled with him from Bataan and maybe a bunch of fishermen who hid him in their homes to date, Pertig's credibility as a commander had been under scrutiny among the Filipino guerilla leadership, to the Muslims specially and likewise among the Americans. He was rumored among fishermen that Pertig was keeping caches of arms and supplies from Allied submarine that surfaced recently in Iligan Bay. Aside from his cook, he also trusted nobody.

Back in December at Dapecol, suspected collaborators were left alone and seemed to be enjoying that the advantage of siding with the invaders was a right decision. Unknown to them, their activities were being evaluated by the newly formed council of selected officers to decide on their downfall. There were too many on the list that Sergeant Guido Agustin disclosed he had, mostly Christians by name. He made the list with the Moros. Rhodora X is on the list. Left nothing to do until Malvo returned, Santos and Cabarles reviewed the said names until only one left, Ruben Pablo. Cabarles could not care less about the man but in the end he just burned the paper.

Rosalia Brown had already acquainted herself with the Boholanos, she was updated of the situation in the province.

In March 19, thirty days since they left Davao, the escapees from Davao were feeling restless in the camp. Though they made their stay in the guerilla camp useful, the plan of continuing the journey was always the topic of talks after a long day. Myra and Rosie helped in cooking meals while the soldiers lent hands in the training of recruits. Cabarles assigned himself in teaching how to shoot imaginary birds with available rifles. Santos and Agustin conduct classes in reconnaissance. Donono remained in the vicinity of pots and pans where he also helped in food preparation. There was nothing that could make his day fulfilled than be where Myra was.

The long wait for the return of Malvo was making Cabarles anxious. In Misamis, Malvo and Damal had finally met with the general. It didn't take too long to commit the man on the nature of their business. Locating him was harder than they thought it would be. Makalintal went back to his headquarters in Negros but gave words of assurance to Pertig that his commander, Captain Macario Peralta, with a twenty-thousand-strong guerilla force would maintain contact with him. Makalintal left for Panay as a lieutenant. His role in convincing the distrustful "general" in the legitimacy of the existence of many guerillas willing to fight in his command was noted according to Malvo. There was one problem—the ten-thousand-strong guerilla camp was in Lanao, in Moro land.

Pertig was cautious of the Filipino officers at first but was told that the escapees were formerly in the unit of the Fifty-Seventh Scout Group commanded by Capt. Ernest Maish; he could not pass up on jumping at the opportunity. He knew Maish well enough—another commander without men to command, currently a major and recruiting. If Pertig would discard the message of ten-thousand-strong guerillas who addressed him as general, then most likely they would turn to Maish for leadership. He knew that the major, was vying for the same glory. In fact, one of them didn't like to be under the command of the other. Maish claimed that he was the commanding officer of Sixty-First Brigade in Mindanao as soon as he set foot in the island. Pertig believed he was. Learning that the Dapecol escapees who wanted to meet him was formerly under Maish's unit, the opportunity was worth the risk for the glory. Suddenly thrilled to realize that the soldiers who addressed him as general were the same soldiers whose unbelievable bravery and heroism he heard from a rival officer himself. They were reporting back to duty to the Sixty First Division, which certainly was an honor; and at the same time he can exceed the legacy of the other. He could have a star for real. Presumed dead but were all incredibly alive and leading a massive guerilla operation in the second largest island of the Philippines, retaining the command of Fifty-Seventh Scout Division. Pertig may not knew the escapee but in no way he would allow them the chance to establish contact with Maish.

What he knew about the escapees was hearsay: "Cabarles giving cover while allowing his commanding officer run from a sure death." His cook was telling events that was hard to believe; he said he would never forget the men fighting intensely at the same time taking good care of each other. He would not expect them to get out of that hill alive, all three of them on a battle that caused the death of many brave men who tagged along on the journey. He knew the story from Maish himself in a meeting that turned sour. By all it matters, the story was corroborated by his cook and personal assistant, Joaquin San Pedro, that such names of soldiers exist, confirming they were the same soldiers he was with from Pampanga. Pertig corresponded with all the request of the escapees a fellow officer had abandoned in the heat of battle but still loyal to the Fifty-Seventh as their command unit. There was nothing he can think of in his possession that he could not give to them considering the urgency of the requests. "Everything we got," he ordered San Pedro who gladly followed. If intelligence was true, he didn't want to show up empty-handed in the adjacent province he was told of tales that many Americans disappeared without a trace.

The escape story was hard to believe, but there were guerillas in the thousands that was up for grab to gain a star. He decided to meet these extraordinary men so much for the respect and honor they had reserved for him. Addressing him as general was enough, but reporting back to duty after escaping undetected from the heavily guarded POW camp in Davao with command of an infantry was hard to believe. He must meet the men himself. How they had done that altogether in so short of a time was not important, but he wanted to see them in person, meet the ghosts of escaped prisoners of Dapecol.

On March 24, the escapees were discussing the next leg of their journey. All was prearranged as promised by the Moros with Rabong to guide their way. Around four in the afternoon, Malvo came back from Ozamiz at a time when hope for his return was exhausted. The "general" himself was leading the group of men carrying several military boxes and supplies. The sight of rifle caches somewhat came at no better time. Inspired and spirit renewed, the guerillas in the background saluted as commanded with the pride and respect to a general passing through. Like real soldiers but all eyes on the boxes.

Informed that Malvo just came with an American by his side, they went out of the shed to see the cause of jubilation. Well, Malvo certainly never stopped amazing them. He was told to contact the man with the message in hand; he came back with the general himself. Pertig was farfetched as to the discipline in the camp; he glanced at every soldier in salute while identifying their rank and names. Donono was no doubt as he was described as his cook happily singled him out among the crowd in tremendous elation, not too much of a change in appearance as he was described. He was most interested with the other two, good-looking and clean-shaven young men saluting him awkwardly. Pertig complied. As always, all the talk would be through Santos.

San Pedro had no other way to express his feelings but cry at the sight of the men who saved his life numerous times. How he became the sidekick of the general is unknown; he would tell his story later to Donono. The escapees turned combat instructors Agustin, Rabong, and Damueg had stolen a moment of attention from Pertig, identifying themselves and brief him as fast as they could of the situation around the camp. Pertig became more confident; he was respected and looked up as the man who could lead them all supposedly. All eight soldiers escaped from Dapecol was reporting back to duty. In his coming, another cow must die.

The next words from Pertig was presenting "all that we have" to the loyal soldiers of the Fifty-Seventh, promising more to come in mutual cause. All were happy for the graces that they thought was not possible in this remotest of a jungle that only the brave American would dare to come. The conference room without walls but palm roofing and long bamboo table that also served as officers' mess hall, conference and accommodation was filled up again with food over banana leaves. No official business yet, just hospitality to the general. Though Pertig brought in all the goods that was causing the excitement, most of the praise were extended to Cabarles, Santos, and Donono who could summon a general to attend to their needs personally at a moment's notice.

"We present to you the command of Unified Guerilla Forces in Mindanao," Santos had told General Pertig, informing also of about one thousand present at the time, many more waiting their turns for a formal training as combatants and needing to be armed.

Impressed and honored indeed, the general was also introduced to elderlies of the Moros led by Datu Benghalid. Having learned how to deal with the locals, he took a special box that his staff had prepared and started distributing gifts of foreign liquors and candy bars, even magazines by himself with a sincere appreciation of warm welcome. Lieutenant Malvo and Rabong had to translate, adding more of unsaid words to highlight the bravery of the men all eager to wage war against the enemy at any time in his order. A generous

American, Pertig made a lot friend instantly, especially when the guerillas were informed that he was a general with communications with Allied submarines delivering supplies from Australia. The Moros could care less about those who came from Makaturing with only arrogance to show.

The little Don was so appreciative to San Pedro who actually spared a box of assorted candies for his friend whom he knew had a tremendous appetite despite his size. "Thank you." He said he had something in mind also to brag about.

"Come with me," he told San Pedro. "I will introduce you to someone."

The dishwasher turned fulltime cook and assistant to a general followed naively to a group of men and women in a makeshift kitchen that made them busy all the time. Feeding a thousand men sure would keep them occupied. Myra and Rosie, making themselves useful, had volunteered on the task of chopping vegetables and meat of newly killed animal for supper. Not commonly seen on the table on ordinary days, the feast coincided with the presence of many officers that the last of the cow had to be slaughtered. A box of Hersey bars were given to Myra who shared them immediately to others. Though looking tired and distressed to the sight of Donono that was becoming inconvenient for her, she showed gratitude to the thoughtfulness of the little guy who obscured his real intention of showing off by introducing an old ally.

AN HONEST TRANSLATOR

The hierarchy of the officers in command was already established even before the arrival of Lt. Col. Randall Pertig. As he was told, he was given the full command of the entire guerilla organizations affiliated to the command of Cabarles. The only hindrance for him was he had a counterpart in the person old Benghalid. Santos and Cabarles had thought that it would be important to establish trust and loyalty between the Muslims and the American. The datu was honored indeed but tried his best to the escapees to stay in Lanao. Pertig also did not approve initially with the plan when he was enlightened that the scouts were leaving Mindanao. Santos was very good in correlating his wit to get out of difficult situations only to benefit Cabarles's intentions. He concealed that purpose into justifying a guerilla operation unified as far as the Visayas islands to Luzon was the main objective. With Boholanos also seeking help of reinforcements in their province, the mission was sanctioned by his officer in command (Cabarles) that help it was they need they shall have. The "general" failed to make Cabarles or Santos stay despite offers of best position in his command of their own choosing. Cabarles maintained he would go back to Inez. Santos translated to Pertig that his order was given before he showed up and they could only keep their words to the Boholanos with what they do best—recruitment and organization, intelligence gathering, and communications to report back in his command. They maintained a low-profile approach, having more qualified officers who could do the job. Lt. Luis Malvo was one, and the rest of the escapees would stay in his command. In so doing, Cabarles, Santos, and Donono could stay together to continue on their interisland ventures that should establish communications among guerilla forces known to exist in southern Philippines. Bohol was first on the list with a self-proclaimed guerilla commander from Bohol who was happy to go back to his province of origin with battle-experienced and intelligent guerilla strategist.

According to Engineer Ysmael, a former public works official turned guerilla leader, in Bohol, the resistance were fighting each other for recognition with conflicting principles, and many disastrous campaign against the enemy had caused them to leave the island for a while as the Japanese had put bounty on their heads. Previously furious against the turncoats, which may have cooled down with the insights of the planners of ingenious Dapecol escape that heavily involved the civilians, Ysmael admitted that he might be wrong to lay all the blame to locals suspected of working with the Japanese.

Ghost soldiers they would be with mandated official missions under the Fifty-Seventh Scout Unit; expressing intentions to sail with them back to Bohol was more than enough help they can get. They were elated that their affiliation with the Filipino resistance movement in Mindanao was taken "very seriously."

In pursuit of recognition as a leader of legitimate guerilla group in Bohol, Ysmael had reiterated his alliance to Cabarles and Santos.

Addressed as *Ingeniero* (Engineer) Ysmael, he was indeed an engineer. Cabarles didn't want to discard the former title as it might be disrespectful to the older man. Agustin and Santos followed suit that when Pertig officially commissioned him as a lieutenant, he became known as Lt. Ingeniero Ysmael reporting in the command of Sixty-First Division. Pledging alliance and loyalty with the Fifty Seventh Scouts, his first order was "refrain killing suspected collaborators, befriend them to help you kill the real enemy, the Japanese."

Pertig express discontent one more time to let Cabarles and Santos go to Bohol. He had tried his best in vain but did not push too much. He already had established himself as commander of a division-sized and well-organized guerillas, what else could he ask for? On the other hand, he was worried that if the escapees would know that Maish was alive, no doubt they would turn their loyalty back to him. He had also noticed that most Filipinos who would be all in his command were showing more respect and confidence to Cabarles and Santos drunk or sober than him, including his cook, to make it worse that could not elude his observation. He decided to let them go as far as they wanted, send them out in a mission; out of Mindanao would be better. He promoted all escapees one rank up, with the exception of Engineer Ysmael who was commissioned as a lieutenant. Malvo became his chief of staff on the recommendation of Santos who was offered first but turned it down, explaining he had committed himself to Cabarles. Cabarles would lead the Fifty-Seventh Reconnaissance and Intelligence command, which Santos had invented, and he would remain his executive officer. Malvo was happy and proud with the new position, which he deserved. With his proven record and expertise in public relations and politics, his official responsibility would give the barefoot soldiers a better representations and share of material supplies. His organizational skills was valued as an important asset of the Fifty-Seventh in addition to his dedication as a soldier, following orders without question and getting things done.

Rabong was the communications chief, which he was very good at. Guido Agustin, also became a lieutenant, was the head honcho of the base camp. Aldo Damueg and Digos Amal were drill sergeants together with a dozen 'cattle rustlers' from Dapecol, all of whom were more interested on the insolent collaborators they knew in Dapecol. Looking for the list that they helped to make, they were informed that

Ruben Pablo was the only one left on the entire lists after Santos and Cabarles reviewed the names. They would not forget that man who told the Japanese guards while a soldier was trying to bring in writing pads and pens for their learning class inside Dapecol. Not only that the same soldier, Luis Malvo himself, was beaten up and denied of food and water for two days. In light of the matter, Cabarles reiterated that all civilian employees in Dapecol including the colonos and all those they had seen wearing red dots should not be touched. Malvo and Rabong were revealed that the health mission in Dapecol before Christmas were all participants and major planners of their escape. Like a bombshelling to hear familiar names that the Moro despise, Rosalia added the existence of another prison where she and Myra came from. They also learned that Rhodora X personally oversaw their escape and also a prisoner in Dapecol in the worse situation. It was more than enough information to disregard the list and never to make another one. Santos also added that Abrina is conniving with American prisoners for a major prison breakout with help of the same group of colonos who helped them.

CHAPTER 15

SUNSET IN THE ROSALIA

Back in the sea, scents of a woman fresh in my memory. Dark horizons, bright stars every direction I turn. I left the south, pride regained. My heart is beating, it is not the same. Stars therein I shall bring few to a place where they can shine again. Brothers come shall guide the way.

OVER DARKNESS THERE ARE STARS

The ghost escapees had finally left the guerilla camp before nightfall of April 4. Displaying Garand semiautomatic and Enfields, they rode on the single farm tractor again, heading to the shore of Lake Lanao as total darkness engulfed the forested canopy of hidden paths only the operator would know. In a few hours, the party was welcomed by two people patiently waiting on two motorized fishing boats to cross the lake. For the night, they camped at Maria Cristina Falls; by noontime of April 8, they rendezvoused with the *Seven Seas* renamed *Rosalia* in Kauswagan. The nervous captain had information waiting for them—a day ago, a group of Americans had escaped from Dapecol with confirming details.

The boat was loaded with all kinds of local crops and products to disguise the passengers as local traders. A man named Fernando Viola greeted them with his juvenile son. Darkness engulfed the shore as the boat began sailing immediately.

In another time, in a different place, Cab was looking back to the shore again on the same boat. At dusk, opposite when he left Manila, he could not describe his feelings as they sailed away—no figures to wave back but overgrown trees and coconuts. It was only darkness he saw, but up above, some stars were becoming brighter over land mass. He stayed watching until he got tired of sitting down on the deck. Knees bent tight to hug as he lay his head over it, a woman in mind, it was not the same name. Only he would know how much he carried in his thoughts to remember Mindanao.

The waters of Iligan Bay from the shores of Kauswagan town were calm as the *Rosalia* gained speed as fast as it could. Weary souls, some fell asleep at once taking advantage of the quiet night and cold breeze of the bay. A few were just sitting reminiscing in mind of several experiences while watching that bulk of land mass standing high above the waters and disappearing in the dark—Mindanao, land of kindness and courage, beauty and the braves. Santos and Cabarles knew that on their departure shall commence a battle that would test the endurance of both sides—the Japanese invaders against vindictive people who were hardened by hundreds of years of oppression. Assorted weapons in hand and with natural bravery that flowed in their blood strengthened from the events of the past wars and endless struggle for freedom, it would begin the resumption of bloody gunfights. Confrontations that would give the Japanese a run for their life if they ever set foot in Lanao.

Anywhere they go should be the same as they were told and it can be the worst. What awaited for them in Bohol was yet to be seen. The Boholanos would not leave their island for no reason.

On the boat were fourteen people, five in continuation of their journey, four taking a ride to Bohol. Three were merchants. The other two alternately navigated the boat. The merchants had many stories to fill the gap. From Davao around Cotabato to Misamis, information was heard from ear to ear until it reached theirs and they were all taken with serious worries for the people they left in Davao.

As it was expected, the atrocities had resumed. Prisoners were at constant threat that execution was imminent as retribution. It could not be discounted that everyone wanted to escape, but still it was sad to know that all they had avoided on their own escape was happening. The American POWs had finally found the balls to break out of prison somehow. A village suspected of helping American escapees were burned to the ground outright.

The ghost escapees could only pray, especially for Rhodora X. If she was able to maintain influence over the Dapecol commander after the disappearance of two concubines in Paradiso, the prison break should not cause serious effect other than increased security and summary punishments by starvation and mental coercion within Dapecol. To actually execute ten prisoners per one escapee of ten is a massacre. The Americans would say arrogantly that no serious harm done on their lines but amid of their knowledge and preservation, who would shoulder the wrath of the Japanese were the civilians. The Japanese would hunt the escapees down in full force, and apparently, it had begun.

Northwest had been established as the preferred route to get away from Dapecol. By that notion, they were heading in the region of Cotabato and Lanao. Japanese in pursuit were armed to the teeth, enraged and insulted that there could be no part of the island the escapees could hide. The Americans were expected to be led to the northern part; however, they were also expected to end up in the western provinces to establish contacts with the resistance.

The commanders of One Hundredth Division of the Japanese Imperial Army were right to say that there will be no successful escape from Dapecol without the help of the civilians, but how could they pinpoint who among them? There was no need to do so, left and right atrocities had doubled in their path to innocents. It would be a long way to Lanao where the guerillas would fight them to the end. How many villages they would pass through? Santos and Cabarles could not erase the imminent results from their imagination whom themselves had experiences of their own about the enemy's tenacity.

At first light in the morning, they found their eyes looking at each other; questions on their mind waiting for who should break the silence. None had spoken, but often they looked back where they came from, dark blue and seemingly peaceful but disappearing, they both knew what was taking place. They lighted cigarettes, and in between puffs they looked up to the heaven; it is easy that way. They didn't know what awaited them. Another land mass ahead, the island of Bohol and beyond that offered no assurance that they could get through alive either. In sharing of thoughts, silence was broken by the talkative Martin Liwanag who seemingly knew everything. He was convincing Viola to dock at the most convenient spot for them in Bohol safe from the enemy. He lived in the island, he should know, added the fact that only few weeks ago since they left Bohol.

LET NATURE TAKE ITS COURSE

April 9, in the middle of the Bohol Sea overlooking Camiguin Islands, they thought earlier it was Ysmael's province already. The morning pensive of the escapees was suppressed by loud gunshots from the Boholenos. They could not pass the opportunity of firing their newly acquired weapons to the migrating wild geese flying above. Good meat no doubt that even Santos and Cabarles salivated at the idea, but it was too late, the flock in V formation had veered to the right and flown away. The hullabaloo had awakened the rest of the people on the boat. Donono and the two young ladies from Davao got scared in the beginning but regained awareness as soon as they got up. No more reason to obscure their faces far out of the Muslim land. A hot brew of locally grown cocoa was already simmering on a kerosene stove, with boiled bananas for breakfast.

Donono was missing the apples, grapes, and oranges from Subic Bay. No more of those, but the food for his thought was that he was noticeably happy, very happy that he could actually postpone eating or forget about apples. With Myra exposing her face in the morning breeze, it strengthened his desire to marry her. He was thankful however that the *Seven Seas* never ran out of food and it was not him preparing. Donono and the Boholenos agreed that the wild geese would have been the best meal. His personal and comical accounts had found audiences who interestingly listened, but no one believed him about the stories of Cabarles from the beginning of the war to the current times. Myra could not avoid shedding tears in silence and feeling an extreme sadness when Donono recounted the series of events that caused the death of her parents and how they knew about her. He said that it was only a grand intervention that all three of them were still alive. The Boholenos would find it hard to believe the rest of his story. Good times in Mindanao, none they could think of; even the sight of Dono dancing with the T'bolis was causing them nightmares, the girls said.

Santos, shirtless and grabbing an Enfield close by, was distracted by Ysmael and Martin, apparently there were some accounts from Donono's that needed corroboration to be believable.

"Can you see this scar?" Santos said, pointing to a scar on his chest. "Right where my heart is. It was caused by the point of a Japanese bayonet that went through that man's body." He gestured to the man standing on the bow enjoying the sea breeze against the boat. Santos left the Boholanos with the same disbelief back to Cabarles while loading the rifle in a hurry.

Another flock of birds in the bright horizon flew low in their direction. Cab inspected the rifle that was just handed to him. Birds were coming fast as he aimed at the targets. Just a moment before they were overhead, he had emptied the cartridge of the rifle even before the first bird dropped dead on the water. Five shots in all, but everyone were baffled by the six geese they pulled out from the water. Donono and the others lent hands preparing the birds for lunch. Cabarles stay by the bow with Santos having a good talk like nothing had happened out of the ordinary. The conversation involved the future of Myra, "Should she choose to stay in Bohol with Rosie is fine with me, but we should give her company all the way to Bicol if she wishes." Cab made it clear to Santos.

"That isn't I worry about. Have you noticed Dono lately?"

"What about him?"

"He is always with Myra, he had forgotten about us," Rod said, insinuating that normally Donono would remind them if they had a meal already. Now the sun was way up without indication that the little guy would still do that.

"Well, I don't know what to say. From now on, we just have to serve ourselves," Cab implied, looking at the girl and Don standing close to each other. "What do you think, does Don have a chance?"

"Yeah, definitely, at the point of a bayonet."

"Why did you say that?" Cabarles asked while lighting up a stick of Lucky Strike looking at the pair in question.

"Look at our Don and your adopted daughter. Look at them closely then tell me what you think," Santos implied of Don's hopeless intention and that it would be better for him not to pursue otherwise he will just end up heartbroken and humiliated.

Cab focused his sight on Don and Myra, trying to grasp what Santos meant. He nodded his head. "Yeah, I understand what you mean." Then he continued. "Well, for the meantime we just have to serve ourselves. Let's give him a chance."

Both of them laughed in conformity; there was nothing they could do for now but understand that someone was taking the attention of Donono. Rosie was very kind to take Don's place, citing that he was extremely busy.

It didn't take too long until the ducks were cooking and everyone was resting and waiting. Back on the bow were Cab and Santos. Their usual conversation always involved evaluating the next step and find a mutual decision, always there was careful study of all possible outcomes of their future actions. Back in prison, they could do it endlessly and they could expect to wake on the same place. The situation changed significantly, every time they look afar, the horizon became different. Bohol is a small island. It was a convenience that there were Boholanos in their company. After all, it was the same island they wanted to go first. It was not for Rosalia alone that they were making a stop in Bohol.

The self-imposed mission to begin in Bohol was discussed several times. It was easy by experience to evaluate the problems causing the guerilla unit led by Ysmael. Although their way of thinking about collaborators had changed considerably, Ysmael and Liwanag were annoyingly persuading the ghost soldiers for help to reestablish guerilla command in Bohol. The clear and present problem against them was the constant threat caused by civilians, so they said. Prominent people in Bohol were also believed to be collaborating with the enemy, and they were running out of land to stay, which explained why they ended up in Mindanao. Their exchange of opinion were discontinued by Don approaching with two cups of hot duck soup. They were not forgotten, however, he attempted to bolt out right after.

"Where are you going?" Cab was quick to halt Don who was noticeably taking advantage of every moment babbling on with Myra and Rosie. "*Paihiin mo naman,*" he commented, meaning "Give Myra a chance to go to the restroom." There was none.

In a boat where there was no bathroom and in the company of twelve men they barely knew, how could the girls, shy and distrusting, do their things? Cab was only kidding, a comment said for nothing, but they all realized it was true. No privacy and by now for sure the girls were holding up themselves in the company of a dozen men. Santos had given Donono instructions how to make them one and fast. While doing just that, he told Donono to let the girls come to the bow.

Santos, having more experience with women's behavior and personal needs, could not prevent a burst of silent laugh as the girls walked awkwardly on the moving boat made worse by waves strong enough at times.

"Don't say anything, we already know. Donono is making you one where you can have privacy," Rod told them right away then gave his appreciation that the duck soup was delicious.

"Thank you, sir." Rosie was elated.

Looming ahead of the blue water was the island of Bohol. Rosie had no clue what happened to his family and relatives; her fear was shared by men whose kindness always made it hard for her to believe. What intrigued him the most was they always spent time together talking, doing things together. Rosie must know Cab pretty well by now; however, Santos was just hard to approach. They both were. In the boat where there was basically nothing to do, all that was in her mind was to take advantage of the moment to express her grateful heart. She could not find another word to say that normally she was good at.

"How are you doing so far?" Cabarles asked the younger girl casually.

"We are fine," Myra replied, having difficulty controlling herself.

"Don is taking care of you well enough?" Santos teased a bit, making the girl blushed. He might as well say it clear. "We think that he likes you."

Catching what the lieutenant meant, in her mind, Santos must have looked at Don again and evaluate about what he was insinuating; he must be dreaming too. She smiled in response but hardly so as not to reveal anything of her dislike to the appearance of the man he was endorsing. Unknown to her, the soldiers she respected understood what she may think about the little man, but there was plenty of time to reconsider tenderly and patiently; otherwise, it may really take the other option.

Cabarles must have considered the idea, but he suggested allowing nature take its course. The rest would be easy. Donono seemingly acted as expected, but as how Santos put it, he always fell in love with every female being he saw including a pigeon. Myra was so pretty and young but skilled in manipulating men, even the Japanese. She could handle Donono very easily. What difference will it make? Her young mind and body, forged by abuse and indignation at the hands of the Japanese, could not be impolite to the people who saved her from hopelessness. Santos was not worried that Don would end up broken hearted. It was just beginning, and he was happy to find a real woman to express that he was a man. If Cabarles's way didn't work, then there would be his way. Donono definitely needed help to pursue his intention to the girl.

The makeshift bathroom was done. Donono commissioned the "talent" of a civil engineer and his men in emergency and bragged about it as he informed them that it was ready for use at any time, exclusively for Rosie and Mira. He was appreciated for his effort.

The meal was satisfying. In the middle of the ocean and in time of war, nobody could be picky of the meat they were eating. It was cooked simply and delicious that they all agreed that the boat captain and his fifteen-year-old son, also guerilla operatives, were good cooks. What followed was a long nap for almost everyone. They were awakened in Mabini at the eastern side of Bohol when the engine slowed down to a halt. Fernando Viola was from Misamis and had captained a large commercial fishing and trading boat that sailed to interislands as far as the Bicol Region and Batangas before the war. He knew his way around the waters of the Philippine Islands. He was approached by Lieutenant Malvo to captain the *Seven Seas* as far as the passenger would like to bring them, most likely somewhere in Bicol Region. The vessel was loaded with enough fuel, food, and supplies for nonstop travel if weather permitting. There were stacks of wooden and bamboo crafts of his own to sell that occupied most of the space on the boat, not expecting Ysmael and his company would hitch a ride. Ysmael and Martin had worked hard to convince Fernando to sail across the Bohol Sea to Guindulman Bay. In so doing, they could disembark closest to the village they left a month ago.

IN THE LAND OF MANY HILLS AND VALLEYS

Rosie's family lived in the central part of the island where she intended to reunite and settle. The escapees was left with no choice but to disembark in the Mabini shore east of Bohol. The whole island thrived the Japanese that should have no difference from those in Davao, according to Ysmael. He let them decide where they could embark undetected. The advantage of being with Boholenos was that they could be guided well to the safest place away from the Japanese and collaborators inland. Again in the cover of the dark, they walked through rugged terrains and boulders of limestone on a narrow path at single file that ended in a small house. No good news welcomed them; wounded men and women including an American revealed the remnants of a bloody battle just recently. Rosie made herself busy immediately with the assistance of Myra to attend to the wounded.

Three days ago, the Japanese had raided a guerilla camp in the outskirts of Pilar. All the casualties and missing were men of Ysmael. Among the unaccounted and presumed dead included the wife and mother of Martin Liwanag that made him greatly devastated, his reaction being one asking for immediate revenge in a burst of anger at the enemy and enormous guilt of leaving his family on their own for a few days that had extended too long. The Japanese were not only interested of their heads; they also wanted to annihilate everyone related to them. His grief and rejection of the truth that his wife and mother were dead was felt and witnessed by everyone. The reliability of that information was verified by the people who were able to run and escape to the remotest region of the island. A man in a red shirt and bright overcoat that could be seen even in the bleak kerosene lamp was the one having detailed accounts of the bloody encounter. He added that he also just rejoined the group a few days ago to find them in great forlorn.

In a sudden change of events, the former prisoners of Dapecol convened an immediate discussion. The concern lay immensely on the ladies, especially Rosie who needed to cross the island to get home west of Tagbilaran. Her home province was no better than Davao. No clear decision was made yet as one of them didn't like the idea of turning their back cowardly from the new allies in the tragic situation. Captain Santos firmly wanted to stay until such time his fellow soldiers had recovered. They had the arms and the means to help the people devastated by their loss. Choosing not to interfere on the grieving husband and son, the former POWs were approached by Ysmael who was also angered and tearful, literally begging for help. He said he was like Martin too when he suffered the same loss at the beginning of the war. His only choice then was to retreat to the mountains until he met some refugees, one of them being Liwanag who was said to be a former policeman. Together they formed a resistance group that became too hard to keep as they were being chased every time by the Japanese even in a hidden forest that they thought no one would ever know as their group became larger. The reason why they hated so much all suspected collaborators was that no one else could reveal their position to the enemy, and the suspicion had grown to the limit. A recent terrible event was blamed on a group of former members of the Philippine Constabulary and government officials now working with the Japanese to keep peace and order in the island in the name of the Japanese Imperial Command. But how would they know their whereabouts when those people were concentrated in Tagbilaran, the province capital? The rationale only meant one thing: collaborators in the province were working for the benefit of the enemy in every town they seek refuge in. Were they? With all respect to the vengeful circumstances, the escapees from Davao remained calm and shared in the grieving of the great loss while listening to Ysmael's ranting.

"I had left sixteen men, a few widows and orphaned children," Ysmael sadly told the Fifty-Seventh Scout soldiers. "I don't know what curse I have, but I don't understand why the Japanese seemed to be on my back all the time." He continued in hopeless resignation as he sat flat on the ground.

Since the enemy swarmed in the province and made it their own, the slaughter of innocent civilians were inconceivable, not counting the local forces who tried to defend the strategic location of the island when the Japanese landed in May 17, 1942. There was no significant opposition.

Bohol was a quiet island province south of the Visayas region; the closest was the island of Cebu in the west and Southern Leyte on the northeast due north. The enemy had established a gun base in a small island in the north edge that scared even the small fishing boats in the Camotes Sea. The actions however began inland when Ysmael's group, then led by a more combat-experienced officer, raised arms against the Japanese when atrocities and degradations among the population followed shortly, then they were killed in battle. The only known resistance group that existed was of Ingeniero Ysmael, and the rest of the locals were not cooperating in a reverse effort to end atrocities. The underlying principles were not complicated to understand; the reasoning of the majority who chose to collaborate with the enemy was to save their own life and interests. Majority of the Christians and peaceful settlers were people who played by ear which side would persevere at the end. Many had already embraced the enemy, which was attributed to the past experiences of war when invaders always won. Nothing could be beneficial to raise arms against the Japanese but only the death and destruction of properties.

Captain Rodrigo Santos, seeing the persistent problems of the guerilla operations in Bohol was there's only one known group that defied the Japanese who can concentrate in annihilating them with undivided attention. Knowing that they were short of arms and skills in combat and retreating all the time, the Japs made them constantly running for their life, leaving trails of death and atrocities on the locals along their path. The resulting feedback from the affected peaceful Boholenos to a hopeless cause was if no one will challenge the Japanese strength, then they cannot be caught in the crossfire thus they can avoid agonizing hours of interrogations and tortures that always resulted to death. The first option was to disclose without hesitancy all possible locations of guerillas on the run. Simply, it was a difference in opinion. Cabarles could only agree with Santos; it was a little bit complicated for him, but he was learning.

The morning came when only Martin Liwanag seemed to be the only one brave enough to launch an immediate assault on the enemy; clearly his mind was fixated on suicidal revenge. He was calmed down by Ysmael who was now leaning to a more logical approach, taking advices from ghost officers that such action was futile at the moment. Intelligence gathering and reinforcement must be prioritized. For the meantime, they should find a safer place where they could establish a base with a better defensive position. As a whole, they could be all wiped out by a single grenade. Cabarles was an exceptional hunter; he would know a perfect place to establish a position where he could see a target at the same time a route to retreat from dreadful mortar fire. They walked five more kilometers deeper inland and upward a place overlooking Sierra Bullones. There was a small freshwater spring suitably located in the vicinity and under towering trees. Looking back south were green sceneries that ended with an ocean view and over that was Mindanao. There was no better place to settle with wounded men as well as children.

Fernando, the *Rosalia* captain, and his son were let go to attend to their business, but they promised to come back at a specific date and time on the same mooring. The first order of discussion pertained to the recruiting of civilians to return to their fold. How? They didn't know yet how it could be done. There was none they could think of, but as of now, a move to spread information that the remaining guerilla group was not crushed by the Japanese and joined by soldiers from Mindanao and Negros was made while telling people that a massive number of guerilla forces were preparing to retake the island. It was a strategy that was learned in Dapecol and proven effective. It was lies that would encourage the hopeless to hang on and the braves to show their color. They immediately got attention; one showed keen interest to when and how it would happen, only to be fed by exaggerated information from a general and a cook.

The Japanese base camp is in Tagbilaran, about forty miles away west and Rosie said two miles west of the town, was where her family lived. There was no available information that would warrant a safe travel at the time to let her reunite with her parents. According to Ysmael, the Japanese were everywhere. Not too many as they appeared, but they could throng the guerillas even before they could retreat. Struggling every which way they turned to go, Ysmael was elated that the ghost commanders of the Fifty-Seventh Scouts whose reputations precede them were actually extending help and expertise on how to deal with the enemy. Ysmael submitted himself to the ideas and knowledge of guerilla warfare of the newfound friends who would not leave him in times of desperation. The first thing that was needed for a successful resistance organization was the cooperation of the civilians. Ysmael didn't have them. His group consisted of the majority of locals who lost one or two loved ones and who joined out of revenge, including him, and their numbers were dwindling.

Martin Liwanag was probably the only real soldier left and was currently vindictive as hell. The American in the group was incapacitated because of the multiple injuries from consecutive encounters with the Japanese. Rosie and Myra were taking care of him since they joined the group, thanks to the medical kit and assorted medicines they brought with them from Davao. A soldier, who was the bravest of them all, was thankful for the kindness of the former dancers. He was Lt. Jack Bradford, a young pilot from the Far East Air Force, Twenty-First Pursuit Squadron, last of the defender of Manila Bay, fought hard in a dogfight until he was hit hard and crashed in the water. Local sea traders fished him out of the water and took care of him for several days; eventually he joined and led guerilla forces in Bohol where he ended up. Incapacitated of several wounds, a few healed while some were still fresh, his determination to live and continue fighting against the Japanese earned him the respect of the ghost soldiers. Nothing else could be done to him but let his courage to live take place on his own. Though the Boholenos always took good care of him, at the hands of Rosie, his spirit floated with fresh courage to live. Rosie said she had done everything she was taught to do; she and Myra stayed with him all the time alternately while attending to about a dozen children who were mostly orphaned.

The men in the lead of Donono made shelters immediately in compliance to Santos's command. He made himself busy without a word until he could not see anymore in the dark, Myra could only share hard work that she had to be reminded by Donono in taking a rest sometimes. He was advised by experienced brothers in that department, to be kind and caring to the girl, that gave a grim hope to the man's heart if his "thing" didn't work.

"I don't know how to do that," he said.

"Don't let her get bitten by mosquitoes for one," Santos suggested.

He did. He did it very seriously. Later, Myra was telling Cabarles and Santos that Donono was beginning to scare her because apparently he kept on staring at her very closely. It took a while before the poor girl understood the intention; they could only laugh.

At the first sign of daylight, Liwanag had to leave and find the remains of his family; Ysmael and another man were going with him. Cabarles expressed his intention to wander in town while Santos and Donono would never let him alone, citing the risks. There were a few letters to be delivered from Dapecol POWs as promised. The coincidence of a letter addressed to a certain Atty. and Mrs. Felipe David in the nearby town of Carmen among a few as far as Tagbilaran was an important undertaking they had to do if they could personally. The addressee was allegedly a collaborator based on the information provided by the guerillas. They chose to do it themselves as letting one of them to come would double the risks presented upon disclosure that the man was long targeted for reprisal.

They would go at night. They took the services of a fourteen-year-old boy as a guide who at first refused if not given a gun of his own. "No one carry guns to deliver a mail," Santos said. The boy was explained of their objectives, and he would pretend to be the son of Captain Santos.

"Why not yours?" Santos would ask, thoughtlessly speaking of the boy's similarities in appearance to Cabarles—tall and dark with thick eyebrows.

"I already have one, besides you understand what he speaks," Cab replied. "Don't worry, boy, when we come back, I will teach you how to shoot guns, but for the meantime, you should learn discipline first and how to follow orders from your officer." Cab continued, turning his attention to the boy that he thought required translations of what he just said.

"Don't worry, sir, I speak Tagalog."

"What is your name?" Santos asked the boy who would be his son.

"Herman Espaldon, sir," answered the boy who agreed to the terms and conditions on his part.

"Do you know your way around this forest to the town of Carmen?"

"Yes, sir," he said, with an awkward salute that made Santos proud of him, then both of them responded to the gesture of the kid almost at the same time.

"From now on, I'm your father and he is your uncle. Do you understand that?" Santos told the boy.

"Yes, sir. I'm very proud to be your son, Captain," Herman replied without hesitation.

"Are you sure you wanted me to stay?" Donono complained after knowing that Cab and Santos were leaving for Carmen.

"Yes, I wanted a good place to sleep for me and my boy when we come back," Santos told Don. "Besides, we know you wanted to stay with Myra." He continued with sarcasm while lighting a cigarette.

THE MAILMEN

In a house one more mile to the town proper, they knocked on the door of David's house. A decent-sized home with a rotting flower garden in the front yard, they thought no one was in the house, but a few moments later, someone opened the door. They introduced themselves as friends of Juan David Jr. The man of the house let them come inside in a hurry as soon as he heard the name of his son. In his fifties so as his spouse, they had been longing for any information about the son they lost communication with since the Japanese occupation. So happy to learn he was alive, though the letter was written in early December, the joy it brought to the couple was beyond measure. The letter was read as soon as it was handed, adding to the extreme gratitude that their prayers were answered.

"Your son is a valiant soldier, we know him personally," Santos affirmed to the couple. "It won't be long and you will be reunited," he added. He knew the last sentence was baseless, but he needed to say it.

"Thank you very much, gentlemen. Would you tell us how you know him if you don't mind our curiosity?"

"We are from Davao, sir. Members of Fifty-Seventh Scout and Reconnaissance Group, USAFFE soldiers. Your son is a prisoner of war in Dapecol," Santos replied. "He is worried about you, as you are for him."

It was only then when the man got real excited. "When was the last time you saw him? How is he, is he all right? Please tell me," David asked. "Please excuse me a second. I'll call my wife, I want her to hear this."

Despite extreme concern about the son, the mother found moments between joy and wiping out tears in hospitality of the guests. The rest of the conversation was all about the son. The mother was truly worried but relieved and happy to know that Junior was alive. They promptly asked information on how to get to Dapecol.

"We have three more letters of soldiers and civilians from Dapecol addressed in this province. As promised, we have to reach these people. As of now, we are looking for help how we can get in touch with them. It will be too dangerous for us to continue such duty, but we have to do it," Cabarles said while imposing something.

"If you can trust me, son, I can do it for you. I know a lot of people in our province that can equally be trusted." Maybe out of excitement or for returning favor, the man volunteered.

"We will appreciate it very much, sir, it will be a great favor."

Well connected in the province as he said, he was in the best position to continue the task of getting the prisoners' mail to whomever it was addressed. Cab and Rod were so thankful of the older man, but what else could they make him do more than he could say? They had to be careful to discuss their real intention.

"Out of respect, sir, how do you look at the guerilla activities in your province?" Cab started a topic presumed not welcome to be discussed, might as well take advantage of the moment while the man seemed to share their commitments.

"Not so good, son. They cannot get support from the locals because people are afraid of punishment from the Japanese if they get caught. In fact, rumors have spread that there was none anymore because they [the guerilla] escaped to Mindanao long ago," he sadly said. "Bad news to tell you, those who stayed were crushed by the Japanese just recently."

"What do you know about that?"

"It's only a rumor, I don't really know. But I believed the sources."

"We are soldiers, sir. Should we worry that we may be putting you in danger too? We were warned that many people in the town is collaborating with the Japanese."

"No, son. You are safe here for now, and that is not true."

"We met the commander of guerilla forces in Bohol, sir. Do you know about him?"

"Yes, of course. He is an American. Very brave man."

So much information from one man, they learned to believe he was truly a collaborator.

"Do you know Ingeniero Ysmael, sir?" Cabarles asked another question.

"Yes, it is a small province. I heard rumors that he is in the guerilla too. Sad to say, he left for Mindanao and abandoned his troops."

"It wasn't true he abandoned his troops, sir. We know the man. He went to Mindanao to get help and material support. He is a very good man dedicated to the cause against the invaders, and he is so devastated of the losses in his troops. So are we," Cab explained in sorrow and after a long silence while weighing the man's reaction to information he was just told.

"So you know Ysmael. I'm glad the rumor isn't true. I know him very well, he is a brave and intelligent man. I condoled to the death of his wife then, I'm sad for the loss of his men. I may have joined the guerillas too if not worried about the safety of my family." He sighed with regret while pondering a serious thought. "I may not be alive today if I did so, my wife too."

"Yes, sir, we know Ysmael. He was commissioned as a lieutenant in the Sixty-First Division and he is now commanding the Bohol resistance. He is a good man." Rod partially identified himself, and the soft-spoken man went out to get the boy that was told to stay outside and watch activities around. "We are glad to know that we're on the same side."

"I'm a father to a soldier, we share the same allegiance to our land. So you also know the legend of Filipino soldiers who fought a battle to death in Davao against the Japs?" the man asked, taking advantage of a story that began to inspire him, forgetting that he didn't even know who he was talking with.

"There were many battles fought in Davao. Yes, sir, I believe it was all true," Santos replied. He was tired about the story he had narrated several times already; he tried to divert the conversation to how many more locals were still loyal to the Philippine flag in the province. Though he found it hard to bring the topic to his agenda, he let the man talk while calculating the extent of his alliance. The purpose of staying longer than planned was that David Sr. had given them the impression of reliability and trust. He may be the father of an allied soldier but they had to follow strict guidelines in civilian contacts as advised by Ysmael. On the other hand, the invitation to a dinner was just hard to pass.

A decent meal on the table prepared by Mrs. David and another woman who said that she was the aunt of Jun David. Both cannot help it but adore and worry at the same time about the young boy when they learned that all his family were killed by the Japanese, much more when the boy said he had committed himself to become a soldier and kill the Japanese who defied everyone of freedom on their own land. A lot of anger was also expressed to those who spied for the benefit of the enemy. He was reminded again to cool down, be not categorized as another vengeful man and be aware the enemy that did not discriminate children. He would die too young.

Though Santos had met a better person to match his wit while Cabarles stayed unspoken to the impressive intelligence and communication skills of Atty. David, both had reached to the point that the older man had to listen to them again. No more other talk but concentrate on the main objective: how to turn the loyalty of the Boholenos to their own people. After all that, their stomachs were filled that would last for two days with more offered to carry back to the mountain. Downgrading the new leadership of the guerilla campaign in the province absent of the likes of Kapitan Domeng and Lieutenant Santos of Mindanao or Macario Peralta of Negros, there would be no successful resistance group to match the strength of the enemy, the older David would keep on saying.

He was explained that the goals for now was not to battle the enemy but to enlist as many possible combatants for training and establish a communications system that they could rely on with confidence, all of which must be done in secrecy from enemy and collaborators.

Santos was firm to say that the guerilla command in Bohol will be under the command of Lt. Ingeniero Ysmael until Jack Bradford has recovered. He added that the lawyer would be appointed as the leader of the intelligence and recruiting operations. He was commissioned as a lieutenant of the Fifty-Seventh Scout Division in the command of Captain Rodrigo Santos with Lieutenant Ysmael as his senior officer. Santos laid down the chain of command. He would oversee the entire process for now as part of their mission until an effective force had been established that could sustain a battle against the Japanese. Further orders included not giving any reason for the enemy to suspect of such undertaking: Do not antagonize nor harass even the collaborators. Show them what they expect, setting aside all grudges and arrogance and they will deal with the turncoats in due time.

Though the lawyer had accepted the tasks, he belittled Ysmael to become a lieutenant.

"Sir, my name is Dominador Cabarles. I humbly apologize for not letting you know sooner. I hope you understand. We are escapees from Dapecol, a walking dead. We believed that letting everyone that we died in prison is for the benefit of other prisoners we left in Dapecol." he said while looking the older man straight in the eye.

"My brother here is Capt. Rodrigo Santos. We are glad to know that you already heard about us, but what is important now is we confirm you are on our side," Cab said to cut where the conversation was going again. "Our mission in Bohol is clear, and we recognized Lieutenant Ysmael as the officer in command of the guerillas in Bohol." He stopped momentarily with the lawyer whose attention was also taken by Santos who had pulled a .38 caliber pistol out from concealment while peeking through the window again. "Letting you know who we are shall remain confidential, we are never here."

"Sir, we will be trusting you with our life and the life of so many people depending on us including your son. If you need assistance with the tasks you said you could do well, we will provide it for you. If you feel comfortable to find someone you can trust better, please do so. We will be communicating with you." Santos had shown irritation too on the fast-talking man. Maybe the sight of a gun would slow him down.

The lawyer finally listened, not clear if it was caused by knowing who he was dealing with. He started to slow down and stopped lecturing the soldiers.

At midnight, they left the house with assurance from "David Sr." that he would do as directed in the recruiting process of the locals and wherever he could be useful to the guerilla effort. His full cooperation and loyalty would be to the Philippine flag as Santos had made the older man recite after him the US Army oath that he had memorized by saying it every morning in Dapecol musters. In the continuation, they cited how the prominent people of Davao had maintained their anonymity while responsibly participating in such undertakings. But what motivated the lawyer most was an indication that the entire civilian population in Mindanao were contributing in a struggle to help each other in their individual capacity. No one hid in their house; instead they evacuated right on the gate of Davao

Penal Colony. They also described the story of a group of children singing the national anthem to the POWs on a daily basis. Mindanao was truly a land of heroes; age didn't matter. Much more, educational attainment, religion, and differences in opinion were set aside to find a way suitable in their capability to help the guerillas and prisoners. It could also be done in Bohol. The night ended with a hopeful outcome. A last word from David, he advised them to avoid a man wearing a red shirt; he was considered to be bad news as he was seen with the Japanese on a few occasions.

Cabarles believed that the people of Bohol must be as courageous as the Davaoenos and the whole of Mindanao. Lieutenant Ysmael and Sergeant Liwanag indicated the difficulties of getting support from the people. Santos maintained that there must be underlying factors that Ysmael must address first. There was also an arrogant sergeant who assumed that he was in command. Those who wanted to join the resistance just didn't know who to associate with.

Cabarles had learned so much in so short a period in the place. He and Santos had a unique camaraderie. He had taken the rank of captain just because he returned from the dead with it. He had suffered so much physical pain because of that damned hat, but he could not deny it also saved his life. However, he always recognized Santos as his superior; in fact, he addressed him as sir all the time. Unlike when his world only turned around talking to horses and buffaloes that must listen to him one way or another, that night was one for the book. He would never forget giving orders to a prominent and respected lawyer. Though humility was natural, he could not help but become proud of himself, thanking Santos who had taught him so well of everything he knew, most important in how to overcome apprehension in dealing with people of high status.

"Sir, thank you very much again."

"For what?"

"For giving me such honor that you deserved."

"You're a major now, and you deserve it. The honor is mine to serve you as my officer in command, sir."

"I like the captain better, sir. Can I just remain a captain?"

"It doesn't work that way, but why?"

"I believe the curse of the captain is all the luck that comes to me now. I don't want to change it".

"As you wish, Cab."
"Even better. You know, I barely read. I'm nobody without you."
"You must remember, I am alive because of you."
"No, we are both dead. And it's a fact. Isn't it?
"Yeah, it doesn't change anything."

CHAPTER 16

STARRY NIGHTS IN BOHOL SHORES

Brothers shared my woes, seen mirages I thought they are. Hills and valleys mold in grand design best view from heaven they. I'd rather stay and watch them on land. I'll take the struggle and face my fate.

A FUTILE SEARCH

It was close to noontime when they reached back on the foothills leading to the camp. There were so many hills that were almost identical to others. A nap along a wooded path was extended to a sleep that none realized it was noontime already. Just cloudy, the unusual land formations and towering trees of assorted varieties was keeping the ground dark. A worried Donono and a man were on the lookout who spotted them from a far distance that released the little man from agony of what may have happened to the captains. The little man expected them to come back before midnight. Relieved in seeing them coming, he chose to stay for a while. Over a plateau of about a thousand square meters, half a kilometer away where they settled temporarily for the night, a flat ground and a good-sized clearing obscured by boulders of limestone around, Donono suggested it could be a better camp.

"Here I can see farther, and fresh water is flowing freely," Cabarles agreed.

The place would be called Camp Donono, declared by Santos from then on, and a new path was made leading to another place they would call ghost camp. The ghost camp must be retained because they exerted too much work to build shelters already, and many exhausted and grieving people would not be happy to move again. As a reward jokingly for discovering the place, he was given a bag full of food to feast on, but he refused to eat if he could not share with the others equally starving, a pretense that they all knew the intent was to show off.

"To Myra you mean," Cab asked him directly, looking into his eyes, anticipating to reveal his stand on the girl from his own words. He advised him to be patient and let free will take place and it would be more rewarding. He didn't mind being responded. "You know, if you will keep letting her see you like that, she will never like you at all. I mean, with your balls dangling like that from that little piece of clothing you tied up around your waist."

"I don't want to ruin the only pair of clothes I have for our wedding. Besides, I am more comfortable like this."

Santos always believed that a grand intervention was necessary for Myra to fall for Donono as he jokingly reiterated it could only be done at the point of a gun to force his intention. Cabarles must lay out his way in detail that was also proven effective according to him.

"Don't worry, Cap, I have a talisman that will charm any girl to like me," Donono reminded them while displaying the amulets around his neck.

"You're running out of time. She's going to stay in Bicol," Santos seriously informed the little man.

"I'm aware of that, sir."

"So you don't need our help?" Santos clarified.

"No, sirs, but I need your approval and blessing," he replied with confidence.

"Well, good luck then. But if the talisman doesn't work, you tell us."

"Yes, sir, I will."

A few more minutes after discussing another change of events affecting their plans and their role in the command of Ysmael, they started to walk back to the main camp. They walked straight to where they left the women. Tearful and quiet as everybody else, another death had inflicted a tremendous loss in the group. The American pilot died, and the grieving for him was added to what there was already—too much sorrow in the camp. The American was a great leader, the bravest soldier, and the most kind human being who would play with the children like they were his. He would lead the women first to safety during enemy raids.

Ysmael returned, which lessened the anguish as he was reunited with a few more of his men who had retreated into different directions. Martin was not in the group; his wife or mother were not among the bodies they retrieved and buried, giving him hope they were still alive, just lost in the mountains. He had to continue the search. Just out of curiosity, they asked each other who would bring their wife and mother to raise arms against the invaders. Ysmael had a good answer; both women were better than Ysmael himself in guns. Besides, they could also cook. Though all had taken the demise of Jack and his burial as another sorrowful event, some had decided to leave the camp again immediately to join the search for the rest of the missing members, in the forest or they may walk back in town, wherever they could be. In the total count, Ysmael buried ten men, a woman, and two children from the raid. More than forty more are unaccounted for in their force.

Lieutenant Ysmael had to stay at the order of Cabarles so that they could work out an effective strategy in defending the new base in case of another enemy attack. He acknowledged that Donono's camp had several advantages while separating the women from combatants. With a clear visibility of the hills and down the brown meadows to northward directions to the valleys of giant anthills, the sceneries of unusual land formation in the month of summer were largely dying vegetation that colored a wide area to the top in brown pastel. Just an accidental green of coconuts, bananas, and clusters of trees highlighted the miles of visibility that ended on another set of brown hills scattered randomly over the island.

THE MAN IN RED

As every minute counts, the soldiers had doubled their effort to share their acquired knowledge in the art of clandestineness and guerilla warfare. What they learned and realized all the time was that the local guerilla would encounter the Japanese on foot patrol in the woods; the reaction was engaged in a firefight, but they were always overrun by hundreds subsequently. All were advised that the Japanese were not stupid to send six men or less anywhere to hunt them; they must be accompanied by many more. Therefore if a group could not sustain a battle against a hundred to death, better to just hide and avoid them because retreating would only result in leading the enemy to their camp full of unarmed refugees. Santos was serious in conducting a sit-in training class with the remnants of Ysmael's troops while Cabarles showed them how to aim and fire their rifles with better results. He also instructed them how to identify a camouflaged enemy and shoot them at a far distance. In perceivable example, he referred to a guerilla in his bright red shirt with overcoat among the rest that it would only make him a clear target on any background. It was known that the enemy maintained camouflage; a guerilla keeping his red shirt on was an easy target. A lesson learned why convicts wore orange in Dapecol. They were shot to kill of any wrongdoing against the Japanese. How this one was still alive among the many dead, Santos immediately disclosed his thoughts to Cabarles.

"I had been wearing this shirt for a long time, I was never shot at in several encounters," the man said, emphasizing it was a lucky shirt when he was asked.

Santos replied on that one, "Yes, it may be a lucky shirt for you, but it is very bad to our brothers. If you don't get hit, they know your next action is to retreat, run away. You already reveal your location?"

"I shot and killed many enemy more than anyone here." The man was bragging.

"Yes, exactly the same thing I will do too. But what you don't realize is they see you clear in the woods and meadows. They know you will lead them to the rest of your company and always you will come out alive again. Honestly, I don't know why you are still alive and unscratched while others died," Santos exclaimed. "Unless you are a spy conniving with the enemy, I suggest you never wear that shirt again anywhere." He continued at a casual rationalization.

"Where were you when the camp was attacked by the Japanese?" Cabarles asked behind the man.

The question raised some eyebrows, which led to a steadfast conclusion. They knew where he was. He just showed himself when they were attacked. These were all desperate armed men recouping from the horrors of a previous encounter, had lost a friend or family, and were tired of being chased by the Japanese. They knew the answer to Cab's question. The man's lucky shirt was ripped off recklessly by another behind while others pointed a gun at him almost at once. Ysmael was quick to resolve the commotion, but he himself had the most ill feeling. The man they trusted in company was apparently guiding the enemy to their annihilation and was getting near to such accomplishment.

The man was called Pusa (cat) known to have nine lives for evading many encounters. His favorite color was red; most of the time he wore no overcoat. He joined the resistance just about when the guerilla was campaigning intensively against the Japs. He said he was a native of Bohol but was employed in Manila until the Japanese invasion. He had found his way back to the island while being hunted for killing a Japanese officer. He also said he was captured and detained in Pilar and escaped while being transferred to another garrison. His story was commonly heard, like the others who all had one heroic or sad story to tell on their own. Not long ago, he was a front figure in the attack of a group of fishermen under strong suspicion of helping the enemy in his proposition. Pusa may not be wearing a lucky shirt at all times; in fact, Santos only made an example on how to be unobtrusive in combat, but his insinuation had already started a string of conjectures. On another thought, they would not expect seeing a man red in the camp as tipped off by David.

Adverse incidents attributed to Pusa mounted instantaneously. In a series of heated questioning from the furious and irate men around him, he was disarmed and presumed guilty as charged even before he could oppose the allegations of being a traitor.

Santos and Cabarles tried to interfere as they set off the commotion; however, as they observed the reactions of Pusa in collective grilling, there was reason to believe he may be a spy even though he strongly denied the accusations. Weary of a longtime suspicion based on a series of unfortunate events leveled to the doings of a traitor, Pusa found himself in serious trouble instead of being hailed as a heroic man who led the guerilla survivors to safety. He became red in the face too. Lieutenant Santos, who started it all, remained in silence as Ysmael assigned a few men to guard the cat. He said he wanted to kill him himself, but the truth was he never had actually shot anyone yet. It was decided that they better wait for Martin who would give him no mercy. Pusa was a known associate and confidant of Martin Liwanag; the majority decision was to wait in fairness for him before any definitive action was decided.

On the morning of the fourth day in Bohol, the lookouts relayed that about twenty men were seemingly lost at a distance from the camp. In their observations, they were most likely farmers, but none in their right mind would dare to travel in a group at any time in daylight when the Japs were still very active in patrol. They may also be the search party on their way back. Seemingly lost in the middle of a clearing putting themselves as good target practice, they should be an inexperienced group of men not familiar with this part of the province. Cabarles, Santos, Ysmael, and some of his men decided to approach the group. In that misty morning hours, the unknown men were identified as volunteers for enlistment in the guerilla. They were welcomed in great elation on sight by the officers of the Fifty-Seventh Scouts soldiers. Unarmed and exhausted men trying to locate the camp, accompanied by Herman Espaldon and Juan David Sr., they were proud to present the brave and determined young men, all of them firm in their decision to join the military of some sort. They were guided at once to the foot of the hills just below the camp. According to David, more would be coming if given the assurance of a fair chance to kill one or more Japanese, an assertion that gave renewed spirit on the struggling campaign to make the invaders know they were never welcome in Bohol.

In a lesson just learned, loyalty should be established as a priority of every recruit. They were evaluated all at once by the ghost soldiers whom they admitted were not much to base any distrust on but enlist all instead. They appreciated the fast feedback from David. In another humble gesture, the lawyer settled his personal dislike to the younger Inginiero Ysmael with a handshake and quick embrace that turned the mood into equitable alliance to each other.

Higher up the hill, Ysmael sadly presented the camp to the new members. "We have no food and shelter but only brotherhood with a single purpose," he said while ordering what was left in his men to show hospitality to the new brothers in resistance.

"What's wrong with that fellow?" David Sr. asked about a man tied up and guarded a few yards away.

"He was wearing red shirt," Santos offered a confident answer.

David came closer then silently looked to Santos with a little nod.

Indeed, there was no way to confirm the loyalty of the new members; only their effort to reach the camp and David's words about their loyalty were considered adequate. But he was not supposed to be in the camp as he was given the assigned duties that required clandestine and cautious movements. The procedure laid down by the ghost soldiers were meant to be followed as they emphasized that his function was too important to the reinforcement of guerillas and the Allied forces while avoiding so many deaths including his own. Citing themselves as an example, Cab and Santos reiterated that they were never in Bohol but would assist with the endeavors up to the time they feel they were not needed anymore. And that would be soon, seeing how the Boholenos were helping each other. They were careful in dealing with David, knowing that his fragile pride and disposition could change back to grudges. The lawyer spelled out that his motivation to visit the camp was to make sure his effort would not go in vain, so with the men who offered their own life and loyalty through him. He added that many more should be coming to join, including women.

David was invited to come to the rear camp. There he met the women, children, and the wounded who had adapted to the life in the run, pushed out to the remotest region of the island, displaced from their homes to live in the mountain, hoping one day they could strike back at the enemy in victory. But the saddest attestation of the hardship of these people was when he was offered food rations that was part of his wife's generosity three days ago. He saw children fetching water in small containers to fill a bigger one, barely clothed while delivering to the men in the forward camp. Deprived of childhood, some had no parents anymore, but none complained. They were just doing what they could contribute despite their innocence. He didn't know who the young and beautiful ladies were, but he revered their serious effort in attending to the wounded and children just after they showed hospitality to him. Absent of self-esteem and regard for the value of life in hunger and hardship, the sacrifices he had seen from everyone touched his honorable personality. Pity on him who chose to stay home in silent loathing for a very long time when others were fighting to regain freedom of them all. It may be a futile effort, but the hope was there for a way of life worth dying for. This was not a case to defend an innocent in a court of law that didn't exist anymore; all were oppressed summarily in their own land judged by a foreign authority to death simply by defending their land.

He was humbled to be introduced to Rosalia Brown, much more to realize they knew each other. They shared information that mostly involved adversities.

Enlightenment and expressions of many thoughts progressing, they all heard a single gunshot that reverberated in the hills and mounds around to where they were seated. They all got alerted, soldiers grabbing their guns, women gathering the children. It was a scary moment that was felt in a state of mind that was getting used to gunshots but never to the results it brought to them. Rosie and Myra didn't know what to do in a panicky situation, since they left Davao, the only gunfire they heard was in the *Rosalia* in the middle of the Bohol Sea. However, normalcy came back as there was no more to follow. Ysmael was not happy of whoever defied his order not to fire their arms in the new camp that may reveal their position to enemy patrols in the area. They continued their talks on several proposals in commanding the armed struggles; as expected, the lawyer had a lot of arguments but backed out when Santos opposed. He must take the task carefully given the specific duty and was commended for his prompt actions. Reliable means of communications must be established above all that only he was in the best position to implement.

When Martin Liwanag returned, Pusa took the heat of his frustration by one bullet. No sight or news at all of his wife even though he searched farthest south to the barrios of Dagohoy and Alicia. He knew his wife and mother in law would not let the Japanese capture them alive. If they were wounded, the possibility of surviving was too small at the time of the year when even wild animals were starving. All he wanted was to give them a proper burial they deserved as human beings. However, a bit of hope remained that one day they would show up together. He bragged about the time he met his wife in a correctional facility due to a homicidal confrontation with someone who tried to take advantage of her dignity. She wouldn't give up that easy. Too much to his story that the grieving husband was noticeably not grieving anymore while narrating many stories about his wife.

No remorse was shown that he just killed a man in cold blood. The next day, he was out again looking for the beloved wife.

MISSION ACCOMPLISHED

The day over, David Sr. was ready to hike back to town taking the assistance of Herman and a few children to bring with him at home. Doubled the courage and certainty to his previously unsatisfying contentions of existing guerilla leadership in the province, he was confident that it should succeed according to the concepts presented by ghosts soldiers. What he had learned in a day in the camp was equal to so many years in law school; after all, no laws applied anymore. Just surviving by any means. He would send as many recruits in arms and combat training; thereafter, they could go home until the time they would be notified for real actions while waiting for arms and materiel support from the central command in Lanao or Negros. The scout soldiers had made themselves real busy in training the recruits.

Donono shared his skills in jungle survival, how to weaponize plants and frogs and importantly eating them with emphasis on how to be one step ahead of starvation. They must eat monkeys if they needed to. He had organized a group of volunteers to do just that but opposed in cattle rustling. He had learned a lot; truly he could be king somewhere in Mindanao.

Donono liked people who would think through all phases against the difficulties of the present situation and beyond, characteristics he had learned from his officers. Accruing confidence in their company and hardship of all sorts, he presented an implausible tale of a man who survived in many days enclosed in a cage without given food. Donono's diminutive appearance unfitting a soldier was reversed by an automatic weapon he carried added by self-confidence he had gained in prison. Myra was impressed.

The discussion was cut short by the approaching officers, Cabarles and Santos. They were proudly introduced by Donono while commanding everyone to stand up and salute.

As Donono continued, the volunteers concluded arms training from Cab and Santos. They joined the men and listened to what the little man was saying. There was nothing else they could do while the sun was setting. They were hungry, but there was no food in sight at all—only discussion of how to overcome that problem. They were fascinated about several ways to find food that Donono had discussed.

"Our priorities are keeping us alive," Don continued. "We begin to tackle food shortage today as tomorrow we have no more. I suggest we all take it seriously." He ended his speech seeing Myra coming and offering him water to drink.

These were caring gestures for each other that were all caught in action by Cab and Santos. "Do you think the talisman of Abu is working?" inquired Santos to the other who knew about it.

"Have faith with our brother, believe in him, will you? See how much he had changed lately?" Cab responded, whispering. He was not going to disclose that he told Myra to do so.

"You mean he is wearing a pants again?" Santos would say, but it was already noticed sometime ago.

Donono could skip meals without complaining; instead, he became generous to another person in dire hunger. It had been observed. His thought made him look his pal in the eye, he did not understand what he meant in its entirety.

"No, not that. I saw him washing his face in the morning."

"Yeah . . . that one is new, I see your point. If he took a full bath, then I would say he's really serious about Myra."

Dono came to join them and was curious why his backers were seemingly talking seriously without him; whatever caused it he wanted to know. Kids and women came; throughout the day, they were also busy with their tasks and errands. They were seated among the grown men while women were making sure all had eaten, distributing hot brews of some concoctions of coffee and leaves, boiled corn grains, and the usual sweet potatoes. Rosie and Myra joined them too.

The guerilla of Bohol was brought back to life, motivated by Davao escapees. Rosie, a native of Bohol, was now in Bohol as she wished. It may not be the exact place and people she wanted to be with, but few claimed they knew her family and relatives. However, no one knew if they still existed. She stole a moment to state her gratitude to the men and women who pulled her out of hell. Rosie gave the example of women in the cause to the likes of sacrifices of Miss Rhodora X and Rina Penafrancia in Davao. "My own struggles can never equal their sacrifices to save lives. I am not capable of avenging my lost dignity, but sure I will use the best I can to support those of you who can." An applause followed and more when she introduced Myra to sing. In the succeeding turn of events, a little food intake for that night was forgotten; all were inspired and encouraged in support of the guerillas, learning that the Allied forces would come eventually.

"There's no more food for tomorrow," Myra revealed. Rosie pulled a couple of cold *camote* concealed from her bandana. "You two share it," Cab said to Rosalia. They both comforted Rosie that tomorrow would be another day. She was looking haggard wearing an old dress a local let her use. Still looking great in natural splendor, she didn't care anymore about her looks but worried how they could survive in the days to come.

The next day came, one more week until Fernando Viola was told to return. Ysmael had an easy way to find food when consulted of the problem. He sent three men to go to the barrios of Pilar where he lived. In the morning, three cows where munching grass in the vicinity of the camp, and one of them were later slaughtered. He didn't care if all of his assets were consumed, but their stay in Bohol would not be remembered by not being fed well. He had stashed animals in the care of trusted relatives; they may be declining in number, but there would be plenty until the problem was resolved. There were many fishermen down the shoreline about three kilometers away; too bad they killed a few of them.

The hospitality of Ysmael to the ghost soldiers was appreciated, and he begged them not to leave the province but lead his forces to kill all Japanese in Bohol. He was happy it had been a week without incidents or encounters; all were conclusive on the reckoning that the man with the lucky red shirt was a traitor indeed. The training continued; the camp was established as a permanent community. Shanties were built in Donono's camp, crude shelters made solely for daily cooking, and one for the women to sleep. Fortunately, no one new became sick, and those wounded recuperated well.

Donono had already assigned a man to take over in the food department. Lieutenant Santos and Ysmael had promoted six sergeants, including Liwanag, to handle the combat training in their supervision. Two were sent back to town to report to David. All precautions were set in place, but they were reminded to never challenge the might of the Japanese until they received arms support from Mindanao. Lieutenant Ysmael was given advice to maintain contact with the central guerilla command and keep on requesting arms and ammunition. Firm directives were given to keep on alert but avoid confrontation with the enemy and the civilians while waiting for the coming of Allied forces. They were just to keep training men and send them back home ready for short notice of recalling them in battle. Martin was advised to keep cool and be accommodating to the new recruits. There may be another "Pusa," but surely the lesson had been learned from that incident.

Exactly two weeks in expectation of a gentleman's words to be fulfilled, the escapees traveled back to wait in the same place where they were dropped off by Fernando and his son, accompanied by Martin and Ysmael who didn't stop convincing they stay longer but respected the ghost soldiers' decision to continue on their mission. Rosie was staying; she had chosen to be with the guerillas until the escapees left the island. David Sr. would take her home to reunite with her family when she was ready.

AN INCIDENT THAT INSPIRED THE THIRD NAME

The waiting was too much to deal with. What if the *Rosalia* didn't show up? From dawn until sunset, they saw nothing like a boat coming back to get them out of Bohol Island. Another day was over then another; they started to think of alternative plans. It was a journey that nobody could stop them from doing. There was another boat they could use to sail across the next land mass in the horizon and over; the capacity was big enough to sustain four people in the high seas. Ysmael and Martin left, assuring they would be back with another boat. Another night fall came, and swarms of bloodsucking insects were buzzing in their ears already. Don lighted a fire to smoke them away. He sure was true to his word that he would not let even mosquitoes upset Myra. He still stared at her most of the time. His affection for the pretty girl had become a devotion absent of actually telling the girl of his feelings but for his revelation that he wanted to marry her. He was just doing what he was taught to do, but he also spoke out that he would take care of her with his life.

In the solemnity of the passing hours, unsure of what would be next to take place, the five escapees from Davao found themselves realizing they were on their own. Rosie took a walk to the shore for the last chance she could in the company of the former POWs and Myra. Though confident that Lieutenant Ysmael and Sergeant Liwanag would not abandon them, they found themselves waiting for everyone. There was complete silence as they kept their eyes on the eastern sea of Bohol for the fourth day. Cab resigned himself to lying flat on the ground, having in mind to take a nap while Santos took over the watch. Closing his eyes while occasionally slapping persistent mosquitoes, he could smell Rosie's scent as she sat by close, inspiring his daydreaming about someone else. He had given a lot of thought to himself; there were really times he would blame himself for not taking advantage what the moment offers that could fulfill a longing and desire in his thoughts. If given the same chance, he should take it at least before he died. With intimacy developed in most difficult times that didn't find satisfaction, what more chance could transpire to yield himself to that other chance? Someone sat close to him, surely it wasn't Donono. In reality, he is one Donono too in that category, only in his imagination he had actually done it all.

Very appealing, submitting, and he's somewhat responding, drawn to fulfill his imagination in forgiving opportunity. He desired Rosalia Brown like Rhodora, which usually caused his wild thoughts. However, it could only come close to reality as the situation always suppressed fulfillment. He opened his eyes in a drowning moment, assessing what could have caused a noise when everyone was supposed to be resting. Santos was scouring the beach from afar. Myra was the first to see who was coming.

"We have company," Myra whispered, partially surprised to witness the seemingly intimate sight she had caught unexpectedly.

They could be the men they have been waiting. Myra saw the people coming and said that they were definitely women. Who could they be?

Cabarles took the revolver out of his satchel. Two shadows came out through dying vegetation to reveal that they were not enemy. Women, also whispering to each other carefully, were trying to locate the smoke they had seen that morning. Rosie understood what they spoke of. She decided to approach them in the same dialect, Cab close behind.

Disoriented and weary, the women just submitted themselves to the voice that froze them. A woman speaking in the local dialect was most likely a local. "Thank God," they said. They identified themselves, saying that they had been running from the Japanese close to a month already, changing locations every time, but maintaining in the general area of the Guindulman shores, anticipating and praying for some people to come back from Mindanao. Nowhere to go other than the nesting grounds of the Japs that kept on expanding, they chose to stay put patiently.

They were offered food and water, instantly relieved to find friendly people. Rosie filled the women in on what they had missed while in hiding. They sure hid pretty good as they were not found by many people looking for them.

Opposite to what welcomed them, they would leave Bohol with a little happy ending, at least for Martin Liwanag. Not yet as it was getting close to midnight and still there was no sight of either boat that would take them out of the island. The smoker was revived, and they fell asleep again. Rosie's attention was taken by the women. Cabarles had to cool himself off with Donono smirking with only teeth and eyes visible in the dark.

Before sunrise on the first day of May, everyone was awakened by guerilla officers with other two men carrying a fresh batch of food, mostly fish. Martin promptly recognized the voices that called his name. In the same manner, they let out their emotions as they wept in the embrace of each other. The sight of the couple in such commitment with each other made Cabarles envious and fearful. He knew Inez was not as strong as Martin's wife. She was a plain loving and sweet pretty woman who could not survive by herself. His determination to reach Luzon intensified to a mixed feeling that Inez was somewhere waiting for her rescue or just sadly thinking of him. So much for Rosie, he was resentful to take advantage of that moment.

On the third count of his finger, Rosalia Brown was one lady Cabarles had so much to talk about while recollecting the war. But he would swear on any grave that she wasn't her on his mind at that moment.

On another thought, Bohol was so beautiful. Rosie was equally beautiful and possessed an alluring beauty that had been tormenting Cab's senses since the first time he laid eyes on her. What happened last night may be caused by his intense longing for Inez that he found in the presence of another woman. All the thoughts and emotions were cut off by the sight of a familiar dark hull coming from the ocean. Everyone watched the majestic boat in another voyage, giving confidence to the escapees that the next leg of their journey would be safely in the unpredictable seas of the Philippines. The *Rosalia* was coming after all, timed in the highest tide.

Some familiar faces greeted each other, Roberto dela Cruz of all the people they didn't expect to be one among them. Two unknown soldiers also came down. One was a senior officer accompanied by another Filipino never seen before. Col. Ruperto Kangleon, who was briefed earlier about the soldiers they were picking up from Bohol, introduced himself. He was happy to meet the commanders of the guerrilla movement in the island. Aware that they could not stay long, he ordered a few caches to be unloaded from the boat while keeping conversation with Ysmael and Martin. There was no time to waste as the tide was starting to recede. Fernando was worried that they could not get out of the cove if they waited too long.

Cab was the last one in to board, caused by a long goodbye with Rosie. Of all the time they had together, the feelings of at least one them presumably in endless gratitude that were kept and suddenly brought out in mutual passion was coming to an end. Cab's promising that he would come back to Bohol was the same in visiting Davao again. Rosie let him go in tears. A very familiar sight in the eyes of Santos and Donono who chose not to say anything. Again Dono was grinning, another secret to keep on his own, which was not appropriate to tell anybody but he had confided to Santos already.

"What are you two smiling at?" Myra was curious, noticing that Santos and the ugly Don was watching Cab alone at the stern.

He was exactly on the same spot when they left Manila Bay in the beginning when they left Mindanao. He was lying flat on the deck when he could not see anymore of the men and women on the beach. Same picture, same boat, only different in time, out of respect to himself for the many challenges that he had gone through, tests of his weaknesses that he would deny it never went through. Only the beginning, never finding satisfaction in the ending.

"Nothing," Don answered as he turned to the apple of his eyes.

"Liars! I already know," the girl replied, dismissing the attempt of the soldiers to hide their thoughts.

The casual approach of the girl to the men while munching on the apples was entrusting. Finding herself the only woman in the middle of the ocean while the only man she trust was having a dilemma, it was not the right moment to be bothered yet. She pleased herself with Santos and Dela Cruz. She was an outcast as to the nature of the conversation. It was only Donono left to get relief of nervous thought ahead. There was a considerable change in herself; she can stand looking at Donono directly without getting scared of having nightmares afterward. He didn't look that bad after all; in reality, she had also started to appreciate his thoughtfulness. Knowing the scary little man's real intention to her, she was just compelled to be polite and friendly. Her own feelings beyond that was yet to be determined. There was nothing in her heart that was close to that chance whatsoever. There was no one to talk to but Donono. She conceded that even the funny-looking one would not actually give her time and attention if needed by the other two. It was hard to admit, but she was starting to appreciate the thoughtfulness and caring of the small guy. She turned to Dela Cruz, trying to dismiss the pity from herself by asking information about Rhodora X. There was nothing much he could say other than the last time they all left Davao. The man had other stories worth listening, such as his accounts of going back to jail and then escaping again for the benefit of the American soldiers.

Intelligence and recon officers from Australia needed to be aware of about anything. To hear words in English again, Cab was one lost soul and he let Santos alone to deal with them. On the other hand, experiences could easily bring back senses; he had to face reality as Bohol turned to just another land mass like what he could see in every direction. Beautiful places and people, so many to recollect with a good listener, and he was still a thousand miles to Bulacan.

According to Roberto, Davao was back to being a living hell. As expected, the Japanese were hunting the American escapees, and they were combing every inch of Davao and other provinces, leaving trails of renewed atrocities on their path. From Davao to Misamis, they did not find what they were looking for; instead they met an equally dreadful guerilla force that had been expecting them. Roberto was lucky to be seen by Viola while paddling a canoe to Bohol. Then an Allied submarine surfaced in Bohol Sea close to the shallow waters entering Canigao Channel.

Kangleon was requesting assistance to establish a radio camp in Leyte. There was no better person to relay so much information than the convict, who could give to the colonel information about the situation in Mindanao. The only time that brought Cabarles back to his senses while having an affliction similar to malaria was when the boat was docking again. He felt guilty for stimulating sin he had incurred to himself in the last hours in Bohol. He was then informed that Colonel Kangleon needed help that they could not deny. A week was all they were asking for. Cabarles would hesitate, but the colonel, a very respectable and intelligent personality, could speak Tagalog. He complied and Cabarles gave strict orders to Fernando Viola that a week it would be; he would be expected to be on time. Viola was not sailing away anymore if only a week; he was also staying In Leyte until such time Cabarles and company were ready to go to Bicol.

May 21, 1943, Ormoc, Western Leyte, as he was told. With enough fuel to reach Southern Luzon, Fernando reiterated that he was willing to bring them wherever they wanted when ready. He could keep the boat, which he understood the Fifty-Seventh Scout Soldiers had dominion over.

Cabarles and Santos had evaded an order to lead a contingent to go back to Mindanao to meet Pertig in behalf of Kangleon. They would continue northward, rendering an identical mission to what Kangleon was throwing at them. Their mission was reconnaissance and intelligence gathering while uniting and establishing communications between guerilla factions. They had done it well in Lanao and Bohol. They should be heading north as mission accomplished in those provinces. Cabarles implied that Santos and Donono could stay, dismissing them of their duty in his command saying he could manage himself with dela Cruz. That didn't go well. Kangleon could establish communications in Mindanao with the help of Dela Cruz and Viola. Less than a week when radio communications was made to Misamis, the ghost soldiers left Leyte with fresh intelligence that Gen. Douglas McArthur was "on his way back to the Philippines." It was not just that—they had also acquired ordnance as much as they could carry.

CHAPTER 17

MIRACLES OF GHOST SOLDIERS

I had seen many islands, beautiful places. All in majestic view from the sea in bright day or night. Majestic hills, beware. Whispers of farewell . . . again.

ONLY FOR A NIGHT

May 28, Matalom, Southern Leyte. Destination to anywhere, to any place or shore that was the shortest distance possible to travel by land to Polangui, Albay. Fernando agreed without a word. In the middle of the water passing several islands that they could not get closer for fear of Japanese snipers, the *Rosalia* just kept going, motoring lazily at a decent speed for an old diesel engine as the sea became agitated like it didn't want to go any farther. With a wicked storm that came with heavy rains and strong waves that splashed on board, there was no more to scare the former POWs about the vision of death.

Mira's relatives would be about forty kilometers on the eastern outskirts of Polangui, where Mayon Volcano was at its best view. Though she had already told them what exactly her relationship was to their objective, she repeated over and over every name of her aunt, uncle, and cousin in the town that mainly thrives on farming the rich soil of the land. Living in a cluster not too far from the main road that led all the way to Luzon, she was proud of the beautiful scenery of the place that was equal to the inland formations of Bohol. Santos would take the sarcasm of everyone when Myra mentioned a lot of beautiful women too in Polangui. Donono would remain quiet during such a conversation, but Santos was quick to respond for him that Dono had been seeing one every day already. Cab and Donono swore they were not interested anymore in any woman. Teasing followed, with Myra having adapted already to such kind of conversation. She could respond mischievously when being paired with Don. She could laugh, joke, and make comments together with the soldiers without inhibition. Alone with a bunch of men, she had no choice but to be trusting and accommodating. There was nothing else they could do as the boat was sailing but just talk and sleep or watch the islands and seabirds. A day and a half went by until Viola informed them that ahead was the Bicol Region. The great land mass was within eye distance yet too far.

An overview of Bicol as they sailed along Burias Passage was of long plain green mountains of wilderness. A recent forest fire dotted some spots, still billowing smoke like a dark tube that connected land to the sky. They were careful not to get too close just yet as enemy snipers could be lurking and waiting for who may want to land at daylight. They floated and waited until darkness along the shore of a narrow strip of land in Claveda Island, about fifteen kilometers past the southern tip of Burias Islands. Fernando discussed his bad experience in getting too close in Pilar, Sorsogon, when they were fired at by 50 mm machine guns. Luckily, no damage was incurred on the boat and his crew and passengers were all safe, but he had learned his lesson to be more careful. Though a white flag was on display, he had chosen not to take the risk again knowing the people along the ride were hostile soldiers for the Japanese. Timed to sunset, the *Rosalia* began crossing Panglao Bay to let the ghost soldiers disembark on the beach of Libon, Albay.

Not a single house they could see ahead, just the thick forest and dark clouds after walking a hundred yards off sandy clearing from the sea. Myra would say the last time she was in Polangui was about four years ago taking the road from Sorsogon. It was still a long way to the town, twenty kilometers straight eastward. She would keep reminiscing in excitement about how close she was with her cousins. It took an hour or two to push in deeper by foot in a path made slippery by monsoon rain. The plan was to find civilians that could tell them directions to Polangui. They were bound to see one or more but just not yet. The confidence promoted by many people who helped them reach Bicol from Davao had caused similar opinions that it would be the same in Luzon. People they must meet was meant a help they would seek. In the youth of night fresh from a long rest in *Rosalia*, it was a walk in the park about a mile or so over a winding road that seemed not to end. Headlights of a vehicle took their attention, and it was coming fast to their position. They scrambled to run and hide to the north side of the road. Japanese patrols may have seen the boat docking in the area earlier and were out to investigate. Certainly, not the kind people they seeked.

Four people, one a woman, found themselves in the heavily patrolled area by the Japanese as two dark green trucks passed by a few hundred yards from them. Daylight ended, and they had no idea at all of what they had put themselves into. In a minute, they heard a barrage of gunshots from the beach. They were sure that the *Rosalia* was under fire, but it was nothing to worry about as it could handle small firearms. Besides, they knew that Fernando would speed back to the ocean out of range from the beach. The real problem and present danger was entirely for themselves. Already knowing that the route they were at was no longer viable to the town, they kept walking fast through towering coconuts parallel to the sea. Rumbling in the sky began while they were on a trail that was becoming muddy to heavily vegetated and virgin woodland as monsoon season began. Those were all they saw when everywhere succumbed to darkness, with just an occasional lightning that sometimes could be too bright. They only slowed down as requested by Donono who was feeling tired, not for him but for Myra. Nobody knew the time nor how long they had been running away. They stopped anyway and just hoped that morning will come and they didn't push themselves closer to the enemy's nest.

Going back to the beach was not an option anymore; Japs sure scared the hell out of Fernando and his son that they must have been sailing back to Mindanao by now if it was still afloat. They fell asleep on the worries altogether and hoped for the best when they woke up. Not too long after, they were awakened by recurring thunderstorms followed by rain pouring down heavily through coconut palms and trees. Cabarles and the little man were nowhere to see. To a seemingly worried Myra, Santos said they went out to scout the area. Rod also started to get the same feeling as they might have gotten lost already.

Lightning strikes and thunder were terrifying during the night, but it could also be enemy cannons. Extremely aware of the presence of the Japanese in the general area, most likely looking for them, they could not risk wandering at daylight. Engaging with the Japanese would be a suicide, and the possibility of being captured was truly worse than being dead. Their situation actually was a repeat of their first days in Mindanao; the only difference was they already knew there are enemy in the area that they must be afraid of.

"There is a house about one kilometer east," Donono said to Santos. "Someone in there, but Cab would not want to go."

"You took their bananas already, what else do you want, their chickens?" Cab reminded him of similar events. They would continue going northeast but cautiously. The size of their group could not sustain a firefight with the enemy, and they would avoid being detected by all means. Walking against vines and twigs struggling to thrive under palms and trees as they got taller and bigger, they could see a tended clearing, but the danger of crossing it to another wooded area was in exposing them; even the sun was obscured by thick fast-moving clouds. They would go around staying hidden by wild vegetation as they walk squat by every accidental meadow. By afternoon, they halted at a wide river, the raging waters made it impossible to cross. The rain had weakened however, but reevaluating situations forced them to stay by the riverbank. The whole experience so far was not a picnic like it was in Davao and Lanao or in Bohol. They were on their own, with unreliable directions in their memory. What part of Bicol Region it was, they had yet to know. Nobody had any clue to where they were. The weather was not cooperating. Lightning and thunderstorms were still going. Rain stopped to a mist, but there was not much they could do when they were all soaked and there were still dark clouds above.

"We need to cross that river?" Santos let know of his hunch that the Japanese would also be patrolling the riverbanks. A fresh path leading west to the sea could only mean people were constantly walking through it.

"Yeah," Cabarles said while motioning to everyone to keep down and quiet.

Someone was coming. In the way Santos and Cab could see his actions as he followed the muddy track they just made, he was trying to obscure himself to every lightning strike. They made Myra and Dono hide down lower by the water lilies. Though the man was alone, they could not discount the danger he posed, but they needed directions. It was a civilian armed only with a jungle bolo hanging on his waist while carrying something. Speaking Tagalog amid a petrifying situation, the man surrendered himself at the sight of guns and intimidating voices from Santos.

"I'm not enemy, please don't shoot!" he screamed, begging to spare his life.

"Who are you, and why are you following us?" asked a man kneeling on the ground.

"I'm a fisherman, my name is Anselmo, Emong Labangon, sir," the man identified himself.

"Why are you following us?"

Emong easily gained respect from the soldier. After all, what can an old man do?

"I saw how you seem lost in the forest, I thought I could help. I live about five more kilometers to north upstream of the river," Emong answered. "If you don't mind my asking, where are you heading?"

No one answered but only looked at him straight in the eye; none were convinced yet that he could be trusted. He could be a collaborator.

In his story, he was a native of the place who Had survived on farming and fishing even before the war. He had spotted them while embarking from a big boat, but the distance was too far to reach them on time to warn that there were Japanese patrols in the area.

"There are no other civilians around here?" Cab asked this time but didn't disclose where they were going yet.

"There are evacuees scattered in groups in the interior of the jungles. Mostly from the town of Liga and Guinobatan. The Japanese has garrison in Polangui and maintain a tight checkpoint on the road. You may get in, but there's no way out."

"There is a house at the end of a clearing by the road to the pier, do you know who live there?" Cab again.

"Yes, that is the Japanese quarters guarding the beaches. You may be lucky they got afraid of the lightning strikes—they all retreated in that house before the storm. You missed them by minutes." Emong kept going. "I was atop a tree when you came. I was watching you in the last hours of daylight, but I don't know you yet. All I was sure was you were running from the Japanese. That's when I decided to catch up with you, hoping I can help," he explained.

"Sir, may I ask what place we are now?" Donono asked politely.

"We are in a remote area in the province of Albay, son," Emong replied.

"You said you live here, how far are we from Polangui?" Cabarles asked this time.

"My son formerly lived in Polangui. The town is situated over the mountains about twenty miles north. I heard the Japanese burned many houses there."

"Do you know Tomas or Simon Marfil, Tata Emong?" Myra was excited already. "They also live in Poblacion, close to the church," she continued.

"I know, but my son might know them," Emong replied. "I was never in town since the Japanese took over. My son must know. There are evacuees in the place I live. They may have information more than I can tell you."

"My place is not very far from here. If you are going north, you are welcome to come with me and stay there if it please you—the weather can only get worse," Emong offered.

"Do you by yourself to go fishing?"

"I was with a group of fishermen to try our luck at bringing home some food to eat for our families, but the weather was not good. We could only use spears, the undertow is very strong and I'm too old for it. The rest of us went back to our settlement earlier."

"Why did you stay?"

"I didn't catch any, I have nothing to bring home yet. I was trying my luck to visit an old fishing village about two kilometers south, find something I could still use, but there were many Japanese, then I saw you."

Nothing to lose, nowhere to go. Only for a night until the rain stopped did they take advantage of the invitation. After many exhausting hours in the pouring rain, they were entering a makeshift dwelling over a spot noticeably cleared not too long ago. According to Emong, Polangui was almost four hours' walk over hilly trails and treacherous jungles, which was not advisable at this kind of weather. On the other hand, there was no way to cross the national road to eastern Albay if they intend to search for the people they were looking for. Just as dangerous, Japanese may shoot people for no reason at all. When asked, he said there was no guerilla activity on this part of the province, but they were active in the south. Southern Bicol was cut off from all kinds of communication and supplies from Luzon, and the largest concentration of Japanese soldiers was in the town of Liga. They continued listening to Emong. His wife, an adult son with his own family, and three grandchildren shared an abode that was full of holes dripping of the heavy rain. But they managed to cook what they could offer. Not only them, there were more families in the same condition. Robbed of decent life and future but trying to survive in any way to the best of their ability, they were praying and hoping, hiding in the place in a group where they think the brutal invaders cannot find them anymore.

"Having a permanent shelter is not our priority, we may be moving again," Emong stated, justifying their living condition. "The men are all busy during the day to find food that is very rare at this time. We are depending on wild fruits and edible plants that was exhausted a long time ago and the rainy season has yet to begin." Well, it already began and it was relentless. The sad effect of the long drought had already taken its toll on the assembly of people whose ablest men may have drifted away and were not able to come back, presumed to have encountered a Japanese and was shot dead.

"The ocean where we can fish is ten kilometers away, but Japanese snipers may also be hiding in the bushes, and any of us could end up floating on the water," the old man continued between bursts of coughing with the wife who also contributed to his dialogue. With only hope persisting, their physical strength were waning from old age, and they were trying very hard to be understood.

"What is left for many of us here are souls to keep, hence many we buried already. For two days, Emong was not by my side. I prayed for the last time to give him strength to come back to me so I could die happy," she added to what the husband said. "We are old, we live our life in joy long enough until it ends by evil intrusion. If death it is that shall separate us, so be it. When it happens, I just want him on my side to say farewell before I close my eyes." Emong's wife described her last wish full of emotions but unafraid.

Well, it was a wish that was almost denied by the guests she welcomed to her abode. Santos knew very well he would not miss at a range he was aiming his rifle at her husband earlier. What prevented him from pulling the trigger was he hadn't done it for so long he hesitated until Emong was so close to overpower him with a bare hand. The old woman was given a chance to see the beloved husband again all right.

Stacks of coconut palms could not prevent the rain from leaking through. The house too small to accommodate five more people, there was no poorer description of a living condition than what they saw. Emong could only offer what he had. The same banana bunches he carried back home after two days. The total darkness was made so bright every minute or so by lightning bolts through the wall-less abode that revealed many more poor souls trying to cope up on the effects of thunderstorm accompanied by the relentless rain. Conversations paused with every lightning and thunder, to resume again a revelation that was so sad to hear. There was food they carried from the *Rosalia*, fruits from the gods Myra was saving for the relatives she was hoping to see, but how could she deny a hungry child crying in the care of a grandmother that just didn't know what to do anymore but sing a lullaby?

Soaked and dripping, exhausted of walking miles, what good was it to share a humble shelter that submitted to the mercy of nature? A grace presented by an apple to share, a bunch of unripe bananas for tomorrow, so much hope did it bring to the family of Emong, but there was no more they could offer.

Cabarles, sitting on a fallen trunk of a coconut in the pouring rain, hands over the grip of his rifle while opening his mouth at times to fill it with the pouring rain. He was not thirsty nor hungry. Thunderstorm in the summer reminded him of a time when he was one breath away from dying—that one breath to hold on, to make him grasp for another then one more sustained by angels and people who were all guilty of at least causing harm to life of another and paying misdeeds in jail.

A miracle he was given, his salvation from hopelessness he would remember pounded by lightning and thunder to refresh in his thoughts. Darkness of night, nightmares of hell in hell, it was him who was not forsaken but let to live and regain his strength and awareness so that he could see there are other people around. There were children. There was a man walking with a stick braving the rain to reach an abode dozens of steps away hoping in there he could be spared a bite of food. He was not deprived. He was grateful to receive a quarter of fruit shared to a frightened woman in a sudden burst of bright light. For what it was worth, it was shared to another then the rest given to a child.

What else they had left were seven grenades and hundreds of bullets. They were heavily armed to sustain an encounter with the Japanese for at least a while, but no more food even for themselves. Santos and Donono given it all away.

The heaven stopped on rumbling; the sky was clearing of heavy clouds that swept east to the sea, clearing the sky so bright stars could be seen as he looked up one more time. A frog started croaking nearby and then another one that was followed by many more down the hill and in the far distance. The rain stopped, leaving meadows soaked and ground depressions filled with water.

Rodrigo Santos must have realized their situation. There was nothing else the old man could offer but information to make worse the speculations he already said. There was no room for them in the place; they would find their own until such time they could decide for the benefit of Myraflor Marfil. They would leave the place at once. No more food they could spare. For tomorrow, four more people would be added to the residents in total distress.

He convened with Cabarles. "We cannot stay here any longer, we have to leave now," Santos stated to corroborate the same impression of what they saw around. "These people cannot afford to make us stay, they are struggling on their own in great need of food. For us to hang around would mean more mouths to feed for these people in great struggle."

"We are staying, take a rest," Cab said firmly. He wasn't sure he was heard.

Santos heard it loud and clear. He sat by him and chose not to argue. It was too dark so he agreed to stay until dawn. In the morning, they would leave for what he understood.

THE PIT THAT WASN'T BIG ENOUGH

With dawn breaking, it was time to move as Santos thought they should do. He woke up to see that he was alone. There was no sight of Cabarles. The thought that suddenly came into his mind that Cabarles had deserted them was expunged when he saw Donono digging a hole quietly. He came over to help; somebody must have died last night. The wife of Emong presumably.

The hole was about two feet by two feet square, not even one foot deep when Donono stopped and walked away as daylight began. What was in his mind was that for the hole to bury someone even sitting down would still expose the head on the ground. Santos continued digging; he guessed the old woman might have died in a sitting position as how he had last seen her, but she earned his respect to at least give her a decent burial at the behest of the wit of the little friend. For that matter, he took the deed seriously until he was satisfied that the hole was deep enough. Then came a bright morning.

Soiled to the top of his head, humid morning, he sat down by the hole for a while resting. Myra came with a cup of hot brew. She wondered what the captain was doing but felt that she was not in the position to ask. Myra peeked inside the hole repeatedly; the captain was sad and tired. For what a pit dug so deep was for, she didn't know either.

Santos became aware they were staying more than he thought they would be. The morning revealed that there were more people in the place more than he had seen before. Someone was to be buried. Usually when someone died, immediate relatives wept. Nothing like that, it was a quiet morning. He stopped digging. Donono was back.

"Thanks for your help, sir, very nicely done," Donono said.

"What is the hole for?" Santos asked, still believing someone had died last night, a child maybe after seeing that the old woman was alive.

"Outshack, Dapecol style," Donono replied, revealing that Myra had stepped on feces checking out the surroundings when they woke up.

"Why did you do that for? Everyone can just use the cover of bushes."

"I only do it for Myra, sir. Just like how you taught me to take care of her. Thank you for your help again, sir, Myra will be thrilled."

"What else can I do for you? Where is Cab? I don't see him."

"He should be around, you were in deep sleep. We chose not to bother you."

"So nobody died last night?"

"None that I know, sir," Dono replied. "I need to provide privacy around it." He was determined to finish the work as soon as possible.

They went back inside Emong's house and took another bolo. Higher up the hill, they started hacking young trees to the specifications of Donono. Knowing what else he needed, they cut and dragged coconut leaves too. Santos was scratching his head.

Cabarles came back eventually with Emong's son, Felipe. They had fun for what it was they did all night till morning. Emong was thrilled with the frogs and snakeheads he was handed over. Summer rain comes with a lot of graces.

They were not leaving the place until they could determine what was best for Myra. Cabarles had decided to stay for as long as it took. Depending on the information from Emong and a few residents, it was too dangerous for them to continue uptown or any direction. In an unknown place with an ensemble of people in deep need of help, leaving the girl in their care was as good as dead. It was the end of the line for her. Polangui was thirty miles away, but intelligence did not warrant traveling in town considering the risks of an enemy encounter. The option to leave after having the girl in their company presented the unimaginable hurdle that she would be taking ahead. Unlike the first half of journey from Davao where route had been preestablished by people guiding them, landing in Bicol is opposite. Every step they make imperil their chance to reach any destination. Emong was a blessing; somehow they knew where they were though it was not what they expect to be.

Severely malnourished children were barely moving, noses dripping, human feces scattered around. To the people whose only intent was to survive, out from reach of the widow maker, they felt safe in the middle of nowhere. In the jungle, they found refuge of what help others could give until it was no more but hope and determination. Evacuees in Davao were allowed right at the gate of Dapecol. For what reason these people chose to hide away was definitely a choice made in a panicked disposition to save their lives. All together, the ghost soldiers hit a blank wall too, so as these people who were offering help but clearly they were in very miserable condition.

Hope was shared that they would survive in food terms for the meantime. A river to cross was raging and overflowing. They could not leave just yet.

Another project was in mind. With plenty of bamboo down the hill, they spent all morning cutting down as much as they could; lots of materials would be needed. There was an endless supply around. They would build a shelter for themselves too.

There were not many tools to build a house, five bolos, a few knives, clay pots, and tin buckets that everyone was trying to hide from each other, fearing they would get broken or lost or used against them. Myra had a lot of work to do too; she had learned enough from Rosie, but the prevailing attitudes were entirely different to every camp and village she had been. These were civilians whose priorities were their own selves, stealing from each other to survive, unlike the guerillas and villages in Mindanao who were all generous to each other in a single commune. Not to mention Bohol. What Myra didn't understand was these were the aristocrats of the Filipinos in Central Bicol, not used to any hard work but expecting somebody else doing for them, coming to the jungle with a pocketful of money, some with servants, and retaining their usual behavior that they could still manage to survive by telling their help what to do.

Some families went back to town but were presumed meted out with horrible death as they were rounded up by the Japanese, suspected of being part of the resistance in the region. There was no more house to reclaim. With the unchanged attitude of the Japanese toward civilians, those that survived found themselves back in the jungle, some over a year already in the place that without self-determination was also like waiting for their death. Thirty-one women, old and young. Myra was outraged to find that one girl was pregnant. On total count of sixty-six settlers in all, they somewhat enjoyed the gossips and backstabbing against one another. Looking at the inability of the lesser men to work due to laziness or finding excuses of being sickly and depending on others, inutile as may be the right word, it was just too difficult to gain cooperation from each other as everyone resorted to selfishness in an effort to survive the day.

One woman whose husband left allegedly for a noble purpose told a sad story. The husband had left the camp six months ago and never returned. Another one would despise a young man who tried to disavow that he fathered the pregnancy of a girl. She was sure no one else had the opportunity to cause the sinful deed; others were married or too young or too old. The mother would say he raised his son with a firm belief in God and therefore not capable of such an unimaginable sin. Her son, she said, "just turned fifteen and is in line to be a priest." Such problems of distrust could also be attributed to the fact that they had only known each other in a short period of time. The only thing they had in common was they were all running away from Japanese atrocities and were now equally starving to death as they have exhausted what the land offers in food kind, which was made worse by the dry season.

The first step of remediation was to set aside selfishness and snobbery. The soldiers' strategy began to promote cooperation among the people, but that was not enough. Food must be of priority before anyone listened. Myra assumed the responsibility for bringing the population to a more accommodating attitude toward each other. Donono, at her personal service, was only able to help her part-time because he was needed to train a few men left on how to be resourceful in gathering food. At least what was left of them to perform specific tasks.

The boy who would be priest was credited for his diligence and became personally attached to Cabarles and Santos. He was happy to help; in fact, he took over many chores from Donono. Cab led the adults who were given specific jobs to cut cogon grasses that had grown untouched in the area; some followed, some didn't. Few were really incapacitated by disease. By afternoon, the soldiers had a shelter of their own to sleep at night. Myra had immediately developed amity with a few widows, trying to gain more information about the fate of her relatives. For lunch was frog legs fried in coconut oil. Myra and most women spent a long time preparing them. Added for lunch was several heron eggs Cabarles had brought back with him from the cogon field, which was distributed mainly to children and the pregnant girl. He queried about anyone keeping a gun. A woman hesitantly said she was keeping a .22 rifle that belonged to her late husband. At supper, they had birds to ration for everyone with much of its flesh intact.

The group led by Donono that was gathering vines to make rope said wild hogs were seen in the mountain, bigger and more nutritious; they would find it the next day. Some suggested that there must be plenty of fish in the river; they just didn't know how to catch them because of the absence of nets and fish traps. Renewed of hope with the survival skills and leadership of the soldiers, even the oldest of the people in the camp offered their remaining strength wherever they could help. After all, they only knew just now that the cogon field could yield appetizing and nutritious food.

Basket weaving was initiated by Donono in urgency for the making of fish traps and pouches or any trap he may thought can catch anything they could eat. Lot of bamboos were available. Anselmo's family started basket weaving in the beginning; it didn't take long for everyone to want to give a hand.

Having more people seemed to cooperate in the undertakings, persona non grata to those who would not as they had eaten equal share of every meal. Ultimately, tasting the meat of wild hogs gave them motivation. In that afternoon, all bolos changed hands nonstop in their use to the last of the daylight, including the chopping of another boar. It was a feast at supper. By next morning, energy revitalized, they all woke up almost at the same time, taking chores and work that they had already been assigned. Everything went smoothly in the following days, and everyone were doing something. Even the children found their usefulness to the supply of fresh water from a nearby brook, which was the least they could do.

For the rest of May and June then the months that followed, the monsoon season hit the Bicol Region hard with occasional strong winds that frequent repair of the shelters they had built was required. Patterned to the design of Dapecol barracks, the difference was a four-foot aisle in the middle that made it look more like a chicken coop. However, Santos would be so proud with how it was finished; they were happy they could move the last of the family on the last bay. Myra could have her own exclusive room across an open bay where the soldiers could resign after a day's work. No more fighting for food. Fish, crabs, and snails also became available with a fish trap copied from the Manobos and T'bolis. Sweet potatoes and cassavas were replanted and growing healthy, banana plants too.

Emong had gone back to where he was stealing bananas to get planters. He was happy that he didn't have to travel far anymore to eat the fruit. He was just to take care of the dozen he had planted and wait patiently; he was expected to wait until he died that he cannot eat the fruit of those bananas, but he didn't mind. Cabarles and Santos had already scouted over the mountain in the town of Libon, and the sight of the Japanese had scared them not to push through all the way to Polangui. They were disguised as farmers and merchants, bamboo crafts made from the camp they were trading with necessities, at the same time establishing communications with the townspeople, all of whom presumed collaborators.

Every time they came back from reconnaissance, they brought several items, like blankets, cooking pots, and assorted vegetable seeds and seedlings from untended farms, anything they thought they could use in the evacuees' camp. It was determined that the bamboo products they made could easily be sold in town. Bamboo craft and mats out of palm tree became a valuable source of income from the cooperative indulgence of the civilians. Donono's skill, learned from Dapecol, in managing a conglomerate of black marketing was put into fair deal with heightened inspiration because of Myra's equal initiative in the process. No stolen boots and fake pill to sell this time, but all from hardship and the sweat of the locals.

In early August, the pregnant girl gave birth to a healthy boy. She named her son Jose Dono. She was very thankful of the pair who helped and treated her without abhorrence like the rest of the people including her own family.

The boy who wanted to be a priest according to his mother turned out that he really wanted to be a priest as he confided to Cabarles and Santos during one of their fishing trips. He was already in high school when the war broke and had been an altar boy since he was a little child. He swore he never touched the young girl but disclosed he had seen her behaving obliviously in the woods with a man a very long time ago. That man had disappeared. Freed of allegations of fathering the child as the baby didn't have any resemblance to him whatsoever, he was just happy of the good signs the child had brought to the camp. Now free of selfishness and pride, the camp would survive for a long time depending on when and how the war would end. In the mind of the young boy who would be priest, the ghost soldiers were sent from heaven; he was corrected that they came from hell. Whichever case, he believed it was a miracle that strengthened his faith.

With time to spare doing nothing, by the end of August when the weather was forgiving, the ghost soldiers began to reassess their situation. They had concluded that their stewardship of the civilian evacuees was no longer needed. In bringing back their hospitality and consideration of each other's welfare, people now could take care of themselves. No one was hungry anymore though absent of any luxury that had they enjoyed before the war; they were all happy looking forward that they would have the sufficient means to put food in their stomach. A multipurpose structure was also constructed for the growing attendees of a writing and reading class a settler had started. Myra had long joined the effort herself. Cabarles and Donono occasionally attended and somewhat became amused when Santos would hang out with him to see how they were progressing. Later, Cab would learn that the teacher was bearing another miracle baby. He could not blame the father; the Bicolana was really eye catching who was of the likes of the alluring beauty of Rhodora X and Rosie.

Three long months passed by rapidly; it was blamed on the monsoon season that held them up in the place. Sometimes they actually forgot the country was at war while they were having fun playing with the children. He knew Santos was having the most fun finding a playmate of his own. Donono was losing faith on Abu's talisman for what it was supposed to do, but he continued aspiring to win the heart of Myra the way Cabarles was coaching him.

ESCAPE FROM BICOL

However, the soldiers' objective of finding Myra's relatives still remained undone. Every which way they would think of getting to the eastern part of Bicol suggested a disastrous outcome for them. Many more civilians arrived and were welcomed into the camp, but none could give any information about the Marfils. It was sad to think that Myra's uncles did not exist anymore. On the other hand, traveling east across town was planned, but intelligence only assured that the Japanese encounter was imminent every route they could go through. Determined as only a small possibility next to none that Myra's relatives had evacuated in the eastern region if they were still alive, chances are they would not find them. Therefore, the alternative had to be supported and justified in order to lessen the burden of leaving a promise incomplete. Rod Santos seemed serious with Violeta, the school teacher; truly another child would be born, but the father of this one would known. Donono could not be mistaken that he wanted to stay, as he would be where Myra chose to be. In effect, the reason for Cabarles to leave was exactly the same reason for them to stay—for the love and desire of a woman. The only stance reasonable was for him to leave alone.

Sitting at the edge of a creek high enough to see the ocean view from his favorite spot, he always stared at the spectacular scenery of green until it ended on the water. Over it was the mass of lands separated by a water passage, one stretching to the south called Burias Islands, but his mind was also imagining on the northwest, the southern tip of Tayabas province (now Quezon). In fact, it was part of the mainland, but there was no way he could get there without walking around the Camarines provinces. That would be a long walk while considering reliable information that the enemy was heavily concentrated on those areas all the way and multiplied nearing to Manila. Unknown from his brothers, many days he had obtained general knowledge about Albay. Preferred route to north by foot had been established and memorized.

Donono had repeatedly said he knew the wilderness of Quezon and Camarines like the back of his palm because that was where he came from originally. He was found in Manila, and therefore it was clearly possible by foot to Manila from Tayabas (Quezon). He didn't have the agility of Donono and the ability to adapt to surroundings and disappear. On the other hand, without Santos, he could not discount the fact that he was lost already the moment he made the first step. Alone to journey by foot approximately a thousand miles could not be done if he didn't take that crucial first step. The risk he would be taking for personal intention would not be fair for fellow soldiers to come along with him. Weather conditions change considerably; he had by what his gut dictated to leave as soon as possible. He had a plan—he was going by himself and that he would do. He was just taking the time to tie up loose ends. He wanted to leave in good faith with Myra.

His personal concern with Myra Marfil must find closure. The promise could not be fulfilled as plausibly as it was spoken to the girl as the same promise he renewed to Rosalia when they left Bohol. He believed that a promise forsaken had caused him all woes and bad luck.

"Good morning. May I join you?" Myra greeted from behind. "I'm sorry to disturb your thoughts, but you seem very serious and restless these past days."

"Yes, I realized that we have been in Bicol for a long time, and we cannot find where your uncles are. I'm sorry, it's just too dangerous for you any which way I think," Cab replied with a sad smile.

"I have so much gratitude for you I don't know how to express it. You have done so much for me, I'm sure I had found them already with these people," Myra replied.

Said in a sad voice but with a sweet smile from a pretty face of a formerly fair complexion now turned darker, all she wanted was to thank the man who rescued her from the concubine house, but there was more she wanted to know. It had been a long time, but she had never expressed her gratitude; she didn't know where to begin, and the time was right before it would be too late. Myra was advised beforehand to be short and discreet but still shy and nervous to talk with Cab, having observed that he didn't say too much. She was rehearsed by Santos and Donono of what she was going to say and ask about a specific subject. The respect she had developed for him could not equal to all the men she had known, from the tales of his heroism and bravery and how he handled the most beautiful women who had loved and respected him, most of all the concern he had extended for herself even before she actually knew him.

"I'm glad you say that. If only I can bring you with me . . . the danger is unthinkable," Cab said while looking at her eyes noticeably having trouble of saying those words.

"I know. Don't worry about me anymore please, you have done more than enough for all of us here. I will be all right," Myra said, in tears now that she had confirmed Cab was leaving.

"Captain Santos and Donono will stay, they will all take care of you," Cab said while comforting her. "Don most especially will take care of you if you let him."

"I'm sure he will, he is a good man," the girl answered.

"Yeah, only if you can find a place in your heart for him. Otherwise, he is coming with me," Cab uttered intentionally, making himself sound disappointed.

"I already did a long time ago. It wasn't too hard to fall for him, but I understand he had more important things to fulfill—he is a soldier. I know his loyalty to you, and for that I understand. I wish you will let me come with you too if you're taking him," Myra replied. "Please . . . please don't tell him," she continued after a long silence.

"I won't. Did he talk to you about it? Did he force you into it?" Cab just heard the shock of his life. He just didn't know what to say, but in his mind, it was what he had hoped to happen. Someone to watch over her when he disappeared, and Donono was the only one most likely to do just that.

"No, nothing like that. He is always thoughtful to me, attending to my needs. I admit it was not too hard to open my heart for him. Should I think like that when I knew he is only following your orders for my benefit." It was sadness and pity that she inflict on herself. "I should not let myself fall for him. I know his loyalty to you is more than anything else, even his life. He said to me his life for you to spend as long as he lives."

"I believe you, he is really a good man. I will make sure he stays if you can be honest with me. Do you really love him, or did you just miss too many meals? When was the last time you ate? You look pale."

"Why are you asking me that? We had supper together last night." Myra was smiling to confirm that what she said was true.

"Yeah, I just remember. You didn't eat that much, have your breakfast now then come back to me. I want to hear again about what you say you feel about Donono."

Wiping off tears, she laughed. "I'm serious, but please don't tell him. I may not be the girl he thought I am. You know where you found me. I was robbed of my dignity, but no one had taken my heart until now."

"I'm very happy for him, I don't know what else to say." Cabarles smiled.

"When are you guys leaving?"

"I don't know yet, but it will be soon. I'm sorry to say you will wake up one morning and I won't be around. Please pray for me, I will be alone," Cab whispered quickly, noticing the other two soldiers coming to join them.

"I will, always."

"I wish you the best in life with Donono."

"Thank you very much for everything you have done for me."

Santos had tried a few times to get Cabarles to disclose his next move as Myra understood that he could not be relying on Cabarles all the time. It was resolved indeed; however, Cab would also think that he didn't need to drag Santos and Donono all the way to Bulacan, and Santos made it clear that Cab could not leave without him. The status quo had changed since then; Santos was disappearing many nights, sometimes even at daylight.

Neither Santos nor Donono wanted to ask Cabarles "again," only to hear the "concern that has to be addressed first." The concern for Myra was settled. In their own reckoning supported by what they saw and observed, the pair had reason to believe that Cab was deceiving them from his real intent.

Myra was quiet. She couldn't hide that earlier she had cried. Donono handed her something. "Thank you, I already munched on something. I'll share it to the children. Please excuse me." She walked away.

Santos was saying something. Donono followed Myra with his eyes; sweaty and shirtless, he was happy enough to hear her voice in the morning. Cabarles was staring at Donono like the first time he saw him. He lowered his eyes then reached for that unusual thing hanging on his chest. He touched it with serious curiosity, seeing it in every angle then looking at him again, not saying any word. He then scratched his head.

"What did I do?" Dono asked. No way would Cab know yet where he got those bananas he just gave to Myra. Not yet at this time.

"Nothing. Myra is going to take a bath, you know. Does she have enough water?" he said out from what he was thinking.

"Yes, sir, I did it last night. Plenty," Donono said.

Seemingly the information they wanted to know was disclosed, indicated by the crying of Myra. Santos would guess as to the outcome of that morning conversation between Myra and Cab without being told of the details. There was no sense asking Cabarles again; he will not lie to Myra. "What shall we do today?" he quizzed to start a morning talk that always revealed the same topic: about Inez, how much more Cabarles could prevent himself from pursuing that thought. Weather has been permitting the last few days. The sky was clear though the clouds from afar was a normal sight at this time of year.

"Let's go hunt a boar."

Going to hunt a boar, Donono would not let himself be left out. He was coming too.

Noticeable for being restless and troubled but remaining quiet most of the time, Santos knew exactly what bothered the man he had long deemed more than just a friend or brother, but more likely as an extension of his still-beating heart.

Earlier, Santos had instructed Myra of indulging Cabarles to a conversation that would reveal their next move as his own repeated attempts were proven futile. He could not understand why Cab would remain undecided and secretive the past few days, but his silence or avoidance in discussing their current situation and subsequent course of action remain untold. At the end of the day, the only thing he and Don would know was the one they already knew. They had seen that it was time for them to continue in their journey and they should be ready; it was only a matter of time when Cabarles would say so. Santos was suspicious that Cab was planning to go without them.

Night came, and Cabarles slept early with the two soldiers expected to lay down at his side. They did. No talks anymore about anything they had discussed already. Santos was habitually disappearing at night, and so was a young widow that had become a close friend of Myra. Donono had waked up early to fetch water. He didn't know what time it was yet, but he woke up alone and not seeing his buddies. Nothing whatsoever could change his mind; the silence of the darkness had made him decide it should be now. He had long suspected that the sweet-talking Santos must be wandering under the stars with Violeta and most likely enjoying a beautiful night in her company. He grabbed his satchel and rifle hanging on the bamboo wall and quietly walked away. Just like that, he disappeared in the shadow of the plants and trees in the dark.

"Would you let me embrace you to say my farewell?" a sad familiar voice came out a step behind him from the bushy plants. Apparently, she had been there waiting patiently.

Speechless and guilty of getting caught despite the most careful effort he exerted to cover his plan and preparations, there was nothing really he could think of to say until the woman came closer and felt her embrace.

"I'm sorry I can't find a way that shall clear my throat to say farewell to you and everyone else. Please do so for me."

"I will. Let me express my deep gratitude again for what you have done for me. In behalf of the settlement, Tata Emong and all, we thank you very much."

"I should be going now."

Crying again for maybe the last time she would see her savior, brother, father and mother, friend and a great leader for all of them, a very emotional moment took place. They said prayers and good wishes to each other, promising to see again when the war ended.

Though leaving the place had been planned and prepared to the hours he had found courage to set in motion, the feelings of abandoning her and the two soldiers without any notice was still unjustified in his mind. He only hoped they would also understand like Myra who lessened that culpability. Suddenly finding himself alone in a journey he had arranged by himself, he could not avoid but look back to make sure he wasn't followed or admit in a true sense that he was hopeful that Santos and Donono were behind. It was a deliberate intention to leave alone, but the longing for them this early could not be mistaken as he might have made a decision with disrespect to the two brothers he also owed so much.

So far so good, no sight of them within the first kilometer he had walked, almost running occasionally. He stopped for a while in a cluster of bushes to retrieve his stash of food and other things for the travel then continued without looking back. He didn't mind why his bananas weighed lesser than when he hid them, but he didn't pay much attention. His mind was totally made up to one objective—come back to Inez as promised "'till death do us part." Nothing could stop him now, and every step he made was a step of hope that he would be with her very soon. Whatever obstacles were laid down on his path, and all he had in his mind was the true love he must be sharing happily with Inez, whatever hardship awaited him.

At least on the first two miles, he knew the way; he continuously prayed he needed a grand assistance to show him the way after all until he crossed the river that he had no idea what else are beyond. He knew it isn't only the Japanese he had to be afraid of; there was a lot more and equally vicious to cause death. Disorientation, illnesses, wild animals, snakes, traitors and those friendly who would think of him as an enemy spy were a few to consider. Well, there was no turning back now.

IN THE WATER LILIES

Running three more kilometers to the bank of Bato River where he had hidden a raft made days ago, for one last time, he looked back again in the direction of the camp. He knew that at first sunlight his disappearance would be noticed. He scoured over the last clearing through the darkness of dawn, hoping he would see some shadows running among the cogon and cattails field, hurriedly in motion to catch up with him. He walked back a few steps for a better view, keenly looking as far as he could see, but there was no sign of Santos and Donono. The sorrow that enveloped his thought at that moment caused the tears to come down his face. If only he could let them come.

Nobody would see him crying anyway, and he let his emotion take over the sudden longing of the other two soldiers who had been part of his life and soul in mostly desperate situations. They deserved to have the happiness of their own that they found in the settlement; moreover, the camp needed their leadership to survive. "Goodbye, my brothers," he said sadly after a brief prayer and good wishes to them all. Into the thick plants and vines that grew on top of the other he walked, through an obscure path down the muddy riverbank to the raft.

"Do you really think you can go without us?" said a voice a few steps behind, obscured by leaves. It was Santos talking.

Caught advancing in motion of a plan he tried to cover up and which he denied every way he could for days, particularly from them, he was thankful anyway that it was still dark; otherwise they would see him crying.

Euphoria followed by expletives due to the unexpected turn of events, he underestimated the intelligence of Santos and Donono to detect the uncharacteristic changes of the people around them much more of him. All the effort to conceal his departure suddenly became useless. He was caught in the act that he could not deny he was going alone. He grasped explanations on top of his head. He must come up with something.

"You have women in camp. Stay with them and let me go to mine," he said in reaction to only a justification he could think of being caught red-handed.

"I can have a lot of them in Manila just the same," Santos responded. "He shall stay." He calmly pointed to Donono who was eating perfectly ripened bananas.

Regaining a stance from downright embarrassment and having one of them who sided with him instantly, he took the opportunity of getting rid of one first then dealing with the other later. "Yeah, you are leaving without telling Myra. We talked before I left, and she was crying because she knew she will never see you again. Would you let her cry for loving you and leaving?" Cabarles explained in a bid to make Donono stay. "Do you really like her to be your wife or not?" he yelled.

"Yes, I do."

"Well, come back to her, she is waiting for you."

Santos could not believe what he was hearing; it must be the talisman if it was true, but he went along. He wasn't sure of the reason why Cab wanted to leave him and Donono in the camp, but observing all the hardship Don had been through to win the heart of Myra, he helped convince the little man to stay.

Don was speechless; he didn't know what to say. Whether it was the effect of the talisman or of his own merits, he liked the feeling. He was determined to continue with such dedication, but the calling of his duty to his officers and friends was the most important. The situation had changed worth a lifetime to pursue. Myra was young and so pretty; there would be no more of a chance in his lifetime to meet a girl like her. None of her intelligence and courage would ever come into his prudence anymore. He was a soldier, all right, but the orders he was given were errands for him to follow. Not in the situation that he was about to be left out by the people who took him as an equal. On the other hand, what was at stake was a fantasy only worth pursuing through his imagination. With Cabarles's disclosure, he admitted he would never see Myra again if he insisted to come.

Thinking, Donono peeled some more bananas and filled his mouth; his eyes rolled in happiness, but he could not decide on his own. He was always dependent on Santos and Cabarles. He didn't know what to do without them. Much more of being left alone in a community of people similar to those who used to slave and humiliate him because of his mediocrity and dark skin. Anxiety began to succumb his senses.

"Can I just come with you? Please," he said, the quivering noticeable in his voice.

"*Bugok*, a pretty woman awaits and is longing for you. Go back to the camp and make her pregnant," Santos said, comparing him to a rotten egghead.

"I-I don't know how. What shall I do?" he apprehensively confided like a whole banana was still in his throat.

Santos may have wanted to laugh but he held it in respect to a brother. Cabarles could not say anything because he was on the same situation just before the war and thereafter. He remembered it took horses to give him strength of that kind to get to the closest he could say he had done it. In fact, his own experiences did not warrant a bragging expertise on the subject matter; he let Santos give Don a crash course on how to deal with their common predicament while he also listened and learned, adding some pointers but actually pretending that he knew more than reaching the third base.

Time passed; the tide receded that left the raft in a muddy bank. Donono was not convinced that Myra wanted him to come back; hence he would complain he was discomfiting himself to impress Myra for many months whence in his village all he must do was to bring home a dead pig or deer and a woman would come to marry her. Disbelief and laughing arose when Cab top that, truly he did the same to court Inez for so many years but made a mistake of not telling his real intentions that could make the whole ordeal a lot shorter until the war broke. Don must say something to the girl to advance his interest. How to begin, he needed coaching. Cab picked some water lilies himself that Don must give to Myra and then some words that he had to say while handing the flowers to her. Santos repeated his previous advice to use his gun if necessary. In the end, Donono was convinced, with assurance that an alluring beauty waiting for him had fallen mutually in his desire; he decided to go back to the village.

Though still confused, the last thing he did in farewell to Cabarles and Santos was a salute, making a promise that he would make that girl pregnant and happy for the rest of his life. Before he disappeared in the leafy vines, he came back again. Santos, awfully irritated, grabbed his rifle to scare him away. The Don didn't budge but continued toward the burlap bag that Cab carried and took a few more bananas without any word. Then he said goodbye again.

Don was out in good faith, and Cab calculated what should be an effective reasoning for the other one that he knew any explanation would be useless. In fact, it was being anticipated.

"What you did to Donono is not going to work on me," Santos warned outright while shaking his head.

"What should I do to make you stay then?" Cab asked anyway.

"Shoot me dead," the captain replied seriously. He deliberately said not to ponder useless argument.

"All right then, let's go." Point taken.

The tide was coming back, but they still needed to drag the raft out of the muddy embankment. No one wanted to talk other than tell each other to be careful while crossing the river.

Though there was nothing but rugged terrain and virgin scrublands to expect ahead, planning and setting up rules of engagement was discussed outright. Their ordnance could not sustain a prolonged battle when encountering an enemy patrol; only running away would be the best option. Besides, what could they do against the enemy that came like swarms when provoked? Deliberation on the real issues began. What caused them considerable delay was not the enemy. From Davao to Bicol, since they escaped Dapecol more than eight months ago, both were aware that they consumed most of the time by connecting with civilians and guerillas; therefore they avoided them all as well and concentrated on the objectives. Rule one had been in effect since Dapecol; the second rule was added. There was no reason to hurry up, but they agreed that what slowed them were women who cried every stop they made.

ANOTHER BEGINNING

August 1943 in Libon, Albay, they had to share information about the route they had learned individually, so as to expect about enemy activities as far as Manila. They had gained knowledge about the geography of the region, and they were confident they would reach their destination safe and sound. The first day was a walk in the park; Santos and Donono had scouted miles over the area before. The sun was obscured by heavy clouds, and very soon, darkness fell with heavy rain. They pushed more along a lake going toward east to find a place to rest. An old shack through the dark, they sought shelter just in time as a drizzle started. Walking ten hours straight with more energy to spare, both had spent a few more hours talking while the rain started pouring. There was plenty of water they could drink. When one of them reached inside the bag, he was surprised when all bananas were unripe and not good to eat. He guessed what happened to his stash. The frustration turned to laughter between them.

Shaking his head, Cab spoke. "He is lucky we are far enough, otherwise I will go back in the camp and hurt him bad."

"Don't bother, it will ripen in no time. Here, let's have what he prepared for us—a broiled chop of hog we shot the other day," Santos said.

"Very good, now you make me feel bad for leaving him in camp." Cab switched to another tone, clearly just missing the company of Donono to cause his rants.

Turning the conversation back to Donono, Santos took the opportunity to clear some doubts in his mind with Cabarles. Even though he participated heavily, he was somewhat worried about leaving Don to be in great despair. It was just not right in his thought to let him believe an impossible thing. In Santos's view, Donono could only realize his desire for Myra if she was tied up. With no one to help him now, it was not going to happen. The girl was a lot taller and still growing at seventeen. Don somewhat reached the height that was allowed by his gene. The oddest nonconformity were their looks. There were many men who showed interest in the poor girl. All were intimidated to concede through his authoritative order, one to the point of his gun, leaving Don with the advantage of the only man who could actually come closer to Myra with such intention. There was no one to do that now.

Running errands for her comfort and all what his instinct dictated that would make the girl happy had been done only to impress her, just patiently attending to her needs. Cabarles would say that it was the proper way for one who has sincere intention to a woman. Talking about his prolific experiences to one lady he married, he was also saying that even wild animals could be tame and yield to submission if treated with respect and tender caring. Myra would be no different.

"You know, I don't believe you about Myra truly falling for Donono."

"Yeah, I don't believe it either, but love find its way even between the most unusual pair."

"What do you mean?"

"It is true, it's really hard to believe what Myra said. But it is true. I'm starting to believe that thing Abu gave Donono is a real thing," Cab stated. "There is a great possibility we will never see them again. I wish them a great life."

"I know you will not lie to me, but after trying to ditch us, I don't know If I shall believe you now."

"I swear, I'm telling the truth. I only try to leave by myself because I know there is a pregnant woman back there and you are the father," Cab defended.

"I know," Santos concurred. "You know there are other things you haven't told me yet." Santos took advantage of the moment.

"Yeah . . . what are those?"

"I'd been puzzled for a long time. Abu said you must have that kind of thing too," Santos began. "When he learned how you made Betsy submit to your command in an instant, he said you also have a talisman."

"I already told you I was the one who tied him up on that tree. I was feeding and quenching her thirst for so many days patiently. I had tamed her before the Americans discovered and started harassing that animal," Cab revealed. "And no, I don't have any talisman or thing of that kind. Honestly, I never believed it until Myra actually told me that she had fallen in love with Donono."

"Oh, now I was enlightened. I thought you have a special talisman or magic to also make woman accede to you in an instant." Santos was laughing profusely but suddenly stopped, reminding himself of many more affairs he wanted to know the details of the man's involvement who remained silent about all of them. "What can you tell me about your affair with Rhodora X? I was told by very reliable persons that you slept with her?" He continued demanding an honest response to a mystery playing in his mind for a long time.

"Who told you?"

"Myra and Rosie."

Suddenly, he grasped for words to confide an event he really could not remember. "I really don't know what happened that night. I was drunk, we were drunk," Cab said after a long pause. "It's really bad for me to get drunk. I don't recall a lot of things when I wake up."

"So you are not telling me."

"What do you want to know?"

What took place in that room waking up with a naked woman that most men would choose to die just to have the same opportunity was still a big question in his mind he could not really recall; maybe he was just denying. All that he had pleasure with and could remember was seeing Rhoda in his naked delight a moment before he covered her with a thin blanket when he was awakened. The moment that followed should be regretful if given more time when Rhoda actually got up revealing the temptations of her bareness into his eyes. But time and condition was uncooperative when Rosie herself called their attention, reminding that every second that passed was becoming so dangerous for the man, for them all. Cabarles explained and he repeated that nothing else happened. No regrets. Santos was not pleased, still feeling left out of important details.

His persistence on the subject weakened when he was reminded that Rhodora had contributed an important role in their escape. Santos would express his pity to the woman he hated so much instantly on the first day he saw her. Now he was putting her on a pedestal.

The night was still young, the rain was weakening, and he still had a few more names in his arsenal to drop on the man with no memory of other women but Inez. However, he really liked talking about beautiful women, and there was one more he wanted to know about.

"How about Rina? I remember how upset she was when we left Davao. The kisses and tears she gave to you distinctively meant something else." Santos was implying something.

"You're just thinking maliciously, Rina is an angel. To her I owe my life. She's the most kindhearted woman. Brave and caring."

"Yeah, angelic beauty, I agree. Did you see her naked too?" He was teasing, but he knew that the closest to details he could get was making the man admit seeing a woman naked. Nothing more than that.

"No, but she really is pretty, isn't she?" Cabarles responded to suffice the imagination of the fellow.

"Did you see her naked too?"

"My mind never came close to that thought. She is very kind, really an angel in looks and deed. She deserved respect, nothing else," Cab replied.

"Would you mind if I come back for her in Davao someday?" Santos said in a sudden change of tone, disclosing his own feelings and attraction to the girl.

"Only if you are talking with your heart. Many women have shed tears for you already. I'm not counting the fatherless children who will be born in every stop we did because of you."

"Look who's talking. I'm serious."

"Sure. Begin tomorrow, why wait?"

"Only if you are going back that way, I also know what transpired between you and Rosie in Bohol."

"Sleep," Cab said to stop Santos from discussing further on that one.

They both knew it would be a long day tomorrow, and thereafter, whichever way they go would be of equal danger and difficulties. Santos implied a reason to go back to Davao, he was only kidding. The silence of the night was left alone to the distinct croaking of frogs and occasional unidentified birds and animals. The rain stopped, but they remained so close to feeling the warmth of each other in the cold night. With only the two of them, they had plenty of time to discuss about anything. No one talked anymore. They just continue imagining good things on their own until both were snoring.

Though used to the crowing of the rooster, they were awakened because of one that was so close. Time was told so loudly that both opened their eyes with excitement looking forward to roast chicken for breakfast. Must be ten or twenty feet away, the eastern horizon above the treetops showed the clearing sky, indicating no more rain coming just yet. The tall grasses on the ground indicated that no one had been on the place in a long while. Barefooted, the first feel of the cold wet ground didn't hinder; all the firewood to start boiling water must be wet too. They decided to find the rooster that they were sure was not alone. There must be people close by taking care of them, but they could not see any structure standing around except the one they slept on. Somewhat they were having trouble locating their breakfast; what they saw around were the familiar banana plants overgrown by leafy vines. As daylight began, they walked farther along Bato Lake that were ruins in ashes of once a self-sustaining community. There were no signs of people, only fruit trees around with a scent of overripe jackfruits and guavas. Large bats were distracted by their coming and flew away from the rotting fruit. There was plenty of food around that they didn't need to find the rooster. They munched on the sweet jackfruits piling edible seeds that also tasted good when boiled and could last for days without spoiling. They spent hours to eat and gather food as much as they could carry. Things were looking good for them that morning.

After saying a little prayer to the people who lived and vanished from the place, they left cautiously. Whoever burned down the village may be nearby, and they could be spotted easily in broad daylight.

CHAPTER 18

THE BICOL EXPRESS

Church bell is ringing. It's been so long since I heard one. In prayers I found solace. Laying down still, no one must see us.

RULES OF ENGAGEMENT

About a week since they left the settlement, no one knew how far they had traveled already. The more obscure they could be was in the cover of vegetation, which was the favored route. They would see people in the open field wandering for any reason or tending animals, but the best option was not to engage, rules that must be taken strictly, observing every distance carefully and redirect based on what visible ahead. After swimming across another river and walking a few more miles, they saw a cluster of houses of seemingly peaceful residents. Herds of wild buffalo, also unfamiliar animals on the ground and up the trees in a plain and barren lands that displayed spectacular views of mountain standing alone in the great distance, they would see bushes of noticeable movement heading to their location. No reason to be alarmed; with the courage they shared, they should just keep moving, they said. North was the favored direction all along, but it was time to review the map Santos had drawn crudely of squares and circles from what the Bicolanos could tell him. The mountain was Isarog, and lying in between must be the town of Naga where the Japanese garrison was situated that discouraged guerilla activities in the area.

Just passing through, the indications that they were not welcome to stay even for a while in most places had been thought of very well.

Enemy patrols may be lurking anywhere. As long as they could keep themselves down and undetected, they would be fine. Generally, the directional instruction was to follow the western seaboard going north northwest not to drift across the national road to the east. Still a very long way to go. Cabarles was carrying a Springfield fitted with a scope and ten spare cartridges and two grenades, Santos with a carbine and three hand grenades. They knew it could not sustain a firefight but made a fact they will spend them all without surrender if it came to that point.

Travel by day was becoming too dangerous; a serious reevaluation of their safe passage in the plains of Camarines and thereafter must be done in the cover of darkness. A heavily populated area ahead that they had to get through was indicated by a village shadowed by tree lines over rice fields. They had been walking for several days, gone far enough from Albay, but monsoon rains contributed heavily to the difficulties of their orientation.

"How far do you think we had walked already?" Cabarles asked to release his frustration. Seemingly, they were not getting any farther as the sight of Isarog stayed just the same.

"I honestly don't know, I think we are resting longer than we actually walk."

"Let's camp here, it will be dark soon and drizzling again."

Heavy clouds would obscure the sky day and night that telling the time was almost impossible. The day seemed too short and moving at night in the rocky or muddy hills of impenetrable vines, and plants that would suddenly end into a clearing was almost identical with what they passed through already. They were all equally treacherous, made worse by the new growth over thick vegetation.

"Once we pass over the town of Naga ahead, we should be all right," Santos stated.

The sky was clearing after so many days they know it won't last. They would brave the open range to the next tree lines afar where they saw lights indicating there were people who lived ahead. What lurked behind those trees they didn't know, and one suggested they would know for sure when they got there. They haven't eaten enough the past days, and on their location, there weren't any. They had lightened up their load in favor of weapons they carried to no avail, they learned that food was not available in every mile they pass through.

About a one-mile clearing separated the forest, a tobacco plantation. They began walking again after a good rest. The weather was cooperating but the first hours of the morning they can get soaked because of moisture in the path they make. Dews that usually build up heavily in the morning are already present that early night. In the middle of the field, they heard cocking of roosters again up close.

"What time do you think it is?" one would ask worriedly to the other.

"I don't know. I think the roosters in Camarines crowed before midnight, otherwise very soon it is dawn," the other one replied, already worrying if the sun shone while they were still in the barren land; they were visible in all directions.

"We have to run the rest of the distance. I think we slept too long."

"I think so either."

Not a good time to think anything over. They could only agree that the sun would shine minutes away, confirming that they really overslept. They reached the line of trees gasping for breath, twenty feet more pushing in; the thick tree lines from afar wasn't that thick. It bordered a road, a busy road indicated by tire tracks and footsteps leading to both directions. They hurried across anyway on a grassy embankment sloping down gently to reveal a vast clearing. Tall cogon and wild plants lined along the road; the sky was getting brighter and so were the surroundings. Another mile of clearing. They heard a familiar siren that made them to stop and take cover though they could not pinpoint which direction it came from. They crawled into the nearest bushes tall enough to take cover. There was nothing ahead but newly planted rice paddies. A farmer with animal in tow was walking over the road. There were vehicles coming, and from their position, they could hear the engine roaring over a broken dirt road that would pass only a few yards away. Watching military trucks, some pulling cannons on wheels, they froze; they were bigger than what they had seen and fired at them a long time ago accompanied by a large number of Japanese soldiers inside those trucks. They can't move watching the convoy of enemies passing very slow, so many. Both of them should be dead in a second if noticed. They could hear them talking, and to make the situation most terrifying, there were soldiers on foot coming out across the road spread shoulder to shoulder to form a long line watching their comrades passing through. Japanese soldiers in hundreds; they buried their faces on the wet grasses and hold their breath. If the soldiers crossed the road, eventually they would see them. As the sound of engines faded, footsteps and voices became louder momentarily. The soldiers headed east to form a long tail on the convoy of enemies for the best luck they were given. Catching breath as soon as the sound of diesel engine was drawn out, they knew they had noticed one glimpse from the top of the road. The farmer who was halted to give way with his carabao may have seen them. They were not out of danger yet; in fact, as daylight became brighter, the chances of being seen without doubt by other people was greater and they were also going the same way. It was a very busy road.

Civilians walking by in nice shirts and dresses with children were sure that one must have seen them as he picked up a child on his shoulder. A few more soldiers walked by straight passed them, didn't even reply to morning bows intended for them; they must be trying to catch up with the rest of their kind. Bell ringing, there must be a church not too far. Cabarles missed that sound for a very long time.

Almost two years had gone by since the last time I heard a bell ringing—in my wedding. I may have wanted to come to church that day. Silent praying was all we can do that we get through the day because any movement we make will reveal our position. Civilians were passing by, perhaps all kindhearted, none of those with white and red armbands. In prayers, I spent a moment that no one would see us at all, holding breath as we lay down still.

It was a busy morning for the people who lived in that town; suddenly, they disappeared. The mass must have been started. Vast paddies of young rice crops were barely up from the ground; the greater part was barren, and as it seemed unattended like the other side, they could not run a hundred yards without being seen. The thicker wall of coconuts and trees on the other side of the road was the only option they had; run back to the woods again if necessary. They hurriedly crawled back across, knowing shortly that people would be passing through again and they could not expect the same luck. They picked a real good spot to hide, about two hundred feet west along the road. They would spend the day above a big tree with the last of jackfruit seed for breakfast cut in half to share; next meal, they will sleep it over if they make it until then.

The mass should have ended as the bell rang again; people started to reappear, absent of the Japanese displaying its might in wholesale. People were slower in walking back home. Up high above a leafy tree, they had a greater vision of their location. There were houses only five hundred yards east of the road where they could also see the church steeple. People passed by again until there was none, but one father was taking his time lagging farther back from the crowd, noticeably scouring the roadside back and forth while attending to a child that could barely walk. Frustrated of whatever was in his mind, he simply tossed something on the roadside and rejoined his family.

They were hidden up above the tree, which was not a comfortable place to take a nap, hungry and exhausted envisioning themselves falling to the ground and breaking their bones. They could not take that chance. To the south where they came from was a clearing; at daylight, only grasses could be seen coming out from a gentle slope that created green sceneries as it got farther, which was the same view across to the north. They settled on the cover of wet hays and tall cattails growing undisturbed on the edge of the plantation, hoping they survived until dark. Weakening bodies and senses that they could feel was attributed to days of walking and crawling. No one could say he was hungry knowing that there was nothing they could do in a void between two villages. West to the sea was the only option they had left to get around and continue north, but then there was no guarantee they could remain unnoticed. One great luck a day, they could wait until dark.

There was a man obviously walking back and forth on the road. He would stop on the shade of a coconut, pretentiously resting but conspicuously looking around. The rule of engagement was not to engage at all, and they intended to be bound by it. They had made up their minds to move out until darkness. They kept themselves hidden and tried to sleep when talking could only be done by whispering with each other, better if not at all. Even snoring must be suppressed.

If they could hear the talking of the passersby, they could be heard too.

The longest day was in waiting for the sun to set after many days it was obscured by dark clouds. The irony of their situation came when they could actually tell what time it was but flat on the ground afraid to move does not allow it. They got used to saying that it's nighttime when it's dark, eat when food becomes available. On a clear sky, they know it will be a long day.

Rested and strength renewed for a day that was finally over, ears humming from hunger, eyes having trouble to focus at dusk, they manage to trace the same trail they made crossing the road for the second time. They stopped on the same bush, calculating how far the clearing was to the nearest wood. This time, they would favor west as they believed they had drifted too much to the town of Naga the previous night. In a blessing that came at the most needed time, they saw packages the unknown man lobbed away in the morning, food. There was not much but enough to alleviate the empty stomach. With two slices of sticky rice cooked in coconut milk and brown sugar, ants evidently found them before they did. They were thankful, but a second thought was given to avoiding civilians, here were friendly people. By what it brought, nothing amended the rules. They would keep going with strict compliance. One must recite and remind the other, first not to be stubborn to challenge the enemy, second not to make contact with the civilians. They cannot allow themselves to meet another Tata Emong. The best a civilian can offer is the great possibility that they were spying for the Japanese as Emong himself made them aware. However, the local who tossed food on the roadside could not have been a spy; otherwise, they would have been dead already. They moves out as planned, swearing to carefully watch their direction on the way ahead.

They could not shoot the birds and the monkeys, so why not share on what they were eating? Unknown fruits were abundant in the wilds, but they preferred bananas and wild pineapples. Coconuts were also plentiful, but neither had the skill to climb the skinny trunk of the tree. Those that fell to the ground were dried up and empty of the nutritious core. For another three days, they walked, seemingly none whatsoever the wilderness of Camarines can be more difficult that they cannot get through. Rivers and swamps are not obstacles anymore.

Indeed, they had adapted very well to survive in the jungle. There was no reason to hurry up, but they made it a priority to stack on food and replenish when there was plenty available along the way. The second landmark was on sight straight ahead. Mount Labo, situated in Northern Camarines, was a compound volcano in the Bicol volcanic belt that stood high of more than 1,500 meters on its summit.

"We should be lost if we get any closer to that mountain," Santos would say jokingly who just reviewed his map that only he could understand. He suggested to maintain close to the beaches to avoid heavily populated towns and many tended lands.

Cabarles didn't have to worry where his foot sent him to. If Santos said so, then it should be to follow. Someone to talk with, someone to name places, above all, the mere presence of Santos by his side was unmeasurable advantage he wonder where he is now without him. He was able to advance his reading skill, learned the geography of the Philippines as they moved along. There was also someone to get rid of bloodsucking leeches from his back and more, like scratching his back when having trouble to reach an itchy part. Above all, there was also someone to take charge, making sure they were not lost.

A PLACE CALLED RAGAY

The preference of staying close to the ocean suddenly became laborious. It was too late before they noticed that the swamp they were in seemed not to end, and it was already getting dark. The water that began as just barely felt on their feet on the muddy ground was suddenly up to their knees and getting deeper. One would bravely say they had been into many wetlands already; they would reach the other bank eventually. But they didn't until they were literally swimming; they could not move on anymore trying to keep their carry-on dry. The water was salty, and they could feel nothing at the bottom but only a random mesh of roots of the single variety of plants they were hanging on. Waterlines on the tree itself indicates the highest level of the tide.

It was a virgin mangrove field untouched by humans, one that nobody would dare to get in. The other choice was through a dry land, a road that would make their life easier if there was no Japanese blockade. The only way is to be where the land and sea claimed it belongs to one of them. At high tide, they had to swim with the fish hanging on branches of equal growth; at low tide, they had to walk through the roots.

At low tide, however, the mangrove had plenty to offer—crabs in all shapes crawling everywhere in different sizes. They caught as much as they could, which wasn't too easy because it could hide between mesh of roots fast enough before they could grab them. It was just impossible to get through with rifles that kept hanging over tree limbs. They could only wait till the water was high; then swim forward using a piece of log they found to push the hindering branches. Patiently, they made it to the edge or at least that's what they thought so because the same kind of trees were all they could see around in a small piece of dry land in the middle of a cove. When the water rose again at its highest, they barely fit on the peak of the rock sitting down back to back. In the calm quiet night, the poor soldiers came to another point of their journey that made time seem to stand still again. The starry sky in the full moon of a quiet night was broken occasionally by an unfamiliar sound nearby and which indicate that they were not alone somehow. A sporadic splash of water inside the mangrove from all directions would keep them awake and alert, and they made sure their weapons were ready to fire even though they knew no one would venture in that tiny island they had claimed for the night. One would keep saying even Donono won't fit anymore if they let him to come along.

They are not lost as long as they had each other. After the lengthy bedtime stories, they fell asleep in a position that became comfortable till what time would wake up. Tide receded and rose again, and by the time they woke up, the water level didn't seem to change. The cold morning didn't help either, and it was time to reevaluate their location in a place where none of them could tell how they could get out. The eastern skyline was spreading daylight for the second day where they were having bad times in that swampy land. There was no more map for Santos to consult as he had let it submerge into the water in his pocket. He knew that east was the direction to dry land aside from going back south. Cab was busy trying to catch fish with his bare hands. A school of baitfish was passing by that attracted his attention, but they were so little and agile that he had managed to catch a handful only until they disappeared.

They had fresh fish for breakfast while they discussed what direction they would take. They could not reach decision just yet to get started. Both were hesitant to get into the water in the cold morning breeze. Before they could make up their mind, the cove had uncovered itself of many other life that sought refuge and fed at low tide. But like the anchovies, the stone crabs also refused to be meal by hiding and escaping along with the receding water; however, they were no match to the determination of hungry soldiers already salivating on their fats and meat.

Chasing crabs had led them to the edge of the mangrove field. A very calm bay of blue water ended the fun in the morning sun; suddenly, it was a large area of nothingness straight ahead, just blue water. At a distance on the right was an island visibly high and dry with a few coconuts thriving; a sandy shoreline would lead them into it. The excitement increased, but they had no idea where the crabs led them. They were just thrilled over a dry land they could take a nap on with legs stretched out and back lying on the ground. Food did not become a priority at the moment; their eyes were on a larger piece of real estate where they could cook and rest well.

They were absolutely safe in an island reachable only by boat until they came by foot. After three days of basically eating and sleeping with nonstop talking, they felt they were getting fed up with clams, crabs, and a lot of fish. The truth that made themselves stay longer, however, was they really didn't know how to get out from there and they felt the need to get going. Northwest was the mouth of a river exaggerated to about a mile wide; it was unwise to even think of swimming across, considering the strong current of the changing tide. West was an island that vanished in the backdrop of a bigger one that looped around their location over a wide body of pristine blue waters—if only they could walk over it to reach the land mass on the other side of the bay. The choice of direction was to go back east along the riverbank, but they had to hurry to a certain distance possible only at low tide. Come what obstacles thereafter, they had no choice but to go through it. The fourth day was sunny with a wind so gentle they hiked on a trail they could clear, only to see it go over a cliff down to the sea.

One began swearing that he will give hugs and kisses to the first human being he would see again, contradicting the second rule he made up. They spent another day, and it was dead end every which way. They could only turn their increasing frustration and distress on the bountiful food it offered. Both started to be concerned with dark clouds starting to build up; the weather is not cooperating either.

Getting in was a nightmare; how they got into that place they could not explain.

"I'm starting to believe we are being played by some earthly being who lived in this place," Santos admitted out of self-ambiguity, looking for someone else to blame his frustration. The fact was he was running out of patience, and being the lead person directing all trails, he admitted they were lost.

"Yeah, I know." Cabarles sighed. "In Bulacan, old folks were said to turn shirts inside out when lost in the forest. I suggest you do it," he continued with what he could think that might help at the point of total desperation.

Santos said not a word, but he did what Cab had recommended. "Why not you too?" he complained afterward.

"I'm already lost to begin with. Without you, I don't know if I will get this far," Cab replied. "Let's head straight east and see what happens next."

"All right," Santos replied. "How are we going to do it?"

They had plenty of food but not a drop of water to drink; they slept and wished it would rain in their location this time. But not again. In the morning, they did what they were doing when out of water—collecting drop by drop from leafy plants—and they headed east while the ground was becoming more solid and grassy as they kept going, but the elusive rain had yet to come. There was no sign of people that Santos wanted to hug and kiss. He was complaining after crossing a shallow swamp when a drizzle started. But that was what they were all getting as the clouds would clear and the bright sun would show. Then the mangrove field suddenly ended. Mount Labo was visible again afar from their position.

"Can I wear my clothes back the right way now?" Santos asked, having the impression that they were not lost anymore.

"Not yet."

Following the mangrove lines to east was to move upstream of the river. About three miles from the sea, they found themselves a hundred yards toward a bridge they were trying to avoid going through seven days ago. There were civilians to hug and kiss as promised, but there was the problem it presented at the time. They were lined up on the road with soldiers visibly managing the traffic on a narrow wooden bridge spanned over the river. It had only one lane and could not accommodate two vehicles coming through in the opposite directions. A bus full of passengers must be emptied, making the passengers walk in single file to cross. Visible from the bright noontime, there was definitely more soldiers than travelers and traders. At least fifty soldiers they could see without counting how many more on the other side of the river. For what it seemed, they hit a dead end again. Worse, as it observed rule two, it could not be scrapped just yet as the subject of rule one was there too. They could see Japanese soldiers between leaves screaming and yelling to the civilians. They had to swim across the river down under the bridge, the shortest distance to get to the other side.

Truth or just coincidence in the fact that they actually found the way to solid grounds, Santos believed that reversing his clothes was what make them find civilization. Though it wasn't the kind he wanted to see, they had to get closer because there was no other option to cross the swirling water but on the bridge. Santos didn't argue with a desperate man to whom he passed the command. All he said was this was the time he would not mind for heavy rain to come again as he noticed that the Japanese disappeared on drizzles. The rest of the daylight was spent talking at the riverbank to wait and use the cover of night for the next course of action. They had been warned that the Ragay Passages was impenetrable, and truly it was, made worse by daily rain somewhere else, causing the river to rage. The other choices were going further upstream to find narrower and shallow spans over a mesh of caves and Japanese shanties with an array of cannons and machine guns.

Both of them resigned in good sense, taking advantage of the comfort of hearing many people talking after many days of bewilderment. Raindrops alerted them by late afternoon. Heavily it poured, they knew the current will render the river totally unpassable if they waited too long. By dawn, it was still raining; they had to move, either to cross or go back to Albay.

Away from uninhabited land that refused to let them leave by the offering of abundance of food. They were held up by no one for almost seven days, the comfort they rejected. They looked back and were thankful anyway it let them go alive fattened up. It was a nourishing experience, but outright it was taken away to find themselves a few feet below a bunch of Japanese rushing to find shelter from the rain. They made it under the bridge as planned, then someone suggested why not actually cross over it. The other one didn't comply. The Japanese didn't sleep, they could hear them talking just above them.

"I think we will die either way," Santos whispered.

"Yeah, I know, but I don't want to give the satisfaction to the Japanese," Cab replied.

"I still want to kill as many of them as I can before I die. Would you let me?"

"Sure. How would you do it?"

"I have been carrying this grenades a very long time. I don't think I'll be needing it in heaven."

"Yeah, I believe you. How do you use it anyway? I have been carrying few of them too, and I don't how it works."

A quick lesson and an accord on how to get rid of some of their carry-on. The rain was relentless and steadily pouring; their refuge could only offer a night before they were discovered. On the other hand, the water was rising fast, and it could only be worse than it is already. Having no option, they rapidly got into the water taking advantage of the drifting logs in the turbulent current. A moment later, two simultaneous explosions alarmed every Japanese on the footbridge. As expected, the water current drifted them away into full view of anyone it didn't take too long to hear gunshots from the south end of the bridge. They would never know if the shot were for them because raindrops could also be mistaken as bullets splashing everywhere.

"Hold tight, this is one very tough ride," Cab reminded Santos as he tried to get his legs over the log that turned into circles over the swirling current. A volley of gunfire began to confirm that the Japanese were shooting at them as they lined up over the bridge shooting at every floating debris on the river. There was nothing more they could do but certainly hold on tight with each other in darkness.

In the morning, Santos was awakened still alive. Unsure of the situation, he opened his eyes to see blue sky and birds flying by. White birds that made familiar sounds, some standing by him. His sudden movement scared them all away. Cabarles was not around, and he didn't know where he was. Surely it was not heaven. About fifty feet away where the birds congregated lay another human being, obviously not moving. No other one could it be but Cabarles. Santos randomly shot the stubborn birds that refused to fly away, and only then they give way for him to see the man starting to move.

"The birds are feeding on you, I thought you're dead."

"I thought so too either, I saw Inez. Where are we?"

"I don't know, I don't see her."

It was always momentous to find that they were still breathing. They lay down on the sand and thanked heaven they were still together.

"I told you, hell doesn't like me. Definitely you're not going to heaven. We have a long way to go together," Cabarles commented happily.

"Yeah, I know now. Where do you think are we going eventually? I preferred heaven to tell you the truth. I don't like your story about hell."

"I don't know about you, I'm going back to Inez, and I know she's heaven waiting for me."

"Does Inez have a sister?"

"None. Why can't those birds fly?"

"I shot them. I thought they were eating you already."

"Do you think there's no Japanese here?"

"I don't think they can come this far. Look around. Do you see that island straight ahead? I think it's the same one we were staring at for so many days from the other side of the river's mouth. I believe we were able to cross the river somehow," Santos stated.

"Sure like it, but let's take cover. We don't really know where we are," Cab responded.

They landed back on the beach of Ragay all right. It took them three days to find their way out in only the blink of an eye and a lot of prayers to return. "I think we are lost again," Santos declared.

"Yeah, but at least we know now that we cannot head east no more." Cabarles sighed.

Looking on the bright side, the place should have many amenities to offer. It was very convenient that they also thought it may be their last meal; they took advantage of it again. On another morning, they would try again but pushed north along the shoreline until there was no more solid ground they could step on. The same kind of trees, birds, and situation they were facing. Cabarles would yield to reversing his shirt also.

He had something to add. "You know, there's another story I heard from my father. It was about a man that was lost in a place. It was like paradise just like where we are. No matter what he does, he cannot find his way out."

"Don't scare me. I heard similar stories too," Santos admitted. "What shall we do now?"

"I don't know. I don't know if it's my curse causing it. One of us is cursed definitely."

"Yeah, and one is very lucky."

"No way, you don't. Do you want me to remind you?"

"No."

They spent another three days with the seagulls and crabs mainly debating on that arguments.

SOMEONE TO KISS AND HUG

Over a winding road so destroyed that traveling by foot was very precarious enough, much more for any vehicle to drive through, they kept going, aware that it was the same road leading back to the bridge. In the late afternoon, it was raining again. They were alerted by the sound of a vehicle coming from behind. It may be of people looking to ask directions, but people not blended with enemy. They didn't want to be shot at again. Hiding behind the closest bushes and waiting in a deep depression on the roadside washed down by the relentless rain, for the first time, they got their gun ready to shoot. A passenger bus in front of them, full of civilians, stopped to check the road condition ahead. All passengers disembarked giving them a chance to evaluate each one, but there were so many they could not take the risk of interconnecting for fear of spies. All men push the huge bulk of metal and applauded when it got through, and eventually the bus kept on going.

Two more passengers were added to the bus as it labored northward. Just before total darkness, they saw the vastness of the wilderness where they came from that extended across the river mile after mile, farther than they thought it would be. Bananas of the sweet and seedless kind were among stacks of sacks of kernel and other vegetables on the top of the bus. There may be space inside the bus, but Santos and Cabarles preferred to be up there; even it was raining, they didn't mind. They had free fare and food as much as they could eat. They just hope nobody noticed when they climbed up there.

Ahead was a Japanese checkpoint, and there was no chance to come down and run. A man got out, braving the rain to come to a shack. Japanese soldiers who did not want to get wet stayed where they were. Some Japanese soldiers boarded in, and a few more minutes, the bus continued.

"Del Gallego town," the sign read at the bus station lit by headlights. Many people disembarked from the bus, and some came in. People were speaking in Tagalog, rushing each other up. More large burlap bags and bananas were added up on the top, some of the sacks unloaded. They were seen by a man, but the man didn't say anything and kept doing what he was doing quietly. When he was done, he commanded the bus to leave in a hurry. They must have passed another town for a quick stop. The sight of a Catholic church and an array of houses in decent sizes indicated a populated area along that road. Not long after, it slowed down to a full stop again.

"Sirs, you can come inside now if you want. There are no more Japanese aboard," they heard said.

They hesitated for a while, but they could not turn down the invitation. The rain was becoming heavy again.

There were not too many people inside the bus, mostly sleeping. "There are many vacant seats you can take. The rain can only get worse."

There was no reason not to trust the man, if he intend to betray them, he must have done it in Del Gallego where the enemy were visually walking in groups. In soaked and muddy khakis minus the boots, they entered in view of the passengers, none expecting them, none saying anything either. The one closest to them gave Cab a towel immediately, speaking in a dialect similar in Libon. He didn't say anything but took what the woman offered while another handed them food. Next to her, a man opened a bag on his lap, pulling out a dry shirt, and everyone followed suit. Clean and dry shirts for both of them, food of different kinds from people who would just come forward with something individually. Santos and Cabarles had so much gratitude they could not express that they were seized by their emotions. Two soldiers hardened by war experiences though they had been helped and assisted by civilians before, they would not forget the moment when they were trying to evade these people like the enemy. This may not be the first time they cried as soldiers, but as much as they held it, they couldn't stop feeling pity for themselves but proud.

A little girl quietly looking at Santos while on the lap of the mother. Paused from drinking milk in a bottle, staring at him, then she offered what was left of the milk to the man. Santos could smile in gratitude but he almost cry.

A man in a hat began to say something. "You're welcome. If you don't mind my asking, where are you heading?" he asked in an almost whispering voice.

"We are heading to Manila, sir," Santos replied.

"Not a good place for you to go, so many Japanese in the city. So many checkpoints and gun batteries in and out of every town all the way to Manila. In fact, an hour more is a Japanese detachment, definitely dangerous while carrying guns like you do," the man in the hat explained nervously.

"It is very important we reach Manila, sir," Santos said again.

"I don't know how you can get there but good luck," the elderly man said who reminded them of Emong.

The old man stopped talking with them, but continued with another man alongside with him by the window. After a while and about twenty more kilometers, the bus slowed down to a halt.

"We are sorry to tell you that this is as far as you can go for the safety of all of us," the man spoke again.

"We understand, thank you all," Cabarles said in gratitude to the hospitality of the passengers, but he was alerted when the old man followed. Two more passengers came out.

"I cannot help you all the way to Manila, but my men can give assistance as far as you want," said the old man in farewell.

How could they refuse that most generous offer? The first step out of the bus made by Santos was full of hope; somehow he had proven that connecting to people was rewarding and for their benefit. They would take as much they could in company if there would be more to join, but there were only two. The bus left, and the first difficulty was facing the heavy rain and the strong wind. Indeed, it was a typhoon coming, and the rain it brought ahead was pouring hard. Flooded fields and rushing water were everywhere, but it didn't hinder them to reach the forested area miles away from the road through an open plain. About three days or more on foot were taken off for a few hours' ride on the bus. They acquired company to guide their way too. One said he is a musician, just nowhere to go. The other was reluctant to come.

THE MUSICIAN

Tagkawayan, North Camarines
September 20, 1943

The ghost soldiers definitely needed assistance primarily not to get lost in the jungle again. Besides, their large *bayong* must be full of food and supplies in addition to what the civilians had given them. As soon as they reached the woods, they found a place to seek refuge and rest for the night. Between the roots of a huge tree was ideal for letting the storm pass. The unrelenting heavy winds that made a horrifying sound yielded by afternoon of the next day. Despite the devastation it left, they continued walking in the morning as much as they could. The ground was soft and slippery, and the water was still finding its way to subside. They gave up early for the day.

"What made you decide to join the guerilla, Mateo?" Cab would ask the question while munching on the sweet potato courtesy of the man. "Don't you have any family?" he continued.

"No more, sir, they are gone. I had a wife, but she is missing since the war began," Mateo replied.

"What do you mean gone?" Cabarles was interested. A missing wife. He wanted to know how he was taking it, moreover how he lost her.

"They must be dead, the Japanese took over our town. They burned all houses but a few to occupy their own. They built a garrison in our town." Mateo kept on talking. "We were separated in the chaos, I was apprehended but released after a many days. I tried to find my wife and family but only met frustrations since then."

"What town is it?" Santos said this time.

"Polangui in Albay, sir."

"Would you know the Marfil family in Polangui?"

"Yes, sir, we were neighbors. I have reason to believe they suffered the same fate as well."

"There were many refugees who had managed to settle in the western part of Albay. In fact, we met survivors in Libon. We have information that many more evacuated in the east, in the areas close to the mountain of Isarog. Don't lose hope, they may still be alive," Cabarles disclosed. That moment sent him an intense concern and fear for his own loved ones. He didn't talk anymore.

Santos took over. "We had visited Polangui a few times, hoping we can find the Marfils. The town is heavily controlled by Japanese and collaborators. When was the last time you were in that town?"

"About a week ago, sir. What is your relation with the Marfils, if you don't mind my asking?" Mateo became curious.

"There is a girl very close to us. We were trying to locate and reunite her with her relatives. We are not successful. There is a refugee camp in Libon, we stayed on the place long enough to know every one. Your wife, what's her name?"

"Violeta, Violeta Borja, sir."

The name was very familiar; Santos and Cabarles could only look at each other. They know a woman of that name very well, especially Santos. What coincidence will they meet the husband of a woman who thought she was a widow already?

"You have a beautiful wife, she is alive." Cabarles stated.

"Are you sure, sir? You gave me a lot of hope, I'm very happy to hear she's alive and safe." Mateo was truly excited.

"Yes, I am sure. When you find each other and I know you will, please go easy on her. She had suffered enough."

"Yes, sir, I will."

What a coincidence that it could happen. Cabarles was happy for him. A wife lost and surely he shall find her. A wife separated from the husband who may be believed he is still alive, and he is. He should be happy for Mateo, but he was not. It had been a long time he was separated from Inez. In what condition would he find her?

The other man was Francisco Bolez. He was carrying a *bayong* mistaken to be concealing a weapon, but it was not. It was the tip of a flute. A musician before, now he wanted a gun. His story may not be similar to the other, but he just plainly wanted to kill some Japanese. Learning that the soldiers went through the town of Naga on foot, he was sure they were the same duo he had seen. He supported his story describing an event on a Sunday morning back in town about a month ago. Cab and Santos were speechless to learn that the same man was truly a good fellow. They thanked him for the food anyway. Bolez stated that the soldier must be protected and guided by God Almighty to get through that place alive, which was literally infested by Japanese. He said the municipal building in Naga was only half a mile away, and the Japanese were reinforcing while campaigning against guerillas and sympathizers in towns and barrios at the time they were passing through.

"Would you know of another way how to get through Ragay?" Santos asked for what good it could do for them if they chose to converge with Bolez in Naga, Albay.

"No, sir. I have trouble passing through Ragay Bridge too. The Japanese was attacked by guerillas, and there were rumors that scores of Japanese were killed."

"How did you get through?"

"By luck, sir. I was traveling with my family."

"Where are they now?"

"They were in the bus, sir. The girl you hold and kiss is my daughter," Bolez replied.

"Why did you leave them?"

"I am a soldier, sir. I had given orders. The man you are talking with is Lt. Martin Esguerra. He is my commanding officer," Bolez disclosed.

"What happened to your family now?"

"My wife understood, she knows what to do."

"We appreciate your assistance, Bolez. I am Captain Rodrigo Santos." He paused.

Santos evaluated the current situation; there was no better alternative but go what fate dictated them to do. They were still soldiers with legitimate and important missions. Reneging from their oath at this time was impossible. They could not let the agonizing experiences in Naga and Ragay happen again because they refused to get assistance from the civilians. Both unshaven and haggard looking, they could be mistaken as renegades anyway if they did not display rifles and grenades while still wearing khakis. The new company had shown reliability and courage despite the musician was having second thoughts since he learned his wife was alive.

Their guns had been soaked in salty water and rain. Santos had an idea of preliminary training for Mateo, cleaning the guns that had started showing discolorations in the metal. The neophytes complied in excitement. But then before Borja could actually get started, Cabarles grabbed the gun, loaded and aimed for a shot. A hundred yards, he spotted a wild hog wandering down the slippery hill. The animal was so calm and confident, but before Cab could pull the trigger, it ran away and disappeared from his sight.

Something or someone must have scared away the pig; he knew that. He made everyone aware and take cover while keeping aim, waiting. Santos joined at once.

"What did you see?" he asked audaciously.

"I'm sure I saw a boar, but it bolted away. Someone is coming."

"Not Japanese patrol?"

"I hope not. But whoever he is, he is following our trail. Can you see him?"

"No, it's getting dark. Do you?"

"He is coming toward us, look where my Springfield is pointing."

"Yeah, I see him now. There is only one I can see."

There is no reason to be alarmed, as he was seemingly not a hostile individual, with rifle on his shoulder trying to trace the footsteps they made on the grassy hill very carefully.

"One of us, you think?" Santos uttered.

"I think he is," Cab replied.

Before dusk turned into darkness, another one was added into their fold. The soldier identified himself as Sgt. Marcos Agustin of the Twenty-First Division, Philippine Army, when frozen. He was of no relation to Lt. Guido Agustin of Davao. Exhausted and scared upon learning he was almost shot in cold blood, he was jubilant somehow to know that he was again in the company of his kind for so many months of straggling in the southern region of Tayabas. He was a remnant of the defending forces against Japanese landing in Atimonan on December 12, 1941, and since then, those who did not surrender was pushed to Camarines. Finding themselves in the wrong side of the region to no avail, his unit meted out severe losses either by the sudden death in combat from the pursuing invaders or from their wounds and illnesses in the jungle until he was the only one left. He said a year and nine months to date, his account of survival in the forest for that long alone may be exaggerated, but the soldiers from Mindanao believed it was true. It was just that by himself for a very long time surpassed their own experiences, way over the top, only for a reason they could not understand. Why did he chose to stay in the jungle that long.

Agustin said he had a stash of rifles formerly owned by dead comrades, also that needed cleaning and ammo, but Cabarles refused to take them. It was bad luck to own anything from the dead, he said. Besides, he didn't like the idea of retrieving the weapons almost ten miles back south.

After a night of listening to more stories of new allies, Santos and Cabarles found a break away from the storytellers, discussing the impact of the growing company on their plans. In the morning, the Springfield fired a single shot that reverberated in the woodlands of Southern Tagalog. A very large boar died on the spot. A few more hours that morning, they were roasting pig but having trouble starting a fire. They were in the jungle surrounded by firewood but with everything still wet.

CHAPTER 19

THE LEGACY OF HOMBRE DONONO

"I SEE NO ONE"

Agustin would run out of patience. He started slicing and eating the meat as it slowly cooked on the stubborn fire. He said he could not wait anymore as it smelled so good while he was having trouble chewing. Looking thin and malnourished, he was let to enjoy eating as it befitted him. Mateo and Borja took over in maintaining the fire very patiently.

Santos and Cabarles scouted around the proximity. They were sure the gunshot was heard in the far distance. Neither wanted to be discovered by the enemy patrol just sitting and waiting for a meal that looked like will never be cooked for just a day. They could wait till the meat was well done, talking over about scrapping rule two that certainly brings many benefits but also presents foreseeable outcome unfair to the Bicolanos especially to Mateo Borja. Santos's conscience was eating at him for taking advantage of a woman in a time of her weakness. It may be nothing for him at the time, but to learn that she had a husband looking for her desperately was something else. He was regretful in the sense that Mateo would find the wife bearing his child.

Cabarles could only keep his silence; there may be similar things he had done that could have resulted the same. In his understanding, he had committed many sins that had forsaken his vows to his one love. His continued desire to Rhodora X was one that was made worse by a farewell night with Rosie. Both were memories that were not easy to forget; actually he liked remembering those moments than anything else. The regrets were incomprehensible because it presented both ways. He could have taken advantage of both and die happy and fulfilled. He still could not find in his memory what else transpired that night with Rhoda; it was not easy to forget about her.

There was silence in the jungle, that even the talkative Santos was quiet. There was less to worry about their situation in gaining fresh information, there were people to guide their way, and a boar cooking. Their eyes were wide open to begin daydreaming. Cabarles noticed another movement over a cluster of bushes not far away. He immediately took cover and observed.

"It must be another hog, a family of wild hog." Cab relayed what he was seeing to Santos but doubtful because no animal would peek through leaves and branches just like a human.

Santos would still say he could not see anything. Cab certainly saw something. "I think Donono followed us, or I must be dreaming in daylight."

"Why did you say that? Where is he?" Santos suddenly became excited. Cab would not joke seeing Donono; actually he never did make fun about anything. He said Donono was somewhere down the hill; it was just that he could not see what Cabarles was seeing.

"Give me a cigarette, let me think it over before I shoot that bastard," Cab said. He was sure it was Donono. "Look between the trees two hundred yards down, I can see him clearly through the scope. He was peeking over the bushes. I'm sure he had seen us but still doesn't want to come out."

Santos did exactly how he was told. He was shocked to see a dark man behind the bushes, shirtless and very cautious, patiently hiding behind the bushes, very thin. He lighted up another cigarette for himself courtesy of the people at Bicol Express while looking at Cabarles in the eye like he was asking how he got there but equally aggravated. "He is making faces at us too."

Cab turned back his sight to where he saw Donono while aiming seriously.

Santos got nervous. "Don't shoot him, I want to do it."

"I don't know what I ate earlier, I'm having double vision. I'm seeing two of them," Cab murmured while reorienting his eyes, opening and closing them repeatedly.

Santos could not take it anymore. Cab may shoot but was having trouble with his eyes, Don might actually get hit accidentally, and he could not allow that even at the remotest possibility. As loud as he could, he yelled, "Don, come out. We know you're there." Then he turned his worries to Cab. "Are you sure he is down there?" he queried.

"I don't know." Then he looked again in the same location. "Sir, look, he is coming out. One, two, three." He stopped counting and waited for what Santos would see.

"Yeah, I think those *camotes* are bad. I ate that thing more than you, I counted more than three Dononos," Santos commented in agreement, suddenly becoming anxious. "I hope we are not being played again." He was insinuating previous experiences of unexplained events that led him to believe that some folklore maybe true.

"Agustin, come here." Cab could not discount it either. A third guy could confirm what kind of affliction they were both having. Any unexplained event on the place, Agustin should know.

"Yes, sir." The man reluctantly crawled down and stopped ten feet away.

"Over here, come here," Santos called.

"Go look at those bushes and tell us what you see," Santos commanded.

He sneaked a quick look to where he was told. "I see bushes."

"Aside from it, there is something else. Look again."

"I really don't see anyone."

It was a good five minutes that all of them stared at the same location and saw no one. Agustin returned to his position eventually, where the roasting was taking place. In the thick forest of unusually large trees and wild plants, seeing Donono in multiplicity at daylight led them to share different theories. One said they were having a mirage because many lush vegetation could actually be moving from the gust of the wind. One was repenting for he agreed to leave Donono behind. Together they sat back again and talked about Donono.

"We could let him come with us, you know," Santos began. "Instead we obliged him for something that is truly hard to believe."

FOLLOWING ORDERS

Back in Libon, Donono had been giving flowers to Myra as he was told he must do. Sitting miserably on the same spot that Cabarles usually did his contemplations, he was confused as there was only one command he was able to accomplish. As the sun rose, he spent time looking at the last place he saw the only two persons who treated him as equal despite of who he is—friends, brothers, saviors, and all that gained him so much confidence and knowledge. He was respected and equally treated without any sense of pretention. They were gone, so many nights and days ago.

They were the most kindhearted people and the bravest of soldiers. He was tremendously honored to be in their company all throughout the time he met them. He could not forget he was one lost vagrant in the city, a lowly being that only Cabarles and Inez showed mercy for among many people he met in Manila. Through him and Captain Santos, he became a real soldier. However, he started to believe that he was tricked summarily. The reward that came along with giving flowers was none other than female mosquitoes so persistent in biting him even at daylight. A pretty woman he worship was told to be falling in love with him and wanting him. It was just bloodsucking insects. Myra was given the lilies, not just once but countless times but nothing happened.

He was looking on the north horizon where he guessed Cabarles and Santos should be at the time. Camarines was where he was born by the boundary to the next province, in Tayabas [Quezon] where he knew every inch of wilderness that should be the only route to Manila. A very treacherous jungle and not considering wild animals and crocodiles, he was much needed to ensure their safe passage on those provinces. He should follow and catch up with them, a sudden decision that got him, up nullifying priorities and orders. All that rushed in his brain came to a fixation that he would be very effective in guiding his brothers, ensuring their survival in the jungle at his home province. He got up and gathered his things while laying down another bunch of delicate lily flowers that was ruined already while on his way back from the river. He didn't care anymore. In Quezon, where his village existed, flowers grew everywhere and were stepped on, with nobody caring if they weren't edible. He would be welcomed by a willing mate therein to suffice his dingdong that kept going up every time.

The lessons learned from Santos were getting vague, and nothing was happening yet. He had patiently followed the way of Cabarles, and it was somewhat working but to no avail; nothing happened either. He had also lost faith on his talismans altogether

He kept the respect of the settlers, but it was a thought too that he worked very hard for a meager share of food in a village he didn't belong. The reward, Myra, was somewhat more caring to him, and the water lilies were more appreciated than the first time. Every day and nights, he was waiting, but the girl, already in her right age and magnificent shape that surpassed a woman to choose a husband, has remained distant from his compelling needs. He had reason to believe that the scarring never impressed Myra; giving her flowers worked, but only to some point.

"Can I join you on your thoughts?" Myra said.

Always a music to his ears that could put him in a trance especially when a few feet away, that was the nearest she would come to him. Hence, it never happened that he was approached by the lady alone until now. Usually she was with the teacher whose belly was getting bigger as many days had gone by since Cabarles and Santos left.

He looked at the northern sceneries as he sat down again, knees trembling, they should be far away by now somewhere in that direction.

Myra should have accepted that Cabarles and Santos were never coming back and she was sensing that she was about to lose Donono too. It was a foggy morning only a short distance that they were allowed to see yet on usually beautiful sceneries of greens and blues. Donono used to watch the horizon, estimating by his timetable how far they had traveled through the greens already.

"I'm sure they are safe and far away by now," Myra said. "I was looking for you, I thought you'd left me too."

Donono remained in silence. Every night, he was waiting for her to come into his abode he had built by himself so nice that even Myra said it was. She never went in.

"Are those my flowers?" she said, showing appreciation for a routine that began her day.

The flowers may not look like what it was called anymore for being destroyed totally for being sat on. But the young woman was so used to it already.

"Thank you very much." Myra should have known her feelings were already revealed, but she had to maintain her self-esteem. She was sure that she had done more than enough for a man to make his move, but nothing happened. She was close to giving up and admit that Donono's real intention was not her but to follow the footsteps of his fellow soldiers to whom his loyalty remained intact. "You didn't answer me."

Caught in all kinds of thoughts playing in his mind, added with the fresh scent of soap, He would fetch water for her again. He would fetch water for her forever if every time she would come this close to him. He was so confused.

"What makes you so quiet this time?" Myra tried again.

"I was told to make you always pregnant and happy for the rest of your life, and nothing has happened," Dono said but he doubt remembering it in that order. In fact, he had forgotten a lot of what he was supposed to say and do. His steps faltered, and he was always grasping from his memory the proper order that he must say.

"What did you say?" Myra was almost thrown out from her seat.

"Do no, no. Please forgive me. Here are your flowers." Finally he remembered the first thing that he should say.

"Thanks again." The woman smiled. She looked up to Don as one of the three bravest men she had known. She knew how much he had shown his dedication for her, clearly showing submission to her realm. What else did she want to prove? The man was lost by the customs and traditions he was brought up, made worse by opposite opinion from the men they both respected. It was only a matter of time that she would lose him too.

"All right, I believe you're misconstrued. Just make sure the next time you give me flowers, they are not destroyed. Will you do that?" She moved closer.

"Yes, I will," Don replied in compliance. That was an easy thing to do as so many water lilies were blooming everywhere.

"And just so you know, I hate water lilies."

"Yes, I will remember that."

Her touches suggested strikingly that his very intention is reciprocated. However, something was wrong. He finished the abode they would share together and the moon was dying.

"What are you thinking now, do you still want to go with them?" Myra asked, noticing the precipitous changes in the soldier's sentiment by her touches.

"No, I just realized that the man who shall marry us is gone," Don said, full of emotion.

"Who is he?"

"Cap."

"You will marry me?"

"Yes, I always do."

With the most beautiful woman leaning on him, so close it make his heart pound in the beat of a marching band, all there was that must be adapted was the way of Santos. He grabbed the girl and attempted to begin. He was let a little then pushed back.

"You know that's not what I'm expecting you would do right away. Who taught you that, Captain Santos?"

"Yes."

"Wait . . . tonight," Myra whispered.

Donono recovered from frustration out right. For what he was assured, he was getting it finally but to wait a little bit. He wasn't deceived; Cabarles didn't lie to him.

"You know you'll have to marry me first."

Well, the "boy who would be priest" married them before noontime. For the rest of the day, Donono was waiting for the sun to set. He sat back again on the same spot after the wedding, Myra was on his side.

"What are you thinking now?" Myra joined him in his thoughts.

"I made a promise to the birds and all the coconuts and trees my eyes can see, I will find and thank them. I wish they are still here," Donono declared.

"That will be two of us together to fulfill that promise," Myra said while she guided her arms around Doe's and laid her head on his shoulder. Donono was in tears. Myra justified his weeping begets of a woman aside from what the moment had created. "You should not be crying. You know they can take care of themselves whatever the situation led them to," the woman said to calm down her dearest.

"I'm only in tears because you are. I feel the need to cry too." Don must have remembered details of how to impress a lady by words. He had learned so much in that riverbank and all to that effect.

"Now I remember most of what I should had been said and done in order," Don said.

"What is that?" Myra asked curiously.

"I have to kiss you after you receive the flowers."

"And what took you so long to do that?"

The long-awaited night came eventually. He didn't care if it was a moonless night. Don had applied all in every details of what he had learned in that muddy riverbanks of thick water lilies. With two different approaches put together, the end result was immensely satisfying. He was the happiest man in the world. No lily flowers that morning, or anything of that kind. To hell with fetching water and letting her take a bath. He couldn't get up.

THE ENLIGHTENMENT

Not too far away yet, in Camarines, Cabarles would rub his eyes and face repeatedly. He would look at Santos who was doing the same thing to himself. They could not believe what they were seeing. They were resting their backs on the roots of an old tree where they resigned in dispute of what would happen if they had let Dono to come with them. Whatever reasoning to suppress contradiction always justified their individual intention. They didn't cast off Donono. "What we did is what I believed is the best for him and the refugees," one would say, the other one could only agree.

Seven in all was the total number of Dononos they were seeing; the rest would just follow what the first one did in the same fashion— all sniffing the air from certain direction, cautious and excited.

"The leading one must be the real Don, he looks exactly like him in all angles." Cabarles murmured in submission that they are being played by whatever being resided in the vicinity.

"Yeah," Santos agreed. "The second one looked like him when furious."

"The skinny one is when he is hungry and haven't eaten for days, isn't it? Something is really wrong with us. Maybe this place,"

Cab would say without looking, diverting a total misperception to amusement. He declined to look no more, but relied on Santos to keep him informed. Otherwise, what they saw were unarmed to be alarmed. There were seven, and he had seen them all. Cabarles in resign to end the thought about Donono. They had confirmed already that none among they saw down the hill was Donono.

"Do you remember the first time he saw Myra and days after?" Santos kept uttering. "One of them is what he looks like. Mouth open and drooling." He paused, seemingly thinking. "The fifth is when he is worried sick waiting for you. Do you remember when you went to Davao City and didn't come back on time?" Santos intentionally chose that event, sensing guilt taking over Cab.

"Oh really? I didn't know he can change his face that much by worrying about me." Cab sighed.

"At the time, he also stepped on the feces of an American prisoner." Santos stood corrected. "The next one is how he reacted when we learned that you slept with Rhodora X," he continued, smiling.

Cab had seen them all in clear view. They were tribesmen on the hunt for food in the likes and behavior of Donono. But he continued to play along with Santos.

"I may get drunk, but I do not remember sleeping with her," Cab argued. "How would you describe the last one? He looks different."

"He looks like he is smelling something very good," Santos commented on the one sniffing the air intensively, clearly tracking a certain smell for real. Changing its head direction, the random movement prompted Santos to believe differently. "Do you know what I'm thinking now? They are real persons. Let me shoot one and see what happens," he suggested, noticing they were interacting with each other. The Dononos were talking with each other obviously in excitement over something.

"Sure go ahead, but shoot the sixth one. I don't like that kind of look," Cabarles consented.

"Why the sixth?"

"I don't like that look you described about that one."

It would have been a clear shot, the dead branches that fell to the ground by the past storm were the only obstructions. The Dons had no clue they were being observed while cautiously advancing toward them. Santos may not be serious to actually shoot one of them, but at one hundred yards away, he could not miss and Cabarles was allowing him.

Voices calling from behind scrambled the Does to disappear at once in the blink of an eye. Roast was ready, and they could smell the burning fat. They walked away anticipating a good meal. Real or not, what Santos and Cabarles had seen posed no danger.

They sat side by side on the roots of another tree, facing the new allies and the burning pig. The first taste of meat since leaving the refugee camp was delicious, Santos commented.

Cab was getting answers about the people inhabiting the land from Agustin; he was alerted in the act of his first bite. Quietly, he used his elbow to get the attention of the man sitting next to him.

"Look," he whispered.

They both watched for a few moments, the Dononos were in the open. In single file, the last one would stand up and walk to be the first in line and repeated the same manner by who would be the last until they were up close in file, all heads turned to the same direction. They sat and stared at them, no sign of trying to hide. Santos took his gun very slowly, the seven dononos were carrying weapons of some sort.

"Make sure you take down the sixth," Cab advised.

"I can't remember which one, they all look the same to me now," Santos would utter.

Their actions were noticed by the others, especially when Santos started aiming. They all looked behind them and nervously stopped Santos from shooting altogether.

"Sir, don't shoot! They are Abiyans."

Agustin described the Dononos as friendly, the native people that thrived along the boundaries of Tayabas and Camarines. Agustin said he had known them for a long time. They should be looking for him and must have tracked down his footsteps to find him. He said a long time ago that he could share food with them, but since he ran out of bullets to hunt, he seldom saw them anymore. In return for favor, they were the one who supplied him food. They must have been on a hunt and heard the gunshot.

The ghost soldiers looked at each other; finally they had proven they were not deceived by their own eyes, but they still felt the guilt and worrying they laid down upon themselves. Unmistakably hungry, but not afraid seeing their friend Agustin among the group of five people busy eating and talking, they settled fifteen feet away in the direction of the wind, all staring at them, perhaps on the roasting animal.

Enough had been said to be educated about the *Abiyans*, meaning "friends" in Tagalog. Santos chopped a whole quarter part of the meat from cooking and walked to them with the help of Cab, offering the meat. They were obviously elated and gratified to the soldiers. Little Doe was not unique after all. They wanted to see them up close and try to communicate, but they talked differently. It may be a natural act of kindness or missing one of their kind, but they sat and ate with them, watching and refreshing all the said resemblance to a man they knew. Virtually identical to demeanor and appetite, they agreed that everyone however had their own unique features. The soldiers invited them to join the group through hand signs and motions, but they just remained staring at them. They tried to ask if someone would know Donono, and the response they got appeased them. "Don no, no eh." They gave up, both knowing the name was invented for the character of Donono. In fact, they just realized they don't know the real name of Donono.

The Abiyans assembled themselves around and ate as the meat got bloody after slicing.

Cabarles and Santos continued listening to the story about the Abiyans from Agustin and what the Bicolanos could contribute about the tribes. Not quite long, the natives joined them. Apparently, they like their meat well done too. They helped rejuvenate the fire with competent skill they had seen only from Donono. The longing from his absence was over; suddenly, they had seven. In a few more minutes, the natives were done slicing their share of meat to the bone and wanted more. Cab let them to have more as much as they wanted. Agustin knew the Abiyans' dialect very well, and he could translate their conversation. Indeed, they were thankful for the meat to begin a friendship.

"I WOULD LIKE TO HELP"

So much with the Abiyans, they fell asleep with stomachs full as the sun cast shadows opposite them when they woke up. The ground was still slippery, and extreme humidity was taking a toll even on the shadows of the trees. They continued moving northwest guided by two of the remaining Abiyans with Agustin translating. The others had disappeared hours ago. Before night fell, they reached a community noticeably devastated by the recent storm. People who were almost invisible in the dark patiently tried to reconstruct. Every activity in progress was paused with the coming of the new company, and in a moment, the colony of Dononos—male, female, and children—all together with a few they had met earlier leading the pack inundated them. Dead animals they had shot on the way were attended right up.

The villagers' home was obliterated that the only place they could see fit to rest was by a creek overlooking another jungle interposed by a line of rich vegetation drawn like a giant serpent from their location. They would learn it was the Hiwasayan River they needed to cross to keep going, not different to many of the rivers they had crossed already except that giant pythons reigned along most of its banks. Signs of life from afar could also be seen as an orange glow started to adorn the night view. They were told beware of those spots as it may be enemy garrisons.

Getting educated with enemy activities in the province, Atimonan would have the largest concentration. Agustin would recount his story of the battle against the Japanese since they landed in town in December 12, 1941. Their defenses were no match by all accounts as the invaders came with serious might, overpowering the Philippine Army forces. There were so many deaths, mostly among civilians who were thought they would not be harmed for not meddling, but they were wrong. However, such kind of atrocities were similar in almost every place they had been. Some would collaborate to the fullest extent, betraying their own race; some would seek refuge in the mountains; some would stay and bow; and a few would organize and joined the resistance. Many would just sit and just continue surviving as they let their faith take over.

Mateo Gallego and Francisco Bolez were among those who set aside their faith. There were many more of their kind, but the hesitation were mainly suppressed with the absence of communications and leadership that turned down weak motivation to negative thinking. Any effort would remain futile with only bare hands to wage war against the invaders. The journey of the scout soldiers heading back to Manila was given serious reevaluation one more time. They could not adopt rule two as permanent guidelines on their travel because they clearly needed help too. They conceded that the nightmares in Ragay would have been avoided if they made contact with Bolez back in Naga. It could have been easier, but the change of events the man may have contributed could not be discounted that they may also be dead too. They were surviving together, and the luck they were having must be maintained while determined on the ultimate objective that could not be discussed at all.

They could still be prisoners of war or sitting somewhere else. Though having no guarantee of surviving further ahead without help from civilians, the likelihood of keeping alive was a lot greater for just the two of them. For the only reason they adopted rule two, they found themselves surrounded by them. The situation must find immediate solution. Bolez and Gallego had exhausted their expediency. The information they could share individually was valuable before leaving Albay, and no more would they know beyond where they stand. A few things they could add up about the guerilla raid in Ragay Pass in the middle of the storm. Cab and Santos were interested in the destruction caused by the two grenades but not on exaggerated story of local guerillas who raided the Japanese in their stronghold at the footbridge. Very interesting accounts, however, for what the story was worth, there were five more in their carry-on that must be handled very carefully.

No guns to spare and grenades they wanted to keep with them, the baggage they carried were proven to be handy at desperate times. However, Bolez and Gallego must go. They served no more purpose for them. Anything that would happen to them would be innocent blood on their hands. They needed no glory nor honor to claim the heroes in their story. Cabarles would have an elaborate scheme that required immediate compliance and more decisive wit. The Bicolanos may be good butchers and could translate the dialect spoken in the area, but they would do better with Agustin. The Abiyans were still amusing them.

Cabarles discussed with Santos what he thought. After all, amending the second rule was his domain. He made it, they adopted it, and he scrapped it without opposition from the other who made the first one. On the other hand, Santos was very good in diplomacy and association with civilians. As he was presented the proposal, it was collaborated and done even before they could taste the specialty of the Abiyans—boiled meat with some kind of stalk so rough they could not even chew it as they tried. Later, they were told it wasn't meant for eating, just to spice the soup up that was really very good, so they said.

In the morning, Bolez and Gallego were heading back to town on a clandestine mission concocted by Santos. The order was real, but the real purpose was to get rid of them. An overnight course in recruiting and communications and bring guerilla sympathizers into readiness of a grand battle against Japanese in a moment's notice was enough to increase their motivation. Agustin made a commitment to the soldiers he only knew by name and the other addressed as sir. He bragged about his former unit he wanted to reunite, pitching great support on the mission of the soldiers he just met. If he could make contacts with his mother unit on the Twenty-First Division most likely operating in the town of Lucena or the province of Batangas, he said he can provide battle-hardened soldiers in their company.

There was an underlying problem to his proposition. The Japanese had a base in Atimonan in the north shore and a garrison in Agdangan along Tayabas Bay, and the enemy patrols were spread in between fifteen miles of land strip across that connected Bicol Region to Luzon. About seventy more miles to walk to even worry about the Japanese. From the village of the Abiyans, the first ten to fifteen kilometers was a crocodile-infested swamp and the next would be fifty more through heavily patrolled area. Agustin would come with them, and having attempted the feat in the past without success costing the life of his unit, it didn't mean he would not try again. Having reliable intelligence and exact locations of garrisons and checkpoints, the soldiers made up their mind they will push as much as possible and deal with enemy threat as it came face–to-face. It may be simple as it may seem, but not when the whole Abiyan colony is begging to come.

"WE WOULD LIKE TO HELP"

Men, women, and children, the whole village, had gathered what was left to their belongings. There was not much, as most of it were blown away by the storm like their homes. The Abiyans had decided to abandon their village. Reconstructions were deemed worthless when resources in the area could not sustain life anymore. On other consideration, crocodiles and pythons had infiltrated around the vicinity of the village, consuming other animals and their own young at times. They may have food to last two days courtesy of the passersby; after that would be no more. The war may not affect them, but it was time to move to a sustainable location somewhere where they could make ends meet without losing their child and devoid of rivalry for food with stealthy crocs and large snakes.

"Ta toy himunengat ka," one would say in their dialect, meaning, "I want to help," repeated by the other. That was last night after supper, with understanding that only the seven Dononos would come. Taking seven abled individuals out of the colony in time of calamity did not justify the need for guides that many. One or two should be enough for their convenience, but they had something else that made up their mind by morning. They were all going.

"I think the women like you very much, Cab," Santos would say, having noticed that most of them were staring at the shirtless captain that morning.

"Why would you say that?" the unaware soldier responded.

"Look around you." He laughed.

Taking the gravity of the situation into amusement, Santos had observed an unusual show of interest from the inhabitants over Cabarles, especially the young women. Likewise, the elder men that displayed self-inflicted scars identical to Donono were also staring at him.

Scrapping of rule two had taken consequences much more than they could imagine, a feat they haven't done yet before, relocating a whole village. Santos preferred looking at the benefits it presents over wearing his clothes inside out to find their way. On the other hand, he already knew what Cabarles would say, "These are Donono's people." So much to think what Little Don would do, but both agreed it may be the curse inflicted to them by Donono himself. The one they lost that afflicted their guilt and senses was replaced not by another one or seven Abiyans, but the whole colony. Well, the curse of one was more than they could handle, they will take them.

Who was helping who? On the first leg of the hike, they were guided east upstream of the river. The more favored route straight northwest was not rational—freshwater swamps and lily ponds filled with crocodiles, leeches, and venomous snakes or the dreaded tree pythons, not counting quicksands. No one got there and came out. Agustin would corroborate several accounts of disappearances toward the opposite direction as the Abiyans maintained. They would go around five miles and back by way of Calauag outskirts to Guinayangan jungles. Rafts were already waiting to cross the river. Obviously, the Abiyans had traveled the route more than once. Though they were informed that enemy patrols slacked for quite a long time, the natives would scout ahead to make sure. The movement may be slow, but the soldiers found amusement to practice on their bow and arrow. Cabarles must have proven his gifted skill in any weapon while Santos had settled on the blow dart. He showed his talent in blowing that skinny long tube; in fact, he gained audiences when he did it on a flute formerly owned by Francisco. He was matched by a tribal man with nothing but bare hands in a tune that allowed others to participate in lyrical version.

No incidents of enemy encounter in a long stretch, they got through dangerous passages in Calauag to the northern sea where the Abiyans settled on a beachfront overlooking several islands. They were home, they said, originally they came from Calauag until the war forced them to relocate and now they were back. A few more miles was where their former village stood; they hoped it was still there after the storm. Parting ways in good faith with developed friendship in such a short time, the soldiers had no reason to stay longer. They pushed west after being provided with three natives as their guides into the highlands of Guinayangan and Buenavista. They camped in the hills of Macalelon overlooking Tayabas Bay. Known to be in the middle of enemy territory, they did not cook anymore, which could create smoke to reveal their location. Wild pineapples and fruits from abandoned home yards composed the principal diet. A pair of water buffalos frolicking in the wilds along the route were added to the group. Showing tamed behavior, everyone looked at them as nutritious food though slaughtering poor animals at the time was not a choice to consider because the animals eventually became a means of transport. In some way they also looked like carabao rustlers because they knew someone owned the animals for farm use.

Relying on the advance scouting reports of the three Dononos, travel became smooth even in broad daylight. They kept going until they heard a loud explosion ahead. Scouting reports between Gumaca and Pitogo on twenty kilometers of dirt road that ended in water both ways was not good for seeing enemy activities; they were alerted by the explosion. Farther ahead was a clearing, possibly untended farmland or just barren land with isolated trees and coconuts. Nothing looked out of the ordinary other than sentinels and snipers maybe hidden on those trees aside from the fact that the Japanese had booby-trapped the area according to Agustin.

Only two Dononos came back; sad to say, they could only guess what happened to the third one. Courage intact, they suggested to move, favoring southwest by way of Laguimanok (now Padre Burgos). The soldiers agreed without protest in a hurry. Another incident blew up their carabao. A quiet town showed itself up after dark. As they got closer, they put out their kerosene lamp immediately when dogs began barking as they were passing through. Dirt road heading west, they walked straight over in darkness and cut through to the jungle still heading west until Agustin made known that he was already familiar with the place. They should be safe for the moment, and it was suggested that they should take a rest as the sun broke the fifth morning from Guinayangan, Quezon.

From the southern edge of the Sierra Madre called Pagbilao, Agustin continued southwest to Batangas with the Abiyans; the ghost soldiers would be heading north. They had successfully drilled their way through the forbidden land despite sad incidents. Before parting ways, they wished each other the best of luck and gratitude.

THE LEGACY OF DONONO CONTINUES

Owing their life to the Abiyans who guided them through several miles of known enemy strongholds in a short time, they had proven that kindness and courage stay naturally within the Filipinos in every way of life, their despite individual ways to survive. Whether they were the neatly dressed bus passengers or the curly-haired and sweaty natives, all civilians they met had in fact aided them in some way.

Just the two of them again, they would be seeing more of the so-called Abiyans. They all looked alike on their eyes, they had seen another colony with real dark skin and curly hair wandering in the forest. They may also be friendly, but they avoided contact with the absence of a translator. Knowing those blow tubes were weapons with poisoned darts, they could not take the risk of getting close and mistaken as a hostile people. The main objectives remained—one, to keep going until reunited with the wife, the other one was to make sure that the same man is alive when it happened.

In the month of November, nights were becoming colder. Though it did not rain for weeks, they could get soaked in their own sweat. The terrain could suddenly become treacherous over boulders of rocks with jagged edges, but the most difficult was getting through bamboo forests that had thorny stalks spread thickly. Nothing could be tougher anymore than they had been through, they said. Only at daytime could they keep moving to find a path with lesser vegetation. Being aware of tripwires that could kill a buffalo, it was impossible to see them at night. Two days on their own, they found themselves surrounded with coconuts, just coconuts everywhere. They didn't need much effort to bring them down. Triggered by thirst and hunger in a place they called coconut paradise, not a single soul around, they took advantage of the graces the land could offer. They could eat as many young coconuts they could; they had all the time in the world. Strange as it may seem, they found themselves still surrounded by coconuts after a day's walk except that they were tall, way taller, and neither of them had the skill to climb. They resigned under one with overgrown bushes around its trunk for the night, eating matured coconut again that were scattered on the ground.

Another day came up, and they were awakened by people talking aloud. They could not see them, but they were coming closer. It was a mix of kinky and curly-haired Dononos in the crowd led by a couple of men in large sombreros and armbands they had not seen for a long time since Dapecol, giving orders, yelling. It was too late to move, but afraid to be seen, they lay down on their stomachs and watched what the commotion was all about. People were climbing the coconut trunks like it was nothing, harvesting and dropping brownish clusters to the ground.

Suddenly inundated with coconut pickers, any more movement they would make could be seen. In fact, a fellow high up the palm tree had seen them already as he noticeably halted from what he was doing. He may have frozen for a while, but he kept dropping coconuts like he had seen nothing, taking another one to climb without a word.

About two hundred feet and closing, another group was gathering the harvest as they threw it in a pile, creating mounds after mounds. One elderly with curly hair must have done something wrong. He was being yelled at up by a supervisor so mad and loud though they didn't understand what the man was saying. What could have the worker done to suffer the repeated slash of a cane so merciless and strong that sent him down the ground? The Doe on his knee was begging, maybe apologizing, and was about to receive another swing in full force when a gunshot was fired close by, very close to Cab's ear. Before the stick landed on the target, the man in slow motion fell to the ground. The workers ran away and disappeared while the second man in sombrero met the same fate after the second shot was heard from the same gun while he attempted to return fire with his rifle. Wounded or dead, both stopped moving.

"Why did you shoot them?" Cabarles complained, with ears ringing.

"I see you hesitating," Santos replied, realizing they should run too.

Two bodies of people on the ground they hated most, pickers may be elated, but they were aware what it would cause them. Some looked around where the shots came from; only those up on a tree would know the location of the shooters as they came down swiftly to attend to another that was still recovering from pain and shock.

And they ran toward the soldiers, saying something nervously. The sudden decision to run away was made in a split second with the Dononos, nonstop until they reached the end of the coconut plantation. Obviously, they were saying to follow them. They had no reason not to believe the Dons except that it was a tobacco field they were heading and not the direction of choice, to the east. Downed by strong winds recently and no means of cover whatsoever other than a clusters of few that remained standing in rows, following jumpy-curlies was the only option they could make in the panicky situation. About eight hundred yards, they sprinted over the leafy clearing and didn't look back to race the coconut pickers toward the wall of greens ahead.

Even the agile Dononos were resting and catching their breath when they stop. Santos began to complain of a stomachache. Cabarles knew how serious it could be.

Down on the cover of cattails and similar grass in elevated expanse, a few minutes to spare looking back, Cabarles saw that they were being pursued. About a dozen uniformed Japanese with the signature camouflage of leafy twigs had exposed themselves over the tobaccos, scattered on formation on the same path they made. He knew for a fact that it wasn't easy to run with a finger on the trigger of heavy rifle. Perhaps an accidental shot had reveal more enemy distinctively over the plots.

Hidden on the edge of cattails so thickly grown undisturbed, Santos was taking a moment of silence on his own more than just catching his breath a few feet away from Cabarles.

"Do you have to do it now?" Cab asked.

"Yes, I think too much coconut is not good for me," he said.

"Well, hurry up, they are coming fast."

Given no other choice but let his buddy get relieved, he turned his attention back to the pursuers and made sure he had a full cartridge in his rifle and ready. Still a far target at five hundred yards, he would not fire but only observe. At four hundred, Santos was not done yet. He could take a shot, but it was the Japanese he would shoot. Cab could see no more other than fifteen or twenty on the same location. He stayed put and ready; otherwise he would not fire anymore and keep running when Santos got done. The natives were restless; Cab understood that they were trying to say to keep running, and every second counting, knowing that what they saw on the field should not be all of them. One tried very hard screaming to the soldiers, but there was nothing else he could do when seemingly he could not be understood.

Cabarles fired at a target within three hundred yards in rapid succession. Not a second was wasted in reloading, but it was enough to alert the enemy to drop to the ground, Cabarles could still see them clearly. Five more shells were spent by the time Santos was pulling his pants up.

"I'm done, let's go," Santos calmly said in the spur of the moment.

Two more shots, and they rushed up the small hill to find what the Doe was telling. Over was a frequently traveled road; they saw a large vehicle slowing down from the north to give way to others behind. Military trucks coming. Instinct dictated that the only direction they could go was southwest to the nearest woods that further revealed a mountain so tall that white clouds concealed its peak. In body motion and all, the Dononos directed the soldiers southwest, heading to the mountains.

CHAPTER 20

SINNERS AND BELIEVERS

A clever man who had sin, sins of all sinners in one man. Tell me your heroes, he is one of mine.

THE REVELATIONS IN MOUNT BANAHAW

Standing 7,100 feet at its highest peak, Mount Banahaw is an ultravolcano located along the boundary of Quezon and Majayjay, Laguna, eighty kilometers southeast of Manila. Mother Banahaw, the tallest, lies south-southwest, San Cristobal on the west. Banahaw de Lucban is on the northeastern slope that creates a valley of debris and rocky formations with many springs that support overgrowth even in the driest season. Overtime since the last explosion in 1843, it hosted varieties of flora and fauna untouched by men, wild animals, exotic fruits and trees that support life; but a wanderer must beware because it also cost dearly to so many who got lost daring to try in shedding light to many legends and hearsays. Emanating from people who have unexplained experiences on the mountain and enriched by conjectural conclusion beginning back hundreds of years, Mother Banahaw was one place avoided by people.

From the soldiers' eye view, it was just a mountain they could seek refuge in for a while if they could make it at least to the foothills. Heading south-southwest, they knew that the enemy would tore them into pieces without mercy if get caught up with them. What lay on their path were gentle hills and valleys with many clearings with no guarantee that they could not be seen as they saw enemy moving in pursuit like swarms that blended on bushes. No stone unturned, like a hurricane passing through, the Japanese were coming with a vengeance in two companies or more.

Thirteen bullets spent, Santos knew for sure, had hit its target individually. In effect, rule one had been broken, and they could not face the consequences other than run away from it. Mount Banahaw may look close, but it was about twenty more kilometers to reach its foothills. Nonetheless, it was noontime on a bright day. Running the distance was nothing under normal conditions. When one of them was suffering from lingering stomach pains, it was not the same. The last of the Dons they saw were waving pieces of clothes altogether to follow them, perhaps waving goodbye. They changed directions suddenly to northwest, noticing thicker greeneries that was opposite to where the natives were leading them. They found that it wasn't woodland at all, but uphill of thorny vines and accidental clusters of trees between paths that were heavily walked on. Many boulders of rocks that changed the surroundings abruptly, fields of ferns over volcanic debris cut-off by plain green grass - two bearded men lay down gasping for breath to rest. Soaking in their own sweat, they didn't know how far they had able to run away. It could not be too far with Japanese on their tail. To make the situation worse, they didn't have water to drink.

In a place where the sun would set over the peak of Mount Banahaw, the shadow that was created by the mountain led them to believe that their vision was depriving them of hope that they would not make it through another day. They didn't know that they were being watched. They could only be farmers, passing through from a day's work might have wanted to help but refrain from doing so for understandable reasons. They remained standing in the far distance just staring at them, afraid or just didn't want to help, one would kneel down in prayer, which made the others to follow. Cabarles became aware of their presence eventually, but the people continued what they were doing. At the same moment, sporadic gunfire that became intense was heard from far southwest. On their estimate on the distance of the battle, they should be there if not diverted by instinct. However, it was enough for the locals to disappear and for them to move out. They only managed to go a few hundred yards and stop again; Santos was extremely exhausted, worsened by a serious pain he blamed on the coconut, his vision spinning and totally disoriented. They made several stop until they reached a small flat ground on the hill, only to discover the mountain they intended to retreat was not where they are at yet. Mount Banahaw was still a view from their location, unreachable given the conditions at the time.

The turn of events was a blessing. Three civilians approached from nowhere and offered them food and water, which they gladly took. They may be brave enough to do such a deed being women while the audible sound of gun battle was going on. They were noticeably scared but gladly spared water to drink.

"Can you tell us where we are?" Santos asked a woman who offered him water.

"You are on 'the Hands of God,'" she said very calmly and moved back to join the others in prayer.

He wasn't sure if he heard it right, but for the hope and relief it brought, Cab repeated where they were to the oblivious soldier, "we are on the hands of god."

The help they were offered came in unusual way; people were kneeling, they appeared to be praying solemnly while Cab attended to Santos as he helped him lean over his lap. What they were witnessing was pure kindness in the fashion they had never seen before.

Likewise to the women that came to their aid: the weakened man was being fed by the one with the long hair partially covering his bearded face while revealing the scars from lashes on his back.

"We have plenty of food, sir," Cab whispered. "Keep eating." What he said was a lie, but intentionally made to a man whose eyes may be open but who was not responding.

Santos would eventually eat and drink, not a drop wasted on the precious water they were spared by the women. He refused the last of the bite of food that was put in his mouth. Regaining senses on the dwindling daylight, he had known they were equally hungry; water should be good for now. He may be sick, but the other must have drained his strength carrying him. In both cases, however, he would rather let Cab remain able and strong. He apologized for his ineffectiveness at a time needed most.

After having rested enough for an hour or so, Santos declared, "I'm feeling better now, we have to keep going" while proving that he was strong enough to stand by himself.

Pausing with one knee on the ground, calculating if he could stand up by himself without assistance, he looked up ahead; and before he knew it, the same helping hand got him up on his feet. They could not afford to stay idle while knowing that the place was also swarmed with the enemy.

"Are you sure you're all right now?" Cab worried, but he had no choice. He would carry him again if necessary.

"Yes, I will be fine. We have to get out of here," Santos replied.

Recovering from severe dehydration, he concluded that he would not die yet as strength was added to every step, at every single random gunfire he could hear. He could hear Cab uttering words, praying for the souls of those people whom he was sure met their death in the most ruthless way. Somehow he was aware that it could be them. So did the three women tailing them who would do the sign of the cross every time he glimpsed at them. He had no clue what was on their mind or their prayers for, but in a remote corner of his senses that was slowly coming back, he had seen that scene before. "Thank you for the food and water, and for the prayers," he said.

Halfway uphill, they thought it was already safe and obscure to spend the night. The sun set over Mount Banahaw was creating shades at general locations, darker under the canopy of trees, but the sky still blue. A few more civilians were present at the site. After a quick look around, Santos sat exhaustedly at a certain spot, confidently taking advantage of the solemnity of the moment, Cab putting down his rifle on a protruding rock over his head where a little tree were growing. After stretching his arm sideways and yawning assertively, he lay down slowly. He inclined his slender weary bulk, letting his buddy partially feel his weight as he adjusted himself so that his head rested on Santos's ribs until eventually he put down his back on the ground comfortably.

"You stink real bad," he said.

Santos inhaled deeply then exhaled, stomach growling accompanied by the passing of gas. "I feel very sick again," he said.

The battle had long been over, not a cricket was making a noise. What was visible around was only the profile of trees and the people in front of them, just staring at them. Santos would remain holding his gun with right hand standing on its stock on the dirt, forming the reflection of a cross with the Springfield while allowing his left hand freely over Cab at a moment's notice to pull the trigger.

Looking at the sky, Cabarles would not be bothered when a woman would offer them more water and something to chew on. He was occupied with watching the bright white clouds passing from northeast as the western horizon reflected its light over Mount Banahaw, creating different colors in his eye view. The rays found their way through the canopy of trees that brightened up and glowed over their very spot for a few seconds until the light disappeared. There was nothing so special about it in Cab's mind; it always happened in the farms and meadows in Bulacan, but to the perspective of all other people who witnessed the event, they believe what they saw was out of ordinary added to their presence. A ray of light, a miracle had just transpired in the eyes of believers. Cab had seen many animated people when he looked down.

"We have to leave this place, Cab," Santos suggested. "I think this is a sacred place for the people. Look how sincere they are kneeling and praying. It is a disrespect if we stay any longer."

"I noticed that too. Are you feeling all right now?" Cab replied while trying to get on his foot, having trouble a bit to let free of the weight of Santos comfortably leaning on his right side.

"Yes, I'm a lot better."

"We should follow the trail uphill, would you be all right?"

"Yes. Just hold me. I'm not seeing any. It's too dark."

Very slowly, they reached the top of the hill. Someone must have been buried on the place to put a cross where Santos said to stop awhile. His vision had come back from the tormenting hours going up the trail. They stayed until total darkness and vanished swiftly over the nearby bushes that led them to nowhere. They didn't see mountains anymore; they were on it.

Santos was allowed to take five again. Cab scouted about twenty yards ahead, trying to reestablish his orientation. He knew that the Japs were relentless, and they were not done yet to take vengeance for their fallen comrades that died in the coconut plantation and thereafter. In that regard, they would not even the score with the coconut pickers alone, who were mostly Dononos. They would find the real men who dared to shoot their comrades in broad daylight. Anyone breathing on their way would die, and they would not distinguish if they were civilian, women, or children seeking refuge and solace on the mountain. At first daylight, the enemy would resume looking for them.

A NEW SPIRIT

The five became hours to take advantage of finding themselves alone again. In "the Hands of God," they sought refuge another day and reevaluated what went wrong. It was an ordeal neither one won't forget.

They hovered away from the favored Sierra Madre route too far in the east. It was a big mistake. There was no option for now but to find a secure place where they could stay alive, until such time the Japanese tired up looking for them; the enemy could get hungry too. The most viable decision was to get in deeper into the foothills of the volcano complex and above if necessary. Rules were decided to be reinstated, rules that were meant to be broken. It was still a long way they would hurdle to Bulacan.

Aided by the full moon in a starry night, they spent all of their strength regained from the hands of the devotees. About eight hours of patiently concentrating that every step counts away from the enemy, they reached a wall of vegetation so thick that it prevented them from moving further. On a small ground high enough, all they saw was the top of the trees waving back and forth to a midnight breeze reflected by the northern sky. Facing east was the Sierra Madre Mountains where they were supposed to be. To blame the Dons who led them west could not be discounted since they owed them their life too. The most important was they were alive. They just didn't know how deep they went, and by from how it looked, the wilderness of Mount Banahaw was entirely different from any other jungles they had been. How to get out was a different matter with only one thing in mind—stay away from the Japanese.

The foothills of the mountain was also a sanctuary of exotic plants and wildlife aside from its legends. In times of war and for men with guns running away for dear life, it was where they would seek refuge in for a little while. They may wanted to keep moving but they woke up without knowing how they get there, figuring how to get out was simply they could not figure out yet. In the succession of random events since passing through 'The Hands of God', one was worried, very worried. The other was confused, very confused that made the other to worry. Santos was never heard talking about faith and religion. In Lanao, he converted to Muslim in a ritual that also earned him the title of a Datu in the Order of Benghalid Clan and a name that Cabarles could not remember anymore. Being together for a long time confiding with each other, there were so much accounts a clever city boy could tell than a farm boy. Suddenly, it became so quiet that Cabarles would not get any response at times.

Santos was reflecting. He reevaluating the purpose of his own life during the time he survived the war before becoming a POW with Donono and thereafter when reunited with Cabarles. So many incidents had happened when he should have die, and all those times the only one who would be on his side for salvation was the same person who already died for him. Earlier, while running away from the enemy, he was sure he could not see at all. He was blinded; should he reveal it to Cabarles at the time when his only hope was the same person he had sworn to serve and protect yet the one still taking care of him? Lest to admit when his senses came to a point when he lost his vision going up that hill, he was afraid to die. That feeling of someone carrying him was the only thing he could remember until he found himself on the lap of the same man who would not let go of him. In that same period when all he saw were the profiles and figures in a solemn moment of their faith, how could he explain that he remembered clearly he was one among those figures witnessing a man on the lap of another in "the hands of God"? He disclosed to Cabarles that his soul actually left his body to witness the light that showered them both for a moment. In continuation of his revelation of that delirious moment, he was with many people praying for the man in the cross.

So many times he had observed Cab on the same manner, leading him to believe somewhat that he was really a blessed man. Not just a sharpshooting soldier with extraordinary skills in many more other fields. He could keep calm and be decisive in all kinds of danger, not afraid to die and never lose courage. In the absence of Hombre Donono whom he could turn his attention to with disrespect when the other was seemingly in a sincere moment of faith by his belief,

Santos declared he had found himself in faith. To the faith, Cabarles observed in his most earnest way—he knelt down in the same motion of what he saw when his vision and strength almost miraculously came back up that last hill. A sinner and most evil one as he described himself, he had no right to be up that hill. He had felt himself burning; the heat was unbearable though he was cold until kind hands gave him water.

His long conviction of "bad weed never dies" was repealed. The good just doesn't die either, and the only reason he was still alive was because he was in the company of one of the most kindhearted and selfless man who called him sir, the most humble man. To redeem himself of sins and serve him best righteously was to be with his faith.

Still intact in his mind that became mundane was he should not shoot those collaborators in the coconut plantation. The workers should also bear retribution, and he knew it before he squeezed the trigger of his rifle. In so doing, he endangered his own; worse, to the man he swore to serve and protect. Somehow, he was sincerely repentant of his actions and sorry for those soul that met their own demise as a result. In his recovery to full strength given the unusual change of behavior, he was happy they were both alive and no enemy was in sight. It was nighttime, and they really could not see much. The stars clearly indicated that a better day awaited, but tomorrow at first daylight when the wrath of the JIP recommenced to advance, even the praying mantis on their path should die. He was hoping those people that congregated up that hill had gone home already if they had homes to go. Otherwise, they must have hidden themselves by now.

Cabarles was truly worried. He had listened enough to a fellow that talked an entirely different opinion than he usually did. However, they had to keep moving.

An unexpected outcome of events had to be addressed. First, the most unusual one: Santos kneeling and mumbling words not heard before, uncertain of what his friend was trying to say or do. He looked at him, choosing not to interfere with a lot to worry. Should he not be showing off nor truthful to the sudden grasp of faith; otherwise, something had gone really wrong with Santos. It wasn't the effect of the coconuts anymore for sure, but what could have suddenly transformed the brave and fearless one into revering with a grand display of emotions and a lot of dialogues in the realm of the moonlight? He let him do whatever it was the man was doing until he calmed down by himself. Santos may be sincere to his spontaneous awakening into faith, but Cabarles was afraid. He had seen such kind of behavior many times in the Davao Penal Colony; they ran amok afterward. Although he had to admit Santos had scared him a bit for a while, he remained hopeful that Santos was mentally normal when the show was over.

"What was that all about?" Cab opened, trying to prevent his sleepy eyes to close with a man who obviously needed reevaluation.

"I am a new man. From now on, we will pray together," Santos stated.

"You know, you scared me there for a while."

"Did I? I apologize, I got carried away. I honestly tell you a new spirit is in my body now," he replied.

"All right, sleep now."

A new spirit? Maybe that new spirit had made a mistake which body it took over. Cab was hoping by tomorrow that whatever that affliction was, it should be gone after a good rest. He never had a problem with the old spirit of the man, so much to say he got used to that spirit comfortably. He slowly slipped his hand inside his satchel, made sure the .38 was still there as the man with the "new spirit" moved closer. Nothing out of the ordinary, they slept close to each other all the time.

"Drink a lot of water, we don't know where we are. Tomorrow might be as bad," Cab said, referring to the Japanese soldiers looking for them.

"I am not worried. Hey, Cab. In Bulacan, do you think I can purchase a farmland and settle close to your place?"

"Yes, of course, you can."

"Is it close to a church?"

"Yes."

"Very good. In Manila, I had stashed a lot of money. When the war is over, I am hoping I can settle down and find a good-looking Bulaquena and get married. We will be neighbors, and our children will play together, grow together."

"Yes, sure. I'm happy looking forward to it."

The newly spirited man somewhat had inspired hope forthcoming. Cab liked the idea and easily adapted to the concept of a new spirit. Instead of holding the revolver, he pulled his hand out of the leather with Alhambra and lit up. They continued talking about the future, a change in the usual topic of daily strategies on how to survive and avert the enemy. This time, they planned way over the mountains, dreaming. None of the lavishness, but a simple life without the Japanese pursuing them or them shooting back at anybody. The happiness they had imagined was inspiring, simple, and attainable to the same life that one of them had it on his grasp and let go. The other one had expressed his enthusiasm to come down to that esteem and leave the life of luxuries and all with his friend and in his faith. It may be unlikely and cynical considering that Santos's way of life paused by the war was entirely opposite to his, but he was profound to the certainty it would happen.

Riding on each other's credence that what was said was true and serious, the concurrence rendered a common goal that upheld solidarity enhanced by common faith. Punctuated by dawn breaking up to another hot and humid day after a cold night that warmed each one's malnourished body, neither wanted to bring the topic to an end, but they had to face reality. And the reality was they needed to sleep, forget the Japanese hunting them or wherever place they were at. But one was not satisfied yet with a notion that was too stimulating to sleep on. Too scary to sleep comfortably in the company of a fragile new spirit.

"Does Inez have a sister?" Santos asked with no intention to sleep just yet.

"None."

"So we cannot be like real brothers?"

"We can still be. She has a mare she treats like a sister." Getting irritated but realizing that his words was not appropriate, he said, "Don't worry, you will not believe how beautiful Bulaquenas are."

"I know, they are thoughtful and loving, very traditional, and honors vanity until the day you marry her."

"You bet that is right. How do you know that?"

"I heard it before, and Donono had proven to me it is true."

"How could that little man so clueless think about that?"

"That's what you know about him. He is one horny dumb male too. Do you recall when we left you at the Manila Yacht Club? He was supposed to stay on the boat."

"Yeah."

"Well, he confided to me he didn't stay on the boat. He was by the window of your room all night."

"What? That little maniac. Why did you just tell me about that?"

"Because I know you're going to hurt him. He said it was too dark anyway he must not have seen anything."

"That bastard can see through the dark. You're right, I might have beaten him up. Worse, I would've nailed him up that cross we did for his bullies."

"Will you find me a Bulaquena?" Santos said in an attempt to calm down an obviously fuming Cabarles.

"No, you will get a mare with a grown-up offspring. Sleep."

"All right. But I have more to confide to you. You have to listen very carefully."

"I'm listening."

DEERS IN TRANQUILITY

In the cold night of the mountain, they both fell asleep eventually while the sun revealed the blue sky and scattered fog in the lowlands down from the mountain. Dew dripping was shared by plants hosted by another in magnificent bloom of wildflowers as it recycled back to the atmosphere and condensed again in the cold breeze of December nights.

Southern Philippines is so beautiful that poets call it the land of all beauties while visitors plainly call it paradise. To those who get confused, the mountain is enchanted. To those religiously inclined, the place is miraculous, enlightening to the faith.

From their location, the land was covered with greenery gently sloping up and down just like any other place they had been into. This time, they had the opportunity to relish it from above. And from above, they could see a flock of black birds circling afar on the sky, the kind that would feast on a decaying body. No one would comment about those birds as they knew that a battle just took place were roughly on that spot just a day ago. To add to already unpleasant thoughts, gunfires broke again about half a kilometer downhill. They could not pinpoint what direction it was coming from because the sound echoed before it could reach their ears. One thing they were sure, it was close. Their shadows told them it was past noontime, reviving rule one; and in the emerging possibility that the enemy were closing in, the only option was to get into the thick wall of leafy vines and bushes behind them.

At the behest of instinct, and maybe because there was no other place to go but around a long way with similar obstruction, they went into the unknown. They would not see daylight for an unknown period of time.

Vines and stem the size of a finger that became bigger as they moved in deeper, there was no reason to be alarmed. They had been lost in many virgin forests, places they could rest freely when tired, and appreciate the wonder of nature and look at the sky. This place had only became dark as they pushed in. Moistened roots, soft and old, had entangled with each other that it became so difficult to get through, especially when carrying a rifle. Their bolo was useless as there was no leverage to swing and cut rigid obstacles. The only way they could move was pushing them with their own bodies to make a hole just enough to move inch by inch and then spring it back like no one had ever been through. In pitch black, nothing could be seen, not even each other; one had to say something to know that he was there and breathing. In a situation like that, they did what they do best—take a rest, sleep, and hope that when they wake up, they can think of something else on how to tackle the problem. After all, they wanted to hide.

They would never know how long they had been sleeping when they were awakened by the sudden outbreak of unidentified noise like the stampede of animals, causing the surroundings to shake the silence and halted all the humming and rattling of presumed insects and nocturnal beings. A familiar sound, however, stayed—flowing water, somewhere in the vicinity. Their next movement was directed to the source of such water, six length of their body when they felt the ground becoming damp. Thick roots covered a pile of rocks that they felt was designed by nature and was perpetually releasing fresh cold water as it spread down in multiple directions. The glow of the Zippo aided them in evaluating the site. It was a trunk of a giant tree that fell off and was still thriving to create a wall of darkness covered by fine roots. Indeed, it was high enough for them to stand up, but around were the same thick undergrowth, some reaching the ground, many just hanging like curtains in fine and smooth texture racing down to a void of space and offering rich moisture at any climate that was sometimes hard to come from above.

They may have water to drink, but the longing for daylight stands. Which way to go when totally disoriented? Follow a hole made by rats, but no one wanted to scare the other, not to mention that it may be a home for big snakes. Having no clue what place they got themselves into, one would suggest to take a moment for prayers. The other would say he was already praying all the time. Then it was suggested that they should pray together from then on. One reversed his shirt again, showing frustration of the many hours they were crawling under seemingly the same curtains of roots they could see every time they lit up the Zippo. The last of the guavas and coconuts had been consumed already, and they were becoming irritated of by insect bites and thorny vines.

However, the toughest situation was not a reason to give up. They would talk about the experience in Ragay and compare the current situation just to have something to talk about. In reality, they were only trying to divert their attention from the horrific agony of slow and insignificant death. Only the company of each other were keeping their courage as it was from the beginning. An effort to find their way back where they got in was as unachievable as just wanting to get out anywhere through. The Zippo could only give sparks, they cannot see each other no more.

"Hey, Cab, shall we pray again?"

"Sure we can."

"Would you mind praying together with me now?"

"Sure. OUR FATHER, THOU ART IN HEAVEN—"

"Shall we kneel down?"

"You should if you can. HALLOWED BE THY NAME—"

"Don't be playing with me now, I'm serious."

In Ragay, they can see the sky, birds flying up above. White clouds, dark clouds, and the stars at night. The man who endlessly cursing in Ragay, he was praying.

"ON EARTH AS IT IS IN HEAVEN"

There is no place that could be more terrifying. Knowing it only took them a few steps to find themselves in total darkness, finding their way out were hand over to their faith. Total disorientation was made worse by hunger and exasperation, which was alleviated by exhaustion. When they got tired, they slept to gain strength for the next agonizing hours to wake up in the dark again and move inch by inch and repeat the same process.

From a nightmare, Santos would be stimulated by a dream. "The war is over, I was tired of taking care of my own rice crop—tiring but an honest way of living. At the end of the day, delicious dinner can be smelled on the air cooking. Thoughtful hands wiping sweat and splatter of mud off my face with a warm towel. So pleasing that the wonderful feeling would lead me to think that no more can I ask for from this world. A beautiful lovely wife so tender with her hands, making me feel tickled with that damp and warm cloth on my face, on my neck, under my shirt while looking at her beautiful face." He was not alone in the same dream.

"Inez is so delightful and kind, of the likes of Rina Penafrancia with the determination of Rhodora X. So thoughtful but bold and playful, comparable to the sensual and voluptuous Rosie Brown—and all the flirtatious and submitting Bicolana widows put altogether."

Nothing unusual, only that it felt real. Santos closed his eyes again to take advantage of the moment, and that wet and warm feeling touching his face went on. This time, it came with a gentle breathing as he became aware that he was not dreaming anymore. When he opened his eyes again, the colors and shapes of the surroundings were back the way it should be on ordinary days. Daylight that protruded through thinner vegetation on a grassy ground excited him more than anything else, but he wanted to make sure he didn't lose it all mentally. He heard some giggling,; he never heard it that way, but he knew who it was, only Cabarles. Very slowly, he turned his head to see Cabarles, clearly unaware that an animal was licking his face.

A four-legged animal so close he could jump on it and break its neck for food was the first thing that came to Santos mind. He touched his face to feel that same slime dripping from the mouth of the bigger deer as its long tongue retracted back to its mouth. He prepared himself anyway to overpower the animal, but the sight of a smaller and nearer one changed his mind. It was so close it was just an arm's distance looking at him. He immediately devised a strategy; he knew that a deer is an agile animal that he could not outsmart so easily. He closed his eyes, assured it would come again and taste the salty sweat that dried off on his skin, waiting confidently to focus that he started to salivate on the foresight of meat; it should be very tasty and ample.

Cabarles had also awakened, suddenly aware that he could see light above and ahead. They found the way out.

Santos was waiting patiently until there were some movements. He felt a gentle tap on his shoulder, but he let his composure intact on a plan that he knew he only had one chance to be successful. At the second touch he felt on his face, he wasted no moment. He tackled the animal to the ground even before he could open his eyes. Bigger from what he thought it would be but in frustration and setback, he was so apologetic to find that it was Cabarles he had overpowered and strangled. There was no sign of a deer anywhere to justify his action and must be forgiven.

In the mind of a man who had just averted a sudden death by strangulation from the other who had been loyal and trustworthy, he had no reason not to believe the regretful explanation of such an action. But with the prevalent question about his sanity that had been building up, Cabarles's hypothesis was becoming real. From an instantaneous change of faith with a clear attempt of slaying him, he was becoming really worried for Santos, much more of himself in effect. Should he disarm Santos, which would clearly reveal his doubt to his mental state? Santos had two grenades, a loaded .45, and a semiautomatic rifle in his possession. After what happened, should he sleep well anymore? He pretended to believe Santos's excuses until such time he could take those weapons from him without impairment. The best move for now was to show emotional and spiritual support and find food that may put him back to his normal senses.

With likelihood, they had reached the edge of that dark and cursed place alive. He let him lead the way in a more forgiving path until they could actually walk without crawling or bending. There was no way he would allow him behind.

No words were said anymore until they stepped into an open plateau of bright morning light. Around were exotic trees abundant of yield that was so overwhelming to hungry beings. Santos would kneel down for gratitude in a manner he understood his newly acquired faith and spirit that was put to test, crying while on his knees bent to the ground again with spoken performance, increasing the suspicion that only a thread was holding grip of his mind. Cabarles said a short prayer likewise, could be longer, then worriedly attended to the pacification of a comrade exhibiting a present danger and may do fatal harm to either one of them. He swore it would not happen. He would be by his side at the hour he was most needed, more important than the calling of a growling stomach.

It was really such a beautiful place. On the ground were fine grasses like soft carpet as they walked over it. To the west was a domelike natural structure with the leafy branches of trees touching each other over a waterfalls cascading down on layers of rocks, creating a tiny pool at the bottom and splitting the flow equally to separate directions. Trees were adorned with wildflowers and ferns on both sides of the spring, concealing the steep rocky hill where the freshwater was coming from. They were in heaven, one would say. The other would disagree because no guns were allowed in heaven.

Up on a plateau at bird's-eye view, the place was bounded around an unrestricted growth of trees and other plant life a mile or more down to the lower slopes. On its own, old and fallen trees were overgrown by more invasive plants that intertwined on top of the other, causing leaves and broken twigs to dry out without reaching the ground. Thus, a new layer of dirt was made, letting new seeds to germinate and grow to maturity, creating a hollow underworld rich with moisture fed from a spring that dispersed water around the land they called heaven.

Being on the wrong side of the town of Tayabas, crossing back to the Sierra Madre in the east, was still in mind, but it was deemed impossible, estimating the distance between two mountains ruthless Japs and collaborators proliferated. An agreement was reached without opposition, stay in heaven— to recoup strength and courage. Santos may not be really getting crazy, but his physical condition was seriously affected by the aftermath of defying rule one and two at the same time. For Cabarles, it wasn't the heaven wanted to see. He immediately look around.

The first day on that "magical place" was to get rid of slimy bloodsuckers that attached to their skins. So many had fattened up for an unknown number of days, each one sucking their blood. Weakness and disorientation was blamed on the critters, not on a deer though Santos maintained that he had seen a pair. By nightfall, he seemed to act normally. Stars added to the magnificent view on the eastern landscape of Tayabas, at best when the full moon shone, causing different shadows and figures of random formation of land highlighted by hills and trees in the vast domain. One that would stand out was the "Hand of Jesus," illuminated and shaped distinctively from a distance. They had been there sometime ago, the place they went through while being pursued by the Japanese soldiers, where kind people were praying devotedly and offered food and water for them. It was the place where Santos had reclaimed his faith in religion. What he was describing was yet to be determined in the eyes of the confused company. Cabarles was thrown out of comprehension in figuring what Santos was seeming to say that could be seen in the distance was really the "Hand of God." There is sincerity, no doubt about that, but to have faith in God back in the fold of Catholicism for a man who was also compassionate in the call of other religion was truly beyond his grasp. The man was admired so much for his intelligence, he could also count to thousands like nothing.

Santos had yet to find those deer to redeem himself from suspicion that he was getting crazy. Cab may agree with him to say they were truly in heaven, seeing clouds lower than the place they were in.

Because of genuine respect for the intelligence of the man, Cabarles could not reject Santos solely for a fact of improperly exercising faith according to his own opinion. On the other hand, a state of mind that sees things that aren't there is becoming antecedent to what had piled up already. One that was hard to ignore is being strangled only to say that he was mistaken as a deer then telling the man was seeing the hand of God in the vast expanse of Lucban, which was just conflicting. Cab was still thinking firmly of taking all the weapons decorating his body, but such an action may be offending to the captain's authority. Generally, what worried Cabarles the most was the psychological condition of Santos. In the end, all he could do was to defer the worrying but remain aware of what the situation presented and hope that being in "heaven" enlightened both of them with the many amenities it offered.

Clearly it was an impossible feat to climb a steep hill to the top; otherwise, they would go through the same undergrowth of hellish experience to restart the journey. About three hundred fifty kilometers more to their final destination and the first mile seemed to not want to let them go easily. By any means, they couldn't stay. The obstacles offered the ordeal in Ragay offshores the same effect, but given more precursor to consider, delays were disregarded considering the abundance of food and comfort on that small real estate. The first day was all right despite the conjuring concerns that was hard to overcome. Cabarles awakened the next day having food ready by his side. Santos was nowhere in sight that it started him to worry at once, Cab found him taking a bath in the spring, so excited to tell that the water was warm and soothing. The day went on with them just enjoying the place. None would start talking of a plan to leave just yet, wondering who would be taking care of that place with such diligence and loving hands. Papayas thrived by themselves, likewise the pomelos of the sweetest variety planted in tandem at a selected spot; bananas occupied a larger parcel sloping down to the edge. More exotic fruits around grew in the lowlands that could not have been brought up there by nature. Floral plants of the wild kind were spread meticulously by helping hands, noticeable by their arrangements and varieties. But in general, the place had been unattended for a long time, making nuisance vines to grow over freely. Somewhere around, there must be a trail leading in and out, made by whoever was taking care of the place, only obscured by invasive shrubberies.

The third day was tiresome. All day they cut and cleared invading plants in the northwest side, but they found none of what they were looking for. They were amazed to discover that the plateau was larger than they thought, exposing more fruit-bearing trees as they munched on fruits while keep working alternately with the bolo. The familiar stench of overripe jackfruit somewhere eastward motivated them to continue, but daylight was running out that they had to stop and rest.

Unknown to them, they were being watched. Supper was a smorgasbord of fruits and casual chat that involved the firm belief that they would find the way out eventually, encouraging each other to continue the task at first daylight. The outcome of the day may be tiring, but one had confirmed that he was wrong to assume that the other was losing his grip. Likewise, the other thought that he was pardoned; indeed, both wished for the deer to show up.

Cabarles was born a farmer. Clearing unwanted growth out of his farm was what he enjoyed the most while daydreaming at the same time—endless thoughts of a woman that could continue without talking at all until falling asleep. Santos was the opposite, but overtime in their alliance, he had learned how to respect the silence of Cab. He already knew that something was playing in his mind when looking up with a grin on his face, and he also knew that was what kept the man going strong. In the most scenic and inspiring place, he had no reason to bother him, but he wanted to know how he can do that, setting aside all tormenting experiences and dangers ahead, which were not easy to disregard in a matter of seconds. In addition, he had developed fear since his transitory blindness was worsened by agonizing events that followed. Much more of the embarrassment he incurred to himself by subduing the man and which he was inclined to believe was hallucination caused by leeches and dehydration.

"Cab . . ., are you with Inez?" He was hesitant but naturally affable. "Would you spare more time to me before you fall asleep?" Like a kid, he slowly inched himself closer, cautiously, trying to get attention. "I'm so cold," he said.

It was really cold to feel, set off by the December breeze halfway to the top of the mountain boosted by the northeastern exposure. Cab welcomed him with the usual embrace, pressing the better part of his body to feel the warmth of the other, lying comfortably by the spring under the canopy of an unknown leafy tree bearing big fruits similar to jackfruit but which taste nothing though its shade offered shelter from fog and morning dew.

"You're shivering, you must be having fever," Cab noticed, immediately reaching in his satchel to find those pills from Davao. He remembered them with the instructions of what they were for, but they were of two of previously three different kinds. He could not remember which packet is for fever. He had the same trouble when he gave Santos a packet of white powder for stomachache in a rush down in 'The Hands of God'. He took one of each and put it to the mouth of Santos. "Here, these will make you feel better." He then gathered dry wood and set them up on fire. It wasn't totally dark yet, but he could not think of anything to at least make the water warm for Santos to drink. They had left everything including the canteen on that coconut plantation, maybe on the roadside. He took his shirt off while thinking and put it over the man. For two days on that place, he didn't see anything they could use as container other than a banana trunk. He stripped some of it anyway and let it heat up over the fire and carefully covered Santos one piece after another.

Santos was obviously sick again. The initial diagnosis would be that he stood up "against bad airstream," Cab would say, pertaining to what he knew when someone got ill of any cause. If the person died, he "forgot to breathe." A strong reminder to the captain was to keep breathing and the bad air would dissipate eventually. With a simple knowledge, a simple remedy to everything, there was nothing else he could do but wished for a pot to boil water in and some leaves around that he knew could relieve illnesses. Hopeless for such a object, he gathered guava leaves and the big ones just above him, warmed them up also in direct fire, inserting them all inside Santos's shirt afterward. It was a long night for Cabarles who would stay by the sick man, constantly checking his condition. Not shivering and seemed calmly asleep, he decided to take a nap also.

A foggy morning, Santos was awakened to a ton of leaves that enveloped his body from head to foot, noticeably taken one at a time and patiently warmed in the fire before it got around him. He was feeling well but chose not to move at all. Through the thin fog, he could see an animal staring at him, the elusive deer. He was sure his eyes were not deceiving him like the first time, but what was standing alone was not an animal. Startled and confused, nothing came out of his mouth in an attempt to get Cabarles's attention. He blinked his eyes so many times. What he was seeing stayed on his sight, looking at him also like waiting for him to wake up, to get up. It was a clear figure of a human being, old and odd looking, out of this world. The old man disappeared from his sight as the fog got thicker, leaving him dumbfounded and immobile. Gathering self-awareness and perceptions, he managed to get up and pull himself a few feet from Cab who was awakened at once by the rustling of leaves on his naked body. The fire kept on giving heat from a big log in orange glow. However, he put on his shirt seeing that Santos didn't need it anymore while trying to comprehend what the man was saying while pointing at the fog.

In some ways, he understood, and they both waited what the vanishing white clouds would reveal. There was nothing as the morning sun brightened up the surroundings without signs of any being Santos was trying to describe. He swore again that what he had seen was real. He ended up demanding to leave the place as soon as they could, acknowledging that he may not be welcome in "heaven." He was made to take more pill that made him fall asleep again. Cab finally got it, Santos was not welcome in heaven.

"GIVE US THIS DAY OUR DAILY BREAD"

To find the way out was a top priority; there was no reason to get carried away in clearing the whole area that only led to a steep hill. He could see the edge, very treacherous and almost vertical, down to the dark bottom marked by a pile of rocks in some spot. He would never go back down there, a maddening place that added to the deteriorating health and sanity of his most beloved friend. Two hundred feet back was a rise so steep it was impossible to climb after a short distance over a lower creek that obscured the spring and only led to the top of the mountain. In thought and visual replication of the surroundings, there was no way out but the same way they got in. If that was what it took, they would do it. The only option left was to get Santos back in shape.

With a last glimpse around, something seemed to be moving on the place he had cleared the other day. Some animals were reaching for the fruit trees that were now exposed to the bright sun. The deer— the tale of the elusive animal was somehow true—were roaming freely and feeding confidently. He surely regretted he didn't carry his gun at the moment, but it was clearly proven that there was such kind of animal in the area. Santos was not crazy. The first instinct was getting his rifle. There a few more deer in the garden place, but what surprised him the most was about ten feet from Santos was a man sitting on a rock holding a cane out of a branch with both hands. He was just sitting there, staring at the man lying on the ground. Cabarles dropped what he had in his hand and rushed a few steps closer facing the old man. Befitting as to how it was described, he was old and bearded. He was sitting where they had laid down their weapons and satchels. They may be in heaven, but whoever that man was, he had an apparent interest in the grenades.

Santos had been awake a long time ago. He just didn't want to move, frozen, immediately regaining audacity when Cab showed himself. From behind, he slowly got up on his knees and whispered to verify what he was seeing was true to the similarly bewildered brother. Indeed a scary moment at the hands of clearly the resident of the place they assumed their own.

"Please, have mercy. We don't mean any intrusion," Cab finally said something worthy in the call of the situation.

The old man had actually taken one of the grenades and was playing it with his hand with curiosity. In the eyes and minds of the soldiers, he must have known what it was. Like a small pineapple but smooth and heavy, he tossed it lightly, calculating its weight.

"No, please. We don't mean any harm. We will leave this place right now," Cab said again.

And again for the second time, the long-bearded man put the thing in his mouth, leading Cab to just close his eyes, turn, and embrace Santos waiting to die. Minutes over, there was no explosion. The old man was still sitting comfortably, himself confused with the reaction of the soldiers for only trying to take a bite of the odd-looking thing he just found out must not be food. He was not given a chance anymore to play with it when Cab grabbed it from his hand and gave him a banana instead. Santos took away everything else. In an attempt to communicate, they failed all effort and dialect they knew, but only a hand and body motion was the response they got. Just the same sound of *oh* and *ah* every time, leading them to believe he could not speak.

The old man didn't show any reaction at the sound of the gunfire either, but he displayed gladness at the sight of a dead deer. He stayed in the company of the soldiers for a day and also exhibited excitement over a roasting animal in front of him.

With all indications, the old man was mute and deaf. Cabarles could use some basic sign language of his own. Asking if he had company in that place by indicating himself with Santos hugging him to demonstrate what he was trying to say, his response was of a deep emotional expression and sound of grief, pointing to the animal now brown and dripping of its own fat, indicating that there was his companion roasting.

There was a reason to be afraid. Six years ago, Santos was a young student among a daring group of hunters from Manila. Tayabas was known to host a heavy population of game animals. Mount Banahaw was forbidden by superstitions and unexplained mysteries since the Spanish era and beyond. So many that it was left untouched, avoided, and feared. However, the temptation of sure success of the hunt had inspired the group of unbelievers on a scheduled trip. Santos would remember that they killed prized bucks, but the cost was unforgettable. They lost a member of the group and who was not seen since then. The legend of the mountain had incurred in his mind, and in truth, the sight of Mount Banahaw even from afar had given him the creeps. A memory he wanted to be forgotten, but it was on his mind like it just happened a day ago. He disclosed seeing the old man then. Bald to the top halfway around his head, the remaining hair indicated that he lived without seeing a scissor his entire life. To see him up close, the legend of the old man of Mount Banahaw was coming into light. In the company of the bravest man he knew, he had no reason to be frightened despite hearsays that this man possessed powers to do harm to anyone by words alone when he spoke. Afraid of what would be the outcome of their stay on the mountain and apprehensive of his own physical capability to continue the journey to Manila, he left the decision to Cabarles, expressing his desire to leave the place as soon as possible. According to the story of the old man, he really didn't talk, but when he did, it could make boulders of rocks tumbling down and roars could be heard when he got mad from a distance. He didn't want to wait for that to happen.

In the mind of Cabarles, he was an old man that needed respect and gratitude for having them in his place. He was sure the old man had the same inborn affliction like his barber back in Bigaa or he had suffered the same fate like a POW in Davao who didn't recover from shell shock or torture. Nothing really to be afraid of. He didn't talk, all right; Cabarles could communicate with him. The old man was given the honor of having the first bite of the meat while he was trying to communicate, making him feel confident of their presence. The taste of deer would extend their so-called marvelous conversation that would add to the long list of Cabarles's skills through Santos's eyes. Somehow, Cabarles could understand something else other than Tagalog. He gradually overcame his fear; Cab could relay the answer to his queries. The day ended in the fruitful acquaintance with the old man. So many of what he tried to convey may not be truly understood; however, other than a direction to the other way out, nothing really would interest either one of the soldiers about the rest.

By the end of the day, Cab was toured around, including into a small cave behind the spring, around narrow stepping-stones, and through two large trunks of trees. That was the old man's abode, more prolific of exotic plants by the entrance. Inside were accumulation of many things of assorted kinds piled in many spot close to presumably where he slept. About ten steps ahead was a stone wall where the old man led him through a tapered hole and a small ground fit with an old hand-made chair. He thought he had seen the best sceneries ever from "heaven," but there he could see heaven and beyond exclusively. Other than a scratch on the place they cleared while looking for a way out the other day, everything else was spectacular at the time when the mountain partially shaded the site but so bright in the blue horizon of the southern region. Dissented on such view, the place truly got dark early. In the dark, he was told of a trail down stony steps to a three-pronged path, one leading to the northern slope of the mountain where they wanted to go. Detailed to specific landmarks, the trail would end overlooking a large body of water ahead. But they were warned that it may look so close but there were miles and miles of wilderness in between. The old man revealed that there was a way going south, the way they got in. Cabarles would like to know, but the old man was not physically fit to show the trail. As Cab understood, the man had never come down the mountain for many years.

Santos was so excited to learn that they could leave the place as soon as possible. Cab would postpone to another day.

A full day was spent eating and picking fruits, many of which would be carried up in the cave knowing the man was so old in misery and pain. Alone, he could not serve himself anymore, just waiting for 'any moment'. The legend of a formidable old man residing in Mount Banahaw would continue in time. There was no reason to carry too much food or water because they would be found along the way. Given the time to know more about the old man who became comfortable in the company of brave men who discovered his place in a hundred years, after so many years, he found kindhearted men though they carried weapons of war, not like the others who usually ran away in fear. The soldiers would leave at dawn the next day though they were told they could stay as long as they wanted. The decision was made by the insistence of Santos who was still experiencing unexplained hallucination. They left the old man who still believed that the Philippines was still governed by the Spaniards.

"OUR DAILY BREAD"

A large body of sky-blue water lay pristine from afar above Mount Banahaw. According to Santos, it was Laguna de Bay. Cab was excited to know that the far end of the lake was part of the Rizal province. Make it to the north end and make a left, and they should hit Manila through the lake. The other route was west by land that led directly to Manila. Nothing on the west was visible yet from where they stood; traveling by land on the west side should also mean they would let go of their weapons early and move out as civilians. Santos also said he knew of a few people in Cavite who could help them across Manila to Bulacan. Imus, Cavite, it was they were heading. Coming down from the mountain was the first obstacle.

Rule one was in effect strictly, come what may with the civilians. It was civilians they should seek help in Cavite. On daylight, they were to begin the first step with a new set of rules about the people they saw along the way. At daytime, it would be a lot faster especially when being pursued by the enemy who would not give any warning to shoot them on sight. Japanese encounter during the day, mosquitoes at night. As in the beginning, mosquitoes were favored in any situation as defined by simple rationalization—there was better chance at surviving malaria but not a bullet wound that could be fatal in an instant. Taking all precautions deciding which way to take, they should move northeast. The first civilian they met was in a hot springs of Liliw, Laguna. Also visited at times by Japanese patrols and based on information they gathered, guerilla activities in the area were concentrated higher up in the volcano complex deeper in the mountain range of Lucban, where they were many hours ago. At least they knew what place and date of the month it was—December 14, 1943.

Seven days later, they were awakened at Nagcarlan Cemetery. Inside a circular brick wall, they realized it was also frequented by the living as well. Two living souls in the company of the dead, afraid of revealing themselves from hiding because too many people mourning, so many buried that day. It was not until midnight of the next day that they were able to leave, guided by a local saying they could not go in Imuz because the Japanese was maintaining a garrison in that town. It was also gathered that the Japanese never exhausted in reminding people that Philippines is under the domain Japanese Imperial Army in the most terrible way. The intelligence they gathered was that from Sta. Cruz, Lauguna through a long stretch of road to the eastern seaboard was heavily patrolled by the enemy looking for actions. They got a bit of that action in Lucban, and they were sure as hell they didn't like it anymore. They kept going east by foot, bypassing another mountain, Mount Makiling, in the south. For at least fifteen days of walking from Mount Banahaw, one could feel weaknesses.

Dragging their feet away from the scenic view of another solitary mountain, the symptom of dreadful disease made intense by severe exhaustion was not easy to disregard anymore. Cab had run out of those pills that could make Santos sleep like a baby. The feeling of weakness accompanied by denial of such to keep going, until it was felt severely was the price he had to pay. Deprived of rest and sleep in constantly varying weather conditions added by days of starvation was to blame. As his health compromised objectives, the situation was the main concern. They conceded that they had to find help. Several miles' stretch that defied human feat nonstop from Nagcarlan had brought Cabarles to the limit. Attributed to illness similar to the common affliction at the POW camp in Mindanao, Cabarles succumbed to malaria. Not clear if Santos had survived the same capitulation in Tayabas (Quezon), but the emergence of the situation had brought them to rely on faith where they could find help immediately. Deciding that their fate was based on tribulation, Captain Santos's best option was only to seek help at the nearest town. In the middle of nowhere mixed with disorientation, tenseness, and a sick man, he would do all it took to make sure Cabarles lived. Otherwise, they both die.

CHAPTER 21

"FORGIVE OUR TRESPASSES"

There was a place not too far where ruthlessness, deceit, and betrayals became the way of life at the time I was passing by. Church bells were ringing. Into faith I seek refuge, holy men, saintly women. In defeat and illusions, I was taken by caring hands. Faith there was, it was forsaken in grand pretense.

BELLS ARE RINGING

A quiet town in Cavite, so quiet they could walk in the middle of the road with less to worry heading to the dim light that in total darkness from afar, the first thought was someone must be awake in that house to keep that lamp lit at night. Past midnight, Santos thanked God for the coincidence the first house he had seen for quite a long time was obviously occupied.

"Cab, look. There must be some people who could help us there," he uttered to the man barely able to walk. Actually, Cabarles could not walk on his own anymore. The response was an audible hum—good enough.

To carry a man bigger than him was not easy, but there was a rush of hope to see that it really was a house, a big house. But a beam of light from another direction had alerted even the sick one to take cover by instinct, dragging his comrade to the bushes, knowing there was no one else confident enough to travel at night. Two familiar vehicles turning off their headlights as they stopped completely by the so-called house revealed its occupants. A group of soldiers disembarked, and it could only be the Japanese. Clearly, they were staying for the night or so too. They had to keep moving to somewhere else.

They could not go back up that hill again, as they already had trouble coming down. It was a typical road on the country: if one side was a hill, the other was a creek. There was a distinct path heavily used down a grassy plain leading to a tended farmland. Half a kilometer more, they had to hide as dawn was breaking. Roosters had been crowing, and the only place they could remain hidden at daylight were the thick bushes lined uniformly along a big leafy tree upward the trail. The volume of audible sounds in a normal morning also indicated they still thrived in the general area in abundance. It also indicated that nearby was a populated area. "I think we can finally have chicken this time. How do you want it cooked?" Santos asked a barely conscious buddy shivering and unresponding. They could say one that just made the loudest was so close above the tree that also extended its limbs over to their position.

With wild fruits and water that filled their stomachs in the past few days, the possibility of a chicken meal was very encouraging most especially to a dying man. Shivering indicated that he was alive and fighting whoever was knocking his door again, no angels to hold his hands and give him comfort and encouragement. What he saw when he closed his eyes was a dark hole that spun around, waiting for him to jump in. He would keep his eyes open all the time, watching webs and droplets of water as they shone on the reflection of the morning sun until they disappeared through intervals of leaves and twigs.

Santos came back with a large cup of hot brew and hard-boiled eggs. He said the chicken was on the pot boiling to tender. It may not be the rooster, but he was damn sure they would have chicken very shortly. He was cheered; it was the town plaza of Dasmarinas, Cavite. A blessing, there was in fact a *carenderia* (small restaurant) that served cooked food nearby, best it offered on a Sunday. It was just too early that nothing was ready yet. In a bid to find medicine most importantly, Santos was also told there was a pharmacy not far away in the town where he could buy them. It was the best time to go now while the town was still asleep. Everybody was still asleep other than a man who gave him the shirt he was wearing, who would also accompany the soldier in making sure he found the right place immediately, the only place in town that perhaps had a stash of such pill, and it was only dispensed to select people. Santos wasn't one of them. To a desperate man, to get what he wanted was certain, but it would require desperate measures at desperate times. He needed to literally point a gun at another man to get what he needed. It took a while before he left that house. The church bell rang to their ears, to the ears of another man that suddenly awakened from oblivion at daylight.

On the way back from the said house, Santos stopped by the church that just opened its large door to the assembly of people; it was not on the plan, but the calling of the faithful to enter was so hard to pass, especially in full view of Japanese soldiers disembarking from two military trucks. Two civilians in armbands stood out among them. Nothing special, he had seen a lot of them, heard so much about them, and shot them too. It was just that they parked right on his way back to Cabarles, very close to where he had left him shivering. Going inside the church for a while was the only choice he had left.

Santos blended in with the churchgoers, and for the sake of his understanding to Catholicism, he saw how it was done rightfully. People so solemnly praying, with the exception of a few children playing, dressed neatly, and men likewise, shaved and hair combed flat to the skull with pomade that he could not remember when was the last time he did. Suddenly, he realized he didn't fit in. His appearance must be getting attention as he felt people staring at him, whispering to each other while waiting for the Mass to begin. He noticed few men not as neat also uttering words to others sitting on the sides and behind. Surely they knew each other. Nothing to worry about, but on his nerves and thoughts – he had already attracted enough attention.

Too much time he had wasted, it had been hours that he was away from Cabarles that coming back to him could not be justified by the danger he was in for both of them. He could only pray for Cab that he was still shivering; otherwise, he could keep praying for his soul. By the door were Japanese soldiers. Only a few he could see, but there must be more. There must be a back door, but he didn't know where the back door led to. For all he could think, if the entrance showed some Japanese, there must be more around. Then the touch of hand on his shoulder followed by a mellow voice distracted his thoughts.

"The confessionary is available, son," a man in a white gown calmly said.

It was a priest, and not the first time he felt natural kindness from a man, a man of God. He felt the rush of faith that the priest could offer more than what he said. What was a "confessionary" anyway? He gladly went into a little door as he was guided, and to his disappointment, it was so small leading to nowhere aside from an opening he wouldn't fit. He sat in resignation, better than on the atrium where everybody could see him. In his thoughts and appearance, he truly didn't fit anywhich way it was, more so inside a church. So many sins he incurred to himself.

"You may begin, my son," the voice from the other side of the thin wooden wall said.

He remained quiet. He thought seriously for a while, sweating. He lost wit to an uncomfortable feeling that debated reality and holiness of that small place. The call of deliberation needed rationalization of the situation. To confess all his sins must not be a future deterrent to his status; the priest didn't know him, and he would be gone as soon as he could get out of the church. Otherwise, he must be dead anyway. There was a problem however—he didn't know how to begin, where to begin, which sin it was to tell first. What else could he do in the most frightening hours?

In the ravine, Cabarles was awakened by the church bells ringing. The sun was noticeably higher than when he closed his eyes since Santos left him. Immediately, he felt the worries of not seeing the man on his side yet. He gathered his strength to crawl upward. Not too many to see as he peeked through leaves that concealed his presence. A few people, a horse pulling a cart with a neatly clothed woman in white that disembarked gracefully. From a hundred foot away, he could see military trucks to obstruct his sight of the church. His weakened body could not permit more to move even a little; coldness resumed to overpower his senses, worse than earlier. He could do nothing but cover himself of another soiled shirt Santos had left to keep him warm. The khaki just added up to the enormous concerns that he tried to disregard with his own physical condition in futile effort. Where was he? Very improbable not to see him on his side at the most needed time. No chicken meal yet as promised.

No angels either. The best effort to concentrate in imagining good things about Santos at the moment only led to strange effect. Strange and scary nightmares increased by being forsaken and abandoned, to die alone in a ravine with unwanted plants and vegetation that grow wild and green, also dying. Much more in a place where garbage was thrown and accumulated overtime. *I'm so sorry, Inez, my everlasting love. I'm so sorry, my friends. I can only wish to see you all again . . .*

And he closed his eyes, submitting to all unknown creatures so persistent and impatient; he had seen them already, and to meet them again at the same moment when he was totally helpless, even his own body was not responding at all to any effort of resistance. He let them touch him, carry him to a darker place that gleamed with an occasional glow just enough to see the weirdest faces of unusual happiness to see him again. In a place where he could be thrown upward so high to see flames everywhere, but it was so cold in the vastness of indescribable sight while he fell down spinning into the same hands, many hands he had seen before, extended upward and celebrating.

"Let us pray for him together," the priest told the man in the confessionary. As a man of God and hearing all kinds of confession, he couldn't believe what he had heard so far. Sins of all sinners in one man, and he wasn't done yet. He who would be so concerned about the soul of another, so troubled he would weep and yielding to the punishment of his sins; not asking for forgiveness but begging to extend help to a man dying somewhere. And they prayed together.

THE WARM AND SOOTHING WATER

Under an old mango tree by the end of a garbage pile spread by chickens and stray dogs, two people were conversing. Nothing unusual, but in the company of Japanese soldiers, something was going to happen and they would be part of it. Talking casually, naturally like nothing out of the ordinary by two people on a beautiful day who have the same interest. Jesting and laughing with the enemy but clearly, they were Filipinos speaking in Tagalog.

They were laughing, all right, very distinct voices he never heard before as they walked closer. The church bell rang again, this time louder and longer. *It scared all other creatures to suddenly disappear.* Voices become louder, a lot closer.

Warm fluid rushing down from above was felt immediately by the man in delusion, cold fire extinguished by a warm feeling of being soaked with presumably holy water as it was pouring down like the spring of Mount Banahaw. Very soothing as he felt the water drip on his face that traveled around his neck through his bearded face. And it stopped a little while, then it poured again, this time more forceful flow that soaked his body.

A wedding was transpiring inside the church. Such a celebration was uncommon at wartime unless the pair was from an influential family. Though the ceremony didn't take long, a wedding in a church was all that mattered to the newlyweds. Traditional celebrations were observed through the big door of the holy place in jubilation of well-wishers and bystanders and also onto the eyes of Japanese soldiers who were picking up people randomly among the crowd with the help from collaborators. More people were holed up and taken from inside the church. The bride and the groom had left, leaving people who just realized the quick transformation of events. The soldiers were not there to attend a wedding. They were assembling men in a lineup.

The water may be warm and soothing, but it didn't taste good nor smell. However, it made Cabarles return to his senses. Hearing people talking just above his head, they were real. Immobile and holding breath, the only movement he could do was open his eyes. He saw people, one still draining of what more to the last of drop he could give off. A few drops left to end with a sudden motion of the body that made an unusually large thing to dangle a bit where it was hanging down with its pair. The other man holding an empty *bayong,* pressing to its roundness as he fit it to his head with holes cut to match his eyes and mouth. A little bit tight, he took it off and did it again. A Japanese was speaking impatiently, giving orders, making the other one turn around in a rush and together they all walked away.

Cab was left undetected after all, left wiping urine off his face. It may not came from heaven or similar to a pureness of a spring that could relieve his thirst, but sure it gave him relief stimulated by anger and disgust for a little while. Seeing Japanese and those people would make him back to worrying, afraid. There was no sign of Santos. He didn't know how long he was gone; he should come back. Alleviated from delirium, he closed his eyes with the smell of a horse shack. The agony continued. He let his thoughts run, thinking of horses, lying over damp hay where he would daydream many times after making sure the animals were fed properly.

Civilians were lined up on a grassy patio on the north side of the church. A pair of bayong men did what they were expected to do. Simply point to some people among faces they should have seen before. The chosen ones were separated from other; they were not given any moment to say anything when the soldiers also lined up in rapid motion and fired without warning. All six people fell to the ground lifelessly.

It was ten o'clock in the morning when a volley of gunfire alerted Cabarles; intense palpitations of his heart added to the shaking of his body. He wanted to reach for his rifle but chillingly reverted. It was only a stick he could reach. Wet clothes wasn't helping. Back to the same feeling, there was no strength to move his body, and the shivering would be transferred to the bushes and be noticeable to prying eyes. Luckily for him, it was expunged by the gentle gust of the wind and trees. He would hear voices again, the same people who peed on him. He may look at them again if he could, but it was just that he couldn't move at all. He recognized the voices, the same people that were there hours ago, faceless men who were talking like nothing had taken place in continuation of what was interrupted earlier. The last of his awareness was spent in picturing them on his mind. Added to the insult of their dreadful deeds, one threw away his *bayong* that landed in full view. The thing was so light that it didn't fall to the ground, prevented by bare twigs repeatedly succumb to the heat of burning unwanted refuse. Though empty and old, it created a scary sight, it was staring at him. For many hours, they would stare at each other, neither able to move except that one could blink his eyes. With stick in hand, he tried to reach the thing, but it persisted.

His eyes were becoming tired, yet the fight must go on. He must not give up. He had a weapon to defend his ground. For long hours, they would clash with each other.

Weapon in my hand, I'm sure I hurt the enemy, but he keeps getting up. Every time I attack, it can easily pose back up with the same dark and hollow eyes. The enemy is powerful. He is already decapitated, just the face I see, but I shall not be defeated. I attacked again only to be laughed at. The laughing I won't forget, the enemy has a weakness. I laugh back, my nemesis has balls, uneven, and it should not be that way. I know there's another one like him, terrifying as this one. In triumph and defeat, I shall not forget his face, at least one of them.

Leaves and twigs submitted to the gentle force of wind. Whoever lived close by threw away more refuse, and the smoke was augmented. Dry leaves and papers burned.

The battle continues. I am weary, my weapon is not effective against an evil nemesis. I can only keep him where he is but he keeps on moving. Only a matter of time I shall be defeated, no more strength to keep him away.

A stronger gust of wind displaced the *bayong* from where it was; it was blown closer to the feverish man. Stable to where it was held up, smoke entered its wide opening and exited through the holes for which it was made.

My weapon breaks in a forceful attempt to impale the enemy. It made the thing furious, dark smoke coming from his eyes and mouth. I am tired and helpless, body aching, very thirsty. The surroundings is getting hotter. Flaming background behind the thing. The enemy is raging, flame is coming out from his eyes and mouth. I closed my eyes in surrender. It is too hot, very hot.

The immediate vicinity was on fire. Darkness fell lazily, but it was lit by the blaze. Someone was calling his name.

Two men, almost losing hope that they could not find the unresponsive soldier, probably dead already, tried to push at every inch of the bushes. Finally, one found the man they were looking for, rushing and stepping over a discarded thing that fell to the ground and burned, which ended a horrifying battle. Cabarles was still breathing. A man came at the time of defeat. He pulled a man out from the blaze. A soldier stricken with malaria just few inches away from being burned had lost consciousness. He may be victorious in the end, but he was drained of all his strength, there was nothing left.

As promised, chicken soup was offered to his palate. Cold as a cadaver but eyes wide open, the soup was taken with a smile of gratitude as it spilled out of his mouth. The man who pulled him out of the bush tried again. Cab was not responding.

"Cab, get up. We have to get out of here," the voice said repeatedly with a tap on his face.

Cab must have been back one step from hell again. Only one person would call him Cab; only one had the bravery to help him defeat the persistent enemy. His savior and hero, Capt. Rodrigo Santos, is back at the most needed time. He never let him down. He blinked his eyes in the dwindling light of day. He could not even get his arms up to help himself in an effort to embrace the man he was longing for, so happy to see him again. He had so much of a difficulty to swallow the sudden wetness in his tongue; he coughed slightly—a sign of life that he will live for the man whose lap he was leaning on. And in resignation of what he had been through, to the comfort of a trusted ally, he closed his eyes. He could to take a rest; he was tired.

When he rose, Santos was ready to continue with their long journey. They must eat first. So much food was prepared and cooked, chicken mostly as promised. So much that there were more live ones wandering around waiting to be cooked if they wanted more. No more words was said; they enjoyed the food on the table. In such a feast and abundance, there was no reason to hurry but take advantage of it. However, nothing could change their mind to reach the journey's end. Vigor replenished and route established with confidence to reach the destination, each one waited for a cue to get started after a long while. "Let's go," they said exactly at the same time.

Hands over each one's shoulder to begin the first step, they had such confidence with no worry whatsoever that they will encounter the enemy along the way. No weapons only their satchels, they kept on walking on a path so beautiful made aglow by dawn, the birds flying, singing in the wonder of a place similar to the plateau of Mount Banahaw except that the place was a continuous marvel of nature all around. Abundant fruit trees that obscured another one next to it and more, Cab could not identify what was behind them.

Dictated by intuition, he reached for his gun, and it wasn't where it was supposed to be.

"Wait a second." Cabarles ran back to where they began to grab their weapons. "Just in case, it's still a long way to go," he said to the man waiting.

"I don't need it. I never fired it anyway since I had it. You can keep it," Santos said when he was handed the pistol.

"How about this one?" he asked again.

"Yeah, maybe." He took the pistol and put it together with the one he had.

He responded with a smile. "Come with me, I'll show you a place," Santos said.

And they continued walking, no constraints, no worries of enemies and snipers hiding in one of those trees. Into the wide plains as the trees became one, there was only one tree ahead. It was a vast clearing, with only signs of peace around. A cross field that became clear to one's vision even in the dark. On a chosen spot, one sat on the ground. The other followed, having no choice but to do the same and feel the peace as he was told. Indeed, it was so peaceful and quiet.

"I have to ask your forgiveness, my friend, my brother," Santos started, sad.

"For what?"

"I failed the first time when I could be worthwhile to you. I didn't know what to do."

"Why did you say that? We are alive, aren't we?"

Silence. The birds stopped chirping, insects paused from buzzing. "That's another thing. I cannot continue anymore to our destination, I'm sorry."

"Why not?"

"I found peace in this place . . . I cannot come with you the rest of the way. You don't need me. You will be safe without me. It has been arranged depending on your discretion. You and Inez would be reunited very soon, or very long. Which way you choose, there will be people who will help you along the way no matter what route you take. You will be with her in the end. I regret my decision, but it is as far as I can go. Please forgive me."

"You are forgiven. Are you sure you want to stay? You know I want you to be my neighbor too like how we talk about it," Cabarles responded.

"Thank you, I know you do. But I only became a baggage for you to carry for so long, you saved my life so many times. I thank you very much. I thank you for leading me to this place where I found peace with the faith you had led me to. I feel I belong to this place. You are not—Inez is waiting for you."

"AS WE FORGIVE THOSE WHO TRESPASSED AGAINST US"

The church help woke up early. Two days passed, two unclaimed bodies. Time for them to be buried. The priest, who would make sure they were given proper rites, like the first one, was also coming. It won't take too long as holes had been dug out already. As soon as it was over, he would attend to another he was keeping down the basement. The man was alive and hopeful to recuperate.

The burial was over earlier than he thought it might be—no mourners. There was time to spare to visit a fresh grave along with another and say a little prayer.

A man, all flesh and bones, lying on his stomach, one leg and arm over the mound of elongated fresh dirt, caught his attention. Who might he be? Beyond belief, it could happen. It was the same man—the priest was sure. How he got there on his own could not be explained. Even he had waked up last night and left the church, he would not know who was buried on that spot. He was audibly in a delirious state; the soldier was calling "sir" unconsciously. Sir who? He knew for sure who that person was; he met the "sir" himself before his demise. These were many unanswered thoughts he chose to keep in his mind, as things had happened inexplicably. He continued praying for the soul of the ones who died and for the betterment of this one who didn't want to die. Obviously, he not only needed medical attention. He also needed a constant eye to keep him in one place. He was still breathing but barely. He made a swift decision to bring him back to the church. For another two days, Cabarles was responsive but dejected. Great sorrow found solace in prayers with people he had just seen. No Captain Rodrigo Santos by his side.

His swift recovery was taken astonishingly by people who were taking care of him. By faith, it was Cabarles who submitted himself. The priest would say he was a missionary who spent life in remote areas of the province and had caught malaria in the performance of his devotion. The priest and his help who was also the gravedigger would know already who was the man by deed. He carried guns and ordnance that could blow the church to ruins, but it was a secret they had to keep seriously. The priest had foreseen that he could not keep the soldier without detection by the people, and therefore he was let known as a man that also spread the Word of God.

Given medical attention in the privilege of wealthy people, the physician who attended him were given a large amount of money from the belongings of a dead soldier. Also in addition to the good care of the church keep, prayers and food donated by the townspeople led to the rapid recovery of "Father" Dominador Cabarles. Cabarles may not remember what happened and how he became one, but when he woke, he was dressed as a priest. Before another Sunday came, he could walk. He was devastated when told that a soldier in the description of Santos was executed, picked from the lineup in a chain of events that was petrifying and inescapable. In grief, he could be seen not on the bed but in a corner of his room silently weeping and mourning. Though he would recognize the farewell of the friend in his dream that seemed real, he swore he would take revenge against those men who ended the life Capt. Rodrigo Santos.

With constant advice to be calm and forgiving, the real priest highlighted the manner on how Santos had found peace and faith in God before he died. Recollections of the last hours of the captain was relayed step by step, from the moment he stepped inside the church and how he was held up. He didn't choose to fight because so many innocent could die in the crossfire. The soldier's satchel was turned over to Cab with two hand grenades and a pistol left in the confessional seat. As his last word, he disclosed the location of another soldier in desperate need of help. Santos was begging for help from the priest, but not for himself. In his foreseen downfall with no alternative but to remain calm, he surrendered himself instead to faith, not to the enemy, to prevent a battle that could end costing the lives of many civilians. Nothing else could compare to such sacrifice, the priest added.

Pulling through from another death call, Cabarles recuperated to full strength with only one thing going in his mind. Find the *bayong* tandem of evil men and kill them. They may have been forgiven for making him as a urinal but learning that they were the principal participants in the murder of Capt. Rodrigo Santos was not pardonable. In a vindictive change of heart to whom he previously said - in time of war, everyone had the right to side where they feel they should survive, his stance toward collaborators had changed. He would kill them all to serve the opinion of Santos; anyone could be a collaborator, just don't do harm or cause any harm to others. Those people had done the unforgivable. In the principles of the man who perished, to his grave he swore he would seek retribution. Vengeance for the death of the man who had taught him how to read and write, to count and the "one minus one," and many more.

However, he settled on clenching his fists and grinding teeth whenever he saw one. It was suicidal to attack a collaborator in broad daylight. The following days, he could be seen talking with Mulong who was also very informative. Being tired of burying victims of Japanese atrocities, he offered his allegiance and services to Cabarles and showed interest in guns. Also to Cabarles's surprise, the gravedigger also shared a similar hatred toward the collaborators. The man about the size of Hombre Donono and as agile and hardworking became his willing cohort who addressed him as Father Cabarles, sometimes sir. His role in the recovery of Cabarles from the affliction of malaria was sincerely acknowledged, the same to Father Faustino, the parish priest. The most credit, however, was given to the physician who attended to him that he had yet to meet. Angels in his dreams, he was confused.

Romulo Soler or Mulong had also displayed trustworthiness. He was one of the two to know that the new priest who would roam around town carrying a Bible and a rosary was actually an Allied soldier out for vengeance. Soler was also appreciated for being a skillful barber. Cab was looking good like a real priest with hair trimmed and beard clean shaven.

HAIL MARY

Many days gone, many times he had been in the cemetery to renew and express his promise. Romulo continued what it seemed he did best—bury dead people. Cabarles showed no intention to renege what he swore over and over at the grave of Santos. He would not leave the town until his revenge was fulfilled. It wasn't easy, later he would admit, as all efforts to describe either one of the men he was looking for with Romulo was futile. He didn't know the *bayong* men; in fact, he wanted to identify them too. Actually, one fit the description of a prominent figure in town, but it was impossible that he could be the one. Aside from not being seen in town often, he was the kind doctor who visited and treated him when delirious and unconscious. Romulo would thought of the man absolutely as not even close to a traitor; the other one would require a more intricate way to identify. He didn't see his face. However, some collaborators would be found dead, which began when the new priest arrived in town. One suffered the most retribution when his body was found, pants down with his armband shoved down his throat. Cabarles began praying the Hail Mary, sometimes many Hail Marys.

Come third Sunday, "Father" Dominador was given the task of reading a phrase from the Bible. He knew how to read from lessons at the school of the damned in Dapecol but given a heads-up. When the moment came, he could read it very well. He didn't need to actually look at the Book to recite what it said, even when suddenly his heart pulsated faster and louder, when his attention was taken by a couple coming late for the mass, walking through the aisle until they got seated on the first row. Right in front of him.

The very elegant young woman was dressed in hand-embroidered clothing matched with fine satin over the head down to the shoulders. She was so graceful and aristocratic looking while she opened her folding fan and moved it in a back-and-forth motion to her face and occasionally to the spouse on her right. She appeared to be a caring, loving, and idyllic wife in the eyes of everyone. Their age difference quite noticeable, they must have belonged to the wealthy clan in the province or some of those who were not affected by the war. It seemed that they were proud and were enjoying themselves when everyone paused on the solemnity of the moment to glimpse at them.

Cabarles was conspicuously held too in distress, not by the woman but by the man. Rapidly, his calmness was precipitated by a rush of blood, and his bony face became more pronounced as his jaws were clenched in fury. He would never forget that man.

The reading had ended, but he was still standing, hands on the open Book without realizing that he had torn its pages when he clasped his hand over it. Father Faustino walked by in repose, whispering to Cab to be seated. He had to do it twice before he was noted, aware that the man's blood was boiling.

Instead of going back to his seat, he went directly inside a room down to another where he stayed. When he came back, his waist was bulging with pistols. He didn't know how many rounds there were still in the .45, but at least the other had one. He was damn sure one bullet would be enough.

As the Mass progressed, the praying subsided his anger, but it didn't change his mind, just taking some consideration. Who would shoot a man who appeared so earnest in faith kneeling down on the front row and in the presence of many people?

It may be his only chance; he was sweating profusely. His thought was broken as the priest offered the Bread customarily, which he accepted. "Body of Christ," he heard. He closed his eyes and opened his mouth, asking for forgiveness for what he was about to do. His plan was to walk as close as possible and shoot the man point-blank.

The Mass had ended, and he was still kneeling down. People had left the church except the chosen few with the special privilege to ask for more blessings from the priest, also those who believed that an extra time and more prayers could make them go straight to heaven when the time came. Some only wished to get acquainted with the new priest, mostly women, but deprived of such because he himself appeared to be occupied with the sincerity to his faith, praying, staring at the cross and all the saints in front of him who were staring back at him. In reality, he felt as though his knees were glued on, no strength to get up, no courage to murder a man in the house of God.

There was a gentle tap on his shoulder. "I'm sorry to bother your devoutness, but someone wanted to see you," the parish priest uttered.

"Sure, *Padre*," Cabarles replied, not knowing how long he had been on his knees.

It could not have come at a better time. He prayed for strength, for that moment to halt and let God's will to take over, clear the evil from his mind. He submitted himself to where he was led to. Guided by the priest, they walked a few steps right in front of the devil.

"I want you to meet Dr. Bernardo Moran, the man who brought you back to life," Padre Faustino said.

The woman stole the moment before he could respond. "You really are good looking up close, Father Dominador," she commented. "I'm happy our town is blessed with another priest at this time the people is losing faith in God." She kept on talking.

Not understanding any more words, the mind of the fake priest was playing on which pistol he should pull out—the revolver on the left that had one bullet or the .45 on the right, which he wasn't sure would fire. But upon learning that he was the doctor who attended to him, he hesitated. How could he kill the man who saved his life?

"I'm glad you had fully recuperated. Not too many pulls through malaria," the doctor finally found the chance to talk. "You really are a blessed man."

"I believe he really is. I wish you can bless us, Father," the woman requested.

What more blessings could this couple wish for? Evidently, they were living in certainty while everyone else was in poverty and literally scared.

"He will, but I suggest you two go through the sacrament of confession first," the real priest suggested to the husband and wife.

"That's a very good idea. The doctor can stay with me. I would like to take his confession myself if you would allow me, *Padre*," Cabarles expressed his intention to be alone with the husband. He was responded with silence. Father Faustino nodded slightly; he would not interfere. He had the same sacred 'thing' to do with the wife also.

There was an indecision to let the man alone with a priest who was noticeably concealing handguns. Padre Faustino was an intelligent man, a serious man of faith in dire need of help from another with a similar devotion. He would not mind letting Cabarles perform a sacred task, but how he would do it was what he worry about the most. There was a serious attempt to prevent such a rite, but there was an opportunity that was so very hard to pass; there may be no more other chances that could be as forgiving as the progress at the moment. He instigated the soldier to pose as a priest; however, "Father" Dominador carried information that he alone could prove by himself. Let it be by his judgment to find a resolve to what his integrity dictated. He was allowing him to do just that and find a closure about the same thought that also bothered him.

"God bless you, both of you," the priest said. He led the man's wife somewhere else.

The young wife had been in confession so many times in the past with Father Faustino; the husband was not at any time seen inside the church for a very long time. The call for confession was perhaps only to avert suspicion that the "new priest" was a fraud through the eyes of the faithful as they waited their turn to get acquainted with him.

"Yeah, God bless us all," Cab responded seriously for what seemed he was natural at rendering a duty he had no right to perform.

The wife was excited, submitting herself to the priest at the confessional or wherever she was led to. She was obviously more comfortable with Fathe Faustino to whom she got used to telling her sins while committing anew. The presence of the husband in town since the Japanese incursion of churchgoers had prevented her from seeing the priest, or the priest to see her.

"I will take his confession right here, *Padre*, in front of the altar," Cab declared with seriousness in his mellow voice, referring to the doctor who was sweating profusely from obviously many sins he had incurred to himself.

Father Faustino showed opposition, but there was nothing else he could do. He could only attend to one, and the wife was restless and seemed not able to wait anymore to do her own confession. God, she's so beautiful.

So it began.

"Bless me, Father, for I have sinned. The worst kind none would believe I have done such things," the doctor began and lingered.

"Go on."

"I know that the child my wife bears is . . . not mine," the man stated in sorrow, very disappointed. "It offended my manhood so deeply I had been longing to find and kill the man who did that to me, whatever it takes."

A very young, pretty, and alluring wife he had. To walk in the eyes of many knowing she was not all his was really not a good feeling. The "priest" would think about that, but it was not enough justification to what he had done to Captain Santos and the others. He was still a dreadful collaborator of the Japanese army. Cabarles had already taken one steel out, occasionally making a quick look where the spouse and the priest went in. Not coming out yet. He would have knowledge why—that the woman was as sinful as the husband. A long list to confess and repent. She also knew she might be committing another one. It will take long.

"Keep going." His left hand was on the revolver; he was sure he wouldn't miss point-blank.

"I corroborate with the enemy to suit my anger, but the one man I was looking for may still be alive and many have died already because of me. I know you're not a real priest, but I also believed you're a blessed man of so many miracles to be sitting with me at this moment and still alive. I treated you, I don't know how you had recovered from that affliction. It was not all because of me but of grand intervention. I had seen the shrapnel scars and all around your body and it would've been beyond any human can recoup." He paused to look at the soldier directly in the eye, repenting and looking for consolation.

Silence, both made a glimpse at the altar.

"I am a soldier. You're right, I'm not a priest. I know you're a traitor. I had seen you fitting that *bayong* over your head with another man. I had seen him too and I will kill him too. I have nothing against collaborators. Only to those who betrayed the one person I respect and honor the most. The one you betrayed was a great soldier, a hero. He had nothing to do with your own resentment. All he wanted was to find food and medicine for an ill-stricken comrade, instead he died uselessly because of you. You have to pay for it seriously."

"I'm asking for forgiveness." The man started crying. He didn't need to tell his sin; it was already known.

"This gun was given to me by a true kindhearted doctor who saved my life with his own blood caused by many of those scars you had seen on my body. There is only one bullet—only one of us must live," Cabarles stated. "I will let you choose who. Take this gun, I will turn my back from you and make your decision, but I assure you it cannot be me. Wherever your soul is destined to be, on your way you'll meet a man, his name is Captain Rodrigo Santos. He may have forgiven you while I haven't yet." He distanced himself, making it known he had another gun, moving away leaving his burden to the man already tormented with his own.

The man was truly repentant for what it seemed, tearful as Cabarles watched silently. He stood up to walk in the aisle closer to the altar where he had just received communion an hour ago. Cabarles knelt down; he prayed again that he was about to murder a man if it was what he had to do.

A few moments later, a loud pop reverberated inside the church. A few minutes after, Father Faustino showed himself out, sweating, gasping for breath. He looked around to see an undeterred man kneeling; then he rushed to attend to another lying down on the floor, blood gushing out of his head, a revolver still on his hand. It was done.

Then the beautiful wife come over. The horrifying view of the lifeless spouse caused her to burst into tears and find comfort in the arms of the priest who attended to her with an embrace of thoughtfulness and noticing right away that her dress was still halfway unbuttoned. The priest must know that it needed a second person to undo, much more in closing it back. Father Faustino had come to her rescue, a shoulder to cry on over the horrific end of the husband. It may be out of grief or for goodness left in her and the priest. Cabarles had reason to believe that the tears and sorrow were not of a grieving widow. The fake priest watched quietly, his knees shuddering, thankful that he didn't need to make sure the man was dead. One bullet was enough; it was one that he had carried all the way from Davao, in the chamber of a gun he had given for himself when the time came. There was plenty more bullets to spend, none for him until he found the second man.

The wife was extremely horrified; she was led out of the scene immediately. She was turned over to a few devotees coming for a chance of blessing from the "new priest." They understood it wouldn't happen anymore on this day. They witnessed how the doctor walked in the center aisle and shot himself.

"I usually tell you to pray after confession," Father Faustino would say. "What did you made him do?"

"He had committed a sin without absolution."

"SAVE US FROM EVIL"

Well respected, wealthy, and a doctor with a young and beautiful spouse, why he shot himself was incomprehensible for the witnesses. The news of his death had spread in all corners of the town in no time—and into the ears of the enemy who also lost an important asset. The next day, Japanese soldiers and turncoats became more visible around as the sun rose. One more was added to be buried when a local commented to notorious collaborators, peacekeepers, or constables who said they were. It was his biggest mistake to suggest that they (collaborators) must kill themselves too. The Japanese were mad, very furious.

The gunshot alerted Cabarles who had been hanging out in the cemetery, talking to the mound of dirt. Romulo came frightened with news that the enemy were shooting people randomly. He was accompanied by two unknown men who immediately introduced themselves as part of a resistance group, which was substantiated by the church help. Cabarles undoubtedly trusted the men.

Mulong was looking for him to get him aware and advise him not to come back to the church anymore. Too many enemies. With two self-proclaimed guerillas presumably being chased, he had no choice but also to run with them.

Making contact with brothers in arm couldn't have come at a better time. For exactly four weeks that passed since he was rescued, he had relied on the kindness of the priest and his help. Aside from saving his life and giving a decent burial to Santos, his gratitude extended to the many assistance that they did for him especially on the last ten days. Two more men familiar with the jungles of Cavite and Laguna would be a great help, but not just yet. One other reason he stayed in the church was having no idea which way to go by himself.

The town was under siege by enemies who would have no opposition other than the vocal cord of a few braves left and the suicidal. The Japanese would not hesitate to end their misery. Many events of Japanese raids that incidentally occurred on Sundays was discussed while running. For some reason, the Japanese had developed a habit of coming to town when people from the barrios were present, looking for a little hope guided by faith above in the sanctuary of the church. But that day was different; there was another reason that made the Japanese mad. Later they would know that the enemy would be staying in town for good.

Somewhere in the woods that surrounded the cemetery, Cab would not go farther away. He had no plan to leave town just yet. He would find one more and kill the bastard even if he should come back and hide in his mother's womb, and there was no other place to look but in town where he was seen, in the fold of enemies. Showing recklessness in hopeless intention, Mulong was patient to cool him off with the promise that the guerilla organization of the whole Cavite and Laguna would be happy to unite with him for such purpose. He was told it wasn't just him who wanted to kill the *bayong* man, the gravedigger too and many more.

In the accounts of aspiring guerillas, they were given orders to stay inside the church, but with previous acquaintances of Mulong who had chanced upon them, they were directed to a carinderia for a cup of coffee. It gave them the chance to run when they heard people screaming scared, with the truckloads of Japanese that only brought bad news and to make a fresh one at the expense of the civilian lives and those who drifted into town.

Herminio Eleazar and Matias Amoranto, poor souls who had just joined the armed struggle, said they belonged to the unit led by Zacarias Baldonado, a former professor of the University of the Philippines organizing his own band of fighters. They were sad to confirm that the said man had just died. They also said that their mission in town was to establish contact with Captain Nestor Leonidez of Cavite. They admitted that none of them had ever met the guerilla commander, but many had heard about the gallantry of the man. More names of people were mentioned, including colonels and generals. However, nothing other than taking the train was the only way they knew to go to Bulacan, and it came with an extreme warning—Philippine National Railways or what's left of it was operated by JIA exclusively. The former POW had yet to find the usefulness of the new allies.

Displaced from the church and stripped of title he liked best (being a priest), Cabarles was frustrated with the result of his own doing. The Japanese were staying in town indefinitely. What prompted them to do so could not be for the sole reason that another collaborator was dead. They occupied an old Spanish house as their own, fortifying the building and burning an adjacent few to make more space. Not a little respect was shown to the owner of the house who had served them until he killed himself the day before. The whereabouts of the wife was unknown, and the saddest news of all was that Father Faustino was believed to be apprehended and executed at the same time the rumors and gossips began that Baldonado was confirmed dead, shot multiple times together with a few more. Talks from those left alive, the Japanese are looking for the other priest who is not a real man of faith but a saboteur. The only preference left for Cabarles was to go deeper into the jungle. End of the "priesthood."

Romulo Soler conspicuously had a sudden change of interest; he would not care anymore in burying the dead. He carried a gun of his own instead of a shovel and a pick while informing Cabarles that Father Faustino was alive and had left earlier with a few people in company. They would be meeting him in an undisclosed place. The only other person Cab trusted despite the broken respect in his reverence was the priest and the gravedigger. Cab agreed without hesitation. Weighing the current situation with the new company at hand, he needed the priest who could keep his calm despite the most discomfitting hours by praying together. His expertise in buttoning up the wide-open blouse of a woman at the blink of an eye should have other skills that would be beneficial to him. He could not be knowing how to be a priest alone; something of the reverend reminded Cabarles of someone, and somewhat all thoughts dictated for him to see the priest for one last confession. His objectives remained the same until he could devise another disguise to blend himself back into town; otherwise, he should be going if it was the train he would take to Bulacan.

Four excruciating hours of walk back in the jungle, Romulo decided to take five. Five minutes that extended to sunrise. Missed breakfast and nothing for lunch, Cab would not complain. The chain of events that caused the gruesome day was his doing. He was aware of it, but he didn't care. There was one more to kill. He could not explain how the first one just walked in front of him at a time his desperation was reaching the top of his limited comprehension. His endurance and courage was restored in every step, but to see that they were heading to Mount Banahaw was not a good sight nor thought. He was going back south.

"How far more we have to go?" he asked.

"We should be close, sir. Another hour maybe," Romulo responded.

"You know, this place is heavily patrolled by the Japanese. There is a town two kilometers northeast, I suggest we don't go that far."

Before anyone could say more, gunfires were heard. It was a distinct sound to the ears of Cabarles—Aritake rifles about five hundred yards. He had heard so many of those. It only indicated one thing—trigger-happy Japanese. In the jungle, they would shoot any moving thing on sight. Always in a battalion-size patrol, they had no reason to get scared engaging in a battle. In fact, they were always looking for it, hunting tireless guerillas that would not stop antagonizing them. Noontime, one Aritake shot that became intense and clearly winning with noticeably lesser response of Enfields and Thompson and the sound becoming louder, closing in toward their position. Before he could make any suggestion to divert direction and run away, Mulong informed him of the worst scenario he thought was happening.

The Filipino guerillas under fire must belong to his unit. Mulong immediately found position and, wasting not a moment, started shooting. It left Cabarles to do just the same, only with greater accuracy. Two hundred yards, every bullet counted, his preferred distance that surely he won't miss even on a quail. Concentrated to aim on his targets, his attention was distracted to see the same young and beautiful woman who became a widow just a day ago. To see her again running away from the Japanese with the guerillas instead of mourning for his husband distracted his mind-set for a while. Women always surprised him. Of all the women he met personally, this one was different in the sense that she was returning fire to the enemy with a handgun considering that she was last seen weeping and grieving for a dead husband—and she was pregnant.

The Japs kept in the offensive. Cabarles needed a reload after a cartridge was spent. Romulo just kept on firing his semiautomatic. The enemy must have realized they were losing many of their comrades. They ceased firing but remained on their cover; their front line was lost, but the determination to annihilate the retreating

Filipinos was unbroken. They kept coming more cautiously with a change of strategy. They could not take cover from Cabarles well enough they could not be seen through the scope of his rifle. Five more lay dead consecutively.

Romulo had gained high respect from Cab, from previous events together in town and currently displaying exceptional bravery and effectiveness in combat; he was sure the gravedigger was more than what he said he was.

The Japanese split their troops, realizing their disadvantage while passing through a narrow waterways made difficult by volcanic rocks on one side and grassy hill on the other. The Filipinos had established a better defensive position, concentrating their aim on the center, confidence regained to notice that they had reinforcement. Cab could see the enemy crawling above the hill like a line of crocs trying to reach either side while blending with the vegetation. Vengeful to what they did to Santos, he waited a bit to let them crawl more while making Romulo aware where they were lurking. Cab would not need to fire but only to the few that Romulo missed. More on the right that could not be seen from his position, the guerillas would be more willing to shoot them all, gaining momentum to return fire. Those that survived in the middle had started shooting again; some tried to run back, but it was not a good idea—they would fall down dead. The following silence indicated that the enemy had retreated.

There was jubilation while mopping up—no prisoners. The Japanese soldiers suffered equal brutality on their defeat. None are spared alive. Too early to do such, there should be more enemy left alive and unseen, firing weapons with great accuracy, causing another one to add to the guerilla casualty. Cabarles knew from experience that it wasn't that easy to defeat the Japs—they multiplied.

Life for life, the guerillas had suffered many casualties on a mile-long path of shoot-and-retreat engagements. They were not capable of sustaining a prolonged battle, and not many were left; they were on the brink of annihilation when Cab and Romulo chanced upon them. Those who had avoided raging hails of bullets from adversaries had reasons to show no mercy in the sudden change of momentum—just plain savagery and fury to take advantage of a little edge they were given. Instead of running away like what they were doing a while ago, someone was giving orders to take on the offensive.

Too early for the Filipinos to say they were winning the battle. There were enemy snipers successful in taking down more of them. Back into cover.

Cabarles was not distracted by the persevering shots coming from nowhere; he was distracted by the man giving orders—remarkable bravery and gallantry of a man he would not expect to see also in the middle of the battle as to see the woman crying on his shoulder when they were last seen. Pinched down from a single bullet that killed another by his side, he found himself helpless trying to return fire with a pistol on unseen Japs.

There was a little movement over the rocky hill of mixed green and brown leaves. Cab would see it clearly. He called the attention of Romulo to come over, who was shooting invisible snipers indiscriminately. "I'm out, give me a clip."

"I'm out too, only a few left on my rifle," the man replied.

"Give me your rifle then."

It would not make any difference. Any long barrel was fine, with scope or none. He aimed immediately and fired; a body fell off and rolled down the rocky hill. One more that met the same fate after the second shot. No more for the third shot. Then silence, a long silence that only made Cabarles pray because he could see more enemy. He returned the borrowed rifle and grab the .45 pistol he knew was useless in the far distance. His prayer was answered; the remaining guerillas were able to run where he was with Romulo without trouble. Remaining rounds were shared, and command was given to move out before any jubilation started again. Wounded comrades not capable of moving on their own was attended to.

"You are not a real gravedigger, are you?" he asked Romulo out of curiosity after seeing that he was as good in firing a weapon as digging holes.

"Lt. Romulo Soler, Philippine Army, Twenty-First Infantry Division at your command, Major Cabarles, sir." With proper salute in attention, the man was suddenly transformed into a remarkable soldier and an officer.

Cabarles saluted in return the way he knew how. He owed his life to this man and the one down there rendering a duty entirely opposite of what he believed who he was. His attempt to be clarified through Romulo was halted by exhausted comrades who was shocked to find only four people in their rescue, two of which were unarmed. A fresh load and a spare cartridge was given. For what it was worth, he wanted to be enlightened but with the man and woman still under fire two hundred feet back. Cabarles was going for them. He wouldn't let them die just yet; the couple owed him a lot of confession. Romulo was coming with him.

About halfway, splinters of rocks began simultaneously from a volley of fire clearly intended for them. The unrelenting enemy was causing immeasurable tension, sending them flat to the ground. Follow-up shots just barely missed Cab by a few inches while crawling for better cover. Another went through his satchel, grazing his belly. The sniper was a good shot and had sighted at him. It was coming from the south; he regretted not staying on the same spot he was before. The couple he intended to retrieve was pinned down on a layer of rocks. They could not return fire anymore with her pistol but were moving trying to peek through his cover, calculating the time and distance to run where Cabarles was or the nearest possible loaded weapon of the dead. Romulo was left behind about thirty feet back, firing at a certain target that gave Cab a chance to locate the Japs who had no intention to retreat, very determined with their advantage in position and camouflage. Cabarles saw them, however, but a moaning wounded Filipino called his attention. The one that joyed too early, he was begging for help. Not much he could do for him at the moment.

A show of extraordinary skill in sharpshooting was done in slow succession; body falling from a tree, over a cliff, and a few who were attacking from the trail like clusters of leaves would not move forward anymore. Cab took the moment to pull a wounded guerilla by his side, trying hard to prevent blood flowing through the hole on his chest, barely moving.

They didn't know each other. The man could only hold up to his last breath, eyes staying open to the shaded afternoon sky. Then he said, "Thank you." A short prayer for him, made real short by Romulo bitching and cursing about the enemy.

Suddenly he realized he could suffer the same fate at any moment on that spot; the better way to say it is he may not be able to get out of there alive. The enemy was capable of reinforcement, and there was no way to tell that there none lurking in the trees and boulders of rocks around anymore. A few more hours to sunset, he took the rifle of the dead, superstition set aside. He was a priest anyway; he could bless himself, but he gave it to Romulo to calm him down.

"Give me cover again."

Cabarles rolled down and crawled over uneven ground made worse by hard rocks of different sizes hitting his ribs and elbow. Carpets of thorny *makahiya* plants added to the difficulty, but he could not stop. His mind was set to reach two people hopelessly held up by a volley of fire from the persistent enemy. One at a time and distance closing, Cab would fire back five more times until he resorted to using the rifle from the dead Japanese. Better a grenade, but he didn't know how to make it work; they looked different from the ones he had carried for a long time. He wished he still had them. He let the priest do the job; somehow he was damn sure he was not even close to be the man he used to know, the one who denounced the killing as unforgivable sins during the day and who did it himself at night.

"Good afternoon, *Padre*, ma'am." They all knew that the greeting was not appropriate at the time, but for what it meant, Cabarles knew there were three of them now to pray.

"What are you doing here, I thought you left Cavite already?" Faustino asked. He never thought he would see Cabarles again.

"Not yet, someone told me that you have many sins to confess. I have come to do my duty," Cabarles responded while taking aim then firing his last round.

"Why would I do that? You're not a priest."

"So are you," Cabarles replied then handed him a pistol.

"Yes, I will if we make it out of here alive."

"You have a lot of confession to make, do you know that?" Cab said, watching the man checking out the gun. A glimpse to the woman. "And I suggest you take care of her very well. She is pregnant with your child."

"What?"

A very loud explosion nearby cut short the random chat. It would cause the return of the humming to his ears. One more, closer that could not make it worse anymore.

He could not hear anything that was said with fingers on his ears anticipating more explosion. He knew how stubborn the Japanese could be; they were just not afraid to die. Romulo, helping from where he was, sent a few running away. He was ordered to assist the woman out.

One fake priest's fury was more than enough to annihilate the enemy held down on the path where they climbed up. A steep creek as he looked over it, none was running or hiding other than the lifeless bodies who would not survive the fall if able to dodge a bullet. A stony brook of little water flowing in the months of no rain was fed from springs scattered in the area as it seeped back on the ground until it made its way to a place known as Sapang Bato. The water was not crystal clear anymore; there were more dead bodies as Cab looked further upstream where the battle began. Romulo and the abled remnants joined them, securing perimeter. They could see two men standing, of about the same height with one skinnier, both sweating and red of other people's blood, lighting up cigarettes in the open. And they sat slowly, inhaling nicotine out from unfiltered homemade sticks. One managed to talk after a little while upon realizing how much loss had incurred his troops at the end that bloody day.

"I am ready for my confession." He sighed in resignation, calming himself down between puffs of smoke.

"Yeah, I can see you had sinned as much as I do. You can start now by telling who you are." Cab agreed with the man who was clearly not a real priest.

"Nestor Leonidez, Captain, Philippine Army, at your command, Major Cabarles, sir." He made the same salute that was akin to trained soldiers, which was done standing up in attention.

Cab didn't pay attention; he had seen it before from Romulo, and it didn't excite him anymore. However, he acknowledged the gesture with a cigarette sticking between his fingers sitting down on the ground. He had knelt before this man so many times believing that he was a man of faith. He may be telling the truth this time, but he was not engrossed. Orders were given to leave the place immediately while they could.

In another place three hours after the battle of Borol (the Hill), Dasmarinas, the "confession" resumed.

"Who is the real Father Faustino?"

"He was my brother, killed by the Japanese for having a brother who is a soldier," Leonidez stated while sitting back down closer to Cab.

"You are the one killing the collaborators in town?" Cab asked.

"I knew it was you," Leonidez replied.

"Not all mine, three were not my doing. I wanted to know if there was one among them with one testicle way bigger than the other."

"How would I know that? They were all traitors to me."

"Are there more of those kind in town?"

"There always are. Every place, every town." Leonidez sighed in disappointment. "Why are you interested with the one with hernia, does it matter?" he continued with curiosity.

"He was the other man who betrayed Captain Santos. I didn't see his face, I can only rely on his balls to identify that bastard."

"Yeah, I understand. But how did you know?"

"He peed on my face, a lot. The last thing I remember was when I woke up in church. Thanks again for looking for me."

"Now I know why you smell so awful when we found you. You don't need to thank me. I owe you my life today and the rest of us."

"So we are even, you don't mind if I ask you a favor?" Cabarles stated.

"Say it, and consider it done."

"I want to find that man. I swore to a grave that he shall die too. Will you help me?"

"With pleasure, sir."

"Thank you, Captain. Shall we move out of here now because this place will be swarmed with Japanese very soon . . . ? I'll take the rest of your confession later in a safer place," Cab worriedly suggested. "And one more thing, don't call me Major. I kind of likened my luck as a Captain. Cab is better."

"Sure, Cab, let's go."

The officers both moonlighted as a priest. They helped each other get up from the ground and hugged each other with a tap on the shoulders. Another day was concluded at midnight in the life of Dominador Cabarles, who just barely escaped death. The hole in his satchel would remind him of that event extended to the friendship and brotherhood that would last a lifetime in his memories.

CHAPTER 22

"AND DELIVER US FROM TEMPTATIONS"

One Hail Mary, I know, wasn't enough. I made it twice. There were times I was told to make it five. I keep praying. For what I did, for what we did, a thousand prayers will never be enough.

ANOTHER REVELATION

There are no more jungles that could excite his wildest imagination for the adventures he had dreamed of when he was a young boy. All he wished for was to be as accurate as his father on how to shoot a bird or tin cans and later to impress a girl in making a hole on the center dot of a circle around many circles. He never imagined he would keep shooting anything associated with that red dot. In full view of a short line of people who must all have sorrow after realizing the previously long file was not as it was anymore but a dozen left half were wounded, fed from food packs taken from the dead. The horrible sight was covered by darkness of the night when the moon shyly rose to lit the surroundings. It reminded him of life in prison camp. Stolen food to share with ill-stricken prisoners wailing in pitch-black barracks that was denied of hope clinging on fingertips for dear life even if they would wake up to lament pain again the next day.

The burden he would keep for the rest of his life was blaming himself for the death of Santos. He should have still been alive if he decided to remain in Bicol a little longer. If he complied with him to stay in Leyte, then they should still be in Leyte. He should not have vanished pointlessly. Many more people would still be alive today in retrospect. He made many unopposed decisions for personal interest, and the situation did not change a bit. Too late to be remorseful now.

Wherever the place he was walking on, his mind was still fixated on going back to town. Being a priest was not in mind but seemed to work well while blending into the general population. He firmly believed the other *bayong* man lived in Dasmarinas close to the church. Vengeance to one more he blamed for the killing of Santos. It was always refreshed in his mind every time he was bitten by a mosquito, every time he had to urinate. Added to the thought of being back in the forest toward Mount Banahaw, Santos was most needed. No one to argue with on the rules of their journey, and without him, he didn't know how to proceed northward. He was lost in many ways. His stay in the church posing as a priest by day and killing collaborators at night satisfied his day after a lengthy confession and short prayers for absolution. To learn that the real Padre Faustino was long dead, he had reason to believe that he was actually encouraged to kill more people, ultimately lodging all five grenades simultaneously at an enemy detachment that led the Japanese to take over the town.

The "divine priest" who turned out to be a sinful captain pledged to help many, but the hour of mourning for the devastating loss surely needed time for him to redirect his next decision. In addition, he was busy attending to a woman. It all added up—that woman had visited him on his sickbed a few times. He respected the man when he was a priest, more to find he was a soldier, a brave one who was not afraid of death. Countless times, he really knelt before Leonidez repenting sins he had accrued. Enlightened to the true identity of the man, he hated him so much but also admired his dedication as a soldier. It reminded him of his first confession. "Forgive me, Father, I am repentant for I murdered a man."

"Who was he?"

"A collaborator."

"Was he the man you're looking for?"

"I do not know, it was dark."

"Pray the Hail Mary," the priest said casually. At the time, a beautiful woman in line waited for his attention.

On a few more occasions, he did the same act of contrition; the absolution was always easy and the same. The last was on a Saturday.

"Pray three Hail Marys this time."

"Why three, it's only one I killed?"

"There were three found dead this morning."

"The other two were not my doing," he argued.

"Pray for who did it anyway."

One lazy morning within that week, he was told to pray again on one occasion even if he hadn't left church all night. As a result, there were no more wearing white-and-red armbands in public. On Sunday morning, a man took his own life inside the church. Around two o'clock on Monday morning, someone blew up the Japanese barracks about one kilometer entering the town. He wanted to confess that one, but a series of events prevented it to happen. He realized that all of his confessions were all invalid. The priest was so liked and respected by churchgoers that Cab was deceived, a blatant disrespect on the vestment and reverence while dealing with serious people in obligations to their faith. One of those people was a pretty woman who was also thought to be a devotee coming to the church regularly. A very unfaithful woman, and she had a sister.

WHAT WOULD SANTOS DO?

He was awakened by a familiar sound: loud explosions of bombs and Zeros banking while spraying .50 mm on the ground about ten kilometers from their location. No reason to be alarmed, they had walked far enough and were obscured by heavy tree canopies that even he could not see the sky. He was served of the morning chow courtesy of Eleazar. The neophyte was useful in his first taste of battle, proving his significance having experience in clinical practice. First to apply his skill was his buddy Maximo, or Imo as he was called, a superficial wound, but the shock it incurred took a little while to recover. Redeeming himself from embarrassment, he made sure everyone had a meal that morning out of his cooking. He even offered to wash the shirt soaked and dried with blood of the men he imagined either one he should be. He was appreciated very well on his efforts to be useful.

The captain was having a consultation with the man who wanted to be called Cab, both shirtless, talking while roaring airplanes were passing overhead. This was the time when he would need the wit of Santos. He was always following him how many Hail Marys to pray when he believed he was truly a priest; obviously Leonidez was turning the tide in favor of the USAFFE soldier. He knew from the beginning he was a senior US Army officer of a very high intelligence, one rank higher than him.

"I present to you the command of my battalion . . . what's left of it," Leonidez said.

Romulo had ordered the men in formation. A few could barely stand, but their courage was intact as they saluted to the two shirtless officers who had shown them farfetched bravery and soldiering capability. Likewise, all these men were equally valiant and fearless guerillas. Cabarles would show them he can salute competently like that of a real officer as he heard his name mentioned each time from the start of the line.

"Facifico Moran, Staff Sergeant, Philippine Army. Reporting for duty, Major Cabarles sir."

"Corporal Juan Velasco, Philippine Army, reporting for duty, Major Cabarles sir."

Privates First Class Mario Ruiz, Roman Tupad, and Benigno San Miguel. Privates Renato Canlas and Emilio Cervantes. He could not understand why they said their names followed by numbers.

Renato Abad, Alberto Banal, and Martin Pulido in civilian clothes. Herminio Eleazar was the eleventh man rendering a salute awkwardly with rifle on display like the rest.

Very straight line formation. One more, late to join trying hard to stand straight squeezing a shirt with his hands was Amoranto. He could have picked up his own weapon too, but assisting a wounded prevented him.

"Matias Amoranto, *tagaluto, tagalaba* (cook and laundryman), Major Cabarles sir." The last one on the line who just got there honestly said of what he could do competently that burst laughter among others. Cab may have laughed too, but expressed gratitude while taking what the twelfth man was holding. It was his shirt; though still wet, it was a lot cleaner than before.

Cabarles was speechless, overwhelmed of the honor he was given. So much for the rifle salute from Lt. Romulo Santos. "Company ready at your command, sirs." It was spoken in English. Then he was joined in the same manner by Leonidez, his muse on the side.

"Captain Nestor Leonidez, Philippine Army Twenty-First Infantry Division, at your command, Major Cabarles sir," he said loudly.

He remembered when he was presented of the same drill formation of Filipino POWs in Davao minus the weapons. "You have to salute back and it'll be all over," whispered Lieutenant Santos. That was what he did again and turned his back to spread a laundered clothing. Certainly, it was clean, and he looked back at Amoranto to thank him again then sat to where he was lying down. Indeed he didn't realize he had left everyone in shock to see gruesome marks on his back. Not one, not even Leonidez or Soler, managed to say anything about the horrendous sight. They only knew those battle scars in front while lying on his sickbed, but they had not seen yet what was behind in full view until now.

"What kind of hell have you gotten those scars in your back?" the army captain seated back with him said.

Cabarles tried to look over his shoulder as much as he could. He couldn't see anything. He could only assume there were scars on his back as people said. "Many kinds. Some a few steps away from another," he replied. "I had thought for a while I was in the care of God's disciples in the sanctuary of the church, but then I was wrong. It's the devil himself I met. You know you have a lot more to confess to me, right?"

Leonidez could not say a word anymore.

"Sir, we are waiting for your order." Romulo cut down the conversation, getting restless from Zeros flying by that were spraying .50 mm on any discoloration of the forest from above.

Cabarles knew they were being hunted. Five kilometers was not a safe distance to the advancing enemy while sitting down.

"How is she doing?" he added, referring to a worried woman in company who was seated beside Leonidez.

"She is fine," Leonidez replied.

"She looks so tired, we should stay here for a while. If you guys intend to go any closer to that mountain, I suggest let's think over the other options," Cab stated.

In the northwestern tip of that big mountain, Cabarles would know he was back in the foothills of Mount Banahaw. Going further deeper would mean reexperiencing what he had been through in that mystical place. Enchanted was how he described the mountain. He may have made friends with its one resident and he also knew a place they could hide forever. But finding his way back to Dasmarinas would be very difficult by himself maintaining an objective that could not be done by hiding. He also knew by fact that somewhere around the mountains were equally vindictive Japanese who may still be looking for him and Santos. He was told that the western side all the way to the south was mostly steep hills and treacherous volcanic rocks ready to tumble at any disturbance with many clearings caused by forest fires. Therefore, there was no place to go but play hide-and-seek with the enemy right where they are until a logical plan was decided. Besides walking on daylight it was never advisable even on the remotest of jungles.

Seeking revenge for Santos's death remained a priority, but he had to reconsider that he was not alone, and the benefits of a new company at present was a great advantage back in the middle of nowhere; however, he would not allow to drag them all further to his personal sentiment because many had innocently lost their lives already with such inconsiderate actions he had done. On the other hand, he would not let them bring him back up that mountain again.

Cabarles had no one to argue with about breaking the rules of engagement anymore. He actually broke them both left and right without regard to the consequences because of Santos's demise. He would never know how many more civilians would pay and had paid already in carrying a sworn statement to a grave. He insisted he had nothing against collaborators, but as long as the man whom he blamed on the execution of Santos lives, he would not discriminate anyone in the fold of enemy. He will not leave Cavite alive until it's done.

Certainly he missed Santos, he needed his wits to deal with people along the way, finding himself in the company of people who were not what they led him to believe they were and a dozen more who had shown extraordinary respect to recognize him; what he can talk about is mainly about Santos. Their exploits together from Bataan to Mindanao then back in Luzon was a never-ending story. The

Cavitenos shared his emotions and expressed all the help he needed to identify the *bayong* man.

Close to darkness again, no enemy was sighted. Men were called in, and they started to move out after a long speech from their captain. Rested and invigorated, most were happy seeing their family given long liberties while rendering new missions. By morning when Cabarles woke up, no one left except Leonidez and his girl, Soler, and Eleazar and Amoranto who stated that they had no family to go and so were sworn in as guerillas. Amoranto also swore he would be at their company at any errand they would make him do. He noticeably needed some fixing. Leonidez was a native of Cavite, Soler was from Angono, Rizal. He said he had been away from home too for a long time.

Herminio Eleazar is given the rank of sergeant unofficially who also chose to stay with the captains instead of going back to Sangley Point, a former US Navy vase and ship repair and supply depot, now under the control of JIP. Working against the enemy was what he always wanted than identified with arrogant Japanese soldiers and collaborators known in the Southern Luzon as Sakdalistas. Disclosing association with too many stories about Sakdalistas, his loyalty remained under scrutiny by Soler imposing that he trust him otherwise.

Down to five and a muse, they would go back to Dasmarinas as insisted by Cabarles. Leonidez must concur, but ensuring the safety of a very important person was a priority. For Cabarles to resume what was avowed until then, he had no alternative plan but to continue north. For Soler, wherever his captain is, he shall be there.

THE TALE OF THE FAITHFUL CAPTAIN

Barrio Salawag, Dasmarinas. January 10, 1944.

Two consecutive days without incident traveling by foot, it was a quiet morning. Cabarles would wake up from his usual nightmares. What was left of the party were already awakened in a place he was informed should be out of reach of the Japanese. In the backyard of a house, he found a bench to sit on while looking around. Leonidez came to join him; the alliance developed between them forged by many near-death situations, brutal struggles, and salvations in so short a time was beyond measure. They found each other in profound brotherhood that could not be forgotten in a lifetime. *In Cabarles's accounts, "Captain Leonidez was similar to Capt. Rodrigo Santos in many ways except that he had shown immense affection over one woman."*

On the other hand, this man had desecrated the sanctity of the church and priesthood in every manner there could be. Twisted and incomprehensible to the guilt it had created with his limited rationalization to why he also submitted himself in the same actions, the burden was just too difficult to be relieved on his own.

"I have a question for you if you don't mind," Cabarles started to begin conversation.

"What is it?" Leonidez complied.

"How do you sleep well at night?"

"Never easy, I usually don't."

"The first time you wear the vestment of a priest, did it come into your mind you may burst into flames?"

"No, did you?"

"I just woke up in it, but I had thought about it afterward. I prayed not to, every morning with a Hail Mary."

"I never thought about that. What can I say? I became comfortable with it. Why did you ask?" Leonidez passed on the curiosity.

"Because that morning, that moment I felt I was going to . . . when I was about to shoot that man from the pulpit," Cab revealed. "How about when you took the wife away, don't you feel any remorse?"

"No, I take it off. How would you know about that?"

"I connected the dots. I'm still waiting for your confessions, you know."

"Where do you want me to begin?"

"What transpired inside the church that day? It was a setup, wasn't it?"

A long silence ensued, the Army Captain pausing to respond. Despite the crowing of roosters close and afar, the surroundings was generally quiet. For what logic he should conceal anything from this man when the reason he lived was because of him, finally he found words to begin. "Lieutenant Soler described to me about the man you're looking for. We were trying to identify that traitor for a long time, but I never thought it was him. The only way to make sure was to let you see him face-to-face. Yes, it was arranged to bring him inside the church, to make him sit on the first row. It wasn't easy, I never suspected it was him. I always wanted to shoot him too for personal reasons it would be a burden on my conscience for the rest of my life if I did. I just couldn't do it."

"Why? Because you are having an affair with his wife?"

"Yes, but I was just reclaiming what was mine and always is. Aurora and I are sweethearts when I went to military school up north, in Baguio many years ago. The man you killed was an avid suitor who resorted to take her by force when all efforts failed to win her heart. Her parents could only agree to let them get married to regain her dignity," Leonidez explained.

"So you knew I will shoot him at any moment."

"I was aware of that."

"Why did you stop me?"

"I can't let you do it during the mass, too many people. Did he really shoot himself?"

"Yes. What's up with the open blouse?"

"It was taking you too long, what do you want me to do in the privacy of a woman I'm always longing for?"

"Yeah, I understand. She's really pretty." Cabarles sighed in agreement, watching the woman of the subject matter. Aurora was on her way to join them, very appealing despite the circumstances. However, it wasn't her that had caught his attention; there was another.

"Good morning, good morning, Father Cabarles," the yet-unnamed woman greeted, attempting to take his hand for the traditional respect bestowed to a priest.

"He isn't a real priest, you know," Aurora reminded her. "Meet my sister Carmelita, sir."

Like a real gentleman to a graceful beauty that suddenly caused palpitations of his heart again, Cabarles kissed the back of her hand instead. "I'm greatly privileged to see you again."

"Same here, Father, I mean, sir," she replied. "Pardon my intrusion, I want to welcome you in Salawag, welcome to our home."

"Please call me Cab, I'm kind of used to that name already."

There were no more words that could come out of his throat. For what it seemed, his knees were trembling to see Carmelita; in time, he was contemplating his redemption to the faith he disregarded. There was always a sin that kept on coming in many different ways, instigated by thoughts that were evoked from a truly seductive widow constantly alluring her man, a sudden burst of desire to think that he had one better waiting for him in Bulacan. With eyes on Carmelita, going home was jeopardized.

A decent-sized house surrounded by many trees, the backyard overlooked a wide array of unknown exotic fruit trees through a thin wall of coconut palms. The next neighbor was half a mile away. Facing the sunrise, he could see a couple coming with an animal in tow in the shadow of passing clouds.

Sweet rice cooked in coconut milk and wrapped with banana leaves, hot coffee, and fresh buffalo milk. The ordeal with Carmelita seemed over for the meantime in that morning hours with the best of view the house offered. That unusual feeling that took place a long time ago was happening again. He had forgotten what he had been through for what it seemed. Compelled with a longing for Inez, he found that she was right in front of him. So beautiful with all the resemblance to the one irreplaceable in his heart, it was the same feeling. He may look busy with the food, but he was imagining something else. Bulacan was still too far away.

"What you desire is what you see right here in Cavite. A beauty in perfection, what else you could ask for?" he heard whispered to his ears from a very familiar voice that caused him to look over his shoulder. He might have avoided any involvement with all other women who had shown interest in him or the other way around. But this one, the last count of finger in one hand, he may not be as strong as he thought he was. A botched honeymoon with Inez, a night with Rhodora X in the spirit of hard liquor, the inviting and submissive fairy of the cornfield, the aggressive Rosie in the moonlit shore of Bohol. He was also counting the severely malnourished Bicolana widow whom he admitted had become a looker after a while, most persistent than the first three altogether, but that one he had suspected Santos played a great role to manipulate the poor woman in getting into him.

He was proud to say he had kept his fidelity to one love as they had vowed together. Two years they had no communication; two long years he had nothing in mind but to reunite with her. In the period that halted such desires and totally forgotten with rage of vengeance, Carmelita could not have come at a better time in his life when he said he had incurred many sins on himself. Everything was justified; he had no assurance he would reach Bulacan alive nor reunited with Inez. God knows what had happened to her. He had truly been in hell many times because of that sole endeavor, in near-death situations and many times he actually thought he had died already. Too many obstructions along the way, and currently he traveled backward only to be reunited with Carmelita; his steps were guided into her arms, and it was just too much for him to resist thinking of her in the most sinful way. The time had come to reevaluate himself: was it all worth it to still keep his fidelity? The influence of Santos in his personal views, alive and dead, had become a comparison of his inadequate knowledge about most things, and he was starting to believe that Santos's evil wisdom was reasonable after all. Carmelita in mind, he would just have to overcome the trembling knees and all would be fine.

Naturally soft spoken and reserved short of an education to balance himself in front of new people, "what would Santos say?" "What should I do to begin?" He did fill up his mouth with food and remained quiet for as much as he could. A few souls joined them eventually; he had never said a word to Carmelita but listened to people equally taking concerns on how they would make his stay in the place a comfortable one. The drink that goes around comes generously to refill his own glass when it is emptied.

What he would know about West Point they say he is from? He had heard about Sangley Point; he thought they were brothers or cousins. He didn't consider it wasn't Carmelita alone to deal with. Her sister Aurora and the rest of the Cavitenos who were also eager to hear one or a few words who he really was, definitely not a priest. They didn't believe he just wanted to go home to a remote rice-farming village where he grew up. The curse of the captain that he thought he had overcome already returned to bring him good luck instead. There was no more Santos on his side to take over a situation that always caused him anxiety.

In a setting with no Americans to deal with, but a lady in front must take her eyes off him. He needed Santos, and for what it seemed, he never left him alone.

It could not be explained that he was just passing by on his way to Manila. But he could say a few facts about Gen. Douglas McArthur and the current war effort to win back the Philippine Islands, about many nice people he met along the way from Davao. He explained that his mission was to establish communications, train, recruit, and organize resistance to support the Allied forces in taking back the Philippines from the Japanese. He said he reported to a general in Mindanao and a colonel in Leyte, with ties to guerillas in Bohol, Bicol region, and was also successful in establishing communications with guerillas in Camarines and Lucena. He cited the involvement of many civilians including women and children in covert activities helping the resistance and POWs in Mindanao. Suddenly all ears were to him quietly.

"I had laid out my mission to Captain Leonidez. I am sure that in his capacity and intelligence, all will be done accordingly. However, the undertaking requires the cooperation of all. It may look like we had triumphed, but the battle is still a long way to the end. Retributions from the enemy do not discriminate. Women, children, they see us all as targets of their weapons and bayonets. The Japanese will seek vengeance. I suggest we cool off for now and maintain loyalty to each other while expanding our forces. Take notes of names of those who sided with enemies and their crimes against Filipinos—they will be held accountable in due time. Be careful who we judge. Some of them may be hated and despised, but their sacrifices and courage are unimaginable to our redemption." Every word said was listened with seriousness. A USAFFE officer with proven gallantry, he already earned the respect of everyone in the crowd even before he had set foot in that barrio.

The ensuing dialogue was more on stories of heroism and the bravery of many people he had acquainted with. Over a refill of *lambanog* that kept on poured, he kept on talking. "Many died, a few stayed in certain provinces to carry on the general scope of the mission and God help them." He cited the brave women of Davao, about Rhodora X, the mistress of a Japanese officer whose influence over the commandant had changed the treatment of POWs in the Davao Penal Colony. Nurses and doctors smuggling medicine out of hospitals for the benefits of detainees and so on. But a lot of credit were given to bamboo communications established systematically that was material to the escape of POW prisoners and ultimately out of Mindanao. With great sorrow, he let everyone know that a great soldier, Capt. Rodrigo Santos, to whom he fought with in many battles from Northern Luzon to Mindanao then back to Luzon would die pointlessly by the deed of an evil traitor. His burden lessened a bit to let them know that another soldier in his unit was forced to stay in Bicol to ensure the safety of refugees with help of a convict and a former Japanese concubine who stayed courageous despite the death of her own parents from the hands of the Japanese who raped and abused her. Sad stories of many sacrifices, courage, and heroism of people who did not lose loyalty to one another. He excused himself after a while. He could not avoid stopping the tears and weep in attempt to describe Captain Rodrigo Santos, the last man standing by him.

The daylong feast of no occasion but plain hospitality to the guests became a quiet day while people spoke to repeat what he said. People miles away would come with food and a sack of rice or fruit that piled up, expecting to see many guerillas. There were not many but they were honored to meet Captain Leonidez and Lt. Romulo Soler. The noted Bulakeno who was knocked down by the liquor found a place inside a shed.

(The kindness of Cavitenos in the remotest barrio would be told and retold to a small boy many times while he was growing up. Highlighted were the names Captain Nestor Leonidez, Aurora Molina, Lt. Romulo Soler, and Maximo Amoranto. On the side, the name Carmelita always themed the inspiration of many events that ensued.)

CARMELITA MOLINA

He chose to sit on a bench for two after a quick moment to be relieved behind the bushes. Severe thirst, head spinning, he could not explain why the sun was setting already. He missed the rest of the day. He could not remember anything but a beautiful lady in his dream; it wasn't Inez. He swore he would not drink *lambanog* again. He could see that there were no more people around, but for the same lady that complicated his imagination drunk or not.

"God she's so beautiful," he said. She's certainly coming to where he was. Trembling knees would not allow him to run away; it could only permit him to stand up and say a greeting. Hangover would be a good excuse, but he was not mistaken—this woman was causing his heart to beat erratically that was felt the first time he laid eyes on her. He may have previous experiences with her kind, but still he had to find where his tongue was on this one.

"You may like hot soup before dinner, sir," Carmelita said while putting a bowl on the table.

"Thank you very much, ma'am. Where is everybody?"

"*Kuya* Nestor is yet to be awakened, sir. I understand you are all exhausted," she said.

"Please call me Domeng, my name is Dominador Cabarles. You're very kind, I'm not worthy to be served by a most beautiful lady like you. I'm overwhelmed."

"The honor is mine, sir. Can I really call you Domeng?"

"Yes, ma'am."

"Domeng it is, only if you call me Carmelita." Her smile was accommodating, inviting.

"My pleasure, Carmelita. I hope my stay in your place is not too much of a burden to you."

"You're welcome here for as long as you can find any reason you may choose to stay."

"Thank you. Should I tell you already that I may stay In Cavite because you gave me a reason?"

"Now I believe you're really from Bulacan. Poetic, it is said that Bulakenos are also romantic."

"I don't know if it is true because I believe I'm not. I usually froze in front of beautiful woman."

"Clearly you're not . . . I'm not as pretty after all?"

"I apologize if you find me rude. You're the most beautiful girl I had ever seen in a long time. I feel like I have known you before today, you were holding my hands and praying. I thought it was real then I thought I was just delirious, but since then, in many dreams and nightmares I always see you."

"I think you missed too many meals, sir. Have your soup, dinner shall be ready very soon."

Cabarles may still have borne the effects of moonshine to be wordy, but he was also really hungry no doubt. "I think you're right, ma'am," he agreed. "But I'm used to not eating for days. I can miss another meal if that's what I need to express my appreciation on all the prayers you devoted for me."

"You're welcome, I had visited you once when you're in the church with my sister. I don't know you, only with my prayers I could help all those people compelled in taking care of you," Carmelita revealed. "I had already known you more than you think I do. I believe you're a kind man. I thank God you lived, but it is another life you are given. I suggest you spend it in faith to God."

"I had thought about it many times. Should I lay down my gun and be done with it? I don't know any more what else to do. I'm not an intelligent man. It was faith I believed that led the way to all my salvation, but I cannot discount the help of many people that led me ultimately into your arms. Is it fate for us to meet again so I can renege from my vows to hell and heaven? You're a very amicable and fascinating woman, I had fallen in love with you in my thoughts and it's stronger now that I know who you are."

"Please don't complicate yourself as it is already. You're lost in many ways. I can only guide you through faith and prayers," Carmelita stated.

"If that's what it takes, I can honestly tell you that my faith relies on my rifle to keep me alive. If there's a way to redeem myself back to God, I'm doing it. Should you let me in your heart is also a beginning I had already taken."

"I understand. Please do not commit yourself when you know it will be very difficult for you to yield back on the terms of faith. How sweet you talk, you made it too easy like you know what I already feel for you."

"I do. I will cherish it in my heart."

"We will see about that. Please do not take advantage of my weakness when you will leave me heartbroken. Promise me you'll not do that to me," Carmelita pleaded to hold his hands with tearful eyes.

"I cannot make promises that would mean breaking what I made before. It will be a promise I can express to you we both know I cannot keep."

"Then I can only keep praying for you."

Over dinner, it was a pleasant conversation. Leonidez and Aurora were overjoyed to finally have times together without constraint. Cabarles was uneasy; the temptations of staying in Cavite was real and very enticing as the bright light of the Coleman and candles. On his right was Carmelita to whom he cannot avoid to take a glimpse from time to time.

Plenty of food worth a lengthy word of grace; in war or no war, he had never seen so much prepared for four people. All looking good, he didn't know what to get. It seemed once in a lifetime like the last supper in Pandi when he was invited to dine by a couple who would be officially his in-laws the next day.

It was December 6, 1941. The most beautiful girl was on his side also fresh from crying; it was exactly the same setting, absent of lectures and reprimands intended for him. He was also a guest with the option to eat as much as he could on the same table, foreseeing a future to spend with the most alluring lady for as long as he wanted in fulfillment of his dreams. Two years had almost passed and over halfway to reclaim that spot again that he didn't know if still there, his mind deliberating.

Silence, it seemed that time stood still. He could not swallow the first bite he put in his mouth. All that he saw was what he sought, and it was real, presented to him just at arm's reach.

"Please make yourself at home, sir, I mean Cab (Son). You now belong to our family," Aurora (Mrs. Sandoval) broke the silence. "If there's anything more I can offer, please don't hesitate to ask. Just don't make my sister (daughter) cry," she added.

Whatever Aurora meant by he "belong to the family" may need clarifications; however, he was afraid to complicate matters by replying by mouth different from what he would do later. One terrible mistake he did he swore he would not do again.

"I am your guest, I can't thank you enough for allowing me to stay," he replied with chosen words. "I'm overwhelmed, a great honor I don't deserve." Cab added with a quick glance at Carmelita. If only he could stay to make that sad smile happy. Too many sins he had accrued, he didn't want any more. "How far are we to the town, to the church?" It was an attempt to divert his mind out of imagining himself to stay.

"It's too far and dangerous, I suggest we stay for a while," Leonidez stated. "Most people in town should know who we are by now."

"How old are you, sir?" Melinda asked the question out of the blue.

"Twenty-four. Please you can call me Domeng."

"You're very young."

"Yes, sometimes I don't want to think of it."

"Of what, the war?"

"No . . . that I'm going to die very young," Cab said, looking serious.

"I believe you will live long if you stay in Cavite," Leonidez suggested.

"I'm seriously taking that into consideration."

"We will be brothers . . . for real."

"I believe we are brothers already."

"Then stay in Cavite."

"I'm seriously taking that with great concern. Perhaps if I can be priest again."

"That's not going to happen, Carmelita won't let you. She is so pretty, isn't she?"

Very tempting, where was he going with this anyway? He was being held up. In Bicol, it took him more than four months to find the courage to move out. How long would it take him to leave Salawag when every time he glanced at Carmel, she was like a quicksand—he was getting in deeper, and he was letting himself in. Leonidez was not helping get him out, he was pushing him in instead.

"What are you two talking about?" Aurora caught up to what Leonidez was insinuating. "I don't like my sister left heartbroken like what you did to me," she added in protest.

"I think it's too late for that."

Ensuing talks were about revelations on how Carmelita and Aurora had known Cabarles in the beginning. Aurora, being married to a doctor was called into church by no other than Leonidez posing as a priest. She was accompanied by her sister. In the care of the priest and his aide was another priest. Helpless as she was, there was nothing she could do with her limited knowledge in clinical care, unlike her husband who was the doctor. A doctor he was, he could only say that God would save the man if there was one treating after him. Then he was prayed for by Carmelita who took care of him on his bedside all night and day until Cabarles regained consciousness. He and Carmelita had met already beforehand until they saw each other again in Salawag. Though it was disclosed later that Cabarles was not a real priest as she was led to believe, compassion had already developed into the heart of the young woman. Carmelita, whose faith and kindness overbore the sister by a long shot, had maintained empathy on the soldier who became a good shepherd by day in the flocks served by another and disappearing at night.

Through Aurora and many farm help that went to town from time to time, she was happy to hear how Cabarles had recuperated and was well liked by the townspeople. She continued a personal devotion to pray for his soul upon learning that he was not who they said he was. She offered many more prayers that became intense when she learned that his brother-in-law had taken his own life, which resulted in the Japanese takeover of the *poblacion* and the church. She was devastated by the disappearance of her sister and the priests, much more to be informed that the church was set on fire by the Japanese. All her prayers were granted indeed that included seeing the man that became the object of her affection. She was happy to find him sitting by her side, a soldier and an officer. A gentleman, respectful, and admirable without the beard despite the harsh effects of war.

Leonidez was right—it was too late. The young lady had fallen in love with the lost soldier, aware of the consequences it may inflict upon her despite discouragements from Aurora. Not real but pity, she said. Nevertheless, Cabarles was a drifter whom no one knew who he really was. But Aurora could only say so much that was credible enough without backfiring on her. Due to complications of her own love affair that she would choose to remain untold rather than justify as to how it succeeded, she relied on the sensibility of her sister in handling the situation on her own. Carmel was not just beautiful and caring, but she was also very smart. She could handle her many suitors who were all rejected to extinction by herself; Aurora was sure her sister would behave properly if Cabarles made an indecent move. To think otherwise, the man could protect her sister more than she could. Also, it was deceitful of her to meddle, she was greatly in love to a soldier and "priest". The affections that she didn't deny herself in the harshest opportunity she was given was a joy she could not deny for her sister. She excused herself with hands ostensibly cuffed to Leonidez.

What would Cabarles say? Nothing, his tongue had receded as he ate, heartbeat increased in thinking of any reason to excuse himself too. Pretending to like the *biko* (sweetened rice cooked in coconut milk) even if he was bloating with it already, he wanted to run away after he ate them all, but his legs were trembling again to be left alone with Carmelita.

"Do you want more?" Carmel offered, stumped of an unusual passion for the sweetened sticky rice by the soldier.

"Ah, ah . . . no more. Thank you very much," he replied. He felt like he was going to throw up. His jaw locked in again while he looked at Carmel, and his eyes stayed there.

"If you want more, I can get you more. Just don't look at me like that, you're scaring me."

"Ah . . . ah . . . I'm sorry." He froze.

Time up, Aurora came back, which coincided with the end of the suppressed moaning and deep breathing sent into Cab's ears amid the noises of crickets calling for their mate. She had in fact wandered around a long hour already with her own captain; she must have been perplexed at seeing a pan with only banana leaves left on it.

Why was he so quiet? It was an ordeal Cabarles wouldn't forget. As delicious as the food he ate, he regretted the sudden intake of a large amount of sugar in his intestines, which was not good at all. In the presence of an exceptionally beautiful and enticing lady who must have recognized the flaw over his bravery, his nervousness surged, looking for an excuse to say later. The desire for Carmel that was building up must be liberated; there must be something in the *biko* that changed his way of thinking. Maybe it was instigated by the background a while ago; it could also be the atmosphere. The Coleman ran out of kerosene and only candles were left to light the room. He didn't need a ghost to tell him what to do, but definitely, he was taking many lessons on evil outlook from the late captain, leaning toward rationalization of the dead over the woman he was yielding to. He had rehearsed so many things to say and do in his mind; all he needed was courage, a lot of it. He forgot that he was still in the dining room, glued down on the seat.

"Would you care to join us praying the Holy Rosary?" Aurora broke the silence again.

"Sure, I will," he replied.

It was an intriguing leap of conviction for how he had known this woman. How could she? They were also joined by Leonidez. "In the name of the Father and the Holy Spirit, amen."

It was over.

"I didn't know you could actually recite the Hail Mary," Leonidez commented afterward.

"I can," Cabarles replied. "I just cannot concentrate this time."

"Why?"

"I was afraid one us of may actually burst into flames."

"Yeah . . . let's cool off outside."

Outside was very calm. The darkness around was compensated by the gentle breeze and the distinct sounds of insects and nocturnal mammals. He followed the man who chose a bamboo shed about fifty feet from the house. It may be dark, but he had a good idea what Leonidez had laid down on the table—a gallon container of virgin moonshine. In southern Luzon, Lambanog was a product that never ran out.

"It's not every day we survive. I suggest we take advantage of a little pleasure that come to us."

"I agree, Lord have mercy." He was staring at the liquid while it was poured into a couple of glasses. He had just sworn he would not take any more of it, but a few shots should help him sleep off his dilemma. "Where is Soler and the men? I don't see them," he asked.

"I sent them to scout back in town. Eleazar believes he knew the other guy we're looking for."

"I should have come with them."

"It's dangerous, you're the most wanted man in Cavite right now. Certainly you've made the Japanese real mad when you blew up their detachment."

"How do you know it was me?"

"It's only you who could have done that if not me and Soler."

"Yeah, those grenades are heavy to carry, might as well use them before I leave. How many Hail Mary do you think I should do for that?"

"Don't worry, I did it for you already. That's the least I can do for saving us in Sapang Bato," Leonidez stated.

"Well, I can't thank you enough for saving my life too."

"Salud."

Aurora was coming with a fresh candle, also with plates full of goat meat, leftovers of the day.

"Thank you very much."

There was a pause from talking until things were set up.

"What shall I do to make you stay in Cavite?" Leonidez declared.

"Right now I don't know what to decide, so much to think about. I wish I can stay here longer. My heart dictates me to stay forever. This is a very beautiful place, very beautiful and kind people. What else should I wish . . . but my mind says different things. I have an oath and promises to fulfill . . ."

The three-day widow of no sorrow shown whatsoever found herself quiet for the meantime, listening. The man was leaving eventually, leaving her sister heartbroken.

"If I follow what my heart says, I'm afraid it will affect someone very much. It won't be fair for many people."

"Why did you say that?" Aurora was as intrigued as she found the man so reserved in expressing his feelings of love.

"Because the greatest reason for me to stay shall be your sister. The same reason I should leave. I have promises to fulfill." Domeng paused. "Don't ask me why it is her because I cannot explain. All I remember is it began when I was dying . . . When I saw her the first time, it's not because she's so beautiful why I've kept her in my thoughts. I had been loving her since then."

"The promises you have to fulfill, is that also for a woman?"

"Yes, to a woman I married, the same day I left her tearful to become a soldier. I haven't seen her since then. In the beginning, I had been longing for her so intensely to be blessed with courage that I will see her again. Many things have happened to me since then . . . many events that involved mainly of my struggle to survive so we can be together again until I haven't thought of her. I had learned not to think at all about her because it only led to terrible things I'm so afraid to think, but I have to know. I'm compelled to know what also happened to my family."

"I'm hoping she is safe, they are all safe, and I'm sure they also worry the same about you," Aurora said.

"I hope so either." The soldier sighed with tears obscured by darkness.

"I understand. Your compassion made me admire you more. We pray you find peace in your soul," Aurora said resignedly in tears.

The dogs were barking, indicating people in the vicinity. The voices told them it was some people they knew as the help let them into the property. Leonidez needed to check who it was and what they wanted. Aurora stayed on her seat. Every moment was on alert.

"I was told you are looking for a man with *luslos* (hernia)." It was Eleazar saying something over a shot of spirit.

"Yes," he replied. It was true for so many days, but his fury was already calmed down by Carmelita. Praying together and certain desires with her was influencing many concerns to change.

Over the years, Herminiano Eleazar was consulted by many who had cases of hernia. He revealed that a few fit the description about the man under suspicion of wearing a *bayong* in town. One among them was an aspiring mayor before the war who got the job in cooperation with the Japanese. Outspoken and believed to be a Sakdal leader, no one could corroborate the accusation though, the man considered as untouchable, wealthy, and presumed to maintain his own bodyguards. It wouldn't be easy to just shoot him. He was seldom seen in town though he welcomed visitors in his house as a select peer.

The next subject of conversation was visiting the man one day. In light of the identity of the man and the distance to walk back in town taken over by the enemy, the danger didn't warrant pursuing any activity against him at the present time. An elaborate planning was required; besides, the officers could spare more time on their personal affairs. One had his established and going while the other was imagining how it would feel to go beyond than just the softness of a woman's hands. The opportunity was real and the time plenty. Cabarles could set aside his revenge to give chance to the evil in his mind motivated by a ghost; the vague outcome of travel by himself and the prospect of getting laid once and for all became a priority even if he stayed in the province for the rest of his life.

Romulo and Maximo were ordered to scout the barrio where the Sakdalistas were said to conduct meetings and recruit members. Eleazar was given the mission, along with the continuation of his deeds, being a guerilla officer and health practitioner. He was given authority to recruit his own unit and maintain communications with Capt. Nestor Leonidez in Salawag, which became the command center and sanctuary for many guerillas in Cavite.

Meanwhile, Cabarles retained the hospitality fitted for a dignified guest, which he refused. Used to hard work with a lady already impressed, he helped in the chores and harvesting tropical fruits and vegetables in the disguise of a farmhand to the wholesale buyers who also carried information on road checkpoints and Japanese concentration along the way to as far as Paranaque to Manila where they retailed their commodities. Every bit of information was deemed important, but in the end, it was decided that the route was not viable by all means.

Several days went by, and Romulo and Imo came back to the barrio confirming that the Sakdal was politically in control of civilian affairs in Dasmarinas and over the adjoining towns of Cavite. The *luslos* man had gained authority by his serious cooperation with the Japanese. He was allegedly committing atrocities on his own without apprehension toward civilians. With henchmen of turncoats who were allowed to carry arms in a joint effort with enemy to find the priests dead or alive, he ruled the town that became peaceful somehow; cases of kidnappings became rampant. Disappearance of many fathers had also begun. Many would say were executed under an old mango tree behind the school building after hours of questioning and abuse, one of them believed to be Maximo Eleazar. They also reported that it was impossible to get close to the person of interest, as he stayed in a house with armed guards around its perimeter.

A CHANGE OF HEART

The soldiers could not come up with a well-defined plan to kill the Sakdalista leader, Totoy Redoble, as his name turned out to be. In reality, Cabarles himself was dragging his foot. He was more concerned in applying many "evil" lessons he had learned from the late Santos and shoot his other rifle that had been aimed quite a few times but never fired yet. Many days surely he had the chance but were left in aversion because of many reasons he would confide to a conniving "brother" who had begun to foster a confusing respect for the manhood of the bravest man he had ever met. He said Cabarles was rightful to be a priest if not a saint because he was letting many opportunities go in vain.

Romulo Soler had expressed his boredom and decided to spend some time with his family in Angono, Rizal. Switching the guerilla effort in organization, postponing the aggravation of the enemy, he decided to go home for a while like everyone else. Learning that he lived in the north shore of Laguna Bay, Cabarles could possibly take a hitch a hundred kilometers closer to his destination by way of eastern Luzon. But he had to turn his back away from an alluring woman that though had shown signs of submission into his evil desire, he could not take advantage of because she was very saintly herself. One reason that had imposed guilt on his conscience was of a sin he had not done yet, which was leaving Carmelita in the hopeless remand of her heart when truly he could exert no more promises. However, he had let his emotions take over, articulating his gratitude to the Cavitenos for giving him the chance of another life and accommodating him like a family. Everyone expressed that the honor was theirs as he had shown the characteristics of a man so fearless yet so rational and gentle he could not have hurt a fly. All he could say was if he would have a chance to see the war through and over, he would definitely come back to Cavite.

A man who would show concern for his safe passage through the rest of the Cavite province despite failed efforts to convince him to stay was Leonidez. He was coming with him by way of the town of Dasmarinas to give Cabarles a companion of the same intent to pay respects one last time to the graves of fallen brothers, Capt. Rodrigo Santos and the real Father Faustino Leonidez. There was so much to say about all times and emotions that Carmel and a former priest allowed to themselves at the last hours. All details of the relationship that transpired between each other would be told so many times at the count of his fingers in one hand. Save the best of endless memories, the most unforgettable of all his experiences throughout the war.

IN THE NAME OF THE GRAVES MARK BY TWIGS

The route plan was made to suit Cabarles's request, simply concerning a visit to the graves before he left. Two hours to midnight, they were ready. Romulo and a few men would go in a different group directly to a certain location to meet Cabarles and Leonidez who would all go through town by way of the cemetery. Maximo, who was now brandishing a weapon of his own, would be in the company of senior officers.

Back in town successfully under the strict rules of one and two after a swift three-hour walk from Salawag, Cabarles was kneeling at the foot of the mound of dirt. Quietly, he prayed before the tomb of a man he could not avoid but be reminded of how much debt he owed to the name on the grave to surrender a life to save his. The pitch-black night could not hide the tears, a shame to himself to leave the man six feet under in vain and forget what they had been through together, forget all that he swore over this grave.

"How far is it to the house of Redoble from here?" Cab uttered to the man on the next grave.

"I thought you'd never ask. About half kilometer. Maximo can lead us there."

"I cannot leave without paying him a visit. Do you mind?" he said.

"My pleasure," Leonidez replied.

Both knew the consequences of executing what had suddenly come up on his mind; clearly Leonidez had something planned on his own already. As soon as the exact place was sighted, Maximo was given orders as if he knew what he had to do.

It was not too far a walk in the plain of mostly farmed land until they entered the premises through the backyard of a big house partially covered with trees and palms that towered over it. It was three o'clock in the morning, pitch black around that they could not see any living soul until the dogs started barking, which revealed the presence of strangers around. Very persistent animals that met their own demise by the swing of a solid bamboo trunk, at least one of them had alerted the others to distance themselves while barking profusely, alerting everyone in the house too. At the front where the dogs had diverted their attention to attack without provocation, shooting started.

Shadows went through the back door in an attempt to escape from the hostile visitors. Cabarles and Leonidez were covering the backyard. All three were dead in an instant at point-blank from a Thompson. There was no way to tell who they were, but Leonidez would not let anyone run away out from that house.

The firing continued. In the dark, Cabarles could not tell who he would shoot as he was informed that friendly troops were covering the front who may have entered the house already. His weapon remained cold as the other was setting the house on fire. Made mostly of wood, the place was ablaze in a minute. None would survive as the last person inside the house would come out in front, identifying himself and begging for mercy. Mercy or not he was given but taken with them in the jungle as prisoner. There was no time to waste as the surroundings lit up. The man of interest was in custody, but who would know if he really was Totoy Redoble? The man they came for could not be confirmed by killing him. Cabarles was only interested on the *bayong* man. Whoever he was, a Sakdal leader or a high-profile politician or a day laborer, what they did was massacre. None of the dogs had escaped alive.

"What are you doing here? You should be waiting somewhere else," he asked the man whom he thought was far away and waiting for him.

"I was ordered to hang out nearby just in case you change your mind," Romulo responded.

"And these people?" he added, relating to about forty fully armed guerrillas rushing away from the burning house that became intense as it greeted the morning.

"Some of them you already met, the others not yet. Members of our force that can be summoned at a moment's notice," the lieutenant explained.

"Captain Leonidez thought you may raid the place after all by yourself. We owe you too much we cannot let you alone to do it, it's a suicide. We valued your importance as an Allied intelligence officer, and besides, we hate that guy as much as you do," Romulo kept on talking.

Cabarles would learn that the raid was planned in Salawag. He was told that if he choose to stay in the barrio, it could be postponed to another date. Along the path they walked on, men who took part in the raid started disappearing. They bestowed salutes and best wishes to each other, more to him as they all knew he was leaving. One would say they could not let him leave Cavite in rage; he may not come back again.

A man in his late forties, good looking, and of Hispanic descent. Noticeably not used to any physical work. Fine complexion and well shaven, other than a trace of a healed abrasion on his thumb, every nail was perfectly manicured as he put them together while begging for mercy. He acknowledged many actions made against his own race. Adding insult to injury, he was trying to justify his actions, conceiving arguments like a lawyer in court. He admitted that he was collaborating with the Japanese by expanding the Sakdalistas, justifying that he was actually saving lives while keeping peace and order in town, dealing cautiously with the Japanese chain of command. He blamed the guerillas when the Japanese ultimately camped in Dasmarinas, a normally quiet and peaceful municipality in his domain since the war began. Redoble mentioned many names of wealthy and prominent individuals who sided with the Japanese while keeping discontent against American colonization. Duran, Esguerra, Lisazo, Aquino were among the ones Cab could remember; but he wasn't interested nor could he grasp the talk of politics. He was only after the one collaborator who betrayed Captain Santos, and he wasn't even sure if it was really him.

Unlike Captain Leonidez who also wanted to know the place where those people lived, he was running out of patience to learn that most those mentioned lived in far-flung provinces in exception of Duran. He made the man say names of people in his organization that only lived in Cavite. Too many, he was terrified at the thought that Leonidez might actually kill them all. Cabarles exhumed his worry over a cigarette until the man took a pause, asking permission to relieve his bladder.

"Yeah, sure, help yourself," Leonidez replied.

Cabarles followed him to do the same while keeping on guard. He deliberately stood a few feet to his side and took a peek at the man's privates but failed to see anything. Redoble must have noticed his unusual interest, turning back a few degrees to discourage the soldier of whatever his intention.

Embarrassed at realizing what could the man be thinking about his actions, he pulled his pistol and just told the poor guy to drop his pants down. From behind, Cab could still not see what he wanted to confirm as the man kept on turning when he tried to step in front. Ashamed of his manhood or scared to face his death, the man would die anyway for being a traitor, but for the benefit of the doubt, Cabarles wanted to justify what he was about to do.

CHAPTER 23

THE RECKONING

If all it takes to find peace, a thousand times I did. Hail Mary, mother of God, pray for us.

PEACEFUL PLACE

In another dark night, left in the company of Romulo, they reached the shores of Laguna de Bay. In a small fishing community in Binan, Laguna, where two farm help of the Molinas were waiting, he remained in silence since he parted ways with Captain Leonidez. A pact was sealed with a single shot of .45 for a brotherhood with each other that should last forever, so they say.

Little time was spent on the kindness of the people. Food that was broiled or fried from the morning catch were wrapped in a basket prepared hurriedly as time was crucial to reach the north shore before next dawn.

Laguna de Bay was a large freshwater lake east south east of Manila. The lake itself, at 98,000 hectares in its vast expanse, was pristine and unobstructed of large-scale fishing industries at the time of the Japanese occupation. Shores around were mostly virgin vegetation that extended to muddy swamps and lagoons as the land gradually transformed to higher elevation, ultimately into Sierra Madre wilderness in the east to north. Romulo was familiar with the Lake. They would paddle on a wooden canoe two kilometers to an island in the middle, then another six kilometers along the shallow shores of a long uninhabited island bypassing the town of Binangonan to Angono, Rizal.

A very calm, cold night as January ended, two restless souls were braving the water in an overloaded boat across the lake with weapons and supplies. Approximately an hour per kilometer at synchronized movement to prevent capsizing, two different things alternately played in Cab's thoughts, one full of worries to what awaits him in Barrio Pandi. In over two years since he left home, he had many reasons to get scared. What happened to Inez, to all their loved ones? He would not think his stubborn old man would succumb to any degradations and cruelties of the Japanese, same as his in-laws, without a fight. They shared the same opinion if not the arrogance that they could also arm an army to fight against the Japanese. Knowing what could end up to anyone that didn't yield to the Japanese authority, he could not avoid all frightening thoughts. However, any which way he tried to disregard the bad thoughts, it always put him on that regard. Bulacan lies between the north provinces and Manila, and his hometown is the only viable route by highways and railroad to the city and back to the northern provinces.

Inez Sandoval was raised and fed in a silver platter; there was always her a mother or father or aunts and the hired help who would do things for her. She should be fine, and he was coming home. To reminisce the joy that her love caused him was immense no doubt, and to say again it was that love and thought that kept him breathing. Imagining good things inspired by a bright star just above the north horizon giving him hope, Inez must be waiting for him right down that bright star. Inspiration started to flourish; good things began to occupy his mind. He hoped there was no more to test his will.

"Sir, it's my turn to row," a voice came from another dreaming soul by the bow. He may have noticed that the previously swift voyage had become slow.

"Sure," Domeng replied, caught from deep thoughts and realizing that he was on Laguna de Bay. He handed the oar to Romulo.

The boat turned, and suddenly there was no more north star but many not as bright that highlighted the silhouette of the land and mountains of Cavite, Laguna, and Quezon, a privileged view that stirred his mind. To think that Captain Santos would find peace in any of those places was not agreeable, only in the cemetery with the dead maybe, but not for the living. The man who caused his death was in hell, suffering more than he deserved in his last hour. Reminiscing back to the massacre of his family and everyone in the house they burned to the ground was something that would stick to his mind. He had nothing against those people but one; even the dogs were not spared. The captain, a man of faith and kindness as he would know him, a brave and dedicated soldier, a compassionate lover, friend, or brother, was also ruthless and fierce beyond belief. He admitted that he was blinded by vengeance, maybe pride or simply he really just wanted a closure from merciless legacy at a place where betrayals and retributions had become a way of life. It was true to some respect that he was let to proceed on a furious crusade without intervention. A priest there on whom he relied his faith and salvation, only to find later that the same priest was an officer as ruthless as the enemy, literally encouraged him into committing collective sins. Indeed, it wasn't easy to just disregard the consequences afterward; the onslaught he had witnessed had created a turmoil in his conscience due to the fact that he consented it. He may not have fired a single bullet to lessen his burden, which may justify his participation, but it was him who had instigated the event. He should have let it go; now he carried the horrors that surpass everything else he had seen.

There was another concern—Carmelita, the unconditional love and prayers they shared together, saying he had found peace and forgiveness in leaving Cavite in faith, were all lies. By fate they would see each other again. He lied about forgiveness in particular. Seeing the man he spent his life in constant struggle and many close calls of death was down under a mound of dirt. For the man he had become, there was a time he admitted to question his decision and integrity, but Santos didn't deserve to die helplessly by betrayal. So much for forgiveness. Most of all, the love that endured with Carmelita, strikingly the same feeling with the one that was already in his heart, would be determined in time if leaving her also in tears was the right thing to do. For love of a woman it was, he was leaving another so thoughtful and kind.

He looked upward, only to see those stars above brightening up and any which one he locked his eyes on offering vividness. Many thoughts that caused him to light up a cigarette in a bid to clear his head and concentrate to what would randomly come. Carmelita was like those many stars bundled altogether; every moment that transpired between them since he laid eyes on her was a lifetime of memory. *"Should you find peace and free of all burdens, when your heart is full of sorrow, please find me on your side. I'm praying with you . . . I'm joyful with you,"* she had said to him.

A very profound love and thoughtfulness that he had no right to take advantage of even in the most forgiving hours, the solitude of every night after an inspiring day of sweet smiles and allures from the young woman were all worth extending a stay of another day or more. *"Let me hear the kindness that still beat in you, for a moment take out the rage and sorrow and feel my heart within."* That was the moment he felt her chest, tight with the trusting embrace, her own heartbeat pounding against his, feeling the warmth of her breath on his skin. Her scents was so satisfying, leading him to loosen both arms and let them rest around her soft body very carefully while letting his face get closer to a very charming face, somewhat submitting, very alluring. *"I will let your thoughts go free, free as I offer myself if it gives you happiness for a time we can steal. Feel my warmth if you cannot hear my thoughts but beware you will leave with another bleeding heart to comfort the one who need you most,"* Carmelita had whispered.

"Sir, let's take a rest here. My arms are sore," the poor lieutenant suggested. He steered the boat on an islet in the middle of the lake called Talim Islands. Known to be uninhabited, Soler also thought it would be safer to wait till dark to continue along the shallow shores of Binangonan. Aside from growing up as a fisherman himself, it wasn't the first time he went home rowing through the lake. Romulo had educated him on the geography of the lake. Fort Mckinley and a Philippine army base was a few miles from the eastern shore. He was stationed at the base before the war until it was taken over by the Japanese Imperial army. No cause to be alarmed as long as they were in the cover of darkness. Plenty of food they had to bother the people that were also seeking refuge in Talim Island, which was not necessary. For what they had, it did not give them a reason to wander away from their boat.

However, their coming was already noticed a kilometer away. Other fishermen in the area, already notified of their coming, somewhat offered the fresh catches one by one with greetings and exchanges of information. One would offer to bring them into their destination with his motorized boat, which they gladly took advantage. Hours before midnight, they were in Angono at a predetermined spot along a narrow river thrived by thick palms and bushes on both sides to end miles of water into a small cove.

Another half kilometer on foot, by morning, they reached an assembly of old bamboo houses, one of them owned by the lieutenant where his family welcomed him with tears of joy. He had a wife and two adorable children, all evidently denied of valuable nutrients on a regular basis, but as long as Romulo kept on coming back alive, poverty was not a hindrance at all to survive. They were joined by very happy old folks from the nearby abode and a few more to share a load of milkfish, fruits, and dried meat from Laguna and Cavite. A professional soldier, a gentle father, and provider, at the time of war, only that what he could provide when he came from a tour of duty didn't pay anymore. Only donations from friends and the money he had accumulated posing as a gravedigger and church help, some courtesy of the Molinas including old clothes and many more. Now he understood why they took the risk of overloading the canoe; he would think that Romulo could load more if he didn't take a ride with him. Well, he helped in carrying many fishes from Binangonan, trying to sell them to some people they met along the way, so many that were also sold in town that morning for valuable cash. And come to think what followed, the lieutenant tried to share with him the profits aside from the hospitality he was given.

The old Soler, bold and proud of his son, would dig out a gallon of *lambanog* he said he buried from a long time ago that was saved for special occasions. The time had come to taste its greatness with the USAFFE officer, talkative as the son. The topic was Japanese activities and the safest route to the next province. Cab would not remember any as he was knocked down by the liquor in so short a time. By the afternoon, he was awakened to be revived by hot coffee while recollecting his whereabouts. Added to *biko*, he swore once more he would never drink *lambanog* anymore or any kind of alcoholic beverages for the rest of his life.

About the same time, he revealed to Soler his intention to keep going. It was arranged that anytime he saw fit, the old man would give him company to Antipolo close to the border of San Jose del Monte, Bulacan. If there was anyone who would know topography and enemy movements in the region, he was the man. Before sundown, he left Angono with the usual gratitude and well wishes.

A FAITHFUL FATHER

The last of his account he was in the company of a fellow soldier in his bid to come home was with Lt. Romulo Soler selling fish. As soon as he left Angono, he understood that he was officially a deserter. Capt. Rodrigo Santos had explained to him the consequences, but at this time, he would not care anymore; his mind was set on reuniting with his own family just like Soler did. The cheerful celebration that he just witnessed gave him hope, a lot of it to wipe away his worried mind to what awaited for him in Pandi. He had his own beautiful wife to hug and kiss, father, mother, and siblings so joyful to see him again.

For countless days, he struggled against all odds and still did. Back with thoughts of the past, the longest time he had been away from home was overnight, trying to catch the biggest shrimps for Inez, to impress would-be in-laws. That impertinent fool of a father-in-law, who, with unexplained anger, resorted to have him marry his daughter when all he saw he was doing was trying to kiss her daughter. A real fool he maybe because he had kissed Inez many times long before that, and he was sure they had been seen on one or two occasions. Why had he waited in the brink of the war before he decided? The old man should have had a grandchild by the time of the Japanese invasion, and he wouldn't be an insignificant soldier who was only good at shooting loads of his rifle over and over again. Not a single time of experience how to unload his cannon. There were many occasions he came real close. At the count of his fingers, he would remember each time.

He was blaming himself not to follow the way of thinking of Rodrigo Santos or Captain Leonidez. He confided to the late Santos who could not understand his explanation to resist all the chances he was given. Then another evil captain who would lure him to stay in Cavite at the expense of Carmelita. He was coming home to Inez without guilt in the name the love he had promised and bestowed upon her. Despite many call of temptations, he is still a gentleman truly faithful to his wife. Despite all, he was happy to preserve his vow and fidelity to Inez though he admitted it was very close of him to not even come back to her because of Carmelita.

He looked back to see tall cattails, the same ahead and all around. By himself, he was lost already. His guide, Amang Fernando Soler, would say they were in Teresa, Rizal; about five miles was a Japanese base that was also a known POW camp. Darkness was falling again; he wanted to rush away as he felt he as if he were escaping another prison. Indeed, he was excited; the downside was he could only follow the pace of Tatang who was leading the way. They traced a short path, crossing the outskirts of Taytay to avoid checkpoints and detachments then favored the east straight to Antipolo from Marikina. As he was told, Tatang had maintained a devotion visiting the Church of Immaculate Conception and the Shrine of Our Lady of Peace and Good Voyage regularly on foot. A longer stint on duty that was usually three months, the longest to come home, was the most terrifying three months of his life to worry about his son. The reason for going to Antipolo was also as a thanksgiving that his prayers were granted.

"Will there be a real priest in that church?" he asked the goodhearted father of the soldier.

"Yes, of course there is," Amang replied. "Why did you ask, if you don't mind?"

"From where I came from, basically anyone can wear the long vestment and people will call him Father."

"Really, how would you know he wasn't a real priest?"

"I was one of them, and before that, I was many times in the sacrament of confession to a fake priest whom I got the idea—an evil one," he stated with remorse. "I always wanted to do it again, but this time to a real man of faith, to a true priest."

"I understand. My son, the church I'm heading surely had a real priest that I know personally. Indeed it would be best to continue where you're heading in peace and you will also be in my prayers. Many Japanese soldiers and collaborators proliferate in the church, too dangerous."

"I see, thank you for the concern," Cab responded.

"In about a mile, there will be another path that will end to a brook. Refill your water supply as it will be difficult to find another this time of year. Do not stay there too long, the enemy has claimed it as theirs. I heard story about a man shot at by just drinking water out of that spring. Make your own path in the light of day. At night, you will be guided by those lights down there in the distance—that is Manila. The clusters of lights end at the northern tip to Caloocan. The next town is Valenzuela, Bulacan. I believe three or more town is Bigaa. Do not come any closer to the lights at night. Only Japanese has the capability to let the lights on all nights. From here, all I can tell you is what I always tell Romulo." Suddenly, Amang became quiet, thinking.

Out of curiosity, he asked what he usually said to his son every time he left for duty.

"Nothing, I just realized other than asking when he is coming back, there is really nothing else. We missed him on Christmas Day, and many days after. I am a religious man, how can I tell my son that God shall be protecting him, guiding him to safety when obviously he is killing human beings left and right? I can only pray that he comes back to us, and I'm very grateful to be heard again," the man in his sixties stated, full of emotion, sadness, surely tearful if only Cab could see through the dark.

"Romulo is a good man, I'm sure he will keep coming back to you and his family," was all he could say to a penitent man in behalf of his son. "He was very lucky to have a father like you."

"I'm sure you have yours always waiting for you." The man regained his composure as if he had any reason to hide his feelings.

"Yes, sir, I believe they all are. I am excited, it has been a long time," Cab responded.

"How long?"

"Since the war began. I can't wait to see my wife. Two years had gone, I hope I still have a place in her heart. Honestly, I'm afraid. I had never been away from home for more than a day until I left to become a soldier. A soldier I became, the war broke and I didn't have a change to leave in good faith with my own family."

"I understand your worries. All right, be careful now. You are on your own. My prayers will also be with you."

About nine in the evening of March 13, 1944, he made the first step into another wilderness all by himself. Over the hill parallel to another down to many alleys of narrow rock formations, he chose making his own path on the top where he could see the orange lights from vast plains. There was no reason to slow down; no mountain range was treacherous for him anymore. No more darkness could hinder his motivation.

In no time at all, he was in Montalban, Rizal. In another no-man's-land, trees and bamboos competed with each other to occupy every square inch of earth atop the cool climate of the Sierra Madre mountain range. He kept on walking amid different sounds he could hear, nocturnal animals, birds of prey, or insects until he could not make a step anymore. It was a deep creek and no way would he go down there in total darkness then climb back again after a hundred yards. He blamed himself for not refilling his water jug as he was told. Now he had no more and was very thirsty. He had to wait until morning. He spent the last of the moonlight to walk around down the hill toward the light of the cities, watching the moon as it disappeared. He called it a night and just lay down on the ground until he fell asleep.

THE RENEGADE

Take away the fury. Clear your mind of revenge. You'll find me in your heart but I believe it's not me who you really want. I'm happy to think I am as you say because you're in mine.

His plan was to wake up at dawn when leaves produce condensations that would relieve his dry mouth. He had fallen asleep too long, only to be awakened by machine-gun fires followed by simultaneous explosions that caused the side of the opposite hill to crumble down the valley. Mortar fire, he thought at once, making him take cover immediately then crawl to investigate when it suddenly became quiet. The Japanese all together showed themselves to appreciate what they just did. For what he could see, they had no visible protagonist, but one who tried to escape in vain was made to kneel on the ground and was mercilessly shot. That fellow must have done something really bad against the Japanese for immense destruction they caused on the mountain. He could only watch them begin heading west, toward Manila.

Through the scope of his rifle, two hundred feet down was a point-blank shot. He could get one or two, but too many he would not be able to sustain a firefight. Should he pull the trigger and run? Sure, it wasn't really a good idea. Nowhere to run but a deep creek behind. Besides being alone, the enemy was more than the number of his rounds. The risk is way too much to be killed. He waited for long hours until they were out of range, out of his sight. He later decided to come down after making sure the enemy was gone. Heavy green vegetation in the browns indicated that there must be a spring on the site; he had to check it out.

He was right; at the lowest part of the hill where he came down was a small pond of water enough to drink and fill up his jug. For some reason, the flow stopped to a residual drop just barely managing to make its way down. He followed where it was coming from. From about one hundred feet to the site of explosion, he came closer out of curiosity to check what the hill had done to the Japanese to blow it up and leave. They must have some kind of dislike to the spring that was previously there to bury it into a rubble of rocks and debris. For a while he also believed they tried to a build a ramp of debris to easily come down and up the steep rock formations for their troops in patrol. But all his conjectures didn't make any sense. Up the hill was nothing but a little plateau that ended in a wall of thorny bamboos as the elevation got higher.

In a deep depression on the ground, he laid down the body of the fellow soldier and sympathetically covered him with rocks and dirt from the rubble. To the last rock, he noticed that the water had started to find its way out as it suffused the dry ground on a new path until it flowed freely again, filling another pond. He rinsed his hands heedlessly as he glimpsed at the tomb he made then closed his eyes to wash his face of as much water he could fill both palms together. In his mind, he recited his favorite prayer, the Hail Mary, short, prudent, and relevant. Many Hail Marys as he also blamed himself for not shooting that could have saved the man's life. It was clearly like peas in a pod compared at the last time rule one was defied; he hesitated but Santos took a shot and all hell broke loose—the lesson was learned in the most difficult way. In memory of a brother, many more Hail Marys were recited while kneeling, letting the water drip down his burning and exhausted body. Then he slowly opened his eyes to find that he was soaked in blood. He was bathing in blood. Looking for the source, he was terrified to see blood bursting out like a fountain. He made sure he was awake while grabbing his belongings very slowly, watching the water as it splashed out between rocks, forcing its way out. He could only watch a few moments; he ran away from that place as fast as he could. Miles and miles till his legs crumbled, crawling to as much distance he could make until his body refused to the last inch he could make, then he passed out.

Hell binding was the only word he could describe that hill. He had seen most horrific scenes in reality and nightmares; that day was on top of the list. He would not discuss that day to anyone as he himself could not believe it was real. (That place and event would take him a long time to find the rational explanation for with the help of a young boy who had read many stories about the history of war in the Pacific. To establish the fact, he drew it on the ground with a stick as his sixth-grader godson did it on paper with crayons. The narration continued.)

He recounted that he was already in Bulacan when he woke up. He estimated it was somewhere in San Jose del Monte where he was licking dews from stalks of grasses and leaves before the time roosters started crowing from afar, indicating he was near where there were people. Far away from the morbid sight that was still fresh on his mind trying to recover his sanity, cautiously he peeked over brownish stalks to see that he was in the middle of an unirrigated rice field that was harvested a long time ago. Wild grass flourished, new greens had been thriving indicating it had rained down not too long ago. He may be in Bulacan already as he wanted to believe, but in a vast meadow of assorted growth a few inches higher than his knees, he had to run fast again before sunrise. East back to the mountain was the best option. Immense creeps succumbed his mind every time he glimpsed back to make sure the woods ahead wasn't where he had been before. Over long meadows sloping up and down gently, passing many bamboo fields that towered over most trees as they bent down on their tips, was a familiar environment.

In many brooks and rivers where freshwater flowed all year long was where he cleaned himself up of the blood that had dried up on his skin, like the one near home where he would dip himself *"afloat even if the water was only waist high, daring himself to hold his breath for the longest time after a whole day in the rice paddies, washing himself from mud and oxides that stained hands and feet, then going home to change clothes, put pomade on his hair, a little baby powder to the neck and armpit, and he would be ready to attend to the horses."* The daydreaming continued.

"Horses they are, a mare he talks to often, making sure she was fed well because Inez is riding that damn animal, he could express his envy knowing horses could not talk anyway. He hears gunshots from the range, must be his old man and Mr. Sandoval in serious target practice, both insensitive and tough to admit there is someone else better than them. It's an ordinary morning and gunshots is normal on a certain day, it must be a Saturday."

The guns continued firing, many guns of distinct sounds that he became aware of a battle going on. He didn't care, he concentrated on washing himself. By the time he reaches Pandi with approximately three rivers to cross and many more streams, he could get rid of the dead skins that were left unscrubbed around his body. He planned to soak himself in every one of those, to be fresh and desirable when Inez opens the door for him.

But he wasn't home yet, and the world was at war. The fighting subsided to sporadic fire that was getting close to the stream. He may be alarmed but more of aggravation to repulse the fantasies that had been going on his mind. He hid on the embankment, upset to be muddy again.

The firefight was over, and in jubilance, fighters came through screaming and cursing, alive and victorious. *"Mabuhay ang Pilipinas, mabuhay ang Hukbalahap!* (Long live the Philippines, long live the People's Army against the Japanese!)." He heard the shouting of people he knew were Filipino troops. "Mabuhay si Joe Taruc!" He would have decided to come out and establish contact with comrades of the same fold, but a volley of fire suddenly burst again, on the air, mostly aimed at the thick vegetation along the stream right where he was that caused him to pray for his life again at the very moment. Hide as much as he could was the best option. He didn't know who Joe Taruc was, nor which division of the army did the Hukbalahap belonged to. The rules of engagement must be strictly observed. He was alone. Whoever they were, they were coming closer. The screaming subsided with loud talks that he could understand. He realized that any movement he may create out of the bushes could mistake him for an enemy; besides, he decided not to make contact. He chose to stay hidden even when the euphoria had settled down to loud bragging and self-glorification. Too close, he could hear them over; he could just assume they were "so many" as footsteps and voices took a while until it dwindled to splashes of water into silence.

He had to leave that place too; the Japanese reinforcement would swarm the area as always was the case, but he didn't know what direction they would be coming from. The safest choice was to follow the trail of the Hukbalahap troops; the downside was they were heading east to the mountains. Northwest was Pandi.

Coming out of limestones protruding from the ground, crawling to institute other options in the clearing than what he thought the best there was, he discovered that he wasn't alone to take cover in that spot. There was also a Japanese, wounded and gasping for breath.

Cab hesitated to pull his trigger because the enemy didn't fire his pistol that was aimed at him first. They stared at each other, eye contact held without blinking until one gave up to just face his imminent death bravely. The Jap let go of his weapon, attempting to get up, but he could only kneel and bow to him. Bleeding and exhausted, the Jap remained nodding, likely waiting for that one gunshot that would end his life. It didn't come. Instead, a canteen of water was handed to him. He could use one hand in futile effort as the other right was incapacitated. Cab lit up a cigarette then drank water out of the same container, eyes glued on the frail enemy as he tried very hard to stop more bleeding from his wound. The day was at the hottest; he could see and feel in severe pain the sweat and blood mixing. He could end his agony or let him suffer more; either way, he would die if he didn't do anything that would help the poor soldier.

He chose what his conscience dictated. He found something in his satchel to help the man bleeding. It was buried at the bottom of assorted things, mostly that were not his. A cap was most notable to remind him of its origin and a .45 caliber handgun. He helped him, even shared a puff of cigarette. The Japanese soldier was an officer indeed. He realized that the bar was similar to the one who halted a furious soldier from stabbing him once more with a bayonet a long time ago. The one who sent him to a hospital, only to slap his face many times until he couldn't feel his jaw, the same one who ordered and watched while another was pulling his fingernails out. He grabbed the handgun, stared at the enemy for a long moment. With many blinks and sighs, he thought, should he kill this man in retribution for what his comrades did to him in Mindanao, did to Santos in Cavite?

"If you arr not kirring me, saramat (If you are not killing me, thank you)," the Jap said later.

Simple English that he understood. He had actually wasted precious time realizing that the sun was giving shadows, indicating that it was already past noon. Well, if he was not shooting the Jap after helping him, he must leave. There may be more to come, and they would not consider his helping one of their own.

His direction of choice was northwest. He didn't know what group the Huk was, but being Filipinos, they must be friendly with the same cause. His instinct was commanding that he follow them. With them, he could gather vital information knowing they came from northwest where he was heading. Similarly, to trust an enemy was not reliable by all means, but he may be trying to explain his company was coming to hunt down the Huk. At the very least, there should be more Japs who retreated and were coming back for their fallen with reinforcements.

On the other hand, he realized that the Japanese didn't shoot him because it could disclose his position. They would both die either way. For him not to fire was a life he owed and he shall be indebted. Life for life, he wanted to keep his, and it was given by an enemy who wanted to keep his too. After a long moment of indecision, he was cut off by the enemy's salute. They parted ways in opposite directions.

Running again, he would not know what town it was; about time to find a civilian who could tell him before it got dark.

HOME AT LAST, BLUE HOUSE NO MORE

Hungry and tired, but the notion he may be in Pandi already created mixed feelings. His concentration to find the way was always distracted by excitement whenever he saw a blue painted house. A blessing he must say was to see a farmer rushing up to avoid the incoming darkness, but he ran away at the first glimpse of a fully armed man. The surroundings could be mistaken as his hometown, where the houses were a kilometer apart. A river he just crossed that bared a wide clearing of dry rice fields over narrow banks of palms and vines, wherever he may be, it should be damn close to Malibo. Long lines of trees that bounded his view over another clearing, a cluster should indicate a house therein. The topography was all identical to where he wanted to be.

Avoiding many bamboo forests and clearings, he drifted farther westward. As darkness fell, so did the display of kerosene lamps and torches began to light and aid the last chores of the day. As fast as they were lit, the faster they disappeared. There was a bright light that stayed about a kilometer away, and it was moving fast toward the north. He may not have been on a train but he had seen one many times. It was a train indeed, and that railroad would lead him to Bigaa without his asking for directions. He estimated that he was in Marilao, Bulacan, sixteen more kilometers to home. Farther over the railroad should be Highway 54, and in the vicinity were many houses. An incredible excitement began for him. His feet was adapted to all kinds of terrain barefooted almost his entire life. The plains actually felt like he was running on thin layers of hays. Then on the railroad where he would dare the train to slow down by not taking off from the tracks until it got real close to him when he was young. He may not be home yet, but felt that he was already.

That's what he thought; he had forgotten that the tracks was no different from the one in the south. In northern Luzon, every bridge and railroad crossing was heavily guarded aside from the railroad itself, which was constantly foot patrolled day and night. At the rate of his steps, he was about to bump into them. Thanks to the clear horizon, he saw their shadows a hundred foot away, but he was seen too. Without warning, he was shot at, and the only choice he could make was evade and run again for his life. The Japs wouldn't bother to leave their post and chase a lost individual walking on the railroad. They forbade anyone to walk on the tracks. Cabarles would change routes going back east. He was happy to find himself in a more familiar place, the town of Santa Maria. This time, he followed the riverbanks until he reached a bridge, a steel bridge he had crossed many times years ago but on all occasions he was over it. He should keep going under, a gorge full of overgrown cassavas and bananas. Across the river was the town proper, a densely populated town catered to by traders and merchants once a week. Pushing more forward was the town market.

There was another bridge one kilometer ahead connecting Santa Maria to Pandi where the riverbank was a lot lower. He was almost home. The bridge was still there, which was very narrow that even horses would refuse to cross if not guided on a tight rope by his handler. Even Inez would not dare to stay in the carretela when crossing it. He didn't know exactly what day it was; he was taking a chance to buy *pasalubong* (gifts) for the family and all, especially to Inez who loved to munch on fresh *jicama*. Well, the thought was good, but his appearance did not warrant walking around the market. Sniper rifle on his shoulder and a satchel with a bullet hole, he must be inviting a shootout in a place full of civilians, but he was not showing himself home empty-handed. About three o'clock in the morning, retailers must be setting up already.

Aside from being a farmhand before the war, he also steered horses for the Sandovals when they went to market, so much to say that it made an influence by impressing a lady and his folks. On a grassy lot near the market where the horses could mingle with each other so as with their owners and caretakers, it may be too early, but he was sure there must be someone he knew. Someone he hung out with before the war must be there. Only a few hundred yards, he would stop by.

At five o'clock, he passed the crossroad leading to the three towns—Sta. Maria, Bocaue, and Pandi, Bigaa, also known as Daang Krus. He was anxious to meet a man laden of different things worth one peso; heavy it was, the excitement was too much that he would take them all. On the last five kilometers of the thousands he had walked, the excitement was unbearable. Who wouldn't be? Very excited and inspired, the weight over his shoulder was way more than he expected for a peso. Hungry, there were plenty to eat. Surely everyone at home would be very happy as he was.

In no time at all, he reached the streams where he said he would bathe again. He chose the deepest part, but in dry season, it was only as high as his knee, but good enough. He could see their old house through trees and palms. Not far ahead should be the Sandovals' house, obscured by lines of tall bamboos along the streams. His heart started pounding in relief, from Davao by foot, it took another year of unimaginable horror and obstacles that he was finally home and there it was. So quiet though, but it was still early. Everyone must be sleeping yet.

But there was no one home. It had been untouched for a long time. Dried leaves on the ground indicated that no one was taking care of the property anymore. He dropped his belongings and rushed inside, calling anyone. "*Tatang, Inang!* (Father, Mother!)" No one replied. No brother and sister to welcome him in a burst of joy. The house was empty, including utensils and all he could remember that was there. Aside from birds chirping, there was no indication of life all around.

Most disturbing, the big blue house towering over orchards of fruit trees through the window was not there anymore. Maybe he was looking through the wrong window; he tried every one of them. there was nobody to tell him anything about what happened in his absence. He rushed back down on the ground and walked on a path. He was sure it was the same he had walked on a thousand times that led to the Sandovals' residence. No blue color, all green—the house must be obscured by overgrown trees. Many times he closed and opened his eyes as he kept on walking until he was by the gate. The house was burned to the ground except for the bathroom that retained the blue he wanted to see, made of concrete walls and tiles that would be left standing for a very long time. Only charred remains could be seen where wild vines and weeds had started to occupy the premises freely. There were no doors to knock on, no one to welcome and hug him happily.

At that moment, he yielded to an immense lonesomeness, alone and exhausted, deprived of sleep. He could not begin nor think of anything that would give him any more courage. He felt his body shaking, his knees trembling as he let himself fall to the ground.

CHAPTER 24

THE BEGINNING

April 8, 1965

"Ninong, what happened to the house that was there?" the boy asked out of curiosity.

"Oh, that was the old house that belonged to your ninang's family," the man in his fifties replied.

"When it was burned down. It must be a big house." The boy needed more to know the fact therein.

"During Japanese occupation, yes, it was a big house."

Then the story began. The five-year-old boy got more than what he asked for, events after events that lasted many years narrated in many beginnings, some finding the end, many didn't. Many events that was narrated in details and became most interesting in every bit of comprehension of the listener as he grew older.

"When I saw that the house was burnt to ashes, I thought I died. Your ninang was missing . . . everyone. For what I had seen, I certainly wished I didn't come home anymore."

"Where did you go?"

TOO MANY BAD MEN

April 8, 1944. An abandoned house and the one that wasn't there anymore but charred remains was the sight at the end of the line. What else was left for him when all that gave him courage and reason to live had vanished? The end of the hurdles was also the end of reason, the end of hope. The sanity that seemed lost too for a while was regained to feel the solid thing that was pinned between dirt and his ribs was the only barrier to call him dead. The only thing that was left in his possession, to find logic why he had taken it back and carried that pistol from a dead man justified its significance. He pulled it off from its holster and made sure there were bullets in the magazine then slowly let its point touch his skull. Numbness of body and mind for many hours just lying on the ground was all he felt, numb to the bites of ants and mosquitoes that feasted on what was left of him. He just stopped thinking; any which way he could reflect only led to the most horrifying ordeal. All his loved ones were gone, how much had they suffered?

He suddenly heard a loud sound, very close, that he reawakened himself to get hold of sanity—the neigh of a horse as its wet snout forced that heavy metal assembly out of aim felt that he wasn't alone somehow. Opening his eyes at that very moment, he was putting pressure on the trigger, halted of what was about to ensue. Eyes locking on each other, the animal let the same hands that took care of him touch his face as it reached down to a bony face of another stud that he grew up with.

A thousand miles he walked, indeed to be welcomed by an animal who survived whatever happened in this part of the world, which could not be explained by the horse. Somehow it had managed to survive healthy and strong on the loose.

In the presence of a company to cry on, to talk with, and ask the whereabouts of everybody, perhaps if the horse could talk, he may have answered already. However, it made him get up to his foot to feel the warm and bubbly suds that exuded from its mouth to his face. Withdrawn to self-starvation, the hope that the horse brought was good enough to start anew. If the horse lived, then the others should. He took many deep breaths in desperation to establish his mind to a propitious approach as difficult as reliving the sight of the grave of the first important person he lost in his life, the man from his grave who told him he would be reunited with Inez. If only he didn't die and made it with him to Malibo, maybe he could tell where they were.

So if the horse that played a great role in the reality of his dreams and fantasy was alive, then the object of such must be somewhere. He just had to find her and announce that he was back as promised.

It took him the courage of an animal to get up on his foot to revive himself of strength he needed to begin again at the end.

He went back to the family house to share the *pasalubong* with the only living thing who welcomed his coming. Though it could only respond with neighs and whines, occasional kicks of the back foot may be that he was trying to tell something too. He kept on talking until another darkness fell. To see more signs of life can be told by smoke from neighbors that was half a kilometer at the nearest, but it was surrounded by thick bamboo clusters that hid the house itself from afar. Could it be burning too? Burning refuse maybe, but to think there were people still thriving in the sitio, was it the sign of hope he needed? He had to wait till dark; the rules must be applied even in the place he was born and grew up in. Obviously the war also dispensed atrocities on this remote place, and it was not over yet. There was a house on top of the hill toward west, and over lay a chapel blocked from view by a little woodland. There were kerosene lamps moving in that direction along the trail from north.

"Put down your guns, you are also protected just the same in faith. It will help clear your mind. In faith to God, you'll be relieved from resentment. He will guide you to find the love you're seeking. What you seek is not what you see in me. What you feel about me shall give you strength. You'll find me in your heart as you are in mine. In the hours of anguish and torment, think that I'm with you, praying for you," someone had told him that. Truly he was thankful to reach home safely, but for what sense was he allowed to live just to find the reasons of coming home had vanished altogether.

The chapel he helped to build was not far. Two days and nights he spent in agony, he had lost everything as it seemed. A little bit more left in his sanity. He put away his guns as he was told. He would enter the chapel that was built in pure faith, kindness, and goodwill. The chapel where he said he would be married, but which happened somewhere else. He would find his bride inside and waiting was what he would like to believe. Otherwise, to begin his quest for her should begin where he could find himself first. Indeed, he had given deep thoughts to just walk back to Cavite.

For a long time he had gone, so much that he missed the place where everybody knew his name. So much was coming back in his thoughts. Domeng Mapangarap (the Dreamer) was what he was known in the barrio. Well, he never discounted he was, but if needed to be a dreamer again, he would find that dream that he kept on dreaming. He knew it was real then and now.

He was grasping reality from two and a half years ago. The memory was getting clearer with every step he made to the houses that he saw were still standing untouched. A hundred yards to the chapel was the large house of the Santoses where he used to visit with his buddies, not because they owned a store that sold gin and others but because of the beautiful sisters Loleng and Luring. They were close friends of Inez. Together they had also put so much effort in the construction of the chapel that also justified an excuse of many young ladies and dreaming sonovagans to take a glimpse of the one they fantasized. Only a glimpse from a distance because every one of the prospects is accompanied by a menacing mother or father who stood in the middle at all times, standing guard for their daughters. It wasn't easy to court a girl at the time, the worst of which was to spinsters if he was known to have nothing to offer in wealth or prominence. For Dominador Cabarles, to keep his eyeballs at the most beautiful one, rich, smart, and all good things put together in one, he earned the name *Mapangarap* that became synonymous to his existence in the barrio.

Domeng Mapangarap has returned, and for what it was worth, he could keep his head up to the people who used to belittle him. He had what he dreamed for, and no one can took her back from him. There was one problem; he didn't know where she was after a long period of time.

Mid-April 1944, a few bachelors were nearby the chapel, and in the dark he must know them all. Children played, adults prayed, mostly women. Something was going on in the chapel that he was forbidden to come inside.

He was noticed without a doubt, but none would spare time for him. He was still the Domeng that presented no significance at all to anyone but subject to shameful sarcasm and degradation that wasn't forgotten in time. One person to whom he gave the credit as the most irritating human being was Fortunato Hilario, also known as Ka Tato. His wife was in labor, and to what joy it seemed to welcome a child, he was happier to embarrass him in front of many people that had gathered around.

"Where are you hiding, the war is not over yet?" he said. "We are all starving here already, we have no food for you to spare."

He had learned to keep his patience for this man then; now was of no difference. "Your father died and you have no courage to show yourself until now!" Ka Tato screamed, making sure he was heard. Many more said, screaming the name of his father in vain.

He thought he had put away his guns too early; he could just shoot the man and call it even. However, strangling was what played in his mind at the very moment, mixed with grief to know that his father had died. Truly, Ka Tato had a point in his unsolicited ranting. He was not by all it means for the firstborn to mourn at his father's wake if there was any. He still wanted to strangle the bastard. Someone held him back timely upon the crying of a newly born baby in the background.

Adriano Guzman came to the scene. Similarly in disbelief was another young man with him, Ambrosio Gonzales. The reunion with best buddies could not have come at a better time. Eventually, there were many stories; none were happy to tell and fill him the gaps of time he was away. It was a sad beginning. His father had died, all right, buried just behind the chapel alongside with Ambrosio's father and mother. Domeng was relieved to learn that his mother and siblings had evacuated to the main chapel two kilometers afar. Neither knew what happened to Inez for she was never seen in the barrio since the war began. None could tell the whereabouts of her parents either. The rumors were that they were apprehended by the Japanese soldiers; some would say they were taken and held captive by the Hukbalahap for having ties with the Americans. Over his father's grave, he was briefed about the Hukbalahap with information that they may be camping in Batia, the next barrio in the eastern part of the town of Bocaue. Literally, it was situated in their backyard. The speculations was that it was the Huk to be blamed for the burning of the Sandoval residence.

Ambrosio was left orphaned caused by Japanese atrocities. Living in poverty to begin within a family of six siblings, his parents didn't make it from severe punishment of the Japanese when they had nothing to offer to them, food kinds or anything else of value. The sister, in her teens, was taken instead and later made it back; but the trauma and abuse she had suffered had caused her young life to suffer a horrible demise. What happened to Adriano's father wasn't clear, but he had also died in the confrontation with the Japanese in a separate incident. His mother was a midwife currently taking care of the woman who almost became a widow upon her child's birth.

The Sandovals just disappeared. His father-in-law, known to be holding an influential position in the provincial capital of Bulacan and pro-American, was rumored to be taken for those reasons. Otherwise the family was in hiding somewhere safe. The accounts of his father's death was known; certainly he was killed for being stubborn not to cooperate with Japanese or the Huk as folks who could laugh despite the effects of war. His more diplomatic mother who would do anything to ensure safety of his siblings was spared but had left their house at constant raid of "many bad men." They evacuated their house on separate locations, most likely on the main chapel one kilometer away.

Other than the Japanese, the people also worried about cattle rustlers and the dreaded Hukbalahap whom later he would learn forced the civilians to provide food for them. Money or sacks of rice were acceptable. The other disturbing information about all of them was they didn't like Americans and USAFFE soldiers whom they also shot in sight. The Huk camped at their property sometimes in the past until it ran out of food resources, and there were reasons to suspect that the disappearance of his in-laws and death of his father was to their doing.

Moving constantly from place to place, they must be the same combatant troops that annihilated the Japanese patrol by the border of Santa Maria and San Jose del Monte. He had witnessed their brutality, and their numbers of combatant forces was impressive. It was premature to wage war against them based on hearsay. He had nothing against them, but any actions that caused harm of any kind to Inez in their exploits would be dealt with teeth for teeth. He swore to hell and heaven that connived and refused to let him die yet.

On the same night, he visited San Isidro Church of Sitio Malibo. People were sleeping already. A large warehouse and rice mill nearby owned by the wealthy Hilario family was still there. Nothing had changed since the last time he was trading rice harvest for milled grains. So quiet at a night when all people living scared and displaced from their own home would lock every door and window that no way could he get in to wake up one silently. Through a broken window, he could see many people like sardines inside. Warmed with each body heat in the quiet midnight hours, broken by the persistent barking of dogs, it was somehow peaceful inside. Many families with two or three dogs each, so many around join forces with intent to bite, barking at the same time, but one would come tails wagging, whining of happiness that rescinded the others to calm down. The animal still remembered his master, indicating that the Cabarles family was among evacuees in the church. Some people were awakened eventually; cautiously, he relayed the purpose of his visit. In no time despite the hardship, to see each other was the happiest moment that rarely came by.

Though the fate of his father in the hands of the Japanese was confirmed, he was wrong to say it was out of stubbornness. He had sacrificed himself to buy time so that her mother, two sisters, and a brother could hide. In another incident at the account of his mother, Monique, she had to dance and strip for the Japanese in taking their attention so that they spare her daughters from evil intention. The saddest thing was none of them had information about Inez for over a year since the disappearance of his parents. The last time they saw her was also on the day of their wedding. The last of the word they had from the Sandovals was that Inez stayed in Manila since the Japanese occupation upon the advice of his in-laws who were frightened of rumors that many young girls were being taken and abused by the invaders in the countryside.

The decision to seek refuge in the church and abandon their home was for the safety of her juvenile sisters. Their house was situated at the edge of a thick woodland where said to be visited by many bad men. A circular-shaped forest where it got its name, *Batia* (portable water basin used in washing clothes), it was about two square miles beginning from the Sandovals' backyard past the town boundary of Bigaa and Bocaue, also the site of endless gun battles. Aside from different kinds of uncanny beings that lived in the place to begin with, there were other groups known to camp on its elevated expanse. Allied guerillas on the Pandi side, Hukbalahap in the Bocaue part, and all over were cattle rustlers and bandits that preyed on the people of three towns, Sta. Maria, Bocaue, Bigaa, and the barrio of Pandi. Poor farmers of Sitio Malibo were caught in the middle. A constant clash against each group and the determination of the Japanese to annihilate them all in land and air was never successful until they relented. Many clearings caused by forest fires, lit mostly by bombs and gunfights, had reduced the size of woodland by many prairies and meadows.

In the end, it became a Hukbalahap stronghold who was later alleged to be the same people who stole and slaughtered missing farm animals. It became a no-man's-land literally for a long time for whoever wandered in it could not find his way out, enriching legends and hearsays that the place was proliferated by unnatural beings that were traced back during the Spanish era. Throughout 1945 and toward peacetime, the Americans bombed the area in an effort to suppress the growth of communism in the Philippines. Military operations by land followed only to reveal villages of civilians inside the woodland. However, the fight continued between so-called subversives and the Philippine military that was reinvigorated during the Ferdinand Marcos regime in 1970s in the same area. Upon declaration of martial law that inundated Batia with constabulary personnel, it only began to cease on alleged disappearances and murders of its own residence.

ONE HORSE STORY

The only reason Cabarles escaped from Davao Penal Colony was an intense longing to reunite with Inez. He admitted however that he had lost the thought of her many times along the way. The only motivation to reject countless death calls was only because of her in general. Not to see her where she was expected to be was truly devastating. Given last hope she was holed up in Manila throughout since he left her crying in Manila Bay shore somewhat revived his inspiration to live. He didn't know how to go to Manila alone. Back to talking with a horse while reminiscing many happy moments that transpired right in that crumbling shack were all happy moments to relive. Back to daydreaming until he fell asleep, the horse would wake him up. For some reason, it wanted to say something to him that he could not understand. Perhaps it was thirsty. He gave the horse water as he also needed to drink, but it didn't stop showing unusual behavior. Every time he tried to touch it, it would step away and stop then look at him again until he understood what it may have wanted him to do.

He followed the animal about three hundred yards on a certain location by the grassy bank of the stream veiled by a fallen large branch of old acacia tree still clinging on the trunk. Still thriving with green leaves as it lay downward. Normally, cows and buffalos loved to munch on acacia leaves, but it was evidently untouched for a long time, indicating that there no more large animals around. An overgrowth of weeds browned in dry season surrounded other kinds of vegetation in vines as they gradually thickened to the center. The horse wanted him to get in as it seemed. Afraid of snakes, the reluctance was opposed by the persistent animal that he must go in as curiosity mounted over increasing impatience and perspiration.

About fifteen feet to walk into the thickest growth where the horse led him in, he noticed faded clothes on the obscured ground. Pushing down vines to make a path in the rush of blood to confirm presumptions had made him forgot about cobras and sharp thorns. The horror of war sure never relented to make his day. Two skeletal remains in the same position intact as they may have said their last prayers, without question, he could tell they were the missing in-laws.

A busy afternoon, from the ruins of their own house, he was able to make boxes where their remains were carefully placed. By sundown, when Adriano and Ambrosio came to him with a few information and food, he was done to the last shovel of dirt burying the boxes.

"Domeng, where are you?"

"Adring," he called the man from the dark. "I'm here." A call of instinct that he was actually hiding.

"Here, you eat first. I know you like it very much," Adring said. "Who are buried there?" Adring asked right up about the obvious human grave in sight.

"Mr. and Mrs. Sandoval, my in-laws. I found their remains," he replied.

A pot of *dinuguan* (pork guts, fats, and blood) sauteed in garlic and vinegar until tender came with rice wrapped in banana leaves. There was nothing better than the moment having a favorite thing to eat when hungry. Adriano also brought a rooster tied up on its feet. Later he let it loose after rubbing it three times.

"Why did you do that, it will be hard to catch it again."

"For good luck, thank you for bringing it."

Like the old days, they would talk of girls. Daydreaming together in that horse shack now crumbling and empty. No more house to view nearby, and missed was the girl who would come out so gracefully to join them for a little talk with plates of sweet rice and cold drinks. Two crosses staked down in full view instead added to the horror of what happened in that place. Domeng Mapangarap was still talking about the same girl, but this time they were discussing of finding her.

"I have reason to believe Inez is in Manila. I only had been there once, I don't know what to do," Domeng revealed what had been bothering him all day aside from digging holes.

"This place is so creepy, do you want to stay in our abode by the river? It's a safer place for you," Adring stated. "I'm sure we can find a way to go to Manila if necessary." He continued. He knew the friend was a "no-read no-write" man. All odds were against him to do such by himself. Manila was a big city.

"Yeah, thank you for your concern," he replied. "I really don't know what to do yet."

That same night, he moved to the east bank of Bigaa River, a horse to follow. Another half mile, they passed the chapel that revealed many crosses behind. It wasn't there two years and a half ago. In no time, he was appreciating a better place. None had changed on the site where he spent many hours fishing. His father's canoe was still usable, and the river still flowed with crystal-clear water though he was told human bodies floated occasionally.

"I have a net stretched in the water, do you want to come with me?"

"Yeah, sure," Domeng replied.

For a moment, he had forgotten about the war. The simplicity of life in abundance of the food, courtesy of the river, many other places like the vast rice fields that comprised the entire Malibo and beyond; many exotic fruit trees everywhere, tamarind and mangoes and many more along the riverbank, there was no reason to get hungry in exception for those who were extremely lazy. This part of the town of Bigaa was a paradise still, opposite to the eastern side that was turned to a no-man's-land. He would as well enjoy the feeling of home and forget about how the war had changed his outlook.

It wasn't easy. Inez was all that his life gave meaning to live. Where was she now? Every time he asked that question, it was associated with her teary eyes and a promise to fulfill. Any time he blinked his eyes, a different kind of fear would be depicted in his mind. A renewed kind of fear that any which way he thought of it, he wasn't capable to overcome. At least he didn't know how to begin. He had to go back to the evacuation center; his relatives might have more information they had forgotten to tell. They must have also known that he found his in-laws and that he had given them a temporary resting place.

For now, he let himself busy pulling out slimy fish from the gill net while listening to what more could Adring say to fill the gap during his absence. Later, he got tired of the same macabre stories he had experienced on his own.

"Would you please tell me something good that happened when I was away?" he grumbled.

"I really have not much to tell of anything in that category," Adring replied.

"How about the rest of our buddies?" he suggested. "How are they?"

"You already know what happened to Ambrosio. Serafin Gimenez is now working in the town administration under Japanese supervision. Things are all different now. Nothing can be told that will not end Japanese intervention," the fisherman replied in sorrow. "Do you remember Badong? Our competition on about anything? He is a collaborator and still the same arrogant bastard. He is a policeman in Poblacion," he continued.

"Have you been to Manila lately?" he had to ask. If he could not get away from it, might as well turn it to what he wanted to know.

"Never. Manila is the headquarters of Yamashita. The farthest I had been to since the war is in poblacion."

"The bus lines to Manila, is it still going?"

"Yes. You seemed thinking of going to Manila. Why?"

"I believe Inez is there somewhere."

"I suggest you plan it very carefully. In town, I met a girl whose parents go to the big city regularly. I'll see if I can gather some information for you about the situation in Manila."

"A girl, another one?"

"Yeah, a fish vendor. She is pretty, you know. I'm in love with her," Adring stated.

"Uhm, I believe you fall in love with many. Does she know you like her?"

"Not yet, the world is at war. I don't know what it would bring to us."

MORE THAN FISH TALKS

To brave into Manila required a specific place to go; otherwise, he would just become a lost vagrant if not shot in the middle of a Japanese domain. Domeng remembered Espana Avenue where Inez stayed in an exclusive boarding house fitted only for foreign students and the wealthy. Manila was bombed selectively in the opening of war. Should that place still exist remained to be seen. How would his mother learn she was in Manila may come with more valuable details. Should they be just afraid and worried of telling him the truth of what really happened to her? He set foot back to San Isidro church that same morning. They could use a basket full of fish too.

Something to go by, his sister Loretta was keeping a letter from Inez written on December 7, 1941, stating she would be staying in Manila. The second letter indicated a return address, no stamp, telling it was hand delivered. Full of emotion and horror, afraid. A reply after learning that his parents just disappeared one night with their house and horses. However, the return address on the letter was mind-blowing, which he would have to face: "University of Santo Tomas, Espana, Manila." As far as what he knew, only the wealthy and majority foreign students were studying in the university, all of whom were aspiring doctors and educators. His anxiety began to come back.

He discussed his intention to Adriano. He would begin looking for her in Barasoain, Malolos, in her aunt's residence. The fisherman was willing to help any which way he can be beneficial; the problem, however, was the farthest he had been also was to the fish market of Bigaa where his new fling retailed the catch of the day. Having many connections in poblacion, on the other hand, Adrian would find a way to establish communication with Aunt Rita Sandoval. Public transportation operators that plied to Malolos would be perfect.

With a garnish of fish for fast delivery, the driver complied. He extended his willingness to help by also providing information about Japanese activities on Highway 54 all the way to Malolos of which he could relate readily. A detachment camp in the town of Guiguinto that displayed tanks and cannons was very intimidating to passing vehicles if they didn't stop at checkpoint. In the availability of a willing cohort, the friends had labored a day to write a message to Aunt Rita.

The messenger came back with sad information—Inez never made it back to Malolos. There was no more Rita Sandoval as she had passed away a long time ago. However, a survivor of Aunt Rita indicated that they had information about Inez; in fact, a letter she wrote dated September 16, 1942, confirmed her location—UST, which was converted to interment facilities by the Japanese. Though a Filipina, her looks could really be mistaken as an American brunette, and in the company of them, she was one of them. It was indicated in the letter that she was constantly afraid she would be discovered as not a Texan as her classmates made it known to the Japs when they were captured summarily. Having reason to believe that a beautiful Filipina would not make it a night by herself, her friends would not let her alone on her own. She indicated that there were Filipino internees she had met and acquainted with in the campus, with the exception of some strict Americans who were appointed in the administrative committee that reported to the Japanese. She said she was fine and would stay safe until she was allowed to go home. She would complain about a shanty of bamboos the interns had built with diligence and resourcefulness of the Filipinos that when it got completed they occupied it as their own exclusively.

In light of the situation despite the elapsed time to date, great hope was established that Inez was in Manila. Domeng would go to Manila no matter what. But how? He had no money and didn't know anybody in the big city other than Inez. He couldn't even remember how to go there for he had only been on the place once.

One fish at a time, every minute and hours, day and night to raise funds. He could walk to Manila for sure, but there was no way in without getting the attention in checkpoints. The city was the kind of jungle he would be lost in with every step without company. All places were identified by the name of the street and landmarks of houses and buildings side by side, not by the name and kinds of trees and crops growing. Assuming he got in somehow and found Inez, taking her out of internee compound was not an easy task. He needed a place to stay. So many more things to consider.

The urgency of the matter was not easy to disregard. Inez was in an internee camp, and as he knew the life under Japanese dominion, she had been suffering to an unknown extent for a long period time.

In a week, he had gathered enough information; and through Adriano, he found former acquaintances willing to help. They could use more they could trust. Double the fishermen, twice the catches, more fish to sell, more time to spend with the girl of interest for Adriano. Her name was Pacita Salvador. Aside from exceptional beauty, she possessed all the characteristics of a true Filipina lady. Used to dealing with customers in a public market, she could be firm but most of the time accommodating, but not to Adriano's intention to whom she played hard to get. On the other hand through slimy fish, close friendship has long been established in the process with the fisherman.

Pacita was also studying in Manila before the war. As real as Adriano's intention to win her heart, the need to make connection with her required immediate resolve more than fish talks. For a man to show serious intent of heart to a woman, he must visit her at home. Pacita lived in Panginay. To get there was to go through the town passing a garrison that also served as detention center for captive Filipino insolents. Unless they were going through in collaborator's uniform, the possibility of getting apprehended was real. It was a fact that to be seen and disliked at any time was a reason to get the attention of the Japanese. Domeng knew who he was; he could not take that kind of risk. In fact, he chose not to disclose any of what he had been through with anyone. Adriano knew that Domeng was a soldier for what happened to him during the time he was gone; only a few he would ever know. His story about Dominador Cabarles began on the chapel of Malibo. Thereafter, many accounts to tell about him that happened on Bigaa River, with a few other names mentioned— all stood out in the effort to find a safe way for Domeng to travel to Manila.

In the newly formed alliance included Donato Peralta, another gentleman who visited his girl on a regular basis through the river. Well respected, influential, conscientious, and wealthy, he shared the sentiment of the troubled man with a missing wife. Having been to Manila himself a few times since the Japanese occupation, he would not discount the danger for Domeng to brave the city alone. Donato played a great role in getting things going.

As money became available so as exhaustion of all suggested options, most imprudent to the most sensible, all were deemed possible depending on the courage of the main participant. Each suggestion was alike to the mind of the determined former soldier who would do just about anything.

CHAPTER 25

AMERICANS ONLY

A TRIP TO MANILA

On a dark morning of June 4, 1944, after mumbling a short prayer at San Lorenzo Church in the company of Adriano they met with two town policemen: Baldomero Tobias and Serafin Gimenez. Though Adring had close associations with the men, it was Pacita and Renato who made their participation possible. Baldomero or Badong was an arrogant and opinionated man so fragile of a pride that needed to be treated with importance and distinction. A basket of fish was not enough a garnish to obtain his loyalty and cooperation. Serafin was quiet and always assumed that one word should be sufficient to explain what he was trying to say. They were both promised of land rights to till in the event that Inez was brought back from Manila. There was nothing else to worry about their loyalty except that both displayed the Japanese flag on their uniforms. They were serious collaborators as they were known in every corner of the town; the chances of leading Domeng to enemy firing squad could not be discounted.

Traveling to Manila undeterred by the Japanese could only be made by showing he is enemy friendly; nothing could be done better than wearing the armband. Domeng would wear one of those, and he would remind himself of a time when he was furious at anyone displaying them. His indication of refusal not to display a red dot met instant opposition. He would be explained again that it was part of the plan he must take. A pair of decent clothes was provided by Badong, only to his dismay that Domeng was barefooted. He complained that he had to give him his pair of boots too. Serafin secured identification papers that he was a policeman under the JIA of Bulacan Provincial Command.

Drizzling with heavy dark clouds indicated real bad weather coming. The first step out of the church required taking a deep breath again, to the fact that he was assisted by men clearly employed by the enemy. No carretela waiting, just a couple of men by the river standing by, Adriano and Donato. The second time he would take a trip to Manila in his entire life with only one thing in mind was to retrieve the woman he was with the first time. Same route to the bus station except that he would walk with noticeable changes on the surroundings. There was a gun battery in front of the municipal building held by Japanese who were also manning a checkpoint crossing Bigaa Bridge, and across the road was a Spanish mansion they had also taken over. About five hundred yards to the direction of Japanese headquarters was the bus stop along Highway 54.

In the company of collaborators, he hate the most added extreme concerns; at least he appeared to be one of them. There was absolutely no excitement of happiness this time, only apprehensions he could not deny he was walking to his death. The palpitation of his heart was entirely different to the fact that at any moment he could be betrayed or he could be led straight to the end of that narrow street where the Japs executed their prisoners. There was bounty on people like him, and rumors had been that the men he was walking with side by side had collected for a few they had betrayed. Added to the fear when Badong split right by the municipal building to report for duty, he could not discount the fact that Badong may also report that there was a fake policeman heading to the bus station. Although he knew only Serafin would come with him, the trepidations mounted to what was already in his mind. All he could do is keep on walking while looking for the best route to run back at the sight of any approaching soldiers. Another one hundred yards to walk along the highway walking straight to the elementary school ahead that served as the Japanese soldiers' quarters.

On that lazy morning when people chose to stay at home because of bad weather, only vendors and retailers walked by in rapid motion along with them. Every step multiplied the fear as he walked to the center of the town where there was no more possible escape he could take. On the little overhang that provided a shelter from the rain, they stopped and waited for the bus with other people. The fear may have lessened, but the shame increased, thinking that everyone stared at him displaying the enemy flag on his sleeve. Pacita Salvador was waiting as she was expected to come; she had committed herself to assist in the undertaking while having in mind to pay a visit with her relatives in Manila.

Dominador Cabarles could not count how many Hail Marys he had muttered already. He had overcome the first leg of the trip. He could breathe better while entering the bus for not seeing any Japanese. They picked seats about halfway to the back. He didn't try to say a word anymore; the reason caused by the moment rendered an awkward feeling to act confidently as the bus moved forward very slowly to a complete stop before crossing the bridge in courtesy of a big sign that said STOP.

There were no reports of atrocities against civilians along Highway 54 that involved passengers going to Manila for a long time. Though security of the only viable route from the Northern provinces was tight, the Japanese had learned to slack on passengers and merchants vehicles plying through the highway. The best time to travel was first trip in the morning right after the curfew. By chance, the rain also contributed to the sluggish morning that sleepy guards would not like to get wet to board the bus for inspections. Broken roads made worse by the monsoon rain was compensated by many vacant seats. No other choice he could make but let fate take its course on a moment he could do nothing but pray and be alert. He was sure he would fit through the window when it came to that point; he just didn't know how fast he could do it. In his mind, he rehearse many times how to bolt out through that window when the time came.

For the first checkpoint, he must hold his breath right in Bigaa Bridge, where soldiers must be the same soldiers who shot the fishermen down the river. Three of them boarded the bus, rifles talking silently to tell passengers to give courtesy. They walked in at the narrow alley between seats to occupy vacant ones two rows from the very last where he was, then the vehicle started moving again. *"Arigato,"* Serafin greeted. He said it too as they locked eyes with each other. Pacita on his left had to stand up and bow to let a skinny arrogant one sit right across the aisle. Two sat behind them. He could hear his heart beating profusely again; the closest distance he let these people to him since he escaped from prison was fifty yards when he could aim right between their eyes. Now just an arm away, he could do nothing, not even turn his head. About thirty kilometers when he was relieved, the Japanese disembarked at a crossroad in the town of Valenzuela when the bus is fully loaded with some passengers standing on the aisle. The longest thirty kilometers he traveled despite sitting down and only took about an hour. Normally, it would take him a day for a couple of miles. Another fifteen to twenty more miles to reach the destination.

Caloocan was the farthest they could make by bus. Many calesas were available who could only bring them to the remaining distance. The *kutsero*, Macario Noble he said his name was, found out they were not the usual egotistic collaborators. He agreed to bring them all the way to Espana revealing he had a friend periodically visiting the camp to bring food and material supplies to the internees. He became informative to the advantage of Domeng who also developed confidence to the good nature of the man. The topic that started about horses progressed how life was a struggle as it was, made worse by the intervention of war. Domeng could only listen with occasional inquiry about places they passed through. "Where could be the Japanese lurked at the hour?" Macario replied they were everywhere, many in plain clothes that could summon a swarm at any time at the sound of a gunshot.

Noontime when they reach Espana, two bags full of assorted supplies on one, food on the other they carried with them. Time could not be wasted because Macario would be waiting for their immediate return to Bulacan as soon as they retrieved who they came for. Serafin knew how to deal with the guards being fluent in Nippongo, and with a bribe of imported canned products courtesy of Donato Peralta, they were attended to without trouble and the guards let them in. They were referred to the Americans congregating inside a bamboo structure the closest distance from the gate. The trio were halted by an internee who expressed unwaveringly they were not welcome in that structure citing excuses they were soaked and wet with feet muddy; otherwise they must understand what it says on the board at entrance: AMERICANS ONLY. The Filipinos were sure that was only one reason to find listeners; they understood what the sign meant, and they had no intention to cross the line. Aside from being clearly collaborators on the footsteps of American domain certainly would be refused or perhaps being Filipinos was the only reason. Pacita would take charge; she spoke English fluently and for that purpose she had come to state the nature of their business by a woman looking for a woman that should not belong in the camp. Only she was let in, to be attended by uncooperating Caucasians who would not know anyone by the name of Inez Sandoval.

Either they would not betray one of their own into the hands of conniving collaborators who just showed themselves up to claim an internee was a Filipina after long years of interment or there was really no one by that name among the population of about four thousand in the campus. The fact of the matter was none would really disclose any information at all. Pacita could only express disappointment when she came out; none of the Americans were helpful, citing many underlying facts admitting all rational indeed. They could not bring Inez home as easily as they expected. In an area of about fifty acres of large buildings and scattered shanties obscured by trees and bushes, Inez should be somewhere within. The rest of the wet day wasn't enough to locate her with uncooperating people and the limited liberty they could be allowed to look on their own.

Domeng would not like the suggestion of coming back another day from Bulacan if they end-up empty handed, Inez should be somewhere in the compound and he would not give-up that easy. So close he is, the ordeal of coming this far should have no difference what may come tomorrow. He shall stay and find Inez whatever it takes. Time is becoming valuable, the last bus trip to Bulacan is six o'clock in the afternoon and they should be at the terminal earlier to be boarded. Well, they cannot blame the horse of Macario it cannot trot over many pot holes on the road.

Serafin had relatives in Tondo; Pacita had a cousin in Azcarraga (now Claro M. Recto), which was closer. Each one originally intend to pay visit on both places respectively, the real purpose of their coming was manifested on many meetings in Bigaa prior to the trip. They swore to facilitate assistance to Domeng at fullest extent and if it is his decision to stay in Manila, so be it.

At the Bautista residence in Azcarraga, they were welcomed by Victoria, the housewife who is happy to see Pacita in an unannounced visit. Despite getting alarmed to see her in the company of a man in police uniform, the short reunion brought happiness between the cousins. The nature of their visit was discussed at once apologizing she could not stay any longer but promised she would come back another day. Pacita left immediately to rejoin Serafin waiting with Macario on the street, and they left back to Bulacan, leaving a woman who depended on her words that Domeng was a good man. Alone in the house with two children on the street and a husband away, she had reason to worry about a complete stranger who hardly talked.

There were vacant rooms in the house previously rented by students before the war, Domeng can occupy one as long as he wanted. The head of the household, Crispin Bautista, was not present at the time on a week stint of employment to make ends meet in the struggle to feed his family. Victoria, on the other hand, helped in keeping a little business going by selling fried bananas and sweet potatoes with the help of the two children. Pacita's visit was by chance the best of time in the absence of Crispin; there were baskets of food that came in time that her husband had been away longer than he was expected.

Though it was disclose that Domeng was not a policeman but only a fisherman from Bulacan, Victoria knew it would be a lot of explaining to do when her husband came home; for a few days, Domeng was welcome. Having told in the company of a collaborator is only a disguise cannot wipe out Victoria's doubts though she trusted her cousin she would not put her and children in uncertain situation. Few days they agreed until things had been resolved. Until then she has to live nervously with a stranger, few hours in distress alone by herself until the kids come back from peddling on the street.

Petrifying hours she would show hospitality somehow trying to break the monotony with the man who was occupied of his own predicament. The setback of the day could not make him worry more than what he could imagine himself how he would find Inez alone among the entirely English-speaking population in the internee campus. He started very hard to recall all English words he had learned at the POW camp and by all means only a few coming up clearly aside from yes and no. "I will miss you," a phrase whispered in his ears by Rhodora X, stuck in his mind, inspired by recollecting all the times he thought about it highlighted with a kiss that made it unforgettable. In fact, he had rehearsed that phrase in his thought visualizing he will meet Inez that day.

The silence was broken shortly by the coming of two talkative boys, Paul and Fidel, age eleven and eight years old respectively. They were not happy with the many unsold snacks, blaming the weather. After a customary display of respect to their mother and visitor to whom they were introduced by the proud mother, they helped each other doing routine chores in the house. Very pleasant and responsible children, they learned how to cope with the hardship of daily needs to survive. Leftovers of their sale for dinner with no complain at all saving some of the same thing for breakfast. They are upset to miss the visit of Aunt Pacita, however the graces in food kind she brought for them shall be consumed eventually some other day.

THE BIG CITY

For the first time in many years, he will sleep on a bed, the convenience his room offers does not equal the freedom of grassy meadows where he could see the stars or the clouds. Where the wind breeze flowed freely with owls, frogs, and insects continuously making sounds over the night. He has to let the window widely open to hear those instead of the high pitched sound that returns humming in his ears reminding himself in a cage. He felt that he was suffocating. Inside a small room that fits the bed and a narrow space just to walk thru felt he is back in prison, he is soaking of his own sweat he cannot find comfort.

Imagining things that next day will turn out for the better, dreaming while eyes wide open into the excitement of visualizing tomorrow somehow she will find Inez. He is inundated of so many things to think about but cannot concentrate on any. He had seen the internee camp, the big buildings and the wide campus, the iron gate and fences that were lined of cardboards and palm leaves for some reasons does not indicate tight security as in POW camp that was surrounded by barbed wires. He can sneak in easy enough but the problem to communicate in English always lead him to abandon that idea. What would make of him at next daylight was bothering him tremendously that even going back to Bulacan was not an option anymore. He will die, but he will not dare to display enemy flag again, better be shot at by Japanese than abhorred by his own self. Another desperate hour, he could only rely on what a dead man always said: *"Calm down, we sleep it off then when we wake up. We know we are still alive."* Words from Lieutenant Santos who could sleep well at any situation, who would tell him exactly what to do in total desolation. *"We lived another day is more than enough to be thankful."*

He would not remember if he fall asleep but hearing people talking had alerted him. Through the open window, he observed people passing by casually in both directions, some jesting while speaking in loud voices he could not believe how untroubled they are. Children playing, adults laughing in the tune of vendors yelling their commodities to the passing crowd. *"Puto, kutsinta." "Balut, penoy."* First sunrise in the city, somehow he liked some *balut*. He went out of his room to see a worrying mother who would not let her older son alone peddling on the street. Normally she did it too, but the younger child was having a fever she could not allow him to even go out of the house.

With nothing he could decide to do just yet, he took the opportunity to wander around in the company of Paul. He was sure he could blend in in civilian clothes without problem among the people. Carrying one large bamboo pan each of fried banana on stick, he let himself follow the footstep of an eleven-year-old boy in a city proliferated by people freely walking on the streets of Azcarraga.

"My mother told me you're in the city to find your wife," Paul started.

"Yes," he replied.

"What does she look like? Is she beautiful?"

"Yes, very beautiful."

"There is a place not too far ahead, many beautiful women lives there. Do you want to check it out?"

"Sure, you lead the way," Domeng replied. He was delighted. Paul may be just a boy, but his display of concerns and intelligence had earned him respect. Immediately, a rush of hope could only be expressed by touting their retails. "Banana, everyone buy my banana. Large and sweet."

Business was slow; they had missed the influx of people. They hung out a while at an intersection to get him oriented on directions of the street. Straight up going to Tutuban Train Station, north to La Loma and Caloocan. South going to Intramuros, now home to

Japanese Imperial Command one kilometer away where they stand. Paul is really a smart boy. All he got to do is don't get separated from him.

"How far away are we to San Marcelino Church in Ermita?" he asked nonchalantly, trying to disregard the passing truck loaded of Japanese soldiers.

"Not too far away. Pass Quiapo Bridge, down thirty minutes more by walking." Paul pointed to the same direction where the soldiers are heading.

Just what his instinct dictated, it wasn't a priority at the moment but something he will find time when situation is cooperating. It wasn't a promise but he consider it is now, finding himself in Manila, he shall visit the Church one day. It is imperative to be accustomed first in the heart of a city also inundated with garbage every corner that gives-off foul smell and million flies that lingers everywhere. Pan handlers and fellow peddlers occupying the sidewalks with occasional sight of soldiers on passing vehicle. Carretelas rule the streets that are proliferated with animal feces and urine added to unbearable scent of rotten market refuse scattered by scavenging children competing with stray dogs.

Passing a few more blocks, they turned left to a narrow street with many signboards and establishments mostly not open for business just yet. It is the time he totally let his fate at the hands of the boy who just kept on walking, announcing their product. If anything he was afraid of happening, surely he could not find his way back to the same house he was staying by himself.

"Please buy our delicious bananacue, miss beautiful," Paul touted to a voluptuous woman they crossed paths with along the sidewalk.

Very nicely said even though the woman had an uncanning resemblance to Betsy, the interactions initiated by the boy to the young woman he called Ate Delia paused the anxiety building up in mind, suddenly diverted to the amusing kid but only for a little while.

Around were not trees and bushes but people and establishments. He could admire the architecture of concrete buildings and bold signs but the trouble lies on understanding those and anything written that kept on attracting his attention altogether, intervened by a woman who could maintain her size despite many are deprive of nutrition. Delia is about his age and shown despicable interest on food but the good looking peddler caught her palate most. Domeng can only respond with a smile appreciative of the woman's pleasantries on him over fried bananas so not to botch his first customer of the day. Delia has many hungry friends and there are truly pretty ones. Paul knows many things for sure, there are many beautiful girls he is seeing. Nervous or shy in the presence of many all making jokes and interest of his banana, his lips froze in good riddance it stayed to smiling mode while staring at every one of them. They are all beautiful confirming how Paul described them. One stand out over the rest, she is really beautiful to the like of Inez, very close his eyes locked on her. The heavy weight lady saying her name is Delia with a teaser about his silence for keeping his eyes to the one named Gloria. If only beauty he is after, he won't mind taking this one home instead. In fact he toyed the idea for a while, how easy it is to just take her home instead.

"I was already thinking all the hardship I was incurred was a curse of heaven. But how could I blame myself for easily showing interest on someone so beautiful then I cannot find courage to begin a simple talk. Always something my heart dictates for the one I keep longing for. Two and a half long years, I should say I have suffered enough. There is another I see who smiles just the same."

Actors and actresses, aspiring ones and bit players whose dreams and source of living were suppressed by war could only afford banana for meal without losing humor. Though it was revealed Domeng is a married man, he allowed frivolous conversations gaining new acquaintances on a background so different from what he was used to. Meeting many people in a new environment normally caused him anxiety at the effect of being illiterate, inspired by another pretty woman moving the count to first finger of another hand, he had forgotten about the first and the latest for a moment. When his effort to find the one in his heart become fruitless, there is another he can put on a pedestal just the same.

Walking back on Azcarraga St. whilst conceiving such notion, he would realize his search for Inez had actually just begun. Very premature to even think about that woman whom he can really take home for a night at a price. Shame on him he would even let it play on his mind at this time when he believed it is only a matter of time he would be reunited with Inez. The apology blown by the wind was genuine, indeed he would not dismiss his Inez could also be in that area and therefore visiting the place again is justifiable. In all what it seemed, Manilenas are friendly especially the women.

Not too far yet they walk when Paul is called in by group of boys his age. They are happy to see him all sold out and plenty of time till dark, they can play for a while. Cabarles didn't mind at all, he is fascinated by colorful signs he have trouble reading. ODEON and LOTUS written vertical, he is proud he can read but he doesn't understood the word below it that says THEATRE. Paul could not resist the calling of playmates he let Domeng knows it would not take long. Many more to attract his attention, many passersby at opposite directions starting to build up in the afternoon he is entice by entirely new world for him. Despite all the struggles of every Filipinos in the countryside, the killings and atrocities in rural areas; generally the city is calm with many people surprisingly looking neat and confident. Children can play, people can talk freely greeting each other's as if there's no war.

No signs of war in that corner street, just file of garbage. The battle that takes place almost immediately is against annoying flies that's just so many. Giant commercial board he dares himself to read what it says, a cowboy smoking clearly said it was an advertisement for a cigarette brand. Next to it is more interesting he had to be seated to appreciate a blonde woman in the picture he didn't care what the billboard says, he is charmed again by her beauty he started day dreaming about Inez while waiting for the kid. Eventually number of people increases blocking his view across the street.

What are the odds of seeing Inez among many women that catches his eyes, perhaps none but in his mind there is possibility. Seating on the ground with arms over bended knees, his eyes would not blink every time he saw a woman from a distance as they come closer then repeat the process only to find she isn't her. He is very grateful somehow when a lady handed him a penny in his disbelief. It can buy a pound of meat or loaf of bread. The kindness she displayed only prove angels can be found anywhere. Many more angels followed same suit, and many evils too he could not dock when he was thrown at with a concoction of liquid that made his hair sticky and stained his shirt. Why he was given pennies or why he was thrown at with refuse he could not grasp at the moment, nothing yet would break his hopeful prospects Inez is one of the people passing by. He remain seated on that spot patiently probing everyone thanking those who gave him alms while despising the unkind ones. Hours had elapsed he would notice the volume of people are diminishing to only few while the day is concluding. Suddenly he realize he is in the company of a boy. Where is that boy? He nervously look behind to see neon starting to light up the street but there is no sight of Paul. Distress succumb his senses immediately he would think he was left alone. There is no reason at all why the boy would left him behind and therefore he should look around.

Over the shrouds of cardboards and filthy burlaps are assemble of kids taking advantage of the last daylight having fun of their game, he approach them closer he could not understand what is the reason they are throwing coins in the air. Paul is one of them in the inner circle. Another boy who answers by the name of Big Boy is calling the game. As he approaches unnoticed thrown three big pennies he was able to catch two by reflexes that simultaneously break the fun making almost everyone running away at the sight of a grown man. Left an anxious boy who would not stand up, frozen as he is seated on the dusty ground after a glimpse of the man he recognized at once.

"Let's go home now, it's getting dark," Domeng suggested clueless of what trouble bothers the boy. What kind of child play involved throwing money in the air? Why everyone suddenly run away?

Paul look at him nervous and speechless, could not find a word to say in total apprehension. Domeng just grab his hand, alarmed of the incoming hours he knew only few left before the curfew. "Let's go back to the house now. Your mother shall be worrying by now," he repeated.

"You don't understand, I-I cannot go home. My mother will beat me real bad this time," the boy uttered refusing to make any step toward home.

"Why, what did you do?" Domeng asked, having no idea what Paul did to be real afraid.

"I lost all the money in heads and tails," responded the worried boy. "Mother will kill me this time. I should not gamble again." Seriously regretful as he explained that wasn't the first time he did it. As it was hard to earn by peddling, the money he lose included the capital and profit that would feed the family at least a meager meal in the following day aside from bankrupting their business. He is truly afraid he cannot handle the wrath of his mother the only choice to avoid the consequences is not to show himself home anymore.

"Yeah, what you did is very bad." Domeng sighed in agreement to the boy's worries. "It needed severe punishments that killing you by starvation won't be enough. I will hung you upside down while lashing you repeatedly with a large bamboo trunk if I am your mother, it could be worst if your father is home," he added.

"What could be worse more than what you said, that's exactly my mother said if I do it again. I really cannot go home anymore."

The situation needed a quick resolve, it is really a matter of life and death not for the boy but more critical to himself. If he would allow Paul not to come home so did he. He cannot find his way back and without Paul, Victoria already handful of the sick one at home then come this one who wanted to stay on the street is too much for her.

"All right, I will not tell. Let's go now," he restlessly said. "How much did you lose?"

"I said all of it," Paul responded. "Just tell my mother how sorry I am. I will not go home until I win my money back."

"Let's go back to the house now and I will take care of your sorry."

Rushing home did not help the kid to know how his misdeed can be taken care of, at that moment he had let his fate to the hands of an adult he just knew by name. The man is seemingly sincere to get him out of deep trouble he is in. How, he doesn't know yet. Her mother cannot be placate easily when it comes to their finances especially at this time of severity. By the time they reach home, his rear was stuffed with things he thought would deflect whatever his mother could grab to beat him in dire anger.

THE PEDDLERS AT THE IRON GATE

Paul get out of bed early that morning. The mood somehow indicates nothing that involved him seriously; only for coming back home late last night. Domeng is still taking all the heat from her mother about the worrying they had caused to caring mother. "Please come home early this time, don't make me worry that much again." All she said intended to both of them. Between cooking and attending to his sick brother, none of a moment she had stop from nagging as if she is talking in the presence of her husband. The poor man who saved his ass keep apologizing and accommodating at the scolding woman justified to her endless ranting. Paul remain quiet, her mother is not as mad as he expects.

"Thank you for taking the heat from my mother."

"You're welcome, but something you don't understand."

"What is it?"

"I handed your mother all my money to save your ass. You owe me and I intend to collect with interest otherwise I will tell her you are gambling."

"Please don't, but I have no money to repay you."

"You'll work for me."

"Deal."

About nine they are back on the street, not so many to peddle but they both agreed they have to get out of the house fast as they can. Though under strict compliance to be home at certain time, they walk north through a street that ends on Espana Avenue. Across is UST compound situated many buildings known to house thousands of English speaking prisoners. Domeng knows the difficulty of finding a way to get in and establishing communication with the internees is unachievable by himself but it can be done.

"Do you know how to speak in English?" he asked Paul.

"A little."

An answer he would not expect, on the other hand he blame himself he didn't took advantage of the chance of learning the language when he was in prison with the Americans. He might had known few that he was proud of and 'a little' of the boy put together may somehow make a difference. It isn't enough, the arrogance of the Americans to Pacita and Serafin who both speak English fluently suggested a different approach must be employed. What is it? He cannot think of any just yet. He is basically on his own in a new environment full of enemies ready to shoot him on site. No arms he carried but a basket of fried bananas, he concede this day maybe his end before he made that first step to cross Espana road.

Another question just to break the increasing qualms while looking at the long fence lined with mats, cardboards or sheet of rusted tin intended to isolate the camp populations from the locals. There are people, many walking on the side street, many peeking through the fence with packages or basket and bamboo pans just like theirs. The setting is cooperating, they can blend in. "Have you been in this area?"

"Yes," Paul responded.

Barefooted and clothes noticeably not his, an old pair loaned to him by the boy's mother fitted well. His shirt is soak of sweat already while he duet with the boy touting their sell on the air. They both rest down on a spot cautiously trying to find an opening they could peek inside through rotting bamboo shields over the iron fence.

Being a former prisoner himself, he knows the people inside are all eager to make outside contacts and the display of assorted coverings along the fence cannot deter majority of internees. Unlike Davao Penal Colony where a vast open range still separated the civilians from the POW Camp, at UST campus only a fence divides the passersby, visitors and vendors from internees. However he was warned that brutality of Japanese guards are just the same as they constantly reminding prisoners by punishing those who defy their authority. Bad for the internees who are forced to follow rules lay upon them, worst to the Filipinos who proliferate the outside premises as there are no rules applied to them, they are an open target of an Aritake rifles. He will learn none that serious ever happened but many instances the Japanese beat people on both sides by the butt of their rifles.

He befriended another vendor who occupy the only shady spot on that long walkway that parallel the fence. In her long stint of peddling in the same area, she had many information to share. In dull hours that almost no other soul walking by, their first customers by no respect are a group of Japanese soldiers and Filipino counterparts. Normally, Domeng would loathe at the sight of fellow Filipinos eating with Japanese, laughing with them, and obviously collaborating; now no more as he got this far by the help of one not mentioning he was actually in their uniform two days ago. However it didn't prevent him from getting agitated, "the bastards were trying to get snacks for free". Later he would know to get a business space on the area, they must have to pay. For now no sell yet but bananas they offer, they eat as many as they can. Half of their commodity are gone even before they can sell a penny out of it. Despite knowing they are getting bankrupt, they secured a right to peddle on the area at any given time.

Another desperate mission required desperate measures, many thing he had learned in prison by no means he had to do it again where it applies. Only this time he wanted to get inside. Peeking through holes could not allow him a better view of the campus, he knew the urge of getting in at this time does not justify the risk. Observe and evaluate, he has plenty of time. Fixated in believing Inez is inside, it is only a matter of time to see her. To renege when only a fence divides them is not an option until at least he could have a glimpse of her.

No sight of Inez, all he could see through are green bushes and leafy trees. Many shadows of skinny human being not even close to who he is looking for. In thousands of internees, he would have seen a couple of hundreds. There are a lot more to go on. The frustration of the day just built hope for another day. They left for home with empty baskets and no money, added by guilt it created into his mind of two centavos he turned over to Paul's mother is humiliating despite the baskets are empty when they came home. The woman is already burdened of a sick child she spent her savings in the black market for medicine, now worried of what they will eat the next days until the husband comes back home hopefully paid a week earnings.

Back to daydreaming or perhaps planning his next move, the silence of the hours inside his room made to accommodate two people with empty wooden bunk beds reminded him again of another place he had been. Where there were more than four systematically arranged so that the building can shelter many people that outnumbered the bunks. Staring on one, he would imagine people sitting there. People who would stay in silence, carefully exploring a suggestion while the others already asking permission to execute. Too bad, none of them are real except the background of crickets and crying of a sick kid. He could not sleep, his mind alone cannot resolve his situation to pursue an objective taking the help of a kid again when the sun breaks up. Normally he could imagine of good things when hope seemed moving towards what he seeks, he tried all the best his simple thought could put together and he should fall asleep from there. That night is not the same, what awaits tomorrow isn't clear but the will of God he shall rely.

Restlessness made him go outside the house. He had scoured the backyard few times. Thick grasses richly growing over the open land bounded by tall trees around he wasn't sure what's in it, the rainy season had made the nuisance weeds growing rapidly over the dried ones his instinct said a good place to play hide and seek with the Japanese soldiers when it comes to that point. He laid down at the end of property and rest. Where is Inez? He hope and pray he will find her very shortly.

CHAPTER 26

THE WAR ACCORDING TO INEZ S. CABARLES

(Excerpts from an essay written in 1975 by a senior student of St. Lawrence Academy, Balagtas, Bulacan, and published in the school paper the same year. Originally titled "Three Years Apart" by the same author.)

SUNRISE IN MANILA BAY

Left crying alone as she watches a boat swiftly moving away from the docks of Manila Yachts Club, she cannot bear the sorrow that suddenly enveloped her body and soul. Tearful, the man she love and married is disappearing from her eyes while wiping the tears as if it could give her a better vision through the morning haze. If the sun could shine faster she could have given the chance to see him furthermore waving that small piece of cloth, the only thing she could give more than kisses she bestowed at a time when fear suddenly took over the joy they shall share. Many hours she stayed at the very end of the mooring, praying; wishing the boat to come back. The joy that built up in her heart for so many years just vanished together with the person that kindle every beat of it. The love she endures is a love yet to fulfill, to whom she chose to share he is gone.

The morning view of Manila bay from the shore is vast blue sea where it meets the sky. Braking from the clouds ahead is a mass of land revealed by shadow thru haste that tails off from the mainland. Her husband of a day is heading somewhere in that island. Bataan for what she was told. Where he is going is not what worries her but going back home without him. Totally inadvertent of the occasion she was caught in sudden reflection of her love story that seemingly ended as soon as the boat disappear on the horizon. Sadness rises as tears suppressed to face the reality of unexplained trepidations that has been frightening her since Domeng took a pledge as a soldier. Only few hours had passed since they marry each other. Another day the chaos began, Japanese Zeros raid Manila.

With minimal resistance, the occupying forces under General Yamashita quickly took over the city; earlier declared as open city by General Douglas MacArthur before he retreated to Corregidor, later to Australia. Predetermined indefensible from the Japanese invasion, the moved justified to spare Manila from total destruction so as to save many lives of civilians. American and Filipino military forces left the city to Bataan on December 26, 1941 where they fought hard on a futile effort against the Japanese until they surrender and met their fate in the infamous Bataan Death March. Left in the city are civilians, locals and foreign nationals, and small contingents of soldiers and local police either dumb or brave enough to stay but the chaos created by the absence of government didn't last long, the Filipinos must accede to even worst scenario. The bulk of Japanese forces, heavily armed and displayed undefeatable strength occupied the city in January 2, 1942. They came unopposed but lines of curious spectators on the street. Inez Sandoval, also called as Niza with a friend are among them. They are heading in Intramuros from another attempt to reach her husband only to find a barricade at the street leading to No. 1 Victoria Building. Advised to go back home immediately while there is time whatever their reason to visit the place, it was too late the only option is to get into the building to take cover. A fighting that she could not recall how long it lasted, she and her friend found themselves attending on the wounded. Two weeks later she was transported to UST among truckloads of civilian employees of the former headquarters of American Forces in the Far East. Intramuros was easily toppled by the Japanese and reestablished operations and security immediately under their authority.

The establishment of new government in Manila followed while fierce battle to depend the island is being fought in Bataan Peninsula and Corregidor. Terror rule the city as soon as the Japanese took over.

Curfew was enforced outright and executions of civilians follows in payback of Japanese casualties that meted their death from defiant civilians and pocket gun battles with remaining allied soldiers who surrendered eventually.

It didn't take too long to feel the effect of Japanese occupation, hoarding and lootings started. Starvation begun as soon as they came as supplies of food were halted from the North and South. Hardheaded Filipinos keep defying orders to stay home as they also started to inflict murderous harm to the invaders who subsequently took advantage to enjoy what was left in the city, the women. Worth a life to depend by Filipinos, the young daughters, sisters and wives. Vengeful fathers and brothers took their bolos and started hacking soldiers when they see one randomly. The results was unimaginable but it was forewarned. The Japanese proven many times they would kill as many as they pleased in retaliation to their one that perished. The rapes and abused of Filipina women continues to the very eyes of those lucky enough to live and tell the tale, atrocities surmounted. Though many men opted to hike on the mountains, many are left and among them many chose to yield on the new authority. The rests of the population learned how to survive despite indignity and humiliation incurred upon them. Life moved on, lucky still breathing the next day to bow on the invaders.

Though internees had been detained in many facilities taken over by the Japanese in the progress of occupation, UST became a compound of choice to consolidate foreign nationals of hostile countries because many had been taking refuge already in the school buildings since the Japanese started bombing Manila. The swift takeover of Japanese Command of the University increased the population in the compound estimated to two thousands to begin with including Filipino evacuees. At the end of the same month they are estimated more than eight thousands including those that are not qualified internees. Refugees boasted majority of population for reasons like many have nowhere else to go; or afraid to leave because of unsure conditions outside the campus. Many locals walk in to escape atrocities that immediately felt throughout the city hoping they can be safer with people by whom they learned to embrace after another war. The Japanese kick them all out from the compound and UST became exclusive to foreign nationals from hostile nations.

Americans consists the majority. Less work for the Japanese as all voluntarily stepped out from the campus at their own cognizance with a promise of no wrath shall be laid upon them if they just go back to their home.

On the other hand, the captives that were sent in was given strict orders to stay or they shall be shot at. Inez Sandoval is among them and confused, she is a Filipina but taken in as an internee among civilian employees from the former USAFFE headquarters. A school identification cannot prove nor denied she is a Filipina and by looks she's more of a foreign national otherwise she is lying about his country of origin. The purge of the population to strictly citizens of enemy countries reduced the number to three thousands. In the beginning of February 1942, legitimate internees are documented and at their own effort a mini-government was established in corroboration with their captors.

Food shortage was under all circumstances felt eventually, however many Filipinos come together to support the internees with gifts of foods and supplies. Steady flow of such from thousands of Filipinos from outside the fence on a daily basis had been manifested throughout Japanese occupation. As early as the internment camp was established, the Japanese announced the Philippines is in total control of Japanese Imperial Army under the supreme command of General Yamashita. The announcement also came on a daily basis that the remaining Allied forces are being annihilated in battle front and only surrender can save their lives from the might of Japanese Imperial Army.

Eventually the Allied forces surrendered in the aftermath of the battle of Corregidor and Bataan. In early May of 1942, indeed Japanese loudspeakers keep on broadcasting the humiliating defeat of the Americans and it's allied and therefore only futile to anyone in defying orders of Japanese Command in the camp and anywhere in the islands. The internees had became adverse of unsure future they can only embrace the life inside the campus at the mercy of new authority in Manila and the entire Philippines. Escape is punishable by death as it was proven the Japanese are serious of what they say when two interns were captured attempting to escape along with few Filipinos who allegedly helped them. Bamboos and palms huts begun constructions for many who dread the heat and humidity on the overcrowded school buildings only for those who can afford to procure building materials supplied by enterprising locals. In all those time that passed, many individuals remain inside the school buildings afraid and terrified. One who had seen and experienced the brutalities of occupying forces in person can only pray and hopeful her loved ones are safe, especially Inez Sandoval who has a husband in battle front. She is yet to cope up of what her life suddenly became and it's only the beginning.

"Niza, please try to eat your food. There may be no more after this," a truly concerned and caring friend said.

"Sure. Thank you very much Ann." Inez blankly received a bowl of cold soup. She had to hold it with both hands. The shaking of her hands somewhat becoming pronounce in many cases she cannot control. Very nervous, not just the mind even her nerves indicates extreme worries.

"All we could do is pray and take care of ourselves, the Japanese ordered to close down the campus. We have no more communications outside." Ann disclosed of their current situation.

One scared women among others who had seen so much how to be a soldier is the most scared of them all. Still shocked of what they personally experienced in battle field and the harsh treatment of Japanese soldiers. Being held captives is not what worries her. All that had been playing in her thought was Dominador Cabarles and the news about the fall of Bataan, so much effort she had done to get information about him, so much prayers she devoted. Only she could perceived what more to hope for. Tears had been drained clinging on the courage left on her, inspired by a promise he will come back for her.

With only faith to rely on, she had more to worry at the hours of weakness. Her trembling knees were capable to stand-up but she chose to remain seated on the floor with fist clinch the tightest she could make to contain the shuddering. She prayed earnestly: "Oh God Almighty, I can bear all the adversities, but please spare no harm to Domeng and send him back to me." Many times over and over, her prayers and thought are concentrated to one person; two or more she includes. The fate of an unknown soldier that ended on her lap gasping for the last breath in a pool of blood was intact in her mind. So disturbing she could see his face that of a man that own her heart.

The siege of Intramuros left a terrifying agony that would remain in her mind. Dealing on many nightmares since she heard that last word of love from her husband is always so intense she could not learn to accept the fact that he is dead. It wasn't easy to forget that scene.

Ann Shelby, a classmate and loyal friend is one she can depend on, the courage she had shown and extended to her is unforgettable. She told many stories they shared together in early times of war, all were sad. In July, Ann mediate the release of Niza with fellow half bred Filipinos to work at a hospital in Pasig, Rizal that accommodates civilian patients; many plagued with different kind of diseases attributed to hunger, loss of sanity, and many more that seemed irreversible. Many would die denied of nutrition and medication. Beginning that month and many more to follow, she admitted less prayer she devoted for Domeng because there was no more time available to pray even for herself.

GIFT FROM HEAVEN

In December 24, 1942 of the same year she was transferred to another hospital in Mandaluyong in dire need of staff. As engaging her work would be, the more she would like it as she found success to conceal her own malady. Her new job is expectedly more engaging but assured minimal death. She took the job.

An outstanding beauty to volunteer for the care of mental patients would make speculations to many she is also one. Truly no one on her right mind would ever dare to step in the premises of a mental institution at her own cognizance. To those who were already insane, she was an angel came down from heaven on that Christmas morning. For the sane, she is also insane yet to prove she is not. A very filthy environment, human feces and refuse everywhere. Unattended patients running around as filthy while chasing flies, all and those few who attend to them paused to watch her walking immaculately.

The words of the guard still ringing on her ears. "Madam, if you're not crazy wherever you came from, go back now. This place is definitely not for you."

Where else is the right place for her? Where she came from, most people were lying on death bed, those that were not are weeping relatives already mourning even their love ones are still breathing. There are no madness can toppled that experiences. When a message from Bulacan that her parents were missing, presumed dead and their house were burnt to the ground, she had dried out herself of tears. She is no more of a weakling who will cry in burst of emotion and sadness. She needs no one to do and decide things for her. In constantly tormenting grief and sorrows she adapted herself to be resilient; she said despite all, her faith is intact and hope that a promise she was given would someday be fulfilled. She never stop hoping for the return of Domeng. Hope that she never let go of her thought though she admitted many times she just lay on bed tired she can't find time to pray for him.

The first step behind the shielded gate of Mandaluyong Mental Hospital is definitely not a walk on the flower field. She regret turning down the offer of the guard that she be assisted to the office of administrator. "It's a short distance. I can manage. Thank you very much." She said to still astound gentleman.

In no time she was approached by a man, by first look he is crazy. He really is, Caucasian looking in his late twenties. He will play a great role to the end of her stay in the hospital. One of many abandoned by his own people in the heat of retreat. No identifications, he carried nothing but a pocket full of metals when found. Sick and starving, some Filipino peacekeepers pick him up from the street and dump him in the Hospital after getting caught taking shoe off a horse feet.

"Good morning, miss beautiful," he said without inhibition having pre-warned what she is up to.

Genuinely polite into the like of a sane person, however a string of different kinds of metal parts, door hinges and nails around his neck and belly clearly indicate he wasn't. "Good morning too, my name is Niza," Inez responded. A handsome man despite his ridiculous appearance he said his name is John. She added a sweet smile and greetings of happiness that coincide the day. The guard ran to the rescue in anticipation he may do harm. "It's all right," she said. "John would you be kind enough to show me the administrator's office?"

"At your service, Niza. Follow me," John complied.

Mental cases frolicking on the morning sun after a good breakfast courtesy of visiting relatives, all attention to the new comer announced by clinging man so proud she is already known to everyone even before she could meet the head honcho of the facility. "The greatest gift of all, an angel came. Be joyful everyone." He definitely attracted the attention of everyone even those who are totally out of their mind.

A short distance that became too far. Naturally kind and accommodating, she would spent a moment greeting with anyone on the path. Older and younger, men and women she could not distinguish who is mentally ill. An older woman would not let her go as she embrace her like a movie star or maybe she also believe Niza is from heaven.

"How are you, young lady?" Niza greeted to unresponsive and sad looking girl close-by, she remind her of her own situation in the beginning of war. The girl only stared at her to confirm she is the patient, maybe both. Though unsure what kind of harshness caused her affliction, Niza hold her hands trying to reach whatever glimmer of sense she had left. A gleam of a smile, perhaps the little shudder of her fingers send a shockwave to the brain of the girl causing that response. In many instances the most she got from many individuals from the place she came from were blank stares of their eyes that were left open even though they already died. Her spirit afloat immediately, liking the place already.

"Merry Christmas everyone." She greeted loudly. No marching band but there is metal man who ran back and forth and around posed the most heartwarming welcome while singing to the tune of Jingle Bells. Well, he didn't had bell but the metals he carries did the job.

An older lady, dressed simply like many people that greeted her, catching up in the fun of early morning rendition of Christmas carols. She was presumed to be one of the employees, indeed the only person that looks having stable mind in the facility by how she is dressed neatly. Having sacrifices of her own, she could not hold it but express her admiration to Niza; more to be informed she is going to work in the premises. Niza could not describe nor knows what kind of work yet but any would do. She thank her for the assistance, and show equal esteem to the people that join them until they get inside of an office.

"My name is Dr. Fatima Abella, I believe you said you wanted to see the hospital director," the woman said as conversation became possible in the silence of the room. "For what purpose you come to this place?"

There she showed a recommendation letter from another doctor. The woman read it quietly while looking at Niza making sure the letter matched what it says to the person sitting before her. Not even close. Peeking over her thick eyeglasses in unequal raised of eyeballs without moving her head, she stayed quiet just looking at her even she finish reading, then looked at the paper again. Her behavior was expected; Niza would think prematurely she might be slightly unbalanced too having heard of forewarnings about her. Tenacious and strict administrator, yells at everybody; her reputation is substantiated though no yelling yet. Absolutely quiet and confounded, walk by the window and look outside for a moment without a word then walk around her table taking the other seat across Niza. She look at her closely then reach the same paper again. Niza started to get nervous.

Finally she said something while taking off her eyeglasses. "Your name is Inez Sandoval?"

"Yes, Dr. Abella," she responded. On her table lay a woodcarving that said it all. "Dr. Fatima Abella, Administrator."

"I'm sorry for my silence, but I have to make sure you come here as a staff, not for other reasons."

She understood what the doctor meant. "Definitely not to consult, Doctor," Inez replied.

"You make a good impression on your first day, I hope you really knows what you're up to. You are in volunteer capacity here. No one gets paid. We only rely on donations by Red Cross and kindhearted people."

"Being in a place that people can still observe the spirit of Christmas is a lot better from the place I came from, I'm sure my service here would be for my benefits too."

"I do hope so and you find it you're right. God bless you, Inez."

A short list of do's and don'ts until the conversation progress to personal matters. Admiration and respect between each other were developed in that short period over sad stories made understood in few words. The doctor was reminded many patients waiting for her attention. Dr. Fatima Abella is also the only doctor in the hospital, she assumed the responsibility of the administrator when the American who previously held the job was hauled out by the Japanese. Others just ceased showing up including most Filipino staffs and through her effort she kept the facility going with the help of volunteers. She also emphasized that she cleans bathrooms too among many of the chores in the facility. Understaffed and undersupplied of food and necessities, her coming coincided with many Filipinos bringing gifts. She also stated Inez is the greatest gift of all.

"Will you assist me on my rounds already?"

"Sure I will, Doctor."

The first day is witnessing an acquaintances without prejudice, half of the people may had forgotten who or what they are but still many others care for them in the spirit of family bonds. On this place, at least many can laugh and happy on their own world. Making reasons to be merry individually as they are clapping hands when Niza and Dr. Abella came out of the office. Niza is given a welcome so heartwarming appreciated very well even though she knew the people are mostly out of their mind. Amidst assembly of insane, one keep himself stand out with the noise he is making. Rejoice continues when it was announce Niza is staying to help oversee the hospital.

Mandaluyong Hospital was about a mile and a half from UST. A walking distance, Niza had found time to visit Ann Shelby. In a condition that became worse since she left the university, she is happy to see a friend surviving, barely. Beginning first few months of 1944, the security in the compound also began to relax. The Japanese knew there may still be internees who wanted to escape, but none have enough strength to do such. Food supplies they provide to the internees are very little it never sustain the population. The dry season produce poor harvest on the vegetables that already drained the soil of its nutrients and many simply turn to selfishness to ensure their own welfare. Though Filipinos didn't relent on donating packages of food and supplies, it was never enough the entire population became a nightmarish sight of thin and hopeless soul who also lose interest at almost anything other what they can put in their stomach. For the Japanese, the advantage of starving and sickly internees are clearly on their favor, the command of less than a hundred soldiers are more than enough to secure order in the compound.

In another account after the war, Inez narrated that the university was once proliferated by neatly uniformed students in whites on a well maintained landscapes were chaotically converted to a city of shanties and refuse by worst appearance of men, women and children. A panoramic view of people to remember all waiting until the guards were done inspecting packages of donations. She also said that in April 8, 1944, she visited the compound after few hours in Quiapo Church. The date cannot be forgotten in her mind as it was the same day she had seen the man as the object of her many prayers.

CHAPTER 27

MISS "U"

There was a moment I felt I was so close to her. I can't understand the feelings. Like a wind that carries her scents to refresh my memory of our happy times; it restored my strength and the greatest hope I will find her. She is always within my grasp, I can feel her so near.

A DAY TO MISS, SHE HAS NOWHERE TO GO

Falling asleep on the ground under the banana plants, good weather could allow him of good dreams he could sleep well in the backyard of the house comfortably. Continuously on that night till morning of the fourth day he is in Manila, an embarrassing morning to wake up hugging a fallen banana trunk as he gets exposed on the burning sun. He moved over on the shades trying to grasp what had just transpired in his fantasies. No more but a feeling of being rested well, the best sleep he had for many days. Inside the house is quiet, none of loud voice of a woman voicing out concerns on a boy about to peddle on the streets. He went in to see nothing, no one cooking but an empty table and a pot of water already cool down. He quenched his thirst anyway seeing a boy so quiet in one corner of the house.

"We have none left to sell, we have nothing to eat. My brother is gravely sick and my mother doesn't know what to do," Paul said rapidly.

Domeng would not know what to do either, as he enter the room of a sleepless mother who remain on the side of precious child quietly caressing his face wishing he would wake-up rejuvenated. Afflicted of lingering fever for three days, he suggested of bringing him to the hospital. The pills she spent all her money apparently didn't help. Without the husband and no money Victoria cannot decide what else she can do, she herself look sick.

Afflicted with a disease similar to many soldiers in prison who would die shortly, he immediately told Paul to find a plying carretela on the street of Azcarraga. The nearest hospital is two miles away in San Lazaro, along the way the worried mother lost consciousness. To make matters worse, as slow the horse could make, they had to wait until Japanese soldiers, Kempeitai, and their prisoner could climb up a truck blocking the street. The first instinct is to get off and run but Victoria passed out leaning on her shoulder he could not move with the boy already on his lap, He closed his eyes, holding his breath pretending he is attending to a family of his own. Only few feet away from the bastards already displaying brutality too early in that morning. Immovable and helpless against sudden rage, he followed the cool of kutsero who isn't saying anything either. Later he would reveal to Domeng he always wanted to run them over with his horse and *carretela*. Keeping quiet in the loathing of the man, *the probinsyano* could only agree while at the corner of his eyes he was trying to remember every landmark on the streets. He knew they have no money to pay the ride, most likely they will walk back to Azcarraga.

At the hospital entrance, he was surprised how they were attended instantly. Victoria seriously apologizing when she woke up complaining dizziness making the mother and son admitted for treatment. In the following event, he was later informed that his 'wife' is pregnant but the boy would need to stay in the hospital for observation of possible dengue and he could die. The kind *kutsero* must be waiting his fare and that he had to deal with nothing in his pocket.

"Can I pay you later? I have nothing—" he started to the man feeding his animal patiently.

The man looked at him then continued caring to the horse. "Is your family all right?" he asked casually like he was expecting what would come to hit him.

"The mother would be fine, the boy is not . . . A doctor gave me a list of pills to buy. I don't know what to do. I really don't have any money left," he replied. "Actually they told me the boy would die if not treated immediately." He deeply sighed.

"I only have a *piseta* (half peso), this may help you for now. I don't know how else I can help you," the kutsero offered.

"Thank you very much. I don't know how to repay you," he said, thinking. "How far from here to Ermita?" It was a long shot and unsure of how much more help the kind man can extend but running out of option he must visit the church now if possible.

"Very far, but my horse could take it. Where in Ermita if you don't mind my query?"

"San Marcelino Church, I have a friend who promised me help if I can visit the church," Domeng replied.

"Well, let's go."

No promises how he would be paid, just a random act of kindness to the man he doesn't even know. "My name is Juan, I live in Arranque," the kutsero said.

"My name is Dominador Cabarles. I'm deeply indebted to you. You're a saint."

"You are too. I know they are not your family but yet you're as worried."

Someone he could trust indeed, Juan Kutsero is the first man emerged for his aide in Manila. The man remind him of a gravedigger in Cavite who turned out to be courageous guerilla leader, a valiant soldier who also maintain the love and duty to his family and one of many whom he owed his life. At the moment he told him his name, he knew his life is at his hands too. He implied he was not the real husband of Victoria; he could deliver him into the nest of the enemy instead of where he wanted to be.

The emergence of the matter as the day transpired had prevented him to hang out at Espana Avenue. The previous day he was sure he had seen few into the built and like of Inez. She may lost weight but who didn't, a day to postpone their meeting would not hurt. Something came up that needed his time and attention. If any of those women bathing on the sun is Inez, she is not going anywhere. Besides he needed more resources and meticulous planning to get over the fence. He is afraid if discovered peddling nothing but a basket full of banana leaves could cause him lots of trouble. In between occasional conversation with Juan, he is imagining Inez coming forward by the fence where they can see each other. He had strong feeling as he woke up in that morning, it must be the day he would find her. That was his belief every hour, everyday it became intense. Not as intense for a worried mother who surrender to helplessness watching his son motionless and unresponsive. "I'm afraid, very afraid." Victoria said. It wasn't just the boy she was afraid of. For herself too.

THE BALDING MAN

"I usually pray short but it may take a little bit longer this time. Please don't go," Domeng said.

"You shall find me here waiting for you anytime you come back," the kutsero replied.

The biggest church he had seen, no bullet mark anywhere just yet. He made the sign of the cross, then say a little prayer even before he gets in. Only few people inside by the altar, with the lights provided thru many big stained glass windows he knelt down immediately on the last row of seat locating a certain spot on his right. "*Find a statue of a saint holding a rosary, the other hand raised expressing peace to the world, he is standing in painted white and gold platform. That is hollow and inside you'll find a bag. Take the bag. What's in it is yours if I'm not with you, there is more.*" As he was told, a wooden statue of a balding saint was there; he was having trouble reading the inscriptions of the name but he extend his prayers for someone's soul in great gratitude. He stayed for a while citing whatever comes in his mind in a hurry. The bag is full of money. Capt. Rodrigo Santos never let him down.

As slow as the carretela rolled down San Marcelino Avenue back to San Lazaro Hospital, his heart beats faster than the sound made by the horse when its feet touches ground one at a time. He doesn't stop praying, he locked his eyes on the beads of wooden rosary decorating the horse cart. First time he saw it, so as noticing Juan is balding on top of his head creating a shiny reflection at noontime on a busy street few hundred meters from Intramuros. The man is also quiet concentrating in commanding his animal as it steadily maintain its speed over broken and dusty road of San Marcelino then to Sta. Cruz. An occasional "hoh" and "hah" broke the silence of at least one of them at a time. Domeng remained in total silence, so many things playing in his mind, back in the thought of first time he was in the street of Manila, back to condition of Victoria and her child; and way back to the character of deceased man who dedicated his life for him.

"Did you meet the man you wanted to see?" Juan asked as they were passing into array of business establishments along Sta. Cruz.

"Yes, he never changed. Very prolific and kind," Domeng replied.

"I know a place where we you can buy all the meds that you need, I suggest we buy it now before we go back to the hospital."

"Yes sure. I appreciate all your help very much. I beg you to extend it to the fullest if you can. Honestly, I don't know much around here in Manila," he revealed.

"I will be at your service as long as you need me."

The truth he is afraid at every moment added by the fact that he is having in possession a bag full of money. All paper bills he didn't have the ability to even estimate how much considering his comprehension in numbers had exceeded over the count of his fingers. Sweating profusely, he needed someone to tell him what to do next. Long enough along the road he may had gotten an answer until the steed slowed down indicating they reach back to the hospital safely.

Paul is waiting by the door looking weak and worried. Domeng realized aside from just eating fried banana soaked in rain water a day ago; they all missed too many meals already. At the bedside of the young son she found Aurora almost unresponsive but awakened in rush of hope to see box full of prescribed drugs, vitamins and food.

"How are you feeling now?" he asked casually spoken with genuine concern. "You have to remain strong, for your children. God is helping us."

Many more encouragements with each other's until Domeng aired his intention to go back to the house with indication of coming back accepting a request to look over for Paul. Domeng is informed the younger boy is in better condition and it isn't the dreaded dengue fever that is making the boy sick. Something else, otherwise he is dead already, but the worries lies on the mother so weak the fetus in her womb may not survived.

Back in the house, his palpitation had subsided already as he is sitting in his room. The day full of tremendous trepidation somewhat ended without any incident. Truly he is being guided by the One up there he said to himself. The indications he will find Inez is not remote, his intuition dictates she is not far away. He missed a day but there's a lot of tomorrows coming. With a new acquaintance who implied willingness to help, the confidence surmounted. The meeting with the *kutsero* is a blessing as information flows while developing trust with each other short of disclosing what he is aside from a name he wanted to be called.

"My name is Juan, Juan Tavera," the balding man said as they had liberty to occupy the Bautista residence with only Paul present.

"My name is Domeng, from Bigaa, Bulacan."

"He is a fisherman and lost in the sea for a long time. Now he is looking for his beautiful wife," Paul cut in.

"I had seen you the day you came in Manila. We thought you're an enemy collaborator. Are you?" Juan needed to be enlightened.

"I swear to you I am not. The boy is right. I only come here to find my wife. I believe she is in UST."

NIZA SANDOVAL CABARLES, AN ACCOUNT OF AN UNFORGOTTEN DAY

Earlier on the same day, April 8, 1944, around nine o'clock in the morning, two women and a man were walking down in Azcarraga from Plaza Roma. One of them was Inez accompanied by Fatima Abella. From Quiapo Church where she offered prayers for the soul of many lost loved ones. She also witnessed the people being apprehended by the Japanese. Though she had seen many similar incidents in Pasig garrison, what caught her attention was the man inside a carretela. Only a few feet away, she was sure the man resembled someone she knew very well. Only a shout away to call his name, but she was frozen in the midst of frenzies by people who were momentarily distracted by the scene that halted the horse. Her heart pounding in unexplained reaction she maintain her eyes to the man slightly sideways and looking down from view where she stand. She just prayed for the man on this a day he was born truly miraculous to see him alive. However, the sudden gradient of hope were immediately turned to disappointment when a woman lay down freely on his shoulder then to his lap seeing the children in her full view.

It wasn't him definitely, but she was damn sure if she saw the same man alone; even in the crowd, she could not have prevented herself of what she would do in a leap of joy. All night she devoted many hours in thought and prayers in memory of the man that will always in her heart and mind. More prayers for his soul again while they kept on walking towards the direction of her former school.

In that morning, Inez and company went directly to Espana to revisit a few friends. It was a planned trip out of the asylum. Gifts could only get through the gate after thorough inspections by the guards, though they stayed along the iron fence in hope of Ann Shelby may come out of the building. They left after buying some snacks from the woman under the shade of acacia tree.

With them was a handsome man dressed on dark brown pants and shirt matched with Irish hat, handed down by Fatima Abella formerly owned by deceased husband. The same woman who also adopted Niza a daughter of her own the very first day they met. Together they share the effort of identifying who really John is, he had shown considerable recovery since Inez set foot in the mental institution.

John Bakal (metal), as he was known, was looking good in the absence of metals around his body in new attire, however he said so many things about himself. He chose to stay in the asylum he already called home, generally harmless and useful in many chores in and around the hospital, his hard work made the yards free of unwanted debris and refuse. The surroundings was neatly maintained by his effort. Niza was credited significantly in containing a nuisance man in the benefit of everyone. Meanwhile, John is still habitually fascinated on metals, lessened discreetly to turning his affection to Niza. He never missed a simple occasion without gifts for the pretty Filipina. Niza was always accommodating, she just doesn't know what to do in her drawers overflowing of different kinds of used hardwares.

In the beginning, reactions from other staff were unstoppable laughter on the unusual relationship. In many days that moved on so as noticeable changes in the personality of John who never disappear no more from the compound. Her conduct became noble and they too had change attitude towards dealing to John, to all patients in general. John in many cases was also useful assisting in patient care focused mainly in Niza's consolation that sometimes she would really take advantage of him to run errands for her.

Improved to almost normal lucidity but not remembering any about himself, the reason why he was taken with them on April 8 was also an attempt to reestablish his memory. John may not comprehend the importance of the day for Niza, in his mind a special day for someone special needed a special gift.

Back in the hospital before the day ends John approached on her desk. Looking haggard and sweaty, he was carrying a medium-sized box. "This is for you, today you deserve a special gift my lady." He declared with unusual satisfaction on his face that was likewise responded with always accommodating and sweet smile.

"Thank you very much John. What is it?" she said while receiving the box.

Normally it was a visible thing unwrapped and rusty, the box is heavy and having unknown content Niza got curious somehow on what's inside. A hundred nails, a car part maybe.... a door knob taken from one of the rooms needed to be reinstalled? She breathed deeply then she opens the box. It was a brass padlock shined to perfection lay on top of chain links where it is lock in.

"Happy Birthday, Niza." he said proudly.

"John . . . it's not my birthday. Today is my husband's birthday," she clarified while taking out the chain and the padlock in full view.

"Oh God, this is the security chain at the UST main gate." Inez sighed. The fear suddenly took place if he was caught. The Japanese had clear warning against pilfering acted upon a secured facility, the punishment could be death without pretext.

PRISON IT IS I MUST ENTER

Domeng had missed a day hanging out at the iron fence. Basket full of freshly bake rice cakes increased his confidence as a peddler when he reached UST, sufficient to last all day he wasn't worried if it sell or not. The idea is to establish a presence until he can devise an ultimate plan to retrieve his lady out of the compound. First thing he must do is to make contact with her or someone who may had known her. A former prisoner in Japanese domain himself he knew how much as he wanted to get in, it's just the same the internees wanted communications from outside. All he needed to do is to find a willing partner, someone who can speak Tagalog from inside. There is none. In a conspicuous change of convening internees in the campus, they avoid getting close anywhere by the fence. The drawback is frustrating.

Friday as he was told the day was. Security on the gate is evidently fortified with additional guards. A vendor would tell him someone stole the padlock that secure the iron gate. The influx of people along the fence begin at seven o'clock that subsides after an hour. Coming at ten is definitely bad for business. Walking with eyes over the fence most of the time hoping to get a glance of the same woman he thought was Inez two days ago. He passed the gate a couple of times, noticing additional guards manning the entrance that is now permanently close. Too late to disregard the call of one, perhaps buying but only wanted to inspect his basket covered with banana leaves. He was let go eventually but not after taking some to munch on for free. He went back to the house with chest still palpitating he could have apprehended. He can handle the talking but to no avail only on situation he fully understand whom he talked with.

Paul would remind him by saying "I told you so." Obviously Paul is a smart boy advising him to stay home while he pick up his mother and sibling from San Lazaro with Juan. He didn't listen; he went on his own.

With the alliance of Juan Kutsero, a new strategy was formulated. A package and a letter shall be sent to Inez Sandoval Cabarles and from outside the fence they can watch who shall pick the package. Simple as it may seems the letter is not allowed and the package is subject for inspection. Peddling by the gate continues, visiting locals are restricted by just dropping off their packages. Gifts are collected thru bars inspected and stockpiled until a certain hours it shall be claimed by group of Americans who in turn pass them to the internee. Juan Kutsero is one of them making sure his package is labeled with a name on it. Far and obscure from eyesight, they cannot see who is picking one with Inez name on it.

Sunday, too bad the profit was lost again even before he could sell any, but Domeng didn't care; in fact, he offered as much as the guards wanted. Too bad he took advantage too early of seemingly elated soldiers to let them peddle inside by sign language. The futile attempt was a test; he knew these Japanese couldn't be any different than the guards at Dapecol who can be bribe with just about any. If only he can communicate in the like of Pops Abrina or the wit and courage of Rod Santos, he may have said something or offer something the guards cannot refuse for a little favor but his lips remain sealed the whole time. Two words he knew, *bakero* and *arigato* better than nothing but bowing is proven safer to deal with the Japanese. Few English he learned from long time ago is better not said at all, best not to say anything at all especially in dealing with enemies with bayonets attached on their rifle. Let the kid do the talking. As far as the guards knows, he cannot talk.

On Monday, the gate had a new chain and padlock. The same day, fourth package to Inez S. Cabarles came with short message: "Miss u very much." All day he waited for Inez but was only disappointed when someone else picked it up, not even close to the likes of the person he wanted to see even at far distance.

In the mind of persistent and determined person, he believed what he wanted to believe. He believed Paul suggesting Inez may be sick inside one of the big building and may not be capable walking out of the building. The urgency of the matter suddenly require a bolder approach. They could not think of any aside from peddling and hope one day they will see Inez among the people bathing in the sun, no sign of the beautiful wife. As he became a common sight by the guards who always got free snack, he was finally let in but only on specific spot that indeed inched inward as days go by. In many cases he would share his profit to the guard even though there was none. The presence of a peddler who needs someone to do the talking for him became tolerable to the Japanese, an insignificant mute they said about him. In fact, Domeng was missed at a day he doesn't show up at the UST gate. By the same people he used to shoot when he was a soldier who had likewise did the same to him many times over.

Needless to say, bribing the Japanese did not give any result. He knew the risk of getting caught was real, just a matter of slight mistake. The soldiers will not hesitate to kill him for sure and the consequences would be the same to an innocent boy and his family. Maybe the neighbors also for harboring an allied soldier on the loose. The Japanese won't need to ask question who he really is, just stripped him out of his shirt and they will know.

Many days passed, the desperation increased significantly. He blamed himself to let his emotion and impatience to take over when he saw someone he really thought is Inez. The subtle effect of obsession eventually turned to paranoia. Many woman in the campus would look like Inez in his vision, a lady he embrace tightly who instinctively resist from his apparent burst of joy isn't the one.

"I miss you, miss you," he said.

The consequences certainly ended his earned privilege inside the compound. He may had established himself as friendly and generous but internee police still kicked him out. He was nobody but incoherent man with outstanding interest on pretty women, who doesn't. He was told several times no Inez Sandoval among internees, but his perseverance went over his head indeed. He knew the time and effort he put up to find Inez among the internees shall make its way to conclusion. But where else he is going to look. Where else he could find her but at former school that is filled with many resembled to her likeness. Somewhere she must be lurking inside one of those big building, maybe sick and confined. His persistence did not end yet, he just had to reevaluate his approach. He firmly believed that someone inside that campus is Inez, someone at least must have known her.

Added to self-pity is wasting a phrase he rehearsed saying, instead it got him into trouble. He would turn the blame to Paul for not warning him she wasn't Inez he was hugging and kissing.

"How would I know she isn't her?" Paul defended himself. "All I know is you're looking for a pretty woman. I thought too she is her. A picture will help, you know."

The boy was right, name was not enough. The kutsero seconded. He lost the one picture he had a long time ago, and the damn Japanese burned down her home where there were plenty. The only description he could rely on is what was on his mind of her, happy and sad. After so long, she definitely look different now.

A WHOLE CHANGE OF PLAN

On a candlelight that night, Paul worked hard to make a letter. Not only writing, he was also translating in English while Domeng dictated. He wanted to redeem himself of the very bad thing he had done. Not much written as both were having difficulties in composing. The letter must be in English.

"To whom we should send our letter?" Paul said as he was rewriting what they had composed.

"I don't know. I don't know her," Domeng replied. "Miss you, miss you . . .," he suggested.

"Okay." He paused thereafter from talking, writing seriously.

After a long moment, Domeng just looked. He was amazed observing how the boy could move that pencil so fast. If only he didn't cheat in school when he had a chance to learn, he could have done it himself.

"Your parents must be so proud of you. How old are you?"

"Eleven. I was in fifth grade when the war broke up, but I never stopped learning with my mother's guidance."

"You're so smart, here I am finishing sixth grade, and I don't know much in reading and writing as you are."

"My mother started teaching me when I was five. How old are you when you started school?" Paul was just curious.

"Twenty-two."

"How old are you now?"

"Twenty-four."

"It takes one year to finish a grade regardless of your age. How did you do that in two years?"

"In my school, I actually did it in one year. I may have finished high school if I didn't quit."

"Yeah, how did you do that?" Paul repeated.

"I have special privileges. Besides, my teachers and the principal were my friends."

"I don't understand."

"Don't try, you won't," Domeng replied, lighting up a cigarette to the last glow of a candlewick. "Go to sleep now, you'll deliver that letter tomorrow."

"What will you do tomorrow?"

"You know I can't go back to the campus anymore. I'm thinking of going back to Bulacan."

"You're quitting?"

"No, I will try to find a picture of Inez."

"Good idea. Try asking her parents, I'm sure there should be at least one in their house," the relentless kid suggested.

"Their house was burnt in ashes, only the ghost of her parents I can ask," he said in despair.

"All right, I will go to sleep now."

Eyes open all night even at his favorite spot on the grassy backyard does not give him comfort anymore. A fallen banana trunk that gave him company on which he also rehearsed the "miss you, miss you" every night became what it is supposed to be. Arm over his forehead as he lay down flat looking up in heaven partially obstructed by leaves, he is still thinking what went wrong with his mind during that moment. That bony freckled brunette was a tough lady he can still felt her strength pushing him back. He could not discount she's pretty, but to the likes of many widows in Bicol Settlement Camp. Many women refreshed his memory again but none of those his heart is longing for. Faces after faces intact in his thought, within three years span he won't forget the one but should he had mixed up what she actually look by now from many others. He admitted many times each one had taken his thoughts considerably. Should he had allowed to just submit himself to Rhodora X the first time, should all affection he allowed his mind for others is taking effect over his head? He could not discount should he stay in Mindanao, in Bohol or Bicol most likely he was dead by now or in the embrace of another woman. She may not be Inez but it will do as well. Same thing in Cavite where he was so close to take advantage of an alluring and irresistible Carmelita—so lovable, very kind and understanding. Should he take Gloria Villa home in Bulacan and be done with it?

Any one of those women in one way or another always came at a time he could not avoid to reminisce that there were many moments any decision he make would change his fate. He wanted that one woman he vowed to love forever. He honestly admit that he saw Inez in every women he can name at the count of his fingers, somehow they all worth to think over when all effort seems failing. Should he just come back and stay in Bulacan to wait until Inez show up by herself one day looking for him instead? What if she is really at the internee camp, sick and oblivious?

The humming in his ears had returned, this time caused by a slap so hard it brought him back to his senses when "miss you, miss you" was spoken to the wrong person. Too much for the mute peddler he acknowledged his objective cannot get a result that way. He cannot just park himself in the campus and look at every woman who come his way and hope one of them would be Inez. Much more to think his eyes could deceive him, doubting himself even he may not recognized Inez for not seeing her for so long.

THE PHOTOGRAPH

He went back to Bulacan the next day; the frustration could only be shared by Ambrosio. A new mission at hand but finding a picture of Inez won't be easy. He could visit her mother and siblings again, also see how his crop doing. As expected they were not much help. He could only put his desperation to what he knows best.

His rice plants grew unattended. Water lilies and weeds had overgrown most of it. The rice paddies is situated on a trail going to Batia and to Sta. Maria for that sort. However not too many people go there from the barrio. Maybe just one, he cannot understand why the man found amusement in humiliating and mocking him when he should know he is already troubled. Ka Tato knew his father, he may not know his landlord is also his in-laws and their missing daughter is his wife already. All he asked for is a little compassion if he cannot shut his mouth up.

"Oh, Domeng, where did you hide this time? The Hukbalahap are looking for you, you know," the man said rapidly in succession. "You have no more right to till this land, it doesn't belong to you no more. You must know that." He laughed, which could be heard maybe a mile away when he was standing only ten feet in the rice pad.

He thought he was right; the land was abandoned for two seasons. The man is also known he can interpret land ownership and seen in the company of land surveyors before the war. For what it is known, he also tills few hectares of agricultural land for the Sandovals.

Fortunato Hilario, twice his age, may deserve to be buried in the mud, but respect to older people runs in his blood. He understand Ka Tato and his old man had many altercations before the war but putting it on him in the name of Hukbalahap is what he cannot grasp. Well, whatever he said he tried not to listen; whoever the Hukbalahap is? His priorities cannot be influenced by Ka Tato. Just weeding the paddies for he have nothing else to do yet losing all hope to find a picture of Inez. Definitely higher than the crop but not taller than him as what Ka Tato said, he keeps on weeding disregarding the man who added more insults before he walked away. In an attempt to picture Inez clearer in his mind without others interfering he didn't stop weeding until darkness. Appreciating what his rice field turned into, the ambiance could have been best if Inez is with him. She just cannot get out of his mind and he felt he is getting crazy if he stay any longer by himself on that very lonely place. He feel someone is telling him he is not welcome in the property until Inez is home.

Talking to the horse again was futile, the same result over the grave of his in-laws. He left the place afraid he may get a response from both then he shall be truly crazy. Thru the brother of Adrian, he had learned that Adriano had eloped with Pacita. That same night he swim across Balagtas River to meet them. To greet and support the friends in devoted affection with each other into an enduring bond fulfilled in time of hardship. He was indeed happy for them, not needed to say his true intent to visit them is for another favor,

The pair could only listen to his failed exploits in Manila. He disclosed his dying intention to come back while implying his search could be just the same without a picture. He told them many beautiful woman in Manila but none he seek. One he thought she was while daydreaming his frantic actions resulted unpleasantly.

"Why? What did you do?" Adrian asked interestedly.

"I hugged and kissed a girl, I really thought it was her. Well, she wasn't. If only I could speak in English I can explain my action maybe. I was close to getting mauled if wasn't able to run away," he replied.

Came a time the story would be funny but not at that moment when everyone knew such mistake could cause his dear life. Adrian can only shake his head. He knew Domeng could not read and write, hanging out in an internee camp full of Americans and guarded by Japanese is way out of his league. He was truly courageous, lucky.

"What are you planning now?" Pacita broke the silence that suddenly took the moment.

"I'll find a way to visit Aunt Rita's house in Malolos. She may had kept a picture of Inez in her house," Domeng replied.

"Don't do it yourself, we can send the same man we sent before, he can do it for you," Pacita suggested.

"Thank you very much again, I want to go back in Manila as soon as I can."

In the 1940s, personal pictures were only taken on very special occasion; in fact, only the rich could afford to have their pictures taken. Inez Sandoval had posed for a studio portrait when she was eighteen. Domeng was given a copy he cherished for many years. He could not remember how he lost it but so much to say he lost everything he had in the heat of the Japanese occupation. What was the chance of having one more in her Aunt's possession is possible, by a long shot. His prayer was heard, there was one.

Staring at it all night, new spirit afloat he would not waste time. The next morning he is on a bus travelling back to Manila alone. He is afraid but the excitement drawn all worries, most valuable in his possession the eight by ten photograph. A thing he will protect with his life. The closest he can hold and look for now until he found the real one. With two inches border under thin glass framed in metallic gold color, the thing he carries is huge but he kept it that way for protection against weather. Excited, he knew when someone in Manila saw the picture till then he can prove her existence.

Ten days he was gone, the Bautista family is doing well in health and noticeably the business of selling snacks progress to a little food stand. Now they sell regular cooked meals. Aurora's husband decided to extend his weekend longer from wayward employment after learning what happened to his younger child and pregnant wife. During Domeng's absence, Crispin Bautista came home finally. Even though he was told of a man from Bulacan is boarding at their place and ultimately became their savior, Crispin remain apprehensive towards Domeng because he had discovered a Japanese collaborator's emblem and identification hidden in his room. Likewise the attitude is mutual, Crispin is employed in Japanese controlled power generation facility in the outskirt of Manila which in every way required trust of the JIP to keep the job thus he is believe to be a full pledge pro-Japanese, conclusively a *Sakdalista*. On their first meeting, nothing else are said with each other but Crispin express gratitude on how Domeng took care of his family during his prolonged absence. Domeng could only say about the beautiful family Crispin had, must be proud of the boys especially the smart and hardworking Paul. However, distrust with each other continues as jealousy mounted on the side of Crispin. Paul and Fidel would seem to become attached to the *probinciano* in the eyes of their own father made worst to see his wife Aurora wholeheartedly attending to the handsome "spy" despite she knew only days he would stay at home to deserve more attention.

The picture was shown to everyone eventually, true to how she was described in details.

"How did you lose her?" Crispin asked.

"I was lost in the sea for so long, when I found my way back she wasn't home."

"What were you doing in the sea?"

"Fishing," he replied. What else one could do in the sea aside from fishing, definitely he could not tell how he was lost for so long but at least it is close to the truth. "I have no other purpose in Manila but to find my wife."

Being a fisherman was dubious but looking for a wife is genuine as Crispin was told how much effort he had exerted already. What choice he has anyway? As much as he wanted to quit his job, he cannot support his family by sitting home. He has to go, leaving a promise of weekends to spend at home.

When Domeng woke up in the morning, Crispin was gone already. He rose up with no clear plan in mind. He never had anyway, he only depend what the day turned into. On that day Juan Kutsero is standing by on the street. He had a glimpse of the photograph. "I may have seen her," he said.

The problem was, he could not remember where and when. The hope it gave to Domeng was tremendous. It was possible thinking Juan is at best occupation to meet a lot of people.

The previous night, rain was heavy enough to make water puddles on the street. He carried the picture like the real person holding it with both hands as he walk over the muddied road. In Espana, he show it to Bertha, the stall vendor asking if she had seen her inside the campus. "Yes. I did see her inside a very long time ago," she said. "As a matter of fact, she also resembled a young lady with a Caucasian man and elderly woman not long ago walking by."

Now what to do, the information he was getting was mixed up. Inez is everywhere, he had proven he wasn't crazy. Crazy like the man coming, filthy looking adorned with shiny metals hanging on his belt. The man may attract his attention to remind him of someone tormented of the same affliction at POW Camp. The difference is the man he knew in prison was collecting talisman of different kinds. Different object that also adorned himself. There was another, the medicine man who adorned himself of leaves.

Recalling POW camp in Davao, in his thought made him seated on the ground leaning his back on the fence. The picture of Inez only complicates his search. Missing an Abiyan who can really do many things, he always wondered why Donono was never caught stealing from the American POWs. If he is with him at the moment, he could have just tell him to go inside and find Inez.

This man of strictly metals adorned his body passing back and forth is in similar ways noticeably lost his mind. Staring at his direction every passes is giving him a reason to think he is being recognized, maybe this man is also a soldier. Was it possible an American POW escapee from Davao somehow had also found his way to Manila and recognized him? He looked down to slightly obscure his face by sombrero attempting to light up a Lucky Strike stick. From his lap, he place the picture frame on his right side to free his hands just as how his back is leaning on the fence. Disregarding pair of legs coming closer, thinking he would not understand what he is going to say anyway, he remain quiet. Paul is far away. In his mind there's only one thing this man can possibly caught his interest, him. He was wrong. John Bakal snatch the picture frame.

It may be the shiny frame or the picture itself that made the man interested, there is no way he will let him get away with it. Too late to react and get up from the ground, by the time Domeng caught up with John was in a muddy crossroad where they wrestle for the precious thing. No one would give it up, the scuffle continues. One must be bleeding from the broken glass or from sharp metals as the fight progress rolling over with it in puddle of water. In a matter of seconds, the photograph he would protect with his life was destroyed while the metal man was taken away by bystanders who break them up. Wet and muddy himself, he tried to wipe off the dirt out the soaked photo as the image disappear before his eyes, tears fell right on it as no more Inez smiling back at him but smudge of dirt all over a piece of thick paper. So angered he wanted to kill the iron man but he is gone. Insane or a former soldier from Dapecol just picking up on him is no excuse. He did a very bad thing it deserved a payback.

Dubbed as *taong putik* (mud man) while taking the road back to Azcarraga, all people avoided getting close to him to realize another one added to the long list of peculiar characters frolicking on the streets of Manila. At first look, Domeng was someone carrying an L-shaped thing that look like a weapon. Obviously, he meant to do harm at anyone who crosses his path. What they thought was probably true, the man was bursting in anger and no more is more important for him but to hunt down another man who caused him so much loss. What is left of the thing he shall protect with his life is half of the frame, hacking the air how he will whack another nemesis. Well, who would not be afraid seeing him like that? Some people speculated he was a mental asylum escapee; others suggested to get the authority to bring him back where he came from. Block by block he walk around frustrated, for many hours on the humid climate of August that already dried out his clothing. Only a moment to pause seeing military vehicle coming by. Instinct dictated immediately he had to hide. Japanese soldiers driving around with some collaborators looking for someone disturbing the peace. He had seen them more than twice over a short period of time. He had reason to believe he had blown his cover and therefore there is no reason to still act mute and deaf farm boy or lost fisherman. He had expressed a lot of swearing out of anger and many should have known he is not also a harmless peddler.

He made it safely back to Azcarraga, he didn't come into the house but went around to the backyard. From his favorite spot, he scoured the meadows again to predetermine an escape route. What lies over those line of trees and houses was unknown yet but there is no other place to run if he needs to.

"Where have you been?" Paul asked from behind. "I was looking for you around earlier, the soldiers were everywhere looking for a mud man. Have you seen him?"

"Yes, I do. I had seen him," he replied. Darkness made his appearance unnoticeable. "Paul, what's on the other side of those tree lines?" The boy should know for sure; he was casual.

"Houses," Paul responded quickly.

"Would you find Juan for me, please? Anyone asked you about me, you don't know anything. Can you do that?"

"Yes sure, but why?"

"I'm putting you and your whole family in danger. I cannot be staying in your house anymore," he spoke. "I am more than what you know about me. I am not a policeman nor a fisherman."

What he should have done is yet to determine, his only trusted allies are a boy and a *kutsero* both considered to disclose his whereabouts under Japanese pressure. Though he had kept his real identity from them, being a dangerous crazy man wanted by the authority would not make a difference if get caught. He started to rethink of his objective, there's always something that held him up. He decide to just go back home, he is giving up.

Lucky for him, earlier the authorities had apprehended another man wrapped in mud aside from the metals that would confirm he is crazy and detrimental; he is the man causing disturbance of peace. As he fits the descriptions, he is also carrying piece of picture frame thought to be a weapon. He is send back to mental asylum where he belonged. John is receive by worried staff, he was somehow missed from his disappearance in many days. With amusing story to tell taken unconcernedly about what he had been through, his safe return is anticipated only not in bloody condition. Cuts and bruises are given treatment while the worried Inez herself despise the person who did such injury to harmless and thoughtful man. John should not be let out of the hospital premises anymore upon Niza's remand.

Meanwhile, Domeng received a message he was forgiven from malicious conduct he did to a female internee. In fact, Paul told him she wanted to meet him sharing hard luck of a man who just wanted to find his wife got slapped on the face instead. She offered help that if Inez was in the camp, she would find her. The meeting was arranged, and they met in a discreet spot along the fence with Paul translating.

Packages of food and supplies addressed to Miss U resumed, coming through discreet locations along the fences on a daily basis with steady bribes to the guards. Despite a serious and expensive effort, nothing of solid information would lead to Inez Sandoval. There were speculations she might have been transferred to Los Banos, Laguna in April the previous year or was released in early days with many Filipinos but the search keep going. Communications in trusting ways were established with many information that changed tongue and ears. As it was requested, a transistor radio was smuggled inside the compound eventually. Just as hopeful to know someone from outside had endless resources and capability to help them.

In no time, the Japanese security was tipped off that a radio existed in the campus and the search proved there was one. It was confiscated and destroyed by the Japanese connecting intelligence that "miss u" was somewhat a guerilla spy operation. Timing to favorable outcome of the war for the Allied forces in Europe battlefields, the discovery of the radio by the Japanese in the university and counterspy reports of communicating with resistance network dubbed as "miss u" resulted to heightened security; the worst of the situation began in effect among internees. By Japanese propaganda, it was not a legitimate guerilla network but a conglomerate of serious gossipers and rumor mongers. False believers who would drastically spread any information that came their way. The Japanese reminded the Filipinos that they must know all the Philippine Islands was a domain of JIA under the name of the emperor of Japan. Atrocities heightened to the point Domeng is advised to stay out of the streets of Manila.

Inside the campus, alleged participants were rounded up and punished severely, and the effect to already starving internees were felt harshly as food shortage became at its worst. Packages to "miss u" was halted eventually, and Juan Kutsero had long disappear into thin air. All civilians who instigated the effort also disappeared. Bertha who may have contributed in some ways also vanished from the sidewalk. Vendors were not allowed no more any place near the fence. People on the streets took the heat as punitive atrocities made them to stay in the safety of home. The Bautista family was evacuated in Bulacan in a continuous ride of *carretela*. The man who started it all, frustrated and otherwise hunted also disappear. The monsoon rain in early August of 1944 had aided them in safe travel to Bigaa, Bulacan though reluctant to leave their house. The danger to their lives was seriously taken as priority. In many ways, Victoria Bautista with children Paul and Fidel had supported an enterprise that became a household dialogue. In deeds and in thought the courageous pregnant mother of two and her children themselves had personally took part in the "miss u" network at the command of the soft-spoken *probinciano* who was obviously not a Japanese spy as they thought he was in the beginning. They confirmed, however, that he was a fisherman indeed.

Juan Kutsero who exerted a major role in the "miss you" effort remained in Manila; through him, the network was extended to the resistance that consisted of former soldiers and Filipino professionals. He had long speculated that Domeng was a senior Allied officer. However, the mystery of another man in San Marcelino Church that they visited one more time was never known. In fact, Juan and his unknown associates had speculated that there was no missing wife, rather she was dead. There was no *probinciano* nor a fisherman who would know so much intelligence about the coming of Allied forces nor one who organized and financed the "miss u" effort that turned eventually to guerilla network. Upon reaching Bulacan, Tuvera would learn that Domeng was truly a fisherman looking for his wife. He didn't believe instead he revealed to Pacita that the man had established himself as a high-ranking officer in the Manila resistance. Adriano would deny any knowledge he was a soldier, but one thing he could confirm about Dominador Cabarles: the woman in the picture was truly his wife. He was the best man at the wedding.

CHAPTER 28

HOPE REGAINED TO LAST FOREVER

THE LAST TEMPTATION

At the nipa hut, he used to daydream together with childhood friends, and many times alone, the relentless downpour forced Domeng to seek refuge. No one in his right mind would go out fishing in the already raging current of Bigaa River. Out of tremendous frustration, he refrained crossing the *sitio* just yet. He decided to stay overnight in the shack. Tired, disheartened, and alone, he felt that the wrath of heaven came upon him. The guilt it created in his mind to cause trouble to many people for his personal interest was eating at his conscience. He wasn't a soldier anymore; his wanting to become a soldier one more time and die one was an option considered most at that moment. But being down frustrated and exhausted in bad weather, hanging himself, was another thought that came in mind. Without Inez, it was just too hard what to daydream. It was time to give up; the surrender was very hard to accept, blaming himself of the unknown fate of Inez.

No one could see him crying, bursting his emotion and the loud prayers that draw in the sound made by the wind against tree lines were useless. Soaked and cold at a time daylight is starting to yield to darkness, there was something else he can do. He dug out from the wet ground a secret stash of moonshine, leftover a very long time ago. It's still where he buried the bottle. No one had touched it since the last time he and his friends drank half of it. Aged underground with some additives of local fruits just fit his taste, unlike the fresh one that made him drunk in Cavite.

The rain continued; he started gulping *lambanog* straight from the bottle. So dark nothing he could see. Obscured from his visibility was a raging river starting to overflow. He keeps on drinking, screaming regrets and repentance over Inez that if she is in heaven already, she must take him. Feeling warm eventually, so much to recoup on his thought. Frustration was undisputedly taking over his senses to the gory impact of war in his life, letting himself to ponder what freely come up in his mind and begin when he find good memory. Many things, trying to concentrate of any happy moment he had that is still fresh in his mind. The agile and funny Little Don who shall found happiness with Myra somewhere in Bicol. Nothing of such kind he could remember with Capt. Santos, nor of his own existence with him in the past years. His mind brought him back in Cavite.

What would he become in the guerilla force of a sworn ally and brother for life who instigated his suicidal vengeance for the death of Santos? A priest, an officer, and a great lover whose intelligence he admired and hated most for arranging to meet a traitor for him to kill inside the church where they posed as disciples of God. Capt. Nestor Leonidez, a.k.a Father Faustino, a very reverent priest, intimidating and murderous as a soldier. They both were. The most rewarding thought worth a lifetime to reminisce at anytime was the glorious Carmelita. He imagined between raising the bottle to his mouth a pleasure just the same if he stayed in Cavite. Too late to be pondering another mistake he did but all worth the thought, the other choice was a woman he dedicated his heart and soul now admitting she may be dead. Another woman who offered the same inspirations, kindness, and splendor; Carmelita is a woman that possessed the characteristics of the other. He may had her yielding, very understanding. As much as he wanted not to lose hope of fulfilling a promise despite all failed effort, the image of Inez overwhelmed his mind. The wind gust so strong he almost fell to the ground. He was not destined for heaven as Inez and his parents could only be. They were very kind and humble people.

Hours passed, almost midnight already, he could not feel the cold nor the splatter of rain against his soaked and numb body. No more of the *lambanog* could he taste as he kept pouring it in his mouth. At the last drop, he would try standing up, but he couldn't. Nothing else could form in his spinning mind even if he closed his eyes. They just stayed close he would not have any idea how long it was until he was awakened.

"Domeng, Domeng," someone calling his name as he lay flat on his back, arms and legs spread out. It was repeated he could not remember how many times before he responded.

The sky was blue, his clothes had dried. There were no more punishing winds, nor rain or dark clouds, no roof on the hut either as he open his eyes directly to the blinding sun.

"Oh my god!" the man said, seeing a gallon bottle empty. Seeing the young man alone and thought dead for a while, he was shocked and confused to see there were no other footsteps in the vicinity except his after the typhoon and the great floods that came with it. "How long have you been here?" The river was not passable for three days. How many days he was passed out he could not tell, and Domeng had no recollection there was even a flood.

Complaining of a severe headache, muscle weakness, and thirst, Domeng noticed the downed trees and branches. The debris that managed to get collected over the floor of the hut indicated how high the flood was. Any higher, he would had been swept away by the current.

THE LEGACY OF THE DIMWITTED FARMER

Another chance he was given, countless times he was spared even at a time he wanted otherwise. He cried like a child and asked for forgiveness from his Creator. He abandoned the woman he vowed to protect and be with; instead he committed many sins, in thought and in deed. He deserved all the sufferings, he could not get away from what he had done without atonement. All wrath from heaven was a punishment he would take and from then on he would hold dear his own life for whatever purpose it was saved again.

Needless to say in the mind of many people in the community, he was hiding on the riverbank all the time. Speculations that originated from the mouth of Fortunato Hilario who for some reason despised Domeng. He believed that Ka Tato resented him for botching the bid of his brother to secure an engagement with Inez by arrangement while equating their wealth to the Sandovals. The old man could not accept embarrassment that his more-deserving brother was dumped aside despite his serious involvement of courting the lady. Domeng possessed absolutely nothing to deserve a beautiful, educated, and wealthy lass. Working in the rice field all through his life that originated in the family blood line, Domeng was an insignificant farmboy, poor as a rat, fit only where he should belong: in the herd of water buffaloes or in the horse shack or in the river where he could keep hiding all his life. Now added to Domeng's reputation was a coward bloke who would show up and disappear every time there was a threat of enemy. Rumors were that Domeng was a soldier who did not change his attitude; in fact, it got worse to assume he deserted. He may be right on the latter.

Of all the many people who should not be at the chapel of Malibo, Fortunato was there among elderlies for after-storm chatting. Recent natural calamity added to already scarce source of food is the topic of conversation highlighted by destructed homes and crops. In addition to war evacuees, many more added in the crowded occupants of the chapel because of the storm.

"There is no more room here for you, go back to your hole!" Ka Tato screamed, overheard by many.

Domeng went inside the chapel anyway; no one could deny him to practice his faith. A short prayer done quietly, but the mocking of his manhood continued that hindered the sincere intention.

The truth about his stints and whereabouts during the Japanese occupation was there was no one who really knew aside from the Sandovals who was survived by Inez hence also missing and also survivors of his own family who chose to deny he was a soldier because they believed the retributions for being related to a soldier was what was making their life miserable. In general belief, Domeng reneged on the call of duty in the military; instead he eloped with Inez.

"He is a soldier, all right, what is he doing here now. I'm sure if he is, he deserted—a coward." Ka Tato had made sure his words bore into the mind of his listeners, young and old.

Dominador Cabarles could not have chosen a better time to pray in the House of God he help to build. He uttered many prayers at same spot he was always kneeling down. Same prayers asking for guidance for what he shall do for another chance he is given. One more prayer added, to acquire self-control so he would not strangle that man who seemingly had serious despondency against him. "Oh God, please tell me what to do, I want to kill that man when I get out of here." He said silently. He was heard immediately, someone opened the side door letting wind breeze felt like cold water. He went out that way and around the meadows he took the path going home, a home that is yet to rebuild.

His crops were not seriously damage by the flood compare to those on the riverside that was planted earlier. In fact, it was healthy enjoying bath of sunlight. He has something to keep busy. Well, as long as he wasn't visited again by Ka Tato, he shall be all right. In many times he would see someone coming from afar, he had learned the best move is just hide until they disappear. He said he might not be able to keep his promise to cause any harm against another person. August ended with the news of massive Allied forces closing in to the Philippine Islands, then long September begins as WWII in the Pacific Theatre is dominated by the Allied. A horse gave him company every day with all restlessness put to clearing the unwanted weeds in the paddies again. There was something to look forward for food when his mother and siblings come back home. He also repaired the horse shed, which he used as his own shelter temporarily; later he would build a nipa hut hoping one day he would see Inez from a distance coming home. She needed a place they will both call home. No Japanese in sight for many days but he hears bursts of gunfire frequently over the woodland. No reason to be alarmed as his surroundings look like a jungle too, many places to hide. He still hang out by the river where he could listen to the radio with fellow fishermen at night, he just never drank lambanog nor of similar kind.

On the last week of September, he received a message from Manila. Miss U had been located, and he was needed to decide the next course of action. The information came from very reliable source, in fact it was Tuvera himself brought the message from Manila. Timing to heated battle echoed from the highlands, he would be seen running across the meadows and untended rice fields of sitio Malibo. In the eyes of Ka Tato and company, a cowardly act not worth for a man his size, one who can't defend a wife from a fly running away from his turf like a dog with tail inserted between his legs.

The excitement brought upon by a message from Juan Tavera was enough to begin a new hope. He knew Manila would be under siege any time in the coming of Allied forces, he also knows the Japanese would not give up the city without a fight and they fight persistently. If Inez had been found anywhere she might be, he wanted to be with her when Manila is liberated.

Juan was sure about his information; the problem existing was it was clearly suicidal to go to Manila at the time where every crossing along Highway 54 was a blockage of Japanese soldiers. Fortified sandbags and machine guns in heavy alert. Going out of the city may be permissible but surely not going in. According to Juan, Manila was just the same, many Japanese positioned in places just shooting people at their sight. He was not interested in the Japanese; he just wanted to get Inez safe before all hell broke out. It had already begun.

RELIABLE INFORMANTS

A man so hopeful anew and desperate could not be scared by raging bullets alone; air raids were a different matter, but clearly it was not from Zeros. Allied planes had flown over Manila. For two nights, Juan and Domeng reached Manila by foot through the railroad that was clearly sabotaged in many spans. At least one of them carried a weapon; the kutsero was armed and didn't mind if he left his horse and carretela in Bigaa. A survivor of many battles against the Japanese, he believed that adopting rule one was the only option to reach Manila alive. Juan was advised that in any situation, he could not shoot back nor could not risk getting caught, which was worse than dead. Back at the Bautista residence in Azcarraga, people were awakened on their coming. He was introduced and greeted as well. New faces he was not comfortable with, but he took hold of Juan's association with them. Manuel Kalaw, brothers Ramon and Rosendo Tiglao, and two young women he had encountered in his earlier stint in the city, all were major players in the Miss U undertakings that expanded in the greater Manila area.

He got so excited when he thought that one of the women was Inez herself, but no, just as pretty. The same girl he laid his eyes on while selling bananacue across the street where the Odeon and

Lotus theaters are, she must be exalted as well to be reacquainted with Domeng. A few times they had met, she could not understand herself for longing to eat bananas the soft-spoken vendor was selling until he disappeared. Meeting the man in another identity of noblest personality be it known he is the elusive leader of the guerilla network in Manila made her put the dignified Domeng on a pedestal than just missing his banana. Gloria Villa and her friend Delia Tagle, both performing artists in Manila theaters, could only make their lips tight in knowing that the man they were making fun with and could only smile very timidly was also a man on the top ranks of the resistance.

Domeng was desperate to find the wife, not another pretty girl or a fat and talkative one. Though he had at one time imagined bringing Gloria home instead, he didn't want to think of such idea anymore. He looked at Juan who was waiting for the true story why he had to come in Manila if not for Inez. He appreciated being served with a hot meal by another beautiful lady, but he wanted what he came back for. It wasn't easy to run sixty-five kilometers.

"Would someone please tell me why I should be here?" A little impatience showed in his voice while grateful for the cup of coffee handed to him by Gloria. A short glimpse of her with a smile calmed him down somehow, then he took a long deep sigh.

Juan had previously informed Domeng that Inez was in a hospital; he was not able to elaborate more of her condition nor what kind of hospital because he actually didn't know the details yet. Tuvera had relied from an information, verified and substantiated by the source of the information, that it would be for the best that Domeng saw her himself.

All attention was taken by someone who barged in before anyone could say a word. For all the people present, they knew who was coming. They were used to him just coming and going as he pleased. Domeng did not easily forget; he knew him too very well. His intent to kill that man still stood. At any given condition, he would do just that. A rapid surge of blood in his already frantic disposition, he did not waste a moment. He tackled the man who stole and destroyed the photograph of Inez. Pushing his head on the ground then strangling him so hard, the man was gasping for breath before someone reacted to break him out. Domeng was ultimately thwarted to an unsuccessful attempt; all the men didn't allow him to get close to him anymore, saying he was mentally deranged.

He apologized and calmed down indeed when someone said that John was a friend of Inez. Domeng could only justify his sudden outburst of anger by disclosing the story about Inez's photograph.

"We believe that Inez is in the mental asylum in Mandaluyong where he was staying," Manuel Kalaw revealed.

He didn't respond. Instead he reached inside his pocket for a cigarette, trying to recompose himself. He sat down, eyes still on the poor white man who was still grasping his breath. He did understood eventually John should know Inez, explained why he tried to steal her photograph from him. It all make sense.

A common sight in Manila streets, John had somehow eluded his watch in the asylum. No one could explain why he is still alive considering he basically live on his own. He was taken from the streets and seek refuge at the vacated house by Juan Tuvera five days ago during an air raid over Manila. In the house he had seen the other half of a picture frame proudly telling the woman on the picture that was there is a sweetheart he called Niza. Juan eventually became interested, the information was worth pursuing. In that effect, the intelligence that came back to him was certain; there is Niza and or Inez verified as one person in Mandaluyong Mental Institution. Someone would be very happy to hear it. They were looking in the wrong place. Wasting no time he went to Bulacan by himself to relay the news knowing it should be a one way trip for his beloved mare and carretela. Air raid in Manila had begun and radio information spread that the liberation is imminent. The other reason for Tuvera to summon Cabarles to Manila is following an order, given by Cabarles himself that any development in the "miss u" effort must be relayed to him at once. For Cabarles, his sole intent is to find Inez, lest he didn't know 'miss u' also expand to combatant group of Filipino guerillas in very large numbers.

THE BOMBING OF MANILA

The succeeding air raids in Manila prevented the civilians from remaining on the streets; however, many would defy the odds of getting killed while jubilating as they counted formations of Flying Vs dropping bombs at selected targets, but many errant shells drifted down randomly. Many times exactly where they stood or were seeking cover. Added to the many casualties were from the Japanese turning their guns on the civilians in sight. Burning of buildings held by the enemy had begun in early September as they vacated each one they occupied to either join Yamashita in escaping to Northern Luzon or to fortify the strength in Intramuros. The bulk of the Japanese Imperial Command had already left Manila; what was left to defend Manila against American and Filipino invasion forces were Yamashita's faithful soldiers hardened by their own murderous occupation of the Philippines.

As the Allied was advancing from the south by land and the Japanese navy was taking defeat in the Philippine Sea from Allied invasion forces, the Japanese seriously continued setting Manila ablaze. Many buildings and businesses they previously occupied were set on fire before abandoning the place while fortifying defense against the inevitable. Many Filipinos in Manila had started their own campaign of reprisal against small enemy contingent frolicking the streets. Many collaborators began to switch sides; many suffered payback from people or relatives of people they abused and betrayed even before they could throw away their Japanese emblems. The casualties begin to mount unimaginably on the side of the Filipinos taking heat from three sides. One was against each other, the Allied bombings that caused death summarily, and random killings of the Japanese. There were no safe haven for those who wanted to live. Only faith could they cling on and luck—a lot of lucks to survive a day. The liberation of the Philippines is in effect at the time Domeng started a nipa hut in August 1944. The air raid in Manila began in September 21 thought to be a precursor to warn the Japanese to leave the city otherwise. Yamashita and the bulk of his forces had long retreated to northern Philippines by then but left contingents of loyal fighters with orders to defend their post at all cost. The September air raid also gave signal to the guerillas, the time of payback begins. The Japanese maximize atrocities and will die than surrender.

As the bombing got intense, Domeng and company was held up in the Bautista residence. Domeng would not touch a gun especially from a dead Japanese; he was concentrating on a plan to journey further to Mandaluyong. By himself, he knew he could not find the way. At the urgency of the matter, the only one available to help was the metallic man whom he would not dare to trust after an attempt to kill him. Least of the problem, intelligence sources indicated a fortified enemy defense and gun batteries in Mendiola and Sta. Mesa, the only known way to the next town. In fact, it was a suicide to even get out of the house at daylight. View at the backyard, cattails had been burning from every direction, and it was just a matter of time the flame could reach their location if it doesn't extinguish itself. Smoke billowing everywhere from all direction of the city and afar.

His desperation could not be satisfied by just waiting. He turned to Juan Tuvera for help.

"We are more than willing to follow your orders, sir, that's why we are here. Sergeant Juan Tuvera, sir. Meet my officer in command, Lt. Manuel Kalaw. Our intelligence officers, Sergeant Ramon Tiglao and his brother Rosendo."

Salutes were responded with salutes instinctively.

It wasn't a surprise to know who they said they are, handguns bulging in their waistline and displaying submachine guns. The gentlemen were guerilla leaders with units consisting of former soldiers and civilian volunteers who took part and benefited on the Miss U effort, put together and spread out initially to determine who were the suspected enemy corroborators in Azcarraga and around from Espana to Sta. Cruz and beyond. So that one person can move freely less worried of his steps being watched and get caught. They know the man who said is a fisherman from Bulacan cannot be what he said he is. His initiative in the Miss "U" effort, and having an endless source of fund to expand guerilla communications and reinforcements in Manila had gain him respect from idle units. As it expanded in the methods of bamboo communication system in Mindanao, it was conceived swiftly in heavily populated city where people can exchange information every corners. The involvement *carretelas* and peddlers also played a major role to spread the words on the streets. In addition, a bag not so full of money entrusted to Juan before his return to Bulacan for Inez photo also contributed in many good ways at the disposal of the kind *kutsero*.

There is one more needed clarification before venturing across the city. Domeng would need assistance also in returning to Bulacan.

His enthusiasm had already been replaced with tension; nervousness had been inhabiting his disposition for many reasons. Inez was located, but not how he expected she would be found. The absence of replies upon inquiries had made him expect for the worst of her condition. Only an escaped patient from the asylum could recognize Inez from a picture who indicated that she was there for the same reason. Whatever the case, he would get her out of there while he began blaming himself for what had happened to her.

He could not hold on to the tears when all promises he spoke had resulted to unimaginable sufferings. What he had done was unforgivable enough. Whatever caused Inez to lose her sanity could have been averted if only he was at her side since the war began. The guilt mounted and burdened his mind when they left the house. If he was to take care of her all his life in any condition she would be found, then so be it.

His silence was respected. As planned, at two o' clock in the morning, three people ran over the burned meadows. Fresh ashes stuck on their clothing while rushing through burning field and across Mendiola. One kilometer or so, they would be in the hospital in no time if they avoided shootout with the Japanese. In his company were Juan Tuvera and Manuel Kalaw, both of whom displayed bravery as soldiers to the likes of Leonidez and Soler of Cavite. Along the way, they were joined by a dozen of armed men following orders from Kalaw. In the backwoods one hundred yards from the asylum, they would wait for Domeng and Juan. It would be an easy mission—an extraction of a mental patient from a compound presumed that no Japanese presence was expected to go smoothly. The problem was getting them back to Azcarraga and ultimately to Bigaa. In the last strand of hope to a place where people had succumbed to insanity, all was good to go to take Niza Sandoval out from the asylum in the heat of air raids over the city.

MISS U IN PERSON

The perimeter was quiet, only shadows of bushes in the dark as they walked around to the front yard. One building on a wide ground of bushes and trees concealing evacuees lying on the ground, no movements at all. About two hours more until sunrise, too risky to create the attention of many souls resting on the yard. Aside from its known functions, the hospital compound was also accommodating refugees, treating the sick and the wounded. Makeshift shelters of cardboards and coconut leaves occupied the yards, indicating that the intelligence was right. They sat and rested by the wall of the building closest to the main door. It was locked from the inside when they tried to get in. Tired and deprived of sleep, Domeng was extremely nervous. Another moment would come that he was longing for—this must be it. Just a door dividing them that would open in time, he was truly nervous and afraid. The assurance of minutes away to be reunited with Inez was clear; the worries was on how to be recognized and forgiven. Whatever her condition was, he would take her home and take care of her. His mind was set on that notion.

"Juan, do you think she can still recognize me after those long years?" he asked Juan, trying to scout as far as he could see on the premises.

"Yes, I'm sure she will. Relax, everything will be fine," Juan replied.

"I can't relax. I can't stop blaming myself of what happened to her," he said worriedly. "I feel so sorry for the death of her parents. I feel so bad to think I wasn't with her at the time she needed me most."

Time was plenty to extend the agony. He may have thought of breaking in already, but the trembling of his knees and strong palpitations of the heart could not be overcome by imagining the love of her life in the most glorious days they shared in the barrio. This must be the end of his nightmares, another nightmarish hour in the view of many people lying on the ground; for what they looked like and seemed to be were like dead bodies in the aftermath of a battle.

"I always knew you're not only a fisherman. Who are you, how did you get separated from Inez?" Juan Tuvera was always mystified of Domeng's character. He was taking advantage of the opportunity to be enlightened.

"It was a walk of faith I want to forget. There is no more sufferings and struggle that can top what I had seen and what I had been through. Please don't deprive me of a moment where I can finally think there is an end to this madness," he said.

In the sky were Allied planes passing by in an early morning air raid in Manila. People suddenly got up and scrambled, some snatching little ones to take cover. Some watched in jubilation. The yard suddenly burst into life.

"I apologize. I know how much effort and concern you bequeath for Inez all this time. You never say who you really are, but I know you're also a soldier. I just want to take this moment to express my pleasure of knowing you."

"The pleasure is mine, Sergeant. There are many people I had known, soldiers like you, civilians in selfless sacrifices and good deeds offering their life for others they don't even know. I'm happy to keep meeting people like them, like you," Domeng stated.

"It had been a long time. I believe what happened to me is the wrath of heaven for I wished the heaven to come to me, only to walk away when it was granted," he added. "So much has happened to me since I left Inez in tears, so many miracles one after another I am happy to be given this chance again." He was in tears.

Juan was stunned. He had heard enough from a man so courageous, and now he was weeping. He may have so many questions; however, he refrained for more but one. "We are taking orders from you. My commanding officer saluted you. Should we?"

"You don't need to. Once the liberation is over, we are back to nobody. Our sufferings and struggle as an individual or a soldier in this war shall be a story worth telling under the tree on a lazy day. I had seen many deaths, many I buried myself. Who would remember them? Perhaps those men who in some ways offered a little prayer and grieved for them, only to end in the same fate. The only thing that mark their shallow graves was a piece of rock, a cross made of twigs. They are the ones worth every generation to be saluted, not me," he replied.

About six thirty in the morning when the door opened, he was among the assembly of people standing by, eager to see their loved ones. Eventually, many got in until he was the only one left. He froze again. A person standing by the door called his attention. "Sir, we only allow immediate relatives of patients to get in. May I know who you are visiting?"

"Niza, Inez Sandoval Cabarles. Would she be inside? Please let me in," he asked politely.

"May I know your relation to her?"

"I'm her husband."

"Oh, I'm sorry, sir, you can get in, of course. I suggest you wait in the lobby. She may still be asleep." In the mind of the custodian, he was another one claiming an intimate relationship with Inez. He must be let in. Suitors came into the compound looking for Inez with gifts. Many had claimed her as a friend and a few as a sweetheart. This one was way out of his head in saying he was the husband. But he had to let him in; he was trained on how to accommodate retards. Laced with ashes on the face and clothing, filthy as hell, this one was evidently worse than John Metal.

"WHISPERS OF LOVE AND PROMISES, I SAID THEM ALL"

Well, Domeng was allowed inside after given instructions to take a seat and behave while waiting. It was too early to be attended to. He followed courteously by the rule. Only moments away, the pounding of his heart became louder and faster than it was already. He breathed deeply while watching people coming out from a hallway, starting to assemble in the big room adjacent to the lobby where males and females mixed up together. People started coming in, started attending to others that obviously needed caring. A similar sight was still fresh on his mind, only in a worse condition. He was on the same situation lining up for porridge or any concoction on the menu. These people weren't lining up for any but for another human being to give them care, hoping they would get better someday. He observed intently, making sure nobody would pass his way that he could not recognize, some taken directly out in the sun. The instructions were clear—take a seat and wait, exactly what he was doing until the march ended from the hallway to the lobby into a big room where noises began simultaneously. No way he shall miss her; no one was taking care of her presumably. The march of patients and relatives subsided. There was no one he could see but the likes of Inez.

He blended into the crowded room, checking each one closely. She wasn't there. Nothing really ever came easy to his favor. Back on the seat, he clasped his palms together on a hectic moment; he was becoming agitated, leaning over a bit regularly so he could get a full view of the hallway. There was no more coming out. It was possible that Inez must still be inside left alone because there were no relatives to attend to her. He could not take any more gripping. There must be one more inside so sickly, not capable to walk by herself like a few he had seen assisted by someone. Long hours had passed already. He was told to wait a second time. One whom he asked about Inez said she was Inez, but she was not even close as he may recall. He could not wait anymore. He took off to get her out himself as she must be still inside.

He checked every room, every occupied bed. There were a few more poor souls left not capable of adhering basically on about anything. None he was looking for. He won't give up that easily; the desperation was tremendous that she be found in this place.

He noticed a movement under one of the beds, the last of possibility; his mind was set to believe that she was the long-lost wife at last. There could be no one else but her.

"Inez, is that you? Please come out. I'm here to take you home," he said very kindly. In prison, soldiers behaved the same for many reasons as shell shock, severe starvation, complications to illnesses, and tortures. Sometimes just fear of tortures could cause such a kind of behavior. He had seen them all. There was a chance of recovery though the percentage was small than those who eventually died. He could not deny that once he had been in that kind of situation.

From the main gate, Fatima Abella and Inez Sandoval Cabarles were just entering the premises. The sight of refugees that they were already used to seeing around had doubled up in number, but what they could do? Only sad regards like another day, hoping they could all cope up. But the morning was different from any other day. She spent a little bit of time in the mirror than usual. It should be another long day or maybe their end altogether.

In the room, Dominador was having a hard time convincing the woman out into the open. "Inez, don't you recognize my voice? We are going home," he said. Intimate persuasions, cherishing the love that they shared, promising anew.

"Huhm, huhm," was the only response Domeng got.

"Inez, I'm Domeng. Thank you. You still remember me?" Definitely a young woman under, face covered almost totally of long and thick hair. "Please give me your hand, we are going home." No response. "I came back for you. Don't be afraid, I won't leave you anymore." He peeked under the bed to reveal a poor girl afraid, perhaps of him, the shelling, or daylight. She remained unresponding but yielding when Domeng touched her hand. He may have shed so much tears for Inez that at that moment, he could not prevent shedding a lot more.

The woman seemed reluctant to reply, somewhat the persistent voice calling her "Inez" and gently holding her hands in a very comforting manner had eased up whatever she was afraid of. She crawled out, long hair obscuring her face. For how he was sitting to convince the woman to come out, he hugged her and wept a long while to what "Inez" had become. Very light, severely malnourished, and also crying profusely. She said, "Don't ever leave me no more."

"I won't, I'll never leave you anymore. I'm bringing you home," he responded.

He assisted the wife he thought she was to stand up, and they walked out together through the long hallway. He kept on whispering to give her comfort, then silence. Complete silence so as those few who followed them.

By the door, Niza was being informed that a new patient had come. He was not John Metal but worse, laced with black ashes for where he must have been rolled down in—well, in ashes. This one was severely afflicted because he was claiming he was her spouse. It was true that so many would try to get her attention on a daily basis, considering the status of people she took care in the asylum, but no one had dared yet to be her husband. She prayed all night for him; she prayed that the war would end. There was always hope that they would see each other again. As the man was described, he was likely another deranged human being. Nothing out of the ordinary.

Domeng was seriously comforting "Inez" in his embrace and whispers, bringing her outside like everyone else did. She was very submitting though no more could he hear from her talking. Many whispers of tender sorry and promises of a new life he had expressed already in the distance, they walked through the aisle, and he was in fact very serious. He kept on whispering, "The horse is home also waiting for you, and I already built a home just for the two of us . . . You'll see when we get home. Please be strong, we are going home."

"Thank you for the heads-up, Mr. Alfredo. Where is he?" Inez asked casually as she entered the building lobby. No one was seated anymore where the man was told to stay, but what caught her attention was a man leading one of the patients out of the door. A woman that nobody ever convinced out to see the light of day in the worst condition of mental affliction.

A man managed to walk her out somehow, looking down at the floor very carefully, assisting the woman as they walked toward the door. Niza could not explain the joy that just struck her for her patient who had no known relative that ever walked in for her concern.

Juan Tuvera instantly recognized Inez from the photograph. He greeted the woman outright to steal a moment before she could turn around again to the pair heading out the lobby. "Ma'am, you are Inez Sandoval Cabarles?" he asked.

"Yes, I am, sir. May I know who is asking?" Inez said in confusion. She could not see the man claiming he was her husband, but her heartbeat was already increasing in view of an armed soldier.

"I am Sergeant Juan Tuvera, Philippine Army. I'm greatly honored to finally meet you in person, ma'am. You are also known as Miss U and subject of a search dedicated by the most kind and noble man I had ever met."

"Are you the man who said to be my husband?"

"No, ma'am, he is," Juan replied, pointing to another man.

So much confusion suddenly colliding, she looked at another man Tuvera said he was. The man was dearly occupied in another woman. There was only one coming her way with a woman, a patient in her care. In his appearance in the bright morning sun, the man was looking down, watching every step carefully, not aware that all eyes were on him. He was very concentrated in his comforting ways for the deranged woman in his arms.

Niza froze. The man walking away taking the patient out was the subject of her eternal prayers. By all extent, he had changed considerably the last time she saw him. She was sure of who he was. She remained standing at the rush of an unexplained feeling. The man walked past her a few steps, so close. As close as it could get between them, almost touching each other, she uttered his name. "Domeng." Her voice so soft, body trembling.

It was heard from an expected source, and Domeng gently uncovered the woman's face. "Thank God you remember me." He caressed her sticky hair then gently cleared it over the shoulder to reveal the face that was stooping down. He touched it, hands tenderly finding the chin with intent to raise it so he could see her better.

"Domeng . . ." Softly as the first time. Heart pounding.

Lips tight, she could say his name clearly. He genuinely shared her anguish with a tighter embrace. "Yes, I hear you, Inez. I'm here."

"Sir, she's not Inez." The voice of Tuvera.

The voice he heard was real; she was calling his name. He could not be mistaken; he heard her saying his name a couple of times. He was taking her home to take care of her personally. He looked up to Juan right in front of him. The sad realm on his face could not be described as everyone else had kept silent.

Juan quickly motioned with his eyes that there was someone else standing close by him. The episode of a life story he was witnessing made him almost speechless. There were tears in his eyes. "Look over your shoulder," he said. He was ecstatic to have taken part in the triumph of the greatest love so sincere it had found each other back in the most unusual way.

"I'm here, Domeng," Niza said as their eyes met each other. A little smile to express an overwhelming feeling like in many dreams, in many bad dreams.

Domeng could not say a word; he had said it all already. Whispers of love, renewed promises, and all he could think of.

"Inez."

It may be the most awkward moment, one that could smile over the one saying his name without opening her lips. He let go of the one from his arms in a swift transformation of emotions. He stepped closer.

An immense joy it was between each other, no words could explain the feeling. Warm hands they felt, just hands as their eyes met. Tuvera was confused about the one they were about to bring back to Bulacan that he suddenly found in his arms.

Three years had gone by when he left her in the cold morning of December. The longing had ended, but the literal madness to see around that day was real. There was so much insanity around, the struggle to keep theirs was proven intact with ecstatic emotions that the love therein remain in their hearts.

"Please don't leave me again," Niza said.

FAR TO BE HAPPY

The Allied bombing of Manila continued. The south had won, and the liberating forces were in tandem with Filipino fighters in the battlefront closing in to the city. The northern troops was delayed encountering serious resistance from the Japanese who retreated in the stronghold of their defenses in Bulacan, Bataan, Tarlac, and Pampanga. The more organized and decisive southern forces with better air support was racing against time. Manila kept on burning. The casualties among civilians were already mounting as the Japanese would not take their fingers off their rifles, shooting people indiscriminately.

In another call of duty as a soldier, Dominador Cabarles would not budge in a decision made and strengthened by what he called "answered prayers." The very last of his function as a soldier was turning over the command of Manila resistance to Lt. Manuel Kalaw. It was paradoxical because it was a command he didn't know he had. The soldiers were appreciated for their contribution into "Miss U" undertakings as it achieved successfully the very objective it was formed. As it expand to an organized network of resistance indulging civilians, it also recruited and united combatants in clandestine operations while launching retribution to the Japanese. Following an unanticipated turn of events, there was a considerable change of plan. Inez was clearly capable of expressing reluctance to go back in Bulacan just yet. The couple may have overcome joy and excitement of their reunion, but there was also a sad reality they had to face.

Domeng shall stay in the asylum until such time the situation eased up or until Inez said so. Under mitigating priorities and prevailing situation, there was a commitment that each one must consider. Inez simply spoke to Cabarles that she could not leave the compound just yet; Domeng likewise didn't need to be explained of the reasons. They sought help from Tuvera and Kalaw to provide assistance to the needs of the facilities and growing numbers of evacuees in the asylum.

"We need food and supplies, medicines of all sorts. Can you extend your kindness and allegiance for that matter?" Domeng stated.

"Consider it accomplished, sir," Kalaw proudly replied with a salute.

Domeng chose to just shake his hands same with Tuvera and a few others before they disappeared into the woods. Inez, who was present in the accord, was equally pleased of cooperation by benevolent soldiers. Miss U wasn't asking for more; what the guerillas brought for her that day was immense, immeasurable happiness that could not be expressed by words. There was nothing more she could ask for.

For quite sometime, she and Fatima Abella were indeed wishing for a certain miracle to overcome the hardship brought in by evacuees to already starving "insiders" of the institution. Earlier that morning, nothing was out of ordinary except that she stayed longer in front of the mirror, something she hadn't done in a long time. It was one of a night she chose to come with Dr. Abella rather than stay in the office where she used to sleep at night. Dedication at work was taking most of her time, in fact she was told she was looking like one of the 'insider' already while also attending the care of the "outsider." The terms were long established to differentiate the patients and the sane respectively. However she used to stay in more often than in the Abella residence.

The decision of Domeng to stay for the time being was made earlier. To find Inez in good health and capably persuasive was the main reason. "Please try to understand," Niza uttered. "I longed for this moment to come. In my dreams, in all my prayers and in my heart I always know you will come for me. For the years we're apart, my survival was made possible by many kindhearted people whom I shared hope that the war will come to an end eventually. Every day we are at constant struggle how to ration food that was hard to come by hoping the next day donations in plenty would come." She paused for a while and let go of her tight hold on Domeng's hands. "I cannot come with you just yet, you had seen the people under our care here. Caring relatives deprived of safety on their own home who chose to stay with us for a son or daughter or mother or father, for those who cannot distinguish blood from water; a fly to put in their mouth to say it taste better than bees that stings. The situation could only get worse, only God knows when it will get better."

She sat back to where she was, grasping again the callous hand she had let gone for a while. No tears but a sign of serious heart strengthened of many sufferings and agonizing hours, she continued. "How could I turn my back and deprived them of little help I can. We are blessed Domeng, I know we will live happily someday, please don't leave me again." Then she became tearful.

"I'll never leave you anymore. I still have nothing to offer you but my love. Take this thing that I kept with me. I believe it guided me back to you as I promised and it is with you I shall cede that once I was a soldier.

For what it is worth, only a glimpse she made of tiny pin on her hands. It is worth the future between the two of them. She closed her hands and hold it tight.

"I am happy now that we are together. That's all I asked for. Happier to find you're not drinking blood or eating flies. I'll take you home when you're ready," Domeng reiterated. "Please tell me what to do."

"Nothing, just stay with me please. I don't want to lose you again."

"I am too, but I can do better."

THE LIBERATION OF UST

A few minutes before another sunrise, a group of people came. Among them where Gloria Villa, Delia Tagle, Pilar Kalaw, Crispin Bautista, and five gentlemen carrying sacks of rice, bananas, sweet potatoes, and boxes of canned foods. The woman carried the weightless assortment of breads and their personal belongings who didn't waste time to find Domeng and Niza Cabarles. Before they could locate the pair, they were inundated by hungry people many of who were not eating for days. They found themselves busy even before they could take a rest from a long night of preparations and travel by foot from Manila.

From November 1944 to end of January 1945 when Manila and surrounding towns were being bombarded from air, land, and sea by the Allied liberation forces, the asylum was inundated by refugees seeking meager amounts of food in any kind. Eventually, the compound was also converted to a field hospital that outnumbered the mental patients. Though many other Filipinos volunteered on the same effort, difficulties were felt mainly when resources were exhausted in the influx of refugees during those months. Thanks to donations of many Filipinos, money may still be at hand, but food to buy was just hard to find.

When the full force of Allied forces entered Manila in January, guerilla forces and vindictive civilians were already waging war against the Japanese one on one. Casualties mounted among Filipinos to discover that large numbers of Japanese remained in the city when it was known that General Tomiyuki Yamashita had fled north already. A wounded soldier came among others by the name of Juan Tuvera. The wound was not serious but incapacitated him to remain in the battlefield. Lots of death, he said, but he would not know what happened to his commanding officer, Manuel Kalaw, as Tuvera was given command of his own unit in the front. In January when aerial bombings subsided to nothing but mortars and tank shelling, many refugees started going back to their own homes.

In the beginning of February, there were rumors that civilians and a few armed men attacked Intramuros. Their fate became clear when the liberating forces discovered their bodies lying everywhere in an offensive campaign to retake the former USAFFE headquarters. About the same time, the liberation of the UST internee camp was in effect. The entire city of Manila was not liberated until March because there were many Japanese who remained defiant to surrender and had chosen to continue fighting, taking civilians as hostages and executing them before they killed themselves. In many cases, they were held up helpless as the wind turned in their demise. There were indeed many vindictive civilians waiting for payback in the most horrific way. No mercy was shown in retribution to the atrocities the Japanese committed over the years.

In more dramatic events, the news of a standout between the Japanese command and the American forces at UST had made its way to Mandaluyong. One of the stronghold of Japanese forces in greater Manila area, they held hundreds of internees in the main building as hostages then announced their intentions to kill everyone without surrender.

There were many Filipinos concerned with the safe release of internees. Niza was one among many others. The long standout and general opinion that the Japanese would be toppled eventually out of the university, she spoke out her thought to pay a visit at the same time meet a few people in the campus the moment they were freed. She only needed to say the word. Domeng had also expressed his decision of going back home to see the family, but he could not do it without Inez coming with him too. Most refugees in the facility had left but those who stayed were kindhearted locals to volunteer, and there were many of them. As a situation that seemed permitting, the time had come for discussing a plan of going back to Bulacan as soon as possible. In the morning of February 4, Inez and Domeng left the asylum in good faith with Dr. Fatima Abella and many friends they made, one at best in the person of Juan Tavera, who had healed his wound but still complained of pain. Time to attend to their loved ones, to give a decent burial on their death and gather those that were spared of their lives. Along the way to Bulacan, they would also pay their respects to Ann Shelby.

To begin as a couple leaving the premises, a few more joined. Crispino Bautista and Juan Tuvera were also coming. By the gate were dozens of them on foot to UST. About halfway, there were thousands to join thousands more of Filipinos gathering a few hundred yards from UST southeast of Espana road, thousands more behind the Allied forces. Many were waiting for the conclusion of the siege so that they could get closer to the compound to deliver packages of food that was halted in many days. Many were just onlookers jubilant to witness the fall of the most hated Japanese troops in Manila; the rest were waiting an opportunity for reprisal on their own way if given the chance. Altogether, the angry and furious mob impulsively found the tides had finally turn in their favor.

For Niza, she wanted to have one last contact with a friend presumably still in the compound. She lost communication with Ann Shelby for so long that Domeng could not oppose. The time for love is also the time to pay tribute for the people who loved them. He also wanted to see Bertha and proclaim his own triumph.

The iron gate was blown off by liberating troop;, many internees awaited the end of standoff while negotiations were taking place in the release of hostages along with the surrender of the Japanese. They were among the mob many carrying packages patiently waiting to move forward to the main gate. Loud jubilations inside the campus indicated the internees were freed somehow. But where were the Japanese? They were led through their way by American troops, as part of whatever deal they made that shall spare their life. Domeng and Inez found themselves in front rows clearing the street to give way to seemingly proud-looking Japanese soldiers.

The march of the surrendering Japanese was somewhat in order, until one of them recognized a familiar face among the crowd—a man who helped and let him live sometime ago in the aftermath of a firefight with Hukbalahap. Without thinking, the limping Japanese officer approached Domeng while reaching for something inside his trousers. It was passed discreetly to an incoherent man who by no mistake also recognized the Japanese. It was an outright fatal blunder; the chain of reactions was swift. Domeng's immediate response was to protect Inez as he was outbalanced to the ground. Tuvera and Crispino tackle the Japanese that started the inevitable. From both sides of the street, thousands in the angry mob ended the walk of terror by the Japanese. The atrocities, and murder they committed in and around the school did not need a trial. Their American escorts could not do anything but watch. As they tasted blood of the enemy, increased the thirst for more and so they shall find more. It was substantiated that Filipino civilians would wage attacks against the Japanese even unarmed. The fighting continued with stubborn Japanese snipers in many areas in the city as stubborn as the Filipinos who seek vengeance.

Highway 54 to Bulacan was cleared of enemy but the province itself was where many of the Japanese was holed up retreating to the jungles. The last stand of the Japanese in their three years of authority in Manila. Many surrendered and many were pushed to eastern towns to Pandi, Sta. Maria to San Jose del Monte and up to northern provinces ultimately where they met their death against many factions of guerilla forces already engaging a battle of their own against each other. On April 2, they decided to come home with Crispino Bautista. In Bigaa, they paid a visit to Adring and Pacita. Crispino eventually rejoined with Aurora and children. Several days more to stay in Sitio Dalig because the woodland in their backyard was burning while intense gunfight was going on. Inez was prepared of what he would see, but she was still devastated. One happy horse welcomed their coming; surely the animal had many sad stories to tell on his own. Nevertheless he could also tell his master who harvested the rice crops Domeng planted if he can talk. Domeng could only renew promises to Inez they will rebuild in no time.

Awakened from a very bad dream, they wanted to think it was. In their mind and in their bodies bore the marks that will remind them forever that it was not a dream. Together they watch the western horizons as the sun timidly touched tree lines from afar. Deep red sky, the bloodshed wasn't over yet; it would never end.

They leaned with each other over the meadows where promises were made. Their eyes met, no more words needed to be said. They were sure of one thing—they have each other, they can feel each other and it's not a dream.

EPILOGUE

Throughout 1945, the war endured a mopping-up campaign against the Japanese who retreated in remote areas and to the mountains. The effort of the Americans to contain and annihilate the stubborn Japanese was achieved in the capture of General Yamashita and his top officers. All were tried for war crimes and executed by hanging and sorts. The Philippines was liberated. Continuing operations in the countryside was halted upon realization that they were confronting a new breed of armed fighters. More intense and dreadful than the Japanese. They were Filipinos themselves; many factions of displaced civilians that sought refuge in the mountains and chose to embrace the life they found with each other on the same sentiments. No more homes to go back, and those that still had were aware that they could die in hunger as well as rebuild on the land that was not theirs to begin with. Adapted to the life they were accustomed to for three years of war that was prolonged by the concept of idealism that the Philippines may have been liberated against the Japanese, but it still remain under foreign rule, the only option became clear to just stay in the mountain. The general opinion was similar in some respect originated from poverty and land bondage since the Spanish era. The failure of new government installed after the war to resolve the problems only get worse as the rich became richer, the poor became poorer. The latter continues the struggle, resorting to extreme measures to do what they do best, farming. Men and women, illiterate and of pint sizes, found camaraderie with each other in the same retrospect. Filipinos in the countryside rebuilt on their own in the tradition of self-reliance and perseverance. In Pandi alone, thousands of hectares of land were exposed by the burning of woodland and converted to farmland. The forest land behind their backyard became an unimaginable sight of ashes and dead trees for quite sometimes. It was reduced back, almost a kilometer away from the Sandoval property.

Sitio Malibo, which was only accessible by foot for many decades, can only suffice in the same antecedent as children of war matured to adulthood. Bigaa (Balagtas) River, that was originally lined with hundreds of yards of embankment, a sanctuary to all kinds of exotic fruit trees and bird species, was reduced to bare lands. In the seventies, the river itself became polluted upon the construction of industries that dumped its waste into the river; upstream mushroomed large-scale piggeries that totally killed the source of living by poor families that depended on the river. It was only until the eighties that the benefit of education was realized.

In the aftermath of the liberation, the Philippine Constabulary was revitalized to pledge allegiance to the Philippine flag as part of the national defense force solely to maintain peace and order in the rural areas, to contain widespread looting, cattle rustling, and ultimately to quash the spread of communism comprising of former comrades and guerillas added by the serious recruitment of young blood. All Filipino soldiers who served with the Allied forces were recalled on active duty together with the new recruits in the infancy of the Philippine national defense forces under the presidency of Sergio Osmena.

Throughout those period, the realization of redeeming himself was considered, but priorities was seriously established; no way in a second lifetime would Dominador Cabarles go back to active duty in the Philippine Army or Constabulary. No way would he touch a gun again, not even for shooting quails and cranes. Aware of his situation, there was truly never a time he would be at ease thinking he would be arrested for deserting or defying another call of duty. On the other hand, he had closed that episode in his life that he was a soldier, denying he was ever a soldier to avoid reprisals from the Hukbalahap known to camp just a kilometer from his backyard.

However, he revealed that there was a time he could not discount reporting back to duty with encouragement of no other than his wife, Inez. The time coincided with the unburying of the bones of his in-laws to be given a decent burial in Pandi cemetery; it also unburied the memories of war to the sight of his rifle and belongings he carried from Mindanao.

On April 8, 1946, Inez gave him the noblest gift he could not forget in his entire life. She handed him a gold pin. It wasn't the thing but the thought of selfless regard to offer himself redemption in a burden that shall clear his name attributed to his disappearances in the time of war.

"I can come with you back to Manila if you wish" were the words that came with the thing.

"I regret the first time leaving you for such reason, and it will not happen again. The rest of my life I will spent with you," he said.

"Thank you very much."

Ka Tato never relented to self-imposed commitment to harass him making threats of many kinds. He admitted he was caught off guard at one time as he slipped on the dike of muddy rice pad, leading the old man to believe he was really afraid—well, he was. He disclosed he was truly afraid in a long period of time. He revealed he was so tempted at one incident to dig out his guns and just shoot the old man.

In 1948, Inez gave birth to a beautiful girl, the happiest of their life together, then a boy after three years. Two more years passed, and they were blessed with another girl. He said there was nothing he could ask for more and never will; he was the happiest man. He started the construction of a bigger house identical to the old house of the Sandovals. He also painted it blue, and from a distance, the color stood out in the background of bamboos and acacia tree to the eyes of the increasing population of Sitio Malibo. The earliest I could remember being associated with him was when I was about four years old when I started to recognize his generosity, especially on Christmas Day. Then sometime in early 1964, an old man died of natural causes and life became better for him. No one reminded him of deserting anymore, a relief that lessened his burden for quite sometime. It didn't last long. Another challenge came into his life, a fight with his own ghosts. None of his children wanted to go to school, only the youngest. He could not be happy enough, but then Anna became afflicted of an unknown illness. Then it began. Praying for one last miracle, they realized that nothing more could be granted because they had already used them all up for themselves. "One more miracle we pray." They didn't give up.

In May 1965, the couple and their daughter visited a monastery in Batangas, a place known to heal many illnesses miraculously. They had visited many similar places in the north then back to Southern Luzon; again, never they lost hope down to the single penny left in their pocket to also consult the best medical practitioners in Manila.

On September 19, 1972, he asked me a favor to give him company in Cavite. Taking a ride with the visitors and seemingly endless accounts of Japanese occupations and people they knew, the long trip was as thrilling in listening to many stories in addition to those I had already heard. We spent a long hour in a cemetery and visited the church. They were all sad memories to reminisce along with the detailed recollections of specific places around the town of Dasmarinas. He said there's lot of difference than he remembered the town. Many residential houses and establishments had been erected. An old grand house stood out; he could not prevent himself from knocking on the door. Unannounced guests given a brother's welcome of more excited woman about his age. He didn't need to introduce himself, but I did so and so did Dononos. For many hours, I was caught at the dining table listening on their conversations. More than a little was talk about her sister Carmelita Molina who became a nun and survived the war to live in a monastery in the Batangas Province. So much to talk about a man who was not present at the time. A promise was made to visit Cabarles in Bulacan in behalf of the husband.

In August 1986, I made time for him to visit Davao. Counting fingers while mentioning many names that had long begun, he said he just wanted to pay respects and gratitude to all the people who helped him during the war. We only made it to Bohol with a specific address stated in a letter from Bicol a very long time ago. Bohol became a priority because it was closer, and I had my own reason to visit the place. We ended up both frustrated for wasting our time; we didn't meet people we wanted to see. He never made it to Davao. Through this book, I want to convey in behalf of Major Dominador Cabarles, USAFFE, that there was one man that never stop expressing his endless gratitude to the people of Davao, the whole Mindanao as well.

Sometime after that month, finding amusement in cockfighting, he was approached by a man in Balagtas Arena. His name was Roberto dela Cruz. For all what it brought in their accidental meeting was another inspiration that added to many more accounts confined within that three years of his life and over.

THE DESERTER

CAPT. RODRIGO SANTOS
Oct. 28, 1943

MYRAFLOR M. DONONO
1925–2013

LT. HOMBRE DONONO
2008
****

ANNA SANDOVAL CABARLES
1953–1968

INEZ SANDOVAL CABARLES
1921–1983

DOMINADOR CABARLES
1920–1996

AND ALL THE GRAVES MARKED BY TWIGS AND STONES

ACKNOWLEDGMENTS

A burden passed on is a burden to find closure, lest to find peace and redemption to the survivors that carried the liability and inconvenience. Four years it has befallen. Four decades to tell, it was a long pause to be buried in memory for another two. The book is written, but the people to whom it is dedicated to had long gone; the acknowledgments they all deserved can only be expressed by simply praying for their soul. "You are not forgotten." To the living whom the author owes as much and for those who inspired the writing of this book, all gratitude cannot be expressed by only disclosing your names. I simply thank you all.

THE AUTHOR

Edwards Brothers Malloy
Ann Arbor MI. USA
August 3, 2017